Ethics in an Age of Terror and Genocide

❧

D1563477

Ethics in an Age of
Terror and Genocide

∾

IDENTITY AND MORAL CHOICE

Kristen Renwick Monroe

PRINCETON UNIVERSITY PRESS

PRINCETON AND OXFORD

Published by Princeton University Press, 41 William Street,
Princeton, New Jersey 08540
In the United Kingdom: Princeton University Press, 6 Oxford Street,
Woodstock, Oxfordshire OX20 1TW

Library of Congress Cataloging-in-Publication Data

Monroe, Kristen R., 1946–
Ethics in an age of terror and genocide : identity and
moral choice / Kristen Renwick Monroe.
p. cm. —
(Pt. 1. the puzzle—Introduction—The Holocaust and genocide—
Pt. 2. a study in contrasts—Tony: rescuer—Beatrix: bystander—
Kurt: soldier for the nazis—Fritz: Nazi propagandist—Florentine: unrepentant
political Nazi—Pt. 3. cracking the code—The political psychology of genocide—
A theory of moral choice—Conclusion: the psychology of difference)
Includes bibliographical references and index.
ISBN 978-0-691-15137-3 (hardcover) —
ISBN 978-0-691-15143-4 (pbk.)
1. Terrorism—Moral and ethical aspects. 2. Terrorism—Moral and ethical aspects—
Case studies. 3. Genocide—Moral and ethical aspects. 4. Genocide—
Moral and ethical aspects—Case studies. I. Title.
HV6431.M655 2012
172'.1—dc22   2011009533

British Library Cataloging-in-Publication Data is available

This book has been composed in Minion Pro

Printed on acid-free paper. ∞

press.princeton.edu

Printed in the United States of America

1 3 5 7 9 10 8 6 4 2

For my beloved children
Alex, Nik, and Chloe

But what else could I do? They were human beings like you and me.

—Rescuer of Jews during the Holocaust

But what could I do? I was one person, alone against the Nazis.

—Bystander, World War II

CONTENTS

∾

ACKNOWLEDGMENTS

∾

WE ALL HAVE MEMORIES of events so important that we can identify exactly where we were when they happened, who was with us, what we wore, or where we sat. I remember the day my father told me about the Holocaust. We were sitting in the car—an old Chevrolet Biscayne, blue, with plastic seat covers that cracked in the cold, made you sweat in the heat, and crinkled whenever you moved—driving from the small midwestern town in which we lived to St. Louis for my weekly piano lesson. I can no longer recount precisely what my father said, but my memory remains fresh with a sense of horror so overwhelming I could hardly breathe. And then Daddy told me, "You must always remember that there are no depths to which man cannot sink, but there also are no heights to which we cannot soar."

My father was a judge who took seriously the majesty and the integrity of the law and believed passionately that law should serve humanity in the search for justice. I adored my father and, for many years, intended to follow in his footsteps and become a judge. Eventually, I took another path, but much of my father's passion and his concern for moral values nonetheless are reflected in my professional life, as in this book. Daddy loved people and was never happier than when talking about important issues with them, and this, effectively, is what I have built my career on: talking with people about what matters in their lives, trying to understand how ordinary human beings respond to the suffering of others, how they make sense of the world around them, and how they navigate the moral terrain of both the everyday and the unexpected events that sometimes challenge them to reach moral choices. I am grateful to my father—to both my parents—for giving me this awareness of the important issues of the world and for encouraging a young girl to believe she could play a small part in that world, and that her involvement might matter. It is a gift I wish for my own children and for my students.

I never dreamed I would meet the kind of people I have been privileged to know as part of the research for this project. I was privy to intimate conversations with an extraordinary and an extraordinarily wide range of people, from those who rescued Jews to bystanders and Nazi supporters. Effectively, these people allowed me to walk around inside their heads as they reflected on what drove their moral choices. The conversations were close-to-the-bone and extremely personal; I hope I have honored the trust of the speakers, most of whom have since died and have left their stories with me. To protect their privacy and that of their families, I can thank them only anonymously.[1]

The first interviews for this book were conducted in 1988, and I have thought and talked about this project a great deal over the years. My thanks to all those who listened and shared their insight thus must be extensive, and I apologize that space constraints restrict my ability to mention all of those who were so kind and helpful.

I have presented numerous papers on parts of this book at meetings of the American Political Science Association (APSA), the International Society of Political Psychology (ISPP), and the ISPP's Caucus of Concerned Scholars: Committee on Ethics and Morality (the Caucus). Parts of this book were presented as the 2010 Ithiel de Sola Pool Lecture to the APSA, the 2005 Guetzkow-Heyns-McKeachie Lecture at the University of Michigan, at a series of visiting lectures in 2010 at Uppsala University (Sweden), and as my presidential address at the annual meetings of the ISPP in Paris, July 2008. Parts of chapters 8 and 9 appeared in two separate issues of *Political Psychology* or in *Political Research Quarterly*; I appreciate the journals' permission in allowing me to reprint parts of these articles here. A version of the Pool Lecture will appear in *PS: Political Science and Politics*, and the APSA plans to stream some of the videos via the APSA website. Special thanks go to ISPP members Janusz Reykowski, Suzanna Smolenska, Tereza Capelos, Cheryl Koopman, Bruce Dayton, Radell Roberts, David Winter, Jerrold Post, Ervin Staub, Gerd Meyer, Catarina Kinnvall, Rose McDermott, Shimon Samuels, Sam McFarland, Paul Nesbitt-Larking, Anne Birgitta Pessi, Fred Alford, David Sears, and Jim Glass for generous comments. Chloe Lampros-Monroe, Alexander Hart Lampros, and Jane Guo gave invaluable technical assistance in many of these professional presentations, and Nicholas Lampros generously edited his mother's deathless prose.[2]

I received valuable feedback on my work during several other public talks, including talks at the University of Nebraska, the Holocaust Memorial Museum (Detroit), the University of Michigan, George Washington University, Duke University, Trinity College Dublin, Simon Wiesenthal-Pepperdine University Institute for Law and Ethics, the Yale Interdisciplinary Center for Bioethics and Yale's Genocide Studies Program, and the University of Southern California.

As always, I owe a special debt of gratitude to my colleagues in the departments of Political Science, Philosophy, and Psychology and Social Behavior at the University of California at Irvine (UCI). Members of the Political Psychology Program and the interns and faculty at the Ethics Center provided stimulation and challenging questions: Adam Martin, William Chiu, Bridgette Portman, Lina Kreidie, Ted Wrigley, Kristin Fyfe, Beth Riley, Alexis and Stephanie Etow, Maria Luisa Martinez, and Priyanka Ghosh challenged me as students and Jerry Tobis, Mahtab Jafari, Francisco Ayala, Gloria Mark, Shawn Rosenberg, Kevin Olsen, and Manuel Gomez were supportive faculty colleagues. I have drawn on joint work with Adam Martin and Priyanka Ghosh in chapter 9 and with Molly Patterson in Appendix A. Sandra Cushman, program manager for the UCI Interdisciplinary Center for the Scientific Study of Ethics and Morality, and Edna Mejia aided in the preparation of the manuscript and generally (tried to) keep me organized. Dean Barbara Dosher and professors David Easton, Etel Solingen, Kamal Sadiq, Cecelia Lynch, Mark Petracca, and Roxane Cohen Silver are owed special thanks for their constant encouragement, stimulating conversation, and friendship. Rose McDermott, Lloyd and Susanne Rudolph, Joseph Cropsey, Fred Alford, Jim Glass, Joanna Veccharelli Scott, Claire Kim, Janusz Reykowski, Gerd Meyer, and Jennifer Hochschild provided inspiration and friendship, as well as comments on the manuscript at various points. If I have failed to respond satisfactorily to all of their suggestions, their generosity and advice are nonetheless appreciated.

Funding was provided by the Biosophical Institute, UCI's Citizens' Peacebuilders, and the UCI Center for Global Peace and Conflict Resolution. Two anonymous readers for Princeton University Press offered valuable comments, and the staff at Princeton University Press performed its usual fine job of editing and bringing the manuscript through production. Special thanks go to Karen Carter and to Chuck Myers, surely one of the world's most sensitive and caring editors.

As always, my thanks and love go to my mother, Gertrude Renwick Monroe, and to my wonderful children: Alexander, Nicholas, and Chloe, to whom this book is dedicated.

PART 1

∾

The Puzzle

CHAPTER 1

❧

Introduction

I BEGIN WITH A PUZZLE. When I asked people who had rescued Jews during the Holocaust why they had risked their lives—and those of their families—to save strangers, rescuers invariably responded with bewilderment. "But what else could I do? They were human beings like you and me." When I asked bystanders about this same time period and inquired whether they had done anything to help Jews, I came across the same baffled looks. "But what could I do? I was one person, alone against the Nazis," was their reply.

The same puzzlement. The same lack of choice. But different perceptions of themselves in relation to others, and vastly different behavior. Identity, it seemed, influenced moral choice. But how, and why? I considered the fascinating complex of relationships among identity, choice, and moral acts in my analysis of the political psychology of rescuers (*Hand of Compassion*, 2004) but was unable, because of space and time constraints, to give it either the documentation or the systematic consideration it merits. This is my purpose in this book.

In particular, I ask if the psychological process of categorization I found so important in explaining altruism among people who rescued Jews also exists—albeit with a different focus and outcome—among bystanders and among those who tacitly or enthusiastically supported or engaged in ethnic, religious, and communal violence and genocide. In broader terms, this book thus continues my exploration of moral psychology by presenting data designed to capture the full range of behavior along a moral continuum.[1]

My initial intellectual objective was to explain the psychology of genocide, determining what made some people rescuers while others actively supported Nazi policies or stood by and did nothing. A scholar dealing with the Holocaust, however, cannot long remain involved at only an intellectual level. The human anguish is too great, the emotions too universal, and most of us who write about this dreadful period do so in the hope that, in some small way, our work will help end the kind of pathology that lay at the heart of the Holocaust. I have been disturbed more times than I can recount when, lost in the daily newspaper, I find myself uncertain whether I am reading about current events or my academic research on World War II. The past seems to repeat itself with a vengeance that still catches me unaware. Worse, while the locale changes and the geography and specifics of the political groups involved shift, man's inhumanity to man seems to remain a constant.

Nor is it only the news that blurs into my research themes. Pieces of literature and films about places far removed from the Holocaust—*The Cellist of Sarajevo* or

Hotel Rwanda, for example—describe psychological processes that feel eerily familiar to me. Identity and, more particularly, our sense of self in relation to others, play a powerful role in our responses to the suffering of others.

I thus became conscious of what should have been obvious all along: the themes found in the Holocaust resonate with other periods of genocide, other instances of ethnic cleansing, other acts of prejudice, discrimination and group hatred, and animosity, just as they resonate with other instances of compassion, heroic altruism, and moral courage. The psychological forces at work during the Holocaust partake of the same political psychology underlying other political acts driven by identity. The same need for affirmation, and the relation such validation can have to group identity and to those who are different, lies at the heart of other important political behavior, from prejudice and discrimination to sectarian hatred and violence on the one hand and forgiveness, reconciliation, and amazing acts of grace on the other.

I slowly realized I faced two challenges. First, I had to untangle the puzzle presented by participants of World War II, constructing the diverse parts of it into something that made sense in the hope that my interviews with rescuers, bystanders, and Nazi supporters were representative enough to lend insight into behavior of others in similar wartime situations. My goal in this part of the analysis was to reveal the political psychology of genocide and to determine whether the altruistic perspective I had detected earlier was part of a broader framework for thinking about ethics that all people share. Second, however, understanding the psychology of genocide meant I had to link my analysis of archetypal behavior during the Holocaust to deeper themes that run throughout other political periods, other instances of prejudice, discrimination, and group hatred that deteriorate into a wide variety of evil acts, from apartheid in South Africa or ethnic cleansing in Bosnia to civil war and political rape in the Congo or Darfur. Doing so resulted in using my analysis of Holocaust interviews to construct an empirically grounded theory of moral choice, one I believe accounts for influences on moral behavior that traditional theories—such as Kant's or Utilitarianism—leave undetected.

This book thus has two closely related goals. As a piece of political psychology, it tries to explain the psychology surrounding genocide. As a work in empirical political theory, it uses the examination of genocide as an analytical lens to bring into focus a critical foundational theme in ethics and normative political science: how we treat others. These goals worked in tandem, and I found making sense of moral choice during the Holocaust helped me appreciate how moral psychology influences our daily lives in a wide variety of situations, producing choices that are sometimes morally commendable and at other times morally neutral or morally repugnant. Ultimately, I developed a new theory of moral choice. Essentially, this theory argues that our sense of self in relation to others shapes and delineates the range of actions we find available, not just morally but cognitively.

This theory begins by assuming we each have a moral framework through which identity sifts and filters perceptions to set and delineate the possible choices we find available and thus can act upon.[2] The ethical framework is the cognitive scaffolding—akin to an innate ability for language—that is filled in by life experiences. Its key parts are our self-images, worldviews, and the integration of particular moral values into our self-images. Identity works through the ethical framework to produce an ethical perspective, unique to each individual and situation and developed in phenotypic fashion according to the individual and external influences that frame the situation demanding a moral choice, the person needing help, and so on. It is this ethical perspective that helps us make sense of the ethical situations presented to us. The way we categorize and classify others, our perceived relationship to the person in need, our idealized cognitive models, and our canonical expectations about what constitutes appropriate behavior all work through the ethical perspective to produce both a cognitive menu of choice options we find available and a sense of moral salience, the feeling that the suffering of others is relevant for us and therefore demands action to help, not just a generalized sense of concern or sympathy. These last two factors produce the acts that affect others, whether these acts are morally ethical, immoral, or ethically neutral. The sense of moral salience provides the impetus to act; the menu of choices determines the type of action taken.

Organization of the Book

As with my previous work on altruism (*The Heart of Altruism*, 1996) and moral choice (*The Hand of Compassion*, 2004), I begin by listening to ordinary people as they speak about their behavior. Their words are important, for they reveal the minds of the speakers, their self-images, and their way of seeing and making sense of the world. Although I spoke with many people who lived through the Nazi period, some informally, some in formal interviews that were taped and transcribed, I focus on one remarkable and especially rich set of interviews, broadening my own prior narrative interpretive analysis of altruists to also include bystanders and both tacit and enthusiastic supporters of Nazi policies.

Chapter 2 reviews the literature on genocide to define it, ask what scholars already know about it, and provide a context within which we can analyze the stories that constitute the heart of the data section of the book. This chapter is important for it makes clear that my findings are not simply about the Holocaust; these findings also suggest how people react to moral challenges in a wide range of situations, extending far beyond genocide. We often think of the Holocaust and World War II as so horrific that they become unique. This is not the case.

Chapters 3–7 contain the interviews in the form of first-person narratives. Parts of Tony's narrative were printed in an earlier book,[3] and occasional quotes from other narratives appeared in journal articles.[4] This is the first opportunity, however, to print all of these narratives in full. I do so for several reasons, some familiar to readers of my earlier work on moral choice. First, the stories constitute a particularly rich data source, one I hope other scholars will be able to utilize to better understand World War II, the psychology of genocide, the importance of cognitive frameworks for choice, and the process by which individuals accord moral salience to the needs of others. As our scientific knowledge of human cognition on moral choice. I thus chose these five interviews for my published, in-depth analysis and because they serve as an approximate match, designed to control background characteristics as best we can in real-life situations. Certainly, it is striking how, despite their many background similarities, these five individuals' actions locate them at quite different points along a very rough moral continuum. Yet their narratives suggest identity works to constrain choice among all of them.

Chapter 8 also presents other findings I found striking. First, I discovered what I call the ethical framework. I define the ethical framework as the cognitive scaffolding consisting of an individual's self-image, worldview, agency, and the integration of particular values into this self-image. Once filled in by life experiences, each individual's framework produces a particular way of seeing the world and one's self in the world. This creates the individual's ethical perspective. Second, I found knowledge of the critical parts of an individual's ethical perspective are far more important than background characteristics, early childhood socialization, or even traumatic events in explaining the variation in wartime treatment of others. This is true whether the treatment was good, bad, or indifferent. Third, the route through which the critical psychological parts of the ethical perspective exercise their ethical pull is via a process of cognitive classification involving the speaker's expectations about what is normal behavior toward others. The classification schema and categories used by these five individuals as they negotiated their way through World War II accounted for their dramatically different actions during the war and yield insight into other rescuers, bystanders, and Nazi supporters I interviewed.

In chapter 9, I step back from the immediate analysis to contemplate the broader themes and implications of the work and to construct a new theory of moral choice. Doing so suggests there is a critical gap in existing moral theories, especially those that tend to emphasize deliberative reasoning. Utilitarianism, Kantian ethics, religious admonitions, indeed, most existing theories designed to guide our moral behavior and help us understand the ethical acts of others fail to adequately capture what appeared in my analysis to be the critical importance of psychological factors. In chapter 9, I thus propose a new, empirically based identity theory of moral choice. I sketch the outlines of this theory and relate how it was derived from my empirical analysis. I then note important literature in a wide range of fields, from linguistics and cognitive science to primate behavior and neuroscience, which offers scientific underpinnings for the theory. Finally, I suggest how this theory can usefully help us understand other forms of ethical political behavior.

My conclusion presents some thoughts about the implications of this study for our understanding of ethics, moral psychology, and other work on prejudice and genocide. A methodological afterword considers the ethical and methodological issues involved in the research. Appendix A considers the reliability of narrative interviews as a tool for doing social scientific research; a glossary (Appendix B), contains key concepts utilized in my discussion of moral psychology.[8]

life experiences. Its key parts are our self-images, worldviews, and the integration of particular moral values into our self-images. Identity works through the ethical framework to produce an ethical perspective, unique to each individual and situation and developed in phenotypic fashion according to the individual and external influences that frame the situation demanding a moral choice, the person needing help, and so on. It is this ethical perspective that helps us make sense of the ethical situations presented to us. The way we categorize and classify others, our perceived relationship to the person in need, our idealized cognitive models, and our canonical expectations about what constitutes appropriate behavior all work through the ethical perspective to produce both a cognitive menu of choice options we find available and a sense of moral salience, the feeling that the suffering of others is relevant for us and therefore demands action to help, not just a generalized sense of concern or sympathy. These last two factors produce the acts that affect others, whether these acts are morally ethical, immoral, or ethically neutral. The sense of moral salience provides the impetus to act; the menu of choices determines the type of action taken.

Organization of the Book

As with my previous work on altruism (*The Heart of Altruism*, 1996) and moral choice (*The Hand of Compassion*, 2004), I begin by listening to ordinary people as they speak about their behavior. Their words are important, for they reveal the minds of the speakers, their self-images, and their way of seeing and making sense of the world. Although I spoke with many people who lived through the Nazi period, some informally, some in formal interviews that were taped and transcribed, I focus on one remarkable and especially rich set of interviews, broadening my own prior narrative interpretive analysis of altruists to also include bystanders and both tacit and enthusiastic supporters of Nazi policies.

Chapter 2 reviews the literature on genocide to define it, ask what scholars already know about it, and provide a context within which we can analyze the stories that constitute the heart of the data section of the book. This chapter is important for it makes clear that my findings are not simply about the Holocaust; these findings also suggest how people react to moral challenges in a wide range of situations, extending far beyond genocide. We often think of the Holocaust and World War II as so horrific that they become unique. This is not the case.

Chapters 3–7 contain the interviews in the form of first-person narratives. Parts of Tony's narrative were printed in an earlier book,[3] and occasional quotes from other narratives appeared in journal articles.[4] This is the first opportunity, however, to print all of these narratives in full. I do so for several reasons, some familiar to readers of my earlier work on moral choice. First, the stories constitute a particularly rich data source, one I hope other scholars will be able to utilize to better understand World War II, the psychology of genocide, the importance of cognitive frameworks for choice, and the process by which individuals accord moral salience to the needs of others. As our scientific knowledge of human cognition expands, such data constitute a valuable historical archive for future analysts to probe using superior methodological tools.[5]

Second, the stories themselves are rich in human drama. They engage the reader's imagination as they reveal the speakers' cognitive frameworks and how the speakers think about ethical issues. Such data present a rare opportunity for the researcher by demanding that the reader engage with them sufficiently to reach an independent judgment concerning the material. This reassures the analyst that there is a natural corrective for the inevitable selectivity inherent in excerpting passages to illustrate analytical points. For this reason, it is important that the interviews precede my own analysis and thus are presented first with no commentary on my part.

Third, narratives provide a unique insight into the human mind, suggesting how decisions are made and how the individual interacts with cultural forces to create the moral life.

Finally, and most simply, the stories are exciting to read. So much scholarly work is dry and analytical that it is a treat—albeit sometimes an unsettling one—to be able to leave behind the world of academia and try entering another time and worldview, even when that worldview is deeply disturbing. I have tried to recreate the experience for the reader in the narratives. To do so, I print the stories with minimal comment and save my analysis until after the reader has had a chance to form an independent impression of the speakers. Only then do I put forward my analysis of the narratives. By placing the stories before my analysis, I hope to provide the reader the opportunity to form an independent judgment and to have a richer context within which to understand and evaluate the analysis I present.

The stories begin (chapter 3) with an interview with Tony, who was a young Dutch cavalry officer when the war began. Tony was extremely articulate, and I had the opportunity to spend time with him over a number of years—from 1988 to 2004—so his interview is both lengthy and insightful. As with all my interviews, I present Tony's narrative in as unadorned a form as possible, with limited editing and no analytical comment. I do so to facilitate the reader's entering into Tony's head, to understand how Tony's ethical framework, and particularly his perceptions of himself in relation to others, worked to limit the choices Tony found available.

The rest of the interviews presented here were selected via a respondent-driven sample because of the speakers' relation to Tony. Chapter 4 presents a narrative interview with Tony's cousin, a woman I call Beatrix. I interviewed Beatrix in her apartment in Rotterdam in 1992. Since the two are related, Beatrix shared many background characteristics with Tony, and she spent much time with Tony's family after her mother died. In terms of behavior, however, Beatrix would be classified as a bystander, whereas Tony was a rescuer.

The most elusive person I interviewed was Kurt, a German soldier whose interview contains fascinating insight on how identity constrains choice. Kurt matched Tony in many background characteristics. Both Tony and Kurt were the only children of affluence, both were in the military, and both saw heavy fighting. Although I never asked directly, and Kurt never volunteered information about his personal participation in Nazi activities, he did express what seemed to be clearly racist

views. At one point Kurt appeared even to question the extent to which the Holocaust existed, or at least to suggest that the magnitude of the Holocaust has been
greatly overstated. I classify Kurt only as a soldier who fought for the Nazis. But I
found his interview extremely helpful, precisely because it reflects so much ambiguity, dissembling, and—to my mind, at least—self-deception. I present the chapter on Kurt (chapter 5) as reflective of the moral psychology of many Europeans
whose support—implicit or militarily—kept the Nazis in power.

Through Tony's contacts at the National Institute for War Documentation, I was
able to interview a Dutch collaborator named Fritz. Fritz shared many of Tony's
prewar conservative opinions in favor of the monarchy and traditional Dutch
values, although he was of working-class origins, unlike Tony and Beatrix, who
were Dutch bourgeoisie. But unlike Beatrix or Tony, Fritz joined the Nazi Party,
wrote propaganda for the Nazi cause, and married the daughter of a German Nazi.
When I interviewed him in 1992, Fritz indicated he was appalled at what he later
learned about Nazi treatment of Jews but that he still believed in many of the goals
of the National Socialist movement and felt that Hitler had betrayed the movement. I thus classify Fritz as a disillusioned Nazi supporter who retains his faith in
much of National Socialism. Chapter 6 is presented as illustrative of the psychology of those who once supported the Nazi regime but who were disillusioned after
the war.

Finally, in the summer of 1999, I interviewed Florentine, widow of Meinoud
Rost van Tonningen, one of the two top Dutch Nazis during the Hitler period.[6]
Asked to head the SS (Schutzstaffel) for Holland, Florentine's husband instead
turned over the position to Florentine's brother. But Florentine's husband served
as the Dutch plenipotentiary to the League of Nations during the 1930s and as
head of the Dutch National Bank during World War II.[7] Offered the chance to be
secreted to South America after the war by the Nazi leadership, Florentine and
her husband elected to stay in Holland to "tell people the truth" about the war.
Florentine never knew how or when her husband died, and believed he was beaten
to death while imprisoned by the Allies immediately after World War II. Florentine remained an unrepentant Nazi until her death in 2007, traveling as much
as her health permitted to speak in favor of the Nazi cause. She was extremely
proud of her job as former leader of the Dutch Nazi Youth Movement for Women
and was devoted to the memory of her husband. Although the interview is chilling, the chapter on Florentine (chapter 7) makes fascinating reading and offers
rare insight into the mind of an unapologetic supporter of genocide, racism, and
ethnic cleansing.

Chapter 8 focuses directly on the puzzle that initially intrigued me. Why did
all of the participants—rescuers, bystanders, or perpetrators—claim they had no
choice in how they treated others during World War II? What caused this feeling,
and what accounted for the dramatically different responses toward others? Since
my earlier work suggested psychological factors were the critical determinants of
altruists' treatment of others, I wanted to try to isolate the psychological component as much as possible, while still utilizing data from a real-world situation.
Obtaining four narratives that are so well matched with Tony's offered a unique
opportunity to conduct a more systematic analysis of the psychological constraints

on moral choice. I thus chose these five interviews for my published, in-depth analysis and because they serve as an approximate match, designed to control background characteristics as best we can in real-life situations. Certainly, it is striking how, despite their many background similarities, these five individuals' actions locate them at quite different points along a very rough moral continuum. Yet their narratives suggest identity works to constrain choice among all of them.

Chapter 8 also presents other findings I found striking. First, I discovered what I call the ethical framework. I define the ethical framework as the cognitive scaffolding consisting of an individual's self-image, worldview, agency, and the integration of particular values into this self-image. Once filled in by life experiences, each individual's framework produces a particular way of seeing the world and one's self in the world. This creates the individual's ethical perspective. Second, I found knowledge of the critical parts of an individual's ethical perspective are far more important than background characteristics, early childhood socialization, or even traumatic events in explaining the variation in wartime treatment of others. This is true whether the treatment was good, bad, or indifferent. Third, the route through which the critical psychological parts of the ethical perspective exercise their ethical pull is via a process of cognitive classification involving the speaker's expectations about what is normal behavior toward others. The classification schema and categories used by these five individuals as they negotiated their way through World War II accounted for their dramatically different actions during the war and yield insight into other rescuers, bystanders, and Nazi supporters I interviewed.

In chapter 9, I step back from the immediate analysis to contemplate the broader themes and implications of the work and to construct a new theory of moral choice. Doing so suggests there is a critical gap in existing moral theories, especially those that tend to emphasize deliberative reasoning. Utilitarianism, Kantian ethics, religious admonitions, indeed, most existing theories designed to guide our moral behavior and help us understand the ethical acts of others fail to adequately capture what appeared in my analysis to be the critical importance of psychological factors. In chapter 9, I thus propose a new, empirically based identity theory of moral choice. I sketch the outlines of this theory and relate how it was derived from my empirical analysis. I then note important literature in a wide range of fields, from linguistics and cognitive science to primate behavior and neuroscience, which offers scientific underpinnings for the theory. Finally, I suggest how this theory can usefully help us understand other forms of ethical political behavior.

My conclusion presents some thoughts about the implications of this study for our understanding of ethics, moral psychology, and other work on prejudice and genocide. A methodological afterword considers the ethical and methodological issues involved in the research. Appendix A considers the reliability of narrative interviews as a tool for doing social scientific research; a glossary (Appendix B), contains key concepts utilized in my discussion of moral psychology.[8]

CHAPTER 2

∾

The Holocaust and Genocide

IT'S NOT OVER AND IT SHOULD NOT BE FORGOTTEN. The conflagration we call the Holocaust—the systematic state-sponsored extermination of six million Jews by the Nazis and their collaborators—involves us in much more. The Holocaust itself also entailed the systematic murder of between eleven and seventeen million additional people from other targeted groups: ethnic Poles, gypsies,[1] Slavs, prisoners of war, the disabled, homosexuals, other religious minorities, and political opponents. The sheer enormity of its human loss makes the Holocaust primus inter pares, a genocide that is the first among equals,[2] with an import extending beyond its uniqueness as an isolated, terrible historical event. If we approach the Holocaust this way, we can use our knowledge of other genocides to inform our understanding of the Holocaust, and we can use what we learn from close examination of the Holocaust to help explicate other instances of genocides and related political evils that grow from the same roots: prejudice and discrimination.[3]

My first task in this chapter is to define what is meant by genocide. I next note the importance and extent of genocide, citing other instances of genocide and ethnic cleansing. I summarize the existing knowledge on the causes of genocide and describe my research methodology to suggest how my work will lend insight into critical questions about genocide, especially how it will increase our understanding of behavior by rescuers, bystanders, and supporters of genocide. Throughout this discussion, I try to remain conscious of the extent to which understanding the human psychology surrounding the Holocaust can lend insight into a far wider range of related, important, and ongoing political behaviors that emanate in forces deep-seated within the human psyche: prejudice; discrimination; ethnic, sectarian, religious hatred and violence; and all the specific embodiments these evils take, from sectarian civil wars in Lebanon and apartheid in South Africa to ethnic cleansings in Bosnia and Rwanda-Burundi or military conflicts in Darfur and Sudan. If we can crack the psychological code of rescue, bystander, and perpetrator behavior during the Holocaust, we will have gone a long way toward unlocking the door to understanding a far wider range of related and important political behavior involving moral choice.

WHAT CONSTITUTES GENOCIDE?

The act is ancient; only the terminology is new. To understand genocide and the psychology surrounding it, we first must be aware of what is meant by genocide, in both everyday language and scholarly work.

The term *genocide* is widely attributed to Raphael Lemkin,[4] a Jewish Polish scholar (1900–1959) who drew on the Greek root *génos* (γένος) to refer to family, tribe, or race (*gene*) and the Latin *cide* (*occido*) to refer to massacre or kill, thus capturing the essence of what we now know as genocide: killing members of a tribe or race not because of their individual acts but rather because of their group identity. In an essay titled "Crime of Barbarity" (1933), Lemkin first called for an international convention to outlaw what he termed *acts of barbarity*, defined as "acts of extermination directed against the ethnic, religious or social collective."[5] In 1944 Lemkin coined the term *genocide* to describe such acts and argued they constituted crimes against international law.[6] In developing this particular concept of a crime into the idea of genocide, Lemkin used as illustrations the experience of the Assyrians massacred in Iraq on August 11, 1933, equating this with "the slaughter of Armenians" during World War I.[7] Lemkin tried—but failed—to have such "acts of barbarism" outlawed by the Legal Council of the League of Nations.

Lemkin's *Axis Rule in Occupied Europe*, published in the United States in 1944 by the Carnegie Endowment for International Peace, ties Lemkin's extensive legal analysis of Nazi rule during World War II to the concept of genocide. The international community accepted Lemkin's use of genocide as an offense against international law, using it as one of the legal bases of the Nuremberg trials. (The indictment of twenty-four Nazi leaders in Count 3 of the Nuremberg charges states that the defendants "conducted deliberate and systematic genocide—namely, the extermination of racial and national groups."[8]) Lemkin continued to work for an international resolution against genocide, encouraging countries to cosponsor a resolution for consideration by the United Nations General Assembly. When attempting to define genocide, Lemkin wrote:

> New conceptions require new terms. By "genocide" we mean the destruction of a nation or of an ethnic group. This new word, devised . . . to denote an old practice in its modern development, is made from the ancient Greek word *genos* (race, tribe) and the Latin *cide* (killing), thus corresponding in its formation to such words as tyrannicide, homicide, infanticide.[9]

Lemkin went on to write:

> Generally speaking, genocide does not necessarily mean the immediate destruction of a nation, except when accomplished by mass killings of all members of a nation. It is intended rather to signify a coordinated plan of different actions aiming at the destruction of essential foundations of the life of national groups, with the aim of annihilating the groups themselves. The objectives of such a plan would be the disintegration of the political and social institutions, of culture, language, national feelings, religion, and the economic existence of national groups, and the destruction of the personal security, liberty, health, dignity, and even the lives of the individuals belonging to such groups.[10]

Genocide is defined further—and condemned—by the United Nations Convention on the Prevention and Punishment of the Crime of Genocide. This international agreement was approved for signature and accession by the UN General Assembly on December 9, 1948, and was entered into force on January 12, 1951. Article 2 of this convention defines genocide as

> any of the following acts committed with intent to destroy, in whole or in part, a national, ethnical, racial or religious group, as such: killing members of the group; causing serious bodily or mental harm to members of the group; deliberately inflicting on the group conditions of life, calculated to bring about its physical destruction in whole or in part; imposing measures intended to prevent births within the group; [and] forcibly transferring children of the group to another group.[11]

Like other important concepts in social science and international law, genocide as a term is utilized in different ways by both scholars and political groups. Among scholars, for example, we find slightly different definitions of genocide, such as the one expressed by Helen Fein, executive director of the Institute for the Study of Genocide and author of nine books and monographs on genocide and collective violence, including two prize-winning works, *Accounting for Genocide* (1979) and *Genocide: A Sociological Perspective* (1993). Fein defines genocide as "sustained purposeful action by a perpetrator to physically destroy a collectivity directly or indirectly, through interdiction of the biological and social reproduction of group members, sustained regardless of the surrender or lack of threat offered by the victim."[12] Fein's sociological conceptualization is slightly broader than the United Nations' definition. Its importance lies in noting critical aspects of genocide. Genocide is sustained action, not merely an isolated massacre or pogrom. It is purposeful in the sense that the act itself demonstrates and effectively proves the intentions of those who committed the act. Genocide is not uncoordinated, unorganized mob violence. The intent is the physical destruction of group members, not merely the destruction of their culture. The method of destruction may be direct (murder) or indirect (the slow starvation or removal of children from their biological families of origin). Finally, genocide is one sided. The victim group cannot defend itself successfully because of an imbalance of power.[13]

Other scholars offer additional, minor variations on the conceptual definition while accepting the core concept as advanced by Lemkin and the United Nations. As a commonly accepted core concept, then, genocide refers most simply to the deliberate and systematic destruction of a people, frequently through murder but also involving the obliteration of other aspects of a people's identity, including attempts to eradicate the social institutions, culture, language, folklore, and even the history of a people.

This still leaves variation in the concept as used by political groups, many of whom frequently shift the meaning according to what is politically expedient for their cause. Political debates over the definition of what constitutes genocide become especially heated when military and/or political repercussions follow from an event being classed officially as genocide. Does a government have to be complicit in these acts for them to be classed as genocidal? Need we find official documents specifically ordering genocide? If so, whose orders are relevant? What distinguishes genocide from other forms of mass violence and murder? Should we distinguish between genocides that are ideologically based on blatant racist ideology (such as the Holocaust) and those that are couched more in terms of retributive genocide, the by-product of perceived threats posed to one group by another, as is often considered the case with the Hutu-dominated state by the Rwandan Popular Front?[14] In practice, these distinctions blur, and we shall learn in later chapters that many Nazis viewed their cause as one righting wrongs, taking back things they believed were stolen from them by Jews, Slavs, and others the Nazis considered *untermenschen*.[15] As this one aspect of genocide illustrates, it is precisely because debates on genocide are so heated and tinged with political exigencies that they become difficult, if not unfeasible, to resolve into general principles.

In practice, two important additional concepts that have developed over time frequently enter discussions of genocide. The term *white genocide* has been developed to describe attempts to eradicate a people by means that do not involve murdering group members, but which instead focus on acts such as the transfer of children from one group to another or the eradication of cultural traditions.[16] *Ethnic cleansing* is a term developed in the early 1990s to describe events in the former Yugoslavia; it usually refers to the different military policies and practices designed to achieve security during war through displacing members of an ethnic group from specific territory.[17] (*Ethnic purification* or *nettoyage ethnique* and *epuration ethnique* are other frequently used terms to describe this same phenomenon.) The United Nations defines ethnic cleansing as "rendering an area ethnically homogeneous by using force or intimidation to remove from a given area persons of another ethnic or religious group."[18] Ethnic cleansing usually aims at the removal of stigmatized ethnic groups from a given territory, not their complete eradication, although mass murder frequently does occur. This locates ethnic cleansing somewhere between genocide and nonviolent but still pressured ethnic emigration.[19] International law offers little formal legal definition of ethnic cleansing.[20] However, ethnic cleansing in the broad sense—the forcible deportation of a population—is defined as a crime against humanity under the statutes of both the International Criminal Court (ICC) and the International Criminal Tribunal for the former Yugoslavia (ICTY).[21] The obvious human-rights violations that are part of ethnic cleansing are usually treated as separate crimes, which often fall under the definitions for genocide or crimes against humanity.[22]

WHY IS IT IMPORTANT TO UNDERSTAND GENOCIDE?

The question almost seems too obvious to need answering. The wanton destruction of even one human life simply because that person happens to be born in a particular race, religion, sect, or ethnicity upsets and offends the sense of decency held by most of us. Yet it is when we consider the scale and waste of genocide— some estimates suggest up to over 262 *million* people during the twentieth century alone[23]—that we feel the full sense of urgency that accompanies discussions of genocide.[24] To remind ourselves of the unbelievable devastation of genocide, we need consider only the most general statistics from the events that gave the world the word *genocide.*

The Holocaust (*Shoah* in Hebrew) involved the destruction of approximately six million Jews by Nazis from 1939 to 1945. We then add to this the Roma/Sinti Porrajmos (The Devouring), the Roma word for the destruction of approximately half a million "gypsies" by the same Nazi government. Jews and the Roma/Sinti were victims because they fell into what the Nazis considered a "stable" category of race. For the Nazis, such "stable categories" denoted a characteristic that one could not change—such as race or ethnicity—and were different from categories that could be changed by the individual, such as political affiliation.[25] Other groups who were persecuted by the same regime but who did not face inevitable destruction because they were not in so-called stable categories included male homosexuals, Jehovah's Witnesses, political opponents (especially Communists and Social Democrats), priests, habitual criminals, and other national groups, such as the Poles. Further targeted groups, persecuted and frequently subjected to murder, included members of the handicapped or people with genetic diseases. (For example, the Nazi T-4 killing program began on September 1, 1939, and continued for several years, leading to the deaths of approximately 300,000 individuals in hospitals, wards, and gas chambers.) All these deaths should be considered part of the genocide we refer to as the Holocaust, and constitute victims apart from those killed as part of the lamentable but more routine wartime destruction.

The Holocaust was neither the first nor the last genocide in the twentieth century. Classed by most scholars as the first twentieth-century genocide, the Armenian genocide occurred before the word *genocide* was termed, and remains a hotly debated point of contention; the Turkish government still insists no genocide took place.[26] The Armenians emerged as a people in the sixth century BCE in eastern Anatolia. One of the first national groups to convert to Christianity in 301, the Armenians had an independent country until the last Armenian kingdom collapsed in 1375. Thereafter, Armenia was a part of the Ottoman Empire. By most measures, the Armenians were a loyal minority in the empire until the late nineteenth century, when Christian minorities in the western part of the Ottoman Empire used Great Power support to achieve autonomy and independence. The first attacks on Armenians came in 1881, when between 100,000 to 200,000 Armenians were killed—many in 1895—and others were forcibly converted to Islam. The period from 1895 to 1922 is the controversial period, with the dispute focused on the genocidal intent on the part of the Turkish government. The stable element of the genocide was Armenian nationality and language. Christianity fell somewhere in between a stable and an unstable element, as some Armenians were allowed to live if they accepted Islam. Because of the extent of these conversions, many Armenians today refer to this period as a white genocide.

The core of what is classed as genocide by most scholars, even if still disputed by the Turkish government, began April 24, 1915, and was closely related to Turkish fears of Armenian separatism and disloyalty toward the Ottomans during World War I. The action began with the deportation and murder of the Armenian intelligentsia and civic leadership. Armenians in the army were murdered. Military units attacked communities in the Armenian heartland, with the men killed and the women raped then frequently killed, and children sometimes kidnapped and taken to be raised by Turkish families. "Delegates" (*murahhas*) organized and supervised the deportation and massacre of the departing Armenian convoys, usually in the deserted backlands. There were "Special Organization" (*Teskilatl Mahsusa*) bands in charge of the killings, the majority of whose members were criminals released from prisons. Armenians who survived the initial onslaught were subjected to further forced marches into the Syrian Desert, where they were frequently killed, as at Deir es-Zor.[27] The total number murdered is estimated at 1.5 million Armenians, but the destruction and obliteration of cultural institutions, art, manuscripts, churches, and cemeteries, along with the deportation of an additional 1.1 million Armenians, makes the toll of the genocide much higher. Unlike the Holocaust, the Armenian genocide was surprisingly well reported in the contemporary American and European press.

After the Holocaust, the passage of the UN Convention, and the world swearing "never again," one would think that genocide would be an act of the past. This is not the case, as is illustrated by just a few more recent examples, from events in the 1990s in the former Yugoslavia to those in Rwanda-Burundi.[28] Estimates for the Yugoslavian ethnic cleansing run to more than 200,000 civilian deaths in Bosnia and Croatia, plus tens of thousands of women who were raped, some more than a hundred times, while their sons and husbands were beaten and tortured in concentration camps like Omarska and Manjaca. Although Serbs were the most frequent ethnic cleansers, the evidence suggests this method was adopted by all sides during the course of the war, with ethnic cleansing leaving more than two million refugees and displaced persons in former Yugoslavia during the war in Bosnia. This number increased with the expulsion of Serbs from Croatia and the ferocious atrocities committed by Serbs against the Albanians in Kosovo.

In Rwanda-Burundi, ethnic cleansing resulted in hundreds of thousands of Tutsi fleeing to Tanzania and Congo to newly formed refugee camps. The overall estimates range up to one million killed, 800,000 of whom were Tutsis. This problem remains unsolved as I write, with the spillover from this and the Darfur genocide destabilizing the entire region in Africa at untold waste to human lives and disruption to normal political, economic, and social stability.

Analysts spend a great deal of time discussing whether an event constitutes genocide, with diplomats focusing on applying the law to the facts rather than treating the conflict as an openly political and contentious process in which different parties assert conflicting interests and innocent people are wantonly killed.[29] This semantic and legal deliberation—both tragically and ironically—often results in delays in the allocation of support for victims of what is at the least mass murder, even if it does not technically fall into the category of genocide as defined by international law. The late 1990s and early 2000s saw numerous situations tinged with overtones of genocide and ethnic cleansing, even if they failed to fulfill all of the commonly established criteria. These include the murder of large numbers of civilians in East Timor by Indonesian military and police forces. The central government of Botswana has been trying to move Bushmen out of the Central

Kalahari Game Reserve. The expulsion of white farmers by the Mugabe regime in Zimbabwe in 2000 provides an interesting illustration of how whites can be victims in postcolonial societies. (At one time 270,000 whites lived in Zimbabwe; now there are only a few thousand.) Attacks by the Janjaweed militias of Sudan on the African population of Darfur, a region of western Sudan, constitute a major foreign policy issue for current governments and are widely considered genocide, with some 2.5 million displaced. Less frequently, the Iraq war (2003 to the present 2010) is mentioned as involving genocide, with entire neighborhoods in Baghdad charged as being ethnically cleansed by Shia and Sunni militias.[30] Iraqi Christians represent less than 5 percent of the total Iraqi population, but they make up 40 percent of the refugees (as of 2008) living in nearby countries, leading some analysts to cite this displacement as a genocide. The Iraq war, which has overtones of sectarian violence even though its origins come from other sources, underlines the difficulties in designating events as "genocides."

There are many other instances that could be classed as genocide but my intention here is not to compile a list of recent genocides so much as to provide a feel for the scale of human misery that accompanies genocide and ethnic cleansing and to demonstrate that the problem endures into the twenty-first century. Genocide continues to be a scourge on humanity.

How Can We Best Understand the Causes of Genocide? Literature, Research Methodology, and Data

Traditionally, three sets of factors are found to create the confluence of forces that erupt into genocide. The first includes macrophenomena, such as wars, the breakdown of empires or multistates, economic depressions, and the transfer of political power during revolutions or postcolonialism. A prime example of the importance of macroinfluences on genocide is the Holocaust, with its origins in World War I, the flawed Versailles treaty, and the worldwide depression that ensued. The Armenian genocide occurred in conjunction with a world war, the disintegration of the Ottoman Empire, and the founding of the new Turkish state, just as the Bosnian genocide occurred during the break-up of Yugoslavia and the disintegration of the Soviet or Communist bloc.

The second set of factors focuses on structural-political features, such as the totalitarian aspect of political regimes and the lack of a free press and effective political opposition. Again the Holocaust illustrates this category of influences, with the Weimar regime epitomizing the deterioration in democratic institutions and the political culture that resulted in Hitler's 1933 ascension to power. Hitler's use of anti-Semitism as a tool to gain and expand his power illustrates genocide's tendency to flourish when a state is taken over by a dictatorial elite or a political movement that relies on unchecked violence. Such elites then frequently both create and manipulate in-group/out-group animosity to the elite's political advantage; this transpired under both Hitler and Slobodan Milošević in the former Yugoslavia.[31]

Social scientists have developed sophisticated explanations for both the macro-level and the political-structural determinants of genocide, and I encourage readers to consider them further, even though they are not the focus of my work in this volume.[32] My interest here lies in the third set of forces critical to an understanding of genocide: the personal psychological factors accompanying genocide. These are the domain of the political psychologist. Since these factors occupy my attention throughout the rest of this book, let me first review what we know in this area in more detail. In doing so, I examine the personal political psychology associated with genocide to answer three specific questions: First, what causes ordinary people to support genocide? Second, how do bystanders differ from rescuers and from supporters and perpetrators of genocide? And third, what causes some people to risk their lives and those of their families to save strangers?

Literature

The consideration of the personal-psychological contributors to genocide is set in the context of work on just wars;[33] humanitarian intervention;[34] human rights;[35] and racism, stereotyping, and prejudice;[36] and I draw on insights from this broader literature in my own analysis. Both scholarly works and journalistic accounts[37] of genocide have engendered a lively debate over the rational underpinnings of this seemingly insane behavior. Once dismissed as the result of ignorance and ancient hatreds or psychopathology, genocide now is more frequently explained as having an instrumental component, with the spark that ignites the powder keg emanating from the desire of political leaders to gain power through manipulating or inciting a passive citizenry whose passions are diffuse and malleable.[38] This psychological basis linking leaders and followers to genocide and ethnic cleansing is complex, and scholars do not have definitive answers about the flows of influence or shared complicity. One view is that hate-mongering demagogues serve as malevolent group therapists to their wounded nations, providing explanations for their people's adverse situation, such as those that occurred as the Ottoman Empire lost its territories in the Balkans during the World War I period or as Germany suffered after the punitive Treaty of Versailles and the loss of World War I.[39] Leaders focus the source of their people's misfortunes—whether economic, political, or cultural—onto an external target, such as the Armenians, Jews, or another ethnic/religious/sectarian group. (The intensification of ethnic-nationalist hatred leading to the Bosnian ethnic cleansing, for example, has been explained through the loss of enemies after the collapse of the Soviet empire.) Old wounds are reopened and old enemies are created or revived, providing a fertile climate for genocidal destruction as political leaders find ways to gain and retain their political power through manipulating the anguish and discontent of the population.

The role of bystanders is often critical in this process, with analysts[40] arguing that the road to genocide frequently begins with small transgressions, such as the passage of laws prohibiting a minority from attending school or holding positions in commerce or government. These small steps are critical, however, especially for people who are neither rescuers nor perpetrators. If no one speaks up in the face of the initial steps on the road to genocide, perpetrators—both the elite and the masses—are emboldened. Passivity has a subtle effect on bystanders, too, causing those who may feel sympathy for victims to feel guilty and then justify their failure to respond by minimizing the seriousness of the harm in their own minds. This serves to further distance bystanders from victims and encourages a sense that those suffering must somehow deserve it.

Works linking the psychology of genocide to elite manipulation[41] note three psychological switches concerning the victims. (1) Victims lose their marginal status and are viewed as outsiders and hence people to whom in-group rights and obligations no longer apply. (2) Victims become seen as threats to the political community. (3) This struggle between victims and perpetrators assumes the tone of an epic battle, with groups that are victimized being seen as controlled by powerful outside external forces or as carriers of biological contagion. Genocidalists in Rwanda-Burundi, for example, spoke of "killing cockroaches." Jews during the Holocaust were referred to as diseased. In both instances, as in other genocides, ethnic cleansings or even racism, the legitimacy of a group's claim to dominance or territory[42] originated in the perpetrator's belief in previous wrongs.[43] These are but two illustrations of how members of the out-group become dehumanized and thus may be treated in violation of all existing legal and ethical norms for dealing with fellow human beings.[44]

THE ROLE OF IDENTITY

Much of the empirical work drawing on actual instances of genocidal violence, from Bosnia to Rwanda and Armenia, focuses scholarly attention on the importance of psychological factors, such as symbols and myths[45] expressed in stories that reveal who people believe themselves to be.[46] This work highlights the importance of identity or self-image for ethical behavior.

At the individual level, identity, the self, and character are long-standing scholarly concepts dealing with ethics,[47] beginning with Aristotle's emphasis on developing a good moral character and reflected in contemporary philosophy as virtue ethics.[48] Adam Smith made sympathy[49] the foundation of moral sentiments, and contemporary psychologists concerned with empathy have extensive findings attesting to the importance of putting one's self in the place of another for a wide range of ethical activities.[50] This rich literature on what we might think of as the moral psychology—defined as referring to that part of our psyches that addresses moral and ethical issues—ranges from psychological experiments on justice and altruism,[51] helping,[52] cooperation,[53] whistle blowing,[54] volunteering,[55] and sharing[56] at one end of a moral continuum and extends to work on prejudice and discrimination,[57] ethnic violence,[58] genocide,[59] and evil[60] at the opposite ethical pole.

Some of this influence operates via individual personality factors. (Witness research highlighting psychopathology and sadism among perpetrators.[61]) Other works retain the importance of individual personality characteristics but combine these with social psychological factors—the environmental influences that draw forth certain types of behavior or parts of our personalities[62]—or note the interplay between certain personality characteristics and external social forces.[63] In the move beyond simple microexplanations stressing individual psychopathology (*The Authoritarian Personality*) or group-level explanations that stress mob psychology,[64] political psychologists have increasingly developed explanations based on assumptions underlying a theory called social identity theory, which emphasizes the importance of an in-group/out-group dynamic.

Social identity theory was formulated by Henri Tajfel,[65] a Polish Jew who was studying chemistry at the Sorbonne when World War II began. Tajfel served in the French army and was captured by the Germans, who did not realize Tajfel was Jewish. He survived World War II in a series of prisoner-of-war camps, returning to Poland only to learn that few of his friends, and none of his immediate family, had survived the Nazi Holocaust. One can only wonder how Tajfel's wartime experience influenced his later work, but all of Tajfel's studies[66] inquired about the psychological basis of the kind of prejudice and discrimination lying at the heart of the Holocaust.[67]

Tajfel and his collaborators, in what became known as the Bristol School, based their work in an extensive collection of psychological experiments. Although Tajfel and his colleagues were acutely aware of the importance of social context for human psychology, their experiments tried to isolate these factors to determine whether conflicts of interest were necessary to produce in-group hostility toward others.[68] Participants in Tajfel's experiments were assigned group membership using mechanisms that were trivial. Participants were selected for groups randomly, by a coin toss or a preference for abstract art.[69] None of the criteria by which subjects were assigned group membership was something that would ordinarily be associated with a natural interest that could serve as a basis for group conflict. Once subjects were assigned to a group, individual group members were asked to allocate rewards to members of the various groups, including their own. A classic variant of the Tajfel experiments offers participants two choices. In choice 1, everyone in group A would get $5, everyone in group B would get $10, and everyone in group C would get $15. In choice 2, everyone in group A would lose $5, everyone in group B would lose $10, and everyone in group C would lose $15. As most of us might expect, most participants in group A choose option 1, which gives money to members in all groups. Yet roughly one-third of the participants in the Tajfel experiments choose option 2, the option that gives their group members no money BUT which penalizes them less than it penalizes other groups.

The Tajfel studies were remarkably robust. In thousands of experiments over the years, Tajfel's students found that even these artificially created minimal group memberships serve as the basis for generating rewards of money, trust, cooperation, and affection. Even without any prior common interests to create identity, people prefer their own group members. Further, people like doing better than other groups and will choose this reward structure even if doing so means that everyone in all groups—including their own—does worse objectively. This suggests that even putting aside differences in social standing, economic and political power, or culture, in-group favoritism is a powerful force in human behavior. Identity trumps self-interest for one-third of the population studied.

Tajfel and his colleagues developed a sophisticated theory—social identity theory—to explain these empirical findings through the human desire for self-esteem and the need for belonging.[70] They argued first that people naturally categorize. We put others and ourselves into categories, labeling people as members of diverse groups. These groups then are juxtaposed in pairs, such as men or women, young or old, rich or poor, friend or foe, or, in the case of the Nazis, Jew or Aryan. We eventually identify and associate with certain groups, which Tajfel called in-groups. Doing so plays an important role in our need to bolster our self-esteem, and provides a sense of security and belonging. As part of this process, we compare our in-groups with other groups, and find a favorable bias toward the group to which we belong. Social identity theory thus roots prejudice, discrimination, and the violence that can result from it in an innate psychological need for distinctiveness. We desire our identity to be both distinct from and compared positively with that of other groups. The critical intellectual traction of social identity theory lies in establishing a clear link between the psychological and sociological aspects of group behavior, in effectively linking the microlevel psychological need to distinguish, categorize, and compare groups with the broader, social phenomenon of group behavior.[71] This framework thus provides a valuable beginning point for understanding how important both real and perceived differences can become when encounters between individuals are conceptualized as encounters between group members.

Social identity theory is found at the heart of the classic description of the process by which group identities crystallize into genocide.[72] It underpins later work[73] outlining how this process makes each group the enemy of the other and how groups effectively limit individual choice by setting what is appropriate behavior for group members.[74] More generally, Bar-Tal and colleagues note the importance for shared group beliefs and how these group and/or societal beliefs relate to the sociopsychological foundations of both intractable conflicts and their resolution, including reconciliation. The kind of collective memory and an ethos of conflict act as mechanisms to maintain and institutionalize conflicts, even those going back centuries, as was the case in the Balkans. These group beliefs frequently crystallize into social identity and the development of cultures of conflict.

One contention is that genocide erupts when ethnic identities become reified and boundaries harden into politicized identities, as opposed to less polarizing cultural identities.[75] Still other analysts find that merely the creation of a group can result in members becoming caught up in a genocidal dynamic,[76] with this process heightened when identities are codified into formalized power sharing arrangements.[77]

Research specifically on the diverse responses to genocide breaks into work on perpetrators, bystanders, and those who try to save the intended victims. While it is useful analytically to speak of rescuers, bystanders, or perpetrators as separate categories, in reality the boundaries between the groups are more porous. Hence, as we think about differences among the three groups we must note the extent to which bystanders occasionally rescue, rescuers relate instances when they did not help, and—perhaps the most bizarre phenomenon—stories of perpetrators who save one member of a group while massacring others.[78]

RESCUERS

The earliest work on rescuers was descriptive and biographical, often in the form of memoirs by rescuers.[79] The first social science works[80] to focus directly on rescuers' motivations were correlational, asking about a wide variety of sociocultural influences, from religion and social class to education or gender. Over time, however, sociocultural correlates proved inconclusive; the predictors were too sensitive to the particular instance to be dispositive. Sociodemographic correlates of rescue behavior now appear to serve more as trigger mechanisms, stimulating what are the critical psychological forces driving rescue behavior.[81] This may explain the variance and disagreement in early studies since one trigger mechanism (for example, religion or gender) could prompt rescue acts in one person while another trigger (for example, duty or education) might activate it for another person, or even for the same person at a different point in time.

As analysts zeroed in on the psychological component of rescue behavior, they tended to focus initially on general psychological factors, such as the thrill of adventure involved in rescuing or a sense of social marginality[82] in which the rescuer felt an empathic bond with the persecuted because of the rescuer's own feeling of being an outsider.[83] In 1986 survivor Nechama Tec identified what now seems the key personality factor: the sense of self. Tec argued that rescuers had a strong sense of individuality or separateness and were motivated by moral values that did not depend on the support or approval of other people so much as on their own self-approval. That same year, *The Courage to Care* further highlighted identity and character, arguing that rescuers "had to do it because that's the kind of people they were."[84] Significantly, the Academy-Award-nominated documentary of the same title[85] included interviews from both survivors and rescuers. The fact that both these groups identify the same critical concept is noteworthy. A critical methodological question when dealing with memories, especially of traumatic events, has been whether past action, caused by an unknown factor, may lead to rescue activity that in turn engenders the set of attitudes, personality, or perspective noted years later by the analyst as explanatory.[86] The fact that survivors—people who were there at the moment of decision, as it were—also note the extent to which character trumped choice is reassuring for analysts who arrived at the same conclusion utilizing data collected years after the event.[87]

The first important systematic analysis of rescuers supported findings establishing identity as the critical force driving rescue behavior. *The Altruistic Personality*[88] was the largest survey of rescuers ever conducted, including 406 rescuers, 126 nonrescuers, and 150 rescued survivors throughout the Third Reich, and remains a classic in the field. The Oliners isolated the importance of identity, particularly the kind of broad, inclusive identity that connects to a shared humanity. This particular conceptualization of identity was essential for engendering cooperation and strong communal connections. An "altruistic personality" was defined as one in which behavior encouraged by parents or other significant role models eventually led to habits of caring that effectively became structured as an altruistic personality. This finding supports philosophical work on virtue ethics,[89] stressing the ethical importance of the development of character, and suggests these habits included tolerance for differences among people and a worldview characterized by the Oliners and their collaborators as "extensivity."[90] The psychological importance of reinforcing empathic and humane behavior was reinforced by Fogelman, who found a series of correlational factors associated with rescue behavior but who also stressed psychological factors related to the sense of self.[91] Fogelman found that rescue activity was driven by multiple motives, ranging from a moral code or religious faith to duty or even particular fondness for Jews. In terms of identity, Fogelman found rescuers undergo a transformative encounter that effectively creates a different persona, a rescuer self that allows otherwise normal people to lie, cheat, or even kill if necessary. This transformed self is critical for Fogelman, providing rescuers the ability to maintain the kind of double life Lifton (1976) identified—ironically—as critical for perpetrators. This transformation, however, while designed to help save life, often involved the rescuer in unethical behavior, such as lying or murder.

My own work on rescuers—*The Heart of Altruism* (1996) and *The Hand of Compassion* (2004)—also emphasizes the self-concept but highlights the importance of the rescuers' perceptions of themselves in relation to others, suggesting it was not simply character but also the rescuer's perceptions of the relationship toward the person in need that was critical. I found identity perceptions created a sense of what I called moral salience, the feeling that another's suffering was relevant for the actor and hence necessitated action to help alleviate that suffering. I located the power of this psychological phenomenon in the mind's need to categorize and classify information, with people thus being classified into alike or different, friend or foe, member of an in-group or an out-group, and so on, in the fashion described by Tajfel. For rescuers, the boundaries of this classification system were broad and inclusive, including all humanity. Later analysts developed this concept into a psychological scale that usefully predicted volunteer activity[92] and altruism in both the United States and Poland.[93]

BYSTANDERS, SUPPORTERS, AND PERPETRATORS

The self-concept seems critical for all groups involved in genocide. Ervin Staub, Daniel Bar-Tal, and James Glass each note the importance of the self for perpetrators. Passive bystanders can distance themselves from victims and even subtly justify the acts of perpetrators.[94] Gobodo-Madikizela (2003) reinforces findings[95] on bystanders' lack of choice, linking this to the actor's sense of ontological security.[96] This draws on Brewer's (1999) argument, that the key process driving behavior captured by social identity theory is security more than self-esteem. An individual's feelings of vulnerability appear reinforced by the system's de-legitimization of the "other" and the creation of the enemy as someone to fear,[97] by viewing one's self as a victim of circumstance, poverty, or fear, or by living in an environment that is a high-pressure crisis system, such as South African apartheid or the Caribbean during slavery.[98] In such systems, bystanders find few resources to resist the political repression justified as necessary to control the enemy. Browning's (1992) analysis of non-Nazi reserve order policemen in Poland illustrates how this process can turn bystanders into perpetrators and, unlike Goldhagen's (1996) re-analysis of these data, draws on social psychological theory to explain the police-men's behavior. Browning stresses the policemen's sense of isolation, which was heightened by massive propaganda, and the extent to which the Nazis consciously manipulated the men to instill a strong group identity as members of an alien group under attack by partisans in the neighboring area. This psychological ma-nipulation made it easier for the Nazi high command to encourage ordinary men to engage in mass killing of Jews. Thus did ordinary people become killers through a process of group identification as potential victims who needed to kill others before they themselves are attacked and killed.

Staub's work underlines the evolutionary nature of behavior and the power of bystanders to frame an event so that people do—or do not—take responsibility for another's suffering. If people object at the initial stages of prejudiced legisla-tion and policies, minor transgressions do not develop into genocidal atrocities. There are crucial junctures in the escalation, with the perception of the events, the victims, and the bystanders' ability to withstand the escalating discrimination all being critical.

While there are many factors that contribute to perpetrators' behavior—ideological commitment, misunderstanding the full magnitude of what they're doing, stunted moral conscience, deeply held grudges, material reward, ven-geance, inability to control violent impulses or tendencies, following orders—Neil Kressel (2002) offers an interesting way of classifying genocidal acts, one that relies heavily on identity and the self-concept: crimes of submission versus crimes of initiative. Crimes of submission are more passive, operating out of fear, a weak sense of agency, or role-playing. This allows perpetrators to distance themselves from the acts they're committing and makes them feel more driven by events than by their own initiative. (We shall find this psychological process with bystand-ers.) Crimes of initiative connote a more active role, including a stronger sense of agency, lack of shame, enthusiasm for the job, even idealism. Crimes of initiative also encompass those motivated by hateful ideology and those who have difficulty controlling violent passions.[99]

In thinking about perpetrators, I found categorization theory useful in identify-ing the subtle process of recategorization through which a perpetrator distances a neighbor, slowly turning a friend and fellow citizen into "the other" who is now seen as threatening and against whom violence as self-defense thus becomes justi-fied.[100] Drawing on linguistics and cognitive science categorization theory is more basic than the social identity version, although the basic parameters correspond. It argues that categorization is basic to thought, perceptions, action, and speech. Categorization is automatic, unconscious, and applies to actions (eating) as well as to things (trees). We recognize abstract entities (truth, justice) as well; hence, almost everything we do involves categories, with reasoning closely tied to cat-egorization. Therefore we need to understand how people categorize in order to understand how they think, reason, and function.

My prior work (2004) utilized the concept of recategorization primarily to refer to the psychological process of excluding group members, as when bystanders re-classify Jewish neighbors to make them members of an out-group with whom one has no ties of affection or commonality. But the concept also can work the other way; members of a different group can be reclassified to now belong to the in-group. This recategorization can become an important part of conflict resolution. A positive recategorization occurred when former enemies in Western Europe became part of a European Union in a process that led to peaceful conflict resolution. A recategorization that led to hostility is the breakup of the former Yugoslavia into independent and "different" states in the Balkans.[101]

I found strong evidence of categorization in work on perpetrators of sectarian violence during the Lebanese civil war, where subjects also demonstrated this distancing and dehumanization of "the other" that occurs during war and ethnic violence.[102] We traced a direct line between such categorization and the deterioration of minor felt hurts and underlying prejudice that flares into open acts of willful violence and brutality. Helen Fein's (1993, 2007) work on moral exclusion also highlights assumptions about who belongs and who should be protected. It reinforces the importance of the concept of moral salience[103] suggesting the cognitive process of categorizing others as "friends" or "foe"; this process thereby creates (or fails to create) a feeling of moral salience that requires action, not just a generalized feeling of concern or sympathy. This raises the question of whether a modification in social identity theory might be in order. In particular, we may need to focus on what causes a difference (such as being Jewish or Aryan) to be perceived as morally salient, not simply ask if a difference is ethically and politically trivial or insignificant, as was the distinction for Jews and Aryans for most people before Hitler took power.

The literature thus suggests distinctions between "us and them" occur for both rescuers and perpetrators.[104] It further finds people do not begin with sharp cognitive distinctions. People learn about differences and cognitively create differences by valuing or devaluing others. People who are judged "different" frequently become further devalued, ignored, dehumanized, and eventually even killed because it is perceived as the "right" thing to do. One striking illustration of this psychological phenomenon is provided by the public health officials during the Holocaust. Doctors sworn to save life instead acted to protect what they saw as the good German body politic from the foreign vermin who infested it.[105] Ironically, this insight from the spread of disease may provide the clue to how the cognitive categorization process can be reversed, moving toward more positive views of "the other" as part of a process of reconciliation. Porous group boundaries;[106] an individual's embeddedness in the group;[107] and the ability to separate from, criticize, and deviate from group-proscribed behavior may constitute critical factors in reconciliation.[108]

FROM IDENTITY AND CATEGORIZATION TO COGNITIVE STRETCHING

Society's ability to set the moral tone for individuals is related to what I think of as the concept of cognitive stretching, a process whereby the previously unimaginable becomes accepted as the norm.[109] But for some people, "the horror is so unimaginable that the imagination refuses to accept its reality. Something fails to click and some conclusions are simply not drawn."[110] Individuals who cannot accept the new moral tone either resist (as rescuers did) or retreat into psychic numbing, as did many bystanders.[111] Psychic numbing demonstrates the doubling phenomenon noted among Nazis, experienced as "a form of desensitization . . . an incapacity to feel or to confront certain kinds of experience, due to the blocking or absence of inner forms or imagery that can connect with such experience."[112] The psychological "cutting off of one's sense of reality" fits nicely into the concept of cognitive stretching, the process whereby an individual is confronted with some political act so far outside the ordinary frame of reference that there literally has to be a widening of the cognitive parameters before the individual can grasp fully what is occurring.[113] Perpetrators report being "on automatic . . . in an emotional block. . . . [You] cross the border and enter the surreal . . . everything becomes a sort of a blur, but you have to move."[114] This stretching thus includes the process of "doubling" whereby perpetrators operate as a dual self, with one part of the self disavowing the other. (This process fits with Fogelman's concept of a rescuer self, one that allowed rescuers to kill people in order to protect others.) Cognitive stretching also includes the denial of genocidal events and of the actor's ability to do anything to help. We find this denial among both bystanders and perpetrators who insist they were innocent cogs in a giant machine whose purpose was unknown to them. This may be a critical part of the psychological process that results in what has come to be called the "banalization of evil."[115]

Ironically, a rationalized component of this psychology surfaces in bystander testimony. Wives of both apartheid and Nazi supporters describe happily remaining officially in the dark despite suspicions about what their husbands were doing. They tacitly, if not openly, supported the regimes' terror because their lives were good: "Whites say they didn't know, but did they want to know? As long as they were safe . . . had . . . nice houses . . . third cars and . . . swimming pools . . . they had no problem. . . . [W]hy did they never question this?"[116] Basically, then, bystanders and—to a certain extent perpetrators—live in a "self-willed, protective twilight between knowing and not knowing, refusing full realization of facts because they are unable to face the implications of these facts."[117] Primo Levi noted: "Those who knew did not talk; those who did not know did not ask questions; those who did not ask questions received no answers; and so, in this way, the average German citizen won and defended his ignorance."[118] Both survivors and scholars note that bystanders frequently feign ignorance to dodge responsibility. Both bystanders and perpetrators resort to denial, rationalization, and righteous anger at the victims for causing the mess in the first place.[119]

All these explanations are an advance on the initial focus on only the psychopathology of perpetrators,[120] and help explain the important question: why ordinary people—not just psychopaths—engage in genocide.

Research Methodology

I examine the themes in the literature summarized above and try to advance our shared scholarly knowledge by focusing on six central concepts: the self-concept, worldview, moral salience, ethical perspective, cognitive stretching, and categorization.[121] As I examine the moral psychology of people who lived through the

Holocaust, I ask: Does everyone have a general perceptual framework concerning ethical issues, or just rescuers? If everyone does have a general perspective that relates to moral issues, how does the ethical content differ for bystanders, rescuers, and Nazi supporters? These are central questions that can yield insight on genocide and ethnic cleansing as well as on related forms of prejudice and discrimination.

INTERPRETIVE NARRATIVE

My analysis utilizes an interpretive narrative methodology. What does this mean? A narrative is essentially a story, a term more often associated with fiction than with political science.[122] Yet narrative also refers to the ways in which we collect disparate facts in our own worlds and weave them together cognitively into a design that helps us find order, and perhaps even meaning, in our reality. Since these narratives help us understand ourselves as political beings, narrative becomes an invaluable tool for revealing how people navigate the myriad of sensations that bombard them daily. Insofar as narratives affect our perceptions of political reality, which in turn affect our actions in response to or in anticipation of political events, narrative plays a critical role in the construction of political behavior. In this sense, we create and use narratives to interpret and understand the political realities around us. We do this as individuals and we do it as collective units, as nations or groups.

The stories people tell thus provide a rich source of information about how people make sense of their lives. Narrative analysis is particularly useful in providing insight on the cognitive process and on the role of culture in shaping any human universals. Narratives are increasingly being utilized as both a concept and as a methodological tool in social science, proving especially useful in revealing sites of cultural contestation.[123]

As a research methodology, narrative is utilized in a multitude of disciplines, from anthropology and literary theory to history and psychoanalysis. It is one of the most widespread and powerful forms of discourse in human communication. It differs from other modes of discourse and other modes or organizing experience in several important ways. (1) Narrative generally requires agency. It involves human beings as characters or actors. These human beings have a place in the plot, a role in the story. When narrative emphasizes human action that is directed toward goals, it provides insight on how different people organize, process, and interpret information and how they move toward achieving their goals. (2) Narrative suggests the speaker's view of what is canonical. What is ordinary and right is discussed as the matter of fact. The unusual and the exceptional are what is remarked on. Narrative thus provides data for analysis not only in spoken responses but also in the spaces and silences. (3) Narrative requires some sequential ordering of events, but the events themselves need not be real. The story constructed may be indifferent to extra linguistic reality; it is the sequence of the sentences, the way events are recounted (rather than the truth or falsity of any of the particular sentences or of the events recounted), that reveals the speaker's mode of mental organization. How the speaker organizes events to give meaning to them is what becomes important, for it is the process of organization that reveals much about the speaker's mind. (4) Narrative requires the narrator's perspective. It cannot be voiceless. It thus moves beyond mere reporting; it suggests how the speakers make sense of the commonplace. It reveals how the speakers organize experience and reveals the distinctions people make in their everyday lives. The speakers create the context to be analyzed by drawing on what they consider relevant cultural influences. This makes the narrative contextually thick. It provides a sense of speakers' cognitive maps of themselves, both in relation to others and in the specific contexts of their described behavior.

Narrative is especially useful in revealing the speaker's concept of self, for it is the self that is located at the center of the narrative, whether as active agent, passive experiencer, or tool of destiny. In at least one sense, narratives function as autobiographical accounts given by the narrator in the present about a protagonist who bears the same name, who existed in the past, and who blends into the present speaker as the story ends. The story explains and justifies why the life went a particular way, not just causally but, at some level, morally. The narrator uses the past self to point to and explain the present and the future. This is as true on the individual level as it is on the macrolevel, when groups of people describe a common past suggesting why they have a collective identity that should be recognized by others as legitimate.

I think of the stories in this book as acting like flashes of lightning, illuminating the cognitive landscape and helping us understand how people see themselves, how they see others and the world around them, and how their cognitive perceptions influence their political acts.[124] In this sense, narratives are one of the most important tools for analyzing political data, of special value to those interested in political psychology, defined as the study of how the human minds works to influence our political behavior.[125]

Data

To detect the self-image and empathic worldview of subjects, I thus utilized a narrative interpretive analytic methodology[126] designed to reveal the psychology of ordinary people as they speak about their behavior. Their own words best reflect the mind of the speaker, his or her self image, worldview, and way of seeing and making sense of the world.[127] I spoke with many people who lived through the Nazi period, conducting over one hundred interviews. Some of these interviews were informal, with speakers asking to be interviewed off the record and with their interviews treated only as background; some interviews were taped and videotaped and transcribed. Some interviews occurred in person, others via the telephone. In a few cases, I conducted both telephone and in-person interviews.

To facilitate clarity of presentation while still revealing the complex nature of the moral psychology, I needed to focus on fewer people and reveal more of their conversations. I thus chose one unusual set of "matched" case studies that disclose the intricate nature of the "thick" ethical concepts facing people who lived through the Holocaust.[128] This process produced four related data sets from people whose actions during the war classed them as rescuers, bystanders, or Nazis/Nazi supporters.[129]

BACKGROUND INTERVIEWS

General conversations with more than one hundred people are treated as background data, used primarily to suggest topics on which to focus specific questions in more structured interviews.

FORMAL INTERVIEWS

Thirty formal interviews come from structured interviews that were taped and/or filmed, transcribed, and approved by the speaker for full public quotation.

OFF-THE-RECORD INTERVIEWS

Thirty informal interviews come from an additional thirty plus people who gave structured interviews but who did not want their interviews fully recorded, wanted parts kept "off the record" or used only as background, or who did not want to be quoted directly in print. These thirty plus informal interviews fall mostly, but not exclusively, into the category of bystanders and Nazi sympathizers. (Indeed, I was surprised at the number of rescuers who did not want their interviews discussed publicly, usually because they said they had not done enough and felt uncomfortable being put in any kind of laudatory position.)

TARGETED OR MATCHED CASE STUDY INTERVIEWS

Finally, in this book I emphasize a smaller targeted sample of individuals. I do so because the nature of a narrative analysis necessitates extensive quotations from a few individuals to reveal the full nuance of the conversation, including ambiguities, ambivalence, and statements that show exceptions to overall conclusions. Narrative offers an advantage over surveys—which allow only preset short answers to questions formulated in advance by the researcher—but requires careful selection of case studies to ensure that the few cases presented will accurately capture the critical characteristics in the general sample. The goal is to make the cases chosen truly reflective of the larger groups they represent.[130] To do this, I selected five of my thirty formal interviews to construct a fourth set of data—these I call targeted or matched case studies—and focus my analysis on this data set. These targeted case studies come from five interviews gathered using a respondent-driven snowball sample technique beginning with one particularly articulate Dutch rescuer.[131] I chose these five interviews because the speakers' remarkable sociodemographic similarities allowed better isolation and thus discernment of the influence of personal-psychological factors driving the speakers' quite different responses to the plight of the Jews in the Third Reich.[132]

CREATING A RESPONDENT-DRIVEN MATCHED SAMPLE

I began with Tony, a nineteen-year-old rescuer serving as a Dutch cavalry officer when Germany invaded Holland. Tony was bourgeois, with conservative social values and strong feelings of support for the Dutch monarchy. Tony credits some of his empathic worldview to his wartime experience; he saw heavy fighting during the Nazi invasion of Holland. His unit was guarding the Dutch government and royal family and held off the invaders long enough for the government and the royals to leave for England. Unlike other soldiers, however, Tony's military unit was held captive after the Dutch surrendered because Tony's commanding officer destroyed sophisticated equipment the Germans wanted. During this time in captivity, Tony and his friends began what he characterized as naive and entirely peaceful attempts to get information to the Dutch government in exile. Unfortunately, one of the men in Tony's unit was dating a girl whose roommate was dating a German. Tony's Dutch compatriot told his girlfriend what Tony's unit was doing; the girl told her roommate, who then told her German boyfriend. When the Germans learned of this, Tony's entire unit was rounded up and executed. Tony was one of three who escaped, and only because he was spending the night with his own girlfriend when the Nazis came to arrest him.[133] Tony thus was forced to live in hiding throughout the war, with a standing warrant for his execution. Yet despite his perilous situation, Tony worked in the resistance and saved both Jews and Allied servicemen.

I asked Tony to provide names of people with similar background characteristics. Tony's cousin, Beatrix (a pseudonym), shared many background characteristics and spent much time with Tony's family after her mother died. In terms of behavior, however, Beatrix was a bystander, living through the war as someone politically uninvolved. She told me of her marriage to a Dutch doctor, how her husband took over a medical practice from a Jewish doctor, how she and her husband then moved into the Jewish doctor's large home in Utrecht. Yet Beatrix never seemed to make a connection between her own good fortune and the Jewish doctor's plight, saying only that she didn't know what happened to him and that perhaps "he fled to South Africa" (page 95 of chapter 4). In her attitudes, worldview, self-image, and other psychological characteristics, Beatrix captures the themes commonly voiced by other bystanders I interviewed.

Tony also introduced me to a Dutch collaborator (Fritz), who shared Tony's prewar conservative opinions in favor of the monarchy and traditional Dutch values, although Fritz (a pseudonym) was working class, not bourgeois like Tony and Beatrix. Chance played a critical role in this interview. I was traveling to Holland and planning on visiting Tony and his wife, Susanne. While speaking with me on the phone, Tony mentioned a woman who lived near him and suggested I interview her, since she was the daughter of Dutch Nazis and might be interesting to speak with. "How old was she during the war?" I asked.

"Just a kid, I think. Around six or seven."

"Well, then, she wouldn't remember much," I responded. "Now, if you can find me a real Nazi . . ." I suggested, mostly in jest since at that point I had not planned on doing research on Nazis.

Tony called back a few days later to report that his friends at the Dutch Institute for War Documentation had given him Fritz's name, and we proceeded to set up the interview, conducted in the office of the Institute for War Documentation. Tony manned the camera—with the lens cover on to protect Fritz's anonymity—as I pondered the improbability of these two former enemies discussing the war so openly and with such little rancor.

Unlike Beatrix or Tony, Fritz (also a pseudonym) joined the Nazi Party, wrote propaganda for the Nazi cause, and married the daughter of German Nazis. He traveled widely and lived well during this period, which Fritz describes as one of the best times of his life. After the war Fritz lived in Germany for many years because he was afraid he would not be welcomed in Holland. When I interviewed him in 1992, Fritz indicated he was appalled at what he later learned about Nazi treatment of Jews. Nonetheless, he retains his belief in National Socialism and claims Hitler betrayed the movement. I thus classify Fritz as a disillusioned Hitler enthusiast who remains a supporter of National Socialism and Nazi ideology.

Finally, Tony used contacts at the Institute for War Documentation to obtain an interview with Florentine Rost van Tonningen. I was again visiting Holland and, by that time, had realized that I could better understand the light if I also focused on the dark, that a comparative analysis would highlight the differences and serve to create a kind of contrasting or baseline data effect. Tony told me about Florentine. (Florentine asked to be identified by her real name since she is proud of her Nazi activities; she and Tony are the only interview subjects whose real names are used. At one point, Tony decided he did not want his real name used and I have published one article quoting him by a pseudonym. Tony's wife later convinced him that he should use his real name, so all other interviews with Tony refer to him by his true first name. Except for Tony and Florentine, I have modified details of all speakers' lives to protect their anonymity.)

I wrote to Florentine, explaining that I would be in Holland and was writing a book on the Nazi period and asking if she would speak with me. She responded by fax, saying she would speak with me if we could arrange the right conditions. I naturally—naively—assumed Florentine was ashamed of her Nazi activities and I wrote back to reassure her that I respected the privacy of interview subjects, would protect her identity, allow her to use a pseudonym, modify identifying statements, and so on. She faxed back her response, saying that was all fine and good but that she had been thinking about money.

I was miffed and somewhat self-righteously outraged at the thought that I would pay a Nazi when I had never paid anyone else I interviewed. I wrote to Florentine, explaining I did not pay for interviews and figured that was the end of it. Florentine replied, however, saying, "Well, if you can't pay me, can you get me a copy of my husband's death certificate?"

This seemed an odd request. I phoned Tony, asking how it could be that the Dutch government had never given a woman her husband's death certificate. Tony was not surprised: "He was a notorious Nazi, one of the top two, and he was probably beaten to death in captivity. A death certificate that listed the cause of death would be proof of this, and the government was probably afraid the neo-Nazis would use that against them."

"But," Tony continued, "the fifty-year statute of limitations has now expired so you could probably get a copy if you were willing to pay for it. I'd guess it wouldn't cost more than 25 or 50 Dutch guilders."

I was wary, but figured that if I had learned anything from interviewing the rescuers it was to treat all people well, regardless of how you view them personally. And truth be told, obtaining a death certificate seemed like an act of ordinary compassion, so I offered to pay for finding a copy for Florentine. Tony found someone to go into the archives, search out the death certificate, and copy it. I sent Florentine the copy. She was immensely grateful and when we met, insisted on having her picture taken hugging a somewhat uncomfortable interviewer.

My discomfort came because Florentine is the widow of a top Dutch Nazi during the Hitler period. She herself remained a defiant Nazi, dedicated to telling people "the truth about what really happened." Florentine was head of the Hitler Youth for Women in Holland and was an active Nazi until she married and began raising children. Her marriage provided Florentine entrée to the top circles of the Third Reich. She described leaving her wedding to go to meet Hitler, while on her honeymoon, as one of her proudest moments. Florentine's brother headed the Dutch SS and her husband was head of the Dutch National Bank.[134] Offered the chance to be secreted to South America after the war by the Nazi leadership, Florentine and her husband elected to stay in Holland to bear witness about the war. Florentine never knew how or when her husband died, and believes—probably correctly—he was beaten or thrown to his death while imprisoned by the Allies in 1945. (Not unsurprisingly, the long-awaited death certificate did not make clear the cause of Rost van Tonningen's death.) Florentine remained a virulent Nazi all of her life, traveling as much as her health permitted to speak in favor of the Nazi cause. She expressed fierce pride in her job as former leader of the Dutch Nazi Youth for Women and was devoted to the memory of both Hitler and her husband. Her interview makes gripping, if chilling, reading but offers rare insight into the mind of an enthusiastic supporter of genocide, racism, and ethnic cleansing.[135]

These four cases are Dutch, a national emphasis that is deliberate because it offers an advantage of substantive significance. Many discussions of the Holocaust focus on characteristics deemed particularly Germanic, such as a proclivity for authoritarianism and efficiency, in explaining this genocide.[136] Highlighting Dutch cases underscores the fact that the psychological roots of genocide are deeper and more pernicious than is suggested by work focusing just on Germany. If quislings, bystanders, and Nazis existed in Holland, with its well-deserved reputation for tolerance and humanitarian treatment of refugees,[137] they can exist anywhere. Nonetheless, these four Dutch cases form only a subset of the broader sample. To demonstrate that they reflect findings from the overall sample, I occasionally supplement analysis of the case studies with quotes from formal interviews with other rescuers, bystanders, and Nazi supporters.[138]

I also supplement detailed analysis with an interview with a young German soldier for the Nazis, someone who so closely resembled Tony in background characteristics and situation during the war that he provided a valuable contrast. Kurt thus constitutes the fifth person in the matched or targeted case study interviews. Kurt shared Tony's bourgeois affluence, was also in the military and saw heavy fighting during the war. His discussion of the war on the eastern and the western fronts provides fascinating illustration of the importance of categorization for our treatment of others. Kurt never volunteered information about his political activities, and I never asked directly whether he was a Nazi, but he evidenced what seem characteristic views from bystanders whose tacit support for the Nazis allowed the regime to continue and flourish. I hence classify Kurt as a soldier who fought for the Nazis.[139]

In addition to my own close reading of these transcribed interviews, I employed four coders to review all formal interviews and note the factors they found influential in explaining the subject's wartime behavior. Coders were asked to focus on background characteristics, values, socialization, trauma that might lead to empathic awareness of others, choice, categorization, self-image, and worldviews. Coders highlighted all phrases relating to these key concepts and entered these into the N-Vivo computer program for coding qualitative data. (For example, a bystander might say: "My parents never loved me" or "My mother died when I was 10." These phrases would be highlighted and then placed in the analytical category for "family" as part of a general category of "background." A statement such as: "There was nothing I could do to help the Jews" would be designated as relevant for "choice," and so on. Quotes were stored under every category for which they were relevant.) Once all texts have been analyzed, the N-Vivo program then can list all quotes classified under each category. Each analytical category contains all the separate quotes and their speakers' names, to facilitate analysis. The general categories utilized here were quotes that lend insight on altruism, values, trauma, family background, group identity, religion, self-views, social views, worldviews, choice, and categorization.[140] Only quotes in which there was uniform coder agreement are considered in the analysis.[141]

Beyond the background I have just provided, I believe it is best to let the interviews in part 2 speak for themselves. Such an independent perusal of interviews free of editorial comment will provide a context into which the reader can both evaluate and understand my own analysis of the interview data. I thus encourage the reader to compare his or her reading with my narrative interpretive analysis of these stories, presented in part 3.

PART 2

❧

A Study in Contrasts

Rescuer: Tony (Dutch rescuer)

Tony: We all are like cells of a community that is very important. Not America. I mean the human race . . . every other person is basically you. You should always treat people as though it is you. That goes for evil Nazis as well as for Jewish friends who are in trouble.

Bystander: Beatrix (Tony's cousin)

Q. *Did you know about the concentration camps during the war?*
Beatrix: Yes.
Q. *Did you know that the Jews were being gassed?*
Beatrix: Yes. I can't tell you who told this, but my husband heard a lot . . .
Q. *How did you react to something like that?*
Beatrix: You couldn't do anything.
Q. *There was nothing you could do.*
Beatrix: No. No . . . [Long silence. . .] You could not do anything.

Soldier for Nazis: Kurt

Q. *Do you have a feeling that you were caught up in history? . . . You keep mentioning these other things repeating themselves . . .*
Kurt: Ya. Why do we do this again? . . .
Q. *But I'm hearing you express a kind of futility at doing it again and yet you kept on doing it. Does it never occur to you . . . ? [Kurt interrupted, with some vehemence.]*
Kurt: Can I change this? I have no power to change this!

Nazi Propagandist: Fritz

Q. Did you know much about what went on with the Jews?
Fritz: Not much. . . . I did know that there were concentration camps. But I didn't know what was happening there.... You stick your head in the sand, like an ostrich.
Q. You stuck your head in the sand.
Fritz: Yes, I must say now.
Q. You didn't really want to know about it?
Fritz: No.
Q. You never thought about helping anybody or trying to hide anyone?
Fritz: I hadn't the possibility to help people. I didn't see the need of it at that time. I didn't know what was happening.

Unrepentant Nazi: Florentine

Q. So you think the Christians have treated the Jews too, uh, too well throughout history? Is that what you are saying?
Florentine: We are too nice, I think. We are defenseless against them.

CHAPTER 3

◗

Tony: Rescuer

We all are like cells of a community that is very important. Not America.

I mean the human race . . . every other person is basically you. You should

always treat people as though it is you. That goes for evil Nazis as well as

for Jewish friends who are in trouble. You should always have a very

open mind in dealing with other people and always see yourself

in those people, for good or for evil both.

July 15, 1989

Q. Why don't you tell me a little bit about yourself?

Well, you told me you were studying altruism and I have very strong thoughts about altruism. I'm not talking about the suicidal type of thing. That's totally different. Risking your life, that's not a form of altruism. Personally, I'm not particularly Christian, insofar as men believing in the resurrection of the Lord and stuff like that. But I do believe that one of the most important teachings in Christianity is to learn to love your neighbor as yourself. I was to learn to understand that you're part of a whole; that just like cells in your own body altogether make up your body, that in our society and in our community, that we all are like cells of a community that is very important. Not America. I mean the human race. You should always be aware that every other person is basically you. You should always treat people as though it is you. That goes for evil Nazis as well as for Jewish friends who are in trouble. You should always have a very open mind in dealing with other people and always see yourself in those people, for good or for evil both.

Q. Where do you think you got this idea? Where do you think this came from?

Basically, I've had some very good gurus—I'll call them that—in my life. All very, very different, starting off with my parents. I didn't always get along with them but basically they gave me a good education. And I definitely got a strong sense of right and wrong from my mother. A little too strong, sometimes. I had a very interesting British nanny who taught me discipline and also a very strong sense of right and wrong, perhaps a little too much so in the old-fashioned sense. Then I was very lucky to have a marvelous high school principal who had studied at

Eton. He was very liberal in his teachings, to the point that he refused to get rid of his Jewish teachers in his high school and refused to turn anybody in [during the Nazi period]. Consequently, he himself went to a concentration camp. Later, when the Indonesians had kicked the Dutch out of the colonies, they invited him to set up their school system. This is quite remarkable considering he was basically from the enemy country. The other man who influenced me was my military commander in the School for Cavalry Officers. He was basically a pacifist who saw the military as only a last resort for defense. He was an extremely fine gentleman who taught us simple old things, like you never, ever order a soldier to do something that you have not yourself done at some stage several times. The other thing he taught us is [that if] you want to be an officer and a gentleman, [if] you want to have those privileges, that means that if there is a war, if the country is attacked, [then] you cannot look down on a soldier for being scared or for wanting to desert out of fear. But since *you* wanted to be an officer, you have to be the first one to get killed when that happens. You cannot expect it from others. That is because if you want that privilege, you have to pay for it when the time comes. That's the type of responsibility that he taught me. I guess the other guru I had was a German [film] director who had studied under Max Reinhardt. He was half Jewish and was hiding in Holland during World War II. I became his assistant. We worked together quite a bit in a workshop. He was very proud of being German. And he was *very* anti-Hitler. He was an extraordinarily intelligent man, one of the world's top experts on Shakespeare. We did all the German plays. Remember, this is during World War II, when nobody [in Holland] likes the Germans. He was very proud of German culture and thought that Hitler had betrayed all the great things of Germany. So there was always that idea of looking at "there's the good and the bad."

You cannot put labels of nationality or race on people. Just like today [the late 1980s and 1990s], I'm very unhappy with certain things the state of Israel does. I'm very upset with what they're doing to the Palestinians. I've spoken up about that in the local synagogue when I was invited to speak there. Surprisingly enough, I got a lot of backing from some of the people who were listening.

I guess, too, that a great part of my education came from [the time], during World War II, when I was condemned to death in 1941 for having hidden weapons and being part of the Underground activities and hiding Jews and American pilots and things like that. They didn't catch me. But I suddenly had to leave the wealthy, upper-middle-class family and go into hiding. That was an eye-opener. I was told right away by a friend of mine, "Look, if you're ever in trouble in town and there's a raid on the street and you have to go into a house somewhere, if you're anywhere near the red-light district, go to any of the houses of the prostitutes. They'll hide you. They don't like the system. They'll hide you."

And they would. They were risking a death penalty for that. But those women would always hide you. They were the people whom I had looked down upon socially before that. I ended up working with a variety of much lower-class people than I would ever had associated with in my previous existence. That was a great eye-opener to find that these people were in no way different. It's like the old say-ing by George Bernard Shaw: How do the poor differ from the rich? The difference is that they're just like the very rich, except that they have no money.

Q. So your wartime activities really changed your outlook on life, too.

Yes they did, to a great extent. The war was also very traumatic and very difficult. The war came during my youth. I only did one year of college study, half a year. Then I went right into the army and got stuck in there for two years before the war started in 1938 and 1939. And then I was in the resistance. So I never did get to go to college. I was self-educated after that. The war occurred during the whole time that you normally party and play and have fun. But being in hiding, I could never go to a party, never go to a show, never go to anything. You did get outside sometimes but it was a totally different life. You always have one eye over your shoulder and one eye in the back of your head. On two occasions I got stopped but fortunately I managed to talk my way out of it because of good papers.

Now, remember the place where I was hiding would vary at times. You were on a bicycle most of the time in Holland. So every night that I would come home, you'd ride around the block once, to make sure that nobody was following you. That way, if you did a full block around, you could immediately notice that some-body was tailing you. This is to protect the people where you were hiding. You'd always have a signal. For instance, normally they would have a little glass curtain that would be caught on a cactus in the window. If there was an emergency, if the police were in the building or something, the curtain would hang normally. Be-cause it is very normal for a housewife who is nervous and has cops in the house to straighten out something. But if the signal would have been the opposite, if you were to hang the curtain on the cactus if something is wrong, then any cop worth his salt would immediately notice that. But the other way around, to straighten something out, was normal.

So you would live through very tense situations. It involved a lot of personal things, too. Obviously, with all of us living there, hiding together, sexual libera-tion took place during the war. What the Americans discovered ten or twenty years ago [in the 1970s], we discovered right here in the war. Working very close with women and friends in the resistance opened you up very much to women's liberation.

I started the first women's courier service [in the resistance]. Some of the people in the military were very opposed to that idea of getting women involved. Well, the women wanted to be involved, so why not? They were better at this than the guys. Less obtrusive.

Q. Let me ask you to tell me a little bit about your early life. When were you born?

I was born June 28, 1919. I'll be seventy in a week. My mother was Belgian-born and her mother was French. My father was Dutch. We have a very long family his-tory. For instance, my paternal grandfather was a psychiatrist. I'm mentioning him because he's rather different. He started off as a Navy doctor. He sailed around the

Cape in Navy sailing ships and was in the Indian wars; things like that. He became one of the very first hypnotist doctors. Later on he became a psychiatrist and was a very close friend of Freud and Jung. He translated the older works of Ellison, Freud, and Jung.

My mother's father was a military man who worked his way up from a farm boy to a general. He became the first military commander in the Belgian Congo when that colony was turned over from a private possession of the king. The king was forced to turn it over to the Belgian government. My Belgian granddad was a friend of Stanley, of the Livingston and Stanley. I have other relatives going all the way down the Battle of Waterloo. It's a bourgeois family. The one side had military and the other had medical people. They started off as fairly simple country doctors, all the way back to 1650.

My father was not a doctor. He was a dentist. He was a top dentist but that was already a slight betrayal of the family's medical tradition. Of course, I couldn't go to college because of the war. When the war was over, I wasn't about to go spend another eight years [to go] through medical studies.

I'm the only child. I grew up in Amsterdam. We traveled a fair amount in Europe, mostly going to Brussels and Paris, sometimes to Switzerland, but not much beyond that. In some ways it was a very happy childhood, in others not. I was very spoiled in material things. My mother was a social climber. She would have liked very much to have been part of the aristocracy or the upper-upper classes. But she was not. My father was a wealthy dentist so she always played the upper-class game whenever she could. She had lots of antiques and lots of money and status symbols around. I was never very much into that.

I was a lonely child. Because I was an only child, my mother was very protective and I was a mama's boy for quite a while. To give you an example, when I finally went to high school, which was my first moment of liberation, she insisted I wear my sailor suit. This was as bad as [it would be to] wear a sailor suit when going to high school nowadays! But it had an odd effect. It did teach me to live through situations that are painful. To not give a damn about what people think of you and just do what you think is right. But I had a very rough time in high school in the beginning because of that.

So the army was a liberation for me. It was a chance to outgrow my sissiness a little bit. Then the beginning of World War II was a really odd liberation. I'd always been extremely realistic about matters of life and death and I'd always looked up to all the military men around me who were all bigger and smarter and better, better at horseback riding or whatever it was. When the war started, I was totally at ease with the situation. I was ready to be killed if I had to be. But left and right around me, all these officers that I had always looked up to, so many of them fell apart because they were not very imaginative. They had no idea what the war would be like when it happened. To me, the war was exactly what I expected it to be.

I have always been extremely realistic about life and death. You're born. You live. And it's the game you play, the game of life. You play it as well as you can. Then at the end, you get your reward and you die and you don't have to struggle any more. This happens to be my own philosophy. It's not what you get out of life. It is not the rewards you get. The reward is peace when you die. Life begins like entering a very tough tennis tournament. You only do it, not for the money, you do it for the fun of playing that game and playing it as well as you can. That's my life's philosophy basically. We all know that the game won't last forever. It's like going to see a good movie. You know it's going to end and after that you go to sleep. And that's sort of a time to relax. It's time to rest, like going to sleep.

I guess I believe in an afterlife, though not in the standard Judaic-Christian idea of men today. It's more like the old Judean idea. It's like the one I just described, that you go to sleep. I don't believe in an afterlife of a Heaven or Hell where you sit around on a cloud and play the harp. No. I think that the world is a world of energy that is like a cell in the body of creation. I see the whole world as one living body basically. But not our world only. The whole universe. And I'm like one of the cells. So I'm as much a part of that as others. Without me, the universe doesn't exist any more than my body exists without its cells. So I'm part of a whole and I will go back into that part, in the Indian philosophy sense. Whether any consciousness remains, we'll find out. I'm not convinced one way or the other. It could be. I'm not in a position to judge that. I'll be very interested to find out, if I am in a position to find out.

Where was I? Well, I started doing a study for notary public. My mother wanted me to get a very safe, prestigious job in Europe. In Europe, if you're a notary public, you are an official, like the mayor of the town. You're appointed by the city and it's like a legal job, like being a top-level attorney. All the contracts, all the wills, everything has to go through you. You have the job for life.

I hated the idea. But I did six months of that study. I started it and then I decided I'd rather do my military service first and then finish my studies later on, hoping I could get away from that particular job. I wanted to be in the motion picture business. That was my idea, an idea which, of course, went over like a lead balloon with the family. So I went into the army.

I was actually doing my military training in the School for Cavalry Officers when the war began. This is again a very interesting story. My mother was very anxious that I go into this particular division because her father had been a general, and the horse cavalry is very prestigious. It's like the Guards' regiments in England. I entered during the last year of the horse cavalry. We were mechanized a year later and I ended up in a motorcycle regiment, because the horses were past history. But it was a very socially prestigious situation to be in. This again was very educational for me because I was there with all the "Vons" and "counts" and all that. I was one of only two members who didn't have a title. They certainly let you feel that! So my mother's social climbing in that sense was an unpleasant element for me.

When the war broke out, I was in the 1st Regiment of Motorized Hussars. We happened to be transferred from the German border to just north of The Hague [between Amsterdam and The Hague] the night before the war started because they expected to have a landing of paratroopers. The Dutch knew exactly what was going to happen [when the war began]. It was no surprise at all. There was one regiment between the royal family and the government in Hague, and [the

spot] where some 5,000 German paratroopers landed. Thanks to our good training, we had about 50 percent casualties, but so did the Germans. More important,
we prevented the Germans from reaching the city of The Hague and the Dutch
royal family. It was vital that this be done. Very vital. The royal family had to have
a chance to get away to England and set up the government in exile. The Dutch
Navy and Merchant Marines had to get its ships out of the harbors and to England
to continue the war. The Germans were very anxious to capture those ships. They
wanted to capture all the Dutch Navy, which was still in port. If they could capture
the Dutch royal family then they could have had a hold on them and it would have
been easier for them to govern Holland. Preventing that was our main assignment.
Once the invasion started, we didn't really sleep much for four days. It was constant nonstop combat with these paratroopers. We suffered very heavy losses, but
we won. And the royal family and the Navy and the Merchant Marines got away.

On the fourth day, the Germans finally surrendered to us. Then, a half a day
after that, when the whole Dutch Army capitulated, the war was lost. I remember
that we talked to our German POWs. We said, "Look, guys. Basically now we are
your prisoners of war." The Germans were rather realistic, just like we were. They
said, "Go on home and go to sleep and we'll talk about it tomorrow."

That evening our commanding officer gathered together the whole regiment
and all our state-of-the-art equipment. There was quite a dramatic pile-up of all
the equipment. He just opened the gasoline tank truck and let it drain into the
field, with all the ammunition and everything on it. Then he himself threw a hand
grenade on it and ran. It was one big bonfire that banged all through the night.

When the main German forces reached us (not the paratroopers but the high-
level command), when they got into the area, they called him in and took him
prisoner right away. They told us that we were POWs. We had to go to a place east
of Holland and then they held us there for about two months. We later on found
out they executed our commanding officer. The other Dutch troops were allowed
to go home. After two months they finally released us all and said that since we
were of Germanic blood they hoped we would join in the effort of Hitler for the
Germanic people, and so on. Then we went home.

Several of us, in the short time between the truce and the time that the Germans
completely incarcerated us, buried a lot of our weapons. After we were released,
we went back and dug up some of them. We had other friends we knew from high
school who were army officers. Through them I got to know a group of officers
who were trying to figure out what to do. You know, there wasn't much resistance
we could do at the time. You heard some talk about what's going to happen to Holland if the Germans ever lose and the Communists take over the world. There was
that element. But nobody really had worked anything out.

We decided we should hide some of our friends who were in trouble and dig
up some of those weapons in case. Maybe we should get in communication with
England. Maybe we should get somebody to go over there and set up a code. It was
all very vague at that time. We were so klutzy about all this. We were terribly naive
about that type of thing. Nobody is more naive than army officers. We were only

twenty-one, too. People tend to forget that you're just kids. Then, too, I was not a typical Dutch kid. I was a spoiled little rich boy. I was shy. I was a bit of a sissy.

But I was a careful person and I had read a lot and I was very realistic. I had a vivid imagination. I fully imagined the war to be just exactly what it was going to be, with people being blown to bits and all that. So when the war started, I was not at all surprised, whereas several of the other army officers I was around—real sportsmen who were very much into horse jumping, for example—were totally flabbergasted. They had not expected war to be what war was. They were more the "rah-rah" military. Several of them went to pieces when it started. I was always very phlegmatic about living or dying. I always figured if I got to die, I got to die. I was not terribly afraid of dying. That's maybe a weird thing and I don't know where I got that. Certainly I was never reckless at all. If anything, I was a little chicken and a little overly careful. But the idea of death itself was never something that frightened me.

So this is how we—some eighty army officers—started a very primitive little resistance movement. Mostly we just were talking about it, not knowing what to do exactly. But a girlfriend of one of our guys was rooming with another girl who was dating a German soldier and, well, things leaked out. The Germans managed to get an address list for all of us. We hadn't learned how to do these things intelligently yet.

The Germans came to everybody's home during curfew. I was one of the lucky three who was not at home that night. I was spending the night with a girlfriend. I got a quick call from somebody saying, "Don't ever go home again because they want to pick you up."

The other seventy-seven officers were all executed. So that changed the situation a little bit. Up until then, it was almost a game, you know, this little resistance movement. But the executions suddenly showed us the total realities of what the German occupation was going to be like. It's like the [Chinese] students are finding out now [summer 1989] in Beijing, on a minor scale. So I had to find hiding places, which was not hard because most people in Holland were very opposed to the Nazis. There was only 1 percent of the Dutch population who were in the Nazi party in Holland. For the rest of the people, 49 percent didn't want to get involved with anything one way or the other. The other 50 percent, even if they didn't do anything active in the resistance, their sympathies were very strongly against the Germans. So you had a good 50/50 chance of ringing any doorbell and having people hide you.

After I was condemned to death, I went to various friends whom I knew. It took a while to get false papers. But after a while I had good false identity papers and I could get back on the street. And, oh, of key importance, I had a friend who worked in the National Archives where they keep all the ID cards. In Holland, every person has something like a driver's license, but without being a driver. You have to have an ID card. My friend in the National Archives lifted my master card out of the files. So I didn't exist. We did that with several people in the resistance. On paper, I no longer existed.

Q. So you originally were in a political resistance? You didn't start rescuing Jews and then get involved in the resistance?

No. Originally the trouble with the Jews did not start right away. The Nazis knew they had to play it safe. I'm trying to remember the exact dates when it really started with the Jews. I don't remember, but it started out very calm. First of all, nothing was going to be done against the Jews. I heard a lot of Jews expected that it might continue that way. Then they [the Germans] brought up a form. They said, "Just for identity purposes, we want to know everybody who is of the Jewish faith. We want to know what your background is. Because we know that the Jewish people don't like the Germans. We just want to be sure to know who you are and where you are." The Jews signed voluntarily. Well, they were effectively told [to do it] so it was not really voluntarily. Everyone was given the form that marked how many Jewish ancestors you had, whether you were religious, if you were going to a synagogue, and all that.

I had a lot of Jewish friends because my high school had a lot of Jews and Amsterdam had a population of close to between 10,000 and 15,000 Jews, which is almost something like 8 percent or 10 percent of the population. Right then and there, I told all my Jewish friends, "You don't look Jewish. Why would you turn yourself in this way?" It's one thing if you're very Semitic looking because there was a penalty if you didn't fill it in. You go to a concentration camp. So I suggested, particularly to friends who didn't look that Jewish, I said, "Don't fill the stupid thing in. Let them do the work. Why turn yourself in that way?" Some of them did and some of them didn't.

So in the beginning not much happened. Then inch by inch, the Jews weren't allowed in certain restaurants. Then they were taken out of certain businesses for "security reasons." Then it changed. They were not allowed to use the movie theaters, not allowed to go to a regular restaurant. They had to go to their own restaurants, their own movie theaters. Gradually they lost all their businesses. First they had a German manager with the business and they could still be involved with it. Then they were kicked out. It was all done gradually.

But the most evil thing that the Nazis did was to form the Jewish Council. They got some very wealthy upper-class Jews in Amsterdam. The last one was Mr. Asscher. They put him in charge of the Jewish Council. The idea was that these upper-class Jews would organize the situation of the Jews. They would be the spokesmen for the Jewish community. Mr. Asscher had been a friend of Hermann Goering. He'd sold him a lot of diamonds at the time and they developed a friendship because Goering was always interested in intelligent Jews. In *rich*, intelligent Jews. What the Germans made this Jewish Council do was to encourage all the Jews to follow all the German orders and organize their own departure later on. They'd do it in an organized manner.

First they were going to "country work camps." The idea of the Germans was that the Jews had been too much in the money business and too much into diamonds and jewelry and stock market, all those things that were from a social point of view less desirable. The Nazis said, "These [Jewish] people should learn to be real people and work on farms, work on the land like the Dutch farmers." This kind of stuff.

That type of propaganda was not totally disliked by certain people in Holland. You must remember that like any highly visible group, any ethnic group, there's always a percentage of people who are less desirable, that can be very obnoxious. You know, like 90 percent of the Jews would be very, very well liked, very nice. But then there was a percentage of Jews who were living very high. They had very high-profile lives, throwing around too much money. Too much property. Those are the ones that came out of Germany or out of Russia with quite a bit of money and could be sort of arrogant. There was a percentage of Jews who did that. And, of course, the result was that there was a certain anti-Semitism against those people in the society. Not against Dutch Jews, who had been in Holland forever. Even Dutch Jews were a little anti-Semitic about some of these German and Russian Jews who would come with a lot of money and who had left everybody else behind. So it was a very intricate thing.

But you wanted to know how I got started helping Jews. My parents knew a lot of Jews. My father had a lot of wealthy Jewish clients. When the war started and when the trouble started with them, my father tried to help some of his Jewish friends. A couple that I remember in particular was a lady who owned a big department store, like the Robinsons or Macy's or something like that. We helped them and their kids.

We had an interesting story there. There were two friends of mine. The one was a very fine musician. He had played with The Quintet, The Hauf Club, The France. He was just a young guy. His brother was studying to be an attorney. A couple of years after the beginning of the war, we said, "Look, you got to get out of here. You're going to get killed," because they were to go to concentration camp Westerberg. We helped the one guy to get out with his girlfriend. But the nicer of the two, the musician, said no. His girlfriend has been picked up and she was in this labor camp; he said it wasn't going to be all that bad and he wanted to be with her in that labor camp. He didn't want to leave her alone and escape. So he went to the Westerberg Labor Camp, which, of course, was the first staging area for being sent to German camps, to the death camps. He was never heard of again. His brother survived and ended up going to Cuba, I think. He came back after the war. He never became an attorney; he became a driving instructor. It shows you the strange things that happen.

Now, all of this situation as I mentioned earlier, the stress of those four years during the occupation—always being in hiding, always being looked for, and surviving—but because I was surviving, surviving by being always on my toes and being a good actor the times when I got caught, I had no problem with that at all during the war. But two or three months after the end of the war, it expressed itself in a nervous breakdown. The girlfriend I was dating, she wanted to get the hell out of Holland, too. I can fully understand now. She ended up marrying an American and took off.

A lot of things happened. We'd had such high hopes for the Dutch government. We thought that we were fighting this great cause and that we would have a great country after the war. We'd volunteered to go fight the Japanese, but they [the Dutch government] didn't want us to do this at the time. Then they called us up eight months later to go fight the Indonesians, who were our old best colonies and who had been literally liberated by the Japanese from the Dutch colonial system. The Indonesians didn't want to go back to a colonial system. I was very upset about that. I thought that we should let them have their freedom and work with them as friends. There was a good possibility of doing that. So I was really disappointed in the Dutch government at the time.

I had gotten a medical discharge because of my nervous problems. But I didn't want to stay in Holland and I came to America. So that's how I came here. I never went back to Holland, not until 1958 when I was technical advisor for the movie, *The Diary of Anne Frank*. Except for that one visit, I never went back until last year [1988] when my wife desperately wanted to go. I sort of settled the old account.

The Dutch government, after forty years, had sent me a medal. And the Israeli government, God knows why, sent me a medal after forty years too, from the Yad Vashem. It came out of nowhere. As I said, I was a little unsure whether to accept that or not because I was so upset about what Israel is doing right now to the Palestinians. But I decided that there are good people in Israel and there are bad people in Israel and that I really felt that the medals were handed out by the good people so I didn't want to be rude to them. I certainly didn't want to do anything against them.

Q. So you distinguish between just and unjust causes and just wars and unjust wars?

Not war. I believe in good people. It's very difficult to explain. To give you an example about good and bad, it's so hard to define. I differentiate in my own mind between what I consider righteous and what I consider bad. Not whether it's done by a German, by an American, by a Jew, by an Arab; that's irrelevant. I've been in those countries. I've spent time in Israel; I've spent some time in Arab countries. The people are the same on both sides. It's the culture. It's the education. It's the economies. They could all get together if they wanted to. But education works so strongly against it. There's propaganda in education.

I give you a perfect example. I saw the impact of educational propaganda on the last day of World War II, when the German Army capitulated to the resistance movement. The SS has been pretty wiped out by this time. They wanted to fight to the end but there was only a small group of them left in the Gestapo. The resistance wanted to attack the Gestapo buildings—there were about one hundred guys still in there—and wipe them out. We had a little talk about it and I said, "Look, I think this is nonsense. They're well fortified there. They have plenty of arms. If we attack them, we're going to lose a lot of people. This is the last day of the war. The war is over. Why do we have to do that?"

They said, "Well, they're shooting at people."

I said, "Let's solve it in a different way. They are just as scared as we are. I don't like the Gestapo but why doesn't somebody go over and talk to them?"

They said, "Yeah, who wants to do that!"

"Okay. I'll go. I don't think, if I go alone and unarmed and I dress in such a way that they don't know whether I'm a German or a Dutchman, I'm sure I can get to ring the doorbell and I'll talk to them."

I did exactly that. They didn't shoot at me. I got in. I said, "Look, I'm a liaison officer from Allied Headquarters and I'm here to discuss your surrender so that there's no unnecessary bloodshed either on your side or on our side." I lied a little bit there. I was introduced to the commanding officer, who was a twenty-year-old dressed up as a Gestapo lieutenant.

I asked him, "Hey, where's the commanding officer?

He said, "Oh, Colonel L. He got on a plane and he escaped to Germany." It turned out that the entire staff had escaped.

"Well, what are you doing here?"

He shrugged. "Somebody has to be in charge of the men."

"Well, I think I can talk to you," I told him. It turned out that he was a guy who had been raised in the Hitler movement since he was a small boy. He was totally impregnated with all these ideas of Nazism. He was basically not even a bad guy. He was a little like one of the marines at My Lai. But he was following orders. We made a full arrangement that solved all the problems and when I left, he said, "I wish so much you guys had fought with us. You were Dutch. You should know about this. We could have made this a better world. You'll see. The Americans are going to come here and they're going to take over your economy. The Russians are going to move in and they're going to take all of Eastern Europe."

I thought, "He's absolutely right." I still didn't believe in his philosophy. But I could see how he had ended up being what he was and I could not hate the guy. He was the product of his environment, just like our black kids in the ghetto are. Now, this knowledge doesn't mean I don't think they shouldn't go to jail or be hung if they commit certain crimes. But I can also understand it. It's like a bad dog. You know, you have a dog. You mistreat it and it bites people. You have a dog and you treat it well and he'll grow up to be a loving, caring dog. To me it has nothing to do with race, religion, or anything else. It's people.

So that's how I got involved with the resistance. Living underground, I have a false identity. I formed my own little resistance movement of twelve guys, which was fairly well equipped. Our principles were not to go out and kill Germans but rather to do espionage. We wanted to keep a low profile because anything you did, the Germans would go and shoot hostages and unrelated innocent people. So what we did mainly was invisible: sabotage, espionage. I got then involved with a larger remnant of the resistance and then we got in contact with a variety of other resistance groups. We had the Communists. The Socialists. The religious people. The military people. Students. They all worked separately. We managed from the ground floor on up, because the guys who were the leaders of these groups were all heavy ego personalities and had trouble getting together. So we worked on the lower level. In 1944, just before the end of the war we finally succeeded, together with the people in England, to form a united resistance movement.

My rescuing Jews, that was totally on the side. Essentially, I was doing three things: (1) I was involved with a theater workshop. (2) I was fully involved with the Dutch resistance movement for espionage. And (3) I started not only the girl courier group but a film and photo unit. I thought it was extremely important to document what was going on, photographically, just like we're seeing now in China. There was a lot of opposition to this last activity because the military and the resistance leaders thought it was too dangerous to do that. So we figured out a way so it would not be dangerous. Every photograph you see in any "Time-Life" books about the occupation in Holland are all photographs that came from my photo unit. We had several exhibits after the war. They still have exhibits in Holland with our pictures. That was my main occupation.

Now, on the side of that, separately from that, there were friends of my parents who were Jewish. Or there were school chums I had known who needed false papers or they needed to find a hiding place. There was one, he was a rag and bone man. We still had them in those days, you know. He was a poor Jewish guy who was pushing a pushcart and selling and buying junk. But we'd known him and my grandfather had known him. He was our rag and bone man. He came by one day and he said, "I have some of my savings in silver that I have hidden away. Some silver candelabra. Some coins. I know that if the Germans come, I want to save my savings, if not for myself, maybe for whatever member of my family survives. Could you be kind enough to hide that for me?"

So we hid his things. He had a place he was going to hide. But he got caught. He got killed and later on we turned over his silver to a remaining relative.

Then there's another funny story. It's funny ironic, not really funny. Rudy Meyer was the head of the Amsterdam Film Studios. He was German-Jewish. He was married to a non-Jewish wife and so for a while he was safe because of being married to a non-Jewish wife. Then they changed the laws and any Jew who was married to a non-Jew, unless they had children, would still go to a concentration camp. At the same time, I knew a Jewish family who had to go into hiding. We had found a hiding place for them but the woman was very pregnant and it was very uncomfortable. It was a tight hiding place, like Anne Frank's, where they have to be quiet. It was just impossible to have a newborn baby there because the noise would give them away. So we made a deal. Rudy Meyer's wife started to walk around with pillows under her dress, looking more and more pregnant. She told everybody she was pregnant. And the other lady with the baby, the minute the baby was born, the doctor—who was in on both deals—transferred the baby and gave it to Rudy Meyer's wife. The family went into hiding and Rudy Meyer had a baby.

Now the tragic part is that the parents, the real parents of the child, several months later got caught in a raid. I guess their hiding place was not really that good. Then Rudy Meyer was caught. It was totally unrelated to his being Jewish. He was caught in a street raid for hostages. But they found out he was a Jew and they shipped him off to a concentration camp. We thought he was dead.

Six months after the end of the war—actually it was on a day when I happened to be visiting Rudy's wife and their little daughter—the doorbell rings. Here's a very skinny man with a Russian cap on, dressed in rags. Rudy had been a big fat guy. But this was Rudy Meyer! He'd survived. He'd lost two fingers but otherwise he was intact.

He had gone to a concentration camp that had been liberated by the Russians. He spoke some Russian and that made him a spokesman. He'd been taken to Moscow and held there until there was a chance to repatriate him. Like a good businessman, while he was in Moscow he managed to get the Russian distribution rights for his studio. He came back on a freighter, in rags and with his Russian cap on. He lived happily until he died a few years ago.

I don't think the daughter ever found out who her real parents were. Rudy and his wife just raised the child as their own. They raised her totally as their child. I don't even know if they told her about how she had been born. I left Holland so I lost touch with them.

So my rescue activities were separate. I divided my life into three distinct segments, as far as possible. Mostly the rescuing happened as things came up. It was loose knit. It's not that you have an organization that was that tightly knit, although we all had false identities. I knew people who had good contacts to get people across the border into Belgium and from there into France. I had Belgian relatives who had contact with the resistance movement in Belgium so that we could get somebody to Belgium. I could pass them on to my Belgian relatives, who would then be able to get them from there into the French resistance movement.

It was a very loosely knit group of people that you sometimes knew only by code names. [Sometimes] it was a personal friend. You know, I'd go and check with somebody that I knew and try to find out a place for them. I'd ask if they might be willing to take in somebody—the father of a half-Jewish girl that I had dated for a while, for example. Her father was at first in danger. They thought maybe he would be arrested so we took him in. I took him to a little country home at a lake that we had, which we had rented with a bunch of friends. We hid him there.

Sometimes when I saved people I'd do it myself, alone. Sometimes with my parents, sometimes with other friends. That's what I'm trying to say. It's all very loosely knit. Sometimes you are nothing more than a go-between, trying to find a place where someone could hide. Since I was hiding myself, I couldn't hide anybody personally, but several times I hid people short term in my parents' home. But *I* couldn't live at my parents' home. It was always done over the telephone or through various little messages. Maybe my parents went and visited me somewhere and we'd set up something. Sometimes I would set it up at a home of wealthy Dutch friends who had room. Sometimes it was my parents' home, which we used for short-term hidings. So people would not stay for a long time. They would be there for several weeks, until there was a way for them to be moved across the border.

I myself was moving around from place to place. For instance, there was the wife of one of the top pilots of the KLM. He was over in England. She was in Holland. She was fairly well to do and owned an apartment building. I was hidden there for a five-month period. A British agent from London was hidden there after he had been dropped by parachute. We had a Jewish lady and her daughter. Another Jewish friend I had brought was hidden in there. We had two kids from the resistance who were operating secretly but not underground, who didn't have to hide yet. We ended up with an American pilot and a Polish fighter pilot. We were all staying in what had been the servant rooms in this big apartment building. It was a whole block of flats. This lady didn't own the whole thing but you could move over the roofs from one building to the other and get in one building and go out through the exit of another building by going over the roof. We had people in various apartments. It was a marvelous place to hide people. Then we had hiding places built in [the separate flats]. This lady was one of the coordinators who did that. But it is not an organization as such. It's very loose knit.

Imagine this thing happening to you tomorrow here. Suppose that we end up getting a very repressive government and anybody who had protected the environment is in danger. What do I do? What do you do? You do like the students in China do now [the summer of 1989]. What do they do? They have to get false papers and they have to find a place to hide. But what do you do? You start calling your closest friends, the ones who didn't go to Tiananmen Square, and you say, "Hey, I'm in trouble. I was photographed in Tiananmen Square. I've gotta hide because they're going to pick me up and they're going to kill me."

They can't go to their parents' house because that's the first place where they'd go. So they find a fellow student, for instance, who was not quite as active as they were and whose parents are sympathetic with the cause. Maybe they haven't spoken up much about it but they may want to save this kid's life so they were willing to hide him for a while. Maybe the parents of a friend can't do it but they say they have a cousin who lives in the country and he has a farm and I can write to him and maybe he could work on the farm there for a while. That's how this operates.

Then sometimes, suddenly we'd get someone like this American. I needed a place for this American pilot immediately because he had bailed out and he had a piece of shrapnel in his leg. He needed to be operated on. We had a doctor friend who did that. But we also had to find a place [to hide the pilot]. So the first night the American slept in an office building of a friend of ours and then we moved him to this particular apartment. We pleaded with this lady, asking if we can move one more in here and she took him in. Then the next one was a Polish pilot. They were only going to be there a fairly short time, like a month or so, and then we would try to get them across enemy lines again.

It was much easier with pilots, because with pilots we have the active help of the British and the Americans. The Jews, the British and Americans were not at all anxious to take. Not Jews. The only way for Jews to get out was to go through Belgium, through France. Even Switzerland was not that helpful, though there were some who helped. Then, hopefully, we'd get them across the Pyrenees into a neutral country like Spain and then through Spanish Jews and relatives get some help and maybe go to Cuba or whatever.

The key thing to understand in this is to draw modern parallels. That's why I say Tiananmen Square is perfect example now for people to start learning what do you do. Now it's China; tomorrow it could be us. What would you do under those circumstances? That's exactly what we did. Put things in a context you can understand.

I've always been interested, ever since World War II, in understanding what caused this Nazi monster to come to be. And I finally realized, every time you see the monster, you basically are looking in the mirror.

All over the world, there's a certain attitude. It's not any one nation. It's not because they are German. It worked well in Germany because of the tradition of discipline. It doesn't work as well in Holland because Dutch people are very ornery, and horrendously independent. They'll say "screw you" and go their own way.

People get depressed because there's not much they seem to be able to do about things like the Holocaust. Well, I firmly believe that people *can* do something about it.

August 4, 1989

Q. Can you just tell me a little bit about how you view basic human nature?

I believe in man as an animal and not as a separate creative created being. As far as I'm concerned, we're dealing with differences in culture but not as human beings. I think deep down, every person has animal instincts. Through culture we've learned how to control them. Rape is a perfect example. In nature, rape would be a very normal thing because it's for the reproduction of the species. In a society, however, you cannot afford to have things like that happen. So I think that human nature is to a large extent a matter of culture. As we saw in Germany during the Nazi time, the human nature changed to quite an extent because they had different cultural objectives. That didn't mean the people individually are aware of it. Take the United States as an example. In the last eighty years in the United States, we have behaved like a colonial empire and yet the people in this country are never aware of it. The people on the receiving end think of us as villains.

Human nature to me is very much the same all over the world. It is tempered and arranged by culture. Normally, unless you deal with insane people, there are good and bad people. I think it [human nature] is almost 100 percent cultural.

Q. Human nature is like a blank slate? Is it basically good? Is it basically bad?

I don't think that nature knows good and bad. That's a religious concept that came in with the Christian church. If you deal with Hindus, if you deal with other religions, they don't have that split between good and bad or right and wrong. Nature is there for survival. It's quite right for a lion to kill his prey. But the antelope on the other end will feel very differently about it.

Q. Well, what is the characteristic of this nature? How would you describe this nature? You said survival. Is that the key?

Well, the nature of nature is basically the reproduction of the species of any culture. This again is not acceptable among each other, and you have to gradually make adjustments. I think the nature is changing, because when you reach the point where you're close to the depletion of the planet, your survival becomes different and you have to become less selfish in order to survive. I think that was the great teaching of the time of Buddha and Christ: to teach people that the time of total selfishness for survival had ended and you had to change and adapt.

It's very similar to an egg. If you think of the world as an egg and the yolk is being used up, and if you think of the human being as a cell and you change from the concept of the cell, that now becomes a multicelled animal. So the survival instincts of the cell are very different from that of the multicelled animal that learned to work together. It's a jump in evolution, as far as I'm concerned. We're right in the middle of that process with the whole world.

Q. Am I hearing you articulate almost a Darwinian explanation for how human nature develops? That we have strong desires to survive and to reproduce and that we'll do whatever's necessary to do that?

Yes. And now, through better communications, we are learning that in order to survive [we must act] as mankind and not just as an individual, since the chances of surviving as an individual in modern society are no longer existent. You cannot just go out and hunt and kill something or grab some fruit from a tree. You have to pay for it. You have to interact with other people. So those survival instincts have to be remolded through cultural education. We are reaching the point where in order to survive we must act as a species rather than as an individual, which has always been part of nature. Essentially, it is always the species that had to survive. That's the whole point of death and birth: that the species goes on existing and the individual dies. In society, the same thing is going to happen. We have to develop harmony among each other and as a planet. That's the only chance to fulfill our destiny, so to speak.

I guess maybe this is an evolutionary view that I'm expressing but I have never seen it written up that way because it's sort of the next step beyond Darwin. My background is not good enough to write anything about it. But in many searching ways, different religious leaders tried to come to that same conclusion. Only they expressed it in different cultural mores for their different populations to understand.

Q. Well, how do you explain the cultural variation that you have? If we're all basically members of the same species and we're now at a point where the world is complex enough that we should move away from a crude Darwinian survival of the fittest to a situation where we have to cooperate, how do you explain that some cultures don't emphasize that and others do? The Nazi culture had to come from someplace.

Well, there are two reasons for that. One is that they are not faced by the same emergency. If you live in the hills in Tibet, for instance, your ties with the modern world are so different that you can still operate on a past level. If you're right in the middle of the action, it's also a question of education. All through society, you have individuals who still behave on a Neanderthal basis. We call them criminals most of the time. You have politicians who still operate on the basis of instant gratification and greed. You have corporations who still behave in the way that was intelligent in the 1850s but which is, with any foresight, even as a corporation, very destructive thirty years from now.

But many individuals are still culturally very selfish. That's how you used to make it in the old world, to think of yourself [that way]. They don't mind if everything goes to hell. It's the old King Louis view: "Après moi, le deluge." It's the view that says, "I don't give a damn what happens after I die." And, obviously, with the disintegration of the cultural values of the old churches, of the old religions, as it came in conflict with the Darwinian theories, what has not come up is a new moral religious sense. When I say religious, I don't mean in the sense of worship; I mean in the intrinsic religion. The interrelationship between man and nature, which is man and God, is the need to create a new morality. I don't mean sexuality. I mean world morality.

Q. Is that your concept of religion, Tony?

That is very much my concept of religion. I think it was first articulated in its initial form with people like Buddha and Jesus, who sensed almost instinctively that the time was coming for a change. It's not that you're opposed to the animal way of being. It's that the animal way of being no longer worked. If man wanted to survive in the way in which he was growing, then he had to get into a different morality. Unfortunately, all the time people refuse to face that.

You can see the conflict between the outdated morality and the new one in lots of areas. Take the sexual area. Obviously, man's reproduction is destructive for present society. But with present-day birth control, there's nothing wrong with using the sex instincts in a beneficial manner, in a more loving manner. But here you find that certain people are opposed to birth control yet want to go on procreating in a way that would be destructive for the way the planet is right now.

I'm always struck that so many of the prolife people are also people who are very adamant about wanting capital punishment. They are often also very militaristic. It's contradictory. That's exactly what I mean about the two cultural moralities getting into conflicts with each other. They're not aware of the horror that this overpopulation has created. Many of the moral majority people are not even in favor of birth control. I can see their point about abortion, which is a very sad solution. But, on the other hand, they do not even want to allow the birth control. Yet if they would spend some time in Calcutta or in Ethiopia they couldn't help but see the incredible sadness that this creates. This thinking is contrary to what I would call God's plan. If God gives you the intelligence to have birth control, then use it!

Q. Tony, do you think people are essentially alone in the world or do you think that we have group ties or are part of different groups?

I think that we are as much together as the cells in our body are together. They are individual. They each strive for their own little survival yet somehow they also will sacrifice themselves at times for the whole. Whether that is conscious or not, none of us has any way of knowing. Or they are made to sacrifice themselves. I think it's very similar to that. We cannot today exist as individuals. Oh, maybe one or two of us can go off in the wilderness and exist. But as a modern-day American or modern-day European or Chinese, there is no way to survive in this world unless we see ourselves as part of a whole in some way. The big, big difficulty is to do that without falling into the trap of totalitarian government.

Q. How do we do that though, Tony?

Just the same way the way the body does it. It's almost an instinctive voluntary sort of way, a sensing. Again it's a combination of education, a combination of new morality, of learning love, of caring, of setting your goals so that your happiness is not necessarily based on collecting the most that you can possibly collect. It's knowing that your happiness is based on your sympathetic vibrations with your environment, with nature, with the other mankind around you, and on a certain degree of courage, which I describe as being aware that life does not last forever. It's knowing that you are into this [life] in the same manner that you decide to play a tennis game, for instance. You're going to play the best game you can and have fun doing it, even though you know that the game will end; just as you know that life will end, but you can feel that I was a good team player in the game. Maybe it's more like a soccer game, where you work with a team together and it's not that you want to destroy your opponent. Even sport is not always a good example. You may want to build a bridge over a river with your team.

Q. But is it the pleasure of the process of building the bridge that's more important? Or is it accomplishing building the bridge that's more important?

It's the combination of both. If you accomplish it without pleasure, without enthusiasm and love and pleasure, then it's a very sad situation. So it should always be a combination of both. It's the accomplishment and also not being heartbroken if it doesn't always succeed. You have done the best you could.

Q. Tony, let me ask you a little bit about duty. Do you think people have a social responsibility to help other people who are in need?

Yes, but again within certain intellectual limitations. That gets to be a very difficult point because how suicidal do you want to get? I used to be a very good swimmer and I over the years rescued some eighteen people here on the beachfront [off Malibu, California]. But then I reached a point where I was getting too old and the last time I did it I almost drowned myself. Then it gets to be that heart-rending decision. You see somebody in the water and you know that you are totally endangering yourself. Well, that's fine if you are at that point that you're willing to die. It is also difficult if you have other things in mind, like your own family that you have tried to help to raise, your own projects that you believe in and which may be very important. That's one of the decisions that has to be made on the spur of the moment.

But generally speaking, I think everybody, within those limits [has duty]. Basically, yes, if I can save somebody and I can do so with a relatively low risk, it would be very unsocial not to do that. The degree of risk is a degree that has to be judged for every individual. Unless you make it your profession. Let's say you're a lifeguard or you're in the military, or certain other jobs, then that's part of your decision you make. You cannot join the military just for the money.

Q. But you do think that you would consider whether or not your actions to help somebody else in distress would endanger or harm your own welfare and how it would affect the welfare of your family and the people involved?

It always has to be a balance between those two points, yes. Otherwise, it becomes an emotional decision, which is very often the case.

Q. Let me ask you a little bit about the decisions. When you saw these people drowning off the beach at Malibu, and then again during the war, did you actually go through a decision process in your mind?

Yes. The decision concerned what are my chances of saving them. Because I am a total realist and a firm believer in the lifeboat theory. If a ship sinks, and the lifeboat is full, then one more passenger on board will make the lifeboat sink. Then I will feel totally free to either kill that person and save the other ones that are in the lifeboat or let that person drown. But of course the more humane thing would be to kill them if you are in certain circumstances.

Although it is an emotional decision, it has to be an emotional decision tempered by intelligence. Like in my case now, I know I cannot do it. I could not nowadays swim that distance. I'd be just as dead as they would be. Now, that doesn't serve any purpose. But when I was younger, I would decide yes. I stand a good fighting chance to get them out here and every time I did it, I have succeeded. Sometimes it was very minor and sometimes it was very major.

During World War II also I wanted to save my friends if I could humanly do so. I would try to help if I think I stand a fair chance to save that person. On the other hand, on the first day of warfare in Holland, my scout on the motorcycle in front of my unit got shot off his motorbike by the Germans. He was obviously badly wounded and lying in the middle of the highway. I did not allow any of my men, including myself, to go and save him because it was absolutely certain that if we went into that open street, we were going to be shot at by the Germans who were lying there fifty feet away. That is part of being in the military. In this case, our assignment was to destroy the enemy. So we have to move left and right and advance. I have to protect the lives of my men. To have a strictly emotional reaction and run up and save the guy, the chances were too much against that; I knew that it was 99.9 percent certain that I would lose any other man who would try to do that, including myself. And if [trying to save him] meant I would not fulfill the assignment, then we would actually play into the hands of the enemy. This is a constant military dilemma. You might be in a situation where you have a 50/50 chance. Then you do it.

Q. I see. You don't believe in self-sacrifice just to try to . . .

Well, in this particular military reasoning, self-sacrifice makes you a bad soldier. If we're all getting killed, why then go into the battle in the first place?

Q. Let me see if I understand you correctly. I understand your discussion about the military. You're feeling that there is a different calculus that has to go into play there. But what about the rescue activities during the war? You knew that the risk was very high that you would be caught. You'd already been sentenced to death and were living underground yourself. So you were in rather a risky situation as far as that went.

Yes, but it was a controlled risk. I might be taking a high risk, but I was not taking an uncontrolled risk. To me, that is a tremendously important difference. One becomes totally an emotional act here where you are trying to rescue people. Now, if you rescue people, the only way that you can rescue them is if you save yourself so tomorrow you may have to rescue somebody else. So your long-term achievement in helping people does not help at all if you commit suicide. You are rescuing one person today. But you can rescue many more tomorrow.

Q. Is what I'm hearing you say, then, that your decision to help people was a conscious decision? It was not an emotional decision?

Not an emotional suicidal type of thing, no.

Q. But it wasn't even emotional, you're saying.

Well, you cannot exclude emotions. That's the old thing. If there are two girls drowning, if the one is pretty and the other one is ugly, which one is the guy going to save? There is always an emotion. You cannot exclude emotion. But to me it's very important that the emotions are tempered by intelligence. That still does not mean that you say, "Oh, well, I'm not going to take even one small percent of chance." No, no, no. That's not the point. You have to constantly take risks. If you drive to your office, you couldn't get to work if you weren't willing to die someday in a car crash. Your whole life is based on that sort of decision, and those decisions cannot be totally selfish. You have to think of your fellow man, not just yourself. When you save your fellow man, you save yourself, too.

Q. I see. So what you're saying then is that we're all part of the same people and so, therefore, you should not sacrifice your own life because when you give up your own life, you're losing part of the whole, also.

That's right. You can see that even with some firemen going up a very rickety building to save a little kitten. The kitten is not even a human person. It is not even part of your own species. But it is the principle of life that you are trying to help. You saw that with these people trying to save these two whales up there in Alaska. The Russians and Americans are working together and spending millions of dollars, which is probably the biggest sacrifice any American can make, to save these whales. That's emotional. But to me the emotion is an indication of very deep-lying survival factors. When I said you'd save the pretty girl before the ugly girl, what is "pretty" versus "ugly"? Usually, pretty is healthier, a better body for reproduction. A healthier person basically is the essence of prettiness. So you are more tempted subconsciously to save the better reproducer. You are more conscious very often and your emotions very often deal with *why* it is more important to save a child, for instance. Socially, emotionally, why is it more important to save a woman? Emotionally, because there's a very deep-seated drive for the reproduction and the maintenance of the species. I hate to be so intellectual about it because it's kind of analyzing it to death.

Q. Well, that's what we're doing. I'm asking you to explain it to me. Let me ask you about the whales though. I understand that it's a very complex idea that you're expressing. Now, if we're all part of life and the whales are part of life and they have just as much right to live as you do, I think that the thought that you're expressing is not simply that one very coldly and analytically makes a decision about risking one's own life to save somebody else. It's more that your life is part of the other person's life and so there is . . .

An emotional link.

Q. It's an emotional link. And the link is that you have a right to live also and that that too has to be an important factor?

Yes. If you take the cathedral [as an example], the cathedral cannot exist without the brick. The brick cannot exist without a grain of sand. So by removing a grain of sand, basically you harm the cathedral. You may not notice it right away. But if you remove enough grains of sand, sooner or later the cathedral will collapse.

The American Indian had a good feeling of this. If you kill a buffalo because you need the buffalo's meat and the buffalo's hide for the tent for your family, you are not murdering the buffalo. You thank the buffalo. You are grateful for the fact that you live together with the buffalo family and the buffalo is your friend. It's like the lion and the antelope again. Whereas if you come like the Yankee on the Southern Pacific and you shoot buffalo out of the window and you let them drop dead and just leave them there, then you are committing a crime, emotionally and psychologically.

Q. I understand. Now, let's go back to the example of the whales. Suppose we're spending millions of dollars to save a couple of whales. Is that a good decision when those millions or hundreds of thousands of dollars could be used better to keep alive starving children in Ethiopia?

Absolutely correct. There's always a toss-up, and in this case, if you're going be very high-nosed about it, the toss-up was that for the Russians and the American companies involved with the rescue, it was good high-profile publicity. For the news stations, it made very good news. And the individuals who did it weren't really spending the money. They were spending their time and their effort and they would get that marvelous pleasure and satisfaction that you get out of something like that, that emotional satisfaction of saving somebody. That is your reward.

However, we cannot spend everything on things like public housing or whatever. We also have to think long term. The best example is to consider whether we should send food to Ethiopia, for instance. My idea is that there is nothing that we can do by sending food because the more food we send, the more they will procreate and the worse the problem gets. If we can send that same amount for heavy-duty birth control in that area, we will help them more twenty years from now more than we could humanly help now, when the problem will just repeat itself. Now, that's a hard-nosed thing and if I'm standing there and seeing these little kids die, I'll probably spend my money and send them food. It's this horrible fight that always exists between the needs of the immediate and those of the future. That's why it's so difficult when being a military commander to deal with your emotions. It's the lifeboat theory again. You've got to take that person on board. But if you use your intelligence, you know you're going to kill that person and everybody else [on board] by doing that. So I have two choices. I can jump out and let the person in. That's what I should do if I am a true hero, give my place to somebody else. This happened in many instances. On the *Titanic*, for instance, people did that. Husbands jumped out and drowned to save their wives. You're asking tough questions now. But that is the purpose of your interview.

Q. Let me ask you some easier questions. How would you describe yourself? How do you view yourself? What kind of a person are you?

Oh, about thirty pounds overweight. I'm seventy years old. My body is seventy years old and starting to disintegrate in various places. But my mind, well, that's the peculiar thing. If I look in the mirror, I'm always shocked. I see this old man looking back at me. But the person who is in my thinking and my mind, and even in what I would like to do with my body, I am much younger. I'm just experiencing the frustration of stepping on the gas pedal and the thing doesn't move very much.

In terms of personality, I guess I'm fairly gregarious. At times I can get a little grumpy, mainly out of frustration or under too much stress. It's very interesting when you're married to somebody who's thirty-six years younger than you are, because their goals in life are very different than yours. We work together and I'm very much trying to help Susanne. I've seen my wife's life as almost like a child's in a sense, as a continuation of my own thoughts also. I am very anxious to educate her and see her succeed in all her projects. Yet at the same point in instance, I've run out of time for some of my own philosophies that I would like to get on paper. So generally I'm trying to do more than I can humanly do. Of course, the body is no longer in that great a shape so I tend to have some little conflicts there. I try to work too hard and then I see my clock running out. I'm trying to catch up and finish work that I want to finish. If we were both older, we might both say, "Oh, well, to hell with it. We're going to sit and rock on the porch." I think it is very healthy that she is younger because it keeps me buzzing on some of the things that I would otherwise procrastinate about.

I have two children of my own and two stepchildren of my ex-wife. Unfortunately, my children were a major disaster. They grew up not only in divorce but also right in the middle of the worst end of California hippiedom, in the drug culture. They burned out on acid and on drugs, LSD and every other drug. They got into crime. My son—I haven't seen him for years—he's sort of got it together. He originally became a Jesus freak. Then he joined a slightly less extreme religious group, which helped him. They're a group of rock musicians who had a whole little commune going. They got him back to where he could at least do some work. His brain is pretty well fried but he can still do good carpentry work. He's about thirty-five now and finally, after years, at least he can survive on his own. He married a girl from the same commune and they seem to be working it out. But he was gone so long that, in many ways, he sort of died. The relationship no longer exists. The same thing happened with my daughter, who is about thirty-three. She went through the exact same thing and hit the road. She tried just about everything, from crime to prostitution at the time. Recently, she sent a note for the first time in almost six or eight years. Most of the time, whenever they did that in the past, they wanted money. We decided it was best to leave things being the way they were. We both had learned to survive without each other. There wasn't really very much left. It's sad but that's the way it was. So in many ways . . . [Tony paused].

I hate playing games and pretending. There's nothing worse than being a family and pretending you love each other, pretending you're being polite with each other when really there's nothing there. There is none of that normal warmth that exists between family and children. That's the negative page in the story.

You know, maybe when the old home existed, when you had the old homestead and you were part of the land in so many ways, things were different. But even then, I remember there was a lot of hate. In my case, we don't even have hate. We're living our own lives. But I saw so much hate in the old days, too.

Q. Well, it isn't really necessary that you should have a great deal in common with people just because you're related by blood.

No, particularly when your lives split in totally different directions and you have totally different goals. I will say though that the drug situation is horrible. Drug and alcohol abuse! You know, I love my martini on Friday night. I don't mean that I have anything against drinking. But alcohol abuse and drug abuse is something else. We're in a culture that advertises it, day and night. The beer ads for these fifteen-year-olds and the glamour of the vodka, the deluxe imported vodka in the ads. It's a very strange culture we're in.

August 8, 1989

Q. Do you think people have control over their fate or destiny? Do you think you have to take the initiative to control events?

I think that everything in life is very random, but there are certain things connected with your destiny. If I'm going to walk a high wire across the skyscrapers in New York, for example, I'm really tempting destiny. But outside of that, obviously you have control. You have control over what you do. You can get yourself into situations where normal intelligence will warn you, tell that you could get yourself in trouble. But outside of that, I think I'm a great believer in the randomness [of life].

Again, that goes back to the Darwinian theory. It's not like throwing the dice. But it's totally Darwinian in the sense that things will move in a certain direction. Things will happen through natural selection, through a natural selection of circumstances. So many things repeat themselves every day. The surf is a very good example. Because the water tends to break at a certain place on the sand, the lighter sand gets thrown in a certain direction and the heavier sand sinks away. After a while you get certain lines of white sand in the area. This is not accidental. But it is still totally random. Nature creates certain situations and patterns, things that happen. They repeat themselves in many different places. So it's not totally random but it's also not planned.

Q. What about human events? What about the rescuing? Do you feel it was your destiny to rescue these people or that someone put you there to make sure they were saved?

No, I just happened to be there. It's a little like driving downtown and happening to see a holdup. I might trip the guy if he runs by me with the loot, but if I had had an errand in another part of town, I wouldn't have been there.

Q. It wasn't God or fate or anybody that put you there?

No, no.

Q. Tony, you've talked a lot about your personal ethical values. Could you briefly summarize whether or not you have any personal ethical credo that guides your life?

I think in life there are two things that you shouldn't do. You shouldn't do anything that hurts anybody else unless it's absolutely essential. And, secondly, you should not hurt yourself unnecessarily. That's like love thy neighbor as thyself for very practical reasons because the more you love your neighbor, the kinder he'll be to you, too.

Q. What would make it necessary for you to hurt someone else?

Let's say some guy comes into the living room with a gun in his hand. I'll shoot before he shoots. Or if I see some guy on the beach who's raping some little girl, I would certainly let him have it one way or the other to help that person. I would hurt the guy who's hurting the other person in that case. Maybe two wrongs don't make a right but that's one of these borderline situations.

Q. How did you develop this kind of view? You mentioned different role models before.

From a variety of people I knew during my life. That's where you learn your ideas. What is socially right and wrong is usually conveyed to you through your cultural background, your family, church, whatever.

Q. Was it difficult for you at all when you felt there was a conflict between your own ethical values and the values of the laws of the society in which you were living?

Yeah. It's always difficult. Let's take a very simple little example. I am totally at ease with nudism, for instance. Now it's allowed if it's on your own property. But there were many years that you couldn't even sunbathe nude with your wife and a friend in your own garden. If a helicopter flew over, then they'd send the cops out and arrest you. That was the way [it was] in Los Angeles until about twenty-five years ago. There was one particular person who took it to court, all the way to the Supreme Court, and won the case.

I remember another example, also involved with sex. It really was the most funny thing. Somebody had put up a ladder against the side of a house to look into the window of a one-armed trumpeter. He was fairly well-known at the time. And the guy happened to be in bed with two girls! The guy who climbed up the ladder reported it to the police and the trumpeter was arrested. I thought this was very sad, if only because it's very commendable for a one-armed man to be that enterprising anyway.

Those are just two laws but then there are many other laws which are more tragic. For instance, the German laws against the Jews or laws that would get you sent to a concentration camp for saving the life of a Jew or hiding a Jew. Those are bad laws. I don't have any holy respect for the law, just because it's law. The law is man-made, although generally, for the sake of the society, you should always stick with the laws. The best example of that is the law requiring driving on the right-hand side of the street. If I am here in Los Angeles and I start driving on the wrong side of the street, I might exert my independence but I'd end up in a head-on crash. Yet if I'm in London and I drive on the left side of the street, that would make excellent sense because that's the convention there. So in many ways, laws exist for cultural and practical purposes. They are not there for deep-seated moral reasons.

Q. Tony, do you think you've changed much over the years?

I think I have changed somewhat from when I was a teenager. I was a very conservative, little rich boy, from a family that tended to applaud the mounted police chasing a Socialist down the street when they had a parade. I think I have changed my point of view very drastically in that sense. I'm much more liberal-minded than I was as a kid.

Q. Did your rescue actions change you in any way?

No. What changed me mostly was being condemned to death and having to hide and consequently hiding with very different social groups than I was normally familiar with socially. That had a definite effect, seeing how the other half of the world lives. Then later, traveling all around the world and seeing more [about other cultures was important, too].

Q. What were you like when you were rescuing people? You were between twenty-one and twenty-four. That's an early age for someone to be doing the kinds of things you were doing.

Not so young because I got to be quite realistic about it. I had the added advantage that I didn't have a family to take care of. I didn't have any responsibility. My parents had enough money so I could somehow get enough money to survive on. Had I been married with a wife and three kids, with my livelihood depending on a job and if I did anything wrong that would mean I'd lose that job, I might have had all the same feelings, all the same inclinations, but I might not have been in a position where I could do anything.

Q. So you think that the situational factors are important in rescue activities?

Extremely important. That's why you so often find the most successful revolutionaries, both in America, France, and in Latin America, are so often people like Che Guevara, who came from a wealthy, aristocratic family. Look at the Chinese students. They are not the peasants. They are the ones who can afford to be revolutionaries. First of all, they have the education and secondly, they have the time. If you're a peasant, you are slaving from sunrise till sunset. You just can't take the time off to do things like that.

Q. But you said that even now, when you live in Malibu, that you've pulled almost eighteen people out of the surf who were drowning in some way or another. You have family. You have ties. You have responsibilities. But you still do it.

Yeah, but I am also a very good swimmer.

Q. But you still went ahead and risked your life for other people.

Yes and no. It's not much more dangerous than driving through heavy traffic. Something can go wrong, that's true. And as I got older it got to be a little tougher. You constantly take chances. . . . For some reason, in the minds of a lot of people in the old days who couldn't swim, the idea that somebody would jump in the cold water to save somebody made somebody seem very heroic. But for a person who is a good swimmer, it's very different.

Let me give you an example of something that is really heroic to me. I had a girlfriend in Holland. Her father was Jewish; her mother was not Jewish. We hid her father for a while, until it turned out that he was really not in danger because he was in a mixed marriage with children. So he went back to his home and everything was all right.

A few months later when I was condemned to death, I needed a place to hide. We also had some weapons from the resistance to hide. Now here is a man who is a very scared, very nervous middle-aged little Jewish man, with two children. And he said, "I'm so opposed to Hitler and what he stands for and my son is in England in the 1st Airborne Division. I want to do something, too." So he insisted that I would hide at their house. It was really strange to hide in a Jewish home. But it was a very good place because nobody looked for you there. Secondly, he insisted that he was happy that we hid some of the weapons in his attic.

Now for this man, who was an extremely nervous and a naturally scared person by nature, that was real courage. To me, that man was a real hero because he was not one of these happy-go-lucky guys who think, "Oh, nothing can happen to me." He was totally aware, more than aware, of the chances he was taking. Yet he was a totally unsung hero.

Q. But he had been hidden himself, by you, earlier on, so he may have felt he owed a debt to you.

Yeah. But we also had somebody else hide there, too, one time. It was not just a debt to me. It was more that the man had very strong convictions and he was very opposed to Hitler and he wanted to do his thing.

Q. Tony, some people have said that religious people will tend to be more altruistic.

Okay. Anybody who says that, I would send them immediately to the Middle East, to Beirut, and see how religious people behave toward each other there. The most horrible things in history have been done in the name of religion. So I think that religious people are just like everybody else. They can be very moral, very kind. But they're human. For example, I'm very close to three rabbis in this area. I've spoken in their synagogues and I even have an inscribed book from one of them. But I've also been trying to get some funds for some of the Mengele twins to go on this trip to Auschwitz because many of them don't have the money to go for this last reunion there in Auschwitz. I wrote to the rabbis I knew to solicit their help. None of the rabbis even answered my letter! I had a friend check with one of them and the guy said, "Well, it's a controversial matter, dealing with Israel. I just can't get involved with that." He is moral. He's a nice man, intelligent and friendly. But he'd rather not get involved. Now there's a religious person who is a little like a professor at a university with a lot of tenure. He is not going to make waves.

Q. Tony, do you believe in an afterlife at all?

I don't know. I am an agnostic in that I do not believe we have any way of knowing until it happens. It is obvious that there is a plan in the universe, some plan, some master plan. As an agnostic, I do not believe that we are in a position to be able to judge and to evaluate that plan and how it works. I never have had the feeling that the finger of God points at you or knocks you over or helps you up. No. I have never believed it. And for very good reasons! Because I've seen some of the nicest people totally destroyed, and to me it's like a natural happening that grows by itself but it's not terribly involved in the individual, no more than the grain of sand and the brick in the cathedral. Some grains of sand will get knocked off; some will be added if they have to make some alterations to the church and nobody worries about the individual grain of sand too much.

Q. Any religious beliefs that you may have, were they relevant at all in your rescue activities?

The general Judaic-Christian morality teachings may have been relevant. To me, the teachings of Jesus, for instance, and of Buddha and many others are very, very important teachings. To me, there are two aspects to religion. One is the aspect of worship. Getting down on your knees and in fear, or in hope, praying to some superior being there that will rule your life. The other is the aspect of social morality. This definitely was taught by Jesus, for instance, and this to me is by far the more important part of religion. Unfortunately, the two have been mixed together at times. They're confusing for people.

There's so much superstition involved with the first type of thinking. To me, it is utterly unimportant whether Jesus ever walked on water or whether he walked on the rocks. It is what he had to *say* that is important to me. Jesus came up and said, "Look, I am the Son of God. We are *all* Sons of God. We all have it in us to lead a good, a kind, a moral life. I'm no different. I am you. You can do it."

That to me was the teaching of Jesus. Anybody can do it if they want to. Sure, you may endanger your life. Sure, you may get crucified. But if enough of us do it, nobody will get crucified anymore. To me, that is the initial teaching of early Christians and of all religions. There is no difference. All good religions are saying that if we work together and love, fewer of us will have to be crucified.

Q. So yours is more religion as a morality. Was that relevant in your rescue activities?

At that time, no, because I hadn't studied religion that much at the time. I obviously had some religion through the family. There was a very strong teaching of right and wrong in the family, from my nanny on to my grandparents, my parents, and definitely my high school principal and my army commander.

Q. Let me just ask you one last question on religion. I'm gathering from what you said that religion was not a factor in your rescuing people. You did not do it to buy yourself a better spot in paradise, as they say.

No. No, not quite. [Tony laughed.]

Q. How did rescuing the people you saved make you feel about yourself? Did it affect the way you felt about yourself in any way?

Oh, of course. Yeah, you have fun. It's a twofold thing. The one thing is that you're happy that you succeeded and obviously it's a lot of fun to be able to save somebody, to help somebody. Secondly, in a conflict like we had with the Nazis, it was delightful to pull away one of their prey. It was fun.

Q. Were you surprised that you were able to do it?

No. It's not that terribly difficult most of the time. It's just a question of doing it.

Q. Did you feel that you did something good?

Yeah.

Q. How did you feel about the praise you got afterward? Did you do it in any way expecting praise?

Well, I learned one thing a very long time ago. Today's hero is forgotten the next day. As long as it is socially acceptable, people are delighted to be all over you, to compliment you and all that. If it becomes something that is not totally pleasant, like the thing I'm doing now with Israel, then all the same people will be just as apt to turn against you. I've lectured in synagogues and I'm trying very gently to mention the fact that the Nazi mentality has absolutely nothing to do with your race, with your religion, with your nationality. The same type of totalitarian thinking will crop up everywhere. It'll crop up right here in the United States. It'll crop up in Holland. And it'll crop up in Israel. Everybody can rationalize their point of view.

I was in South Africa and this Israeli who was working there was complaining about those little monkeys down there, referring to the blacks. An Israeli should know better. But they don't. A Dutchman who would be very anxious to send troops over to Indonesia at the end of World War II to recapture the colonies, to me, was exactly the same as the Nazis. For greedy purposes, he wanted to recapture the colonies. To take the freedom away from the people who'd just gotten it! And he was willing to bomb villages to do it! To me, he was behaving in the same manner that the Nazis had behaved. There may be a question of degree but the basic behavior is the same.

I don't feel that the Nazis are monsters. I never felt that way. The Nazis were normal German people who, through education, training, cultural thinking, and greed, ended up where they were. And tomorrow it's our people. And the day after tomorrow, it's somebody else. It's something in history that teaches you that the minute you destroy an enemy, you look behind you and he's standing there in your own ranks. You have to many times look in the mirror to make very sure that he hasn't crept into your head.

We have to watch for the old yellow gooks mentality. It is much easier to shoot at or burn the "yellow gooks" than to shoot and burn at some other farm boy just like yourself. But the evil and the good can be in all of us. The Yin and the Yang. Good and bad is in all of us. You have to look in the mirror. We're always looking in the mirror.

Q. How do you think you came to have this view?

Travel. Education. Being exposed to anything that is beyond your immediate parochial views, starting off with the family, starting off with your village, your street, your gang. I have a program that I used to do sometimes. I offered it to the local rabbi here. I said I would love to organize a group of ten Jews and ten Arabs from the communities here in LA. We will have a meeting and we will reverse the roles. The Jews in a meeting will have to speak up for the Arab problem; the Arabs will have to defend the Jewish point of view. By the end of the evening, you won't know the difference between each other. I've seen it happen. People very vehement defending the new group that they suddenly belong to.

What's fascinating was the answer from the rabbi. He said, "I would love to do it but only as long as the Jews can defend the Jewish point of view."

That is not the purpose of what I was proposing. Far from it!

I felt very strongly about what was happening in Israel. Several years ago I put together a proposal for the Palestinians to advance in a very totally peaceful way rather than through violence. I tried to make it the equivalent of *The Diary of Anne Frank*, to show what the sufferings are for people who are in the Palestinian camps, people who have lost their homes. I want to make it clear that basically there's not that much difference between these things and what the Jews went through. People should learn and get together. The odd part is that in Israel the people who are closest to being in the middle point of view are the military. They've seen both sides. Killing a population of Malays or blowing up a home and shooting teenagers or kiddies in a Palestinian camp, if you're basically a good person, these things really make you feel horrible. Half the trouble with Vietnam veterans is this same phenomenon. They'll talk vehemently against the Vietnamese because they feel sick about what they had to do at the time. Some of them face it and totally fall apart psychologically. Some of them refuse to face it. They may sound extremely violent against anybody who was against the war. Yet when you talk to them in person, you start to realize that the people they're mad at are themselves, that they allowed themselves to be trapped into becoming murderers.

Q. Why do you think some people are able to see this and to reach out across the boundaries of race and gender and nationality and see others as human beings?

Well, there are two things that prevent it from happening. First, some people have very closed minds. They're terrified of letting go of their security, whatever it is: religion, Marine Corps membership, Jewish or Christian faith. Any of these things can separate me. Without them, then I suddenly would have to face my own humanity. It's very easy to employ some marine to follow orders. It's very easy to say, "I'm sorry. I'm a Jew. I'm defending the Jewish rights." Or, "I'm a Christian. I'm going to do this or that." Or a Muslim or whatever. We hear this all the time from people. That is one reason.

The second reason is the lack of exposure. I heard people talking about homeless people, saying, "Well, they're all a bunch of drunks. They admit they don't want to work."

They don't realize that, aside from the alcoholics (who still have all their own problems) there are many homeless people who are simply mothers without a husband who cannot get transportation, cannot get their wardrobe or their hair done sufficiently to get a job and who consequently are totally trapped in homelessness. Yet here people lump them all together and say, "None of these people really wants to work and they're all a bunch of drunks and that's it."

They don't even think of the obvious, that there are mentally retarded people on the streets. But if had they spent one afternoon in downtown LA or even in the park in Santa Monica and looked and learned to see through their eyes, they could not give that same answer. But most of the people look away. They don't want to see because it's disturbing.

I see this now and I fully believe the people who lived next to the concentration camps and say, "We never saw anything." Of course, they didn't see anything! They didn't want to see. You don't want to think of your son sitting there getting his jollies out of torturing people or sticking them alive in an oven.

I have compassion for the people who are little people, who are hiding and don't want to know. But the higher you get politically, if you want to become a president of a nation or a premier, somebody like Kurt Waldheim, if you are aiming for these positions, I do not have compassion for people like that who then still are striving to get into power positions. To me, they are far more evil than even the concentration camp guard who did as he was told.

The kind of people I sympathize with are people like a German acquaintance of a friend of mine. My friend is a German Jew who lives in Malibu. He was in Germany and he went into a restaurant that was full. He had to sit at somebody else's table. They ended up in conversation and they hit it off and eventually ended up corresponding with each other. One was a German man. And my friend is a German Jew. Recently my friend got a letter from the gentleman, who told him, "Look, I have so much enjoyed corresponding with you that I can no longer be dishonest. I want to let you know that during World War II, I was a lieutenant in the Gestapo. I never killed anybody or tortured anybody. Still, I feel terrible about my connections with this. It has been more than forty years ago but I do not feel that I can honestly keep up a friendship with you without you knowing this. Do you still want to stay friends with me?"

Now to me, that's a very, very different attitude than what I see from Kurt Waldheim. To me, I respect that man in the restaurant, the one who wrote my Jewish friend. He's grown. We all can grow. We're not doomed. Again, we go back to the teachings of Jesus where our sins are forgiven. We are not doomed to forever be a sinner. We can at any moment in our lives decide to change things and that requires courage too.

Q. Was it important to you that you actually were the person who saved these people? Or did it just matter that somebody did it and you just happened to be there?

As far as I was concerned, it just mattered that somebody did it.

Q. Let me ask you a few questions about your family. I think you've told me a lot about them. You grew up in Amsterdam. Did you feel you were part of a close-knit society or was it very open?

No. Since my mother was of Belgium-French origin and my father was Dutch, I was not like a typical Dutchman either. I was kind of an only child and lived pretty well by myself. We had family that we saw regularly. We did have a circle of friends and all that. I very much enjoyed the school I went to. Amsterdam is a cozy, fun city. In the resistance, of course, I had a lot of friends there. So I very much liked Holland, which made it so hard when at the end of the war I was so disappointed that so many of our efforts had been frustrated. You know, we succeeded and yet the enemy popped up right in our midst, in the actions of the Dutch government with Indonesia. We had been totally unpolitical in the resistance. Yet there were some people who had very quietly jockeyed for political position there at the end. The people who had done most of the work in the resistance got little or no recognition at all. They were immediately replaced by scheming bureaucrats. People treated us like we were a bunch of Commies trying to overthrow the government, which we were not. The system, the establishment, does not like people coming in from the outside and doing a better job than they did for a while. It's like when a part-time substitute teacher comes in and he manages to teach a better class than the regular teacher for a while. The teacher who normally would be in charge feels uncomfortable because an outsider came and did a better job than he did.

Then, too, there were lots of weird little jealousies. People who had not wanted to stick their necks out and join the resistance but yet who were not pro-Nazi and who were in the police or in the government, they all felt ill at ease with us [in the resistance] and tried to get rid of most of us as much as possible. That gave such an uncomfortable feeling. So since I wanted to work in the movie business, anyway, I decided, "To hell with it. I'm leaving."

I actually left Holland in 1947, as soon as I got completely out of the army.

• • •

Q. Tony, when you were growing up, was there any kind of destabilizing event in your past, anything traumatic that happened?

Oh, not terribly much. My father and mother were always fighting, ever since I was a little tiny kid. My mother was very Latin and very possessive. My father made the mistake once. So many men do it. It's really not in their minds. It's not that important. Just a little fling with some cutie somewhere, which didn't mean that he didn't love my mother. But there's the difference between male and female feeling about it. One has to build the nest, after all, and the other is supposed to go and fertilize the world. Male and female minds, they're two radically different approaches. But my mother found out about it and for the next thirty years, she talked about it constantly. "I should have left you, but . . ."

She was always going on about it to the point that now, in retrospect, it's funny. But at the time, as a kid, it wasn't.

"Look at your father and see what he did to me." She was always telling me that. That's a very Latin approach.

Q. Was it hard as an only child when your parents fight?

It is very hard to speculate. Probably all families are that way so you don't know. Other than this, I was very spoiled. I got all the books and all the toys, which was very nice. My grandparents gave me a lot of books. I guess the major event in my late adolescent formation was being condemned to death and having to live underground. That flipped everything around. From becoming a nice little Republican in Holland, one of the [members of the] establishment, I became a criminal. At the end of the war, I was asked to join the foreign officers. It just didn't appeal to me.

Q. What is your political affiliation now? Do you consider yourself a political person?

Yes. But unfortunately, there's no party that I feel comfortable voting for. I'm a registered Democrat mainly because I try and keep one or two good people in office. I wish I could vote for a party that I really believe has some autonomy. Unfortunately, I don't think that exists now. Right now, I think it's the A team and the B team. When the A team screws up, they put the B team on the field. Like beautiful little sheep, we all believe that we're really voting for something. You used to be allowed to vote and you really thought you were voting for somebody. But that's politics.

Q. Did you consider your activities in rescuing people political or more humanitarian?

Totally humanitarian.

Q. Tony, you said your family was very wealthy when you were growing up. Were they active in politics? Were you a well-known family in Amsterdam?

No, they were not at all active in politics. When I say very wealthy, I don't mean rich like the DuPonts or something like that, but wealthy like a rich doctor is wealthy. My family background is totally unpolitical except that my mother had a certain hate for the Germans as a result of World War I because she was Belgian.

We did not like the Nazis. Now, to me it was more Nazis than Germans, because I had German friends. So I was far more political than anybody else in the family. But when the war came, they [my parents] helped hide Jews, too. Once the war started, they were very political. But before the war they were a good Dutch conservative loyalist family.

It was interesting what happened to them after the war. I left in 1947. My parents stayed, but they lost all their money during the war. They had invested in real estate and the four properties that they owned, three of them were destroyed. The big home that we lived in, in Amsterdam, was very badly damaged. It was taken over by the Germans. The investments my father had in Indonesian stock all lost money. Then, too, my mother lived rather high on the hog. It took a long time for her to let go of her lifestyle. They used to have three maids and a butler, just for the two of them.

After the war there was a housing shortage in Holland. The Socialist government told everybody with a large house that they would be forced to take in boarders. They could keep three rooms to themselves and if they had more rooms, they had to take another family into the house. So my mother was forced to take two other families into the house. There was no more help and the whole lifestyle collapsed. She basically used up too much of the family money. They had kept sending me money as though it was in the good old days. Suddenly one day I realized that they were totally broke. So I suggested they come to America, which they did. They arrived with $500. My father hoped he could be a dentist here, which was impossible. So he ended up in the kitchen of the Santa Monica Hospital and my mother ended up as a nurse's aide. They both lied about their age so they could work. My mother worked till she was seventy-five. My father worked till he was seventy. They managed to get their Social Security and a little pension from the hospital. It was the first time in my life that I remember them not quarreling and really loving each other. They'd walk to the hospital everyday and go to their jobs. My mother was being exposed to all the miseries of the people in the hospital and it made her less selfish. It brought them closer together. I don't want to engage in a cliché like "money destroys." But there is definitely something about having a lot of money that makes you very distant from the people who don't have money. I may have quoted George Bernard Shaw to you before because I like his saying: "The main difference between the very rich and the poor, is that the rich have more money." But it's true. I've seen it.

Not that I'm in favor in poverty, though. I wish I had a little more money to do some more traveling, to buy some more of the books I'd like to buy and help get my wife's show on Marlene Dietrich produced.

Q. Do you belong to any particular groups that play an important role in your identity formation?

Well, I didn't go to college so I don't have any titles. My main interest in the motion picture business was to communicate and to make movies and to express ideas in pictures. But I found out that's not how it works. It's a very closed shop. It's a difficult business to get into. It's very hard to make a living in the meantime. The same with my writing. I have several things I'm trying to write but to have the time to do it and to survive is hard.

Our living situation is interesting because we basically are quite broke but we live nicely. I don't know how to explain that. I have one room in the back of a garage here behind a house on the beach in Malibu. It's one room. It has no heat but we have a little wood-burning stove. There's a tiny little kitchen and a tiny little bathroom. I've built a small separate office with the permission of the landlord. There were two lots next to the house belonging to the same landlord, who is from a huge land-owning family. The public started to cut through the beach over there and it became a horrible mess, with broken bottles and old rusty bicycles and junk. I suggested that it might be a good idea to fence that off and plant it up with trees. He said, "Great, if you want to. Fine."

"Can I use it as a garden if I do it?"

He says, "Sure, I don't care. I'm keeping it for some future development. You do whatever you want to." So now I'm the proud tenant of two huge lots that have an enormous tropical garden with thirty-foot-high trees. It's a little like Gilligan's Island. Then in front, I built sand dunes to prevent the ocean from flooding his property and the empty lot so I have the use of the beach area. But we live very simply.

When I met my wife I was broke. I helped her get into modeling and acting and for a while she did extremely well as a top model and top commercial actress. Then recently, at the tender age of twenty-eight, she started to age out of modeling so finances got a little tougher. But at that time, I just happened to get a small pension from the Dutch military. That helped make up for it. We rent out this silly garden to photographers and motion picture companies who need Hawaiian-type settings. So we're struggling together.

It used to be that I could do it all myself. I'd build everything myself. We chopped the wood for the fire and if I needed a piece of furniture I'd build it. But I'm slowing down. Mentally, I'm still together. Oh, sometimes I have a little trouble remembering names. But in my mind I'm still a young man. In my body, I'm okay.

Q. You seem to be able to live without the kind of security that most people need.

Security is very dangerous. The moment it is pulled away from under you, you can break. You see these guys who work for General Motors for thirty years. Then suddenly it ends. They're totally shattered. There's nothing they can do. That was one advantage I had. I learned to hustle. Somehow you muddle through. If you have to live in a tent, you live in a tent. That's not what I'm aiming for, of course. But I hope and I believe we can do okay. The thing that worries me more is getting physically incapacitated. The worst thing that could possibly happen is that I become a burden on my wife.

Q. Did you feel that you had anything in common with the people that you helped? Did you know any of them before?

Some of them I knew, yes. There were two sons of a very wealthy department store owner. In summer vacation their parents and my parents used to go to the same beach resort and we'd always played together as little kids. So I'd known them for quite a while.

Q. Who were the first people that you saved?

Well, the first person that we tried to save was the father of a girl that I knew. He was the one I mentioned, who hid me in his home later on. We got him out as fast as possible. We got him first into my parents' house and then to a little farmhouse in the Lake District. It was funny because then it turned out that he really didn't have to hide. But he was probably the first one that we got involved with.

Q. Can you tell me what went through your mind when you rescued him? How did it actually happen? Did he come to the door to ask for help? Did someone tell you about him?

Well, before the war I'd go horseback riding together with his two daughters so I knew them relatively well. I was not seriously dating them but we'd go to parties sometimes. At first, his family was safe because the mother was not Jewish. But he was getting very worried. What he was mostly worried about is that something would happen to his family if he was there. He was afraid they might accidentally take the daughters along. His wife was not the friendliest soul. She was a rather cold cookie. A very non-Jewish German. She thought her husband was a threat to the family! I told you she was not the nicest person. She was one of these strange people. She was annoyed at her son in England. They'd sent their son to college in England and he up and volunteered for the army. She thought he was going to get himself killed, which he did actually. And she resented that. Whereas the dad was very proud that his son had done this. There was some tension in the marriage. There were some discussions, and I thought it'd be wise for him to get out of there before they came for him.

So I just went by his house. We got on our bicycles and we bicycled to my parents' house. It was that simple. It was my idea that he needed to be hidden. My parents had a large home. So he came over and we bicycled over and got there safely. We didn't hit any Germans on the way. I guess it was my idea.

Q. Were you living underground yourself at the time?

No, not yet.

Q. So this was when you were still a spoiled rich kid.

This is just before that happened, yeah. Well, maybe I was not as much of a spoiled rich kid as before. There's nothing like five days of combat in the field and losing half your platoon and seeing people getting blown to bits to change you rather rapidly. Plus it gives you a certain degree of self-assurance. This was during the period right after the war but before my colleagues were all arrested. But after the fighting I'd been through, I knew what was going on.

I think I said to this Jewish gentleman, "Hey, why don't you go into hiding?"

"Yeah, where will I hide?" he asked me.

"Oh, I'm sure we can figure out something. Today you can go stay at my parents' home. I'm sure that'll work out. We have this little country house in the Lake District, this little summer shack there. We're probably all going to go for a few days' vacation anyway. Why don't you come along and you can stay there with us? It's in the Lake District. They're not going to come there and look for Jews."

That's how it started, my hiding Jews. Very casually.

Q. When it started, did you think anything about the potential cost to you? That it might be costing you your life?

Yes. But again, that was a couple of months after the war began already, when you've had real dangerous situations, with people shooting at you and bombs dropping. Plus you're playing the big game, too. You're fighting those bastards. If you can do something against their game plan, it's exciting. You don't want to let those bastards win.

This was one case where they were rather clearly the meanies. Things get pretty complicated sometimes, with good people doing bad things and lots of shades of gray. But in World War II, it was great. It was simple. The bullies were over there and the good guys were over here. You had the white hats and they had the black hats. It was one of those rare situations where, for a little while, you could feel rather righteous.

Q. What went through your mind when you were on the bicycle with this man, taking him to your parent's house?

Just, "Be careful. Look out. Keep your eyes open. If you see any German patrols, make a U-turn and go back in the direction you came from."

Q. What about your emotional state of mind?

I didn't have any more [emotions] than I feel driving a car through heavy traffic. You're just careful.

Q. Was it an intuitive, spontaneous act that you did?

I guess so. It seemed like the right thing to do for him.

Q. You didn't think about it?

Why stay at home if there's a good chance that they'll come and get you? Because I'm sure they're not going to come by my parents' home right away. It's only for one night. After that we can go right down to that Lake District, where chances are 99 percent that they're [the Germans] not going to come there, not at this moment at least. They were all busy in the big cities.

Q. Did you go through any kind of conscious calculus where you thought about weighing the pros and cons of what you were doing? Did you think about the costs to you or to your parents, whom you were endangering? Was there anything like that?

I knew that they felt the same way I did, my parents. In that sense, my mother was very feisty. My father was a little bit more milquetoasty. But my mother was a general's daughter and she was quite feisty in that respect. She was not always the smartest in doing it but she was quite feisty. I didn't think there was any great risk connected with it at that time. Later on, we had a situation where there was far more risk involved.

Q. In those situations, did you sit down and weigh the costs and benefits?

Well, you analyze your chances and you have a pretty good chance of getting away with this. It was certainly less scary than trying to smuggle a truckload of guns through a German checkpoint, which I also did.

Q. So you were more frightened when you were doing the political part of your activities than when you were rescuing people.

Well, no. When I smuggled the guns I was in a German SS uniform. We had a German Gestapo member who had wanted to clear his record. This was now near the end of the war. We had a stolen German army truck. We had a lot of Dutch [men] drive along in a German uniform. We had a whole load of weapons that had been dropped out in the countryside. We had to smuggle them into town and we knew we had to pass the checkpoint. We had this German sergeant who was afraid he'd hang. He knew the war would be over soon so he wanted to clear his record. He knew the passwords. So we'd have him sit between the two of us in the front seat. Behind the canvas in back of him, we had a guy with a machine gun pointed in his back. We weren't taking any chances with him. We'd drive up to the German checkpoint and they'd say, "God, it's a German truck with three Germans in there."

I spoke excellent German at the time. But I kept my mouth shut anyway. I just said, "Heil Hitler."

The guy'd say "Heil Hitler" and then the sergeant in the middle would say, "The grass is green," or whatever the password was. The little sentry says, "Oh, good." And you drive on. We had three guys in the back with submachine guns so we had a fighting chance of getting away.

It was a little like in the movies. People really do these things. It does happen and partially it's exhilarating. There's that element in there, too. But that was a hell of a lot more scary than some of the instances when I escorted somebody [Jewish into hiding].

You do stupid things sometimes, too. Once, I hid an American pilot. He was hiding as Captain Franklin Coslet. He's now a brigadier general, I think. He bailed out over Holland and we got him a hiding place. After three months, he was so stir crazy sitting in that little tiny room, he said, "Jesus, I'd love to get out of here."

"Well, I think it's kind of quiet in town. We can take a little chance. Let's get on our bicycles and we'll go to my mother's house and have a cup of tea."

Now, I hadn't visited my mother in nearly a year. It was too dangerous. But that's what we did. It's not always heroism. Sometimes you just feel sick and tired. You want to do something else, even if the risk is great.

Q. In thinking about these rescues, can you distinguish between empathy and what I would describe as a feeling of duty, a sense that it's right, that it's the right thing to do, that it's my obligation?

I think empathy and the feeling of what is right are very closely related. What makes it something right and wrong is that here, by the grace of God, *I* go. That's me. You can even extend that feeling not just to mankind. You see that with some poor dog that is suffering somewhere. It's life. I'm part of life. It's one thing to go hunt for your meal and kill for your food. It's another thing to see some poor animal or a person caught in a trap or being tortured. The closer it gets to you, the stronger the empathy gets, of course. You can step on some ants and you're not going to feel a tremendous amount of empathy. They're fairly alien to you.

Q. Let me see if I'm understanding what you're saying then. Are you saying that it's not just empathy in the sense of feeling another's pain as your own, that it extends beyond that? And it's not just duty. It's more an identification of yourself with the other person?

Yes. I think it is the identification that all around you counts. Again, to go back to my parable that I used earlier: If I am one cell, I can be a little independent cell, swimming around in a drop of water. But at some stage in evolution I become a cell that is part of a body. Now what happens to the other cells around me, happens to me. If something does it to them, they do it to me. I do it to them, I'm destroying myself. Man, by doing this to mankind, is actually destroying and hurting himself. Even in a completely, totally hard-nosed intellectual way, if we drop bombs all over South Vietnam and destroy their economy, we may very happily say, "Ha, ha, ha. We destroyed their economy." But in the long run, any part of the world economy that is destroyed will diminish our own status. It will diminish our own economy. This we're gradually learning with the environment. Sure, you can say, "I don't care. I'll bomb his country." But gradually we're learning that any kind of atomic bombing hurts everyone.

Look, here's a perfect example. For a long time people in the United States said, "We don't give a damn. All the factory smoke blows over to Canada so *they* have the acid rain. That's too bad for them." Now we're gradually realizing that it all blows back to us, and that when we are destroying the ozone over the South Pole that's it's going to hurt us sooner or later, too. It won't just hurt those penguins. It's a sort of stupidity of mankind, a little like an immature child who soils his own nest, who doesn't realize that we're all one. There's an expression in environmental philosophy—I think it's the Gaia theory[1]—that expresses the concept that the world is a living entity. All of it works. All is in harmony. All is in balance. It takes very, very little to throw that balance out of whack, as we are now finding out with the ozone layer, with the carbon dioxide, with the destruction of the rain forests in South America.

I've always felt very sympathetic to the way of thinking that we are one. I think that type of thinking was first discovered around the sixth century BC with Buddha. Then came Jesus. Then there were various philosophers and teachers who gradually became aware that we're *not* just one tiny, little tribal family here and screw the rest of the world. The tribe next to us has the same problems. Why don't we work with them? Then from tribe to country, from country to alliance, from alliance to world, gradually, by opening your eyes, you see that the animal kingdom is part of that, the vegetable kingdom is part of that, the minerals in the ground and the earth itself is part of that. We can poison it or we can keep it alive and live beautiful lives. It starts right with the individual always and my immediate neighbor. You know, love thy neighbor as thyself. Because it *is* yourself. It's the mirror, again. Everyone is you.

If the local skinheads were going to get your neighbor, you could very easily say, "Hey, why don't you come on over and stay in my house for a little while until the heat is off?" That's the kind of the attitude you have for most of these rescues during the war. There were later cases that were more complicated and that involved much more preparation. But initially most of the situations were rather simple.

Q. So it was just spontaneous?

It was quite spontaneous, yeah.

Q. Were you actually part of a network of rescuers at all?

No. To tell you exactly what happened, after our first initial group was caught by the Germans, I laid low for a little while. Then I managed to get some good false papers through a friend of mine who was a painter. He was one of these real artsy artists, an idealistic Communist. He had some Communist friends who got me papers. So that first time I got a set of false papers through a member of the Communist Party. Later on we had our own people specializing in making false papers. But that was the first false ID I got.

Then I lay low for a while. A bunch of friends of mine were in trouble so we all rented a houseboat and anchored among some little islands in the middle of a lake. In Holland this was still a pretty safe place at the time. The Germans hadn't gotten to motorboat patrols yet to check all these outlying places, though they did later on. We basically goofed off for the summer on the lake, having our girlfriends visit us and doing some sailing. But come fall, we had to go back to town.

I found another hiding place and started getting together with some of these friends. We founded our own little resistance unit of about fifty men. We collected some of the weapons we had hidden and brought them into town. Once we had done that, we really didn't quite know what to do. How do you tackle an elephant, which is what the Germans were? What are you going to do? We're not out to go shoot individual Germans or silly things like that.

Through the grapevine I got in touch with another, much bigger group in the Dutch army. They had gotten together a very cautious group. Their main purpose was to see to it that the national security in Holland was safe so if the Germans ever lost the war, the Reds would not take over. Some of the officers were a little more enterprising, and by this time they had gotten a contact over to England. They had a code so they could communicate. I joined up with that group. I was fortunate that the commander of the southern part of Amsterdam, which was where I was living, was a very nice guy. We really hit it off together.

My little group was the only armed unit they had in that whole resistance movement at the time. But we were totally opposed to actually firing guns because it can only lead to trouble. We were not into just murdering people. We started specializing in espionage and collecting information. I did a fair amount of photographic espionage at the time.

Now gradually this resistance movement expanded over the years until there were several parallel resistance movements. There was a student group where the guys in charge happened to have been old school friends of mine so I became somewhat of a liaison between these two organizations. Then later on there were two or three more organizations. The heads of all these organizations could never get together because their egos were so great. One was a Socialist group. The other one was an ultraconservative religious group. The third one—my group—was a very stuffy military group. Then there was the British Intelligence working in Holland, the OSS, the Netherlands Intelligence from London. Finally, toward the end of the war, there were just far too many people.

I'll give you an example that is so typical of how things operate. There were people who specialized in nothing but supplying the resistance and [the other] people in hiding with ration cards. That was a particularly feisty group. The Germans issued new ration cards every Friday afternoon. They printed the cards and then you had to go show your ID card and pick them up. What this group did is every Friday afternoon, somewhere in Holland, they made an armed attack on one of these ration bureaus. They stole 50,000 or 70,000 ration cards to supply the Jews and the resistance people—like myself—who were in hiding. They succeeded every single time, except one time. That time they were all killed. But they had the B team standing by and they then attacked a second bureau, in another part of the country and got the cards.

After a while, somebody finally had a bright idea and said, "This seems like a very complex way of doing this, not to mention very hazardous. Who prints these cards?" They found out that the people who printed the money were the Dutch mints. We figured there have to be some anti-German people in there. So we gradually established contact and found some engineers who were working there. They said, "Oh, sure. We'll run off another 70,000 for you. Then you don't have to make the raids every week." From then on, that's how the cards were distributed.

Q. How do you know whom to trust in this kind of situation?

Strictly gut feeling. Of course, you get as much information as you can from old school buddies, friends of friends who you know how to trust. Sometimes it's very difficult. We had one incident, for instance, with two twin brothers. One was working with me in my resistance unit and his brother was working for the Gestapo.

Another time we had a Jewish gentleman, who looked ethnically very Jewish. We found out he was working for the Gestapo. In exchange, his family didn't go to a concentration camp. But he traded off God knows how many other Jews whose hiding places he'd discovered and whom the Gestapo arrested. I don't know what happened to him after the war.

I know there was one Jewish lady, hiding out with her daughter in one of the places where I was hiding. She found out later on that her son had worked for the Gestapo. She committed suicide when she found out after the war. I have a picture of her laughing and celebrating with us the day we found out Hitler had killed himself. Then two months later, she was dead by her own hand, after going through all this!

So you had people who specialized in making false ID cards. You had another group known as the fight gangs. That was the fighting gang from the student group. They went into the national records and they put the place on fire, so that everybody's ID cards burned up and were destroyed. Then there was another photography group, with whom I worked when I started my film and photo unit. I also worked with the units that collected weapons; the weapons were dropped outside of town by the British and then we would smuggle those into town. So I was part of several different units but none of it was what you'd call a super organized network. Things just came up as needed.

Q. When people talk about philanthropy, one of the explanations that is often given is that people feel they're part of a network. Because other people they know are giving money, they feel they want to give, too, or they feel they should give money. In other words, partly they give money because they want to feel part of the crowd. Was this factor relevant in any of your rescue activities?

No. There was a very, very strong feeling against the Nazis. After all, these people had come into our country. We had been a neutral nation. We had meticulously stayed out of any of these European conflicts. Then suddenly, it's like some gang from South LA comes and enters and takes over your house. They start killing your friends. You happen to have a friend who's Jewish and they say, "Oh, well, let's send him to a death camp." So you build up a tremendous resentment against these people.

At the same time, we were always sharp. In other words, we could tell the difference between the different kind of Germans. There were nice Germans. There were weak-kneed Germans, people just drafted into the war but who were not really evil. But there were evil people, and then there were some of these super evil characters that were involved with this. Also, some of the really bad ones were the Dutch Nazis who were collaborators. But that was a very small percentage.

So that's why I have to explain it a little bit more. It's not so simple. You have to understand this combination of very loose-knit networks. Sometimes many of us knew each other by our real names, because we knew each other from school or from the football or from the army. Then other times, you'd get introduced to somebody but you were always introduced by your code name. Every once in a while, like once a year, you'd change your code name. That's why so often people asked me, "Oh, did you know so and so? He was in the resistance in Holland."

I always say, "It's very possible that I knew him, but I would have no idea what his [real] name is."

Q. So did all of these networks spring up because of the rescue activities and the resistance activities, or were they the cause of them?

They came up by themselves. As the need arose, people ended up getting involved. The young people particularly were eager to get involved.

Q. Let me ask you a little bit about the costs of your actions. Were you conscious of the potential costs for you and for your family?

Yes. As I said, those are decisions everybody makes every single day of their lives. Anytime you drive to downtown LA and listen to the radio you hear that every single day people on that same route get killed or they get shot at if they're in downtown LA. You totally randomly accept those challenges. You don't give it a second thought. Oh, sometimes you think about it a little bit.

Q. But what you did was a little more dangerous than going to downtown LA.

Yes. It is more dangerous, though actually you may not realize how dangerous driving is. Look at the statistics of the people that get killed each year. There are more people killed each year in car accidents than were killed in the whole of the Vietnam War. So it's funny how the mind adjusts. If you're a native in Africa and you've got to run through the jungle, you're not going to give the lions and tigers a second thought. They're there every day.

Q. So you didn't think about the risks?

We were cautious. It's just like you are in driving. You say, "I'm taking a risk driving there. It's dangerous driving at rush hour. Maybe I won't take the freeway." You take certain precautions.

Q. The idea that you could be losing your life for this, it never really affected you?

Oh, it sunk in at times. But it's just like flying. I'm going to fly to Israel. I know we've just had three major air crashes and I really don't like flying. But what am I going to do about it? Not go on the trip?

Q. So are you saying that a calculation of the risks doesn't really have any relevance to your decision to do the action?

Not too terribly much. There are times when things get very risky. Or you have to do something that is very dangerous, like crossing a checkpoint with a load of weapons. Now, in this situation you very consciously know that you may have to shoot your way out of this one. So you sweat it out a little bit. Your blood pressure goes up and you start perspiring. It's a little like going skiing. You're going to try that one slope that you've never tried before. You know that there's a fair chance that you could break your neck.

Q. Let me be sure I'm understanding what I'm hearing you say. Any calculus of the risk or the potential cost just affects the caution that you exert? It does not affect the actual decision to go ahead and act in a certain way?

No. Unless you say, "Hey, the risk is just too damn great. This would be foolish to do this. You don't have a chance of surviving doing that."

Q. But you might *say that.*

Oh, definitely.

Q. Was there ever a situation when you turned away somebody that you could have helped because you thought the risk was too high?

No, not that I remember. I did refuse certain military assignments. They were certain foolhardy ideas some guys had. We discussed it and I said, "No way. That is total foolishness." For example, I remember one instance even sillier than the others. They were shipping away all the meat reserves from the frozen slaughterhouse to Germany. They were shipping Jews away to Germany in the same train. One guy wanted to blow up the bridge. "If we blow up the bridge," he said, "they can't take all the food away from here. Also, if they have trains with Jews, they wouldn't be able to take them to Germany." The guy was a civilian, a student, and very enthusiastic about this [scheme]. He was willing to participate in it himself.

I said, "Look, let me teach you some arithmetic. To blow up a bridge of this kind, other than just destroying a rail, which you can repair in fifteen minutes, but to actually blow up the bridge, there are two or three things you have to remember. It takes about forty-five pounds of high explosives. Then you would have to drill into the basic structure of the bridge and pack explosives inside. Otherwise you'd need five hundred pounds of explosives, which we don't have. To pack the explosives in the bridge would take forty-eight man-hours. That would mean forty-eight men working one hour or one man working forty-eight hours. The bridge is patrolled every twenty minutes. You cannot work on it with more than two men at a time. Therefore, it is physically not possible to follow that approach."

"You could ask the British to bomb the bridge. But this particular bridge is on the list of bridges that the Intelligence has told us they need for the advance of the Allied army. So you cannot destroy the bridge. As terrible as it is that the Jewish trains would go over there, it's not feasible [to blow up the bridge]. It's not a feasible solution."

Q. So this goes back to what you were saying before. You were talking about being a part of the whole and that every part of the whole is valuable. You don't sacrifice yourself. You don't sacrifice any one part of the whole unnecessarily to save another part unless the part that's going to be saved is greater.

Oh, yes. That's right. It's the same thing I wanted to tell you, too, because it ties right in with this. Many people in the resistance, and also people who wanted to help the Jewish population, said the Dutch railroad workers should refuse to man these trains. What was very hard for us to do was to explain why we couldn't do this, without giving away secret information we had. The resistance had made an arrangement with the Dutch railroad workers so they would continue to work for the Germans, be very helpful and active and never do anything wrong against the German army or the transportation. The purpose of this was so the Germans would trust them completely. Then they would not replace them with German railroad workers. Then when D-Day came and the Allied forces moved in, the Dutch railroad workers would en masse go on strike and sabotage the whole system. Each of them was then in a position to do that.

They did this beautifully. This was very well organized. When D-Day came, the German railroad system in the Netherlands was just a total mess, totally out of order. Trains were derailed and everything went wrong. But at the same time it was done very meticulously so we could keep the advance routes for the Allies clear. The routes the Allies needed weren't blocked. So it was a very precise military Intelligence operation.

Now, it was very difficult for us to explain this when there were trains going that were taking Jews to Germany. The reality was that if the Dutch were not the engineers on the train, they would immediately be replaced by Germans. If they sabotaged the train at that point in the system, all they would do is sabotage one unit and then the whole railroad system would be suspect and the whole plan for D-Day would fall apart.

So you weigh a lot of emotional things one against the other. What emotionally would have been great is to blow up the steam engine of the train that takes the Jews away. But it would only have been prevented the departure for ten hours and then there would have been a different train.

Q. Let me be sure I understand you. Is what I'm hearing you say is that there is a conscious calculus that goes on but that it's a strategic kind? But that this calculus does not really have any impact on the decision to help other people, to rescue people? Is that right?

Yes, it is. Sometimes it is [affecting the decision] if you say, "No, it is too dangerous to do this. I would not succeed." Yeah, in that sense it could have a risk. Like I said, my scout who got shot down in the middle of the road, I definitely had to make a decision: No heroics because I'll just lose more men and I cannot afford to get killed myself because I am in charge in the platoon and I have to stay alive.

Q. You don't consider yourself a hero?

No. I always have trouble with that definition. What exactly is a hero? It can be a total lunatic who does something and happens to succeed in doing something that basically was an absolute madcap thing. To me, the closest thing to a true hero is the guy who is really terribly, terribly scared and does it anyway. To me, that is a real hero.

Q. And you were not a hero because you weren't scared?

Well, there were moments that I was scared but I mean . . . This is sort of confusing. When you think of a hero, you think of some Greek god standing there defending the pass against 5,000 Persians and knowing full well he'll be beaten. That is the true hero in the classic sense of the word.

Q. You don't see yourself as that kind of hero?

No. I'm a cautious hero.

Q. Well, most people would say that what you did was an extraordinarily good deed and that you should be rewarded for it. Do you think you did anything unusual?

I don't think that I did anything that special. I think what I did is what everybody normally should be doing. If you were in your best evening dress and you saw your neighbor's little girl fall in the swimming pool, you'd jump in and help her, wouldn't you?

Q. Yes.

That's right. Now, a lot of people, unfortunately, in this world, worry more about their evening dress. That is what is disturbing. Unfortunately, a lot of people are very selfish. It is not that we [rescuers] were so special; it is that they are stupidly selfish. Because sooner or later when somebody will have to help them, nobody will be there, and we all should help each other. If you see somebody rob a store and the guy runs away with the loot and you have a chance to trip him, remember that tomorrow they may rob your house and you'll be delighted if somebody else trips the thief then. It's common sense and common caring for people.

Sometimes people don't even want to take the littlest chance. They don't even want to phone the cops. We run into that attitude: the "I'd-rather-not-get-involved" attitude.

Q. So you're saying that there's nothing unusual that you did. You didn't do any-thing special. It's just that people who didn't help were just extraordinarily selfish?

A lot of them were. Some people, I can see the point. If you have three little chil-dren in your home, you'd better not get too involved because you are responsible for their lives, too. It's never clear-cut. But generally speaking, a lot of people could have done more. Basically, the whole resistance movement in Holland at its height was run by five hundred people. Now then, three weeks before the end of the war, in Amsterdam alone, we called some 15,000 reliable citizens who we knew were not pro-German and who had been in the service or been in the police or some-thing like that. We called them up. Literally. It was voluntary but we sort of drafted them and like little sheep they came. They became, for the last five days of the war, the resistance police units where we needed people to guard a certain place, to guard prisoners, to guard buildings. But they actually were not very involved in any of the resistance activities at all. They never were really active. It's ironic that they are the ones who formed the Resistance Veterans' Movement. It's all run by these people we called up in the last ten days of the war.

Q. How do you feel about people like that?

I think it's amusing.

Q. You have no other harsh feelings towards them?

They are very human, very typical. Well, we needed them for those ten days and so they were in the resistance.

Q. You don't have any bitterness toward people who were bystanders or people who turned in people in the resistance?

Oh, well, wait a minute. There's a big difference between the two groups. Sure, the people who turned in Jews are the people who deserve to hang by the you-know-what. I mean, that's horrible. One time we had requested a raid on the Gestapo building. It got very confusing but we thought it was going to be a ground raid. I even wanted to put up a camera to film it from a home in the neighborhood. I was living a block away from the Gestapo building. In the morning I suddenly see these mosquito fighter-bombers coming in at the rooftop and shooting off rockets, right over my rooftop and hitting the Gestapo building. So we then went in right away. There were time bombs and we went in with a unit of pseudo air raid wardens, supposedly to help the wounded (which we did) and also supposedly to help the Germans evacuate the building, which was partially burning. In so doing, we stole a lot of guns and stole several file cabinets. One of the cabinets was a lucky find. It had the receipts for people who had turned in Jews. The receipts contained their names and their address. Several of the people were later tried on the basis of these receipts. These people turned in Jews for the equivalent of what today would be fifty bucks. However poor you are, that's pretty sick. Then, too, people turned Jews in for grudges. You don't get along with so and so, so let's get rid of them.

Q. If you had known then exactly what was entailed in all of this, would you do it all over again?

Oh, sure. I'm still doing it. I'm still involved with this.

Q. Was guilt at all a factor in your rescue activities? You said you were a spoiled rich kid. Did you ever feel that maybe you had to make it up to somebody?

No, no, no. *Now*, in retrospect, I see myself as a spoiled little rich kid. In those days, I was like all little rich kids. I wasn't at all aware that I was spoiled or rich. You just go to Daddy and Mommy and ask them for money.

Q. Was there any kind of concern that you might lose the respect of somebody whose opinion mattered to you if you hadn't done some of these things?

Not really. No.

Q. Would you have been able to live with yourself if you hadn't done it?

I would have felt pretty weird if I didn't do any of these things. Particularly in the beginning, there were such easy things to do. It's almost like not stretching out your hand to somebody who's drowning. So it would have seemed strange not to do it. Oh sure, maybe they could pull you over the edge. But ninety-nine times out of a hundred, you'd just pull them out of the water.

Q. Did you ever think about the possibility that it might be you someday in a simi-lar situation of needing help?

Of course. But I didn't think about that too consciously at the time. In philosophiz-ing about it, I think a lot of it's basically the idea that you help your fellow man. If you analyze it in depth, it's probably because you feel, "Well, I hope somebody would do that for me, too."

Q. But do you think about that at the time?

I don't think you consciously think of that at the moment, no.

Q. Is what I'm hearing you say that you don't consciously think about anything [during a rescue]? You just do it spontaneously?

That's right. Except that you do use your intelligence. There are people who don't. There are people who just do it [without using their intelligence] but that's where you get a heap of soldiers in the middle of the highway.

Q. Was there a time in your life when there was any kind of a critical moment or an emotional period when you yourself desperately needed help from somebody? During the four- or five-day war with the Germans? Or when you were in hiding afterward?

Well, during the four- or five-day war, there was simply close-knit military action. You had your platoon and you did your fighting. When I had to go into hiding myself, that was no problem. There were dozens of people offering to hide you.

Q. So you weren't desperately alone. You weren't essentially on your own.

No. That's the advantage of a close-knit country like Holland, where most of your schoolmates still live in town. I think finding a hiding place took all of one hour that time. But I'd hopped around from one place to the other. You never stayed very long in the same place. In contrast, the Jewish people had to stay in one place and not be seen anymore if they looked very Jewish. The ones that did not look Jewish did exactly what I did. They managed to get false papers and simply kept on moving around. The more you moved, the safer you were, of course.

Q. Let me ask you one last question. If we would like to have more people like you in the world, what can you tell us that would be useful in doing this?

Oh, I don't know if I'm really the world's most desirable citizen. Let's not get too focused on me. In general, maybe education, motion pictures, books, religious leaders, role models, all these things in life create better citizenship. I don't mean we should get trapped in complex religious things because religion has a way of backfiring. And I'm not talking about sexual morality or patriotism or things like that. I mean simple moral behavior in the classic sense of the word. Simply general international morality. We live on one world. We are one people. We can behave or we cannot behave. To me, behaving means working in harmony with the world around you, harmony in the same sense that a big symphony orchestra is in harmony with each other. By being in harmony it creates something very, very beautiful. If you get one man who plays the wrong note, then you lose it. And yet a good conductor is not a dictator. He is a friend and a guide and it's a pleasure to work with him. And tomorrow, maybe you take over and conduct. You share it all. The most important thing is that it does not become a pyramid with a leader or führer or a dictator or a president who has too much power.

In the United States, we lack the terrible disorganization that is so marvelous in Holland. In all its disorganization, Holland is very organized. It's interesting to analyze the historical origin of that. It comes to quite an extent from sea ferrying. If you're on a boat and everybody doesn't work together, well, sure you have a captain but tomorrow the captain is sick or the captain isn't there and any other guy should be able to take over. Then, too, it comes from the building of dykes. If you had a set of villages, unrelated villages, that in most countries normally quarrel a lot among each other, if the ocean came across the sand dunes and flooded the land (as it did in the year 1404 in the St. Elizabeth flood), all these farms would drown. Their cattle would drown. Their crops would be ruined. So they have to learn to get together and to build dykes, *not* just in front of their own farm but in front of the whole ocean. They have to learn to do this together. Even if they did not benefit from it directly, in time it was important that they all did it together. That's something that really put a stamp on a lot of things that happened in Holland.

Q. Do you think that the Dutch seafaring tradition and the need for dykes was something that made the Dutch extraordinarily helpful in rescuing people, more so than other people, for example?

Well, those are two elements. Certainly the historical situation of seafaring and dyke building is one important factor. The old seafaring tradition and fighting the ocean and working together in a totally unorganized manner, without somebody at the top telling you have to do it, but doing it together on your own, like the kibbutz phenomenon [in Israel], that makes a difference. The other thing was that Holland originally was a marsh at the end of the Rhine. It was behind sand dunes. A lot of people who were serfs in other parts of Europe escaped from their tribe and, for whatever reason, ended up in that very safe marshland, where they could hide with their little rowboat somewhere and build a little building on a little knoll. Nobody would know where they were. They became very independent, just like the Swiss were in the Alps. Nobody could get at them. The Dutch do not greatly like strong authority. They hate authoritarian situations. They are very good at working together among each other. But they don't like somebody who starts telling them what to do.

Whenever I had to do something with my platoon in the army or before an action, I'd always get them together. We'd sit down at the table and say, "Look, guys. We're going to do this because of such and such." For example, I remember one ridiculous situation. I was a very young lieutenant. I was still a virgin, in fact. I had to give a lecture on sex education to this platoon, many of whom were men who had been called up because of the war and were in their mid-thirties and married with kids. I said, "Now this is ridiculous. Who wants to give this class? Some of you guys know much more about this than I do." One of the guys who happened to be a medical student gave the class.

We did the same thing another time. When I came straight from the horse cavalry, we had to have a class on the maintenance of the new motorcycles we'd been given. I didn't know anything about it. I had the book. So I picked one of my best soldiers, a guy who was a mechanic. "Come sit next to me. You teach this class because you know more about it than I do," I told him.

Q. But Tony, isn't it extraordinary that someone would have the strength of character to admit that he didn't know everything? I mean, to stand up in front of a bunch of men when you're a nineteen-year-old and say, "I don't know anything about sex"?

Well, that's why we got along so well. That's why we had a fun team. That was the point. So I was a lieutenant and they were soldiers. Big deal. Working together, basically we are the same. Nowadays the Dutch army does not salute its officers. There is no basic difference in uniform. They have a union for the soldiers. If you're dissatisfied with something that is being done to you, complain to your union. You can grow your hair as long as you want to. Yet each year they tend to win the NATO contest. They do the best job. It's been three years in a row that they won the contest.

Q. Are you saying that you think geographic and cultural factors have made a difference in Holland, shaping the Dutch national character? That there was a long tradition of valuing freedom and independence that was also a relevant factor in the Dutch rescue efforts?

Yes. I am not all that familiar with the history of Holland and the revolt against the Spanish king. But there was in Holland a long-standing tradition for freedom. Holland was the first western country that became a republic. It revolted against the king of Spain and told him, "Thank you but we don't want you as a king any more."

Q. That was a long time ago.

It's so strange. It's seems a long time ago to you. To the people in Holland, to this day, every single incident of that situation is like it happened yesterday.

Q. Is there a great deal of pride in this? Do you think that's an important part of their perception of themselves as a people?

Well, the Dutch are tremendously attached to freedom. That has a lot to do with it. It's not so much the pride. There are little incidents. The city of Haarlem went through a terrible siege with the Spaniards outside their city. To this day, you enter the church in Haarlem and there, imbedded in the wall, is still a cannonball from the Spaniards. There's a little plaque somewhere for this little fifty-five-year-old lady who formed the Ladies' Defense Corps at the time in the town. There were about eighty women who dumped pitch and boiling oil on the Spaniards who tried to scale the walls. Several of them got killed. That was in 1590, I think. It's a long time ago. So it's a little like our pilgrims. Everybody knows those stories. Since people still live in the same little towns, and see the places where it all happened, see the tower on which the old ladies fought and the church with a cannonball still in it, it somehow doesn't seem like it's that long ago.

· · ·

In August 1989, Tony and his wife took part in a trip to Auschwitz with several of the remaining twins on whom Dr. Mengele had performed his experiments. Tony later went on to Israel to receive his medal from Yad Vashem and, like other Yad Vashem recipients, to plant a tree on the Avenue of the Righteous. We spoke about this trip on Tony's return. Tony was troubled by several things that happened during the trip. His concerns underlined some of our earlier conversations in which Tony was careful to stress the fact that the Holocaust was not simply something that resulted from Hitler's evil or from flaws in the German character, but that the ability to do good and evil exists in all of us.

I'd been invited because I had done all the research on Mengele. I also felt that if I went I would represent the five million non-Jews who also died in the concentration camps. I'd even promised a friend on the board of a local gay/lesbian organization that I would put up a little pink triangle for all the homosexuals Hitler killed. Everybody who goes to Auschwitz puts up little signs for relatives, for friends, for people who had died. But when I tried to put up a pink triangle, I was told not to do so. This was one of the very first [unpleasant] things that happened. Two other things came up which caused difficulty. First, there has been a revisionist phenomenon taking place in Israel. I think as a result of the pressure from the Western world, which is quite unhappy about what the Israelis are doing with the Palestinians. Countries like Holland have spoken up quite clearly. The Dutch like the Jews but they have spoken up clearly against the Israeli military approach. The result has been a reaction in Israel, like a circling of the wagons. Anybody who doesn't agree with them [Israel] is now an opponent. So whereas five years ago Holland was always complimented about what the Dutch had done for the Jews during World War II, now suddenly it's the reverse. The Israelis now are saying that the people in Holland are anti-Semitic, that their help for the Jews in World War II was grossly exaggerated and they hardly did anything. This was fascinating in and of itself.

Then secondly, the attitude now is very much that the Holocaust was directed only at the Jews. The other people who died were incidental. This immediately brought up discussions. I said, "Well, what about the gays? What about the gypsies? What about the retarded people? What about all those political people who also opposed the regime? What about the Slavic population?"

Anybody who has studied German history during that period knows that the intention of the Nazis was to destroy as many as possible of what they considered the *untermenschen*, the lower sort, and replace them in time with German farmers. They wanted the Ukraine and Poland to be the breadbasket of Germany. To do this, they had to get rid of the people who lived there. Well, combined with trying to get rid of all the Jews everywhere, it was just impossible to do that and they never got it finished. But what is happening now leads to a straight conflict with the Polish government. Now the Israelis are also blaming the Polish government. The Poles were the second largest helper of Jews. Holland is the top and I think Poland is the second among the nations. But you see, from the Polish point of view, six million people died in the concentration camps in Auschwitz. For them, that means six million Poles died. They do not differentiate between Jewish, Catholic, Protestant, or whatever. There are Polish citizens who died in concentration camps. Just like when there is a plane crash in the United States, you don't split them up into black, Latino, Jews, and whites. You say two hundred or three hundred Americans died in a plane crash.

But Israel is very upset about how the Poles talk about the Holocaust. They want to have it very clearly said that the Holocaust was only against the Jews. The others were more or less incidental. They just died in the war.

This has focused on the name for the concentration camp at Auschwitz. It was [originally] a little village of Auschwitz. The Germans used it. Now up till recently, everybody always spoke of the German concentration camps. But recently, the revisionists started talking about the *Polish* concentration camps. This really upset the Poles. Although it seems minor, you must remember that it was not the Poles who set up concentration camps. The first inhabitants of Auschwitz, the first prisoners, were 19,000 Poles who, without exception, all died there. So after the war, when the concentration camp was set up as a memorial in collaboration with the United Nations the agreement was that it would be a nondenominational memorial. There were not to be little separate chapels for Catholics, Protestants, Jews, or anybody. It would be a monument to the horrible things people did to other people. The area outside of the camp, what was left of the town, was reinhabited by the Poles who returned to their town.

Now, comes *Perestroika*. Now the Jewish pilgrims can visit the camp. So they come in huge quantities. Especially, there are lots of Israelis who are coming from Israel to Poland to visit Auschwitz. Now that travel is much easier and a lot of people can come in very easily, they're coming in huge numbers. But unfortunately the attitude has changed and the attitude is now not to see what horrible things were done by the Nazis during this horrible historical period. The lesson used to be that this sort of thing should never, ever happen again. *Now* the stress is on how the Jews have been persecuted and why we must never, ever give way. "We [Jews] must be strong. We must fight for our independence. In other words, we have to expand our homeland. We have to be as tough as they were and defend ourselves." So it has been switched into a nationalistic thing. Many Jews I talked to are very unhappy about this. But this general attitude was so extreme that I heard a lady say—not a lady from our group, there was another group there from Israel—and I heard a lady say, "Well, this is where they should send all the Palestinians." That was just one woman but it's still frightening.

Q. What did she mean? That the Palestinians should be forced to see it? Or that they should put them in a concentration camp?

No, no, no. She meant that this is where we should put all our Palestinians. This is an American-Israeli. At least she was English speaking. It was just a single incident. And I would never project that [attitude] on the whole group. But that anybody would even dream of saying that, particularly someone who is a member of a group that had gone through this kind of persecution, it was very shocking. There was a fair amount of that kind of attitude.

Then next to that, of course, you have the tactlessness on the other side. A group of Roman Catholic nuns bought a dilapidated old building next to a gravel pit where they used to execute people. This is outside the museum but it abuts up against the outside fence of the museum. This little group of nuns has a special order and they pray for the souls of those who died in Auschwitz. Now, that's fine. It doesn't hurt anybody. But the new way of thinking from Israel, which holds that since Auschwitz was only to eradicate Jews, they don't like the idea of Catholic nuns praying for the souls of Jews. Now, ordinarily, nobody would even have known about this. But the convent was so tactless that they turned the gravel pits, which were the execution grounds, into a normal garden area. It's grown over and has soil in it and it's a grass lawn. It's right next to their building. Then they put up a humongous twelve to fifteen-foot-high cross, right between the road and, behind the cross, you see the walls of Auschwitz. So that worked like a red flag, particularly on the new Jewish pilgrims. So there's a lot of insensitivity on all sides.

It was a very hot, very emotional day when we were at Auschwitz. I was not allowed to put up my little pink triangle because homosexuals are considered sexual deviants and this would upset the conservative Jewish contingent of our group. The people in the group said, "No, we'd feel very uncomfortable about that. That would upset our people because after all they are sexual deviants." I made it clear I was disappointed.

Everybody's very emotional, very upset. There were all these members of the Knesset who came out when we were in Israel. There were all kinds of speeches. For several of the Knesset members, it was more of a photo opportunity. But the others were definitely very moved.

We had interesting things happen. Let me give you one example relating to the twins Mengele did his experiments on, since we traveled with them. The grandson of the doctor who was in charge of Mengele, who was in charge of this genetic research in Germany, his grandson had contacted one of the twins. When he heard that they now suffered from lots of unknown diseases, he offered to go look through all his grandfather's research to see if he could be of any help in trying to figure out what they had been injected with. He asked if he could come along on the trip, because he suffered from the traditional German guilt of people who are descendants of these murders. He's a very nice young man, sort of like a German hippie. We all liked him very much. He had been invited by the Israeli woman who was one of the ladies in charge of our trip; but the rest of the Israeli contingent didn't want to have him stay at their hotel. So he ended up staying with the American contingent. That again was a weird arrangement. The Israeli contingents never socialized with the American contingents. We never had a dinner together. It was totally separate. Only at Auschwitz were we ever together. Then there [was] a very emotional outburst. But oddly enough nobody talked about the Germans. There were a couple of people who started to attack the Poles, who are our hosts there. They attacked the Poles, saying the Poles have never done anything to help the Jews during World War II, saying the Poles are anti-Semites, and even though they try to tell us that they helped the Jews, they never did.

Then the guy went on and said the same about the French, and even the Dutch. "They're always so touted about helping all these people," he said. "But what happened to all the 100,000 Jews that died in Holland? They didn't make any real effort to help. There may be one or two people but there was no real effort made." He said this in front of TV cameras.

When we were through, I took the guy aside and said, "Look, I was there; you were not." He was a three-year-old child at the time. He was not from Holland. He was from Germany. I said, "You have your facts wrong. I know how many people helped Jews. I know how many of my friends died helping Jews." For a tremendously long time we were trying to convince our Jewish friends to hide. From the very beginning when they had to fill in the forms about their grandparents, about how many of their grandparents were Jewish, we tried to convince them to lie. I still have the forms in my possession. I begged them, "Just hide your family bible or tear up photographs of grandparents with big beards. Tell your rabbi to also get rid of his files or hide them because there's no way that without that they can prove that you're Jewish." But no, they absolutely refused to do that. When things got a little worse later on, we tried to convince several of them who were not specifically Semitic looking to join the underground. We told them, "You're going to get into terrible trouble. They're going to end up sending you to death camps. Now is the time to cash in on your possessions. Liquidate your holdings and join the resistance and go underground." No, nobody wanted to do that.

We had this Mr. Asscher, who was a wealthy diamond dealer, a friend of Goering. He was appointed as head of the Jewish Council and he had his whole organization with his people. They were putting out the newspaper and they were telling the Jewish community not to worry. "Nothing is happening," they said. "The worst that is going to happen is that they want the Jewish people who have been into banking and money deals. They think that we should all go through a certain period of time where we work on the land as farmers in Westerbork (which is a preliminary work area there).[2] We'll work on the land in the open air and we will be controlled by our own people. Just go."

Asscher told people this. It was a total lie. Maybe he believed it himself in the beginning but toward the end there was no question that he had to know what the Germans were doing. I'm not sure what happened to Asscher. I know his family survived because they were our neighbors. I think he survived also. He may have been sent to a camp. But only at the very end, when all the Dutch Jews were gone, were he and his family sent to a camp, to Theresienstadt. There they got preferential treatment and they all came back. But they sold everybody else. *This* is the real history. The people don't like to hear it.

Normally, you never talk about it because it sounds anti-Semitic, but the Dutch Nazi Party in Holland before the war had several Jewish members. It was an ultra-right political party. They were not anti-Semitic originally. So there were several Dutch Jews who were ultra-right wing and who were even admirers of Mussolini. When the war came, a few of those ended up working for the Gestapo. A few other Jews in Amsterdam also volunteered to work for the Gestapo, very understandably, in order to save their families or save their own lives. But in doing so they made it very difficult because they were trying to find out about the resistance movement. They'd say, "I have a family of Jews that want to hide. Can you help me?" When you helped them, then you were turned into the Germans. So it was not an easy thing to hide Jews.

Finally the point comes when the Jewish people Asscher's talking about, the bankers and rich merchants, have gone to Westerberg. We sent photographs of the camp to try and tell them, "Don't go. Don't go because you're on your way to death." Then the street raids started. Suddenly, overnight you have 60,000 people who want to hide. Well, that's not possible. There are logistics involved with that. We have food rationing cards. We had fairly sufficient food but not enough to share with another family, so you have to find ration cards for these people. Secondly, by this time a lot of the people's businesses had been taken. They had no money left. Now, the wealthy are not usually the people who help others. It is usually the middle class, the lower middle class, which is more apt to help people. These people often did not have the money to buy extra food or to buy black market food or all the other supplies that people need when they are in hiding. They didn't have the room. Plus if you and your family were caught hiding Jews, they'd all be killed. It's one thing to do it yourself. Like for me, it was easy. I was single. For my parents, they were single and if anything happened they would be the only ones who would be killed or go to a camp. But other families had little children or teenagers and if they were caught, their whole family was killed or sent to a camp. So the percentage of people in Holland that were hidden was the largest percentage that you could expect to be hidden on such short notice under those conditions.

You know, I've never talked about this before. I also feel very upset for having to even apologize for this, because people really tried hard. So when this man said all this, that was a very upsetting situation. The man refused to apologize. I talked to our group leader and said that he really owed me an apology. But I wasn't excited or mad about it.

The group leader said, "Well, it's very, very difficult because he's one of our top contributors from Beverly Hills."

So in talking to this man, in trying to convince him that he was wrong, I reminded him that this is not the first time in history that this kind of thing has happened. When they held my tree-planting ceremony, I read a poem about Anne Frank. It's called "Anne Frank, Stop Looking at Me." It's about the fact that Anne Frank is still alive and is still getting killed every day. Sometimes in a Cambodian terror camp. Sometimes in an air raid. Sometimes in a terrorist attack. Sometimes in a bomb blast. But basically Anne Frank is still being killed somewhere. You know who is killing her? It's you and me, the people who fight the righteous cause for God and country. I wanted to read the poem out loud at the ceremony. But they absolutely said no, that it would upset the conservative Israeli group. So we kept the photo opportunity separate from my Yad Vashem acceptance speech.

I don't want this to sound like a diatribe against the Jewish people or Israel. But there were other unbelievable things that bother me. I read in an Israeli newspaper that there are serious plans to rebuild the Temple of Israel. To do that, they will have to tear down the Mosque of Omar and the Mosque of the Golden Dome or the Mosque of the Rock, which are the two biggest shrines after Mecca. This would create an instant holy war with all the Arab countries. But they're serious about it. They're starting to make the utensils for the temple. They're weaving the cloth for the priest's clothes. They put in an order for red heifers in Sweden so they'll have the animals to use for the animal sacrifices.

Now, all this troubles me. Israel's changed. I was in Israel in 1962. At that time Jerusalem was controlled by the Jordanians. Oddly enough, though, then there was more respect for the international shrines, including the Jewish shrines, than there is now. Now Israel is like a damn police state. It reminds me of South Africa. They have the police cars with all the dents from the stones and the mesh on their windows, and everywhere, the soldiers with their guns at the ready. We were there two hours before the Sabbath near the Wailing Wall. It was getting too hot for me so I entered one of the passages on the side, in the shade. This area is filled with sixty soldiers, all with their belts holding tear gas and grenades. They're there to stop Arabs. There's nothing specific you can put your finger on, but you see them holding onto the guy's arm while waiting to check his ID and they're not letting go. It all has a chilling effect. I would never, ever expand this to say this is a Jewish phenomenon. To me, this is a political thing that is taking place, a lack of tact. It's the same lack of feeling for which they have so long and so rightfully accused the non-Jewish community. But when we were boarding the plane at the passport control, there's an Israeli passport officer who talks to the group leader. He points at Susanne and me and said, "Do you have any other non-Jews in your group?"

Now, if the reverse occurred. If you were in a New York airport and an American passport official said to a group leader, "Do you have any other Jews in your group?" Jesus! The commotion that'd ensue! I know it wasn't meant badly. I know the guy's just trying for security reasons to figure certain things out. But it is *exactly* the same thing. It's the same prejudice that for so long they felt rightfully uncomfortable with when it was done toward the Jewish people. Yet they do not seem to sense that some of the things they are doing now are very peculiar and are very sad.

Q. How did the twins respond to all of this? You said there were ten sets of twins who went back with you?

Yeah. They're not complete sets because sometimes one of the twins died. But we had one very good thing happen, which happened because the young German helped a lot, the one whose grandfather was the doctor in charge of genetic research. When he was at Auschwitz, they went through the file cabinets that are still available. You have the file cards in there and he found the file card of one very nice Czechoslovakian Jew, a man named Peter. They discovered that Peter's twin sister had *not* died in the concentration camp like he thought! She might still be alive somewhere in the world. So he was very excited and he's going to try to find out where she is. It was amazing to discover it, fifty years afterward. More than fifty years. Now the fact that it was the grandson of the guy who was in charge of all these horrible experiments who helps you find it, well, so many weird things happened!

See, my theory in all this, is that there are good people and there are bad people in this world. And there are a lot of people in between, who don't do anything. But the good people should work together. We should fully realize that there are bad people in America, in Holland, and in Israel. There are no God-chosen children, anywhere. Because, that basically is the same theory of the superman of the Nazis. There's an amazing contradiction in the Jewish people. Some feel they have to express their uniqueness in the form of a supposed invulnerability and, as far as I'm concerned, in a racist police state of chosen people continuing ancient cycles of suffering and domination until the coming of the Messiah who will make them all-powerful. Now on the other hand, there are just as many others who have expressed their sense of uniqueness through the spirit of Isaiah and Rabbi Hillel by believing that *because* of their faith, more is expected from them. By giving of themselves, by giving the world love, compassion, education, intelligence, democracy, law and justice, that's paving the way for the day of the Messiah. In my heart, I'm more in tune with those people. This is what I admire in the Jewish people. This is also the spirit of the kibbutz. But there is the split between these groups in Israel now. Which way is it going to go? I don't know. The dime is on its edge.

I've been invited by the rabbi here to speak about our trip to Auschwitz and to Israel. I want to be totally honest and it's very difficult to do that. I'm going to tell him ahead of time how I feel. If he doesn't want me to speak, I won't speak, of course. I don't want to insult anybody. I will warn them ahead of time, because it's not fair if you think somebody's just going to make a nice little travelogue talk. But if he still wants me to talk, then I will tell what I saw in all the kindness of my spirit but as a warning that we have to fight against this kind of thing wherever it happens.

• • •

In 1948, Tony immigrated to the United States, where he worked in the motion picture industry as a technical, historical, and script adviser and where I interviewed him in Malibu, California. In the summer of 1990, shortly after we completed the bulk of our conversations, Tony and his wife moved to Holland, where he lived quietly in a small town near the ocean with his wife, Susanne, and their young adopted son.

The family later returned to the United States and lived in Arizona and Washington State. We visited throughout this time and I was able to supplement our initial interviews, although the portrait that emerged during these later interviews did not modify the basic view that emerges of Tony's ethical perspective. A full story of his life, dictated shortly before his death, is available in his memoirs, The Last Hussar: Resistance without Bullets, published in 2010 by Conserve, a Dutch publisher.

By 2009, Tony's health had deteriorated and he died of congestive heart failure on July 19, 2009, with Susanne holding his hand. Still wishing to avoid public acclaim for what he considered behavior that any normal person would do, Tony had willed his extensive photographic records of the war to the National War Museum in Amsterdam with the stipulation that they plan no exhibits until after his death.

CHAPTER 4

Beatrix: Bystander

Q. Did you know about the concentration camps during the war?

Yes.

Q. Did you know that the Jews were being gassed?

Yes. I can't tell you who told this, but my husband heard a lot when he
 worked in the hospitals.

Q. How did you react to something like that?

You couldn't do anything.

Q. There was nothing you could do.

No. No . . . You could not do anything.

Spring 1991

I am the cousin of Tony and I have stayed a lot with his parents when my mother
died. My mother died when I was thirteen years old. I was born in 1913—here, just
two houses away—in Rotterdam. I am looking at the house as we speak.

I've been from one school to another. I first went to the gymnasium, and at a
time when it was strange that a girl went to the gymnasium, which were then usually only for boys. Then my mother died and I went to school in Brussels, a boarding school. That was because the mother of Tony knew it was a very good school. I
made acquaintance with a Norwegian girl. She spoke a little Dutch and so she was
allowed to come to my home and I was allowed to go to Norway. We went with our
ship to Bergen. I think it is a beautiful country.

Oh, I remember everything of my youth. My father liked very much sports,
cricket and tennis. My mother was always at home. She was always making cloth-
ing. She did everything, including the most beautiful handwork. It was very beautiful. But she died very early at the time. I think she was operated on for gall blad-
der problems. In America you had medicine that could make the blood coagulate
but then she got a little clot and died.

I was not the only child since I had a brother who was seven or eight years
older, but he didn't live anymore at home much after that. He married very young;
when I was thirteen, he was about twenty, and he was at home. My mother was

closer to my brother because I was, at that time, very young. It was hard, and after some years my father remarried and at that time I went from school to school. I had been in Brussels, and I wasn't happy there. Then I came to Holland and I went to school next to my grandmother, who was living in Bussum, next to Amsterdam.

Q. What was it like to grow up in boarding school at thirteen?

You have no choice. I made several good friends who went to boarding school too. But they have all married. One has gone to America and the other one is living in England. Some are living in The Hague. Just when I came here, there was one girl, she came here too, and lived here.

Q. So boarding school wasn't a great time for you? It was difficult?

No. I liked it better than being home.

Q. What was your stepmother like? Did you get along with your stepmother?

Oh, yes. I knew her, and adapted with no difficulty.

Q. Tell me a little bit, if you don't mind, about what it was like in the home. The American family right now is so different from the families that my father, who is more your age, would have been raised in. Children were treated so differently.

Totally different, because when I was twenty-one years old, my stepmother said to me, "If your father heard that you have ever been kissed, there will be some difficulties." That was when I was twenty-one years old. I married one year later.

Q. Did you kiss your husband before you married him?

I kissed my husband just before. That's all. I think now it is much better, that people are living together before they marry. Because it is such a shock!

Q. Did you eat dinner with your father and your stepmother? Did children and adults eat separately in terms of meals?

Oh, no. We always ate separately. I've been, my whole life, very lucky. [Beatrix smiled.] I had a very good life. I always was spoiled. But my husband worked very much. But I had time to go and play tennis. I played squash and all sorts of things. We had two helps in the kitchen and one help for his practice, too. At that time you did your medical practice at home. My husband went to the people to see if they were ill enough to be put in the hospital. Now you telephone the hospital, but at that time you telephoned first our home. Then I had to look to find where he was.

Q. So you went to boarding school and then you came back to Holland. What happened then, Beatrix? Did you go to the university? Did girls go to universities?

No. They had an exam that I took, to learn steno and typing. Then I worked as an assistant in a hospital. Because I had been to Norway, I learned a little bit of Norwegian. I've forgotten all of it now. Oh, I can say some words, but not much. But at that time, I had to type and answer the phone and then she sometimes said to me, "Well, look at that man who is coming. He is for department three." That was the department where . . . I can't say the word . . . it's difficult. But lots of sailors or shipping clerks, maybe you would call them, were sent there because they had some sexual illnesses. My father was very afraid that I would learn difficult things. So he went to the director and asked that I didn't learn too much things, well, things about sex. He didn't want me to know that there was any sex in the world. Those people had an illness of sex. Yes, it was syphilis. That was what it was called. Now I remember. Syphilis. I wasn't allowed to know it, and so my father went to the director and asked that I didn't learn too much of it. He was really very old-fashioned, very old-fashioned.

Q. How did you meet your husband?

Well, my husband was eleven years older and he had a surgeon he knew there. He took care of special things for the women, how do you call it? Gynecology. Then he could get a place to work in the south of the Netherlands, at a place that was on an island. Absolutely an island. If we wanted to go away, we had to take the boat. But there was an old woman and she left all her money to build a hospital, and so they built for us a house, too.

So when I was twenty-one years, I lived in a beautiful house. All grass and grain. Now there are many houses around. That's the way I lived. My husband was the only doctor. There were no other specialists. He was the only specialist. You came to him and then he had to tell them, "Yes, you have to go to Rotterdam to that and that specialist." He couldn't leave the island because my grandfather, Tony's grandfather, too, had always, every year a meeting in Huss, an island south of where we lived. When we came to Huss, came a telephone and we had to go back immediately. He [my husband] stayed there for six years. It was a beautiful hospital. When he came there, they told him he had to buy everything, all his own instruments. Even if he thought, "I don't need it so much now but perhaps there will be one time when I need it," well, then, you must buy it now, because when we are on this island where we are working, you can't buy anything more.

Q. You haven't told me how you met him yet.

Before he went to this hospital, I met him several times. I knew him from playing tennis. Then he came to work on the hospital because he wanted to make, as a doctor, a trip around Africa, for two months. Then he came to work. He came to the hospital and he worked there for some days. So we went out together and he asked me to marry him.

Q. Very quickly.

No, because I knew him from tennis. But then we met at the hospital again. Then he made the big trip around Africa and when he came back he married me and we went to —— for six years. But then my husband felt that he couldn't be up to date. You have to go to certain things to be up with everything, to hear the new things and so, all the updates. So we went to Utrecht. There we stayed in a very big house and we lived next to the bishop.

At that time, the prices were quite different, and the man who sold his practice to my husband asked for his house too much. It was only 2,000 guilders; it's nothing now. But then it was a lot.

My husband said, "The practice will not go. I don't want to go back to the family for money. I don't pay 2,000 guilders; it is too much." So it was bought by the Catholic Church, and we got to rent it for six to eighteen years. After eighteen years he had to go to another house. Also a big house. It needed to be big because he had the practice at home, you see. If you didn't feel well in the evening, if you were ill he said, "Well, come to me." Also in the afternoon, between one and three, he had practice at home, not practice, but he looked after you. Then he stopped when he was sixty-five years old, he lived in such a big house. Downstairs was his practice, we lived on the first floor, and we slept on the third floor. I said, "Well, why don't we sell the house and go and live in a little house?" We sold the house very well and I went to a house that was for sale . . . and there was a man walking and I say, "I want this house . . . I should like to look at it."

He said, "You mustn't do it because I just sold it. I just signed and I am the owner." At that time we had to move, there was no other place, because we had sold the house. So I lived [there] for eighteen years. While it was nice, the sun was beautiful there. But otherwise, it wasn't nice; you had not contact with the ground because this was an apartment on the seventeenth floor, in Utrecht. My husband had a very nice group of people he studied with in Utrecht, and all his friends, who were also older, and all the wives of his friends. They were also older, and they all died. There's nobody living anymore of his friends. They all came to our house, when they studied in Utrecht, and when there was a party, they came to me.

Q. Where were you living during the war, when the war came?

We had just left the island. G——.[1] This is just off the coast of Holland, but it is in Holland. We were living there when the war broke out. We were just arrived in Utrecht and then I lived in the very little house for some months because the surgeon who sold the practice to my husband wanted to help him to get started. Then he fled to South Africa. I am not sure, but maybe he had something . . . Jewish, I'm not sure. . . . So we went, actually just ten days before the Germans came to Holland, we went in the big house in the middle of Utrecht. The day the war started, it was terrible because Rotterdam was bombed. My parents worked here. We heard that Rotterdam was bombed. The middle of Rotterdam was totally lost. We didn't know much how my parents had difficulties. So I went with the typist and we went with a tandem bike to Rotterdam. She wanted to know if her friend was alive because he had to be in Rotterdam at the time. I wanted to see if my parents were alive. My parents had very much luck. My grandfather, and also the grandfather of Tony and other brother of my father, they were all here and the Germans were flying just in a wave, but one of the airplanes was shot down so they didn't hurt this one area. A little bit farther on, yes. But here, not. I went to see on a bike from Utrecht. Everything was all right and also my grandfather and the grandfather of Tony, because he lived in the middle of the town at that time. I don't remember exactly why he was there. We were all afraid of the war because we knew that they would come. We expected them. We didn't know exactly when they would come.

But my house was never bombed. The house of my parents is still here. I can see it here. That's why I live at this side of the apartment complex. The rest of the homes are totally changed.

Q. Then what happened during the war?

My husband was a surgeon, and he went to the country. During the war, he operated for cheese and meat. He would operate and people would give him cheese and meat in exchange because there were a lot of farmers. They all helped and I had several addresses also from patients of him. I got on the bike of my father without the [tires] because if you had a good bicycle, the Germans took it. So we had not much, because when you went away, we were allowed to put the car in the garden of the bishop whose garden was a little bit bigger than our garden. He had a back entrance, so we could put our car there. My husband had a motorcycle, and he worked on a motorcycle. He went to several places on the motorcycle. But when he went out in the morning, he had just one piece of bread, that was all. We slept upstairs, but my mother-in-law was with us and I had a small sort of stove with wood. In the morning my mother-in-law slept there, we took it out and put it in the other room, and then in the morning my children had lessons there. No. One class. I don't remember which of the children. I became mistress and all in that room. We had several places where we could write. It was a very old-fashioned home, and so we had in the attic . . . we made a part where you could go away to hide.

Q. Was there anyone you were hiding?

My husband had been taken away once, for one day. That [happened] with all the specialists, because they had taken their nameplate from the door, [as a protest] and they all, every specialist they took it away, and then the Germans started the . . . arrests for one day only. After one day he could come back home.

Q. Why did they lock up all the specialists?

Because they all took their nameplate off the door, and that wasn't allowed.

Q. I see. So you had built a hiding place for your husband to hide. Did you use it to hide anyone?

He hasn't been there, but our neighbor of the other side, he had to hide for a certain moment.

Q. Why was he hiding?

I don't remember why.

Q. But you did not hide him?

No.

Q. Was he Jewish?

He wasn't Jewish, no. Because if you were Jewish you were immediately away or you had gone to Africa. When my husband made that trip to Africa, a lot of Jewish people were abroad. We saw it already coming.

Q. But you were not hiding Jews in the attic?

No.

Q. Did you know any people who were Jewish at that time?

Yes.

Q. But nobody approached you . . .

No, because there were a lot of Jews who stayed there and didn't want to hide. After some times, they were taken away, too. Because [there were] a lot of Jews who lived normally, and had only to wear the Star of David. Yes. My husband had known in the hospital because there have been several Jews put away so nobody knew . . .

Q. They were hidden in the hospital . . .

Yes.

Q. And your husband knew about this.

He knew about this, yes.

Q. So then the war continued. It was pretty bad in Holland the last year of the war, particularly, wasn't it? The hunger winter . . .

Oh, yes.

Q. How do you get through something like that, Beatrix?

I was very lucky that my husband could always get from farmers meat and cheese. But he operated also in two little places. But then you were controlled when you entered Utrecht. One time he was on a motorbike . . . and then he had on overalls. He bought a ham. He put it here [inside the overalls].

Q. He looked pregnant.

Then he was stopped on a bridge. The Germans asked him, "Do you have any food with you?" He said, "No, only some potatoes." They looked in the back side of his motorbike and said, "All right." When he had to put out the motor, he couldn't bend down. I didn't know what happened, because the Germans were very polite, and he came home.

Q. It's a good experience as a gynecologist, to have empathy for pregnant women, then.

I have had a daughter in the war, but it is not the nicest time to have children . . .

Q. No, it must be very painful. There must be a lot of anxiety, just being pregnant. Your emotions are so high anyway and there are so many fears. You worry about everything when you are pregnant, and then having a war on top of it must have been very difficult.

It was.

Q. Was there anything that helped you get through that time period, Beatrix?

No.

Q. You just had to do it.

Yes.

Q. Are you a religious person at all?

No. Not at all. Neither was my husband.

Q. Was there any kind of faith or belief that this would come out all right? Were you sure that the Germans were going to be defeated eventually, and you just had to hang on? At first it looked as if they were doing quite well.

Yes.

Q. But there wasn't anything in particular that helped you get through the time period?

No, you have to . . . I forgot to say that I was arrested by the Germans, because my husband had to work and I filled the car's gas tank for him.

Q. You were arrested by the Germans?

Yes, but afterward, when I explained it, they accepted it.

Q. Were you frightened when they arrested you?

Yes, I was frightened because at that moment when I did it, my husband was ill, he had a sort of influenza. He was in his bed, and the Germans said they had to come to the house next to Utrecht. I said to my husband, "I am afraid to go alone. You have to come out."

"I am too ill," he said.

I said, "I don't go alone." Then I drive the car; he was sitting next to me. When we entered the house, the men who arrested me said, "Just go," because they saw that he was so ill.

Q. So you were very lucky.

Yes, I was lucky but I was afraid to go alone.

Q. You had children, of course.

I had two children born on the [island], my son of fifty-seven and my daughter of fifty-four and the youngest one, she is forty-nine now, was born in '42.

Q. Did you know what the Germans were doing in terms of how they interrogated people or what it was like? Did people have a reasonably good idea about the methods that the Germans were employing?

Yes. They knew, but that was not very nice. The only difficulty I had was the German directive, and one time they came and rang the bell. My help opened and then went upstairs and they took my husband away. He was not yet dressed. It was very early in the morning. It was seven o'clock or something. Then he was away for one day. But he was not alone. All the specialists were taken there. They were away for one day. That was the only thing I always . . . I went on an old bike to get milk . . . and on the other side of our home was living a very rich German woman who had been married to a Dutchman. She was widowed. She didn't like this from the Germans. All the Germans had to come . . . there were also Germans who didn't like it. Her family came to her and she kept them. . . . It was not very kind what I am telling now. But we knew that she was a good one for us. So I remember I was stopped by the Germans, who said, "Where are you going with all that sort of food?" I said, "Oh, that is for Mrs. so-and-so," and he said, "Oh, then it is all right."

Q. So you basically just tried to lay low and make it through and avoid the Germans as much as possible.

I must honestly tell you that I knew everything on the minute exactly about my news, but in the middle of my life, there was a lot. [Beatrix shrugged.][2]

Q. I understand. Did you know what Tony was doing during the war?

Yes, he came to me. I will remember always. He was in the military.

Q. He was a cavalry officer.

Yes, and then he was in Utrecht. Just ten days before the war, he came to my . . . I lived in a little house where the man who went to Africa, my husband bought the practice of. Tony came to look us up. He told his friends that they had to telephone him so that he didn't have to stay too long. I always remember that. He said, "Oh, I'm sorry. Yes they ring me. I have to go." But I liked him very much, Tony. Tony had not had a very easy youth.

Q. No. So you knew that Tony was working in the underground.

Yes, I knew.

Q. Did he ever ask you to help him in any way or hide him?

No.

Q. Did you try to talk him out of it in any way?

No. When he came to me that was before the Germans. In wartime, I didn't have any contact with him.

Q. None at all. Did you know what had happened to him? Did you have any idea?

No.

Q. As far as you knew he was dead.

No, I knew that he was alive. You didn't know much about . . . if you didn't work with the underground, then you had no communication. Because when you had communication, I shouldn't know something, they could interrogate you . . .

Q. So you didn't want to know anything . . .

No. Tony didn't know anything. It was much safer.

• • •

Q. This may seem like a strange question, Beatrix. If any of these questions are not something that makes sense to you, just tell me that. OK? Can you tell me something about how you view basic human nature? Do you have any thoughts on whether people are good basically? Are they bad basically? Have you thought about this at all?

No.

Q. You don't think much about people. You haven't thought about this.

I don't think I am a very easy woman. Some people I like very much and other people I don't like. I can't say why.

Q. But you don't think that people are basically good or people are bad?

No.

Q. Do you think that most people act out of their own self-interest? Do you assume that people will naturally try to take care of themselves and do what's best for them? Or do you expect people to think more about other people? We all have preconceptions . . .

The only answer I can give you is this: if I had no children, I wouldn't know how I would spend this end of my life.

Q. What do you mean by that?

I told you that my husband was older. So there were older friends. They always came to you. . . . I lost girl friends that I met here and knew from my youth. I don't know where they are . . . they are married or away. I don't know where. I don't know how I started this . . .

Q. You said that if it weren't for your children, you didn't know [how you would spend this end of your life].

Oh yes. I still have friends from my sport in Utrecht. I am always going to their address in Utrecht still. So I always look them up. There were two sisters who wanted to enter the hospital of ——, but they were not allowed because they could talk about the people who were in the hospital. So they went to Utrecht, and got their training. Afterward, one of them became head of the operation room. I always see her. Not always, but sometimes . . . when I am in Utrecht I see her and talk with her.

Q. But you said that if it weren't for your children . . .

When you came, my daughter, who is living north of Amsterdam, had just telephoned me and sometimes I go to her. My son rings two or three times a week.

Q. That's what keeps you going.

Yes. I think next weekend I will go to my son because one of the children has his birthday and . . . I don't know if this interests you but once the children have gone to ski to France. Then one day I was sitting here talking to an older lady, and the telephone rings. I heard a little voice. My grandson is about thirteen years old; he said to me, "Oma, I am in the hospital. I am hurt. I am ill." His father and mother were, at that time, when their three children went to Vienna, where my eldest daughter is living now, and my grandson said, "Do you know the number?"

I was very much afraid, because they told me that he had been unconscious, he had been flown with a special air jet to the hospital. He didn't know the number in Vienna, where my daughter is living. I was very anxious. All is right now. He is going to school again now. When you are alone, you don't have anyone to talk to. Some people say, "Why don't you go back to Utrecht?" I don't know. I mustn't think about it . . . it's very . . .

Q. Disconcerting?

Yes it is. The children have helped me a lot, but still, there is a lot, so much people. When I go I just have a new permission to drive the car . . .

Q. Correct me if I'm wrong. I think I'm hearing you say that we're basically alone in this life, that we just have children that we interact with, but you're alone now.

Yes, I am alone. Because first when I came here when my husband died, he died very unexpectedly. I knew he had always heart pills. One morning he had to go to the doctor, a heart specialist, and I drove the car. He made a little bit fun. This is too difficult to tell . . . but we had fun and laughed a lot, when we got in the lift. Do you call it a lift?

Q. Lift or elevator. We say elevator in the United States.

Elevator. Then we sat there in the room for the specialist, and he came out, the specialist, and said, "Just a moment, I have to go back" . . . Just at that time when he said, "Just a moment," my husband fell down, and the man came back. He was very nice. . . . I could ring the neighbors of my daughter in —— and my daughter who is living in Vienna now, at that time she was married to a South American and she was over for some months, and I lived for fifty years in Utrecht. All the shops know me, and she [my daughter] told me this particular morning, "I am going to buy cheese," and so I ringed the cheese shop, and asked, "Have you seen my daughter," and she said, "Yes, madam. She just left the shop . . . I will see if I can find her." And so, they saw her walking there. She immediately came to the hospital, and my son at the time was for a special course in Maastricht. He came by car. So they all were there. At that time, my husband was reanimated and then looked and said, "This is all wrong." And he died at that moment. So all the children were there. All my children have always been there to help me . . . to support me.

Q. Was this what got you through when your husband died? It must have been very difficult.

Yes. And then my son was living here in the neighborhood, and said, "Why don't you come to Rotterdam? I don't have so much time to come to Utrecht. Come and live here." So I came and lived here. But I had, first from '85, '86 when the children were little, I drove them to tennis training and hockey training. I did a lot for them. Which I liked very much. But then my son his got function, and very, very well. It was too much. If you have . . . a weekend service, a Friday evening, Saturday, Sunday, Monday. He had been here one month because he had to finish one month before he could leave and the telephone ringing at night and you could say, "Do this, do that." Sometimes you have to go to the hospital. But you have no night that you can sleep the whole night. You are always interrupted.

Q. A very difficult life.

Because he comes from a hard family as I call it. I think it is very good . . .

Q. Virtuous, worthy? Let me ask you some other questions. Can you tell me how you would describe yourself? My family will always ask me when I do an interview, "What was this person like." What should I tell them? How would I describe you to them?

I don't like so much to say it, but I am always doing the wrong things.

Q. Always doing the wrong things. What do you mean by that?

Just what I say.

Q. Wrong things. That could mean a lot of things. That doesn't mean you're immoral.

Not bad.

Q. Not good for you?

I don't know how to say it.

Q. Give me an example, a time when you did the wrong thing.

Oh, no. I do so much. I don't know how to explain this.

Q. Are there things you wish you had done differently?

Yes.

Q. How would you feel?

My conversation. Sometime I really say the wrong things. I don't mean it but I do.

Q. But nothing major wrong, like in the sense that you wouldn't have . . . would you have not moved from Utrecht, for example. Is that one of the things you are talking about?

No. Because the first years here I have had a wonderful time, because the children were so young that I could look after them, but now they have the age, if I come there, they look after me. You see?

Q. Yes, and I can tell you, as a working mother, a grandmother who does the kind of things you did, there's a special spot in heaven for you. It's wonderful to have a grandmother who will be that close to the children.

This time you and the children become too old. It is a quiet bit of time, because I have been, well, my father was very old-fashioned, and I think that I am not old-fashioned any more, but still, the life of the young boys are quite different. They go out in the Saturday evening. I can't understand it. Because they are thirteen, fourteen, fifteen, and [in] the evening they go out at that age to discos. Still I think, I'm not afraid of the disco, but I am afraid of what can happen when they come back from the discos by bicycle.

Q. How would you describe yourself? Are you somebody who is a self-confident person? Are you shy? Are you aggressive?

I am not aggressive. I am, shy is not the right word, but I am not very sure, I am not very . . . I don't know how to . . . [Beatrix trailed off.]

Q. Are you a follower? Are you a loner? Are you somebody who marches to your own drum? You do what you think is right? You don't worry about other people?

No, I am worried about other people. Sometimes too much that I . . . all the children . . . some have difficulties . . . you must keep your mouth closed. I don't know how to say it otherwise.

Q. Is family important to you?

Very. But I don't have much family. I . . .

Q. The children . . . ?

Well, yes. For instance, I think to do the right things, and then always do them the worst things. My brother has married two times. At the last years he didn't know very much. If he didn't do what his children wanted, he didn't get his drink, and that's what he liked very much. But at a certain time, there was the daughter of his first marriage who telephoned me and said, "Aunt, I am just leaving for a trip, I don't know. I heard yesterday that they have changed the inheritance of my father. Please help. My father has a lawyer, those big offices, very big, very much people."

So I phoned someone, and afterward, perhaps it was stupid. We must do something about it. At that time there was a case where he [my brother] had to go before the judge. And then the eldest son, he didn't say anything. Then my brother had to come before the judge too . . . The only thing he had to say was "Yes." But he didn't say it. But then my nephew didn't tell the judge that his father is not capable of saying anything else. And now, the whole thing is finished. The children from his first marriage won't receive anything. It's gone all to the second marriage. And I have paid a lot of money for the whole thing.

Q. But you did what you thought was right.

I did what I thought was right. But now they say I have done the wrong thing and because of me, they didn't get anything.

Q. But you were doing the right thing.

I *thought* I was doing the right thing. And I did it for them, because they asked me. If you tell this in America, you could call me . . .

Q. So you're a pretty strong-willed person. You're willing to antagonize people if you think it's the right thing to do.

Yes.

Q. So you're willing to take a little unpleasantness, in order to do the right thing.

I didn't know if it was unpleasantness because I didn't like what they were doing at that time. Because when my husband died, a son of my brother's second marriage was studying in Utrecht. I think Tony still has contact with him. He always came to me and then he had dinner with me when I lived in Utrecht, and he asked for his golf pack and golf things. "Yes, I can do someone pleasure with it," he said. I said, "Yes." He told me who he would give them to. When I phoned him when he came to have dinner, then I got that person on the phone, who had got the golf things. But that man never said to me, "Thank you." First I didn't know. Afterward the son asked for all the ties. He was a man who had a tie; he had a lot of them. Then he asked for the shoes, and I said, "Why not?" And for a blue suit. But he always sold it. I didn't know.

Q. And kept the money.

Yes. And now he is living . . . I didn't know at that time why he came so much to me and why he was so . . . and he is in the second marriage, and he is living in Utrecht . . . He is doing very well I think. Tony met him. Tony's right. He said, "I'll not get involved in all the quarrels. I don't want to hear of the quarrels." And he is right.

Q. And how do you feel when somebody does something like that?

Still, I don't feel very happy.

Q. Did you say anything to him?

No, because this son . . . this other son from the first marriage, who didn't get any money, they are living in —— and his wife has cancer. I went a lot there before she was ill. When I came there I always brought something. I always brought, I don't know what you call it. [A thank you present.] I always came with something. They have been very nice to me when my husband died. But after this, she phoned and said, "It is your fault that we didn't get any money." That was not true. I haven't said very much [about helping them]. But I did it. And now he said I caused them to lose their money. That isn't true. It's just lying. And then she . . . I liked her very much, but still I think she had a very difficult life. She was a young girl, she stood in a kimono, next to fire, and it burned, so she was burned entirely. Then my son, who was already a surgeon here tried to help. Well, she is not helped by the right specialist. This one is not clever and her treatment was not good. My son said, "You must go to the hospital and bring her back. There is a special burn wounds hospital and she should be treated there." So I went. She has been operated on there. Now she can move her arms. They have always been nice to me. And I have always been nice to them and done it all, this business about the money. He doesn't come to me and to fetch me anymore.

Q. Could you just forget about it and let it go?

The only thing is that sometimes she ringed me and she chastised me again, about my interfering. I would still like to know how she is doing, because I have been there before, at times when she was very ill. And she didn't want to be operated on because she said, "I have been hurt enough, and I don't want to be hurt again."

• • •

Q. Can you tell me whether or not you have any kind of personal/ethical credo, Beatrix? Any ethical beliefs in particular that you use to guide your life?

No.

Q. Well, is there anything that has helped you get through life? I wasn't asking you about an afterlife. I'm interested in that too though.

I don't think . . . I would be very happy if there was something, but no, I don't think there is anything.

Q. How about any beliefs that help you get through this life?

I have no beliefs . . . if I don't die tomorrow I would be lucky.

Q. Are you tired of living?

Yes, I have had quite enough of the whole thing.

Q. You're not afraid to die?

I am afraid of being more . . . [Beatrix shrugged.]

Q. . . . senile?

Yes. I don't want to go in a sort of hospital where you are . . . I am afraid.

Q. How about any kind of system of ethics or beliefs that certain things are right and certain things are wrong? Do you have any system of beliefs like that?

Yes. I think that a lot of things are wrong. I don't know if you know it is impossible for the moment to go out with money. If I go and fetch money from the bank, I have two little pocketbooks in my pocket with a safety belt. . . . Beginning when I lived here, it was much too warm here. In the night I heard . . . It was too hot and then . . . it went . . .

Q. Footsteps?

No, not footsteps. My furniture went. I had someone who repaired it, a very nice boy. My children said to me, "He must be a homo, because he is so nice." He *was* very nice. And he said to me, "Mrs. ——, when you go with money, just put twenty-five guilders in your pocket. If they want something, they might make trouble with you so you just give them the twenty-five guilders. It's the only thing they want. They want your money to be able to get drugs."

Q. So, you think that people want money, and they'll do things to get money?

Yes, it is known that as an elderly woman, you can't walk on the streets with money . . . or be with money in the hospitals. If I am brought to the hospital, then I can be sure that I will be rid of all the personal jewels.

Q. Jewelry. So you think that people are basically out for what they can get?

Yes. This is a very . . . for me, it is a very strange time it is going this way.

Q. You don't think it used to be like that?

In my time, no. When my husband was a surgeon, no. You could put in the table next to your bed, you could put your money. Now it is impossible to do that.

Q. Now, if what you're saying is that people were more honest, fifty years ago, does that mean they were better people?

No, but they didn't have the difficulties of drugs.

Q. I see. You've told me about your brothers. You had an older brother . . .

I have only one older brother, yes.

Q. Were you close to him at all?

No, because when I had the first six years of school and he had just gone to the other, and when I got to the other school he had finished that school, so we had a total separate life.

Q. You didn't eat dinner together?

Not much, no.

Q. You lived basically alone a lot when you were a child.

Yes, I was. But I've been in boarding schools in Brussels.

Q. What about your community when you were growing up? You grew up in Holland. I'm sorry, you grew up Rotterdam.

And in Brussels . . .

Q. How would you describe your community life? Did you feel you were part of a closed community . . . or more of a cosmopolitan . . . more of an upper-class . . .

What?

Q. Was it more of an upper-class lifestyle? To go to boarding school mostly?

No, not at that age, because my mother died and because my father remarried and . . .

Q. So that was really why you went to boarding school.

Yes, I think so.

Q. You talked a little bit about your mother's death, Beatrix. Were there any other events when you were a child that were destabilizing for you . . . that were the . . . kind of event that caused your world to get thrown off and reorganized? Was there anybody that you were particularly close to when you were a child, that you lost? You said you really weren't that close to your mother.

Oh, yes, we were close, but I was too little still. But there were lots of . . . neighbors.

Q. Let me tell you an example. I had a friend whose grandmother lived with him when he was young and she was a Greek lady, a very powerful person. She was very important in his life. She was very close to him. She and his mother had a fight, and she basically left the house and he never saw her again. This was a very great shock for him. It was very hard for him to readjust. She was such an important person in his life. Did you have anything like that? Was there anyone that was very close to you, that all of the sudden wasn't there, or something happened that was very traumatic for you as a child?

My mother died. I went a lot to Tony's parents, and I went a lot to my grandmother of mother side.

Q. And that's how you faced the loss?

Yes.

Q. You were close to Tony's mother?

Not particularly, but she has been very, very nice for me. They lived . . . Tony lived as a boy, I think a very difficult life, because he . . . I don't mean it unfriendly, but she felt very . . . I don't know how to say it. She had a beautiful house, and at that time, her guest room, she had already a guest room with her own bathroom and that was not known at that time in Holland. Also her house, it was beautiful. I can't . . . if I could have taken a photograph, but she was very, very nice to me. Tony's father too. But Tony, I don't know if Tony has told you, he had to go to school in Eton boy dress.

Q. He described his mother as being a social climber who subjected him to wearing a sailor outfit when he went to high school.

Yes, and still she was nice to me. I can't think . . . [Beatrix shrugged]

Q. Were you involved in any activities in the community of any kind, in Utrecht for example? Were you part of that community? You said people knew you in the stores and shops.

Yes, but I lived there for fifty years.

Q. Were you involved in woman's groups and church groups and charity?

No. Only . . . I have had a very spoiled life. All the . . . I had several shops . . . and they knew my children too and they asked after my children. I met, a half year ago a daughter of a niece. The niece has to say aunt to me . . . they do their shopping at shops I know. Because it is very difficult to park in Utrecht, and I can't park anymore there, so they say good-bye of me and tell them not to do this because one of them was a very hard working person . . . he had trouble with his life, because of [lifting] heavy things . . .

Q. Trouble with his back.

Yes, and I said to say good-bye to the . . . he said it's not allowed to do that anymore. . . . Sometimes I think, "Well, I have to go there." But, I can't park anymore.

Q. How about politics. Have you ever been interested in politics?

I am interested in politics. It is a thing I listen to.

Q. Have you been involved in any political parties at all?

No, I am a member of a political party, but I am not active.

Q. May I ask what political party? I don't want to pry. I lived in Canada and I was told that in Canada, it is less offensive to ask someone about their sexual activity than to ask them about their political party. In the United States, nobody cares. They'll tell you. There's the old Will Rogers joke, "I don't belong to any organized group or party, I'm a Democrat." If I'm asking something that you find too personal, please stop me.

Name, I can't say the word every moment, I am a democrat . . .

Q. Social democrat . . . Christian democrat . . .

No, I . . . [Beatrix hesitated, searching for the name, then shrugged.]

Q. It's OK. Are you active? Did you ever run for office?

No. Only I vote.

Q. How about during the war. Were you involved in any of the politics that was going on then during the war?

No. There were no . . . there were all the same against the Germans. I am such a terrible woman that still I should not like it if one of my children was married to a German. I always have something against the Germans.

Q. Because of the war.

Yes, because of that. There were a lot of German boys who didn't like it at all and had to do it.

Q. But you didn't get involved in any of the anti-German activities during the war yourself?

No.

Q. You were kind of a normal citizen . . . normal average person if you will. Did you know what was going on? What was your impression of what was happening? Did you . . .

Did I know?

Q. Yes. What did you think was the situation for the Jews? You said a lot of them that you knew went to Africa . . . the man who sold your husband his business, for example.

Yes. And they went to a camp in the neighborhood; I can't say the name. I knew it.

Q. What kind of camp was it?

Those camps. There was no gas, but they had a very bad life.

Q. So it was a work camp?

Yes.

Q. Did you know about the concentration camps during the war?

Yes.

Q. Did you know that the Jews were being gassed?

Yes. I can't tell you who told this, but my husband heard a lot when he worked in the hospitals.

Q. How did you react to something like that?

You couldn't do anything.

Q. There was nothing you could do.

No. No. [Long silence.] All the Jews I knew were already away. [More silence.] No. [Silence]

Q. So there was nobody you knew who was still here. They had all gone.

Basically, yes. I knew no one, but still there were Jews, and they had their sign. But no. [Another long pause.]

Q. Did you just feel that you were kind of helpless in this situation to do anything, to stop it from happening?

You could not do anything. You could hide them. But you have help in the house. We had too much people around because we had a practice at home . . . you couldn't do anything. [Beatrix threw up her hands, as if indicating helplessness.] You could help with food and a lot of people were put out of The Hague, and so I was warned that . . . an aunt was put out of The Hague and was living in B——, and I knew the mayor of B——. I bicycled there. She was with her elderly sister. They had big books . . . that they didn't know what to do with. I could sell it for her.

Q. She was a Jewish lady.

No.

Q. Refugees, non-Jewish refugees?

No, no refugees. You were . . . at a certain moment you had to leave The Hague.

Q. When you were growing up was there any particular group that you belonged to that was important in the formation of yourself, your identity? Did you have any important role models? Role models, any people you looked up to emulate, that you felt, "I want to be just like my daddy . . . or Aunt Louise" or someone like that. A teacher . . . ?

No, I haven't had very much brains. Never.

Q. OK, it's all right. I'm just trying to think if there are any other questions I should ask you about. Was there ever a critical moment in your life when you were very needy emotionally? When you really felt weak and vulnerable? For example, my father died and three years later my brother got cancer, and when he died it was a very hard time for me because my mother kind of folded up so it was a very hard period. You turn sometimes in those periods to certain people or certain institutions or something to get through. Did you have any time like that, other than when your mother died?

Oh yes, I had my grandmother. And I went to Tony's parents.

Q. You said when your mother died, you turned to Tony's parents . . . is there anyone else that you leaned on for support emotionally?

No.

Q. You think basically that people have to get through these hard times by themselves?

I don't think so. You have to accept it.

Q. There was nothing you could do to change.

No. There was nothing to do. But the only thing I remember is that the neighbors where I lived, all the people, it was the last street [inhabited]. They call came to live there at the same time. So we all knew each other very well. And what I remember very well is that my mother was operated on and my father told me that I was to bring her something ... I don't remember what, a book or something like that. But I was not allowed to enter her room. And I did it, [I mean], I did take the book. When I went back, the nurse came and said, "Your mother asked if you would come in." I said, "I am not allowed." "Yes, but your mother asked if you would come in." I said, "I am not allowed." That evening or very early the next morning, there was a telephone call. The hospital told my father that my mother had died. And he went only with my brother. I wasn't allowed to go. I remember very well, they were walking in the garden, the neighbors of my parents. Two wives, they came to me to tell me she had died. I was not allowed to go to her.

When she was dead, I was allowed to see her yes, at that time. And she was very modern. She was very unusual for that time.

• • •

Q. Do you think that people have a social responsibility to help others in need?

If you can, yes. Certainly. But to start, you must be able to help, because I am not very clever. If I can help somebody sometime with money, yes I do.

Q. How about hurting people who are close to you. During the war for example, there were people who had small children who ... one woman told me that she saw a family with their children being hung, because they had helped hiding Jews. What kind of situation is that for you?

I have never ...

Q. You don't think people have a responsibility ... ?

Yes, but I had no contact with the Jews. I had our neighbor for some time. I had still help in the house. She stole something from me and I saw it. She said, "Well, if you say anything, I will go to the Germans and tell that you have ..." I had food in the house and I helped several people with it. Also that school ... how do you call the teachers of my children? I could help with some food, because my husband operated for food. I don't know how I started.

Q. This woman was stealing something from you?

Oh, yes, and I said, "Go to your house, because I know that you are also hiding someone in your floor." If you had a floor made of wood, you could take things in and out.

Q. You don't think that people who didn't help people were bad in any way?

No. We all are close to help each other.

Q. How about wealthy people who have a lot of money but don't give any to charity? Do you think that they are bad people?

I don't know what you mean.

Q. You have a lot of money. For example, there are a lot of people in the United States who are pretty wealthy. They don't give very much money away. Maybe a little bit.

Yes, but you can't look one moment on the television. Every moment, they have requests for some money. I can't tell you how much. They are certain things you must help. But you can't help everything.

Q. So when you make your decisions of whom to help, how do you decide whom to help and . . .

I don't know. Life has become much . . . [Beatrix shrugged.]

Q. So how do you operate?

I don't owe anything from money. I have put what my husband has earned, I put in a bank and they look after it. The brother of my husband is still alive. And he has a lot of money. He is working . . . he has sent me to that bank. He still lives.

Q. So, you give money to charitable causes?

Sometimes. But I am not rich. To live here is very expensive. And the difficulty is that at the time I came here I have to buy this flat. This difficulty is afterward, when it didn't run. They started with hiring. Everybody is hiring. If I wanted to go away, I couldn't because I wouldn't be able sell this flat. And that's what I don't like very much because I haven't earned very much. I've worked for three years. I remember my father working very, very hard, and my husband too.

Q. You think if people work hard, it's their money, they don't have to give it away if they don't want to. You don't see anything wrong with people who don't give money.

If you are thinking you have to help, why shouldn't you?

Q. But there are a lot of people who don't. Are they to be criticized for that?

I don't know. I don't talk about it with other people. Every moment on the TV they are asking for money. For the Indians, Africa, everywhere, everywhere. I don't know if you know about also.

Q. There are a lot of appeals going on.

Yes. You can help certain things, but you can't help everybody.

Q. You take care of your family's needs first. That's most important?

Yes.

Q. Do you have any other kind of guiding principle that helps you decide how you would make decisions like that?

No.

Q. I can't think of anything else to ask. Is there anything else you'd like to tell me?

No.

Q. Thank you.

The difficulty is that I . . . I'm stupid, I can't say certain things at the right moment.

Q. No, you're not stupid at all.

I know I am, but . . . [Beatrix shrugged.]

Q. Thank you.

CHAPTER 5

❦

Kurt: Soldier for the Nazis

Q. Do you have a feeling that you were caught up in history? . . . You keep
mentioning these other things repeating themselves. . .

Kurt: Ya. Why do we do this again? See how often the Goths went over
and pushed the Slavs back from their border.

Q. But I'm hearing you express a kind of futility at doing it again and yet
you kept on doing it. Does it never occur to you . . . ? [Kurt interrupted, with
some vehemence.]

Kurt: Can I change this? I have no power to change this!

1989–90

Q. I'm interested in finding out about your life, and in understanding how you see
the world . . . [Kurt interrupted.]

Very different than people here.

Q. Do you? Why don't you start by telling me about this, about yourself? Where you
were born, what your parents were like, things like that.

I was born in 1914, M——. It's a town in Prussia and I was raised in Berlin. My father was killed in 1914, in action in Belgium. I never knew my father. No. And my
mother was the first to start in Germany a [certain type of business] in Berlin, in
1912. She was an educated woman. Well, she was on her own, made good money,
and then in 1913 she married. She was married for a year and then it was the end.
My father was a grain merchant with a big corporation. We came from the miller's
family, going back to 1559 or 1556. I don't know exactly. We are researching that
because there are still documents available in Germany. So the main family name
[deleted] is a Gothic noble name.
   You know what the Goths are?

Q. [Kurt's accent was heavy and he pronounced the word "Goffs" so I was unsure
what he meant.] No.

These are Germanic tribes, north Germanic tribes, Gothenburg in Sweden. Gotholand. This is where the Gothic people came from. The Ostrogoths and the
Visigoths you call them here, one of the most strongest Germanic tribes. They

conquered their empire from Sweden over to the Baltic Sea, what is today Lithuania, and all this to the Black Sea, and the Iskar River was the border to the Slovak people. Then when the Huns came, in the third century after Christ, 360 AD, they retreated because the Huns overran the whole country and burned the villages and so on. So then they [the Goths] fell into the Roman Empire. They pushed the Romans back into Constantinople and they even penetrated the eastern Roman Empire. Then they pulled back and conquered then the whole world with their empire including Gallia, Spain and then settled in Spain. So this was the Gothics. These are my ancestors. Ya. And all Gothic kings, you have Theodoric,[1] Harmonrich, Roderich,[2] and so we are the family [deleted]. It's a noble family. The Gothic tribes are the first to add a written law code. It was written down I think in 290 or 295 after Christ, and from thereon we had the Gothic Gothorum in Germany. All the other German tribes took that up. Gothic translates into English as a law code. The Gothic code. The other German tribes took it up too, and then there was another Gothic, Aleman Gothic. You know, we Germans are called in Spanish the *alemanes*, and it means all men, from different tribes, they just came together— boys and girls—and they formed a new Germanic nation, Aleman, all the man from all nations. These are the Alemanas, and they came to France into Spain and even over to Africa. They have their empire built, you see.

This is the background of my family. So we're very proud. I was raised always by my aunt. We still have the mill then, which we sold in '22. Our family goes back very far.

Q. You have a great deal of pride in your family.

Ya. And this is connected with being honest and trustworthy and all this, you see. Okay, being raised partially on the mill property and partly in Berlin, I was educated by an older man who was a corporal with my grandfather, who was wounded in the Franco-Prussian war in 1871 outside of Sedan,[3] where the big battle of Sedan was fought. My grandfather got a spear wound from the French dragoon and never healed. He was living another twenty years with this and got cancer in it. The other fellow whom he took back to the mill lost a leg in the same battle on the same place. Both these men, when they were older, turned out to that place where they were wounded and took photographs. I have seen those photographs.

I was raised in Berlin. Then my mother remarried. I was seven when my mother remarried. Then later on I had to go through education the traditional way. We haven't a good school outside Berlin where I went. I just as recently as four months ago showed my wife all the places and the school. It's still standing there.

Q. Do you remember much of the World War I period?

Oh, ya. I remember this. In Berlin, where we lived, our city houses was in an apartment while outside Berlin we have a large property with fruit trees and asparagus planted and all this. I remember the First World War very good because when the Empress[4] went from the city castle to Charlottenburg,[5] she had to drive every morning from the castle to her place where a big park was, and there was a trumpet riding in front, you see. "Ta da da da! Ta da da da! The Empress is coming! The Empress is coming!" All women had to lean down, and I, as a little boy, had to bow. This I remember.

Q. Do you remember how you felt?

Well, I just talk to some old ladies close to where we lived. We were sitting on a bench and we went through that park, and a lady said, "Now young man, are you a Berliner?" And I said, "Ya, I am a Berliner and I visit the first time after forty years." Oh, now what do you think! She said, "You know, I can remember when the Empress came through here." I said, "I can remember that, too." So we talked about this. There's a pastry shop; we were sitting down and we talked about this for a half an hour with these old ladies, and then most of my memories came back.

Q. What was it like when Germany lost the war in World War I?

Well, I don't know this exactly. I will tell you. When I was in M—— visiting my grandmother, they had a friend, Major Shriver. He was an army reserve man, and he had under his control the Citadel of M——. The city of M—— was a fortress. There was a Russian prisoner with a beard there, and he was Piłsudski.[6] Major Shriver and Marshal Piłsudski, they played chess. Later Piłsudski was the Polish leader. I was always standing with open mouth beside that little table, when they moved their chess figures and wondered what the horse will do, where that piece goes now. That man amazed me with his beard. He was not tall but he was bulky, you see, and finally I found out, after visiting a couple of times, that was Piłsudski.

In 1918 or 1919, Marshal Piłsudski became the leader of the League. . . . What do you call that? It's something like the United Nations now . . . Oh, ya, the League of Nations. Then he became president of Poland. I had a little thing with his niece later on during the Second World War.

Q. But do you remember him personally?

I knew him from the chess playing, you see. He didn't look at me, you see, but I was standing beside there or kneeling beside there when they played chess and I wondered why they do this, without any words. When you play chess, you don't have to talk because talk is getting you away from the only way of thinking. Well, that was Marshal Piłsudski.

And then we had a *putsch*. It was a putsch, a revolt of the Communists in Berlin, and I remember there were trucks coming in with trumpets and the red flag and we were opposed by some army units. The army was dissolved already but in Berlin there was another army built to protect the city. There was shooting going on and there I saw the first man killed in my life. I was four and a half, I think. I can remember. He was fleeing in the church. On the steps on the church, he was gunned down. He was not a Communist; just a civilian. He was killed by these of the trucks, by the Communists.

Q. What kind of impression does that have on a four-year-old child?

Well, I dream at night quite often about this and always protected my back against the wall because I was trained when someone is fighting, you go back on the wall, so you are protected from the back and then you fight on the front. Even as a little boy you learn this. Okay. Now, then came the inflation, and I remember my mother buying me a banana from a little fruit stand and she said, "Now, this is the food which we had plenty of here before the war, and it tastes so good." The banana was maybe four or five thousand marks in the inflation and I didn't like it! I liked potatoes, boiled or whatever, and cabbage but not the banana. I didn't like it at all. My mother started crying. "Now, I spent that much money and here there are twenty bananas," she said. "Where can you find them?" And I didn't like it.

Q. *What was your mother's economic situation after the war, Kurt?*

Oh, she had always money. She improved her gymnastic institute from year to year. She had doctors, lawyers, high government officials there.

Q. *So you came from a family that was very old, and had a fair bit of money, and your mother was a very smart lady.*

Ya. Ya, she was.

Q. *I would think in some ways it's kind of unusual to have a woman who had that much financial savvy and . . .*

Ya. She inherited about a million Reich marks from her father when he died.

Q. *What would that be in today's . . . ?*

Well, in gold—I don't know—that's something like $40 million or something like that. It depends what the gold's worth. Today, an ounce is about $390. Well, $300 million.

Q. *So you weren't just upper middle class. You were very wealthy.*

Ya, but despite this we lived austerely in the mill property. We are Protestants, so had no big pictures on the walls. I mean, at the mill. All the rooms were very austere and very protective.

Q. *Protective of what?*

Everybody worked together, you see, and when I had some problems or what with other kids, I ran home to the mill and my aunt always said, "Oh, you sit down in here," and I got help from everywhere at home. Our coachman was G——. This was four generations in our family. Always the same coachman, and the oldest son got the job. So this was all working in a certain frame that was worked out hundreds of years ago, in the same way.

Q. *Was that comforting to grow up in such a stable environment?*

Well, I didn't feel it.

Q. *But you felt secure? Even though your father had died, you were very secure, yes?*

Okay, and then the inflation came and we had to sell the mill because my father was killed and another brother of his, my uncle, was killed, and the third brother he was an architect. He didn't want the mill so it was sold to a large milling company, and then after the Second World War, this property was torn down because this large property was useless for the big milling company. They tore the buildings down. At this time I'm just working . . . I put a man in charge in Hanover to go out to work in B——, which is a town in the former Kingdom of Brunswick and where we belonged.

Q. Where was the mill located?

Close to the Prussian border, but I was raised Prussian on the other side of that. There were no border fences or nothing. The last two hundred years, it was all open. In B——, there's an archive today where all the old documents are on tape, on computer tapes, and they gave me the measurements of the property, the measurements of the houses, but in measurements I cannot understand. So I had to search back. I had to call them up. Give me in meters what this was. And they said, "Well, it's very difficult because this was a Gothic property, beside Frankish property, and they all had different names for certain measurements." It's very, very interesting. This is where I really grew up. Ya. So I had an understanding of this, and when I grew up in Berlin I never went back very often to A—— where the mill was but I went to my grandmother in M——, and her mother was still living, my grandmother, and they were fabricating tins, vegetable tins. He was inventing the tin, the tin can. My great-great-grandfather from mother's side—always from the maternal side—invented.

Okay, now it was the end of inflation. When I went to my grandmother she had a house on the Harz Mountain.[7] It was two days with the coach. The coachman and horses were ordered, and I liked this riding for two days in the Harz Mountains to see my grandmother. When she was a young girl, I think she saw a train accident. The first train running over a bridge from Berlin to Constantinople fell from the bridge, and people were crying and steam came out of the locomotive, and she never rode in a train, and I remember the last time—I can hear it today— she said, "You want to bring me in the train? Then I can kill myself right here!" And four weeks later, she passed away. She was eighty-eight.

Q. It sounds as if you were very fond of her.

Ya. I can remember that, I played train with her so often and she hated trains and she told me and I couldn't understand it. Today, yes.

Okay, so then I grew up outside of Berlin and went to school in K——. Come the strife years, I changed schools. Then I went to a school that was very democratic, in Berlin. We had a branch in England too, the same school, and we had our own judge and a cojudge and a second judge. Oh, I have to mention. My kindergarten teacher was Madame Montessori in Berlin. She came to Berlin during the war to help more because she established this, you know the Montessori system.

Q. Yes.

I had diphtheria when I was four years old, and from that point after the diphtheria I couldn't distinguish between green and red. I was color blind, and she discovered this because we had little buckets or glasses with different colored toothbrushes and I always grabbed the wrong one, and we had to polish our teeth, and she told my mother then, "Mrs. ——, your son has the color blindness developed."

Okay, when I grew up, went to school, finished school at eighteen, what you call graduation, in 1932. Okay, I had to go to the military, and Germany had a restricted army so it was very hard to get in. You had to have a certain degree in sports.

Q. So you must have wanted to go into the military.

Ya, I had to go because it was a tradition. I would have been the fourteenth generation serving in that same artillery regiment.

Q. It wasn't that it was a law that you had to do it?

No, no! It was a tradition in the family. See? This was the artillery regiment. I served during the war in this regiment. I went there for one year and came out as a reserve officer aspirant, as a corporal, and then I had to do two more short servings to become a lieutenant of reserve. So in '32, I went to the military, and it started in fall so I had a half a year. What can I do in a half a year? My grandmother said, "Well, we all like planes and flying and all this, and you will be trained as a pilot. You make your pilot license."

My grandmother paid for it. So I had a hell of a time, you see, flying with L——. He was a fighter pilot in the First World War and he had a Rumpler[8] observation plane from the First World War. The Rumpler was very heavy, a biplane, but we had a restriction for planes only one hundred horsepower so we had to mount a smaller horsepower motor in the heavy plane and it didn't fly very fast. It was very slow. So I trained on this in Frankfurt an der Oder, which is Polish. No, Frankfurt an der Oder is still in East Germany but the other side is Polish today. Okay. Then I did this. I had my pilot license. I had my sailplane license. Then I went to the military for a year, and then came out, and then I had to study two years in engineering at the technical university in Berlin. Professor Meyer[9] was my math teacher. He was an assistant of Dr. Einstein, and I saw Einstein every second day. I showed my wife, just recently, Einstein's room, where he taught. It's still standing. Well, he left then, in the year 1933.[10] Just when I started there, he left. At least, I saw him every second day for about two or three months, and then he finally was gone. Everybody was talking about that.

When I finished there, my grandmother said, "Well, you have to leave this country because, you know, this Hitler doesn't do good. It cannot."

Q. She didn't like Hitler?

Well, there was nothing against Hitler but the system, you see, the program of the system, and we were bound to be under this control.

Q. What was it she didn't like about the system?

Well, we had travel restrictions, the visa, money restrictions to carry out in other countries. My grandmother was very free living and she didn't like to be restricted. So she said, "Well, France, no. Italy, I don't like it. Go to England." England was never invaded since the Normans. So I applied with the British Ford Motor Company, outside of London, and I was interviewed with the Ford Motor Company in Germany in Cologne. So I had approval and arrived in London and then went out to D——,[11] introduced myself to my later bosses, and I was given a man who was looking for a flat for me. I found one with Mrs. L——. I can still hear her pitchy voice and her shouting at me. I was different than she was and I found the same. I worked on an assembly line as an inspector. I don't know what it was. I didn't like it. You see, I was expecting something different. Mostly it was the surrounding. D—— is in a part of London which is very industrial and smoggy and dirty. The houses are row, by row, by row where I lived. I was not familiar with this. You see, Berlin was not the biggest city—the biggest was London—but in expansion, Berlin was the largest in the world by that time. We had a lot of gardens and trees and this was not so in D——. My supervisor said, "Well, Kurt, I think you don't ike it here."

I said, "No, I don't like it here." Saturdays and Sundays, well, I knew what I wanted. I went down to the old city to the Tower Mayfair, Mayfair Hotel. We danced at teatime Saturdays and Sundays.

"So you don't like it?" he asked.

"No."

"Would you come with the company to Romania?"

"Okay." I said I would like to come there. First of all, I knew when we went from Berlin to the railway stations, there was an Orient Express, and it was designed to go through Budapest and Bucharest, and so I go there. You can take off right from Berlin. So the twelfth of June in 1936 I arrived in Bucharest. Before at home in Berlin packing my things and four days in the Orient Express. . . . This was not an express train. To Munich was fast. To Vienna was fast. To Budapest was fast. In Budapest, they said, "Well, you can stay here in Budapest or join the next train in two days. I liked to see Budapest, with all these restaurants and gypsy music. I enjoyed this. I stayed every time I went back to Berlin.

Okay, now I arrived in Bucharest. I was driven out by a taxi to where our plant was still established and being built on a little lake outside of Bucharest. Then I found a flat, which was right downtown on the Colavictoria. My landlady was Madam G—— from L——. She was the drug store owner's wife, middle class. I had all the help from Madam G——. I just showed one of my customers a letter from that house that I got after the war. I wrote to them that I came back from the war and I'm still in good condition and so they answered me that letter. I just showed it a couple of days ago to a fellow here from Bucharest, a Jewish fellow. He said, "Well, Kurt, that's such a good letter. They must have all liked you."

I said, "Have you seen the signature down there?"

"Ya."

He looked at the signature. "That man is Jewish," he said.

But I said, "I know." I wrote to him, you see, and he came from Vienna and had to move out of here, and every time I came through Vienna I took some of his parcels to Bucharest, and they had to escape too.

Q. So you helped them escape?

Ya, I was in Bucharest for two years. My boss was Cooper, Mr. Cooper, a British engineer, and the third year Mr. Cooper sent me to Bulgaria to order to survey roads. The roads in Bulgaria, they were very bad and primitive. There was no cars moving this. All by horse or oxen and donkeys. You met on the bridges to find out how much the bridges can carry because Ford had the Model E and EB, produced in Bucharest and they wanted to expand into the Hucriel,[12] into Bulgaria. They wanted to build filling stations too for it. So I surveyed for one year and that was very interesting. Two years later I joined the war. I went the same roads there. It was my military outfit. So every second week I had to report back to Bucharest through the Bank of Bulgaria, the Bulgarian Bank. This is a state bank, and they wired everything back and they kept also the drawings and all this in a safe. I had a very nice apartment then of two rooms rented from a lady, Popov. The first in Budapest was Gregoroff and this was Popov, and she said, "I hear you like to play chess, and around the corner on Rue Esparu I lived there. Asparuh[13] was the first king of the Bulgaria and so and so. Okay, there is a place where some older gentlemen play chess and maybe you can find a mate." I found a mate, a British older gentleman, and I played with him. He introduced himself as Mr. Donovan, also an engineer, and I was an engineer. He knew I was a reserve officer already, a Germany reserve officer. He never touched anything there, never said anything about it, or asked me something, you see. I had to report to Colonel Hansman. That's a German military mission in Bucharest when I moved. Now, in Bulgaria I moved quite often so I had always to send them a letter because I was in the reserves. Once I had a letter on the table addressed to the Harris Mission in Bucharest, and then he asked me, "What are you doing with the Harris Mission, the army mission in Bucharest?" And then I told him I have to report. Oh, never touch this again. Later on during the war—I have to tie that in right now—I heard that Mr. Donovan was a 5th Colonel of the English Secret Service. My wife gets me a lot of books here from the library and she got a book here about the Secret Service, and there I said to my wife, "Look here. That's Mr. Donovan as I knew him! Exactly." We photocopied this and had it enlarged. No, we photographed this with the permission of the library, and I had it enlarged now. It will go in one of my albums. He was the chief spy there for the British, you see?

Q. Do you think he was pumping you, Kurt?

He did not ask me anything! I didn't notice this before.

Q. He just liked you. Maybe he wasn't going to use you.

Ya. Well, we played chess every second day maybe, you see, and now I wonder what he did. He knew I worked with Ford. This made our first connection, our first contact, for the British Ford Motor Company, and I don't know from where he was. In England, but he was very familiar with the place where I worked for three months and which I didn't like. He said, "Well, I think you did right to move out here."

Then in Sofia[14] in August '39, there was a secret mobilization of the German army. So I had to go to the consulate, and my passport was taken away. I said, "Well, this is my passport. I paid three marks. I own this."

"No, you don't own this. This is owned by the government."

Q. The German government took it away?

Ya. I said, "Well, what can I do with the passport?" Ya, you go in this room, and there are other Germans sitting, a little bit older than I. All together, we were fourteen. After three days waiting there, I could go home and have to come back the next day, and then we were fourteen. We got a ticket, a train ticket, all fourteen on one ticket so nobody could escape, and probably there was an agent with us. I don't know. They didn't tell us. But everybody were not trusting, and this is the system. You cannot ask your neighbor because he may be that agent.

Q. You could feel the distrust in the air?

Ya, and this is what my grandmother didn't like.

Q. Was your grandmother still alive during this time?

Oh, Ya. Well, we were all in Berlin, you see. Now, when we reached Vienna, there was a total mobilization of Germany.

Q. Was this in '39?

Ya, and Vienna was the capital of Austria. Austria was taken over by Germany. They voted this. I mean this was a free vote. They still want to come to Germany. Today, still. Okay, and then I went back to Berlin, home, and then two days later I was already on the road to Poland, in the army. In Poland, I was with horse-driven artillery. It's a horse-driven artillery. We didn't have many motorized units by that time, but the motorized units we had, they were advancing through Poland and then the bombers, you see. So where we came to this, the war was already over there.

It was very quick, a very quick war, you see. We were in Poland only seventeen days and the only one shot fired from one of my guns was in Radom. It was a fortress on the Russian demarcation line. There was a Russian front but there were Russian matters. They took part of Poland, what we have not taken. They had a pact, Ya, and nobody knew about that pact. I mean we did not know this, you see? At least I did not know it. Okay, in Radom I had a grenade exploding in front of the gate of the citadel and then the citadel opened and they surrendered with the white flag. This was all obliterated in Poland. I have seen Poland later, then I went to Russia several times. Terrible, washout, and all this how that was bombed, but we were mostly going through the countryside with Austrian artillery.

Q. Let me just ask you something. Your grandmother has made you very sensitive to the fact that what's going on in Germany is rather ominous, and she wanted to get you out of the country, but you didn't feel like . . .

I didn't feel that way. I had not the wisdom an older generation has. If I tell my boys [sons] about what wisdom I now have, they say, "Dad. That's bullshit. Don't tell us about this." You see? So that was the same, but I couldn't tell my grandmother in the words my sons are telling me today, right?

Q. You didn't feel the ominous-ness yourself?

No. No. I felt it then when I went on leave from Bucharest twice a year, once in summer and once at Christmas. I felt it with my former schoolmates and friends. They were so different.

Q. Were they different? How were they different?

Well, they were not so open anymore. They were holding back something. I had two very, very close friends. I went through France with them when I was fourteen and fifteen, with bikes. We saw all the old castles and the castle where Courteline[15] was killed on the ramparts of the castle and all this.

Q. But basically from 1934 until the mobilization in '39, you were not living in Germany?

No. From '36 I was not living in Germany to '39, but before I had to study. You see, we toured Europe. I was in Denmark. I was in France. We toured the Pyrenees with our bikes and we were accosted by the French population very often as Boches. The war was just over when we bike through France, after about eight years. France suffered from the occupation, but when we asked them to [let us] stay overnight, by saying, "We will help you in the stable. We will milk the cows," well, then they started being different to us. Then the next morning, I remember one woman, she said, "I hate the Boches but I love you." She gave us parcels of cheese and bacon. So we biked there and we had a lot to eat, and wine! This was every day in France. We did not find a family who was against us the next day. The first day, always, yes. First it was, "Oh, let the Boches work and clean all this junk out here." And when we did so, fine. Then this was all different. Okay, and the same feeling is today with France and Germany. We want to unite.

Okay, from Poland we were torn out and brought to the western war, built against the Maginot Line. So I get an artillery position in the Saar district, near an old torn-down castle. That had been the property of the Churchill family from the fourteenth century. The French fought very often in France and then they took properties before they went home. So this was Meinsberg.[16] I put up my observation post up there in the rec tower and from November, December, January, February, March, April 1940.

Q. This is 1940 now?

Every second day I had maybe twenty grenades free to shoot, and I saw something on the other side. There was so much movement over there on the other side of the river. The French changed. We had to go with infantry to get prisoners from the French to find out what regiment is there. That's the normal thing. And then we had the Blue Brigade.[17] They were fighting in Spain before, probably against us. They were Communists, you see, and they were sitting right opposite. Well, they moved out after a couple of weeks and another thing came in. So I was very secure there and a friend of mine, a mountain climber who worked a camera, he was on my tower when I had the twenty grenades free. He said, "I'll save a couple shots for tomorrow and then we have to shoot over there. I can get this very fine. So my mother saw me three times in the newsreel in Berlin and so did my grandmother and all my friends and cousins. So then on the ninth of May we were mobilized and we attacked France.

Now I have to say that we had no intention, no one in the army had any intention to go over to France and fight again because most of our older people in our army units were in the first war. What was it? Twenty years. And the French didn't have any intention. So once a day I went down to the river and was fishing for trout. Fifty meters on the other side were the French and you talked to them. They were mostly talking German because a part of France was as us. So we don't want to fight and they don't want to fight. So what? Okay, so we exchanged chocolates against cigarettes and all this. Now when the war started in the tenth of May, well, we went through Remagen[18] over the bridge into Luxembourg. Before the bridge the blockade was open, I went in a boat, a motorboat over to the other side with my operation with my radios and my two radio operators and we crawled up the hill to the radio Luxembourg Center to the radio transmitter. So we were received with coffee and chocolate and everything. Finally, comes a solution to the Luxembourg problem. Luxembourg was neutral but we went through it, and then part of southern Belgium in the direction of Sedan, and on the right side of us to the north there was the fortress, the French, from the northern end of the Maginot Line and it was the Passchendaele[19] fortress 505 because 505 made us. It was the highest elevation. I have not seen this. It was more than a hill. It was a mountain. But we heard it. For ten hours, this took us within there. Boom! Boom! Boom! You know what a stuka[20] is? Stuka is dive-bomber. So they were going for ten hours. For ten hours, and the next day we were outside of Sedan in the meadow. Artillery from the very heavy artillery the French had like the First World War, and we only heard boom! This I can compare today with the sonic boom. I asked at the regiment and they asked in Berlin, what could it be, you see? We did not know anything about that. So the French shot every hour somewhere into Germany with this big artillery until we found the gun and then the Stuka came in and blew it up.[21]

So then we transferred south of the Sedan, over the miles on a bridge, and I came to a little village, and I said, "Gee. My grandfather was billeted here." We had front and rears shooting at us. Front and rears are the illegal soldiers shooting in civil clothes. And, no, you cannot do anything you want to, you see? The army surrendered to us, and then we had some British soldiers taken prisoner. They were still there from the expedition corps. They did not know where to go! They could not speak French and the French didn't like them. They didn't answer. So they were all captured, and then I found the observation post where my grandfather was. I saw it! That photograph! I saw that photograph my [grandfather] took about thirty years before and I had this photograph in my mind, and I said to my boys here, to my soldiers, I said, "Here was my grandfather wounded and that night after he was wounded, it rained and rained until the next day, so they were laying in the mud." And I could feel it! I want to go over there together with my wife, and sixteen kilometers, forty miles farther north, my father was buried, fallen in the First World War, but I could not escape this. I had to follow this. So then that night, we had to march south in the direction of Verdun. At three o'clock in the night, we had a meeting with our general and he said, "Well, Kurt, you have to go with two guns at the fastest way you can go to village Verdun and there you will find somebody who measured already where the guns are going in positions."

I said, "Verdun?"

"Yes, Verdun."

"Verdun." The First World War. One point four million soldiers were killed at Verdun.[22] Gee, Verdun. And then I came to Verdun in the morning and at six o'clock and there was a lieutenant from the division and he said, "Well, today is no attack; it's tomorrow. So you can take care of the other guns when they come in." They were still bombed by us in this position from the First World War and [made] big craters. So the next morning we had all together, the battery was in position with four guns, and then at three o'clock, they didn't start. It was the sixteenth of June in '40. To my mother I wrote a letter, and to my grandmother, because the advance was set back two hours. And then at five o'clock, the trumpets blew, and Attack! Attack! Attack! Once in a while, there came a shot out from there, and then our general called, "Kurt! You have to take in fog grenades." We have to fog that whole area in so they cannot see. We want to attack immediately. We have to be up there around noon. We attacked this mountain, and the French surrendered here. See they come against us with the white flag. I had to surrender in '44 against the Russian army. We were bleeding out, had no more tanks, and I did the same thing, and that's a terrible feeling, for a man to surrender. It's a terrible feeling. You lost everything. You lost your honor. You lost your responsibility against your family and all this. It's a terrible feeling, and I told our boys when we attacked, "Well, when we take prisoners, think about what their feeling is." Now when we came up to Fleury-devant-Douaumont, you see, they came out of Chattancourt, so we were talking to [the French, saying], "You did a brave job." So this was with France. In Russia it was just killing, you see? See how we talk to each other, we mingle. I took this picture of us together. I had a Leica [camera].

Q. *Even while you're going through this, you have a sense that this is historic, what you're going through?*

Ya. Well, I took pictures as I could get them. I could not always get them, you see. I had much more than these here. This is my observation point [showing picture]. Here's my radio and three operators, and there's a gun here in the back, an infantry gun. When I took that picture I heard [some soaring sound] and then the grenade came and all dead! Right at that moment when I took that picture! These people, right there were killed. It was dreadful, yes. But you don't have any choice.

Q. *You didn't have any choice?*

No. There was no choice. I could have stayed in England but they're the same way. I'd have had to fight with the British. You know that 1.4 million were killed around Verdun. These gray shadows here, in this photo, these gray strips here, these are all graveyards and crosses. So when we advanced to this, the feeling you have when you advance through huge graveyards! [Kurt shrugged.] Eighteen years ago, they were fallen in fighting. French, British, German, they were all put in one grave. Later on, they were separated. There was a French graveyard, a British, and German. The Americans didn't fight here until later.

Q. But your father was killed there?

My father was killed in Liege, outside of Liege.

Q. It must have been very moving, very emotional for you?

Yes, sure it is. Sure it is. Now coming then into Verdun, the next day, you see, there was nothing destroyed. You know Verdun was always a fortress. The first big fights, they took place in 843,[23] between the sons of Charlemagne. There were thousands of people killed around Verdun. The Moss[24] River was a very important river for traffic and going over. The defender of Verdun in the first two years was Marechal Pétain.[25] Herr Colonel D——, my division commander, said, "Well, we have to honor that man. We make a parade right here." Two hours later we had a parade. We as a German division honored the French defender of eighteen years before. That's what I try to explain to you.

Okay, a day later I was wounded here, at the head here. I got hit through my head, through my hard head [helmet], through my steel head [hit by a grenade]. I thought I was dead but I was holding my head together because I had seen two days before that somebody got a hand grenade on his head and the head was blown up and that fellow was running two circles before he collapsed. Those were just nerves. But I thought I was dead. When I came to the place where they bandaged me up, I asked my regimental doctor, "Doctor, I'm still alive?"

"Yes. Smile. I'll take a picture of you."

This the doctor took and he gave it to me later. See? [Kurt showed me another photograph of his head, then showed me the same spot on his head.] So this is what I have here, the cracks and the baldness here. It's broken here. You can feel it here. Just touch this spot here, on my head. This was from a grenade. Then the next day when I was released I wanted to go back to my battery, you see. Otherwise you are lost. What can you do in a hospital? You are lost. You are without your people. You know nobody there. You don't even know if they treat you well. So I wanted to go back and they bandaged me. Now, I could not fight with this bandage so they painted it green. A day later I was back fighting and this was terrible because I had a concussion and had to lay at rest at least two or three weeks and I did not. I fall from my horse sometimes.

Q. Why did you do this?

I wanted to stay with my people.

Q. You felt that the army was your people?

My unit was my people. I was responsible for that part. As a lieutenant, I was not the leader of the battery but I had my observation troop and all this and you feel a certain responsibility because this goes on for generations, you see? When I think back, in my family they all had these jobs and they were all wounded, you see?

Q. It's almost like it was something that gentlemen do. I mean, honoring Pétain, treating the French soldiers well. It's almost like you were fighting in the nineteenth century.

Yes. That was the way I was raised. You see, the air fights. They had the dogfights. They shot one down. They landed beside him. "Are you hurt?" they ask. Then they bound him up and started back fighting another one. But all in those Russian families, they were raised this different way. That's why we could not overcome this Russian butchery in Russia, you see? So that's finished. Here, the war is finished for you. [You] might be a soldier . . . You go in a prison camp and we are treated . . . I know that French prisoners in Germany, they moved free. They ran little farms with the women, you see, or there were factories and they could smoke their pipes and do what they wanted. With the Russians, it was different.

Q. And you didn't know that, of course, at this time?

No. At this time we didn't even know we had to go to Russia. Here, see what the French had. Their arms, guns, these were all from World War I. They had no arms. They had to surrender in Verdun because they had guns in their old settings and metric guns. This British delivered ammunition that didn't fit in the French guns. They had no rifles to fire with. These rifles were all useless because they had no ammunition. In France nobody wanted to produce this anymore after that First World War.

Q. They were sick of it?

Yes. See, and people don't know this today. They had nothing to fight with. That is why that whole French war took twenty-seven days. Marechal Pétain became their president. He worked together with Hitler. And when we came back [from fighting], see how sporty we were. This photo was at ten o'clock. At twelve o'clock we had already sport again. I took that picture.

Q. You were going out like just going to the beach?

Yes. Every day. Every day until the horses were made ready again.

Q. But every day, you'd stop in the middle of the day during the war and . . .

Well, not during the war, no, but when you were in the resting positions, yes. You had to do this. See Hotel de Ville and the City Hall of Nazi Nantes where Patton had his headquarters later on.

Now, all these French soldiers sitting on the trenches, they were all saved. None of these were ever killed. When Pétain made their peace with Hitler, no more soldiers . . . he will never attack us again. And this was the word. If Pétain wouldn't have done this, at least three and a half million of these soldiers would have been killed.

Q. And volunteers, too?

Ya, villages and traffic lanes destroyed and all this. Okay, and then he [Pétain] was tried as a traitor later and executed. Today they honor him. We said, "Why is he killed?"[26]

Then we were moved back to Poland, occupation force, then back on the railroads. Here is the landing in Poland, and that's the end of that.

Q. Now let me ask you, Kurt. Even at the beginning when this war was rather civilized, you know, among gentlemen honoring . . .

Ya, gentlemen. You cannot but say this. Ya, respect was there. Very much respect.

Q. Was it like that on the eastern front, in Poland too?

In Poland it was different because of the sentiment against the Poles. The Poles were different. They wanted our land, always coming back and taking parts of Germany. I know. When I was on the Polish frontier on vacation one year, a Polish train came down and made photographs of barracks, military barracks. This was during the peacetime, you see, and there was always something. It was not a friendship, and when they asked for more land and more land, well we said the French were sitting here. You know that the Burgundy people—what is Bourgogne in France today— they were living before in ponts[27] on the River Rhine, and before they lived between the Vistula and the Oder [rivers]. This was their original home, and the Heroskas . . . Heroskas was a German tribe, and many called themselves Rusks, Heroskas. The Vikings called themselves Rusks. What is a Rusk today? The Russians, you see? So there was always . . . something wrong. So when we came back to Poland to oc- cupy . . . You see, we came right on the Russian demarcation line. There was a big grain shed, where they store hay and grain. How you call this on a farm?

Q. A granary?

Ya. Okay. And their workers talk and I took photographs from when they tended the horses down there. We had 164 horses in the battery. So the owner of the farm—it was a huge estate—was a beautiful young lady, and she was always very snobby to me because I was German. Her husband probably was killed in the war or was in labor camps in Germany or what. I don't know. But she needed help. They had no horses. Everything on this huge estate was done by hand by Polish women. I offered her the horses because here we have 164 horses. They don't do anything. They have to work. We have to move them around every day. No, no, no. She never talked to me, and one day she came and said well, excuse myself and so and so. I said, "Well, you see, you are Polish; I'm German. That's very hard. It's a big difference between us. I am free. But I had seen a Polish marshal when I was about three years old. His name was Piłsudski."

"That's my uncle! This is my uncle! Come in!"

And then she took me in the living room and she said now, "Do you know any other names?" I said, "Ya, he was a prisoner in M—— Citadel, and the Citadel commander was Major Shriver."

She said, "Well, I have to take these books out for my uncle here." You see, and it was her uncle. Major Shriver. Yes. He was a very polite man and we had a good understanding. We could play chess and drink a beer and all this . . . We even had some physical contact, and then everything was all right. We even had a little love romance afterward.

Then when we left on the fifteenth of March '41, and were put on railroads going to Bucharest, close to Craiova through Czechoslovakia, through Hungary into Romania and unloaded in Craiova so I asked my division commander if I could go to France by motor bicycle. "Yes, you can." So I met Cooper, my former director, and they were just packing because they knew we were coming and they had to move out. They had three days of transferring their personal belongings into Turkey and Mr. Cooper said, "I have another position in Alexandria, in Egypt, with Ford, and . . ."

Q. But the war is still on?

The war is still on, but they had to produce, you see? There was no Libya coming up and nothing, North Africa, Roman. There was nothing in sight of that. So [he said], "If the war ends and you are alive, Kurt, you come to me." And I did later on.

Now from Romania we went then through Bulgaria, crossing the Danube on the same position from Georgia to Russia where 1,500 years before the Goths went over into the Roman Empire. Same thing, except they were on floats and we had a big ferryboat. Then the march through Bulgaria. All the rules I knew. Now [showing picture], these are bone houses.

Q. What is a bone house?

The bone, the skeleton from the Russian/Turkish War in 1878, and here was a big battle in Kalafat where Omar de Pasha[28] had to surrender here, and this is the dirt here. They were all cut in rows and rows and rows, thousands in a row, you see, and this was built over them. When I was working in Bulgaria in '39, they opened one of these and I had seen that, you see. Then we marched through the Balkan villages. When the order came to send for our horses, we had to hire oxen, and there we go with oxen over the Shipka Pass,[29] and then here down there and here the British Expedition Corps comes one day. I get through my radio we have to take positions and certain artillery above the valley because the Expedition Corps landed in Salonika.[30] Same as in the First World War, you see? And when they came here, I had two guns this way and two guns this way so I could shoot them up here and here. Block them so they could not move any more, not take more, not go farther. Well, there were more coming from the bank and were more ships unloaded in Salonika. Now this is the famous Truma Valley, where the Roman emperors to the north or to the south, where the Goths came along the same valley, you see, and then I said to my radio operators, "Probably one of my forefathers was here with his troops."

So then we stopped the British here and the landing was stopped in Salonika. Then we had a service [with] an Orthodox bishop. He had a Thanksgiving here [with] the German troops and the Bulgarian troops too. So that was the landing of British landing corps, and then a month later we were in Russia. Well, that's a Russian month. I had a picture here from the first dead Russian I photographed. I said to my wife, "This is the first one out of 20 million." Twenty million killed!

Q. So you were involved heavily in the Eastern War?

Ya. I lead a troop with artillery. I was called back, and two minutes later, Whoom! Whoom! Whoom! Whoom! And here they lay!

Q. And everybody's dead. How does that make you feel? You've talked about these men as if they're your family.

I cried last night. I looked at this fellow, for instance. I shaked his hands in the morning and then half an hour later his hands are stolen away, and this fellow has no more head. His helmet lays here. When you bury them, what do you say? I was crying. I couldn't even say the "Our Father, Our Father" or how you say it, the "Father and Son." I had to write letters to the families.

Q. What do you say in the letters to their families?

Well, I don't know. There was a form, you see. There was a form. And here, there are thirteen men buried. Then two days later I crossed the River Iskar,[31] which was once a border between the Gothic Empire and the Slavs. And this is all history. Most people did not know this in our regiment. You see, even officers did not know this.

Q. Do you have a feeling that you were caught up in history? I'm hearing a strong sense of . . .

Ya. I like history.

Q. But when you were doing this, you keep mentioning these other things repeating themselves.

Ya. Why do we do this again? See how often the Goths went over and pushed the Slavs back from their border.

Q. But I'm hearing you express a kind of futility at doing it again and yet you kept on doing it. Does it never occur to you . . . ? [Kurt interrupted, with some vehemence.]

Can I change this? I have no power to change this. See? And then comes Russia here. We were retreating from Moscow on the twenty-fourth of December, Christmas Eve, and then we had to march seventeen days in 52 below zero in Celsius, which is 52 below Fahrenheit also, with nothing.[32] Now in March, three months later or two months later, we had the coats. Before, we didn't have anything. Like we came from the warm Balkans. The first shelter I got was in [a] bunker after the retreat from Moscow. This is west of Moscow, Rejev. We discovered a village that was covered with thatched roofs. We need these roofs for food for our horses, so we took the roofs off the village, roofs covered as after the Napoleonic war. It was 1813, 1812. A hundred thirty years ago, the houses were covered with this straw and this was now our food for the horses.

Q. And the only thing you could find was straw then?

Nothing. Nothing else.

Q. Were many men dying from the cold?

Ya. Many. I just had a report yesterday. I listen to the German radio station every evening and the French station because it's a different thing than here, and Gorbachev granted that there are two million still missing in Russia. Two million people! 1.3 million civilians taken after the war, East Germany, and 700,000 prisoners of war. Where are they? What happened to them, and so on. So that's all recorded by the Russians, you see?

See [showing picture], this is Refev. Now he is a policeman. I became a friend with him. I gave him sometimes tobacco, you see. He was three years a policeman under the Czarist Empire and then the revolution came in 1917. So he told me about how it was before. He spoke very good German. Many Russians speak very good German. Poparochek was a Russian lieutenant, and we took him prisoner and we tell the prisoners okay, you can stay legally seven kilometers behind fighting lines or you are transported in trains back to Germany to work there, but in the trains you will have no food. They are locked up. They stay somewhere for a couple of days and it is cold, and most worked then behind our lines, and then the Swiss observers came. "Are there some Russians here in front?" This was a lieutenant. He was very useful in everything. Most Russians were very handy. Now here they have to shovel roads. It's a future road to Moscow. We'd started another advance to Moscow but never did it. He had some of my people frozen to death. Here they are buried. Here [describing a photo], this was the food for the Russians and the food for us. The horse came down and couldn't do it anymore. We shot it, you see? So this was left—just the guts, the hoofs.

Q. So you ate horse meat during this time?

Ya. And then I had to go back to Berlin in March for our new outfitting lists. A list had to be done in Berlin.

Q. What rank did you have at this time, Kurt?

First lieutenant.

Q. What was it like for the German soldiers during this Russian period?

Nothing. No thinking. You lost your way of thinking, just defending yourself, survive. Survival. Then we had to retreat and Stalingrad came. I have no more pictures because the pictures I took then I could not get out when I was taken prisoner on the twenty-fourth of August in '44.

Q. You were at the battle of Stalingrad then?

Ya. I was flown out. I had another war. Here, give me your finger. Search. [Kurt asked me to touch the injuries on his head and face.] Feel, this here. My jaw was split. I got another one here. I had three head injuries during the war.

Q. So you were at Stalingrad and you were injured by a grenade?

Ya. I was flown out about ten days before, and then I was given to another division then, later on.

Q. You had to go to the hospital though?

Ya. With this I was about four weeks in the hospital.

Q. They wouldn't let you go out and fight?

No, I didn't like it, you see? After Stalingrad, then I . . . Well, this was only retreats, you see? Then I came to the tank division with artillery and there I was kept shut in hospital. This is north of Balta, where I was fighting before in that Ukraine area.

Q. Was it different for you now because you were losing?

Ya. Well, this was the end of it, you see? We were losing. We lost in this battle over three thousand tanks and the Russians had four thousand tanks, and it was just steel. So I was burying people at first. We had to bury the Russians. It was the twenty-fourth of August, which was very hot, and the bodies, they were green. They blew up in five hours, you see, the bodies. This was in '44.

Q. Did you not want them to end the war?

What can you do? If you retreat . . . the leaders, even company leaders, were tried for treason.

Q. Now, this was after the plot to kill Hitler, which was led by old army people, no?

Ya. Everyone in the army was against Hitler. The army was against Hitler. How many generals were killed? Destroyed in planes. Flying graves we called them cause so many had time bombs in them. Then General Model died and general this or that.[33] They all fall down with the planes, you see. So the pilots didn't want even to fly generals anymore.

Q. They knew that the planes would be sabotaged?

Ya. See? Now, what can you do? Finally you have no concentrated power where you can go to or pray to or think about it. There's none left.

Q. You felt totally powerless?

Ya. You feel powerless. Oh, Ya. We felt this the first day because we knew, when we went into Russia, the first day, we cannot make it. Never. Then everybody had the feeling . . . I mean the officers had the feeling this will never go good. We had not enough men to cover every kilometer by two men maybe. Our army was so small. People don't think about it. Germany's half the size of California.

Q. So you thought you had no power at all?

The power was good-trained, very healthy men, sporty men. See, if I see the Marines here, I feel sorry. These are not human beings for me anymore, in uniform if I see them hanging around here on the freeway hitchhiking and all this.

Q. What do you mean by that? They are not human beings?

They're not soldiers for me. The soldiers don't lift that thumb up. He walks!

Q. Did you conceive of yourself as an army person, Kurt?

No! Absolutely not. As a reserve, we had to do this to defend or to protect, you see. We had to have an army education or a defending education that you call an army, but every family leader or man in the family has to be aware that he has to defend his women, his friends, his younger folk or the older who cannot do anything because it happened so often, you see?

Q. So war was a fact of life for you?

For everyone I knew. My history teacher in the K—— in Tabernik, he spoke old Gothic because he said, "Kurt, you come from a Gothic family. I'll tell you this story." So then he told me this in Gothic, in Old Gothic. My wife had a teacher who still spoke old Franc and old Gothic. So this is what you hear, so your tradition goes back this long.

Q. But this was a tradition that, in the immediate circumstance, because this tradition was so strong, you couldn't break out and do . . . [Kurt interrupted.]

Why should you break out? Why should you? Was the other better? Okay, when the Vikings established their Normanic empire in North Africa—people don't know this here—Vikings came down to North Africa and established an empire there in Sicily. We heard that they got stranded, that they mixed with other populations. Nobody knew after three hundred years about them anymore. I don't want this in my family so I stayed with my tribe. I hope I have good leaders, and we have. We saw to it until Hitler came and this was partly why the German tribes were not united anymore. Part went to Czechoslovakia, part went to Poland, and all this. So then you said, "Well, I have family there and I have family there and I want them back." When Hitler promised this, many came and more came.

Q. So you liked what Hitler was doing in a sense of trying to reunify . . . [Kurt interrupted.]

It was not Hitler. Hitler muscled in there. This plan was before Hitler came. This plan was just established after Wilson signed the peace treaty and cut this from Germany. Wilson did not know how Europe was formed by blood connections. That was a big mistake. . . . Even the British Crown said this. This is not correct. This is not right. This will end bad, and it took just eighteen years. See? Then you press yourself in the foreground and say, "Well, I have to do that actually, too, to protect my family and see my other part of my family and there and there and there." You see?

Q. You mentioned one of the photographs crossing the rivers into the Slavs' land and you said it was fine until you got there. That's where the mistake was, you said. You should have stopped right there?

Ya. Stopped right there.

Q. Because then it was family? It would have worked out?

Well, this was actually part of the Gothic nation, you see? Even if it was 1,600 years ago.

Q. But within this Gothic nation, your grandmother pointed out that there was repression going on.

Ya, in Germany after the First World War.

Q. In Germany itself after Hitler came in. Were you happy with this or you just didn't see that?

Well, I said, "I'll go abroad and then maybe I can survive until this ends." We did not think it would last, you see? No one in Germany would think it would last, but Hitler was just pushing this way.

Q. What about what we now know about what went on with the Jews during the war? Did you know anything about this?

No, we did not know. The Jewish people came from a village to surrender to us to get away from the Russians. We said, "All right. You come over and then you find yourself somewhere where you can stay." We did not know anything. I did not know about concentration camps. This was all taken away from us. When the war ended I came back to Germany. I was discharged in Bavaria by the American army, and with discharging papers, I could go on a train. Before, I could not even go on a train, you see. Trains were just freight trains, and I saw beside me was one fellow sitting with these striped uniforms, and I said "What are you wearing here? Are you coming from Cologne? Are you from Cologne?"

He said, "No. This is the concentration camp's uniform. This is an honor for me now." And he was a priest, a Catholic priest.

I said now, "Why did you come . . . ? What is a concentration camp? Why did you go in?"

He said, "Well, I was Catholic and I was preaching against Hitler."

Q. So the first that you heard about the concentration camps was after the war? Is that correct, Kurt?

After the war. We were never told. You see, we were defending in Vienna. The last days, I was fighting in Vienna against Russians and there some of my soldiers told me, "Well, there are concentration camps here in Austria. Auschwitz." And I said, "What are they? What did you hear about it?" They took prisoners there and they took French people there and they took Italian people there, Russians. So this was a mystery, and the first fellow who really told me was a priest.

Q. You didn't know about Kristallnacht?[34]

Oh, the Kristallnacht! Ya. This was taking place in Berlin and then the synagogue was burned in Fasanenstrasse,[35] but then the Jews lived there. I did never hear that one Jew was taken away, and I still don't believe today how many Jews were taken away because when I came back to my house, which was completely bombed in Berlin, to our city house, I was told, "Ya, the family who lived right below you, they were killed in a concentration camp."

Mr. Louie. Louie was Jewish and even under the Hitler regime he was running a big garage house in the Konstanz working-class area in Berlin. Okay, so Louie was killed. His wife too. Yes? Okay. Okay, seven years, eight years later in Hollywood, we go down. Two of my oldest sons with me. There comes a man, "Are you German?"

"Yes, we are German."

"From where?"

I said, "From Berlin."

He said, "From Berlin? Where did you live there?"

"B——strasse."

"I am Mr. Louie." He lived above me, right? Here they were! I was told over there [in Europe] that they died. So here he was. He invited my wife, my two oldest boys—my wife was pregnant with them—and here they live. Now the aunt is here. They brought them all out. When? After the war. They were hiding somewhere in Belgium, and then they came out.

Dr. Schneider, she was translating for the German Consulate here in '52. She came out. She's Jewish, and she said, "This is terrible to live here. My daughter is on drugs and she has a boyfriend. She doesn't want to marry because she changes [boys] every four weeks. Terrible living here!" Dr. Schneider, she lived on Silverlake somewhere. She invited my wife and myself to tell me the whole Jewish story and from her I heard. Here, not from Germany.

Q. So your impression was that after Kristallnacht when the Jews disappeared, that they just left the country?

That's it. No. Now they are quieting down because after the First World War, we had Jewish families living with us in our houses and in businesses. Nothing happened, but when the Polish Jewish came in, from after the war in Russia, after the First World War from Russia and from Poland, you see, they were collecting garbage and rags and all this, old shoes. They built businesses. Built businesses and cheating and cheating and cheating. We did not know this in Prussia. Our Jewish families, they left there when King Frederick II left. Everybody can be going in Heaven after his fashion.

Q. After his fashion?

Ya. How many Jewish families were doctors and lawyers and all this? My lawyer here is Jewish and he's from Berlin, and we talk so much about, "How you couldn't have known anything about this," he said.

Q. You really didn't know anything?

Well, he says this is ——. It's just over here across the street. See, this is the Kristallnacht. Then we thought, "Well, this is finished." I danced with Jewish girls. They had the Jewish star here when I was on leave. They didn't tell me they were harmed or anything. I never asked a Jewish fellow with a star. Well, when I came on leave to take my baggage here, bring it at home, I never asked.

Q. Was it because you just really didn't know or maybe you didn't want to know?

No. Did not know! I wanted to know what goes on in my fatherland. I wanted to know but nobody . . . [Kurt shrugged.] The Jewish didn't tell us. Even in our houses people didn't tell us. When I came once on leave, my mother said, "Well, above us the people have to move out. They go to this school. There's a school and they have to be assembled, all the Jews out of our street."

So I went there with food and I asked them now, "How can I help you? Can I bring you out?" No, you cannot risk this. Now what do you know what will happen? We don't know. See? There you get stuck. They didn't tell you. They didn't know. They were told different than what happened later on to get them in peace out of their surrounding . . . I mean, the same as what the Russians did when I was prisoner. First, oh, just deliver your arms, you see. When you had to deliver the arms and then something else and something else until you were powerless. That was the system and that worked with Jews, that worked with the Huguenots in France. This was all before. Now, I knew that under the Queen Isabelle and her husband, Ferdinand, that the Jews had to leave Spain but there were no Jews killed,[36] and they had to leave in France, too. How? Who took them up? The King of Prussia said, "You come here and we settle you down." So the Prussians were not anti-Jewish and they're still not except [to] those coming from Russia. They're [the Russian Jews] here. They grab this and they grab this and they have no education. Nothing. Our Jewish had a high education and they're professors and they knew history. Everything you asked them, this was their culture. Cultured Jews.

Q. But it wasn't just the Slavic Jews who were sent to the camps? It was also the educated Jews?

Ya, but we didn't know this, you see? When I came back and the people above us had disappeared, I asked my mother. She told me, "Yeah. They are in this school there." So from there I couldn't get anything out.

Q. When you came to this country after the war, did you have anyone question you about this?

No. Why?

Q. Some of the other people I've spoken with, who were Germans, when they came over here after the war in the 1950s, they said they were subjected to a lot of prejudice from Americans.

Ya.

Q. They said people asked them, "How could you have done this to the Jews during the war?"

Ya. I mean, they called us Nazis. They called my boys Nazis in school and this is just bloody bullshit! I mean, why? I just don't listen to that. Okay, then when we came to the United States, listen. We had a plantation in South America. I grow ——.[37] One day we come back and we go to —— because I had no head office. There. Okay, and the director talked to me and they said, "Kurt, you make an excellent ——. How do you do this?" I said, "Well, if it's so excellent I wouldn't tell you how to do it." You know, he is a chemist. He is a German Jew, Dr. Brunner, and we asked him, "How can that be done better because we always have residue." He said, "Dr. Brunner. He's a German Jew. You want to talk to him?"

I said, "Ya." We go up; I talked to him. He lived on a little hill. He sells soap, liquid soap, in health food stores. You can see his label. He's a rabbi so we went to him, introduced ourselves, and we found from his household woman, running the household for him, that he's blind. So we talked to him and when we got acquainted after two hours, he said, "Well, I think I have to tell you my story. You know I am a rabbi."

"Yes, that's what we heard." I told him my story briefly here during the war and what we did. He said, "Well, my name is H—— and I am a soap maker. I have a doctorate degree in chemistry and I make soap. So when this program started with Hitler, we moved out here to the States, and I offered myself as a soap chemist to Colgate, and I made soap and I told them how to make better soap because the soap here before was awful! You'd hardly believe it!"

I said, "Well, I can believe it because we heard something like that."

"I made soap," he said, "and then I changed my name because it sounded too much like Hitler's. Now my name is B——. During the war, the FBI took me in as a German spy. Took my wife. I was not blind when I came to this country. Can you see the bumps here and here? Okay, the FBI treated me that way. They shocked me here. The FBI in Chicago!"

These are stories that are not told here. Even the radio people like Michael Jackson—he's Jewish—he never will tell this. He knows maybe but he never brings it to the open. There are others, many, many I listen to, very intelligent Jewish people, who tell me the same story as H——. The Americans say they would never do this. But I asked H—— what happened to his wife and she was mistreated so too. I got a notice here that his wife died yesterday. She'll go to the grave taking her story with her. You can check on what I say about how the FBI mistreated them if you talk with one of the FBI agents who lives now in Santa Monica. You can get the name. If you want some interesting story go to H——. He lives in Escondido. H—— may still be alive. This was ten or twelve years ago. See? That's the other side.

Q. So what you're saying is that there are things that happen in this country that are bad too?

Same way. He said, "Well, the other Jews were mistreated this way and some had to die. So we ran from that situation in Germany into this situation in the United States. We run to here and the same thing happened."

• • •

The man I have called Kurt died some ten years after I conducted my interviews with him. His obituary did not mention his wartime activities. I have changed identifying details about Kurt, sometimes using an initial to denote a town or a person, sometimes inserting another word for a name of a person, town, or mountain, and so on. Many of the places listed here thus do not exist. I did this to protect Kurt's anonymity.

～

CHAPTER 6

Fritz: Nazi Propagandist

Q. Did you know much about what went on with the Jews?

Fritz: Not much . . . I did know that there were concentration camps. But I didn't know what was happening there. I believe that they were more or less prisoner camps, and hard labor. This Holocaust, I came to know after the war. That was a bad experience, of course. In Holland, we had Jewish friends.

Q. You had Jewish friends during the war?

Fritz: Yes.

Q. Did you know . . .

Fritz: You stick your head in the sand, like an ostrich.

Q. You stuck your head in the sand.

Fritz: Yes, I must say now.

Q. You didn't really want to know about it?

Fritz: No.

Q. You never thought about helping anybody or trying to hide anyone?

Fritz: I hadn't the possibility to help people. I didn't see the need of it at that time. I didn't know what was happening.

March 1991

I was born in 1921—I am seventy now—and my father was a civil servant with the railways. Middle rank. I am an only child and I grew up in Amsterdam. I was not born in Amsterdam. I was born in the south of the Netherlands. Since my second year I have lived in Amsterdam. It is a bit difficult to say what was it like at that time but I had a normal youth, and I had a good family.

My father was a quiet man. His hobby was philosophy. He was an admirer of Bolland,[1] who was a great philosopher though controversial. That was the reason my father became interested in National Socialism. He was raised an activist. Before the war he was a little bit worried about Socialism, Communism, and he was very patriotic.

As a young boy you like to be controversial. Before the war National Socialism was like the action group nowadays. I also got friends in the National Socialist Party and the youth organizations, and so I grew automatically in this way. I studied accountancy. I became, let us say, sympathetic to National Socialism in the patriotic way. I feel very strong national feelings. I believe in Germany it was more the economic problems that let grow up the National Socialists. But here, for my part, it was mostly the nationalistic side. I wanted a return of the Great Netherlands, with Flanders, and South Africa . . . a bigger Netherlands. I wanted some of the glory of the past. So it was really a national kind of movement for me.

Before the war, I took little part in National Socialist activities. Only if there were rallies for the youth organization of the party I went down with friends. It was a little bit, shall I say, not to be with the normal people? It felt a little bit as if we were a minority group and we were out of it. The National Socialists were a minority group, so that was a natural reaction.

I studied accountancy but I wanted to be a journalist. I got a job before the war at an accountancy office but then the war came and a friend of mine was a journalist and I got a chance to be a journalist too, at the end of 1940, for the National Socialist daily paper. It was a party paper here in Amsterdam. I, for a short time, was a press officer of the unions. I was basically put under the control of the German government. There I was only a year, and then I got a chance to become an editor of the newspaper-magazine of the youth organization. Then I became a member. It meant a great deal to join the youth movement. It was a feeling of belonging. And we believed we were doing a good thing.

Q. A good thing in what sense, Fritz? That you're restoring the Netherlands to some of its former glory?

Yes, or so you can put it. Back to the old glory. Back to the way it had been. It is perhaps difficult for someone who is not Dutch and has grown up in a very Anglo environment, which is what the United States background is, to realize that in the seventeenth century, Holland was a very important power in the world. People don't think of it that way anymore. Holland is seen as a small country; it's very humane and interesting, but it's not a world power. But, of course, it *was* a world power at one time.

In the beginning I was very distressed by the invasion of the Germans. It took too short a time, the invasion. We were very disappointed. Since the youth organization was very pro-royalty, we were very disappointed because the queen left Holland. After the invasion we tried to give the national Dutch feelings away. So at first, we were not happy when the Germans came in. This national feeling grew stronger as we tried to keep Holland independent. We wanted to save what we could, to keep distance from Germany. But we thought Germany would win the war. We hoped that after that, in a united Europe, we would have a better future.

So, before the war, and even in the first years of the war, I was a very strong Dutch nationalist. But we admired Mussolini and Hitler. That was part of the same party of sorts.

I have a very strong sense of the Dutch people. That's important for me.

Our daily life in the war was normal. Nothing much happened in Holland. I worked for this organization and for this magazine, *Stormy Seagull*. That was our Dutch symbol. I actually started working for them, I believe it was 1941. And I joined the party after I became eighteen. You had to be eighteen years to join the party, although in the youth organization you could be younger. I did not belong to the youth organization, not before the war. But I had friends there. But I didn't belong to an organization at that time. Since my fourteenth year, I was in this.

I continued to work for the paper but it was in Utrecht. I still lived in Amsterdam and stayed in Holland until '44. Then it got complicated. Through '43 and '44, I became a little bit worried about the development of National Socialism in Holland.

The SS faction, do you know about the SS faction? The SS direction was the direction who liked to be a part of Germany. We wanted to be, as I said, independent, in a Europe that would be dominated by Germany. That was clear. We knew Germany would dominate but we tried to get as strong as possible, to remain a free country. Well, the SS direction became stronger and stronger, and they didn't like this independent Holland idea. I kept trying to fight them but I wanted to leave this organization.

Then I get the possibility to be an assistant paper correspondent in Berlin. The job was for a big Dutch daily, the *General Business Paper*, like the *New York Times*. I resigned there and wanted to go to Berlin in September, in 1944. Then I must say, we had cooperation with the Hitler Youth in Holland. There was a girl in the press department of the Hitler Youth dependent in Holland. I had many contacts with that girl. That girl became my wife. That is a complicated story because now I was engaged to a German girl and I was in this opposition to the strong German domination.

My wife is German but she was very idealistic too, and believed also that Germany didn't want to oppress other people. The plans were that she had requested to be going back to Berlin, to the headquarters of the Hitler Youth, and she would go together with me, in Berlin, to this paper. We were not married at this point, just engaged. But then came this crazy Tuesday, the third day of September 1944, I believe. The Allied troops came in Holland.[2] There was a panic of the National Socialists in Holland and thousands were flying to Germany. They were afraid for the revenge of the people when the Allied troops came to Holland. The strange side of it was that I wanted to go to Germany and then came this crazy Tuesday. It was chance that they came together. So I went to Berlin and, in the meantime, there was strong separation in the Youthstorm. Part of the leaders didn't go also to Berlin and wanted to join the Hitler Youth as Dutch Youth Organization. We called it the revolution in the *Jeugdstorm* (Youthstorm). Part stayed in Holland and part went to Berlin. This was in September '44.

I resigned, as I was in Berlin but I was asked—ordered is perhaps more accurate—to join the Youthstorm who would go together with the Hitler Youth, to join them. But I refused that.

The leaders of the youth who went to Berlin to separate from the real Youthstorm, they ordered me to join them and make this revolution with them. But I refused and so I got in Berlin with difficulties, [as] a traitor of the German side. So I had some difficulties with the SD, the secret police. But I had good friends in Berlin and they very much helped me. It was a very complicated story. There were differences between . . . I had to be accredited to be a journalist in Berlin. But they forbade me to take the job with the paper. There were strong differences in Germany between the press people of the SS and the press people of the propaganda ministry. The SS forbade me to be a journalist, and the propaganda ministry allowed me to be. I could edit the Dutch paper in Berlin for the Dutch laborers who were working in Germany. I stayed at this daily paper in Germany till the war ended.

The name of the paper was *The People*. It was a former Socialist paper. It became, after the German occupation, a National Socialist paper. We had a German edition. There I worked till April '44. And in April '44, we married.

So we stayed in Berlin. We were really caught in a lot of the internecine politics that were going on within the National Socialist movement. I did not want the National Socialist movement to be more integrated with the German movement. That was the reason I separated from this. I didn't want it to become German. I hoped to get an independent Holland within a united Europe. Europe would be dominated by Germany, that was clear, but we wanted to stay as strong as possible. I was opposed to this side in the German direction, so I had difficulties. But my wife supported me.

We got married on the thirteenth of April. It was a Friday. But it was difficult then since a German woman who wanted to marry a foreigner must be authorized by the SS. But in a strange way, we get the permission, so we could marry. Then my wife got a Swedish passport, for Sweden in Berlin represented the Dutch interests. They gave her this passport so my wife legally became Dutch. She got a Swedish passport that said she was married to a Dutchman. We were under the protection of the Swedish Embassy.

So that was how we were able to escape from Germany, I think it was a week later, with twenty other Dutch friends. We escaped from Berlin. We were afraid to stay in Berlin. The bombs were dropping, and the Russians were coming. We wanted to escape to the American lines. The Americans were at the Elbe and had stopped there. We knew if we could get there it would be better. At the end we were with about three hundred Dutch people in a camp with the Russians, and there we waited about three weeks before we could go to the Americans. We were exchanged and were sent back to Germany, to Germany under the Americans. The camp was the Neuruppin. It was west, sixty kilometers from Berlin. There were about forty- to sixty-thousand people from all countries in Europe. I still wanted to go back to Holland, though, because I was afraid of the Russians coming in, and the reprisals. But I heard that this marriage of Dutch with German woman was not recognized. I wanted to go back to Holland until I heard this rumor, which meant that my wife would be sent back at the border. My wife was pregnant, so I didn't want to leave her alone. So I stayed in Germany with my parents-in-law for ten years, and then I came back to Holland.

I suppose, too, that my staying in Germany was also related to the fact that I had been involved in National Socialist activity. For all those reasons, I did stay in Germany. I lived near Dusseldorf. It was a very little town near Dusseldorf and I was with my parents-in-law. They knew all the people there so I didn't have any difficulties because of my National Socialist activity. There were no reprisals of any kind.

Q. So you went through the last days of the war in Berlin. What was it like there?

We were very lucky; there was very heavy bombing and every night we were in the shelters. But we lived in a part of town that was, all the time, not one window broken. But other parts of Berlin! On the second of February there was very heavy bombing in Berlin. I was in the office, and there I was in the middle of it.

Q. Were you ever injured?

No. Very lucky. Our honeymoon, the fourteenth and fifteenth of April, my chief editor, who was a woman, said, "Now you go to Potsdam for your honeymoon. You can stay there a weekend." There was never heavy bombing in Potsdam and so we [could] have a few quiet nights. Well, in this first night, Potsdam was bombed. In an awful way. In shelters that weren't worth much. We were only lucky that we survived that. Only a few people knew that we were going to Potsdam. So we were very lucky. As an aside, there is a strange life you have in war. You go in town, to the cinema, to the theater. Then there was a normal life. You go to the theater, you go to dinner and then came a bombing and you go to the shelter and after the bombing, you go back to the cinema.

Q. Aside from the normal fear that people have during the war, the uncertainty of being bombed on your honeymoon, for example, this must have been a very difficult time for you because of your strong beliefs and dedication to National Socialism.

Yes.

Q. At what point did it become obvious to you, Fritz, that Germany was not going to win the war?

We feared that after the invasion. But we still hoped that would not occur.

Q. I've heard a lot about the discussions in Germany of a wonder weapon, the secret weapon.

Yes.

Q. Did you put much hope in that, Fritz?

It's difficult. It's very difficult. I was afraid about the future. I didn't want to have a victory of Germany, but I feared the victory of the Allies. I feared both of them.

Q. *You were afraid that if Germany won, that Holland would not be able to have its independence?*

Of course. And, on the other side, the consequences for my personal life.

Q. *Did you suffer any kind of retribution after the war?*

No, because I stayed in Germany. So this whole—how do you say it?—persecution?

Q. *You never had any?*

I never had any.

Q. *You weren't arrested for anything?*

No.

Q. *When you came back to Holland, it was around 1955–56?*

'56.

Q. *Were there any reprisals then . . . any repercussions?*

No. I went to the department, the Hitler Youth Department in Holland, to ask if there were any prohibitions for me to be a journalist. But there wasn't.

Q. *Had you worked as a journalist, Fritz, during those ten years in Germany?*

I worked as a journalist for some Dutch people and I became editor in '46. I started the first German chess magazine after the war and I did that for ten years. But I still wanted to go back to Holland and I got a possibility with a friend to go into the advertising business. So I went to the advertising agency and worked there.

Q. *And that is what you did until you retired?*

I am not retired. But I don't still work for this agency. In '83, I became freelance as a marketing advisor and journalist and I still do this part time, not full time.

Q. *How do you feel now about National Socialism, Fritz? Do you still feel it's a good . . . [Fritz interrupted]*

No! I still feel, I felt it . . . I still believe it was a good thing. But we had to be glad that it didn't win the war. After the war I closed the chapter and I didn't look back, and I made a new life. The only thing that was left is that it became [my] hobby to read everything about the political development before and in the war. So I read all that was written about the war, the political side of the war. I wanted to know what was going on in the time that I strongly believed in National Socialism. What was going on behind the scenes. That was my great interest and is still. I wanted to know.

Q. *Do you still consider yourself a National Socialist?*

No! That was in '44. It was over. If you heard the things that had happened that was at the time, I was very interested. And I don't regret what I have done. I know it was, in my eyes, it was a good thing.

Q. In your readings about what was going on "behind the scenes," as you say, there was a lot that was going on that was not simply wanting to restore Holland to its national glory. There were a lot of other things. What other things did you find out that were going on?

The Jewish . . . the whole . . . it was so complicated . . . the real meanings of all the National Socialist development.

Q. Could you talk a little about that, Fritz, since you've spent a lot of time reading about it?

All the details that happened. There were intrigues and personal things. What happened between the leading people.

Q. If you were trying to explain to youngsters, to young people. For example, I have a son who is nearly ten and he's getting interested in history now, and particularly World War II. If you were trying to explain to someone like him what the difference was between your views and National Socialism, what would you say? It was basically a strongly nationalist movement. But there was also the option of being like Mussolini and Hitler. They had very close ties with labor unions, what we think of as a corporatist state. Were you in favor of that kind of thing, the close ties with labor unions being worked into the government?

Oh, yes. That was a consequence of National Socialism. But you must remember I was only eighteen to twenty years at that time. So you haven't the insight of the big consequences of the idealism you had. And only afterward did you see what happened in reality.

Q. Would you be one of those people who have argued that the problem with National Socialism was not the ideology itself, per se, but how it was put into effect, particularly by Hitler?

Yes, of course. But the real consequences of National Socialism in practice we didn't see in the war. The big consequences would have come after the war, if Germany had won the war. And I believe for myself, I don't know, but if Germany had won the war, and there was a strong domination of Germany in Holland, if Germany would take over Holland, in my belief then in Holland the same development would be as say in Hungary and Czechoslovakia under the Communist regime. I believe that we would be opposed. I believe that in a National Socialist Europe, so as the people in Hungary and Czechoslovakia, I would imagine that I would be on the opposite side . . .

Q. You would be opposed to . . . ?

Opposed to a German domination.

Q. Even though you then have been in favor of a National Socialist Europe?

Yes.

Q. Do you then make distinctions in your mind between National Socialism and what we think of as Nazism? Or was it pretty much the same thing?

Yes. But I learned that after the war that National Socialism wasn't the real ideology. They didn't know by themselves what they wanted. It looked like it, but it wasn't. There were two strong opposition groups in Germany, too: Between SS and the National Socialists.

Q. Do you think the SS really took over the National Socialist movement?

Not then, but the fear was that it would take over after the war. That was a bad development.

Q. What did the SS represent to you?

The real German side, the domination.

Q. When did you learn about some of the other things that were happening during the war? The oppression and the treatment of the Slavic people and the Jewish people—did you know anything about that during the war?

No.

Q. Nothing at all. Did you read Mein Kampf during the war?

Partly.

Q. Did you take it seriously?

At that time too, yes.

Q. Hitler does say there what he will do. He tells the reader. A lot of what he did, he spells out very clearly there.

But it was so . . . at that time, we hoped and gave our trust to Hitler and we hoped that after the war that he would then realize the real National Socialism and not go with the SS in this. It was a little straw, just a little thing to hold on to. It was not real. It was the only hope we had that there would be a different development.

Q. What would it [a victory of National Socialism] have meant for you? Would it have meant having Dutch colonies again, more trade with other countries? When you say that you hoped that after the war, your hope was that Hitler was just preoccupied with the war and that once the war was won, that Hitler would spend his time with the real National Socialism, the real Nazism? What would that have meant for you? Would that have meant restoring some of the Dutch trade, some of the Dutch colonies?

We hoped that Holland would be reunited as before the war with colonies and if possible, with Flanders.

Q. So you wanted Holland to be reunited with Flanders.

Yes. The so-called Dietz Movement.[3]

Q. Would you still like to see Holland united with Flanders?

Not as a united country. With the united Europe, it is not real.

Q. Are you happy with the united Europe that's come? In some ways that was what you were hoping for.

I can't see it. I believe that there will be strong difficulties for a real united Europe. But this small country can't exist by its own; it must be some part of a united Europe. But I believe there will be strong difficulties with the realization of that.

Q. Let me ask you some questions that may seem a little strange to you, but I'm trying to understand the way you view the world. Social scientists call this a kind of cognitive framework. Social scientists love to invent phrases and terminology. One of the things we say is "cognitive framework" to describe how you see the world. Can you tell me about this? Do you have any kind of views about people and what they're like? Human nature. Do you think people are good? Are they bad? Are they self-interested? Are they going to help you? What do you expect of people?

I believe in the general sense of the word that people are very egoistic. They are always thinking of themselves. And I must say that, before the war, as a minority, I had very strong sense of community with our people. We had very strong feeling to be together and to have an idealistic view. But now, people are too egoistic.

Q. I want to make sure I understood you. You said, "I had a strong sense of community with our people."

Yes.

Q. Do you think people are basically good or bad or just self-interested now?

It's not black and white. Not all good and not all bad.

Q. How do you account for the mixtures you find in people. Is it cultural influences? Is it how they're brought up by their parents?

I believe so, yes.

Q. Do you think that people are essentially alone in this world? The kind of existentialist movement that says "we can form ties, but we are basically by ourselves, that when it gets down to it, we have to take care of ourselves . . . we're not members of a group"?

No, I believe that people believe that they are members of a group. But in the group, they are self-interested.

Q. But you said the attractive thing for you about the National Socialist youth movement was that there was a strong sense of community as a group.

But we were in a minority group. If you are in a minority, you always have the strong feeling to go with people. This sense of togetherness.

Q. Do you think that people have a kind of social responsibility to help other people? What kind of obligations do we have? Where do our obligations begin and start? Are they just to ourselves? Are they to members of the other group? Are they to everybody?

You always have obligation to other people.

Q. How far does that extend? Does it extend first to the family? Sometimes you have conflicts. You can't do everything for everybody. Obviously. Or is that obvious?

The family is an important part of your life.

Q. The son comes first before strangers?

Yes. But we are living now alone. We don't have much contacts to groups. We have our friends and our hobbies, but we are not people who have the need to be with other groups, political or economic or professional.

Q. You're not a member of any groups now?

No. A bridge club.

Q. Not a chess club?

No. I do computer chess.

Q. How do you view yourself? My family always asks me when I do interviews, "What was he like? What was she like?" What do I tell them when I tell them about you? How would you describe yourself?

That's very difficult; I didn't give it a thought. I am fairly happy. I have my hobbies, reading. I have my work. And I only do this work, what I like. I don't have to work. What I do, I do with pleasure.

Q. How would you describe yourself though? Are you somebody who takes on a lot of responsibility? Are you somebody who is a leader? Who is a follower? Are you someone who—in America they'd say: marches to his own drummer? Someone who does what he thinks is best?

Yes.

Q. You're kind of a loner. Would you say you are a tolerant person? Do you tolerate people?

Yes.

Q. Are you self-confident? Are you insecure? Are you shy?

A little bit shy, yes; but self-confident too.

Q. Are you an aggressive person?

No.

Q. Passive?

Yes.

Q. Are you an optimistic person?

I believe so, yes.

Q. It must have been hard for you then in the last days of the war, when you be-
lieved so strongly in National Socialism.

But I was already [Fritz hesitated, as if he could not find the proper word] disillusioned, ambivalent. The belief in National Socialism was at the end of the war not
so strong. I was disappointed.

Q. Do you think the war changed you in any way?

The war changed everybody.

Q. How did it change you?

I became a journalist in the war. I had a chance to be a journalist. And it was a
good time. I met my wife. So I don't . . . I am happy with all it came out.

Q. The war was not a bad time for you?

No. I could travel very much . . . throughout Europe. I was in all parts of Europe.
I had a good time. I like to say that I don't regret it. But now I know what was
National Socialism in reality, I am glad that it did go this way. I don't believe that
National Socialism would be a good thing after the war.

Q. But the war itself was not a bad period for you?

No, I was happy. I wasn't injured. I was twenty and I was not a soldier in the war.

Q. You were lucky?

Yes, I was lucky. I was very lucky.

Q. Do you think that the war changed your basic personality in any way?

I can't say it did. I don't know how it would have been if there wasn't a war. I don't know.
Of course it changed me. But I can't say what would have been if there wasn't a war.

Q. Do you think that people can control their fate? Do you think that people can
make things happen in this life?

No, I don't believe so. Everything in my life was accidental. It came as it came. I
met my wife by accident. I survived the war by accident. I got a good job after the
war by accident. I started a chess paper while I didn't have anything to do. With my
last money I started this paper and it lasted for ten years.

Q. Is it still going?

No.

Q. So you don't see yourself as someone who takes the initiative to make things happen.

No.

Q. You respond.

Yes. But I take my chances.

Q. Can you tell me or not whether you have any kind of personal or ethical beliefs that you use to guide your life. . . . Are you a religious person at all?

No to the religious question.

Q. Were you raised in any religion at all? Do you have any system of how you make decisions that guide you, any kinds of beliefs?

No.

Q. How do you make decisions then. A lot of people have a system of rules that they use to follow in making decisions in life.

No.

Q. Are you an instinctual person?

I believe so, yes.

Q. Do you believe in an afterlife of any kind? What do you think is going to happen after you die?

I don't know. I didn't give it much thought.

Q. Are you afraid of dying at all?

Yes.

Q. What is it that scares you about it?

The unknown.

• • •

Q. Tell me a little bit more about your family background. What kind of relationship did you have with your parents? You were an only child?

Yes. I had a good childhood.

Q. I am always interested because I have young children. It seems to me that the way that children are raised in the United States today is quite different from the way that people are raised in Europe. Can you tell me a little bit about how you related to your parents? Did you always eat dinner with your parents?

Yes. When I came back to Holland, we had to start again. We lived for five or six years with my parents. And then we lived alone. I told you my wife was pregnant. My first child was born shortly after the war, September '45. But circumstances were so bad in Germany that it died after three weeks. Then, again, two times my wife had miscarriages, so we could have had three children, and then we gave it up after the third.

Q. *That must have been very difficult for you.*

For my wife, it was the worst. But then, we said after three times that we would make the best of it together. And we had a good time together. We wanted to have children. We were very sad that we didn't have children and so I suppose it was a difficult time.

Q. *When you said that conditions were very bad, was it just the lack of nourishment?*

There wasn't baby food . . . and the baby got pneumonia. At the time, that couldn't be cured.

Q. *Was it a little boy or a little girl?*

A girl.

Q. *I'm so sorry, Fritz. That must have been very hard. We lost a baby a year ago, and it is difficult to go through. I think it's harder for a woman although it's difficult for a man too, I think. Did you have anything that got you through that hard period? Was there anything you were able to hang on to? A lot of people, if they go through a period of difficulty, stress, or death, will find solace in a religion, for example. But you said you and your wife are not religious. Was there anything that gave you hope or strength? How did you get through this difficulty?*

It was '45 or '46. We had each other, and there was the strong struggle of life to survive after the war. We had to start again. I didn't know the possibilities and I was in Germany. It was a difficult time in Germany. We survived that, too.

Q. *My former mother-in-law was married to a man in the army and she came over to Germany after the war. She later told stories about paying people in cigarettes to do jobs for her. She said there were very unpleasant inequities in terms of how people were treated.*

Cigarettes were the currency. It was a strong struggle. It was difficult.

Q. *How about your community when you were growing up? You grew up mostly in Amsterdam. What kind of a sense of community did you have? You talked a little bit about feeling that you were part of a minority community and your parents were also Nazis?*

My father and my mother were never active. They didn't belong to the party.

Q. *But they were supporters?*

They were National Socialists. And my parents were very alone. They didn't have friends. Only family. My father was a loner.

Q. *How about you? Are you a loner?*

Partly. I have my friends and good relations. But my wife and I are alone together.

Q. When you were growing up, did you feel you were part of a close-knit community or a strong society or was it more you felt a minority?

Yes, of course, my friends at school.

Q. Did you have any particular thing happen when you were a child that was especially traumatic for you or destabilizing? A lot of people have had a parent that they lost at an early age for example.

No, my parents were very old when they died. My father was seventy-eight; my mother was ninety-four.

Q. So there wasn't any particular destabilizing thing that happened to you?

I had a very stable and good youth.

Q. Happy? You seem very happy now.

Yes.

Q. Bouncy, buoyant personality? Do you see yourself as a survivor? Somebody who will always do what is necessary to survive?

No.

Q. It was just luck that you happened to survive.

Yes. In the bad times, in Berlin, the last half-year with the bombings, all people who were guarded by the Russians were afraid of what was going on, of what was happening with the Russians. The women were afraid of the Russians. On the other hand, we never laughed so much as in the war.

Q. You have to laugh. Was it that you were laughing because things were actually funny or was it because you were laughing to keep your spirits up?

Yes, the latter.

Q. I can remember when I was a child, sometimes my father would say, "I laugh to keep from crying."

Yes. So you can say it.

Q. How about your political views now? Are you a political person now?

No. No, after the war, I thought that politics was finished.

Q. You don't belong to any political party now?

No.

Q. You mentioned the National Socialist movement, which was obviously important in forming your identity. Are there any other groups that were important for you? Are there any other groups that you belong to now that are important?

No.

Q. Did you have any kind of role models when you were growing up, people you wanted to be like? People who impressed you in certain ways?

No. I wouldn't say so.

Q. Nobody in your family in particular? No schoolteachers?

No. There were historical characters, from the Golden Age of Holland. People we were very proud of.

Q. Were there any particular historical people?

William of Orange, the founder of the Netherlands, who fought the *kampf*, the battle for freedom from the Spanish in the sixteenth century, the George Washington of Holland. You could say that in my youth, they were my heroes.

Q. Who was the other one?

Michiel de Ruyter, who was a very famous Dutch admiral.[4] He fought the British and the Spanish. As a child, they were important to me.

Q. And this was also what led you to National Socialism.

That was the main theme in my writings, to remember the Golden Age of Holland, to help to bring it back in some way or another.

Q. When you were in the National Socialist movement, and you wanted to bring back this time, what were the factors that caused you to be in that movement? The Golden Age of Holland? Was there anything else? You've mentioned the feeling of community? Was that important to you?

Yes.

Q. Was there anything . . . did you want approval of certain people that this would give you, this activity?

It is difficult to say.

Q. Was there ever a kind of critical period in your life when you really needed somebody to be there to help you emotionally, or help you in some other way?

No special moments. In difficulties in our life, we made it together with my wife.

Q. So you don't expect anybody to bail you out or give you help.

No.

Q. Do you feel you have a responsibility to other people if they're emotionally needy or in difficult situations?

There would be some situations. If friends [needed help], I believe so, yes.

Q. If you saw somebody crying on the street corner would you stop and do something? Or would you feel that would be intrusive?

In Amsterdam, you are very suspicious.

Q. What do you mean by that?

It's a little bit exaggerated, but Amsterdam is a dangerous city.

Q. Amsterdam is a dangerous city?

Especially by night.

Q. So you would kind of guard yourself against that. You would be afraid. How about any kinds of charities? Do you think that people should give money to other people? Do you think that it's the state's responsibility? Is it up to people themselves to take care of themselves?

In some ways, yes, I believe that.

Q. Which?

To help charity and so on.

Q. You do think that people have a kind of obligation?

Yes.

Q. How about the state. Should the state take care of people?

For the old people, yes. But not so excessively as in Holland. There is too little responsibility for the people by itself.

Q. So people should take on more responsibility themselves.

In Holland, the state is doing everything for the people. They haven't any responsibility by themselves.

Q. How about young people? You were talking more of old people. What about young people though? Some people talk in the United States, expressing feelings against people who come, particularly immigrants, who come to the United States, saying these immigrants will get pregnant and will have children and will take money from the state. What do you think of that?

I believe in Holland it is too easy for people to get money from the state. There are too many people who misuse it. That is what I mean about responsibility. It is too easy for people to get money from the state. I believe that I am against foreigners that move into the country, as you mentioned. I have nothing against qualified immigrants. But I am opposed to the many undocumented [ones] and the drugs who come in with them.

Q. Let me ask you just a few more questions about politics, particularly during the war. Did you know much about what went on with the Jews? People always talk about the concentration camps and the Jewish situation. Did you know much about what was happening?

Not much.

Q. What did you know, Fritz?

I did know that there were concentration camps. But I didn't know what was happening there. I believe that they were more or less prisoner camps, and hard labor. This Holocaust, I came to know after the war. That was a bad experience, of course. In Holland, we had Jewish friends.

Q. You had Jewish friends during the war?

Yes.

Q. Did you know? Did they talk to you about being concerned . . . about being sent to concentration camps?

You stick your head in the sand, like an ostrich.

Q. You stuck your head in the sand.

Yes, I must say now.

Q. You didn't really want to know about it?

No.

Q. You never thought about helping anybody or trying to hide anyone?

I hadn't the possibility to help people. I didn't see the need of it at that time. I didn't know what was happening.

Q. Is that difficult to deal with now?

Yes, of course. You can say that [it left a] trauma. And perhaps that was also the reason that I don't want to be interested in politics anymore.

Q. Because of the war?

Yes.

Q. Do you remember when you actually found out about the concentration camps?

After the war.

Q. A lot of times people can remember exactly what they were doing during a significant world event—when they heard Kennedy was shot, for example, or something similar that happened. My mother said she remembers she was playing tennis when she heard that Roosevelt died. Do you remember where you were when you first heard about the concentration camps?

No, there was not one moment when you realized what had happened. After the war, you came to hear of it, and then it became still more that you hear. There was no one day or one time when "now I know."

Q. So there was kind of a slow realization.

Yes.

Q. And how did you feel about it?

Bad.

Q. You said it was a trauma for you?

Yes.

Q. What do you mean by that?

That was the ideology. . . . That's when the whole ideology started to crumble.

Q. So the ideology started to crumble, not because you realized that Hitler was losing the war, but because you realized what was involved in National Socialism?

Yes.

Q. So this was really after the war then, when you heard about it?

Yes.

Q. So during the war when Hitler was winning? Do you remember where you were when you heard Hitler had died?

In the camp with the Russians.

Q. Were you upset about that?

No. We had so many other things to think about.

Q. By that time you thought it was pretty much a foregone conclusion. I'm just trying to understand the sequence of events here about your sense of disillusionment. You said your disillusionment with National Socialism came more after the war when you realized . . .

No, the disillusionment started in the war. Since '43, '44. The disillusionment in the National Socialism with the predomination of Germany. The real breakdown of the ideology came after the war, especially with the Nuremburg process and the Holocaust.

Q. Let me make sure I understand this. The process that happened during the war was that you realized the war effort on the part of the Germans was more for German domination rather than for National Socialism.

Exactly.

Q. And that was very difficult for you. But then after the war, as you realized, because of the Nuremburg trials and what you learned about the Holocaust, that was when National Socialism itself as a doctrine began to break down.

Yes, exactly. And then I think I started to read everything I could get about what was happening behind the scenes. I wanted to know what was going on during the time I believed so strongly.

Q. Have you thought at all about how it was possible for you and so many other people to be misled? Have you thought about that?

Oh, yes. After the war.

Q. Do you have any thoughts on that?

No. We were misled, of course. By the Germans.

Q. Do you think there is anything you've learned since you've gone through this experience that would be helpful to others, to young people, in particular? Do you have any thoughts that might help prevent them from being misled?

I have closed this chapter. I don't have the need to make the young believe.

Q. You don't want to think about it now. It's over for you. Is there anything you feel bad about, or guilty about, or sorry about? You said you have no regrets.

No, I don't feel what I did personally, I don't regret it. I have a strong bad feeling about what happened in the same time that I so believed so strongly in something.

Q. But you yourself didn't really do anything that was bad?

No. Indirectly, I feel guilty of course, that I believed in an ideology that was so bad, with the consequences.

Q. Yes, I understand that.

But I would say without this whole Holocaust and this awful [happenings] in the Eastern countries, what the Germans did there, without that, the ideology wouldn't be so bad. These terrible consequences prove that it was a worthless ideology.

Q. So you feel some regret as a kind of indirect supporter of an ideology that, even though you thought was well intentioned, at the time, yet the consequences you later learned were unfortunate. Do you feel any sorrow? You said you put your head in the sand, like an ostrich. Do you feel sorry about doing that now?

No, I couldn't see it then. Also that with the ostrich is not so good of an example. You hoped that after the war it would be normal, and it would be better. All the extreme events that took place during the war would be better after the war.

Q. You knew that these were inevitable costs of the war, basically. So it isn't really that you put your head in the sand so much. You knew.

We strongly hoped and believed that it would be otherwise after the war.

Q. That it would be otherwise after the war.

And that was the belief in Hitler.

Q. So you believed that he knew what he was doing.

But Hitler himself was the only hope, the only man who could make it better in our view.

Q. Is there anything I haven't asked you that I should I ask you? Anything that you'd like to say? That you'd like to leave behind? A lot of people I've spoken to who have lived through the war, now that they are approaching what will probably be the last ten years or so of their lives, sometimes have a feeling that there's something they'd like to tell me, . . . that they'd like to leave behind. Is there anything like this for you?

No.

Q. What was the worst thing that you saw during the war? You saw a lot.

No, only what happened to our children. The real world things I didn't see. I was in strong bombings in Berlin and Munich, but I never saw a corpse.

Q. You never saw a corpse?

I never saw injured people. I haven't. It was the worst, living in the bombing in Berlin. That was the worst experience, and also you were very afraid that you could be hurt. This bombing in Potsdam on our honeymoon, that was, of course, the worst experience, but we survived it.

Q. Really the worst was losing your children after the war then. Thank you. You've been awfully nice. I hope I haven't intruded. You've been very helpful.

Perhaps I can say that it is very difficult, my English is horrible.

Q. Your English is excellent.

It is difficult to express.

Q. These are very difficult things to discuss. I hope it wasn't too difficult. I know talking about the war is very hard for people.

No, it's not difficult for me. As I said, it was a closed chapter for me . . . at home with reading . . . but for a few years Mr. Kok found me. Then I wrote a book with this man. He was a famous Dutch Nazi journalist. They make speeches for the youth. And I bought a book about this. Then for a few years, Rene Kok found me and he wanted to speak with me before his book was wrote.[5] And I did it with pleasure. I find it, how you would say, I believe it is important for you, for the young to speak with people, with our own history. That is very important to know what these people were believing in and how they were living. I believe that is very important.

Q. Did you ever meet anybody who was high up in the party, in the Nazi Party?

I met one time with the leader of the Dutch Nazi Party, and, of course, the leader of the youth organization.

Q. What happened to him after the war?

He was the first executed after the war. He was the Dutch equivalent of the Minister of Propaganda. He was the real symbol. He was a strong and good propagandist. He was the symbol of all the bad of Nazism. Kok wrote a book about him and he was the first who was tried and executed. It would be fair to say that he was the Dutch Goebbels, yes. But Rene Kok wrote this all in his book, when the man was tried a few years later. He would have perhaps spent five or six years in prison.

Q. Did you consider what you did journalism or propaganda?

Both.

Q. Did you know at the time that it was propaganda? Were you conscious of that?

I was eighteen or nineteen. The strong believing came from the inside. I believed . . . I don't know. Rene Kok said it to me too. I don't feel ashamed over what I wrote. And my writing wasn't censored in the war. Sometimes I had some difficulties with the German press officers about articles I wrote. They were too nationalistic. Sometimes I had difficulties with it.

Q. Too strong Dutch? Too pro-Dutch? Do you have any feelings about the queen now?

Good. Still a royalist. Again. It was very disappointing when the queen left Holland.

Q. You thought that the queen should have stayed and worked with Nazis?

These consequences, you didn't think of. But the whole people in Holland were very disappointed and shocked when the queen left. And afterward, people said that it was the best thing she could do.

Q. But at the time, they had felt that the queen had deserted them?

But it is interesting, the colors of the Dutch Nazi Party had orange in the flag. We had these caps topped with orange as a symbol of their loyalty to the royalty. And against German opposition we kept these colors. It was a strange experience for me that I met Mr. Kok after thirty years to see this. Very strange experience.

Q. St. Patrick's Day is a big holiday in the United States, and people always wear green. I'm here with my family now, and they said, "We haven't celebrated St. Patrick's Day." I told them, "The people they were fighting against were men of William of Orange. St. Patrick's Day is not a big holiday in this country [Holland]. Don't wear green."

• • •

Q. This is a picture of you when you were young. Can I take a picture of you when you were young?

You can take this. I don't have a picture of me. I didn't have any contacts with anyone from the party. I didn't want to have contacts.

Q. A lot of people have said the same thing, and they've used pretty much the same phrase. They've said, "I've closed the book. The chapter was over. I went on and lived my life."

I have no interest to meet people, but it was a pleasure for me to meet with Mr. Kok after so long. I've become very interested, and it is important, the important thing for me, the first books and the first histories after the war, they were very shortsighted. Everything that was National Socialism, everything it did, and every person who believed in it was bad. All was bad and every person that believed in National Socialism was bad. The tendency of the books was only black and white. But now, they are more in the gray areas. Not all was bad, and not all the people were bad. This the young men are seeing clearer. Not all is black and white.

Q. You think it is important for people to know that there were people in National Socialism who were good-spirited and did not know what was going on?

Yes. Of course.

Q. So you're saying things aren't black and white in politics.

No.

CHAPTER 7

∾

Florentine: Unrepentant Political Nazi

Q. So you think the Christians have treated the Jews too, uh, too well throughout history? Is that what you are saying?

Florentine: We are too nice, I think. We are defenseless against them . . .

Q. Why do you say that? What do you mean by that? I'm trying to understand your view. . . . Are you thinking that the Holocaust was really made up? That it was not something [that was] real? Is that what you are suggesting?

Florentine: It's the biggest business in the world.

Q. The biggest what?

Young Nazi: Business. The Jews themselves, they call the Holocaust a Shoah. A Show-a. There's no business like Sho-ah business. That's the Jews themselves who say so. And it is.

Florentine: Yes, I agree. I agree.

July 1999

I drove to meet Florentine for her interview at her villa, near the Dutch border with Germany. Tony and his wife, Susanne, accompanied me in case I needed a translator. When we arrived we were greeted by a young Nazi, a clean-cut forty-something man wearing a business suit who was visiting Florentine for the day. Born after World War II, he had "seen the light" and had left Germany to live in South Africa. With the end of apartheid, he returned to Europe, trying to decide what to do with his life, and had made a pilgrimage to visit Florentine. He sat in on the interview, fairly quietly during the first half of the interview while Tony and Susanne were in attendance. But Tony and Susanne needed to return to Amsterdam before the interview was completed so the last half of the interview was conducted without their presence.

Susanne brought professional quality film equipment and tried to film the interview, but the lighting was too dim because Florentine kept a candle burning under a plate with Hitler's portrait on it, as a kind of shrine. The candle was a large red one, with the Nazi swastika in black on a white circle. Susanne took other pictures in the house while she excused herself to go to the bathroom, snapping photos of the bust of Hitler, an extremely large picture of the Nuremberg rally, and—it appeared—holiday cards, taped on the banister, that said things like "Have yourself a very Happy Nazi holiday."

Florentine's daylong interview occurred in several parts. We began in the morning, took a break, resumed then stopped again for lunch and I finished the interview in the afternoon without Tony and Susanne present. The difference in tone is so noticeable that I have marked the breaks, including the portions when the young Nazi spoke but identifying him only as Young Nazi.[1]

• • •

Q. Let me ask you first: What would you like me to call you? A lot of people prefer to be referred to by their first name because they want anonymity. A lot of people prefer to have the last name used, so whatever you would like is fine with me.

Everybody calls me Florentine.

Q. Okay, Florentine. Why don't we start by having you tell me a little bit about yourself, because I do not know anything about you? Where you were born, where you came from, anything you want to tell me. So just tell me a little bit about your life and then we can talk about the war as we get to that point.

Yes. My father was German and my mother was Netherlands. And so we were living near Amsterdam, and I had two brothers and two sisters. I was the youngest. And I, with my brother Wim, we went all together, and were playing together and were working together. Then, when he was fourteen, fifteen, we were very evacuated from Flanders from the [war] situations. Because we haven't had the [war] in Netherlands, and in Flanders you had Jews and all together.

Q. So where were you born?

Amsterdam.

Q. In Amsterdam and what is your birth date?

Fourteenth November, 1914. I'm now eighty-five. I'm in November, eighty-five. So I've lived in a family half German, half Dutch. My mother was very Dutch; my father was very German. So we have lived always together, so you can understand the German mentality and you can understand some Dutch sides.

Q. I don't know what that means. You say there is a German mentality, and a Dutch mentality. What does that mean?

Yes. They are quite different. Holland is a very old family, of course, and always together. We were a very well known, good family, and living in Hilversum. We had a very beautiful house and so that was our situation. But I'm thinking a home has

not appreciated so much with the German people, so my father has a very difficult
position, because he comes from the Kohls. Kohl is a big name here in Holland.
[Florentine listed names of people with the last name Kohl who are well known, to
demonstrate her point.] All the girls, and my father was the only man, so he had
to do it. So he was living in Amsterdam, working in Amsterdam. Kohl and Kohl.
The Kohls are very important. So it is this situation where I was educated. I had a
marvelous time in my youth, a lot of freedom. My eldest brother and I are ten years
different, so my eldest brother used me for all his situations here, all his work on
zoological things. So at ten years old I know already a lot of things. So my brother,
Wim, and I tried to work in the Youthstorm.[2]

Q. When was this, what date?

I think it was . . .'28. But then he was still in school, of course. But he had the idea
to go with other people to know the knowledge from the *volk*, you know. We were
very for the volk. We were very rich, but a lot of people were very poor, so you
understand better when you are working with them. He wanted to know about the
information of the working class, the poor, working class, basically.

Then we went to Flanders. It's a very nice people, very beautiful families, of
course. The difference between Flanders and Holland is that the Flanders is more
a nice, together family, and the Dutch people are very cold, and the Flanders are
very warm, so together is very nice. So you went to the big meetings; you had
the bonds. The bonds there, and you had the meetings from two, three thousand
people, four thousand people. That's also a big situation. Then in '36, Hitler was in
Germany, and he also noticed the difference between Flanders and Germany, so
our looking was to Germany. Then I was one of the young girls to meet Himmler,
who came to see the German young girl.

Q. And how did you know Himmler?

How did I know Himmler? Oh, ya, uh . . . I was working for the Youthstorm, and
lots of people from outside were interested in our work, of course. I was head of
the Youth, of the girls, so he met me. But the very thing was that I came, then I
was . . . eighteen I think, and I was . . . I don't know. My age, I don't know. So I
came there and then you saw the difference from girls. Before, girls were working like a men, you know. In our time, is the Nazi time, you call the Nazi time,
the leader woman, the girl's leader woman was so very beautiful, so Himmler
asked to bring her in. Before marriage, I was very active, very important in the
Youthstorm.

Q. And after your marriage?

*Florentine was seated on a low chair, facing the candle burning under Hitler's plate.
I was seated on the floor, holding a microphone to get better sound. To answer my
question about the role of women after marriage, she leaned back, spread her legs
apart and flipped her dress up signifying, I surmise, that after marriage one spreads
one's legs and has babies. I was taken aback by the act's coarseness, and wish we had
gotten it on tape.*

[Inaudible.] We tried to do it. So we went a little bit away from Flanders. We were drawn to Germany. . . . But I have had high school; I have had my study in Utrecht in biology, so [tape ends].

Q. So you were living in Flanders, you studied at Utrecht.

I was living in Holland. I was just visiting in summer.

Q. Visiting in summer. So then you studied in Utrecht. And you got the ideas from Germany to start some of this youth movement in Holland?

We're both, we were . . . volk, volk. [The conversation broke up then, as everyone began talking together, defining *volk*.]

Q. People. You're saying volk means the people.

All the youth people. Of course you know that our difference exists also, today. Just the same situation today, eh? So we thought that our idea of all together, of getting all together all of the youth, together, to have nice place, nice situations. So I think that it's also possible . . . but I have been a girl perhaps who went away a lot of times, who went outside, went also to East Indes, like Orwell. So, I gave you my book? [Florentine referred to her autobiography.]

Q. Yes.

Oh. So I worked for my study, in Berlin, in Paris, in East Indies, everywhere. That was my study. My free time we used for this situation, to be useful. Then we had a few thousand girls. It was quite a number, heh? I think my boss has boys. Our Dutch Hitler Youth, in German is BDM, we called Youthstorm in Holland. This was the female branch of the Hitler Youth in Holland. So here in Holland there was a small leader. He is calling himself Mussert.[3] He planned to do something for his own people and it started very well, the beginning, but he has no bad side, you know. He was good for his own people. So a lot of NSB, he called it NSB. My husband was working in . . .

Q. Where did you meet your husband?

Ya. You meet each other everywhere, because you are working, all the work you do. But when he came back from India he said he was staying at G—— with my brother. So he called me. But this is a secret. Nobody knows.

Q. So you were dating him secretly? Your parents don't know about it?

Yes. Of course, we had a lot of work, so it was not so easy in this time of course.

Q. And when did you get married?

1940. 1940. I will show you the photos. Then my husband goes to the League of Nations. He was working there. In thirty-something.

Q. What was he doing at the League of Nations?

Working for Holland.

Q. He was the representative?

Yes, he was the representative for Holland. Before there was the League of Nations, Zimmerman, that was the mayor of Rotterdam, he asked my husband to come also to give him the position there. And Zimmerman from Rotterdam was against the Jews. So my husband did not know anything about Holland's situations. He learned from Zimmerman what the Jews are. Then he looked to the League of Nations and then he thought, "Yes, all the Jews, the capitalists, the money, etc., etc., etc., is all together in the League of Nations." And this was not the idea of my husband. He went to Hitler in '36 and had a private conversation with Hitler. Hitler said, in German, of course, but he meant that, "Every country has its own culture, its own situation, like its own weather." And you had to gather the Aryan people together, you know? Not all the people, Aryan people. So, the g——[4] theory is all Germany, Austria, Holland, Flanders, all together, still starting out. That means that they wanted to have the gold standard but that you had to work for your [living, to work for] whatever you have. This was then '37. My husband was finished with Austria.

Q. What do you mean, finished with Austria?

That means he has worked there for five years for Holland. He works for Holland in Austria and while he was there, he thought all Austria is OK. The situation is okay.

Q. When he is working as the representative for Holland, what is his title?

Doctor. Minister.

Q. So he's working for Holland. Does that mean he's an official government representative of some kind?

Ya, representative for Holland.

Q. Like a council, councilman?

He was Representative for Holland for Financial and Economic Affairs.

Q. And you were courting him, but secretly?

Ya. Because I was young and he was older so I had a lot of fights, etc., etc.

Q. How much older was he than you?

He was nearly twenty years older.

Q. Was this unusual during this time period [to have such an age differential]?

No. No.

Then he ended Austria, ended his work. He said, "Austria is okay. You can do it for yourself. He does not need to have me here." He came back here and then he went to Mussert, to NSB. My husband was a man who was looking far ahead, very far sighted, and with very good education and he is speaking two languages. Mussert is a little bit smaller, a farmer type, so it was not so easy, you know?

But my husband saw not only Holland; he saw all of Europe. So for that reason he started in '42, the East Company and he said, "We lost, through the war, our colonies in Indonesia so we must try to get this money to do another situation, to the East." So then that turned us toward Russia for fishing, for farmers, for all kinds of people who were too small to know. This was a very good thing because a farmer, the house of a forge, today all farmers are put away. But at that time, the farmer, he had no volk. So then because he was very good, he was the same as Janushmart [a famous German Austrian minister], and then in '39 the Germans came here, in Holland. We, the NSB, couldn't believe it because Holland was rather small thinking. But the queen was first. The queen! So we are the only party in Holland to have always had the little flag of the queen. Then there was the difficulty with the whole situation, so the queen said, "La Reina never leaves her country." But the next day, she was away from home. *That* we did not understand. For that reason, it was for us finished. When the queen said, "I am staying here, where I am living, where I am queen," and the next day she left. Well, the whole situation! She went to London.[5]

Q. You felt betrayed?

Yes! So then the Germans were here. They came in. Then, Hitler.

Q. How did you feel when Hitler and the Germans came in? Were you happy?

[Laughing.] No, we were not happy! It was also, of course, for our side, as Aryan people, of course, world war. It was terrible, hum? But then, I was of course on the side of Hitler. Sure. So we noticed that English people are already here, to come into Germany. So it was not set [that] Hitler will not think like me. It was our idea.

It took me a while to understand what Florentine was saying as she explained her view of the origins of the Dutch part in World War II. Florentine believes the Dutch Nazis wanted Holland to be independent. According to Florentine the British invaded Holland in order to get to Germany. Hitler asked the British to withdraw and only after the British refused Hitler's request three times did Hitler send in planes to liberate Holland from the British invaders.

Our idea was that Holland had to be Holland. But the English people came in and wanted to go to Germany so the Germans had to go into Holland. It was only five days [the war] and then there is capitulation.

You know, it was after three times that Hitler has said, "Ask, please. Let go your weapons. Put down your arms." For that reason, it was three times. Two times he waits; the third time, airplanes fly to Rotterdam. But the queen said, "Yes, okay. Capitulate."

That was when my husband was in prison, *before* the Germans came in.

Q. Why was he in prison, Florentine?

Well, the Dutch Reina [queen], of course, had noticed that my husband had good relations with Hitler. So he was a dangerous man, of course. There was a move to take him to England, as a prisoner. But it was not possible because the Germans came so quickly through Holland, Flanders, and France. So all those who were outside, it was not possible to take the prisoners to England. So he had to walk to Collette, and there was Rommel already. Rommel was a big [great] man who was making the way inside to France. Then my husband tried to come into Rommel, to let Rommel see his SS ring and [once he did] that, he was okay. That meant my husband was free, and could come back to Holland with his other friends, these thirty-three people [fellow prisoners]. So then my husband came back. When the queen went away from Holland, then we have had Vinkerman, the commander and chief of the forces in Holland. He has approved that E—— was the leader from Holland. So official through Vinkerman, who has said, "I will work through the Reina." Vinkerman was the German governor of the Netherlands. Then they were looking at Mussert and when he came back, so they said to my husband, "Do you want to take it [control] here in Holland? Mussert is away. You can do it." But my husband said, "No. Mussert is a good man. I don't want to have this position."

So Mussert is staying there [as head]. So then Hitler and Himmler asked my husband to be head of the SS.

"No," my husband said, "this is for young people." So he suggested my brother [Wim].[6] Wim was young. My husband was older. So then they asked him to be leader of the Netherlands Bank, the Bank of Holland.

Q. So your husband was asked to be the head of the Dutch SS but he thought he was too old so he asked your brother to do it?

Yes. He said, "You've got to take my [wife's] brother." Wim was the SS man, yes. And my husband was the head of the Netherlands Bank. Of course, he had a lot of jobs, of course. So it was not easy for us. It was not easy for him also because we are a free country. We have free-thinking people but the Germans came in here, also in control of us and it was not easy. Hitler was very well known. A good, intelligent man, of course, but he did not know anything about Holland. All the men came out of Austria. He tried to do the best but it was difficult because he tried to work with the Dutch population and the Dutch people are very feeling a little bit against this. You understand me? So for that reason, the first year was rather normal but then came the resistance against the whole system. Then you had the NSB and the SS in Germany and we have in Holland the NSB and the VR. People had to be the soldier and that is SR in Germany and VR in Holland. [This would be called the German storm troopers and the Dutch storm troopers.]

And so the position of my husband was, because he knows through the League of Nations lots of other people, he was more aware of the whole situation. He was too big for Holland, too cosmopolitan to think only of this little country. He tried to do it but it was not so easy.

So we had our little movements. My husband was a very good speaker so he was going around speaking to the youths, to the workmen. He was the best speaker of Holland, I think. So for that reason, we meet each other. I was head of the Youth-storm [the Nazi youth movement in Holland]. We have once a year a meeting of all the National Socialists, once a year. So they say, thousands and thousands of people are coming. All the Germans are speaking, of course, because the Germans had to work with us a little bit. But we were free. What we did was free. Mussert was a man who couldn't speak German. He couldn't speak English. So from the German people, the Austrian people came here, they did not catch. Then Ratter was from the SS, for the young class. Fishburg was the man from finance. Vimer from culture and NSB was Schmitt. And, of course, how difficult it was to find honest people. Today, I can't find ten honest people today! But I think it is very difficult.

Schmitt was a friend of Mussert, because Mussert couldn't speak English, couldn't speak German. But Schmitt was a horrible man in our eyes. So they put him out of the train in '44.

Q. So, Schmitt was . . .

Schmitt was a man from the NSB in Holland, and friends with Mussert.

Q. And he was thrown from a train, is that what you said?

Yes, and it was '44. He had two meetings, but I know exactly what happened. They put them out of the train.

Q. They threw him out of a train?

In '44.

Q. And he died?

Yes.

Q. And why did they do this?

Because he was impossible.

Q. Because he was impossible?

Yes. Also he did [things] against Holland. That was not good. He was really a hateful man. They had had this situation where all the people knew Schmitt was coming. It was like a crowd. He was like a frog.

Q. Like a frog?

Like a frog. He was like a frog.

Q. And so Mussert had him killed?

No, no, no, no. No, no, no, no. Mussert was normal and he was normal working.

Q. Who had Schmitt killed?

Oh, maybe that he did it to himself because his work was finished.

Q. He killed himself?

He jumped out of the train or we get him to jump to get out of train since there are different kinds of ways . . . [Florentine shrugged.] It was wartime. His work was finished.

Q. I'm confused. Who was it who encouraged him to jump from the train? The Germans? Or . . .

No. He was a bad man. You wanted to work for years and years. Comes the day, it is finished. So you don't know what will happen with yourself. So you have to think about yourself. Have your goals or will you end your life, like this. You see? People like him, aach, they had ideals. Me too, huh? Big ideas. Idealists. We are thinking that Hitler is our man. I think he is still now. Still. Hitler was our man about the whole situation. But Holland had to be free. Holland was not under the Germans but like the [inaudible] Hitler. We have hundred thousand SS men who are fighting against the Bolsheviks. So our blood, we gave to our work. So you had to appreciate our Holland. Of course, all Germans also there were different kinds. Goering. A typical German. Germans had to work, they say it is OK. But if they get too rich, these Goebbels men, before it was good, but then it was, and they took a lot away here, took a lot out of Holland. This, of course, was bad, against Goering. All right. My husband said always, "When we win the war, Hitler will be Hitler." Himmler, SS will so Goering has lost a lot of situations, he was too late for different kinds of weakness. [Florentine began to ramble.]

So I met my husband, I think in '39, with my girls [in the girls Hitler Youth]. So I had to speak, and my husband had to speak, of course. So we decided quickly to marry. But it is not so easy in our situation because we had to have from Himmler the certificate of Aryanship. My parents were very upset. I could not say to my parents, I was marrying but I did not have a note from Himmler saying it was okay. But it took a few weeks, of course. So Himmler wants to have parents and grandparents to be Aryan. [The requirement was that top Nazis in the SS could marry only pure Aryans, which meant there had to be three or four generations of certified Aryans.] We needed to have this certified in the SS. It was difficult to get this certificate because my parents were not happy with my marriage. All the SS could not marry except to certified Aryan girls, you see?

So then we marry in '40, 21 of December. The winter solstice. We had two thousand people. It was a very big marriage of course. It was in Himpelsen, a city about fifty minutes from here. And we nearly missed the train because we had our day and the evening; we were invited to Berlin to the Adler Hotel where Hitler and Himmler wanted to congratulate us. We nearly missed the train but just at the last minute, we catch the train. So we came to the Adler Hotel for the reception that Hitler and Himmler give for us. Then we went on a horse-drawn bridal sleigh to ——, to a wonderful house of Himmler. We went in the snow. My husband and I get a large mountain goat from Himmler. We wanted to get the goat back to Holland but he kept jumping away. It was very funny. [Florentine showed me her presents from Hitler and from Himmler, of which she was very proud.]

Then the work for my husband was not easy. Because he is more German, more with Hitler. What he do now? You have no culture of your own. But we want to have the culture of our own. We want to start the farmers in the East, the officials in the East. That you have to be you. After perhaps eight years, all those go together, the Russian and the German are going together. Because your roots are your own country, of course. You can't put other people in here—Turks and all these people now! See, they have no roots here in Holland. No cultural roots. We are thinking, and I am thinking too that this culture is the most high situation we have, of course.

• • •

Q. *Just as the tape stopped you were talking about culture, and you said that you thought the Dutch culture was the most important thing that you had.*

Yes.

Q. *Is that Germanic culture or Dutch culture? I didn't understand the difference.*

No, it is not that. It is that the Germanic culture or the American culture had to be in Europe. In my eyes—excuse me when I say it—American culture is no culture. Heh? We have culture. You have no culture. For that reason, many people like to be here. Sure. Because, you see, Amsterdam is a beautiful town. Only we have drugs, all these very awful people today, strange people inside, of course, but the culture was wonderful. Berlin was just the same. This you can't take away from the volk, no? You must respect it, the culture from Aryans. So it is very foolish to say that we don't want to work with the Negro, etc., etc. I have nothing against the Negro but he has his own situation. We have our own situation. I don't like to be married with the Negro. This is difficult. Today, living together, having ten children, drugs, etc. [Florentine made a face to register disapproval.] Well, we had our special culture. We had to be pure.

Q. *What is the culture? I don't understand. It would be Aryan culture? Or Dutch culture? Or German? Are Dutch and German the same culture?*

No. No. Aryan culture is, of course, what you have in Germany, what you have in Dutch, what you have in Flanders. Holbein, the paintings in Flanders. The old buildings what you have in Germany. Holland has also the old buildings. You respect your culture, of the Aryan country. When I write to the Indonesians, I respect the Indonesian culture. I have very good friends in the Chinese. They took me into the Chinese culture but as Dutch woman. No more. Nothing more than that. Not that we should marry together or something like that.

Q. *The cultures should be separate?*

Yes. Separate. They should be separate, and respected. You must respect the culture of other peoples. But you must respect that they are not the same. I am thinking that the Jews have no culture so they don't respect us. This is difficult, of course.

Q. *So there are different cultures and they should be separate and most of them should be respected. But there are some cultures that don't have much culture in the capital "C" sense, in the sense of something that is positive. Is that what you meant to say?*

Ya. Well . . . [Florentine went into Dutch. The young Nazi visiting Florentine, much as a groupie would visit a rock star, translated her thoughts in summary.]

Young Nazi: What she meant to say is that the Northern culture, the European culture is the Aryan culture. It is that Aryan culture that we must promote.

Florentine: Ya. Ya.

Young Nazi: It is our region of the world and we should maintain our behalf to protect it against mixing up or getting rid of it all together, which is what they are trying to do now, with some success, I should say. But this doesn't mean we look down on other cultures or we think they are . . . Every country has their own idea about what life is all about.

Q. Let me see if I understand what you are saying. I think you are using culture in two senses. Because you said earlier that the Americans really don't have any culture, that is a kind of culture with a capital "C," I think, or a capital "K" in your language. And that the Jews didn't really have any culture.

Florentine: No. I said that the American people, they are a new age. I was a lot of time in America, of course. But they all like to be all the time in Europe, to see the beautiful houses. They say, "You have a beautiful house." To an American it is very important. This is true. Because it is coming the different races together. I have had last year, last week, the American people here; they say it is nice to be in Holland, the Old World. It is beautiful, since we have culture, Ya? But the difficulty at this time is that it is not so appreciated. I think we are going to a time when it is all going to be about the same.

Q. Which is culture but it isn't high culture?

No. It isn't high culture. That's right.

Q. I understand. You don't want to mix cultures.

Young Nazi: Culture is related to the people. You cannot say "culture of the world" because there is no world culture. Every people has a system. That is their culture. They develop this. White people have their culture. The Chinese have their culture. The Indians have their culture. People that have been in the system for a while, and not just the mix-up for the last century. Or something. But they have been in the system for a couple of centuries. They have developed their own way of life. What they read, what they don't read, that is the culture of the people. The language of the soul of a people, that is culture. It is a question of the soul.

Q. I understand that. But I think she was also saying something more than that, that some cultures have more value than others. Wasn't that what you were saying?

Florentine: Well, we might appreciate some cultures more than others.

Q. I just wanted to understand what you were saying.

When I am coming to the States. Then you say, "My country is Dutch or German, or from England or Ireland." Everybody from the States says, "We are from Europe." . . . And that's a pity. When Himmler has said, "When we win the war . . ."

We were sure that we would win the war, till the end of the situations. Then all the American people who had German blood would come back to Europe, to put them in beautiful housing, or something, farms or something. So you are together. But today, everyone is lost. Everyone is alone. I have seen it. I was in the States, near Chicago. Oomph! Farm, and lots of country. A farm is still a farm. Terrible. I couldn't live so lonely. But you must work together, you must respect each other, you must know your own roots. It is very special, I am thinking. It is not possible for a Kosovar to be at home here. But they put those people here. At home. They are not Dutchmen. Those people, they are Kosovars. But they live here, three years here. They said, "No. Not *our* roots." They are different, ya? So they need to stay the way they are.

Q. So if they had stayed the way they are, stayed in their place, that would be better?

Ya. Yes. That's it.

Q. So let me be sure I grasp what you are saying about culture. You believe in no mixing of different groups. Germans should keep separate from Dutch, etc. The Americans have no culture because we are a melting pot in which English, French, German, Mexicans, etc., all have intermarried, thus producing no pure culture. Is that it?

Ya. Then the war with the Germans, and the war with the German people was very difficult, of course. We didn't like going at all. We didn't like bombing at all. So that is difficult when you are living in an outside country, here in Holland. Goering was the man who made the plan, the Four Years Plan. But this means that some of the material things get out of Holland and go into Germany. My husband says, "No, no. It is not possible."

My husband was a man, the hallmark of Holland civilization. He fixed the exchange rate, and for that reason today, everyone is going to die. La Reina, the farmers, they have problems with this money.

Q. So your husband was an advocate of fixed exchange rates?

Sure. Yes. Yes. Then he has worked for the East Company, the company that was working for the development of Eastern Europe under the Reich. Our people who were living there, he worked to bring them here, to educate them, to change their vegetables, all these situations. And the leader of the people there has warned my husband, at the beginning of '45, "Please go away. [from Holland]." Because [those] against us were rather strong. The German people lost Russia and Stalingrad. But my husband said, "No, no. I did my work all right. I have very well the right to stay here, to tell the next group, who's coming after us, what I did. So they can take it." So my husband was staying. And my husband said to me, "All the SS have to go to Brazil."

But I said, "Oh, no. I don't want to go without you." So we are staying here, with my children. I have two children, and one who's coming. For that reason we were the only people who stayed here in Holland. Then my husband, he was [working] a lot of different kinds of jobs. He was *the* important man of Holland. No one was

so important as my husband. So I went to the war. It was quite near. Because first
you have to win the war. But we lost, and it was finished. So I was not so glad that
he went away. But I had the babies to commend to him.

Q. *And during the war, where did your husband go?*

In the war he was in Finland, and the Germans were here. He was in ——. In the
end of April my brother was found. Just here. Then came the capitulation. Ya. My
husband was a leader. So for our brethren SS, the 2,000, he got together and he
said, "We lost the war. What can we do?" So he wrote a paper for the queen, and
he said, "Our queen, she doesn't want to have our people here in Holland." She
wanted to go out, with her family and her children, so go to London. That was all
right. But Prince Bernhard[7] already has said lies. So then all the witnesses came
and they put away our men. Of course, so that was the beginning of the terrible
situations. So you are lost. So the people, just like there are people who want to
do with you what they want, yes? All these men who had been with my husband,
because he could speak English and French and German, he was the interpreter.
Prince Bernhard came from the other side. Of course, Bernhard knew our name
very well, Rost van Tonningen, and of course my husband knows too much. So
Prince Bernhard says [Florentine slapped her hands together in a gesture, as if saying, "It is finished, just so."], "This man had to go out, he had to go to prison." So
my husband *alone* they took away, and brought to Utrecht in the prison.

Q. *So Prince Bernhard had your husband arrested?*

Prince Bernhard has done it. And so my husband came to Utrecht for three days,
and he wrote his testament [testimony] in Utrecht. The Canadians took that. The
Canadians did that. Then all the people gets money and they put my husband in
prison and said, "You can do with this man what you want but not [let him] alive
back out of prison." He had to go to die. Then they did terrible things, for ten days,
with my husband. Oh, terrible things. Oh, just the same as the Serbians are doing.
Then the thing is, after they put through my husband on the floor, then there was a
shock. Then suddenly all the prisoners, all the prisoners who were in prison had it
much better, after that death of my husband. So they have done such awful things
to our people, terrible things. They would put out eyes, etc. They was telling about
the German people? Yes? Our people did just the same. Yes? It was no difference
between the German people and the Dutch people. This we call the criminal side
of society. Oh, they had money! Ah! My husband has about twenty wives put on
him you know.

Q. *I'm sorry. I don't understand, Florentine.*

Prostitutes. Whores. Laughing, laughing and the music. Oh, you can't imagine
what happened. Put your head in urine, and this messy! In the toilet. But they say
this was what our people did!

Q. *I don't understand. Who were these whores?*

The guards, the women guards invited them [the whores] to the prison camp. To
have fun. And my husband has to suffer this indignity. The president of the Bank

of Holland! My husband has to put out his clothes, and he had to sing the rounds, with this rope on his penis. He had to sing the national anthem, with a rope on his penis, while they dance around him. This was the situation. You can't believe what happens. But [when] you have lost the war, you have lost the war. Then you can't say anything. All the bad things are, of course, [ignored] when you have won. But *I* am saying [this] because I *know* it. Because I am living with all these people, I *know* it. The SS was the leaders. They were the *best* men we have had from Europe, people who expressed our highest ideals. Everybody, we want not war. No. Only we wanted no Bolshevism. When Hitler was not there, and Himmler was gone, then it was finished with Europe. The Bolsheviks would come through the North Sea. Only with Himmler and Hitler we can thank that there was some way to fight against Bolshevism. For that reason, now half of Europe is still free.

Q. So did you see your husband at all when he was in prison during these ten days?

Ah! Oh no! Not at all.

Q. How did you find out what happened to him?

[Florentine sighed.] Nobody knows.

Q. But you were telling me that they made him be naked and sing the national anthem. That they brought in prostitutes to taunt him. How did you know this?

[Florentine ignored the question.] Yes. I have met my husband on the third of March '45 on the front. So that was near the finish of the war. So my husband said to me, "You have to stay here." But I had two children.

Q. And you were pregnant?

Yes, with the third one. So I say, "I have to go." But I stayed too long by my husband. So it was already very difficult to come back here to the house. Then the Polish people came. All those Polish. Oh, it was terrible. Every woman would be afraid of being raped by the Poles. So I was the only woman, all the women had to go to Germany. But I didn't want to leave my husband. So I was the last. I had just come up and my car was taken by the British. So I went to Holland and from Holland to Friesland. I was flying, of course. So I saw the German and he put my two children in the boat and then he put me on an island in the north of Holland.

Q. And that's where you had your baby?

Yes. A few days later. Then I thought [about another problem]. I always have had the anxieties, the fear that they would say it is not a child of my husband, of course. So I want to have a paper that says it was my son [to certify that it is my son with my husband]. But this was terrible. I had only one bottle of gin and we gave this bottle to get this paper. But all the people of this island then knows that I am the wife of Rost van Tonningen, since his name is written down on the pieces of paper—on the Dutch currency—of course. So all the people of this island came to murder me.

Q. To murder you?

Yes. At the end of the war now, they wanted to kill me.

Q. Well, who protected you?

Nobody.

Q. Nobody?

Nobody. Then I was staying there, on the street. My child was only a few days old. And all these island people have these little flags. The red, white, and blue flag of the Dutch monarchy. One of my boys asked if he could have a flag. So I asked these people if he could give my children a flag also. They didn't. No. They didn't. Now it was the last time the German people saw I was in difficulty. This man took his car, and he took me in his car, with the children.

He said, "I can't do anything for you but only the German shipping is going to sea." I went to one ship. It was the only ship that came out. And the captain of the ship helped me.

Tony: May I ask one question? How did your husband deal with the accusation, toward the end of the war, probably from sources within the NSB who were jealous of him, that he was of mixed ancestry? And this upset the Nazis, especially Himmler at the time.

Florentine: That is the only thing my husband was very, very angry about. My father-in-law was general in the Dutch army in Indonesia and my husband was born in Indonesia. But my husband was a leader, then he was a big man, a great man. Then he here came in Holland and the men in politics was not so big as he was. Never mind, never. But my husband has said to Hitler, "Don't bring us into this position," since there is only one movement, only one NSB. So Mussert had to be the highest one. But Hitler knew only one movement, only one NSB. So for that reason, the people were very jealous, of course, of my husband. Then you have the typical bloody thinking, by not Dutch man, that he was half/half, half Indonesian and half Dutch, because of being born in Indonesia. So for this reason, just the last year, I put the Rost van Tonningen genealogy into the Aristocratic Blue Book, to say how marvelous our family was, you know. But you have always, also today, people who are jealous of the people on high and so on, like this. I told you my husband was too big for Holland. It had to be Mussert. No German in Holland. He had to be president, you see, because he knows the situation. He knows all the thinking. I'm sure if we had done that, it would be much better in Europe now than what we have today.

Q. So go back and tell me a bit more. You've just had this baby, on the island, and the people are trying to kill you because they realize you are married to Rost van Tonningen. You get on a boat, and where is the boat going?

Yes, all the German boats were together. They had already capitulated. And they [these boats] were supposed to stay there. Only one single boat was belonging to this German navy man, so this man said, "Then you can leave on this boat."

Q. So you got on the boat?

Yes. There was only one captain. I have never been on a boat like this, with two and a half children. So I took this, and oh my, we were over the water. We were for ten days on water. Then we came at last to —— harbor. That's in Germany. There were American people there, ya? So I was so ill, and the children were so ill, that they put [us] to the hospital. That is the next story, you know? Then we was in hospital. But I knew that we have lost the war. I knew that.

We have all these cards, with the name Rost van Tonningen, on the kids' cards. So I put them away. Then I knew, when I was very ill that somebody—it was CIA, but I didn't know it—asked me who I was. 'Cause all the important people came, from everywhere, of course. You have to think of the situation from this time. Then I said I was the wife of Rost van Tonningen, the minister, of course. I had to repeat it. Then he didn't do it. My little one was in the hospital, where the babies were, thirty-two babies, all already sick with diarrhea. No, not that. Gonorrhea. It was the babies who had infectious diseases, maybe venereal disease, from the mothers. My baby was in with those babies. They had food for one baby, no more. There was a very nice Sister. She said my child is the best thing. She doesn't have to die still. So she gave a little bit of what she had to my child. I was so ill; she tried to get back my milk, of course.

Still it was after a few weeks, when they said I had to go. First it was, I was to go to Russia. Then, no, no, I had to go to England. Then I must fly out of this hospital. We escaped 'cause we did not want to go to Russia. So my children and I put together the bed sheets. The Sister was very, very nice. She helped us escape. We went out of the hospital, on the street. You must think, in these days, only American trucks were there, you know.

She said, "I am staying all the way. You go into the truck with your children. When the truck stops, you get out."

• • •

Late in the afternoon, Tony and Susanne had to leave to return to Amsterdam and I stayed to continue the interview. Throughout the interview that day, the young Nazi in attendance on Florentine had said little and at first took no part in the conversation, except for an occasional translation of a Dutch phrase or concept, contenting himself with helping serve tea and lunch. But he and Tony translated when necessary, or occasionally attempted to fill in details when Florentine seemed to encounter linguistic difficulties. When he learned that Tony and Susanne needed to leave, the young Nazi offered to drive me to the train station when the interview was completed.

After Tony and Susanne left, the young Nazi took a much more active role in the interview, interjecting his own comments and explanations, to which Florentine nodded constant agreement. It is possible that the interview took this turn because Florentine was tiring; she showed no evidence of tiring, however, and declined my offers to discontinue the interview or take a break. The interview eventually was ended by me, not by her. I suspect that the interview took the turn it did because both Florentine and her guest felt less inhibited after their Dutch compatriots had departed. Because the interview became such a duet, however, complete with vigorous nodding

of the head and "Ya's" from both of them, I include the younger Dutch Nazi's discus-
sion along with Florentine's. I identify him only as a young Nazi.

Florentine and her admirer began this part of the interview by showing me a cher-
ished wedding present, a rather ordinary—ugly, actually—candle holder that Himm-
ler had given Florentine, but one that was treated as a treasured icon. This and simi-
lar actions—a candle burned in a shrine to Hitler throughout our interview—plus
the shift in tone of the interview gave me a momentary flash of uncertainty concern-
ing the wisdom of my choice to remain alone with these people. No one but Tony and
Susanne knew where I was, and suddenly I felt vulnerable and isolated. My anxieties
morphed into black humor as I looked through Florentine's wedding album, complete
with photographs of the lovely, young Florentine in a beautiful wedding dress. She
was surrounded by adorable little children carrying flowers as she walked down the
aisle—with everyone giving a Heil Hitler salute. I had the wild thought that Woody
Allen would call, "Cut!" any minute, and my fear was replaced by a surreal feeling
that I had crossed over into the land of the absurd, and a hidden movie cast would
laugh at this naive American. At this point I continued the interview, unconcerned
about my own safety.

This wedding present is a little different. It says, "My wedding present." And
here is the plan for my wedding ring, which has the symbol for the tree of life,
the old religion, which is the true religion, the religion we believed in. This is the
signature from my husband, on the Dutch money because he was head of the Bank
of Netherlands, you know.

Q. Was it difficult to never have been able to have a funeral, to never know [what
happened] to your husband?

Oh, ya! It's a shame to deny access to the people.

Q. Did you have a service of any kind for your husband, a memorial service or
something like that, to help bring you closure about his death?

Florentine: We have had a family situation but I wanted to have a burial in Laren,
to put it away.

Young Nazi: They know exactly what happened to the bastard for sure. But this
is not allowed [to tell]. The government, it is not right that they blame god!

Florentine: My husband was the first man in power [the most important political
person in the country]. So you can't believe what you're reading. You can't trust official histories. [When I tried to find out what really happened to my husband while
he was in captivity], my neighbors said that I was mad. In the official accounts, my
husband's parents are unknown. He has no job. But everybody knows that he was
a leader. In the newspapers though, he's [listed as] unknown. It's a shame. I think a
country who was doing like this is not such a good country, you know?

Before, when the war was lost, we shake hands to each other, and say, "Oh, you
lost. Oh, well. Forget it." [Florentine brush-slapped her hands together, as if signaling *fini*.] But today, it is something else. [Florentine shrugged, as if in resignation.]

Q. That intrigues me. You said at one point that you thought this kind of punitive behavior was normal during the war and that your husband would have done the same thing, had his side won. But now you are saying no, that that's not what is normal. That if you lose a war, you should at least treat the people who lose with dignity.

I think that it's abnormal after 1945. All that is studied about us, about the Germans, it's all lies. It only has to do with oil. Get Iraq oil, Serbia oil. It has nothing to do with . . . [the reality].

Q. Why do you think Hitler and the Nazis are so hated by people?

Because people, because the media made a devil out of Hitler and the Nazis.

Q. The media?

Young Nazi: And who controls the media? You know that! Jews. Why are they so worried about Hitler? Because Hitler came in with completely new ideas, which was against the Jews controlling everything through money and banks. [Florentine nodded assent, "Ya."] He did it without the banks. Remember, they boycotted the Inland Bank of '33? The Jews of the world united. In 1933, there was a big front-page article in the newspaper that they [the Jews] were going to boycott Germany. In Germany they did one boycott of Jewish things *one* time. That was blown up like you wouldn't believe. But no one talks about the Jews boycotting Germany! The Jews inside Germany didn't want anything to do with Jews outside. They were living lonely and they were forced by the outside Jews in trouble. Because if the Jews outside Germany declare war on Nazi Germany, on the SS, they make enemies of the Jews inside Germany. So if you have anyone you dislike—like the Americans did with the Japanese and the Germans—they would lock them up in concentration camps.

 Florentine: Yes, I think it's too light and dark against each because Hitler is, well, [the people] admired Hitler. Ninety-nine [out of one hundred] people was behind Hitler. But people are fickle, of course. Well, when he lost the war, then everybody is thinking, "Oh, I have no job. We had to do this and we lost that," and so and so. Well, it was not very high living. Because Hitler has shown it is possible to live in harmony with family, with work, with woods and with respect for the other. In six years, he shows the whole world that it would be possible, but it is also hard. Not everyone wanted to have it. It's not only the Germans. At least after the war, the Russians were kidnapping German scientists, and Americans did the same. They said, "You are either a Nazi criminal or you work for us, and then you're not a Nazi criminal anymore."

 So you see, now, you see, the Russians come, the Americans come, we have the same. We give each other.

Q. You were talking about the media. You asked do I know who controls the media. Who does control the media? Were you referring to the Jews with that remark?

Young Nazi: I'm afraid that they do control it. That's why I recommended this book to you. Henry Ford, a great American guy. He found out where the Jews were and he called his book *The Eternal Jew*.[8] In 1922 he wrote this book. 1922! Far before Hitler was known, to anybody. This book comments on *The Protocols of the Wise of Zion*. Did you read this one?

Q. No.

Young Nazi: Henry Ford comments on the progress the Jews made, based on the Protocols [of the Elders of Zion] and he proved that, even if the saying is not true, but the proof of the pudding is eating it. You know? This is an English saying. He proved that even if this was denied, it is all a part of a plan. They were talking about world wars when the book was written at the beginning of the century. World wars! They were talking about the diseases they were going to let loose with secular Jews. AIDS is an artificial disease, you know? The KGB said the CIA made this disease. The CIA said the KGB developed this in the laboratories.

Q. Who do you think developed AIDS?

Young Nazi: I don't know. Some criminal mind or immigrant. Now that it didn't work hard enough so they developed another one. The Ebola is another one which is supposed to be quicker, you know. And it all starts in Africa somewhere and then they blame it on the Korean War. Well, listen! The Korean War involved different things. That was invented by somebody else, you know.

Q. Do you think the Jews were involved in inventing these diseases? They invented AIDS and Ebola? Is that what you are suggesting?

Young Nazi: Oh, listen, the Jews! [Florentine shrugged and made a face of disgust.] I don't blame everything evil on the Jews. I blame many silly people who are in the plan, or who want the glory. Of course, even Clinton is surrounded by Jews. He himself. Ya. His wife is from Jews originally. Even the Pope is a Polish Jew originally. You know that?

Q. Well, no, I didn't know that.

Florentine: Oh, there are many things that people don't know! But that's the thing. And it's all nicely kept [quiet].

Now when a Jew would be a Jew, that's all right. But the Jews are German, the Jews are Dutch, and Jews are England, and the Jews are American Jews, that's always two nations. But they are Jews. They are Jews. But to the Americans, they are all American, you know? They are all Americans. So it's inevitable. You are American, Dutchman, so and so. You can't be both.

Young Nazi: You know what Napoleon said? You know Napoleon had some trouble with the Jews himself, so when he was already powerful, because he was put in power by Russia, I think. Napoleon was a small man. But he was pushed up because they saw in Napoleon a great leader. He was going to clean Europe of the kings and things and make it ready for the people. So then Napoleon had meeting with the chief of the French Jews. Napoleon said, "Listen, what are you? Are you French or are you Jewish? You can only be one."

So the guy said, "Okay, we are French."

Napoleon said, "No more Jewish clubs in France. We are Frenchman now. Finished." Then the Zionists came up, from about forty to fifty years later. If you know where the East European Jews came from, they are not even Semites. They're Asians. Did you read the book from Arthur Koestler, *The Thirteenth Tribe*?

Q. No.

Young Nazi: It tells you about the Cossacks tribe. They converted to the Jewish religion, on the orders of the king. They became the East European Jews. They are not even Jews. They have not a drop of Semitic blood in them. But they are now 80 percent of the Jewish population world over, and they are really Asians in origin and they control everything and they became what the Zionists think. The Zionists really are the ones who are controlling business. No? And if you read the *Talmud*. Did you ever try to read a *Talmud*?

Q. No.

Young Nazi: Well try to read it and then you [will] read what they [the Jews] think about us. What in everyday in the synagogue they tell us. They say we are nothing!

Q. We are nothing?

Florentine: Oh no, we are animals.

Young Nazi: We are animals in human form. Of course, the author doesn't like the Jews to suffer too much by looking at animals, so it won't look like human beings. But we are nothing. They can crook us; they can steal from us. Anything. They can never lend us money without getting a credit interest. To a Jew, they are not allowed to do this, but to the Christian goyem, no problem. We are animals. When you understand what the Jewish think of us, then you can understand why they treat us like this. Why this is serious Christians, or whoever a Christian is, they believe that the Jews are the chosen people because somebody put it in a book. *I* never selected them. *My* God never selected them as a chosen people. But a Jew is a highly intelligent person who knows not to work, not to work as the people work. Manual labor is not for them. You won't find them laboring in the countryside. But what they do is they control the farmers through money lending or through the banks. That's how they control the American farmers, how they cut these farmers out of their own farms and then let them work in their own [Jewish] farms later. But, well, you know this, I'm sure.

Florentine: Hitler wanted to give them their own country, to have their own country, Jews. Jew country, that's right. He wanted to give them their own country. The Jews would come here or someplace, or the Jews had to go to live in Madagascar. But as Jews! The plan there was to live in Madagascar. [The young Nazi and Florentine became quite animated at this point, agreeing so vociferously it was impossible to distinguish their words.]

Q. I'm hearing you say that the Jews treat Christians as kind of subhuman. Is that what I'm hearing you say?

We are not humans. We are animal cattle.

Q. Animal cattle?

Human cattle, we are. That's written in the *Talmud.*

Q. Is that the explanation for you, for why Jews should then be treated that way by Christians?

No! By Christians, not by anybody. The Jews have only power where there are Christians. It's funny you know, in other civilizations they have no power. You talk to India, there's no [Jewish] power because they don't believe all these stories.

Q. So you think the Christians have treated the Jews too, uh, too well throughout history? Is that what you are saying?

We are too nice, I think. We are defenseless against them because we believe the stories.

Q. Too cordial?

If you see all the Nuremberg people, all these people hanged at Nuremberg, I think then you know it. So I believe Hitler. I believe in Hitler. I read Hitler. We are *so* open! We have worked with people who haven't been lying, with people who did not spread hate. Oh, it was terrible.

They [the Jews] had number sixteen of Purim. They delay this hanging [at Nuremberg] one, one or two days. They want to hang them [the Germans at Nuremberg] on Purim as proof of their own people's power. They are powerful.

Q. What do you think about the Nuremberg trials?

Terrible.

Q. Terrible?

Terrible. I think they get all the head people. It is impossible to relate what really happened, because they hate the situation. It is the revenge of the winners over the losers. Before, in the Middle Ages, you shake hands when you had won or lost. And today, oof, you bomb! You see Serbia? Nuremberg? Oh, you can't say anything! You can't say anything! Such a marvelous people! Mothers, marvelous people. They did no crime at all. Nix dix crime Dutch.

Q. They did no crime at all?

Not at all. Not at all.

Q. Was the evidence just manufactured, you think?

Young Nazi: Oh! Yah. Did you read that book, *Some Other Losses, Other Losses from Back*? This is another couple of books you should read, heh? That Eisenhower let one million German soldiers die of disease or starvation *after* he had them in their camps.[9] He put them in camps, but because of him they were not allowed to have protection. They were not allowed to have enough food, and he let them die in 1945, in the early spring of '45, which was a very cold winter. He took them, well, it was Patton, which was a *real* general! When *he* caught the Germans or when they gave up, he put the veterans of the Germans on the road and he drove his tanks over it and he said to the Germans, "The war is over. Go home. Finished."

Eisenhower said, "No, no. They must be put in camps." But he did not want all the prisoners of war. He called them unarmed enemy personnel so then he didn't have to give them food like the Geneva Conventions call for. So he put them in camps and didn't give them food. They even took food *out* of Germany. All these Germans pushed out of their area by the Poles because the Russians said, "*This* we keep. If you want some country, take it from the Germans." You know? So they run to the West and chased the people out, throw them out. A million Germans were kicked out of what was before their country. For thousands and thousands of years, they have been living there! And then the Poles, they raped women and children. Women! Two and one half million dies of the four and one half million—*after!*—from hunger, starvation, shooting, hanging, raping, whatever. But who talks about these things? Nobody! And the Jews, what do you think! They made up the Holocaust! But this is a religion nowadays. Ya. Nobody thinks anymore about other people. Only *Jews* died in the war, it looks like. [He turned to lecture me.]

You be careful you don't tell the world these truths or it will be hard! It will be too much for you! [Florentine laughed and echoed her agreement with these sentiments.]

Q. Why? Why do you say that? What do you mean by that? I am curious. I'm trying to understand your view, to know how you felt about this.

Young Nazi: Have you ever saw a film made in Hollywood, which is controlled by Jews, of course. You know about Stalin murdering fifty million people by starvation? Why not?

Why do you only see films like *Schindler's List*? Which is *Swindler's List*! This is a fantasy film. It's a novella, as they say. It's not realistic. The film is based on a swindle.

Q. You don't think it's true?

Young Nazi: No, of course not. It's a novel. Essentially, if you read carefully [the credits] in the film, it, too, is based on a novel. But nobody sees it [those credits identifying the film as based on a novel]. That Spielberg—another Jew boy—is very clever. The violent film is black and white, so all the silly people say, "Oh, there is documentary there." Of course, they don't think. They only get, they get, aaahhhh, they only think it is real, but it's all the simulation.

Florentine: There was a film, in Germany and there was a friend of mine, or friends of mine in the city, and it was filmed against us [Nazis]. Suddenly these men say [to my friend], "Come." So he was in a camp. He was a high SS man. He was outdoor in the camp. One day they had to put all American uniform on. One, two days.

Then they make pictures about this. They change the tone so it looks like the German people have done all the mistakes. And he said, "It's all right. It's only one day."

Q. *It's all a sham?*

Sham, yes.

Q. *So are you thinking that the Holocaust was really made up? That it was not something [that was] real? Is that what you are suggesting?*

It's the biggest business in the world.

Q. *The biggest what?*

Young Nazi: Business. The Jews themselves, they call the Holocaust a Shoah. A Show-a. There's no business like Sho-ah business. That's the Jews themselves who say so. And it is.

Florentine: Yes, I agree. I agree. Afterward [after the war], in this hospital, this doctor showed me something which was made afterward [after the war] which was colored to make with the blood, afterward, to be put [in the concentration camps] with regards to Jews.

Q. *So the gas chambers, some of them were built after the war was over?*

Yeah. The director of Auschwitz say so, to a Jewish [guy]. There was one Jewish guy who belonged to some club and he read this and went there. Then he say, "I want to know now what the Christians is saying about this. This is not true."

Then the guy, he goes. He is one of us, the Jew-boy, he says, "No, no. This is really constructions made after the war."

Young Nazi: They [the camps] could not have been gas chambers because there was a window. There was a shower room. You could see about the walls a way. There was a window, the doors open to the inside. So can you imagine if they put people in there? They put gas in there where there were openings to the roof that were new openings; you cannot smell that stuff. It's very, very poisonous. They still use this gas. They still use now for antibugs, for delousing. It's most efficient. But you must ventilate for twenty-four hours, if not longer. You just can't enter in there [right away]. It's very poisonous. So if I were in a chamber like this, and they put in poison gas, and I know they are going to poison me, you think I just walk like a meek sheep in there? That I wait until they gas me and then I die? No! I try to get out of the bloody window, or whatever. It's the story that you read about, all so-called eyewitnesses, it's all from here. They say, "Oh, then they get killed, and people looked through the window and saw all the people dying." Who wants to see these things anyway? Then if you die, you fall wherever you fall, you know? So a thousand people stay in a room, you cannot imagine! The door opens to the inside, how do you open the bloody door? You tell me! And nobody can answer this?

Q. *Do you really discount the eyewitness testimony?*

Young Nazi: They are all, *all* pure fantasy. There is not one living person in the world, or maybe already even died, who has seen a gas chamber for killing people.

There are gas chambers in Dachau? Have you been to Dachau? Well, they said already in 1967, it was not really a gas chamber. It was never used as a gas chamber, that kind of thing, you know. I'm talking about 1967. It was never used. Of course it was never used! There was *never* a gas chamber. But in 1945, thousands upon thousands of GIs were taken there and shown gas for *feift gas,* that means "Careful, gas." Listen, if I am a Jew and I was told that was what they were going to do to me, do you think I would just walk in there?! This is so silly, so stupid. So all these gents are standing there and, "Oh, we are seeing a gas chamber?" Until now, GIs will swear, "You are crazy. I have seen a gas chamber." No?

Young Nazi: Well, Simon Wiesenthal, there's another clever Jew boy, who was looking for what Germans looked like, but nobody wants to know about it. He admits now, in his own books, there was never any gas chambers in Germany. There *was* in Poland. That was written when East Germany was still under Communist control, so nobody could check anyway. Auschwitz was in Poland, no? So Germany had never a gas chamber. Simon Wiesenthal, now you ask any man in the street, "Gas chambers? Oh yeah, in Germany." They believe in bloody lies!

And Auschwitz had never a gas chamber. It was fabricated. The SS was running Auschwitz. I don't know whether you know, well, maybe you know that the SS had to fund their own organizations. Ya? You know that? They didn't get any money from nobody. They had to make their own money. So they were producing rubber in Auschwitz, which was an artificial rubber factory. They even had plantations of a plant from which they made this artificial rubber. They mixed it with coal, whatever, and that was the rubber for tires and things. This is all, all history. You can read this if you want to. People had their own plantation. They use Russian agriculturalists, because they knew how to do it. People there were working on the plantation, ya, but they were not camps. Just being used on the plantations only. They were the factories. They were the bulging funnels. This was the smoke. The crematoria, they had crematoria, yes. For any dead person. For the deceased. Especially at the end of the war, when *everyone* was shot at by American and English planes and Russians. Anything moving was shot at. My father and my sister was nearly shot at by English planes when chopping some wood here. So there was no movement possible on the roads. There was food, but it couldn't get to the people. The camps were overfull. People were running away from other camps in the far East, or escaping from the Russians. You can imagine Jews running away from the Russians. They didn't like to be in the Russians' power, so they were going to the other camps. Why should the Germans bother by moving them [the Jews] if they wanted to kill them? They would have left them at the blood camp and that's it. No? They were herded to the other camps to keep working if possible. But, of course, that was all.

Q. There weren't death marches? They were fabrications?

I'm sure many people died because of the Russians. Many fought. It wasn't very many civilians died. But there was not enough food. There was no food; there was no nothing. There were shootings. Some of them were old. Some of these people came into these camps and there was no medical supply to clean them.

Young Nazi: But if the Hunger Winter, here in Holland, didn't do the job, the English people did it. The English people tried to kill the Germans in Holland. Because they had no food.

Q. So it was the English who killed these people?

Oh [with disgust] the Americans they did the same! Because they, well, that's the *"nice"* thing about them [about the Americans and the English]. They made the German authorities responsible for the starvation of the people, while they themselves forced the starvation.

Young Nazi: You see if you read these things, you start thinking, "But what were they really trying to do now?" They [the English and the Americans] wanted trouble. I give you one small detail. I'm sure you never heard this. Churchill was very anti-Communist in the beginning. He hated them. Then in 1936 Churchill was only a minor politician, because after the Battle of Gallipoli in the First World War, which was a disaster. You heard about that?

Q. Yes.

Young Nazi: So he was disliked. Nobody liked Churchill anyway. Then he was nearly bankrupt. Churchill in '36 was nearly bankrupt. He had to sell his house, Chartwell. At the last moment a Dutch Jew came and he spoke with Mr. Churchill and soon he [Churchill] wasn't bankrupt anymore. And suddenly he [Churchill] turned, and these Communist was not so bad anymore. Then Churchill wanted war now, because he saw Germany was becoming a powerful nation. The British were always trying in Europe, for centuries, if you know history, to operate the balance of power. They have been friends with the Spanish, with the French, with the Dutch, with the Germans, with anybody, to the Danes. And they'd be enemies with everybody as well, at the time. So they were always trying to get Europe to fight each other. The strongest, they wanted to be subordinated so they supported the weaker. So [if the strong European powers] they were killing each other, then boom! Down comes the danger toward the England for a while. They were always trying to interfere in Europe so that they [the English] would be the biggest and the strongest. Germany until 1870 was not a threat for them, because it was just a divided nation, a state in a state. They never fight inside Europe. Beautiful, no danger. Then Bismarck came along and he decided to unite them, these little German states, heh? In 1870 they [the Germans] go against the French and they won. Then suddenly Germany became dangerous, because this is a powerful nation now. United and stronger, growing like hell, industry-wise. And *that*, England didn't like. So they already schemed to get Germany in war. The First World War was then the first try to head it, [to get this policy in place]. Then you know what happened in Versailles. They make Germany killed because of this war, a war Germany had never started themselves. It was the Serbs against the Austrians. They are the ones who started the war.

Q. The Serbs.

Young Nazi: The Serbs! They killed this heir to the throne, the crown prince, and the German emperor had signed a treaty with the Austrian emperor, saying, "If you were in trouble, then we will help you." Later the emperor said, "That was the most stupid thing I did." He said so. But he went to Holland, this guy. The czar of Russia was nobility for the German emperor. They were related. He didn't want war, as well but he was a very weak man anyway. So that was intrigued by some French guy.

This intrigue against the Germans continued in the second world war. With Churchill. It was Churchill who bombed the houses to get at the Germans and break the morale of those Germans. All these hardships. So there was a resistance in 1944. Germans, against Hitler. Churchill had a whole list of all the pro-elite who were against Hitler. So when it went wrong with this von Stauffenberg—who was a strange character if you know the history, the real history, you know it's not a very healthy family either. You know what he did? Churchill sent the whole list of all the German underground people to the Gestapo.

Somebody in England said, "Why do you do this to these people?"

Churchill said, "For us." He said, "The more Germans killed there, the better." It was Churchill! He was a bloodthirsty bastard. Then he bombed Dresden.[10] First of all he wanted Germany to disappear from the map, you know, because, well, to make sure that in the future England would be the power. You know, it was bankrupt. Of course they spent all the money to the Americas and the Americas, well, ultimately, it was good business. He wanted to make sure that Germany suffered as well. So he wanted to show the Communists, because he knew the Communists were a danger. Even if he had lived, Joseph Stalin, he was a bastard. Churchill wanted to show the Russians how powerful the English and the Americans were, so he said, "Careful. We are still strong. You cannot do what you like." To do that, it took Dresden, a city full of little kids. An open city, no protection! This is war crime, isn't it? This is war crime. That's Churchill. There was a story that Churchill said, "I'm afraid we killed the wrong pig. We should have killed Stalin." You see. Kill Stalin, not Hitler. But then it was too late because then, of course, everybody, they plundered Europe, including the Americans. Twenty percent came back three years later when Stalin didn't want to play the tune, didn't want to play the tune of Washington. Then suddenly Stalin was a danger for us because the idea was that Stalin was going to rule Europe, but [with the] control from Washington, by the boys who control everything. They still control it, of course. Then Stalin said, "No, no. I want war. I'm the strong man." They had to do something to save whatever it was to be saved of Europe. Three years after the war was finished, there is again the [Cold] War. It was not to help Europe.

Q. I'm going to have to stop. Is there any last thing that you would like to tell me that I haven't asked you about? Is there anything that I have not asked you about that you would like to tell me?

Florentine: That I would like to tell to you?

Q. Yes. To say to me or to the world, through me, through this interview.

I think that I would like to add that we have to work for our youths. I think the youth is the future and now what happens to youth is very bad. Through all this not very good propaganda, I should call it, these stories told, these are not good stories about the Jews. But in reality, the youth have to know that they had to work, had to study, had to make a family, a nice family with children and normal positions, not an abnormal life with high living. So I wish the youth good health and very happy.

Q. You wish that the youth will be very happy?

Yes. Morally happy.

Q. May I take a picture of you just sitting there?

Yes.

Q. Thank you.

• • •

Florentine Rost van Tonningen-Heubel died at age ninety-two on March 24, 2007, at her home in Waasmunster, a small town located in the Flemish province of East Flanders in Belgium. Florentine had previously purchased a gravesite and a headstone inscribed with her name, date of birth, and the inscription, "The truth makes free." Known also as The Black Widow, Florentine remains controversial after her death, and some local residents fear that the grave could become an attraction for right-wing extremists. I use her real name at her specific request.[11]

PART 3

Cracking the Code

In spite of the varied possibilities for information, most Germans didn't know because they didn't want to know. Because, indeed, they wanted not to know. It is certainly true that State terrorism is a very strong weapon, very difficult to resist. But it is also true that the German people, as a whole, did not even try to resist. In Hitler's Germany a particular code was widespread: those who knew did not talk; those who did not know did not ask questions; those who did ask questions received no answers. In this way the typical German citizen won and defended his ignorance, which seemed to him sufficient justification of his adherence to Nazism. Shutting his mouth, his eyes and his ears, he built for himself the illusion of not knowing, hence not being an accomplice to the things taking place in front of his very door.

—Primo Levi, *The Reawakening,* 1995 [1963], 215

CHAPTER 8

∾

The Political Psychology of Genocide

THE STORIES WE JUST READ depict similar individuals who pursued vastly different behavior during the Holocaust. But why? And what caused these individuals
to differ so dramatically in their treatment of others? These two simple questions
soon give rise to much larger ones. To name a few: What insights can these stories
yield on the causes of genocide? What causes ordinary people to support genocide?
What are the critical differences between bystanders and supporters of genocide?
What distinguishes rescuers from bystanders? Is genocide the result of ancient
hatreds that simmer to the surface? Is an ignorant, naive populace manipulated for
the leaders' own political ends? What is the role played by bystanders in genocide?
How critical are bystanders? In what ways do bystanders justify their failure to
respond, either through minimization of the harm being done or by rationalizing
it as being somehow deserved? Or are more complex psychological factors in play
with bystander behavior, such as moral insensitivity or different group dynamics?

As our analysis leads deeper into the minds of those involved in genocide, the
questions it raises eventually grow large enough to return to the most general
ethical themes. Indeed, one of our goals should be to ask if understanding individual responses of rescuers, bystanders, and supporters of genocide can help us
understand broader, theoretical issues that surround ethics. For example, can our
analysis suggest whether everyone has a general framework through which they
filter and interpret perceptions concerning ethical issues, analogous to the one we
found for rescuers? If everyone does have a general ethical framework, what accounts for differences in ethical content and outcome? How do ethical frameworks
relate to the association between character and choice? Are our ethical choices
limited by who we are and how we see ourselves in relation to others? And if so,
how does this relate to a sense of moral salience, the feeling that another's suffering
is something that demands our attention, not just our feelings of general sympathy? Does this relate to the cognitive categorization processes of all participants in
genocide? Do we feel more connected to those with whom we feel special bonds?
And finally, what role does cognitive stretching play in responses to genocide? Are
rescuers those who can cognitively adjust to the new reality more quickly and thus
take immediate and decisive action, or does cognitive stretching just as frequently
result in elaborate systems of denial?

Answering such questions is critical in order to understand the psychology surrounding genocide and ethnic cleansing. These answers also can yield important
insight into our understanding of related forms of prejudice and discrimination.
In presenting my answers to these questions, my analysis of the stories we have just

read focuses on six central concepts: the self-concept, worldview, moral salience, ethical perspective, cognitive stretching, and categorization.[1] For simplicity of presentation, I thus group analysis around these six general topics, all of which tell us about the moral psychology surrounding genocide.

My argument in this chapter can be summarized, briefly. (1) Self-image is the central psychological variable, with rescuers, bystanders, and Nazi supporters revealing dramatically different self-concepts. (2) Identity constrains choice for all individuals, not just rescuers. Understanding identity helps decipher the speaker's perspective and reveals how values provide content and moral specificity to a general ethical framework and empathic worldview. (3) Character and self-image are not all. A critical ethical aspect of identity is relational, having to do with the speaker's sense of self in relation to others and to the world in general. Hence, we need to decipher the speaker's worldview. (4) The ethical importance of values works through the fashion in which values are integrated into the speaker's sense of self and worldview. (5) Personal suffering, in the form of past trauma, heightens awareness of the plight of others for rescuers; for bystanders and Nazis, however, it increases a sense of vulnerability manifesting itself in a defensive posture and heightened in-group/out-group distinctions. (6) Finally, speakers' cognitive categorization systems carry strong ethical overtones. The dehumanization that accompanies genocide works through the reclassification of "the other" and is closely related to a sense of moral salience, the feeling that another's suffering is relevant for me.

THE SELF-CONCEPT

Rescuer Self-Image

Perhaps the most evident important predictor of wartime behavior was the speaker's self-concept. Rescuers demonstrated a strong sense of moral extensivity, a feeling of concern for and a desire to help all people.[2] They revealed a strong sense of themselves as people who were connected to others through bonds of a common humanity. This was immediately and strikingly volunteered by Tony (rescuer), in response to my first question. Significantly, my query was only to "tell me about yourself," a question I assumed would elicit a mere factual recitation of demographic facts (such as "I was born in Amsterdam," "my father was a dentist," etc.). Instead, Tony began by saying:

> *Tony*: I was to understand that you're part of a whole; just like cells in your own body altogether make up your body, in our society and community, we all are like cells of a community that is very important. Not America. I mean the human race. You should always be aware that every other person is basically you. Always treat people as though it is you. That goes for evil Nazis as well as for Jewish friends in trouble. Always see yourself in those people, for good or for evil both.

This self-image is elaborated upon in other parts of Tony's interview.

Tony: I don't believe in an afterlife of a Heaven or Hell where you sit around on a cloud and play the harp. No. I think that the world is a world of energy that is like a cell in the body of creation. I see the whole world as one living body basically. But not our world only. The whole universe. And I'm like one of the cells. So I'm as much a part of that as others. Without me, the universe doesn't exist any more than my body exists without its cells. So I'm part of a whole and I will go back into that part, in the Indian philosophy sense. Whether any consciousness remains, we'll find out. I'm not convinced one way or the other. It could be. I'm not in a position to judge that. I'll be very interested to find out, if I am in a position to find out.

Tony's self-image as someone with ties to others captures the self-image I found in all the rescuers interviewed. Moreover, Tony was remarkably consistent, articulating this view many times throughout his narrative.

Tony: So when you save your fellow man, you save yourself, too.

Q. I see. So is what you're saying then that we're all part of the same people and so, therefore, it's not that you would sacrifice your own life because when you give up your own life, you're losing part of the whole, also?

Tony: That's right. You can see that even with some firemen going up a very rickety building to save a little kitten. The kitten is not even a human person. It is not even part of your own species. But it is the principle of life that you are trying to help.

Tony explored this view again in a long discussion in which he demonstrated that his thoughts on empathy, duty, religion, and rescuing all harked back to his sense of self.

Q. Let me see if I'm understanding what you're saying then. Are you saying that it's not just empathy in the sense of feeling another's pain as your own but that it extends beyond that? And it's not just duty. It's more an identification of yourself with the other person?

Tony: Yes. I think it is the identification that all around you counts. Again, to go back to my parable that I used earlier: If I am one cell, I can be a little independent cell, swimming around in a drop of water. But at some stage in evolution I become a cell that is part of a body. Now what happens to the other cells around me, happens to me. If something does it to them, they do it to me. I do it to them, I'm destroying myself. Man, by doing this to mankind, is actually destroying and hurting himself. Even in a completely, totally hard-nosed intellectual way, if we drop bombs all over South Vietnam and destroy their economy, we may very happily say, "Ha, ha, ha. We destroyed their economy." But in the long run, any part of the world economy that is destroyed will diminish our own status. It will diminish our own economy.

This we're gradually learning with the environment. Sure, you can say, "I don't care. I'll bomb his country." But gradually we're learning that any kind of atomic bombing hurts everyone.

Look, here's a perfect example. For a long time, people in the United States said, "We don't give a damn. All the factory smoke blows over to Canada so *they* have the acid rain. That's too bad for them." Now we're gradually realizing that it all blows back to us, and that when we are destroying the ozone over the South Pole that it's going to hurt us sooner or later, too. It won't just hurt those penguins. It's a sort of stupidity of mankind, a little like an immature child who soils his own nest, who doesn't realize that we're all one. There's an expression in environmental philosophy—I think it's the Gaia theory—that expresses the concept that the world is a living entity.[3] All of it works. All is in harmony. All is in balance. It takes very, very little to throw that balance out of whack, as we are now finding out with the ozone layer, with the carbon dioxide, with the destruction of the rain forests in South America.

I've always felt very sympathetic to the way of thinking that we are one. I think that type of thinking was first discovered around the 6th century BC with Buddha. Then came Jesus. Then there were various philosophers and teachers who gradually became aware that we're *not* just one tiny, little tribal family here and screw the rest of the world. The tribe next to us has the same problems. Why don't we work with them? Then from tribe to country, from country to alliance, from alliance to world, gradually, by opening your eyes, you see that the animal kingdom is part of that, the vegetable kingdom is part of that, the minerals in the ground and the earth itself is part of that. We can poison it or we can keep it alive and live beautiful lives. It starts right with the individual always and my immediate neighbor. You know, love thy neighbor as thyself. Because it *is* yourself. It's the mirror, again. Everyone is you.

This self-image of rescuers as being connected with everyone—"everyone is you," as Tony puts it so simply—was consistent with other rescuer interviews.[4]

Bystander Self-Image

The rescuers' rejection of tribalism—"we're *not* just one tiny, little tribal family here and screw the rest of the world" as Tony says—could not have afforded a more striking contrast to bystanders and Nazi supporters, who adopt the language of social identity theory to explain an us-versus-them self-image and worldview. The basic bystander self-image was one of people who saw themselves as weak, low on efficacy, with little control over their situation. For example, although Beatrix (bystander) does describe herself as a strong willed person at one point in her narrative, the dominant impression she gives off is of someone who lacks self-confidence and sees herself as ineffective.

Q. How would you describe yourself? Are you somebody who is a self-confident person? Are you shy? Are you aggressive?

Beatrix: I am not aggressive. I am, shy is not the right word, but I am not very sure, I am not very . . . I don't know how to . . . [Beatrix shrugged and trailed off.]

Q. Are you a follower? Are you a loner? Are you somebody who marches to your own drum? You do what you think is right? You don't worry about other people?

Beatrix: No, I am worried about other people. Sometimes too much that I . . . [Beatrix shrugged.]

Beatrix's self-portrait was colored by her view of herself as inept or maladroit.

Beatrix: All the children . . . some have difficulties . . . you must keep your mouth closed. I don't know how to say it otherwise.

Q. Is family important to you?

Beatrix: Very. But I don't have much family. I . . .

Q. The children . . . ?

Beatrix: Well, yes, for instance, I think to do the right things, and then always do them the worst things. My brother has married two times. At the last years, he didn't know very much. If he didn't do what his children wanted, he didn't get his drink, and that's what he liked very much. But at a certain time there was the daughter of his first marriage who telephoned me and said, "Aunt, I am just leaving for a trip. I heard yesterday that they have changed the inheritance of my father. Please help. My father has a lawyer, those big offices, very big, very much people."

So I phoned someone, and afterward, perhaps it was stupid. We must do something about it. At that time, there was a case where my brother had to go before the judge. And then the eldest son, he didn't say anything. My brother had to come before the judge too ... The only thing he had to say was "yes," but he didn't say it. And now, the whole thing is finished. The children from his first marriage won't receive anything. It's gone all to the second marriage. And I have paid a lot of money for the whole thing.

Q. But you did what you thought was right.

Beatrix: I did what I thought was right. But now they say I have done the wrong thing and because of me, they didn't get anything.

I *thought* I was doing the right thing. And I did it for them, because they asked me.

Yet interestingly, in response to a different question, Beatrix adds an alternate view:

Q. So you're a pretty strong-willed person. You're willing to antagonize people if you think it's the right thing to do.

Beatrix: Yes.

This exchange typifies the conversation with Beatrix, indeed with many of the people interviewed. The self-concepts are often elicited as correctives or confirmations to questions that I posed. The self-concepts are complex, even occasionally contradictory, and reveal variance in the person's self-image, as in the one comment by Beatrix that she was a strong-willed person, a view that is at variance with the general tone of her narrative, in which Beatrix presents herself as someone who is "not a nice person," as someone who is alone, and would not know what to do if her children did not take care of her now. As with other interviews—such as that of her rescuer cousin, Tony, or Kurt's self-description—the self-concept described, albeit complex and multifaceted, is elicited in response only to the request to "tell me about yourself." Beatrix resembles all the people interviewed, however, in having a basic theme to her self-concept, and this concept emerges throughout the interview in response to diverse questions and at different points in the speaker's narrative. Note this with Beatrix, and also the way she describes herself as someone adrift, without direction or purpose, saying:

> *Beatrix*: "I am alone. . . . When you are alone, you don't have anyone to talk to. Some people say, 'Why don't you go back to Utrecht?' I don't know. I mustn't think about it. It's very . . . [Beatrix trailed off, shrugging helplessly.]

Beatrix seemed world-weary and somewhat nihilistic, a sharp contrast with her rescuer cousin, who at eighty had recently adopted a three-year-old child.

> *Beatrix*: I have no beliefs . . . If I don't die tomorrow, I would be lucky.

> *Q. Are you tired of living?*

> *Beatrix*: Yes, I have had quite enough of the whole thing.

From Bystander to Nazi Supporter

Florentine and her enthusiastic Nazi groupie were proud, defiant, unrepentant Nazis, with the most extreme view of the relationship between Jews and Aryans. Perhaps understandably, the two people who fall somewhere between the bystander and the unapologetic Nazi supporters on our continuum have more ambiguous self-images. Certainly Fritz has a more intricate sense of self in relation to Jews, but his sense of identity and self-image is also intimately tied into his treatment of Jews. Basically, Fritz sees himself as someone who makes his own decisions and who is idealistic. He used to feel a strong sense of community, in which the National Socialist cause played a key part. (He speaks of a "sense of community with our people.") But Fritz now describes himself as passive and disillusioned about politics, after being so disappointed after World War II.

> *Fritz*: I believe in the general sense of the word that people are very egoistic. They are always thinking of themselves. And I must say that before the war, as a minority, I had very strong sense of community with our people. We had very strong feeling to be together and to have an idealistic view. But now, people are too egoistic.

Q. How would you describe yourself though? Are you somebody who takes on a lot of responsibility? Are you somebody who is a leader? Who is a follower? Are you someone who, in America they'd say, marches to his own drummer? Someone who does what he thinks is best?

Fritz: Yes.

Q. You're kind of a loner. Would you say you are a tolerant person? Do you tolerate people?

Fritz: Yes.

Q. Are you self-confident? Are you insecure? Are you shy?

Fritz: A little bit shy, yes; but self-confident too.

Q. Are you an aggressive person?

Fritz: No.

Q. Passive?

Fritz: Yes.

Q. Are you an optimistic person?

Fritz: I believe so, yes.

Q. It must have been hard for you then in the last days of the war, when you believed so strongly in National-Socialism.

Fritz: But I was already . . . [Fritz hesitated, as if he could not find the proper word.] disillusioned, ambivalent. The belief in National Socialism was at the end of the war not so strong. I was disappointed.

Fritz's discussion of the war indicates how much a role Fritz assigns to luck in determining people's happiness, revealing a sense of agency in which individual human beings are passive and play far less significant a role than the one we find among rescuers such as Tony.

Q. How did it [World War II] change you?

Fritz: I became a journalist in the war. I had a chance to be a journalist. And it was a good time. I met my wife. So I don't . . . I am happy with all it came out.

Q. The war was not a bad time for you?

Fritz: No. I could travel very much . . . throughout Europe. I was in all parts of Europe. I had a good time. I like to say that I don't regret it. But now I know what was National Socialism in reality, I am glad that it did go this way. I don't believe that National Socialism would be a good thing after the war.

Q. But the war itself was not a bad period for you?

Fritz: No, I was happy. I wasn't injured. I was twenty and I was not a soldier in the war.

Q. You were lucky?

Fritz: Yes, I was lucky. I was very lucky.

Fritz does not see himself as a tough survivor. Indeed, his discussions of the war indicate he shares Kurt's passive acceptance of what will come, and agrees that people have limited control over their destinies, as noted by the role he attributes to luck.[5]

Q. Do you see yourself as a survivor? Somebody who will always do what is necessary to survive?

Fritz: No.

Q. It was just luck that you happened to survive.

Fritz: Yes. In the bad times, in Berlin, the last half-year with the bombings, all people who were guarded by the Russians were afraid of what was going on, of what was happening with the Russians. The women were afraid of the Russians. On the other side, we never laughed so much as in the war…

Q. I can remember when I was a child, sometimes my father would say, "I laugh to keep from crying."

Fritz: Yes. So you can say it. You understand.

While Kurt, Fritz, and Beatrix saw themselves as low in efficacy and weak agents, it is Kurt's discussion of agency and the link between that lack of choice and his wartime behavior that is most striking. It surfaces in his discussions of fighting the Slavs, something Kurt felt was a mistake since it was not historically the German's land.

Q. Do you have a feeling that you were caught up in history? I'm hearing a strong sense of…

Kurt: Ya. I like history.

Q. But when you were doing this, you keep mentioning these other things repeating themselves.

Kurt: Ya. Why do we do this again? See how often the Goths went over and pushed the Slavs back from their border.

Q. But I'm hearing you sense a kind of futility at doing it again and yet you kept on doing it. Does it never occur to you … [Kurt interrupted, with some vehemence.]

Kurt: Can I change this? I have no power to change this!

This exchange illustrates Kurt's belief that he has no ability to change things because "this is all history," and for Kurt historical forces dictate the parameters within which an agent can operate and make choices. Historical forces are the prime agent, not the individual, for Kurt. This is further demonstrated when Kurt makes references to Verdun and World War I and the Franco-Prussian War, as Kurt describes the German invasion of France, noting that he is preparing to go into battle right where his father was killed (World War I) and his grandfather wounded (Franco-Prussian War). Kurt even refers to the Napoleonic wars when he discusses invading Russia. (He seems to make the Germans analogous to the French in this allusion.) Kurt seems to find a sense of honor and worth in being in tune with this sense of history, noting that he is unlike others in his regiment in this regard. "Most people did not know this in our regiment. You see, even officers did not know this." The importance of being in harmony with the greater forces that drive human beings was evident in Kurt's discussion of his own behavior during the Battle of Stalingrad, when he risked his life to be with his men for he was "lost" without them, left "without [his] people."

Kurt: Okay, a day later I was wounded here, at the head here. I got hit through my head, through my hard head [helmet], through my steel head [hit by a grenade]. I thought I was dead. . . . Then the next day when I was released I wanted to go back to my battery, you see. Otherwise you are lost. What can you do in a hospital? You are lost. You are without your people. You know nobody there. You don't even know if they treat you well. So I wanted to go back and they bandaged me. Now, I could not fight with this bandage so they painted it green. A day later I was back fighting and this was terrible because I had a concussion and had to lay at rest at least two or three weeks and I did not. I fall from my horse sometimes.

Q. Why did you do this?

Kurt: I wanted to stay with my people.

Q. You felt that the army was your people?

Kurt: My unit was my people. I was responsible . . . and you feel a certain responsibility because this goes on for generations, you see? When I think back, in my family they all had these jobs and they were all wounded, you see?

Q. It's almost like it was something that gentlemen do. I mean, honoring Pétain, treating the French soldiers well. It's almost like you were fighting in the nineteenth century.

Kurt: Yes. That was the way I was raised.

Unrepentant Nazi Self-Image

In contrast to the passive bystander self-image, the strongest Nazi supporters' self images are—ironically—those of victims, of people besieged by threats to their well being, who must strike preemptively to protect their ontological security and that of their community against Jewish threats.[6] Florentine's Nazi admirer speaks of the Jews as if Jews had been the ones to attack Germany through acts such as an organized boycott of German banks.

Young Nazi: The Jews of the world united. In 1933, there was a big front-page article in the newspaper that they [the Jews] were going to boycott Germany. In Germany they did one boycott of Jewish things *one* time. That was blown up like you wouldn't believe. But no one talks about the Jews boycotting Germany!

He then speaks of the Jews as being clever enough to avoid doing any real hard work.

Young Nazi: When you understand what the Jewish think of us, then you can understand why they treat us like this. . . . They believe that the Jews are the chosen people because somebody put it in a book. I never selected them. My God never selected them as a chosen people. But a Jew is a highly intelligent person who knows not to work, not to work as the people work. Manual labor is not for them. You won't find them laboring in the countryside. But what they do is they control the farmers through money lending or through the banks. That's how they control the American farmers, how they cut these farmers out of their own farms and then let them work in their own [Jewish] farms later.

The phrasing "not to work as the people work" is an interesting juxtaposition, one we will find later when we discuss the Nazi categorization schema and which seems to distinguish Jews from people. Frequently adopting the metaphor of disease, Nazis make genocide a kind of immunology, designed as preemptive action to rid the body politic of unclean elements.[7] In a somewhat rambling diatribe, Florentine's Nazi admirer links Henry Ford's anti-Semitism to the Jews, AIDS, immigrants, and—eventually—the Korean War.

Young Nazi: Henry Ford comments on the progress the Jews made, based on the Protocols [of the Elders of Zion] and he proved that, even if the saying is not true, but the proof of the pudding is eating it. You know? This is an English saying. He proved that even if this was denied, it is all a part of a plan. They were talking about world wars when the book was written at the beginning of the century. World wars! They were talking about the diseases they were going to let loose with secular Jews. AIDS is an artificial disease, you know? The KGB said the CIA made this disease. The CIA said the KGB developed this in the laboratories.

Q. Who do you think developed AIDS?

Young Nazi: I don't know. Some criminal mind or immigrant. Now that it didn't work hard enough so they developed another one. The Ebola is another one which is supposed to be quicker, you know. And it all starts in Africa somewhere and then they blame it on the Korean War. Well, listen! The Korean War involved different things. That was invented by somebody else, you know.

The scope of this sense of victimization in this quotation is quite breathtaking and certainly reveals that the victim mentality forms a critical part of the Nazi self-image. Consider one last quote from our two ardent Nazis, one that captures the Nazi self-image as victims threatened by Jews.

Young Nazi: [R]ead it [the Talmud] and then you [will] read what they [the Jews] think about us. They say we are nothing!

Q. "We are nothing?" What does that mean?

Florentine: Oh no, we are animals.
Young Nazi: We are animals in human form .... [W]e are nothing. They can crook us; they can steal from us. Anything. They can never lend us money without getting a credit interest. To a Jew, they are not allowed to do this, but to the Christian goyem, no problem. We are animals. When you understand what the Jewish think of us, then you can understand why they treat us like this....

Q. So you think the Christians have treated the Jews too, uh, too well through- out history? Is that what you are saying?

Young Nazi: We are too nice ... We are defenseless against them ... If you see all ... the people hanged at Nuremberg, I think then you know it! So I believe Hitler. I believe in Hitler ... We are so open! We have worked with people who haven't been lying, with people who did not spread hate. Oh, it was terrible. They [Jews] ... want to hang [the Germans at Nuremberg] on Purim as proof of their people's power. They are powerful ... They made up the Holocaust! But this is a religion nowadays. Ya. Nobody thinks anymore about other people. Only *Jews* died in the war, it looks like. [He turned to lecture me.] You be careful you don't tell the world these truths or it will be hard! It will be too much for you!

The Nazi victim mentality is reinforced by a sentiment of racial differences and separation, and a belief in Hitler's wisdom in working to ensure this racial purity.

Florentine: Hitler wanted to give them their own country, to have their own country, Jews. Jew country, that's right. He wanted to give them their own country. The Jews would come here or someplace or the Jews had to go to live in Madagascar but as Jews! The plan there was to live in Madagascar.

This self image is heavy with a victim mentality, with Florentine and her Nazi admirer describing the Nazis as people who are "too open," too nice, too good to protect themselves effectively against the tricks of the unscrupulous Jews. Jews are described as trying to take advantage of the Nazis; Nazis are described as "people who haven't been lying . . . people who did not spread hate."

These are the contrasting self-images then. Rescuers see themselves as people connected to all others. Bystanders describe themselves as weak and helpless, low on efficacy, borne along on the winds of history or other forces beyond their con- trol. Nazi supporters describe themselves as people under siege who must take pre- emptive action to protect themselves. Each self-image is closely linked to choice, as becomes evident when we consider our next important finding: the striking ability of identity to influence and set choice.

IDENTITY CONSTRAINS CHOICE

Regardless of how different the self-images of the individuals interviewed were, their identities clearly constrained choice in every case. One way to understand how this process functioned is to think of identity as setting a cognitive menu of options available for each individual. Acts not on the cognitive menu are not considered, just as pizza is not an option in a Japanese restaurant. For everyone—bystanders, rescuers, and Nazi supporters—self-image required them to act in a certain fashion. For rescuers their self-image created the altruistic personality in which the habit of internalizing the suffering of others as something personally relevant became part of a way of life that required not just concern for others but also action to alleviate their suffering.[8] For bystanders their self-image of helplessness meant they were unable to control events around them. This helplessness was the explanation that was stressed for why they did not do anything to help Jews. (The implication that they wanted to help Jews was usually unstated, more something that hovered in the background of the interview while not being explicitly expressed. Only one person gave the explanation I had expected: "I wanted to help but was afraid for my life or the life of my family." This I thought was striking and significant.) For Nazis their self-image as a people under attack led them to engage in what they saw as a preemptive strike to protect the German body politic. For all three groups, then, the importance of self-image is evident; while the actions taken by members of all the groups were very different, all those interviewed expressed a shared feeling of having little choice, and of knowing only one way to respond to the world they perceived.

Rescuer Identity: People with Ties to All Humanity

For rescuers their lack of choice emanated from their self-image, especially their view of themselves as connected to all humankind. Tony employs an interesting metaphor to describe this.

> *Tony*: If you take the cathedral [as an example], the cathedral cannot exist without the brick. The brick cannot exist without a grain of sand. So by removing a grain of sand, basically you harm the cathedral. You may not notice it right away. But if you remove enough grains of sand, sooner or later the cathedral will collapse.

Tony's statement was not unique in its general sense. John, another Dutch rescuer of Jews, echoes Tony's sentiments.

> *Q. You used the phrase, "I had to do it." Most people didn't do it though. How did you feel you had to do it, when other people did not?*
>
> *John*: I had to do what everyone should do. [John shrugged.] I do it.
>
> *Q. But why did you have to do it?*

John: Because I have to help those in need, and when people need help, then you have to do it.

Q. When you say you had to do it that implies to me that there wasn't a choice for you. Did you . . . [John interrupted.]

John: No. There is no choice. When you have to do right, you do right. . . . I had the privilege to be born into a family that had the idea of serving your neighbor. They taught us that ideal. I remember my father say, "There's an old lady. Help her to carry her bag." This kind of thing. At the same time, with my own mind I have the idea that I have the guardianship of my brothers. I have to help others. Don't be selfish. Help others. With this concept of ideals, when the moment arrived that you had to do something, okay, you have to do it. It was my duty. I claim to be a person to help others. Then I do it.

Q. Did you ever sit down and think about the costs and the benefits and the risks involved in what you were doing?

John: I don't think so. I think that it came as a natural reaction from the inside. Like a mother. Normally, you don't teach a mother how to love her baby. She has that naturally. So your instinct that you develop in yourself is to react that way. It was a quite natural development, not, "Should I do it or not?"

For rescuers, any cost-benefit analysis became secondary to the hierarchy of values already deeply integrated into a sense of self, which demanded spontaneous rescue activities. This phenomenon is noted in work on other moral exemplars,[9] and is posed quite dramatically by John as a conflict in which strongly felt values (such as telling the truth) must be overridden by the ultimate value (in this case, the sanctity of human life):

John: I remember my father saying, "Always do what your conscience tells you." For your conscience, there is no big problem, "Am I right or not?" Another thing, I always learned to be truthful, to say the truth, never to lie. But when I came before the Gestapo, it was for me very natural to lie, to say, "I don't know where are there [Jewish] people." Only after the war did I say, "Was it right or not?" [John shrugged and shook his head, indicating he did not know the answer to this question.] My story is the story of many people in Holland. When the Nazis ask—"Do you have Jews here?"—very naturally, you lie. Only afterward do you ask, "Am I right or wrong?" Even now, I ask myself [John shrugged], and I don't know.

Q. But at the time . . . ?

John: No question. No problem if it's right or wrong. It was right! It is right. They are human beings. . . . I wasn't lying to save my life but to save other people.

Q. So there is a higher value for you than telling the truth?

John: Sometime in life you have to make a choice between higher values. This is a very difficult question. I can't say to anyone else.

Q. What was the highest value for you, the value guiding you during this time?

John: Love your neighbor. You have to help.

Bystanders: Identity of Helplessness, Low Efficacy

While the phenomenon is particularly striking when found among people who risk their lives for strangers, it is not just the rescuers who describe their acts as spontaneous and natural rather than the product of agonistic choice. An analogous phenomenon occurs for bystanders. Bystanders also believed they had no choice; this belief was closely related to their self-image as people who had no ability to help. The mechanism driving bystander psychology, however, differed significantly. The bystander self-image is one of helplessness and lack of agency bordering on low self-esteem, as was evident at several points during Beatrix's interview.

Q. How would you describe yourself?

Beatrix: I don't like so much to say it, but I am always doing the wrong things.

This negative self-image was reinforced at several points throughout our interview, including the end, as I thanked Beatrix and, totally out of the blue, she volunteered the same negative self-concept, as if seeking to reinforce this view as we ended our interview.

Q. I can't think of anything else to ask. Is there anything else you'd like to tell me?

Beatrix: No.

Q. Thank you.

Beatrix: The difficulty is that I . . . I'm stupid; I can't say certain things at the right moment.

Q. No, you're not stupid at all.

Beatrix: I know I am, but . . . [Beatrix shrugged.]

The inability to assert herself, to be someone who makes a difference, the self-image as an ineffectual person who must accept whatever life hands her, goes back a long time for Beatrix and seemingly constituted a central part of her identity.

Beatrix: You have to accept it.

Q. There was nothing you could do to change.

Beatrix: No. There was nothing to do. . . I remember [when] my mother was operated on and my father told me to bring her a . . . book or something like that.

But I was not allowed to enter her room ... I did take the book.... The nurse came ... "Your mother asked if you will come in." I said, "I am not allowed."

Q. Yes, but your mother asked if you would come in.

Beatrix: I said, "I am not allowed." That evening or very early the next morning [the hospital called my father.] My mother had died. [My father] went only with my brother. I wasn't allowed to go.

Is Beatrix's low sense of agency in part a reflection of the objective status—and the lesser treatment—of women versus men in European society when Beatrix was young? Perhaps. These statements by Beatrix, however, also illustrate a critical difference among rescuers, bystanders, and the supporters of genocidal regimes. Rescuers exhibited an internal locus of control over their fate; bystanders and supporters of genocide tended more toward an external locus. This locus of control did not correspond to gender differences; female rescuers demonstrated the same strong sense of agency as their male counterparts. The differences in agency—this sense of who it is who makes things happen in life—were striking, with all bystanders, men as well as women, evincing much less sense of being in control than did rescuers. In the case of Beatrix, it was Beatrix's father, and later her husband, who made Beatrix's decisions. Beatrix described herself as someone who was quite happy being "kept," living her life as Nora at the beginning of Henrik Ibsen's famous play, in a pampered, protected dollhouse arranged for her by others. Not all bystanders were so extreme in this regard, but all insisted they had little control over events and hence there was little they could have done to help Jews. This difference was striking between rescuers and bystanders, regardless of gender.

Nazi Supporters: Identity as People under Siege

For the Nazis their victim self-image meant they felt compelled to strike preemptively, to protect themselves because they genuinely felt like a people under attack from vile, base elements in society. We find this self-image in Fritz's narrative as he describes being in "a minority group and we were out of it. The National Socialists were a minority group." Fritz easily adopts language familiar to social identity theorists, both in his in-group versus out-group mentality (in describing how joining the National Socialists provided "a feeling of belonging") and in identifying group identity with belonging (as when he notes how "[if] you are in a minority, you always have the strong feeling to go with people. This sense of togetherness.") In chapter 6, we read how Fritz's identity as a Dutchman cut against his identity as a Nazi. Indeed, Fritz's support for National Socialism was tempered by his fear that the Germans would dominate in a future Nazi Europe and raises the question of the relationship between Fritz's patriotic nationalism and his National Socialism. ("[We] gave our trust to Hitler and we hoped that after the war that he would then realize the real National Socialism and not go with the SS in this. It was a little straw, just a little thing to hold on to. It was not real. It was the only hope we had that there would be a different development.") Fritz's conflicting identities—

Dutch patriot and Nazi supporter—cut against each other. Running like a leitmotif through his narrative was the extent to which his conflicting identities led to his somewhat mixed views on politics during the war, especially in his description of how he wanted the Nazis to win but yet feared their victory out of concern that the Germans would trample on the Dutch. Interestingly, Fritz's central objection to the SS seems to be that they were German in orientation, an indicator of his narrow and nationalist conception of community. He says nothing of the barbarity of SS.

Perhaps the most striking comparison with Nazi supporters such as Fritz and bystanders such as Beatrix lies in this sense of agency.[10] Neither group sees themselves as people with strong agency, with a strong sense of being able to affect things in life. Fritz describes himself as passive, as someone who does not have much ability to control his fate, much like Beatrix.

Q. Do you think that people can control their fate? Do you think that people can make things happen in this life?

Fritz: No, I don't believe so. Everything in my life was accidental. It came as it came. I met my wife by accident. I survived the war by accident. I got a good job after the war by accident.

Q. So you don't see yourself as someone who takes the initiative to make things happen.

Fritz: No.

Q. You respond.

Fritz: Yes.

In contrast to bystanders, however, for Nazi supporters the prime movers were even more removed. The critical players in their lives were often the forces of history. Kurt's tendency to relate his own experiences to a larger history captured something critical about bystanders and Nazi supporters: the different view of agency that they and rescuers held. Florentine and her Nazi admirer spoke frequently of the *volk*. ("We were very for the volk.") She noted how important it was to be in touch with the volk, which flowed like a life force through history. Florentine speaks of her warm feeling when she met with the volk. ("Flanders is more a nice, together family, and the Dutch people are very cold, and the Flanders are very warm, so together is very nice. So you went to the big meetings; you had the bonds.") The idea of community for Florentine was closely tied to the notion of a state as an entity larger than the individual, not merely an aggregate of individuals, but an entity with a life force of its own. This view of community contrasts with the more individualistic view of human agency found among rescuers, which more closely resembles the English social contract view of individuals.

Nazi supporters not only expressed a lack of personal or individual agency; they also seem to suggest possible excuse-making for their lack of responsibility, relying, to a degree, on precedent. Kurt's discussion of the war as a doomed but inevitable part of the historical unfolding is a striking illustration of this.

All the stories in this book reveal people whose choices were constrained morally by their basic identities. It is the identities that differ, and these differences correspond to critical moral stances. Everyone was compelled to act as they did because "that's the kind of people they were," as one Polish survivor explained rescue behavior.[11] Rescuers were constrained by their strong sense of connection with others. Bystanders were similarly constrained by identity, but in the case of bystanders it was because they saw themselves as people with little ability to help and as individuals who were more passive and guided by others (Beatrix). Dedicated Nazis such as Florentine did not see themselves as weak or passive, but they saw their strength as emanating from being in tune with the winds of history, from a community not from individual will. Florentine's sense of agency meant it was not individuals but larger entities that dictated how events unfolded. Florentine's sense of empowerment came from being close to great men (such as Hitler and her husband) who were in tune with these deeper forces. She constantly refers to her husband as someone "too big" for the Dutch political scene, with big ideas and ideals that set him apart from the masses, even from the other main Dutch Nazi politician, Mussert. She praises the SS as "the leaders. They were the best men we have had from Europe, people who expressed our highest ideals." Finally, she speaks with admiration bordering on rapture of being hosted by Hitler on her honeymoon, of staying in one of Himmler's houses and of being given—of all things to convey honor—a goat by Himmler for a wedding present.

So all of the individuals were constrained in their moral choices. Identity was the mechanism that limited these choices subtly but significantly. Interestingly, this is reflected in the descriptions of choice and in discussions of when and what exactly one knew about the Holocaust and the treatment of the Jews. We find great ambivalence and contradictory statements in both Kurt's and Fritz's discussion of what they knew about the situation of the Jews.

Q. What did you know?

Fritz: I did know that there were concentration camps. But I didn't know what was happening there. I believe that they were more or less prisoner camps, and hard labor. This Holocaust, I came to know after the war. That was a bad experience, of course. In Holland, we had Jewish friends.

Q. You had Jewish friends during the war?

Fritz: Yes.

Q. Did you know? Did they talk to you about being concerned . . . about being sent to concentration camps?

Fritz: You stick your head in the sand, like an ostrich.

Q. You stuck your head in the sand.

Fritz: Yes, I must say now.

Q. You didn't really want to know about it?

Fritz: No.

Q. You never thought about helping anybody or trying to hide anyone?

Fritz: I hadn't the possibility to help people. I didn't see the need of it at that time. I didn't know what was happening.

Q. Is that difficult to deal with now?

Fritz: Yes, of course. You can say that [it left a] trauma. And perhaps that was also the reason that I don't want to be interested in politics anymore.

Q. Because of the war?

Fritz: Yes.

At different points Fritz utilizes the image of an ostrich with its head stuck into the sand to describe his situation during the war, to reflect what seems a desire on his part not to know what was happening. But he also retreats from this self-image at one point.

Q. You don't want to think about it now. It's over for you. Is there anything you feel bad about, or guilty about, or sorry about? You said you have no regrets.

Fritz: No, I don't feel what I did personally, I don't regret it. I have a strong bad feeling about what happened in the same time that I so believed so strongly in something.

Q. But you yourself didn't really do anything that was bad?

Fritz: No. Indirectly, I feel guilty, of course, that I believed in an ideology that was so bad, with the consequences.

Q. Yes, I understand that.

Fritz: But I would say without this whole Holocaust and this awful [happenings] in the Eastern countries, what the Germans did there, without that, the ideology wouldn't be so bad. These terrible consequences prove that it was a worthless ideology.

Q. So you feel some regret as a kind of indirect supporter of an ideology that, even though you thought was well intentioned at the time, yet the consequences you later learned were unfortunate. Do you feel any sorrow? You said you put your head in the sand, like an ostrich. Do you feel sorry about doing that now?

Fritz: No, I couldn't see it then. Also that with the ostrich is not so good of an example. You hoped that after the war it would be normal, and it would be better. All the extreme events that took place during the war would be better after the war.

Q. You knew that these were inevitable costs of the war, basically. So it isn't really that you put your head in the sand so much. You knew.

Fritz: We strongly hoped and believed that it would be otherwise after the war.

Q. That it would be otherwise after the war.

Fritz: And that was the belief in Hitler.

Q. So you believed that he knew what he was doing.

Fritz: But Hitler himself was the only hope, the only man who could make it better in our view.

Earlier I asked Fritz:

Q. Do you remember when you actually found out about the concentration camps?

Fritz: After the war.

The contradictions in Fritz's narrative reflect Fritz's ongoing difficulty in rationalizing and justifying his behavior to himself. The contradictions link Fritz's lack of knowledge about the Holocaust to his sensed lack of agency, which in turn links to his lack of ability to help, as reflected in his description of himself as an ostrich, an image itself later rejected. This is a process also found in other bystanders and weak supporters of the Nazis.

Kurt's discussion (chapter 5) of the Jews reflects similar confusion, contradiction, and ambivalence, all of which seem to underline the extent to which he, too, did not want to know about the situation for the Jews and all of which relate again to Kurt's sense of weak agency. (Note Kurt's comment that, "This [knowledge] was all taken away from us.")

Q. But within this Gothic nation, your grandmother pointed out that there was repression going on.

Kurt: Ya, in Germany after the First World War.

Q. In Germany itself after Hitler came in. Were you happy with this or you just didn't see that?

Kurt: Well, I said, "I'll go abroad and then maybe I can survive until this ends." We did not think it would last, you see? No one in Germany would think it would last, but Hitler was just pushing this away.

Q. What about what we now know about what went on with the Jews during the war? Did you know anything about this?

Kurt: No, we did not know. The Jewish people came from a village to surrender to us to get away from the Russians. We said, "All right. You come over and then you find yourself somewhere where you can stay." We did not know anything. I did not know about concentration camps. This was all taken away from us. When the war ended I came back to Germany. I was discharged in Bavaria by the American Army, and with discharging papers, I could go on a train. Before, I could not even go on a train, you see. Trains were just freight trains, and I saw beside me was one fellow sitting with these striped uniforms, and I said, "What are you wearing here? Are you coming from Cologne? Are you from Cologne?"

He said, "No. This is the concentration camp's uniform. This is an honor for me now." And he was a priest, a Catholic priest. I said now, "Why did you come . . . ? What is a concentration camp? Why did you go in?" He said, "Well, I was Catholic and I was preaching against Hitler."

Q. So the first that you heard about the concentration camps was after the war?

Kurt: After the war. We were never told. You see, we were defending in Vienna. The last days, I was fighting in Vienna against Russians and there some of my soldiers told me, "Well, there are concentration camps here in Austria, Auschwitz." And I said, "What are they? What did you hear about it?" They took prisoners there and they took French people there and they took Italian people there, Russians. So this was a mystery, and the first fellow who really told me was a priest.

At this point, Kurt seems to contradict himself on when he first knew, suggesting first that it was after the war, then during the war. He also makes Auschwitz a prison camp, not a concentration camp, in Austria and not Poland. Yet later he says:

Q. You didn't know about Kristallnacht?[12]

Kurt: Oh, the Kristallnacht! Ya. This was taking place in Berlin and then the synagogue was burned in Fasanenstrasse, but then the Jews lived there. I did never hear that one Jew was taken away, and I still don't believe today how many Jews were taken away because when I came back to my house, which was completely bombed in Berlin, to our city house, I was told "Ya, the family who lived right below you, they were killed in a concentration camp." Mr. Louie. Louie was Jewish and even under the Hitler regime he was running a big garage house in the Konstanz working-class area in Berlin. Okay, so Louie was killed. His wife, too? "Yes." Okay. Okay, seven years, eight years later in Hollywood, we go down. Two of my oldest sons with me. There comes a man, "Are you German?"

"Yes, we are German."

"From where?"

I said, "From Berlin."

He said, "From Berlin? Where did you live there?"

"B——strasse."

"I am Mr. Louie." He lived above me, right? Here they were! I was told over there [in Europe] that they died. So here he was.... They brought them all out. When? After the war. They were hiding somewhere in Belgium, and then they came out. Dr. Schneider, she was translating for the German Consulate here in '52, she came out. She's Jewish, and she said, "This is terrible to live here. My daughter is on drugs and she has a boyfriend. She doesn't want to marry because she changes [boys] every four weeks. Terrible living here!" Dr. Schneider . . . invited my wife and myself to tell me the whole Jewish story and from here I heard. Here, not from Germany.

In this section Kurt seems to suggest that he learned of the situation for the Jews only later in the United States, and he hints that the situation was not as bad as Americans say. Yet he also said he knew about Kristallnacht when it occurred, and while he was in Germany.

Q. So your impression was that after Kristallnacht when the Jews disappeared, that they just left the country?

Kurt: That's it. No. Now they are quieting down because after the First World War, we had Jewish families living with us in our houses and in businesses. Nothing happened, but when the Polish Jewish came in, from after the war in Russia, after the First World War from Russia and from Poland, you see, they were collecting garbage and rags and all this, old shoes. They built businesses. Built businesses and cheating and cheating and cheating. We did not know this in Prussia. Our Jewish families, they left there when King Frederick II left. Everybody can be going in Heaven after his fashion.

Finally, in this quote Kurt seems to imply that "our" Jews are okay, that it was just foreign Jews who caused the problem, revealing a categorization process we will note later as significant.

Q. After his fashion?

Kurt: Ya. How many Jewish families were doctors and lawyers and all this? My lawyer here is Jewish and he's from Berlin, and we talk so much about it. "How you couldn't have known anything about this," he said.

Q. You really didn't know anything?

Kurt: Well, he says this is ——. It's just over here across the street. See, this is the Kristallnacht. Then we thought, "Well, this is finished." I danced with Jewish girls. They had the Jewish star here when I was on leave. They didn't tell me they were harmed or anything. I never asked a Jewish fellow with a star. Well, when I came on leave to take my baggage here, bring it at home, I never asked.

Q. Was it because you just really didn't know or maybe you didn't want to know?

Kurt: No! Did not know. I wanted to know what goes on in my fatherland. I wanted to know but nobody . . . [Kurt shrugged.] The Jewish didn't tell us. Even in our houses people didn't tell us. When I came once on leave, my mother said, "Well, above us the people have to move out. They go to this school. There's a school and they have to be assembled, all the Jews out of our street."

So I went there with food and I asked them now, "How can I help you? Can I bring you out?" No, you cannot risk this. Now, what do you know what will happen? We don't know. See? There you get stuck. They didn't tell you.

This statement seems ambiguous. Is Kurt saying he tried to rescue Jews, or help them move out of their homes? Is he quoting Jews who told him he could not risk helping them, or does his statement that, "No, you cannot risk this," indicate his own assessment of the situation? Despite these ambiguities, in one clear respect Kurt's narrative does seem to resemble the narratives of Fritz, Beatrix, and the other bystanders I spoke with: Kurt did not know about the situation for the Jews because he did not want to know. This suggests the importance of moral insensitivity for moral ignorance. The explanation for not doing anything to help Jews is not a cost-benefit analysis in which the person wanted to help but was afraid of being caught and paying too high a price for helping. Instead, it grows out of the sense of self as someone who has no options, who is kept in the dark, who does not know what is going on and—perhaps by implication—is being duped by someone by being excluded from this knowledge.

Values and Identity

Values enter the moral psychology in complex ways. We expect that people whom we find morally exemplary will subscribe to values we share, such as honesty, integrity, and compassion. But a more thorough analysis of the data suggests that most people give at least lip service to many of the same values. Few genocidalists get up in the morning and tell themselves, "Today I will be a horrible person and do vile things." Instead, as Philip Gourevitch (1998) points out in discussing Rwanda: "the engineers and perpetrators of a slaughter like the one just inside the door where I stood need not enjoy killing, and they may even find it unpleasant. What is required above all is that they want their victims dead."[13] This phenomenon—as Gourevitch points out—highlights the role of ideology and values in structuring identity. Recent work on value hierarchies of Holocaust rescuers finds rescuers subscribe to benevolence, universalism, and spirituality more, for example, than do resistance fighters. Rescuers care less about security than did resistance fighters.[14] But significantly, it appears that it is not specific values per se but rather the way in which values are integrated into our self-image that is critical.[15]

Thus when we consider both the differences in agency and the striking fact that identity constrains choice for all people, the question then becomes: How does identity's influence on behavior work to limit choice? What is the psychological process driving this constraint? Part of the puzzle here is unlocked by considering how the incorporation of key values into the rescuers' sense of self effectively created boundaries in their self-images and then limited and foreclosed debate about transgressing these values. The speakers' self-images and worldviews are what appear to account for both the lack of choice and the divergent responses to the suffering of others. But while prior works noting this phenomenon[16] examined only moral exemplars, I found it occurs for *all* people.[17]

Rescuers Contrasted with Bystanders

Consider the contrast between Tony and his bystander cousin as an illustration of how values exercise their influence primarily by coalescing into a self-image that then constrains choice. Beatrix clearly benefited from the displacement of the Jews. One obvious illustration of this gain is the fact that Beatrix's husband bought his practice from a Jewish doctor, whose home Beatrix then moved into when the doctor immigrated to South Africa, presumably to escape the Nazis. Beatrix notes these facts but seems oblivious and unconcerned by them, outwardly unaware of any connection between her own prosperity and this Jewish doctor's misfortune. Because she does not make a cognitive connection between the two situations, she does not feel that the plight of the Jews requires any action on her part. The suffering of others holds no sense of moral relevance or salience for Beatrix, or for other bystanders.

> *Beatrix*: We were just arrived in Utrecht and there I lived in the very little house for some months because the surgeon who sold the practice to my husband wanted to help him get started. Then he fled to South Africa. I am not sure, but maybe he had something . . . Jewish, I'm not sure.

Beatrix expressed the same vague, moral insensitivity toward what the Nazis were doing when she volunteered information about building an attic hiding space for her husband:

> *Beatrix*: It was a very old-fashioned home, and so we made a part in the attic where you could go away to hide.

> *Q. Was there anyone you were hiding?*

> *Beatrix*: No.

> *Q. Did you know any people who were Jewish at that time?*

> *Beatrix*: Yes.

> *Q. But nobody approached you . . .*

> *Beatrix*: No, because there were a lot of Jews who stayed there and didn't want to hide. After some times, they were taken away too because a lot of Jews lived normally, and had only to wear the Star of David.

> *Q. Did you know what was going on? What was your impression of what was happening? Did you . . .*

> *Beatrix*: Did I know?

> *Q. Yes. What did you think was the situation for the Jews? . . .*

> *Beatrix*: They went to a camp in the neighborhood; I can't say the name. I knew it.

Q. What kind of camp was it?

Beatrix: Those camps. There was no gas, but they had a very bad life.

Q. So it was a work camp?

Beatrix: Yes.

Q. Did you know about the concentration camps during the war?

Beatrix: Yes.

Q. Did you know that the Jews were being gassed?

Beatrix: Yes. I can't tell you who told this, but my husband heard a lot when he worked in the hospitals.

Q. How did you react to something like that?

Beatrix: You couldn't do anything.

Q. There was nothing you could do.

Beatrix: No. No. [Long silence.] All the Jews I knew were already away. [More silence.] No.

Q. So there was nobody you knew who was still here. They had all gone.

Beatrix: Basically, yes. I knew no one, but still there were Jews, and they had their sign. But no. [Another long pause.]

Q. Did you just feel that you were kind of helpless in this situation to do anything, to stop it from happening?

Beatrix: You could not do anything. You could hide them. But you have help in the house. We had too much people around because we had a practice at home . . . you couldn't do anything.

In contrast to findings by other scholars that suggest bystanders tend to rationalize their inaction by subtly deriving justification for discrimination and persecution, Beatrix acknowledges the circumstances for the Jews but simply does not make a connection between the Jews' suffering and her own situation. Although some bystanders (Kurt) did exhibit elements of the rationalization/justification explanation, a more dominant factor is moral insensitivity cloaked in a moral ignorance, cushioned by a sense of helplessness. This process—in which bystander passivity is decoupled from any sense of horror at the Nazi behavior—is reflected starkly in Beatrix's sense that she cannot affect change; it contrasts sharply with her rescuer cousin Tony's sense of agency:

Tony: People get depressed because there's not much they seem to be able to do about things like the Holocaust. Well, I firmly believe that people can do something about it!

WORLDVIEW AND VALUES

Fatalism and Agency

Values enter an actor's sense of self directly through the actor's worldview, the cognitive framework by which we all make sense of the world. Values influenced the speakers' worldviews in subtle but critical ways. Differences in worldview between rescuers and bystanders were especially striking. The bystander worldview was tinged with fatalism and lack of efficacy, with individual human beings described as being remarkably lacking in agency. For Fritz, as for other Nazi supporters, what happens in life seems independent of individual, personal strivings, perhaps suggesting that the value of an individual was less important than that of the group. The narratives of Fritz, Kurt, and Florentine reveal a strong sense of community and communitarian values. If the individual is out of sync with the group, he will not be happy. Yet being part of a group can result in fatalism and an overall loss in individual agency. This paradox was poignantly expressed in Kurt's description of the Battle of Stalingrad:

Kurt: After Stalingrad, then I . . . Well, this was only retreats, you see.

Q. Was it different for you now because you were losing?

Kurt: Ya. Well, this was the end of it, you see? We were losing. We lost in this battle over three thousand tanks and the Russians had four thousand tanks, and it was just steel. So I was burying people at first. We had to bury the Russians and it was twenty-fourth of August, was very hot, and the bodies, they were green. They blew up in five hours, you see, the bodies. This was in '44.

Q. Did you not want them to end the war?

Kurt: What can you do? If you retreat . . . the leaders, even company leaders, were tried for treason.

Q. Now, this was after the plot to kill Hitler, which was led by old army people, no?

Kurt: Ya. Everyone in the army was against Hitler. The army was against Hitler. How many generals were killed? Destroyed in planes. Flying graves we called them cause so many had time bombs in them. They all fall down with the planes, you see. So the pilots didn't want even to fly generals anymore.

Q. They knew that they would be sabotaged?

Kurt: Ya. See? Now, what can you do? Finally you have no concentrated power where you can go to or pray to or think about it. There's none left.

Q. You felt totally powerless?

Kurt: Ya. You feel powerless. Oh, Ya. We felt this the first day because we knew, when we went into Russia, the first day, we cannot make it. Never. Then everybody had the feeling . . . I mean the officers had the feeling this will never go good.

Bystanders' sense of passivity, a feeling that the world was run by forces somehow beyond their control, seemed closely linked to the bystander value of community. If an individual needed to suffer so the group could flourish, so be it. In Kurt's case, this value was reflected in his sense of tradition, which stressed family and group identity above the individual's well being.

Kurt: This was four generations in our family. Always the same coachman, and the oldest son got the job. So this was all working in a certain frame which was worked out hundreds of years ago, in the same way.

Q. Was that comforting to grow up in such a stable environment?

Kurt: Well, I didn't feel it.

This bystander worldview was intimately related to bystanders' response to the suffering of others. Bystanders did not believe they could do anything to help anyone because they had so little control. "But what could I do? I was one person alone against the Nazis," was their plaintive refrain. Events seemed somehow beyond them, as illustrated by Beatrix's discussion of the Jews, where she openly acknowledged knowing that Jews were being sent to concentration camps:

Q. There was nothing you could do?

Beatrix: No. No. [Long pause.] No. You could not do anything.

Nazi supporters demonstrated a similar lack of individual agency; but for Nazis it is historical forces beyond human control that drive world events. Florentine illustrated the Nazi view of the world as shaped by blood bonds and forces beyond any one individual's ability to control. Florentine's sense of individual efficacy thus emanates—with great certainty—from her belief that she is attuned to the will of history. Kurt—the Nazi soldier I located somewhere between a bystander and a Nazi supporter—also refers to historical forces in explaining his lack of choice. For Kurt the German creation of an eastern front was a mistake since it violated the traditional historic land of the Slavs. Kurt reveals the same sense of historical inevitability found in Florentine's interview, but he differs from Florentine in arguing that this part of the war was a mistake. When asked about his actions at several points, he became agitated, angrily insisting he had no choice in the matter.

Q. You didn't have any choice?

Kurt: No! There was no choice. . . .

Q. Do you feel you were caught up in history? You keep mentioning these other things repeating themselves. . . .

Kurt: Ya. Why do we do this again? See how often the Goths went over and pushed the Slavs back from their border.

Q. But I'm hearing you express a sense of futility at doing it again, and yet you kept on doing it. Does it never occur to you... [Kurt interrupted, with some vehemence.]

Kurt: Can I change this? I have no power to change this!

This theme ran like a leitmotif in Kurt's narrative. It appears in his discussion of a secret mobilization of the German army in August 1939, when Kurt's passport is taken away and he describes how his individual rights are violated by the powerful state.

Kurt: In August '39, there was a secret mobilization of the German army. So I had to go to the consulate, and my passport was taken away. I said, "Well, this is my passport. I paid three marks. I own this." "No, you don't own this. This is owned by the government."

Q. The German government took it away?

Kurt: Ya. I said, "Well, what can I do with the passport?" Ya, you go in this room, and there are other Germans sitting, a little bit older than I. All together, we were fourteen. After three days waiting there, I could go home and have to come back the next day, and then we were fourteen. We got a ticket, a train ticket, all fourteen on one [ticket] so nobody could escape, and probably there was an agent with us. I don't know. They didn't tell us. But everybody were not trusting, and this is the system. You cannot ask your neighbor because he may be that agent.

Certainly, one can make a reasonable case that protesting the power of a totalitarian state is futile. But Kurt's narrative seems less a reflection of this fact of *realpolitik* and more the manifestation of his sense of fatalism and lack of agency. Nowhere is this more evident than in his discussion of the beginning of World War II, which Kurt views as a repeat of history, even as he notes that this history condemns the Germans to disaster.

Kurt: They did not know where to go! They could not speak French and the French didn't like them. They didn't answer. So they were all captured, and then I found the observation post where my grandfather was. I saw it! That photograph! I saw that photograph my [grandfather] took about thirty years before and I had this photograph in my mind, and I said to my boys here, to my soldiers, I said, "Here was my grandfather wounded and that night after he was wounded, it rained and rained until the next day, so they were laying in the mud." And I could feel it! . . . forty miles farther north, my father was buried, fallen in the First World War, but I could not escape this. I had to follow this. So then that night, we had to march south in direction of Verdun. At three o'clock in the night, we had a meeting with our general and he said,

"Well, Kurt, you have to go with two guns at the fastest way you can go to village Verdun and there you will find somebody who measured already where the guns are going in positions."

I said, "Verdun?"

"Yes, Verdun."

"Verdun." The First World War. One point four million soldiers were killed at Verdun.[18] Gee, Verdun. And then I came to Verdun in the morning and at six o'clock and there was a lieutenant from the division and he said, "Well, today is no attack; it's tomorrow. So you can take care of the other guns when they come in." They were still bombed by us in this position from the First World War and [made] big craters. So the next morning, we had all together, the battery was in position with four guns, and then at three o'clock, they didn't start. It was the sixteenth of June in '40. To my mother I wrote a letter, and to my grandmother, because the advance was set back two hours. And then at five o'clock, the trumpets blew, and Attack! Attack! Attack! . . . Once in a while, there came a shot out from there, and then our general called, "Kurt! You have to take in fog grenades." We have to fog that whole area in so they cannot see. We want to attack immediately. We have to be up there around noon. We attacked this mountain, and the French surrendered here. See they come against us with the white flag. I had to surrender in '44 against the Russian army. We were bleeding out, had no more tanks, and I did the same thing, and that's a terrible feeling, for a man to surrender. It's a terrible feeling. You lost everything. You lost your honor. You lost your responsibility against your family and all this. It's a terrible feeling, and I told our boys when we attacked, "Well, when we take prisoners, think about what their feeling is." Now when we came up to Fluery-devant-Douaumont, you see, they came out of Chattancourt, so we were talking to [the French, saying], "You did a brave job." So this was with France. In Russia it was just killing, you see? See how we talk to each other. We mingle. I took this picture of us together. I had a Leica [camera].

Q. Even while you're going through this, you have a sense that this is historic, what you're going through?

Kurt: Ya. Well, I took pictures as I could get them. I could not always get them, you see. I had much more than these here. This is my observation point [showing picture]. Here's my radio and three operators, and there's a gun here in the back, an infantry gun. When I took that picture I heard [some soaring sound] and then the grenade came and all dead! Right at that moment when I took that picture! These people right there were killed. It was dreadful, yes. But you don't have any choice.

Q. You didn't have any choice?

Kurt: No. There was no choice.

This passage captures much of the fatalistic worldview that is associated with the lack of choice and reflects Kurt's heavy emphasis not on individual rights but on group behavior. Kurt seems to link this lack of individual choice with the power of the group and the group's place in history. For Kurt, this linkage is a source of pride in family but also a sorrowful awareness of being trapped. In contrast, for Nazis like Florentine, being caught up in history conveys a positive sense of pride at being in touch with major forces.

Agency and Lack of Knowledge

This fatalistic sense of agency contrasts with rescuers, whose efficacy resembles the traditional Western liberal concept of individuals who control their destiny, a concept based on the value of individual worth. This difference in value is reflected in a further noteworthy divergence in worldview. Only rescuers had integrated the value of human life into their worldview. Only rescuers felt it was natural that others would help their fellow human beings. For everyone else, the tragic calamity of the Holocaust was something judged so far beyond his or her control that it was not even remarked upon. Primo Levi—a survivor of the Holocaust—suggests the key to understanding what allowed the Nazis to take and hold power was closely related to a silent conspiracy in which people wanted not to know what was being done in their name, by their government. The real powerlessness grew out of an identity perception in which people saw themselves as people who were helpless; a critical part of this helplessness was ignorance. Their lack of knowledge somehow excused people for not acting. Hence, identity worked through a worldview in which people had to obey the state because the state was somehow not just all powerful but also all knowing and hence not to be questioned. Thus Levi describes this as a code that is widespread, saying that "the typical German citizen won and defended his ignorance, which seemed to him sufficient justification of his adherence to Nazism. Shutting his mouth, his eyes, and his ears, he built for himself the illusion of not knowing, hence not being an accomplice to the things taking place in front of his very door."[19] I believe we can crack this code and decipher how the psychology surrounding genocide works if we can understand the link between identity and agency and worldview and, as we shall soon see, the way in which Jews were then recategorized.

We can discern critical parts of this link in the narratives of this book. For example, Beatrix commented that the Jews did not "have a very good life" in the camps; this was the closest she came to expressing any regret or sorrow for the Jews. It was striking how consistently this pattern held for other bystanders. Fritz, for example, denied even being aware of the extent of the Holocaust until the war's end, despite his being a journalist who claimed to have traveled widely throughout Europe during the war. (One wonders about Fritz's journalistic abilities, given his professed lack of knowledge.)

Q. People always talk about the concentration camps and the Jewish situation. Did you know much about what was happening?

Fritz: Not much.

Q. What did you know?

Fritz: I did know that there were concentration camps. But I didn't know what was happening there. I believe that they were more or less prisoner camps, and hard labor. This Holocaust, I came to know after the war.

Fritz's later remarks, however, give the lie to his statement that he was not aware of the camps, especially when he identifies a key part of his psychological routine as simply not wanting to know. Not knowing and not wanting to know—as he says, sticking "your head in the sand, like an ostrich"—are two quite different things.

Kurt's narrative exhibits a similar ambiguity concerning his supposed lack of knowledge:

Q. So the first that you heard about the concentration camps was after the war? Is that correct, Kurt?

Kurt: After the war. We were never told. You see, we were defending in Vienna. The last days, I was fighting in Vienna against Russians and there some of my soldiers told me, "Well, there are concentration camps here in Austria, Auschwitz." And I said, "What are they? What did you hear about it?" They took prisoners there and they took French people there and they took Italian people there, Russians. So this was a mystery, and the first fellow who really told me was a priest.

Kurt's phrasing, "You see, we were defending in Vienna," almost comes across as "I was a soldier; I had more important things to do. I found out about these events in the course of doing my job." Almost in spite of himself, though, Kurt reveals that he knows the psychology of helplessness all too well, though he ironically identifies it in the Jews themselves:

Kurt: I mean, the same as what the Russians did when I was prisoner. First, oh, just deliver your arms, you see. When you had to deliver the arms and then something else and something else until you were powerless. That was the system and that worked with Jews, that worked with the Huguenots in France. This was all before. Now, I knew that under the Queen Isabelle and her husband, Ferdinand, that the Jews had to leave Spain but there were no Jews killed, and they had to leave in France, too.

This statement implies Kurt "knew" what the Jews might have being going through on a psychological level, but this understanding of their situation apparently never translated itself into empathy or action. Did the Russians help to teach Kurt his lesson too well? Or was that lesson already part of Kurt's identity, a reflection of an unexamined anti-Semitic worldview in which Kurt believes "there were no Jews killed" in Spain during the Inquisition and in which "this was all before"?

The linking of choice to identity is close for all people. Fritz's interviews illustrate how important a role identity plays in the moral passivity that accompanies bystander behavior. Fritz's closest group was the National Socialist movement during World War II. After the war, and as Fritz slowly came to feel more betrayed by the movement, he pulled into his family, forging a world of his own with his wife and his in-laws. At this point his previous group identity, focused on National Socialism and the nationalism of the war years, seems to have vanished entirely, and Fritz became primarily a member of his own family group or of his chess club.

> *Fritz*: We got married on the thirteenth of April. It was a Friday. But it was difficult then since a German woman who wanted to marry a foreigner must be authorized by the SS. But in a strange way, we get the permission, so we could marry. Then my wife got a Swedish passport since Sweden represented the Dutch interests in Berlin. They gave her this passport so my wife legally became Dutch. She got a Swedish passport that said she was married to a Dutchman. We were under the protection of the Swedish Embassy.
>
> So that was how we were able to escape from Germany, I think it was a week later, with twenty other Dutch friends. We escaped from Berlin. We were afraid to stay in Berlin. The bombs were dropping, and the Russians were coming. We wanted to escape to the American lines. The Americans were at the Elbe and had stopped there. We knew if we could get there it would be better. At the end, we were with about three hundred Dutch people in a camp with the Russians. There we waited about three weeks before we could go to the Americans. We were exchanged and were sent back to Germany, to Germany under the Americans. The camp was the Neuruppin. It was west, sixty kilometers from Berlin. There were about forty to sixty thousand people from all countries in Europe. I still wanted to go back to Holland, though, because I was afraid of the Russians coming in, and the reprisals. But I heard that this marriage of Dutch with German woman was not recognized. I wanted to go back to Holland until I heard this rumor, which meant that my wife would be sent back at the border. My wife was pregnant, so I didn't want to leave her alone. So I stayed in Germany with my parents-in-law for ten years, and then I came back to Holland....

Q. How do you feel now about National Socialism? Do you still feel it's a good . . . [Fritz interrupted.]

Fritz: No! I still feel . . . I felt it . . . I still believe it was a good thing. But we had to be glad that it didn't win the war. After the war, I closed the chapter and I didn't look back and I made a new life. The only thing that was left is that it became [my] hobby to read everything about the political development before and in the war. So I read all that was written about the war, the political side of the war. I wanted to know what was going on in the time that I strongly believed in National Socialism. What was going on behind the scenes. That was my great interest and is still. I wanted to know.

Q. Do you still consider yourself a National Socialist?

Fritz: No! That was in '44. It was over. If you heard the things that had happened that was at the time, I was very interested. And I don't regret what I have done. I know it was, in my eyes, it was a good thing.

The war not only ruptured Fritz's ties with National Socialism, it also severed his political activities, and Fritz now describes himself as "finished" with politics after the war. He belongs to no political party and no longer identifies himself as a political person, an identity that was so critical for him during World War II.

Q. How about your political views now? Are you a political person now?

Fritz: No. No, after the war, I thought that politics was finished.

Q. You don't belong to any political party now?

Fritz: No.

Identity also is evident in Fritz's discussion of the critical groups that formed his identity and worldview. All of these were historical characters, usually from the Golden Age of Holland, and they gave Fritz a vision in which Holland was restored to her former and rightful glory. The tone in Fritz's narrative implies that Fritz felt both a sense of entitlement to this glory and resentment and a sense of deprivation and victimhood at the loss of this glory. This resembles what many Germans felt after the Treaty of Versailles punished them for World War I, a cultural attitude that historians frequently attribute as a factor in Hitler's rise to power. But this suggestion is slight and I am interpreting here, perhaps overly so. Certainly, after the war these characters and models became less important for Fritz. Nonetheless, the value Fritz placed on the past and on conserving that past played a central role in his identity as a Nazi Party member and propagandist. And there is no indication that Fritz has shifted his sense of agency or his worldview toward one in which individuals make history and therefore can contribute to events.

Q. You mentioned the National Socialist movement, which was obviously important in forming your identity. Are there any other groups that were important for you? Are they any other groups that you belong to now that are important?

Fritz: No.

Q. Did you have any kind of role models when you were growing up, people you wanted to be like? People who impressed you in certain ways?

Fritz: No. I wouldn't say so.

Q. Nobody in your family in particular? No schoolteachers?

Fritz: No. There were historical characters. From the Golden Age of Holland. People we were very proud of.

Q. Were there any particular historical people?

Fritz: William of Orange, the founder of the Netherlands, who fought the *kampf*, the battle for freedom from the Spanish in the sixteenth century, the George Washington of Holland. You could say that in my youth, they were my heroes.... I find it, how you would say, I believe it is important for you,

for the young to speak with people, with our own history. That is very important to know what these people were believing in and how they were living. I
believe that is very important.

For both Kurt and Fritz, their sense of the past was intimately tied to their identity and to the central role that conserving old, traditional values played in that
identity. But in Kurt's worldview, history repeats itself, carrying him along with it
and constraining his choices. He becomes an extension of his heritage, which sets
the parameters for the possible actions Kurt may engage in during the present.

> *Kurt*: You know, we Germans are called in Spanish the *alemanes*, and it means
> all men, from different tribes, they just came together—boys and girls—and
> they formed a new Germanic nation, Aleman, all the man from all nations.
> These are the Alemanas, and they came to France into Spain and even over
> to Africa. They have their empire built, you see. This is the background of
> my family.

The worldview in which historical forces carry along individuals became stronger the closer we moved to unapologetic Nazi supporters. Florentine was the most
extreme, speaking of needing to be in touch with "the old religion" and prais-
ing Hitler for being in touch with these "big" forces. Florentine refers to leaders
as "big" throughout her narrative, including when she describes her husband as
being too "big" for Holland and his rival, Mussert, as being a "small" man. For
Florentine, the value of all these great men comes from their ability to be in touch
with the grander themes and powerful forces in history.

In contrast, for rescuers the value of human life was supreme. Indeed, one of
the touching things about rescuers is their valuing of each individual life, no matter how lowly that person would be in any grander scheme of things in the Nazis'
sense. There is not pride but rather a sense of peace in knowing you had done the
right thing. (In describing why she refused praise for her actions, one German
rescuer noted, "I was only proud inside, just for me.") A sense of pride in the past
might exist for rescuers but it did not anchor them or play a central role in rescuers' identities or worldview. Indeed, we find Tony able to move forward, to break
with the conservative, Dutch monarchist worldview he possessed prewar and to
see that the world was broader and more complex than he had been taught. This
is evident in his discussion of prostitutes and how they would help you if you
needed hiding.

> *Tony*: I suddenly had to leave the wealthy, upper-middle-class family and go
> into hiding. That was an eye-opener. I was told right away by a friend of mine,
> "Look, if you're ever in trouble in town and there's a raid on the street and
> you have to go into a house somewhere, if you're anywhere near the red-light
> district, go to any of the houses of the prostitutes. They'll hide you. They don't
> like the system. They'll hide you."
>
> And they would. They were risking a death penalty for that. But those
> women would always hide you. They were the people whom I had looked

down upon socially before that. I ended up working with a variety of much lower-class people than I would ever have associated with in my previous existence.

So identity also necessitated choice for rescuers; but the values integrated into the sense of self differed for rescuers. This seems related to the fact that rescuers' identity then necessitated a choice to help. Rescuers thus saw opportunities others did not notice. Why is this the case? To answer this question, consider how differences in worldview relate to speakers' canonical expectations and idealized cognitive models, and how these in turn relate to moral choice.

Canonical Expectations and Idealized Cognitive Models

In attempting to understand why the normative behavior of all people—not just rescuers—is influenced by how they see the world, it is useful to focus on two further explanatory concepts: canonical expectations and idealized cognitive models.

Idealized cognitive models (frequently abbreviated as ICMs) refer to the mental representations by which we organize our knowledge. The category structures and prototype effects are by-products of that organization. The idea for idealized cognitive models comes from several sources in cognitive linguistics.[20] Idealized cognitive models explain the general significance of the cognitive process of categorization, focusing on "prototype effects" in categorization. People appear to learn categories from prototypical examples, not from abstract rules or qualities. They then think about categories by referring to such examples. Categories appear internally structured; some members are prototypical, central, or representative of the category, while others are marginal or peripheral. The concept is widely used to explain language development and to suggest people have a mental representation of, for example, a chair and then use this concept to fill in what an armchair is or an easy chair, deck chair, rocking chair, and so on. Culture enters the cognitive process here in ways we do not yet fully understand.

The normative aspects of this cognitive sorting remain largely unexplored.[21] Indeed, the concept of an idealized cognitive model is rarely discussed in ethics; it nonetheless provides a useful concept for further exploration since it is possible that these more primitive representations may develop into more complex schema or scripts about how we should behave in certain situations. The potential political importance of considering idealized cognitive models can be seen if we consider Plato's (370 BCE) theory of forms, which are rough archetypes or abstract representations of the many types and properties or universals of things we see all around us. Plato's work illustrates how the representation of these forms in our mind carries ethical overtones. How we fill in the general form for our concept of justice, for example, differs for individuals, cultures, and polities; these differences affect our dispensing of justice as we conceptualize it. But even simpler idealized cognitive models carry ethical overtones.

Before presenting evidence from the narratives in this book concerning the extensive influence that emanated from the actors' idealized cognitive models of what constituted the good life or of what it meant to be a human being, however, I want to introduce a second useful and complementary theoretical concept: the idea of canonical expectations. I developed this concept in *The Heart of Altruism* (1996) to capture the normative importance of ideas we carry—as individuals, group members, or part of a culture—about what "should occur in the normal course" and by the actor's sense that "such normal behavior is right and proper."[22] For example, we expect our parents to love and care for us, despite empirical evidence that many parents are not capable of such care. Similarly, certain societies historically have deemed it right and appropriate to have astrologers to guide their political leaders, while others have expected to sacrifice their leaders to assuage the gods in times of trouble. We can readily understand the political significance of canonical expectations when we consider what lies at the core of discussions over the citizen's expectations on the proper role of government in regard to providing health care, police, fire protection, education, and the like. For some Americans, health care is a right, something they expect the government to do, just as they expect the government to provide protection against fires or external enemies. For others, however, this is not the proper role of government, and they find policies that require the government to provide health care paternalistic or intrusive. Much of the political significance from these expectations emanates in their subconscious power, causing political actors to be deeply offended, shocked, and threatened when someone proposes a policy that violates the canonical expectations of another.

Both canonical expectations and idealized cognitive models should be subsumed under the speaker's worldview, so I tried to discern speakers' ideas about what is normal and desirable. Doing so revealed several important findings. Of particular importance were speakers' expectations about what constitutes the "good" life and what it means to be a human being. Each of these expectations was closely related to speakers' ethical actions during the war.

Rescuers' Canonical Expectations and Idealized Cognitive Models

For rescuers, the good life is closely related to making others happy. Rescuers consistently articulated similar variations of this same idealized cognitive model for a human being:

Q. You were talking about the meaning of life before. You were speaking, if I may use that term, about what it means to be a human being. What does it mean to be a human being to you?

John: I have some privileges; we get in turn some responsibilities. To have the abilities of speech, of hearing. I am thankful for what I have. My responsibility is to share with others, because otherwise life would not be possible. I have seen in my life people who are selfish, and not happy. People who have power, and money—everything—and they don't have enough. Never enough. They are not happy. I have seen people who are unselfish, and happy, people who don't have very much, and are happy with what they have. My ambition, my aim is to be happy. So, how can you be happy? By being selfish? [John shook his head, indicating disapproval.]

Q. You would not have been happier if you had simply taken all your family and sat out the war in Switzerland? After the war, you could have said, "At least my family is intact. I love them, I've been a good person, I haven't done anything wrong." You would not have been happier doing that?

John: No. You have not only to not do what is wrong. You have to do what is right.

This quote captures a critical difference between rescuers and bystanders: for rescuers, it is not enough merely to do no wrong. As John says, "You have to do what is right." His matter-of-fact tone also suggests the subconscious nature of how this choice has been made; based on his worldview and personal expectations, the decision was already made for him. This statement also carries particular poignancy since John's sister was killed because she worked in the escape network John established to take Jews to Switzerland and Spain. But John's worldview was very clear on how people should act if they wanted to be happy, and this worldview was related to another major theme we encounter in the worldviews of rescuers: the view of life as a gift that entails responsibility, a kind of trust.

John: You have to think about more than yourself. You have to think about yourself, certainly. You have to eat, and have a home. But you must not concentrate on that. It is not my aim, it is not my rule to say, "I, I, I." I have seen others around me—Salvation Army people—they are very happy. Why? Because they are helping. Happiness comes through helping other people. I am convinced of that.

Q. When you spoke of being given certain gifts, and how these gifts entail certain obligations and duties, you mentioned as gifts things such as the ability to speak and hear, things every human being is born with. Yet you speak of these as gifts. Are you suggesting that merely having the gift of life entails certain responsibilities?

John: Yes, I think so. I am happy that I can fulfill my responsibilities.

I was struck by how many other rescuers echoed this description of life as a gift, even using the same language to describe life as a trust in which privilege conveys responsibility. One Danish rescuer showed me his autobiography, written before our interviews and thus a totally unprompted reflection of his worldview and canonical expectations.

Knud: If I was looking for an explanation of life on earth—what's the purpose, or why are we here—my answer would suggest our life experience here on earth is an indescribable, beautiful, phenomenal gift to mankind, a gift to be shared equally with fellow human beings, in peaceful coexistence, harmonious, loving, altruistic, nonbiased, nonviolent, and nonexploiting acts. [Life] is a great gift from nature.

Q. Does the fact that we received this gift carry with it an idea of trust?

Knud: It is absolutely a trust.

Bystanders' Canonical Expectations and Idealized Cognitive Models

In contrast, consider the bystander view. The good life for Beatrix is defined in terms of material goods, servants, and leisure time:

> *Beatrix*: I've been, my whole life, very lucky. [Beatrix smiled.] I had a very good life. I always was spoiled. My husband worked very much. But I had time to go and play tennis, squash and all sorts of things. We had two helps [*sic*] in the kitchen and one help for his practice, too.

As we recall Beatrix's discussion of her lack of choice and her inability to do anything to help Jews, we can appreciate the ethical significance of her idealized cognitive model. In explaining her helplessness, Beatrix said, "You could not do anything. You could hide them [Jews]. But you have help in the house." In this instance, then, Beatrix's model of the good life—having the leisure time afforded by economic affluence and "helps" in the house—meant she could not save Jews. Her concept of the good life led Beatrix to make a choice without consciously being aware of it. Her desire for the good life, and her implicit and unexamined belief that this particular model was canonical, constrained the choice options on her moral menu. This is readily evident when we consider how many rescuers also had help in the house but were *not* constrained by this. Indeed, many rescuers enlisted or worked with their servants in their rescue activities.

Kurt resembles Beatrix in insisting that he had no ability to help the Jews. At one point he seems to suggest that in the midst of his domestic routine, he took the word of those around him, even of the Jews themselves, that they did not need any help. He asserts that he was ignorant of the Jews' fate, even seeming to insist that he would have been willing to help had he only known. His continuation of this thought, however, seems to imply that the form of help he offered was to help Jews move out of their homes as their housing units were liquidated:

> *Kurt*: The Jewish didn't tell us. Even in our houses people didn't tell us. When I came once on leave, my mother said, "Well, above us the people have to move out. They go to this school. There's a school and they have to be assembled, all the Jews out of our street."
>
> So I went there with food and I asked them now, "How can I help you? Can I bring you out?" No, you cannot risk this. Now, what do you know what will happen? We don't know. See? There you get stuck.

It is difficult to interpret parts of this statement. Does Kurt mean that he is offering to help the Jews move out of their homes and into the place of assembly? Or does "Can I bring you out?" mean he wants to help them leave Germany, which seems the more plausible interpretation, especially one spoken in the United States fifty years after the Holocaust. The last part of his statement: "There you get stuck," especially since it follows "No, you cannot risk this," seems clearer, although even it is not entirely obvious whether this statement is Kurt's assessment of the situation or a statement by a Jew in response to Kurt's query.

What does seem more apparent, taking Kurt's narrative as a whole, is that Kurt's categorization schema relates closely to his perceived lack of choice. This is abundantly evident in his discussion of the war, when he describes his attitude to the French and how he did not want to fight them. Significantly, he notes that "a part of France was as us. So we don't want to fight and they don't want to fight." Kurt constantly refers to people who are "different" as inferior. (His landlady in England is described in unflattering terms. "I can still hear her pitchy voice and her shouting at me. I was different than she was and I found the same.") But when there is a bond, when people are alike—placed in the same category—then they are treated with respect. There are numerous instances of this categorization in Kurt's description of wartime activity. Consider his depiction of the Germans honoring the hero of World War I Verdun.

Kurt: The defender of Verdun in the first two years was Marechal Pétain. . . . My division commander, said, "Well, we have to honor that man. We make a parade right here." Two hours later, we had a parade. We as a German division honored the French defender of eighteen years before.

The same correspondence between respect and being in the same category is evident in Kurt's description of how well wartime fliers treated one another when they shared an Aryan identity and how badly they treated one another when they were Slavs versus Germans.

Q. It's almost like it was something that gentlemen do. I mean, honoring Pétain, treating the French soldiers well. It's almost like you were fighting in the nineteenth century.

Kurt: Yes. That was the way I was raised. You see, the air fights. They had the dogfights. They shot one down. They landed beside him. "Are you hurt?" they ask. Then they bound him up and started back fighting another one. But all in those Russian families, they were raised this different way. That's why we could not overcome this Russian butchery in Russia, you see?

Later, Kurt became agitated when describing how he saw a US Marine thumbing a ride, behavior Kurt deems unworthy of a soldier.

Kurt: See, if I see the marines here, I feel sorry. These are not human beings for me anymore, in uniform if I see them hanging around here on the freeway hitchhiking and all this.

Q. What do you mean by that? They are not human beings?

Kurt: They're not soldiers for me. The soldiers don't lift that thumb up. He walks!

This emotionally charged statement, in which a soldier who thumbs a ride is removed from the category of human being, underlines the importance of categorization for Kurt.

Florentine's narrative also suggests the link between categorization of people and how these people are treated. Note Florentine's discussion of the Nazi Schmitt, who was no longer useful and because of that was pushed from a train. Florentine describes him as a frog. Florentine's values are described as the "old" values that predate Christianity, and her narrative evokes the idea of Aryan myths and high culture. As her young Nazi admirer interpreted for her, "The European culture is the Aryan culture. It is that Aryan culture that we must promote." Florentine's categorization schema centers on cultures and peoples (*volk*). She craves cultural separation.

Q. Just as the tape stopped you were talking about culture, and you said that you thought the Dutch culture was the most important thing that you had.

Florentine: Yes.

Q. Is that Germanic culture or Dutch culture? I didn't understand the difference.

Florentine: No, it is not that. It is that the Germanic culture or the American culture had to be in Europe. In my eyes—excuse me when I say it—American culture is no culture. Heh? We have culture. You have no culture. For that reason, many people like to be here. Sure. Because, you see, Amsterdam is a beautiful town. Only we have drugs, all these very awful people today, strange people inside, of course, but the culture was wonderful. Berlin was just the same. This you can't take away from the volk, no? You must respect it, the culture from Aryans. So it is very foolish to say that we don't want to work with the Negro, etc., etc. I have nothing against the Negro but he has his own situation. We have our own situation. I don't like to be married with the Negro. This is difficult. Today, living together, having ten children, drugs, etc. [Florentine made a face to register disapproval.] Well, we had our special culture. We had to be pure.

Q. What is the culture? I don't understand. It would be Aryan culture? Or Dutch culture? Or German? Are Dutch and German the same culture?

Florentine: No. No. Aryan culture is, of course, what you have in Germany, what you have in Dutch, what you have in Flanders . . . You respect your culture, of the Aryan country. When I write to the Indonesians, I respect the Indonesian culture. I have very good friends in the Chinese. They took me into the Chinese culture but as Dutch woman. No more. Nothing more than that. Not that we should marry together or something like that.

Q. The cultures should be separate?

Florentine: Yes. Separate. They should be separate, and respected. You must respect the culture of other peoples. But you must respect that they are not the same. I am thinking that the Jews have no culture so they don't respect us. This is difficult, of course.

Q. So there are different cultures and they should be separate and most of them should be respected. But there are some cultures that don't have much culture in the capital "C" sense, in the sense of something that is positive. Is that what you meant to say?

Florentine: Ya.

The idea of separate cultures taps into Florentine's idea that the soul of a people is their culture and reveals her canonical expectations about behavior, which should reflect an awareness of cultural differences and the resultant keeping in one's place. When I pushed on this topic, Florentine admitted, "we might appreciate some cultures more than others." Ideas of racial purity and the Nuremberg laws flowed naturally from this worldview and originated in Florentine's canonical expectations that group differences were appropriate and natural and should be maintained. The us versus them mentality in Florentine's narrative also emanated from a worldview that divided people into groups, and in which the in-group bias is clear. (In this regard, Florentine's worldview, and the differences in expectations about political and social behavior that flowed from that worldview, can be explained easily via social identity theory's emphasis on group identity and in-group bias as a way to achieve self-esteem.)

This worldview was not as extreme for Fritz and Kurt as it was for Florentine and her Nazi admirer, but the same emphasis on traditional groups and culture remains evident in Fritz's discussion of his heroes from the Golden Age of Holland and in Kurt's description of himself in response to my first question. Note that Kurt's first statement is that he sees the world "very different than people here" see it, and he then links this to his Gothic past.

Q. I'm interested in finding out about your life, and in understanding how you see the world . . . [Kurt interrupted.]

Kurt: Very different than people here.

Q. Do you? Why don't you start by telling me about this, about yourself? Where you were born, what your parents were like, things like that.

Kurt: I was born in 1914, M——. It's a town in Prussia and I was raised in Berlin. My father was killed in 1914, in action in Belgium. I never knew my father. No. And my mother was the first to start in Germany a gymnastic constituent in Berlin, in 1912. She was an educated woman. Well, she was on her own, made good money, and then in 1913 she married. She was married for a year and then it was the end. My father was a grain merchant with a big corporation. We came from the miller's family, going back to 1559 or 1556. I don't know exactly. We are researching that because there are still documents available in Germany. So the main family name [deleted] is that of a Gothic noble man.

You know what the Goths are?

Q. [Kurt's accent was heavy and he pronounced the word "Goffs" so I was unsure what he meant.] No.

Kurt: These are Germanic tribes, north Germanic tribes, Gothenburg in Sweden. Gotholand. This is where the Gothic people came from. The Ostrogoths and the Visigoths you call them here, one of the most strongest Germanic tribes. They conquered their empire from Sweden over to the Baltic Sea, what is today Lithuania, and all this to the Black Sea, and the Iskar River was the border to the Slovak people. Then when the Huns came, in the third century after Christ, 360 AD, they retreated because the Huns overran the whole country and burned the villages and so on. So then they [the Goths] fell into the Roman Empire. They pushed the Romans back into Constantinople and they even penetrated the eastern Roman Empire. Then they pulled back and conquered then the whole world with their empire including Gallia, Spain and then settled in Spain. So this was the Gothics. These are my ancestors. Ya. And all Gothic kings . . . and so we are the family [deleted]. It's a noble family. The Gothic tribes are the first to add a written law code. It was written down I think in 290 or 295 after Christ, and from thereon we had the Gothic Gothorum in Germany. All the other German tribes took that up. Gothic translates into English as a law code. The Gothic code. . . . This is the background of my family. So we're very proud. I was raised always by my aunt. We still have the mill then, which we sold in '22. Our family goes back very far.

At later points, Kurt relates with pride of being spoken to in old Gothic. The past is alive for Kurt, and his sense of what is right within the framework of that past plays an important part in his canonical expectations. He does not like having to fight and be killed in war, but because this pattern is part of a cycle, Kurt respects and complies with it. His agitation about the war on the eastern front comes in large part not because of the horrors of the war but rather because that war violates the past; it is an invasion of what traditionally was the Slavs' land. Kurt's weakened sense of individual agency is closely related to his canonical expectations about what one individual can—and should—do in the face of such historical forces. Ironically, in Kurt's worldview Germany's defeat can be understood as an almost inevitable result of the violation of this historical process; Hitler should have made war only on the West and never invaded the Slavs' land.

The Ethical Framework and the Integration of Values into Worldview

An analysis of the interviews presented in this book both confirms the importance of an altruistic perspective and broadens this finding to suggest the altruistic perspective is merely one end of a more expansive moral continuum. Everyone has what might be called an ethical framework. This framework might be akin to frames for glasses; individual prescriptions for the lenses vary, making one person's ethical outlook humane and another's insensitive, but all people wear the glass frames. The way *all* people saw the world played a critical role in determining their treatment of both Jews and Nazis.

Is it possible that this ethical framework simply reflects the differences in the values that are plugged into the general worldview? If so, are the critical differences in moral behavior the result of differences in values, not worldviews? The answer to this question is complicated, given how subtly values permeate and focus worldview. Values are not critical in the sense that most people pay lip service to many of the same values. (Most people, for example, express pride in family and pride in country.) Among the cases highlighted here, there was little observable difference in terms of religion.[23] Furthermore, all the people interviewed—except rescuers—bemoaned what they considered the deterioration in social and moral values. Few spent time discussing values. Ironically, it was the rancorous Nazi (Florentine) who spoke about values more than anyone else. She described herself as idealistic, and her life certainly demonstrates an incredible commitment to the ideals she holds dear. This highlights the difficulties in thinking about values— in general terms—as influences on moral choice. Ordinarily, we think of being an idealist as a positive thing. But if the ideals are Nazi ideals, this is something most of us would consider negative from an ethical point of view. Considering Nazis and their values thus reveals the difficulty in speaking generally about values. We need to know the content and specificity of values. When we take such an approach, there seems surprisingly little significant difference on the dimension of expressed values among rescuers, bystanders, and Nazi supporters. This suggests the obvious. Most people want to feel they're doing good, even genocidalists. People do not consciously arrange themselves along a moral continuum with the goal of defining themselves as evildoers or people who ignore the needs of others.[24]

We thus must consider the question of fundamental values or, more precisely, the question of which core values one holds dearest. I return to the concept of canonical expectations and to the content of the values that are such a part of the person's life that they are accepted as a given, an unremarked-upon part of the moral terrain. Here we find critical group differences in values, with striking divergence in idealized cognitive models and the values associated with these models. All the rescuers interviewed had one value at the foundation of their ethical system, whether or not this ethical system is consciously held or is merely an implicit part of who they are. That value is the sanctity of life. Rescuers consistently mention this in their discussion of the Holocaust. This core value expressed itself in the puzzled response of rescuers when asked why they risked their lives to save strangers: "But what else could I do? They were human beings, like you and me."

In contrast, not one of the other speakers mentions the sanctity of human life. Bystanders were surprisingly comfortable talking about what they had done during the war, where they had gone, and how the war had affected them. They volunteered information that they knew "absolutely on the minute" (Beatrix) what was going on with the Jews, knew of the concentration camps, and had done nothing to help. But only one bystander expressed any remorse or sorrow at the incredible human tragedy occurring all around them. This seems a significant omission. The kind of moral insensitivity captured in Beatrix's discussions of Jews is typical of most bystanders.

What about the integration of values into one's sense of self, a phenomenon critical for other moral exemplars?[25] I found a sharp contrast here. Both rescuers and Nazis had strong value systems, and both groups had integrated their critical values into their sense of who they are. But Florentine's values are a passionate commitment to the Nazi cause, racial purity, cultural separatism, and to what she refers to as the "old values and old religion," an Aryan way of doing things that excludes people who are judged "different." These values are so much a part of who Florentine is that she gave up her children for a few years after the war, refusing to admit—because she genuinely did not believe—she and her husband had done anything wrong. She also describes her decision not to be secreted to South America, along with other top Nazis, as an act of idealism, one designed to "tell people the truth" about the war. Florentine retains immense pride in her Nazi identity and activities.

Rescuers evidence a similarly strong integration of core values. But rescuer values are different, centering on a commitment to the sanctity of life; indeed, this value plays a key part of the rescuer worldview and sense of self. For all rescuers, the idea that we should value human life is so deeply ingrained into who they are that they assume—despite overwhelming wartime evidence to the contrary—that everyone shares this commitment. Self-image and self-perceptions are critical in terms of rescuers' actions. Because rescuers hold so deeply the value that all life is sacred, they have a commitment to help others. This in turn creates a feeling of responsibility, a sense of moral imperative, or the feeling that we all should do this, we all should respond to others' suffering by taking care of others.

The integration of critical values into one's sense of self—and the content of the values held dear—constitutes a critical part of the moral psychology. Values matter most when they are integrated closely into the speaker's sense of self. But we also must focus on the specific content of the values integrated into the personality. This is strikingly evident when we contrast Dutch rescuers (Tony) with Dutch Nazis (Florentine). Tony's core values center on the sanctity of life. Not just human life, all living things. Tony makes no in-group/out-group distinctions and does not construct separate categories or classifications for human beings depending on their ethnicity, religion, nationality, class, and such. He notes succinctly, "You cannot put labels of nationality or race on people." Like other rescuers, Tony refused even to deny the humanity of the Nazis, saying: "I've always been interested, ever since World War II, in understanding what caused this Nazi monster to come to be. I finally realized, every time you see the monster, you basically are looking in the mirror." Tony's basic values are intimately woven into his sense of who he was and result in his drawing boundaries that include all people in his community of concern:

Tony: To survive, [we must act] as a species rather than as an individual. We have to develop harmony among each other and as a planet. That's the only chance to fulfill our destiny. We are as much together as the cells in our body are together. They are individual. They each strive for their own little survival yet somehow they also will sacrifice themselves at times for the whole. Whether that is conscious or not, none of us has any way of knowing. We cannot today exist as individuals. Oh, maybe one or two of us can go off in the wilderness and exist. But as a modern day American, European or Chinese, there is no way to survive in this world unless we see ourselves as part of a whole in some way. The big difficulty is to do that without falling into the trap of totalitarian government.

Q. How do we do that, Tony?

Tony: Just the same way the body does it. It's an instinctive voluntary way of sensing, setting your goals so your happiness is not necessarily based on collecting the most you can possibly collect. It's knowing your happiness is based on your sympathetic vibrations with your environment, with nature, with the other mankind around you.

In contrast to Tony's view of the world as a cohesive and caring unit, Florentine's values are family and fatherland. To my surprise, Florentine described her values using the language of communitarians:

Florentine: When we were growing up, Father made sure we came to love and value Germany and Austria as well as our own country. All kinds of German youth groups were forming. We enjoyed our endless conversations with the German youth, when we would visit our family or visit elsewhere. They shared so much comradeship, pride and devotion. Everyone seemed happy and full of hope for their country. This kind of love for the nation was missing in the Netherlands. We did have a group called the AJC in Holland. Their members, however, were mainly children from lower-class families who did not feel any nationalism but were taught class struggle and free love. This was something we could not relate to. We also disliked the Boy Scouts. . . . We searched for something deeper. We wished for a strong and positive youth. We longed for comradeship, for the happiness our eastern neighbors displayed, the sense of love and pride we desperately needed here in the Netherlands. This was our dream.

These values were linked in Florentine's mind to her sense of who she was:

Florentine: Within the NSB [Dutch Nazi Party] a group called the Youth-storm was formed. This was a visibly nationalist group, to instill in our youth a feeling of nationalism, love of country, and devotion to their own kinds. As members, we wanted to serve the country with honour and camaraderie, with order and discipline. Our slogan was "With Trust in God, All for our Fatherland."[26]

Florentine viewed the nation as an extended family, with Hitler as an all-knowing father who fosters respect and harmony in society. "Hitler has shown it is possible to live in harmony with family, with work, and with respect for the other. He shows the whole world that it would be possible." The symbolic importance of family, community, and the importance of the group relates closely to Florentine's categorization schema.

How can we reconcile this respectful Nazi world, led by Hitler, with the actual reality? By recognizing that Florentine speaks of the harmonious in-group. Deviants—homosexuals, gypsies, Jews, anyone who opposed the Nazis—are simply relegated to a separate category outside the circle of humanity. While Florentine's was the most extreme, the denigration of out-group members who are deemed different also existed in the narratives of other Nazi supporters.

TRAUMA AND A SENSE OF MORAL SALIENCE FOR OTHERS' SUFFERING

Florentine's claim that Hitler showed the world how to live "in harmony" and with "respect for the other" raises an interesting issue. What encourages such treatment? Can empathic involvement with "the other" encourage people to see the other's humanity?[27] Does our own suffering make us more sensitive to the suffering of others, or does it increase our sense of vulnerability and trigger a defensive posture? To answer this I asked about past traumas to test the idea that experiencing loss might engender compassion in others who also experienced need. I found a mixed impact from past traumatic experiences. Tony's worldview was definitely shaped by his wartime experiences, which Tony credits with opening his eyes and making him reexamine many of his attitudes and preconceptions. But while Tony's traumatic experiences made him respond more sympathetically to other people, analogous trauma made bystanders and Nazis pull into themselves and become more suspicious and untrusting, not more sensitive to others' needs. Consider Kurt's conversation about post–World War I violence in Berlin.

> *Kurt*: In Berlin there was shooting going on and there I saw the first man killed in my life. I was four and a half, I think. I can remember. He was fleeing in the church. On the steps of the church, he was gunned down. He was not a Communist; just a civilian. He was killed by these of the trucks, by the Communists.
>
> Q. *What kind of impression does that have on a four-year-old child?*
>
> *Kurt*: I dream at night quite often about this and always protected my back against the wall because I was trained when someone is fighting, you go back on the wall, so you are protected from the back and then you fight on the front. Even as a little boy you learn this.

Kurt's sense of insecurity seemed unrelated to his objective economic situation, since Kurt described his mother as a wealthy woman and Kurt enjoyed extraordinary affluence even in the difficult economic period after Germany's World War I defeat.

Tony's response to early childhood trauma is quite different:

Q. When you were growing up, was there any destabilizing event in your past, anything traumatic?

Tony: Not terribly much. My father and mother were always fighting, ever since I was a little tiny kid. My mother was Latin, very possessive. My father made the mistake once. So many men do it. Just a little fling with some cutie somewhere, which didn't mean that he didn't love my mother. But my mother found out about it and for the next thirty years, she talked about it constantly. "I should have left you, but . . ." She was always going on about it, to the point that, in retrospect, it's funny. But at the time, as a kid, it wasn't. "Look at your father and see what he did to me." She was always telling me that.

Tony described other childhood traumas, noting that their effect was to make him realize you should "not give a damn about what people think of you and just do what you think is right."

Tony: In some ways it was a very happy childhood, in others not. My mother was a social climber. She would have liked to have been part of the aristocracy or the upper-upper classes. She was [into] money and status symbols. I was never into that. I was a lonely child. Because I was an only child, my mother was very protective and I was a mama's boy for quite a while. To give you an example, when I finally went to high school, which was my first moment of liberation, she insisted I wear my sailor suit. This was as bad as wearing a sailor suit to high school nowadays! But it had an odd effect. It did teach me to live through situations that are painful. To not give a damn about what people think of you and just do what you think is right. But I had a very rough time in high school in the beginning because of that.

Tony's traumas thus did not lessen his sense of ontological security, as Kurt's did. Instead, they seemed to have opened Tony's eyes to the situation of others, engaging him in the kind of empathic perspective-taking that then made him reach out to help. Tony's view of others had tremendous ethical significance, evident when considering the diverse patterns of cognitive categorization exhibited by rescuers, bystanders, and Nazi supporters.

Categorization

We turn now to the final critical piece of the puzzle, one alluded to earlier but deserving more extended discussion because of its importance for ethical treatment of others: the psychological process of categorization. Cognitive categorization is something everyone does, if only to negotiate through the myriad stimuli presented to us everyday. (We sort colors into shapes of objects, for example.) Cognitive and social psychologists[28] concerned with identity have long recognized that all people classify others in relation to themselves. (We group people into friends, strangers, and so on.) Analysts have only recently begun to explore the importance of these classifications for ethical behavior,[29] but it seems possible that this fundamental part of our cognitive make-up as human beings has far-reaching implications for treatment of others.

The cognitive process by which the people in this book viewed others—their categorization and classification of others and their perspective on themselves in relation to these others—played a critical role in identity's influence on moral action. This cognitive process included an affective component that served as a powerful emotional reaction to another's need. This reaction in turn provided the motive to work to effect change.

The ethical perspective links the altruists' self-image to the circumstances of those in need by highlighting the needy person's situation in a way that then accords a moral imperative to the plight of others. By evoking this particular self-concept, the suffering of others becomes morally salient for the altruists in the way the plight of one's child, spouse, or parent would be salient for most of the rest of us. This process appears to work by drawing forth a particular self-concept rather than through clearly defined differences in moral values. A critical part of the process by which perspective influences moral choice involves the manner in which the external environment thus taps into the actors' core self-concept, a self-concept distinguished by rescuers' self-image as people who cared for others.

Rescuers' Categorization

Rescuers adopted superordinate categories, thinking of all people as the same and thus deserving of equal treatment. This extensive categorization process was one in which rescuers searched for the common ties, not distinctions that separated people. The rescuers' categorization schema was one in which all people could exhibit individual and group differences but also could still be placed into the common category of human being. It was this common category that took on a superordinate moral status in which all people deserve to be treated with respect and dignity.

Because the value of caring for others is so deeply integrated into rescuers' self-concept, it forms a self-image that constitutes the underlying structure for their identities. This means the needs of others are frequently deemed morally salient. This self-concept translates and transforms rescuers' knowledge of another's needs into a moral imperative requiring them to take action. Their self-concept becomes so closely linked to what is acceptable behavior that rescuers did not just note the suffering of others; the suffering took on a moral salience. The suffering of Jews was felt as something that was relevant for the rescuers. It established a moral imperative that necessitated action.

The fact that the rescuers felt a moral imperative to help is evident most strikingly in statements that reveal rescuers' implicit assumptions about what ordinary decent people should do, to the canonical expectations about what is acceptable behavior. The unspoken expectations are embedded deep in a rescuer's psyche but are revealed in their description of what is—and what is not—in their repertoire of behavior. As a German/Dutch rescuer named Margot said, "You don't walk away. You don't walk away from somebody who needs real help." To go even further, Margot adds, "[the] ability to help and alleviate the pain of fellow human beings . . . is the ultimate goal of our short existence on this earth." Other rescuers expressed similar phrases, almost as if reading from a common menu of moral behavior available to them. Witness a French rescuer's (Madame Trocmé) question: "How can you refuse them?" Or a Dutch rescuer's (John's) assertion that "when you have to do right, you do right." And all the rescuers' insistence that "there is no choice."

For rescuers, all people within the boundaries of their community of concern were to be treated the same, and their circle of concern included all human beings. This perception of a shared humanity triggered a sense of relationship to the other that then made the suffering of another a concern for the rescuers. Significantly, this extensivity included Nazis, with the rescuers demonstrating extraordinary forgiveness of Nazis. I believe it is this role of the ethical framework to classify and categorize people and then to work through a cognitive process of salience that provides the link between the lack of choice and identity and the variation in our treatment of others.

Ironically, while other scholars have noted the importance of categorization for genocidalists, I first encountered the ethical importance of categorization via conversations with an ethnic German rescuer, whose time in concentration camps provided a contact with the genocidal mentality that was far more intense and personal than any scholarly one:

> *Otto*: I interviewed many SS guards. I was always intrigued by the question: how could seemingly normal people become killers? Once I got an interesting answer. In a camp in Upper Silesia, I asked one of our guards, pointing at the big gun in his holster, "Did you ever use that to kill?" He replied, "Once I had to shoot six Jews. I did not like that at all, but when you get such an order, you have to be hard." Then he added, "You know, they were not human anymore." That was the key: dehumanization. You first call your victim names and take away his dignity. You restrict his nourishment and he loses his physical beauty and sometimes some of his moral values. You take away soap and water, then say the Jew stinks. Then you take their human dignity further away by putting them in situations where they even will do such things which are criminal. Then you take food away. When they lose their beauty and health and so on, they are not human anymore. When he's reduced to a skin-colored skeleton, you have taken away his humanity. It is much easier to kill nonhumans than humans.

Rescuers were quick to note that this phenomenon is not unique to the Holocaust, occurring elsewhere, especially during wars. As Tony commented: "We have to watch for the old 'yellow gooks' mentality. It is much easier to shoot at or burn the 'yellow gooks' than to shoot and burn some other farm boy just like yourself." In contrast, the rescuer categorization process is one in which all people are included in the same category, and because of that, all are treated the same. The power of this was reflected most strikingly in the rescuers' discussions of the Nazis and in their insistence that genocide's roots can find fertile soil anywhere; it is not specific to one culture or one country. As Tony put it, "All over the world, there's a certain attitude. It's not any one nation. It's not because they are German."

For rescuers like Tony, all people are the same; it is culture and education that cause people to do bad things. "Human nature is very much the same all over the world. It is tempered and arranged by culture." Tony then noted his similarity with some of the Dutch Nazis, linking this similarity to his forgiveness of them, under a kind of "there but for the grace of culture or education, go I" mentality.

Tony: I differentiate in my own mind between what I consider righteous and what I consider bad. Not whether it's done by a German, by an American, by a Jew, by an Arab; that's irrelevant.... The people are the same.... It's the culture. It's the education. [People] could all get together if they wanted to. But education works so strongly against it. There's propaganda in education. I give you a perfect example ... of the impact of educational propaganda ... when the German Army capitulated.... The SS has been pretty wiped out by this time. They wanted to fight to the end but there was only a small group of them left in the Gestapo. The resistance wanted to attack the Gestapo buildings—there were about a hundred guys still in there—and wipe them out. We had a little talk about it and I said, "Look, I think this is nonsense. They're well fortified there. They have plenty of arms. If we attack them, we're going to lose a lot of people. The war is over. Why do we have to do that?"

They said, "Well, they're shooting at people." I said, "Let's solve it in a different way. They are just as scared as we are. I don't like the Gestapo but why doesn't somebody go over and talk to them?" They said, "Yeah, who wants to do that!" "Okay. I'll go. I don't think, if I go alone and unarmed and I dress in such a way that they don't know whether I'm a German or a Dutchman, I'm sure I can get to ring the doorbell and I'll talk to them." I did exactly that. They didn't shoot at me. I got in. I said, "Look, I'm a liaison officer from Allied Headquarters and I'm here to discuss your surrender so that there's no unnecessary bloodshed...." I lied a little bit there. I was introduced to the commanding officer, who was a twenty-year-old dressed up as a Gestapo lieutenant. I asked him, "Hey, where's the commanding officer? He said, "Oh ... he got on a plane and he escaped to Germany." It turned out that the entire staff had escaped. "Well, what are you doing here?" He shrugged. "Somebody has to be in charge of the men." "Well, I think I can talk to you," I told him. It turned out that he was a guy who had been raised in the Hitler movement since he was a small boy. He was totally impregnated with all these ideas of Nazism. He was basically not even a bad guy. He was a little like one of the marines at My Lai. But he was following orders.... When I left, he said, "I wish so much you guys had fought with us. You were Dutch. You should know about this. We could have made this a better world. You'll see. The Americans are going to come here and they're going to take over your economy. The Russians are going to move in and they're going to take all of Eastern Europe."

I thought, "He's absolutely right." I still didn't believe in his philosophy. But I could see how he had ended up being what he was and I could not hate the guy. He was the product of his environment.... This knowledge doesn't mean I don't think they shouldn't go to jail or be hung if they commit certain crimes. But I can also understand it. It's like a bad dog.... You mistreat it and it bites people. You have a dog and you treat it well and he'll grow up to be a loving, caring dog. To me it has nothing to do with race, religion, or anything else. It's people.

Classifying people into the same category seems to encourage similar treatment of them. Why? What is the psychological process behind this linking of category and ethical treatment? Psychologically, most of us feel people are entitled to the same rights we are when they are "just like us." Classifying people as different makes it easier to justify mistreating them, just as African slaves were not viewed as fully human by America's founding fathers because of difference in skin color, or as women's anatomical differences meant they were not man's equal and thus needed to be refused the same legal rights.[30]

I chose Beatrix, Fritz, Kurt, and Florentine as interview subjects because each of them had something in common with Tony. It therefore struck me as ironic that in terms of his political psychology it is Tony who is the outlier, the one who offers the starkest contrast with the others on our continuum. He is much more liberal in his political views. He is the only one who seems aware of women as having suffered discrimination.

Tony: Working very close with women and friends in the resistance opened you up very much to women's liberation. I started the first women's courier service [in the resistance]. Some of the people in the military were very opposed to that idea of getting women involved. Well, the women wanted to be involved, so why not? They were better at this than the guys. Less obtrusive.

Tony is the only one sensitive to the needs or rights of minorities. Perhaps even more remarkably, Tony demonstrated noteworthy forgiveness of the Nazis. Instead of lauding culture, as the ardent Nazis and even Kurt did, Tony's discussion of culture suggests an awareness of the politics of culture, as Tony argues that we must understand how culture shapes individual personalities. He notes that the Nazis were shaped by their environment and are not innately evil.

Q. How do you explain the cultural variation that you have? If we're all basically members of the same species and we're now at a point where the world is complex enough that we should move away from a crude Darwinian survival of the fittest to a situation where we have to cooperate, how do you explain that some cultures don't emphasize that and others do? The Nazi culture had to come from someplace.

Tony: Well, there are two reasons for that. One is that they are not faced by the same emergency. If you live in the hills in Tibet, for instance, your ties with the modern world are so different that you can still operate on a past level. If you're right in the middle of the action, it's also a question of education. All through society, you have individuals who still behave on a Neanderthal basis. We call them criminals most of the time. You have politicians who still operate on the basis of instant gratification and greed. You have corporations who still behave in the way that was intelligent in the 1850s but which is, with any foresight, even as a corporation, very destructive thirty years from now.

But many individuals are still culturally very selfish. That's how you used to make it in the old world, to think of yourself [that way]. They don't mind if everything goes to hell. It's the old King Louis view: "Après moi, le deluge." It's the view that says, "I don't give a damn what happens after I die." And, obviously, with the disintegration of the cultural values of the old churches, of the old religions, as it came in conflict with the Darwinian theories, what has not come up is a new moral religious sense. When I say religious, I don't mean in the sense of worship; I mean in the intrinsic religion. The interrelationship between man and nature, which is man and God, is the need to create a new morality. I don't mean sexuality. I mean world morality.

Tony has strong ties to other people, but the group is not a narrow one, as evidenced by his statement that religion is needed to create a new and a broad-based religion of morality toward all people. The primary group for Tony is not one of nationality, religion, socioeconomic class, or the winning side during the war. It is all humanity. To illustrate this view, Tony adopts a biological metaphor to suggest how we are all part of a whole yet still remain distinct individuals, just as the cells of our body are individual but still part of a larger unit.

Q. Tony, do you think people are essentially alone in the world or do you think that we have group ties or are part of different groups?

Tony: I think that we are as much together as the cells in our body are together. They are individual. They each strive for their own little survival yet somehow they also will sacrifice themselves at times for the whole. Whether that is conscious or not, none of us has any way of knowing. Or they are made to sacrifice themselves. I think it's very similar to that. We cannot today exist as individuals. Oh, maybe one or two of us can go off in the wilderness and exist. But as a modern-day American or modern-day European or Chinese, there is no way to survive in this world unless we see ourselves as part of a whole in some way. The big, big difficulty is to do that without falling into the trap of totalitarian government.

Q. How do we do that though, Tony?

Tony: Just the same way the way the body does it. It's almost an instinctive voluntary sort of way, a sensing. Again it's a combination of education, a combination of new morality, of learning love, of caring, of setting your goals so that your happiness is not necessarily based on collecting the most that you can possibly collect. It's knowing that your happiness is based on your sympathetic vibrations with your environment, with nature, with the other mankind around you, and on a certain degree of courage, which I describe as being aware that life does not last forever. It's knowing that you are into this [life] in the same manner that you decide to play a tennis game, for instance. You're going to play the best game you can and have fun doing it, even though you know that the game will end; just as you know that life will end, but you can feel that I was a good team player in the game. Maybe it's more like a soccer game, where you work with a team together and it's not that you want to destroy your opponent. Even sport is not always a good example. You may want to build a bridge over a river with your team.

Religion is not what drives Tony's worldview or his sense of being connected to others.

Q. Tony, some people have said that religious people will tend to be more altruistic.

Tony: Okay. Anybody who says that, I would send them immediately to the Middle East, to Beirut, and see how religious people behave toward each other there. The most horrible things in history have been done in the name of religion. So I think that religious people are just like everybody else. They can be very moral, very kind. But they're human.

Worldview and canonical expectations may be influenced by religion but they also can precede religion, be more basic, even preconscious.

Understanding Bystander and Nazi Categorization Reveals the Ethical Framework Exists for All People

I thus asked whether the way in which we see the world and others in relationship to us in the world is defined by this categorization process for all people, not just rescuers. It seemed clear that differences in this ethical perspective are closely related to differences in behavior. Following the linguistic analysis of Lakoff (1987), I wondered whether the deep structure of consciousness, rhetoric, and cognition results in metaphors that can produce "hot cognition" or "hot buttons" capable of turning ideas into action. I found striking and obvious evidence of this in interviews with Nazis, such as Florentine, who consistently resorted to the metaphor of disease to explain acts against Jews. But more subtle ethical consequences of the cognitive categorization process were evident in all the people I interviewed.

Consider first the genocidalists and their supporters. People such as Florentine see themselves as a people under attack. There is a bitter irony to this, for in the genocidalists' worldview, the Jewish victims of genocide are seen as threats. The following conversation with two Nazis illustrates how Nazis believed the Jews were threatening their world and had to be destroyed, much as the rest of us would destroy cockroaches invading our home. This excerpt follows a discussion suggesting Jews have no culture of their own and are different from Aryans; it reveals a typical Nazi in-group/out-group categorization.

Q. Why do you think Hitler and the Nazis are so hated by people?

Florentine: Because the media made a devil out of Hitler and the Nazis.

Q. The media?

Young Nazi: And who controls the media? You know that! Jews. Why are they so worried about Hitler? Because Hitler came in with completely new ideas, which was against the Jews controlling everything through money and banks.
Florentine (nodding assent): Ya.
Young Nazi: ...Remember... the Jews of the world united. In 1933 there was a big front-page article in the newspaper that they [the Jews] were going to boycott Germany. In Germany they did one boycott of Jewish things *one* time. That was blown up like you wouldn't believe. But no one talks about the Jews boycotting Germany! The Jews inside Germany didn't want anything to do with Jews outside. They were living lonely and were forced by the outside Jews in trouble. Because if the Jews outside Germany declare war on Nazi Germany, on the SS, they make enemies of the Jews inside Germany.

This conversation continued, suggesting Jews tried to isolate Germany during the Third Reich, devised the postwar myth of the Holocaust, and continue their conspiracy today by inventing both AIDS and what the young Nazi referred to interchangeably at different times as "Ebola" [Ebola virus] and the e-coli bacteria.

Q. Do you think Jews were involved in inventing these diseases? They invented AIDS and Ebola? Is that what you are suggesting?

Young Nazi: Oh, listen, the Jews! [Florentine shrugged, and made a face of disgust.] I don't blame everything evil on the Jews. I blame many silly people who are in the plan, or who want the glory. Of course, even Clinton is surrounded by Jews, Ya. His wife is from Jews originally. Even the pope is a Polish Jew originally. He himself. You know that?

Q. Well, no, I didn't know that.

Florentine: Oh, there are many things people don't know! But that's the thing. It's all nicely kept [quiet].

The political significance of Florentine's cognitive categorization was evident in her arguments for separate cultures, in which Jews should keep to themselves and not mix with non-Jews. This cultural separation was critical to the Nazi cognitive categorization schema. Placing Jews in a separate racial category allowed Nazis to psychologically distance themselves from the Jews and then dehumanize and mistreat Jews. Florentine also wanted separate cultures for Asians and blacks, and her conversation about these groups also suggests they are different and hence less valued than the Aryans.

An analogous phenomenon occurs with bystanders. Bystanders' initial failure to speak out in protest against ethnic cleansing and genocide then tends to morph into a justification of this inaction. Part of this justification process involves bystanders distancing themselves from the victims and finding the victims "different" in some way that is then—perhaps subconsciously—associated with the inferior treatment of the victims. We can see this in Kurt's description of the variation in treatment of soldiers on the western front, where they are "boys" just like his own "boys," versus his attitude toward Slavs, who are deemed inferior people.

Kurt's "boys" in uniform have a quality of martial nobility that has a distinctly familial appeal:

> *Kurt*: That photograph! I saw that photograph which my [grandfather] took about thirty years before and I had this photograph in my mind, and I said to my boys here, to my soldiers, I said, "Here was my grandfather wounded and that night after he was wounded, it rained and rained until the next day, so they were laying in the mud." And I could feel it!

Kurt becomes quite agitated when he discusses a military person who does not keep up to his canonical expectations about how military people act, linking the military to an older way of life and to a kind of extended family tradition of protecting one's own:

> *Kurt*: The power was good-trained, very healthy men, sporty men. See, if I see the Marines here, I feel sorry. These are not human beings for me anymore, in uniform if I see them hanging around here on the freeway hitchhiking and all this.

> *Q. What do you mean by that? They are not human beings?*

> *Kurt*: They're not soldiers for me. The soldiers don't lift that thumb up. He walks!

> *Q. Did you conceive of yourself as an army person?*

> *Kurt*: No! Absolutely not. As a reserve, we had to do this to defend or to protect, you see. We had to have an army education or a defending education that you call an army, but every family leader or man in the family has to be aware that he has to defend his women, his friends, his younger folk or the older who cannot do anything because it happened so often, you see?

Kurt was a most interesting person in terms of his identity. He follows this impassioned statement of pride in defending his people with an equally passionate discussion of war and tradition.

> *Q. So war was a fact of life for you?*

> *Kurt*: For everyone I knew. My history teacher ... spoke old Gothic. He said ... "Kurt, you come from a Gothic family. I'll tell you this story." So then he told me this in Gothic, in old Gothic. My wife had a teacher who still spoke old Franc and old Gothic. So this is what you hear, so your tradition goes back this long.

Q. But this was a tradition that, in the immediate circumstance, because this tradition was so strong, you couldn't break out and do ... [Kurt interrupted.]

Kurt: Why should you break out? Why should you? Was the other better? Okay, when the Vikings established their Normanic empire in North Africa—people don't know this here—Vikings came down to North Africa and established an empire there in Sicily. We heard that they got stranded, that they mixed with other populations. Nobody knew after three hundred years about them anymore. I don't want this in my family so I stayed with my tribe. I hope I have good leaders, and we have. We saw to it until Hitler came and this was partly why the German tribes were not united anymore. Part went to Czechoslovakia, part went to Poland, and all this. So then you said, "Well, I have family there and I have family there and I want them back." When Hitler promised this, many came and more came.

Q. So you liked what Hitler was doing in a sense of trying to reunify ... Kurt interrupted.]

Kurt: It was not Hitler. Hitler muscled in there. This plan was before Hitler came. This plan was just established after Wilson signed the peace treaty and cut this from Germany. Wilson did not know how Europe was formed by blood connections. That was a big mistake. .... Even the British Crown said this. This is not correct. This is not right. This will end bad, and it took just eighteen years. See? And then you press yourself in the foreground and say, "Well, I have to do that actually, too, to protect my family and see my other part of my family and there and there and there." You see?

During our interview and—later—reading my transcribed notes, I was struck by the extent to which Kurt almost seems to have taken a script from history books, describing the attitudes of German romantics toward the fatherland. There is a sense of blood bonds, of an inevitability to the historical process that unfolds in some mysterious manner, seemingly free of the agency of human beings. Kurt emphasized a sense of repetition. Of tradition. Of the old languages, the old way of life. Of Hitler possessing some deep understanding of these forces and connecting the German people with the will of history. All of these were nonrationalist, primordial forces that constituted a dominant theme in Kurt's narrative and his system of classifying and categorizing others.

Kurt expressed a view of himself similar to that expressed by Beatrix, as someone who is "always doing the wrong things." Yet neither of them was able to articulate what they meant by this phrase. I asked if this meant they did immoral things, or if it meant they were saying they were inept. Neither was able to clarify this for me, even when they were pushed on the question. I wondered if their senses of being out of sync were related to a sense of failure to take a side during the war, vis-à-vis the Nazi victims. But I failed to ask directly about this—in part due to my own reticence to raise issues that could feel too overtly judgmental—and neither of them spoke directly to this issue. Beatrix's discussion in particular led me to suspect this sense of "doing the wrong thing" was more a general characterization of being an inept or ineffectual person.

Q. Can you tell me how you would describe yourself? My family will always ask me when I do an interview, "What was this person like?" What should I tell them? How would I describe you to them?

Beatrix: I don't like so much to say it, but I am always doing the wrong things.

Q. Always doing the wrong things. What do you mean by that?

Beatrix: Just what I say.

Q. Wrong things. That could mean a lot of things. That doesn't mean you're immoral.

Beatrix: Not bad.

Q. Not good for you?

Beatrix: I don't know how to say it.

Q. Give me an example; a time when you did the wrong thing.

Beatrix: Oh, no. I do so much. I don't know how to explain this.

Q. Are there things you wish you had done differently?

Beatrix: Yes.

Q. How would you feel?

Beatrix: My conversation. Sometime I really say the wrong things. I don't mean it but I do.

Q. But nothing major wrong, like in the sense that you wouldn't have . . . would you have not moved from Utrecht, for example? Is that one of the things you are talking about?

Beatrix: No. Because the first years here I have had a wonderful time, because the children were so young that I could look after them, but now they have the age, if I come there they look after me. You see?

Beatrix is a most interesting person to consider here. She doesn't seem to make the Jews different so much as she transforms them into people who all immigrated to Africa, seemingly because they wanted to for some unknown and unspecified reasons. She neither blames the Jews for their fate nor offers any reason for why the Nazis so disliked the Jews. Any guilt that she herself might feel at their condition or at her lack of help proffered the Jews comes out only in her discomfort as the video camera records her long silences while I asked her if there was anything she could have done. This is not fully conveyed in a written transcript, only on the videotape. But I found it significant that of all the bystanders I spoke with, only one said that he felt bad that he had not done anything to help the Jews. In contrast, many rescuers protested that they did not deserve praise for their wartime activities because they had not done enough, that they could have done more.

Both this sense of responsibility and the sense of worth on the part of the Jews seem closely related to the way in which the speaker categorized Jews. Interestingly, the one person who demonstrated relatively little of this process was Fritz. Whether this is because Fritz now repents of his anti-Semitism and ostrichlike behavior, I cannot say.

CONCLUSION

So what should we conclude from our analysis? In particular, what is the importance of psychological factors for wartime behavior? Findings focus attention on eight critical psychological differences in the diverse responses to genocide, as summarized in table 8.1. (1) Self-image is the critical psychological variable, with rescuers, bystanders, and Nazi supporters demonstrating dramatically different self-concepts. (2) Identity constrains choice for all individuals, not just for rescuers. (3) Understanding identity can help decipher the speaker's ethical perspective and reveal how values provide content and moral specificity to a general ethical framework. (4) A critical aspect of identity is relational, focused on the sense of self in relation to others and the way the speaker views him- or herself in relation to the world. Hence, we need to decipher the speaker's worldview and the ethical significance of worldview, including the speaker's sense of agency and ontological security. (5) The political influence of values comes less from subscribing to particular values than it does from the integration of these critical core values into the speaker's sense of self and worldview. (6) Personal suffering may increase sensitivity to the misery of others, but it also may heighten a sense of vulnerability and encourage defensiveness. (7) A speaker's cognitive categorization system carries strong ethical overtones. The dehumanization that accompanies genocide works through the reclassification of "the other," a process most strikingly evident among the ardent Nazi supporters. (8) Finally, identity works through the underlying ethical framework to produce an ethical perspective unique to each person and situation, thus shaping the actor's ability to imagine possible scenarios for action. This ethical perspective produces a menu of choice options and a sense of moral salience that work together to produce the moral act by determining which act will be taken (menu of choice) and the impetus to act, stand by, or support genocide (moral salience).

My findings confirm earlier psychological portraits of rescuers and perpetrators but deviate from the traditional view of bystanders as people whose initial refusal to help leads to a sense that perhaps the victims of genocide might have done something to deserve it. While I found shades of this, what was more critical was the striking sense of helplessness, the low efficacy, and a striking moral insensitivity among bystanders.[31] Kurt's discussion of his grandmother's dislike for Hitler focuses on the travel restrictions and the lack of distrust Hitler engendered, not

	Rescuer	Bystander	Nazi Supporter
TABLE 8.1			
Ethical Framework → Ethical Perspective:			
Critical Parts And Differences → Moral Choice			
View of Self/Others	All part of human race	Groups, Ostrich	Community, victims under siege, Aryan superiority, elitist
View of Others	Humans complex/ forgave Nazis	Strangers Aristotelian dissipation of moral energy: Psychological distancing → outgroups lesser	Distance = threat Aristotelian dissipation of moral energy: Psychological distancing → outgroups lesser
Worldview	Mixed	Deterioration	World harsh
Ontological security	Mixed	Weak	Threatened
Values, Attitudes	Human well being core of ethics	Mixed	Cultural, racial superiority
Agency	Ability to effect change	Low efficacy Passive, helpless	Larger forces, historical forces provide agency
Categorization Schema	Inclusive, broad porous boundaries	In/out group Exclusive	Rigid, hierarchical Exclusive
Idealized Cognitive Models/ Canonical Expectations	Good life = helping others	Good life = material well being, affluence	Community key Good life = follow leader, group
→ Moral Salience, Felt Imperative to Act			
→ Menu of Choice Options Perceived as Available.			
Identity Trumps Choice			

on Hitler's policies toward Jews, gypsies, homosexuals, etc. Fritz describes himself as passive, tolerant, and not aggressive, explicitly saying he is not someone "who takes the initiative to make things happen." Bystanders' moral insensitivity was expressed in many subtle ways, from bystanders' inability to imagine possible scenarios that might help Jews to the striking fact that only one bystander expressed any remorse for what happened during the Holocaust. (In describing his Nazi propaganda, Fritz says "I don't feel ashamed over what I wrote.") But the bystander moral sensitivity also is reflected in statements such as Fritz's comment that he had read *Mein Kampf* and took it seriously but was willing to ignore the things Hitler said he would do in the hope "that Holland would be reunited as before the war with colonies and . . . with Flanders." Fritz also seems to find their German orientation his main objection to the SS. Perhaps Fritz's most shocking instance of this insensitivity, however, is his characterization of Holland during World War II. "Our daily life in the war [w]as normal. Nothing much happened in Holland." Given everything that we know did, in fact, occur in Holland—and elsewhere in the Europe in which Fritz traveled so freely as a journalist—there seems a critical link missing between the reality of the war and the lack of moral salience on the part of bystanders like Fritz, who simply did not feel the suffering of others was relevant for them.

An examination of the critical concepts/questions designed to explicate the empirical link between identity and moral action, utilizing extensive narrative interviews from the Holocaust, thus highlights several points to consider in future analyses. These include: (1) the desire for self esteem and the need for continuity of self image; (2) core values stressing the sanctity of life and human well being, values that then are integrated into our underlying concept of who we are; and (3) external stimuli that trigger critical aspects of our multifaceted and complex identity in a manner that either does or does not make us notice and accord moral salience to the suffering of others.

These findings further are useful in illuminating the psychology underlying responses to the suffering of others. They suggest it is the critical parts of our ethical framework—self-image (including a sense of ontological security) and the integration of values into the sense of self and worldview (including one's canonical expectations and idealized cognitive models)—that produce a particular ethical perspective, consisting of the actor's cognitive classification, his relational self, and his moral imagination. This ethical perspective works in conjunction with the external world's framing of a choice or a situation to produce both a sense of moral salience and a menu of choice options. Thus does identity constitute the force that moves us beyond generalized feelings of sympathy, sorrow, or even outrage to a sense of moral imperative, a feeling that another's distress is directly relevant for us and thus requires our intervention and assistance. Understanding the specifics of how an actor's underlying ethical framework gets filled in as it does will help us understand the actor's ethical perspective, especially why some people take positive action to help, when most of us ignore others' misery, thereby providing indirect or tacit support for the conditions that engendered such misfortune. This discovery can lend insight into the psychological forces driving responses to both other genocides and to the forms of ethnic violence and prejudice that precede and foster genocides. When such work is set in the broader context of research on moral choice, it can bring into focus the psychological dimension of ethics to shed light on one of the central themes in normative political science: how we treat others.

I encourage other scholars to test these results in different contexts, and I try to develop these ideas into a more general theory of moral choice in chapter 9.

CHAPTER 9

༄

A Theory of Moral Choice

LIKE FLASHES OF LIGHTNING in a dark landscape, our wartime stories illuminate the workings of the human mind during times of terror and genocide, capturing a universal part of the human experience to suggest how people confront a host of questions at the heart of ethics.[1] Why do some people commit atrocities while others turn away and ignore injustice and violence? Why do a few risk their lives for strangers, and what drives *their* moral courage? How do people navigate the moral land mines of wars, genocide, and ethnic cleansings? These questions touch on the foundation of normative political science and inform research asking that most fundamental political question: what determines how human beings treat one another?

With care, our analysis of these stories can inform us about how people think about moral choices in other situations.[2] In particular the analysis can help us construct a theory of moral choice useful in clarifying the moral psychology driving ethical behavior more broadly conceptualized.[3] This is my goal in this chapter.

My theory of moral choice is designed to fill a gap in a literature dominated by ethical theories—such as Utilitarianism or Kantian ethics—that emphasize deliberative reasoning and conscious calculus. It is an empirically grounded theory embedded in the scientific knowledge of the human mind and focused on explaining acts that seem to arise spontaneously, despite their life-and-death consequences. My theory shares virtue ethics' concern with character but differs from virtue ethics in making character both dynamic and relational; unlike virtue ethics, which concentrates on how to best produce a virtuous character, my theory is more concerned with explicating how character—whether virtuous or not—produces ethical acts.

My theory of moral choice begins by positing an ethical framework that is innate and initially largely void of normative content, functioning as a kind of scaffolding that gets filled in via a number of influences, much as specific languages occupy our innate linguistic structures. Each individual's ethical framework is built in a manner unique to that individual. Our individual ethical frameworks in turn produce an ethical perspective through which each of us views, processes, and makes sense of events and their relation to us in a manner that particularizes the psychological influences on moral choice. The resulting ethical perspective is both a general tendency to see the world and one's self in it and a specific way of viewing a given situation at any one point in time. Moral acts are produced by the last part of this psychological process, in which our ethical perspectives determine whether and how we will act by establishing both a menu of choice options and a sense of how another's suffering pertains to us. The theory's goal thus is to provide initial thoughts on how identity might work to produce specific acts.[4]

I begin section 1 of this chapter by reviewing my personal intellectual journey toward the development of this theory. In particular, I focus on how altruism and genocide created an analytical lens through which I gained insight into political and moral behavior and how this process, in turn, led me to develop the theory of moral choice utilizing the concepts of an ethical framework and an ethical perspective. Section 2 describes the field in which I situate my theory: moral psychology,[5] a relatively new field at the intersection of social science, neuroscience, animal behavior, and ethics. Section 3 presents the specifics of my theory of moral choice.[6] Essentially, I argue that our sense of self in relation to others sets and delineates the range of choice options we find available, not just morally but cognitively, thereby producing acts ranging from the morally commendable to the morally neutral or the heinous. Because I believe there is a value in embedding moral theory in the best existing scientific knowledge of how the human minds works, section 4 presents scientific findings on this topic from a wide range of disciplines and methodologies, but all relevant to specific parts of my theory. Section 5 addresses one of the more controversial aspects of my theory: its claim that moral behavior emanates from psychological processes outside the conscious level of awareness and which may be innate. The chapter thus concludes by evaluating empirical evidence concerning the existence of an innate moral sense.

One of my goals is to broaden the way we think about ethical issues, moving us away from the more traditional routes to moral theory, routes frequently developed out of religion or first principles. My discussion of the works I find germane to a scientific consideration of moral choice extends far beyond the literatures traditionally considered pertinent by political scientists. While the linkages among the diverse literatures may not be immediately obvious, closer inspection reveals they nonetheless provide important insights directly relevant for political science and ethics. Indeed, it is precisely these linkages that can fill in critical gaps in our knowledge of the moral psychology. I thus consider work as diverse as attachment theory, terror management theory, internal mental models of politics, evolutionary biology, animal behavior, appraisal and attribution theory, categorization theory, perspective taking, works on happiness and friendship, an innate moral sense, prospect theory, and related works in cognitive and social psychology, neuroscience, and behavioral economics. Even when the reader disagrees with my thoughts about moral choice, I hope I successfully make the case that there is a broader range of literature that can shed valuable new light on the traditionally employed approaches to political science and ethics. Scholars from these fields have much to gain from—and much to contribute to—a sustained mutual conversation about political psychology and ethics. The importance of this conversation reaches far beyond the discussion of moral choice during the Holocaust.

My goal in this concluding chapter thus is twofold. (1) I advance an empirically grounded, identity-based theory of moral choice that can be used extensively in ethics, political science, and moral and political psychology. (2) I hope to broaden the general conversation about the nature of politics to include a wider range of participants and more diverse scholarly literatures.

THE ORIGINS OF AN EMPIRICALLY DERIVED THEORY

A Personal Journey from Rational Choice and Electoral Politics to Altruism, Genocide, and Moral Choice

Because my own professional life reflects so many critical shifts in the discipline, reviewing my personal intellectual journey can reveal how scholars develop new theoretical work.

I was trained as a political economist at the University of Chicago during the postbehavioral period, just as the economic approach was coming to dominate social science via rational choice theory.[7] The basic assumption of this particular economic approach to politics is that human behavior can best be explained by assuming people try to maximize their self-interest, subject to information and opportunity costs.[8] This self-interest assumption lies at the heart of much contemporary social science, including political science and political psychology. Indeed, an equally compelling and complementary argument holds that social science as initially developed in the sixteenth century is rooted in the assumption that self-interest is the dominant force in human behavior.[9] Under this view rational choice theory's excursions into other disciplines were merely the latest iteration in the tendency of economics to establish intellectual hegemony of a paradigm based on self-interest.[10]

My doctoral dissertation and first publications were mainstream analyses of how the economy influences political support, conceptualized as presidential popularity or voting.[11] After I finished my first book (1984) and stepped back to look at the field more broadly, I realized many of the so-called great voting debates—concerning whether voters voted their pocketbook or voted for more general considerations of what was good for the polity (sociotropic voting), for example—were more reflections of the analytical preconceptions inherent in the models than the empirical reality described. I thus began to think about the fundamental assumptions underlying political science. Doing so led me to self-interest as a critical foundational assumption of our discipline, as indeed it was for others, from economics and evolutionary biology to psychology. Yet my empirical work on the origins of presidential popularity suggested voter behavior that emanated from self-interest was frequently modulated by more collective, even cooperative and altruistic, concerns. Since my economic training also had taught me that most of the basic assumptions of the economic model break down in the presence of collective goods and since much of the most important political behavior falls into that category, I suspected the extensive use of the economic model was limiting what we were able to detect and understand about human political behavior. Rational choice theory, a theory fast becoming the dominant one in social science, had developed out of economics and in reaction to the failure of behavioral social science to capture the human decision-making process. Behavioralism had ignored what went on inside the decision makers' minds, positing it as "the little black box" that somehow mysteriously produced inputs and outputs, in Eastonian terms.[12] My interest in understanding how well the rational choice assumptions about decision making reflected the human reality in the political sphere thus turned me toward political psychology, since I viewed rational choice theory as essentially a theory about the human psychology.[13]

Tenure provided the luxury of reading widely about rationality, an enterprise that revealed how poorly rational choice theoretic models explained several important categories of political behavior, especially cooperation, collective behavior, and altruism. Altruism in particular simply could not be explained using the assumptions of the rational model. Interestingly, reading about altruism revealed similar paradigmatic blind spots in fields as disparate as biology, decision theory, and the more usual suspects in social science: economics, political science, sociology, anthropology, and psychology. Both *The Economic Approach to Politics* (1991) and *The Heart of Altruism* (1996) examined the basic hypotheses concerning altruism and collective behavior in these fields, which, despite obvious differences, all nonetheless made the core assumption that self-interest is the major driving force behind human behavior, in some form or other. My efforts to empirically examine the validity and scope of this core assumption led to my first serious research on altruism. In *The Heart of Altruism*, I constructed a survey and a narrative interpretive analysis of interviews with ordinary people whose behavior placed them at different points on a continuum ranging from self-interested actors to altruists. Entrepreneurs were chosen as typifying self-interested actors, and altruists were represented by diverse groups along this conceptual continuum, beginning with philanthropists, moving onto Carnegie Hero Commission recipients and ending with rescuers of Jews during the Holocaust, as individuals whose wartime behavior most closely approached pure altruism. My analysis found altruism was driven not by traditional sociocultural predictors, such as religion, education, or gender, but rather by psychological factors, especially identity and the actor's sense of self in relation to others. Essentially, altruists see themselves as closely connected to others through bonds of a common humanity. This way of seeing themselves in relation to others—a phenomenon I call the altruistic perspective—constitutes the essence or the heart of altruism. This altruistic perspective is activated by diverse factors—including traditional sociodemographic influences such as religion or socialization—which enter the equation but primarily as trigger mechanisms for the altruistic perspective. These activating trigger mechanisms vary according to the individual, the circumstances, and the context in which the moral choice must be made. But what is important is that the altruistic perspective gets triggered, not which particular mechanism serves as the triggering device.

I became fascinated by the psychology underlying this political behavior and, in *The Hand of Compassion* (2004), I revisited and supplemented my interviews with rescuers of Jews. I treated these rescuers as exemplars of moral courage and used their interviews to make the closer examination necessary to learn more about the complex and subtle psychological process driving altruism. In this instance, however, I employed altruism as an analytical lens through which to gain insight into the normative aspect of politics, by examining the moral and ethical issues to reveal how identity constrains choice. I found the critical factor is relational not merely dispositional, although both personality and situation work together.[14] The importance of values is less their stated content and more the manner in which moral values are integrated into the actor's sense of self. (Most of us, after all, claim to subscribe to similar values: trust, fairness, justice, goodness. It is what we mean by those values and how closely we adhere to them that differentiates us.) The actor's worldview creates an altruistic perspective that filters perceptions of the world and the range of choices perceived as available cognitively, not just morally.

Identity thus appears to set a menu of choices, much as a restaurant menu sets and limits the choice of food we may order in that restaurant. (Sushi is not on the menu in an Italian restaurant, just as turning away someone in need of help was not on the cognitive menu for the rescuers I interviewed. That possibility simply did not occur to rescuers.) For altruists, the psychological categorization of others creates universal boundaries of entitlement and a sense of moral salience that creates the feeling that another's suffering requires action, not just sympathy or concern. My findings concerning altruism during the Holocaust were replicated in work in other contexts. Joint research on the Lebanese civil war[15] and work by other analysts who found the altruistic perspective explained behavior in less turbulent times and contexts suggested the concept of perspective might have broader analytical value.[16]

These findings led me to expand my initial analysis to ask if the psychological process that explains altruists' behavior holds for all people. More particularly, is it possible that the altruistic perspective is merely one part of a broader ethical perspective, just as the twelve inches in a foot constitute but one part of a yardstick? To answer this question the analysis in *Ethics in an Age of Terror and Genocide* broadened my work on rescuers to include bystanders and supporters of the Nazi genocide. Although World War II is hardly a typical historical period, much of what I found from interviews collected during this time period nonetheless can yield insight into the importance of identity and can be used to construct the microfoundations for a theory of moral psychology. In particular, I want to use my empirical analysis of moral choice during the Holocaust to develop a broader theory, one that asks how innate human needs for consistency and self-esteem work through identity to create an ethical perspective that provides an underlying analytical framework that affects not just moral choices concerning altruism but other types of ethical behavior as well.

MORAL PSYCHOLOGY

I situate my theory of moral choice in moral psychology, a newly emerging field at the intersection of ethics, social science, and biological science. Like much contemporary academic work, moral psychology traces its origins to classical Greece.

Both Aristotle and Plato, for example, developed empirical work or a priori conceptual analyses about how people make decisions relating to moral concerns. Later philosophers (for example, the Stoics, moral sense theorists, Utilitarians, and Kantians) also considered moral psychological issues. Philosophers were joined by scholars interested in the mind as the new field of psychology developed into a separate discipline in the twentieth century.

Interdisciplinary in nature, contemporary moral psychology was initially narrowly defined to refer to the study of moral development, with the emphasis on the study of moral reasoning.[17] In the last two decades of the twentieth century, however, this conceptualization expanded as psychologists increasingly recognized the importance of emotions, intuitions, and innate predispositions for action.[18] This work caused a critical shift in psychology after the 1980s, and we find approaches—such as the social intuitionist approach—arguing that the initial organization of the mind is structured in advance of experience.[19] Reason still figures in accounts of moral psychology and plays a role in moral judgment, but reason now is frequently said to operate in a space that is prefigured by affect.[20] Works at the intersection of evolutionary biology, cognitive science, neuroscience, linguistics, philosophy of mind, and biological anthropology provide insight into how the concept of a universal moral grammar might explain the nature and origin of moral knowledge. Drawing on the concepts and models utilized by Noam Chomsky's linguistics, which argues we are born with innate ability for language,[21] recent work suggests there appears to be a moral faculty located in the area of the brain that specializes in recognizing certain kinds of problems as morally relevant. Thus innate cognitive structures constitute a kind of universal moral grammar that effectively provides a tool kit for constructing specific moral systems. Researchers draw on experiments in child development to argue that there is a specific dedicated mechanism in the brain that gives us this ability. In doing so, scholars argue that moral cognition is linked to moral intuitions and emotions.[22] Building on Chomsky's work in linguistics and a virtual explosion of work in cognitive science illuminating how the mind works, researchers suggest ordinary language is susceptible to precise formal analysis. By rooting the principles of grammar in the human bio-program, universal moral grammar holds out the prospect of doing something analogous for aspects of ordinary human moral cognition. This work has attracted the attention of legal scholars[23] and resonates with prior work by linguists[24] who use linguistic and categorization theory to argue that humans employ metaphors of morality to parse the difficult ethical situations we face.[25] An important shift in recent work in moral psychology thus is the move away from the Kantian emphasis on logic and reasoning. If the traditional route to moral action is said to involve perceptions, analysis, and strength of will necessary to "do the right thing", perceptions may be the most important, involving the framing of the situation, setting our relations to others involved, and so on. Beyond this, we now believe emotions work faster and more accurately than reason, with the mind resembling a pattern matcher in which arguments and evidence work best when they tap into basic intuitions. This shift in scientific knowledge, and the experiments on which our new understanding of the brain is based, is discussed

CHAPTER 9

throughout the rest of this chapter. What is important is that there are scientific underpinnings suggesting the psychological mechanisms behind the empirical phenomenon noted by many of the rescuers I interviewed. The general phenomenon is succinctly captured in a Czech rescuer's remark, "The hand of compassion was faster than the calculus of reason" (Otto Springer).

All of this scientific work on ethics and morality resonates with the early philosophical work by moral sense theorists who argued that the moral psychology is the most powerful when and insofar as it taps into basic intuitions or sentiments that make up a moral disposition.[26] Moral sense theory was eclipsed by Kant's magisterial work emphasizing the role of reason in moral choice and was not a major philosophical contender in the twentieth-century discussions of moral choice.[27]

Utilizing the concept of an innate moral sense does not deny the important role of cognition. Instead of juxtaposing emotions and cognition, we should think of the two as working together. Perhaps all moral choice is cognitive, but some cognitions are fast, automatic, and more intuitive while others originate in controlled reason relatively free of affect. Emotions influence cognition in ways that are still not fully understood but that include framing, scripts, and schema that originate in prior experience as well as biology in phenotypic fashion. We can think of schemas as "structured parcels of knowledge from memory situating the self in relation to others."[28] These schemas then "give rise to scripts, or conceptual representations of action sequences associated with particular social situations."[29] Even if the actor is not aware of these scripts or schema, their influence still is felt, thus possibly providing the route for behavior that appears spontaneous, as was the case for so much behavior during the Holocaust.

Moral psychology has benefited from work on appraisal theory that addresses the relationship between emotion and decision making and suggests linkages between emotion and appraisal happen somewhere beyond our deliberative awareness. Much of the decision process we attribute to "gut" intuition may be of this variety.[30] Frames consist of a schema or a collection of stereotypes that people rely on to understand and respond to events, hence the term "frame" the event. The frame of reference frequently influences how the event is interpreted.[31] Most individuals are unaware of the frames of reference they bring to an event, but these frames have been found to determine the choice made in critical ways. Framing has an influence over the individual's perception of the meaning attributed to the word, phrase, or act that defines the packaging of an event in a manner that encourages certain interpretations and discourages other interpretations.[32]

The scientific research in the human mind and its unconscious effects on decision making is developing quickly, and I expect much interesting future research to focus on how emotions contribute to appraisals, cognition, and deliberative reflection about ethics. The hard science understanding of spontaneous choice is not yet there, but it is being worked on by scholars like Michael Spezio and Kevin Reimer, whose recurrent multilevel appraisal model of emotion's role in decision making is one intriguing route toward understanding those parts of decision making that occur outside the direct influence of deliberative reflection. Such work complements Jonathan Haidt's social intuitionist model, which effectively makes morality built on intuitions that function as "evaluative feelings at the edge of consciousness."[33] Haidt's work keeps the concept of moral reasoning but makes it the result of a wide range of intuitions that have been catalogued in our memory, thereby giving us emotional sensitivities that get recognized as decisions.[34] Thus emotions aid in producing the kind of quick response appraisals that moral situations often require.

Moral psychology as a field seems poised to take advantage of the intellectual potential in recent work in the wide-ranging set of fields I have just described briefly. Adopting a broad conceptualization thus seems empirically justified, as the experiments cited above suggest. Such a conceptualization is the one most likely to yield scientific advances for our theoretical work. I thus conceptualize moral psychology broadly to include interdisciplinary work drawing on the conceptual resources of philosophical ethics and the empirical resources of the human sciences concerned with the philosophy of mind that inquires about how we think and feel about ethics and morality.[35] This makes moral psychology closely related to political psychology, itself defined more succinctly to refer to the study of how the human mind thinks about politics and how these psychological processes then influence behavior. This broader conceptualization makes the domain of moral psychology include, but not be restricted to: research on moral decision making, choice, responsibility, character, luck, courage, imagination, disagreement, virtue ethics, forgiveness, and work on psychological egoism and altruism and their behavioral manifestations at both the individual and group level.[36]

AN IDENTITY-BASED THEORY OF MORAL CHOICE

How an Empirically Based Identity Theory of Moral Choice Looks in Practice

I ground my theory of moral choice in empirical reality since I accept the premise that there are central and universal tendencies in human behavior that scientific theories of political behavior should reflect. I find two tendencies sufficiently documented to accept as givens, upon which we can construct our empirically based theories.

1. Human nature is complex but there is a basic human need to protect and nurture the self. The implication of this is that both self-interest and sociability are critical but neither is necessarily or exclusively dominant. Our selfish desires are balanced by less self-centered though often still individual yearnings for social respect, affection, membership in groups, and so on.[37] These needs provide limits to the selfishness that may accompany self-interest.
2. People need predictability and control. The vast literature on cognitive dissonance makes clear that a key source of an individual's psychic comport and the maintenance of identity will emanate in the desire for cognitive consistency.[38]

I then draw on findings from the last twenty years of my own research. This research suggests a further fundamental assumption.

3. Ethical acts emanate not so much from conscious choice but rather from deep-seated instincts, predispositions, and habitual patterns of behavior that are related to our central identity. These spring from diverse forces, such as genetic predispositions, social roles, or culturally inculcated norms. Culture provides a range of self-images, but actors gravitate toward the image that strikes a chord with their genetic propensities, with a powerful filter coming from situational or contextual factors. The actor need not be consciously aware of this process; our moral sense is instinctual and powerful, often more powerful than any conscious calculus.

The corollary of the above suggests that by the time we reach adulthood, the main contours of our identity are set and our basic values largely integrated into our underlying sense of self. We thus speak of adults as agents discovering rather than creating their identities or choosing how those identities will let us do certain acts but not others.[39]

Any scholar attempting to construct moral theory must do so modestly and with an acute sense of the shortcomings that will exist in a first effort. For me, the shortcomings are perhaps more acute since I am not trained as a philosopher, and am drawing on work in many new fields. The scientific advances in our increased knowledge of how the brain works may soon make obsolete some of the findings on which I base my theory. For all these reasons, I offer my theoretical thoughts as initial ones and trust other scholars can—and will—correct my inaccuracies and fill in the details and omissions as our scientific knowledge progresses.

With these caveats, I suggest those interested in moral choice begin by looking at two critical components of any one individual: (1) the ethical framework and (2) the ethical perspective. The ethical framework consists of the actor's underlying sense of self and the actor's worldview. The ethical perspective consists of the actor's cognitive classifications, relational self, and the actor's moral imagination. The ethical perspective is determined by both the actor's underlying ethical framework and the way in which events are framed for the actor by the external world. It is the ethical perspective at the moment of action that produces (1) the menu of choice and (2) the actor's sense of moral salience. The menu of choice sets the options from which the actor can choose, highlighting certain options while others are not even imagined. Moral salience is the feeling that causes another's suffering to be experienced as relevant for an agent, thus creating an emotional drive that compels the agent to help or to turn away and do nothing. These two factors—the menu of choice and the sense of moral salience—are what results in ethical acts that appear spontaneous.

The psychological process through which identity leads to moral choice is complex, and I can establish only the general contours of how the influence flows operate. In general, however, we begin with an ethical framework. This underlying framework is innate to all individuals. It gets filled in through some still undetermined process in which innate predispositions are acted on by critical others and the general environment to create each person's individual character, self-image, and identity[40] or, more particularly, our sense of who we are in relation to others. Our self-images include our sense of ontological security and the integration of key values into the basic sense of self. Beyond this self-image each actor has a particular worldview, or way of viewing the world. (Is it a harsh place or one filled with friends? What causes things to work as they do in the world? What do we expect to happen in any given situation? Are there familiar situations that usually play out the same way?) This worldview is made up of our sense of agency, our canonical expectations, and our main idealized cognitive models. Agency is very important. A critical factor in worldview is how the actor sees the prime movers of critical events. Is this a world in which individuals can make a difference? Are we puppets moved about by larger forces, such as economics or geopolitics or religion? If so, what are these forces? Canonical expectations are another critical component of worldview. What does an actor assume constitutes normal human behavior? What does the actor think is correct and proper behavior? For himself? For others? Under which circumstances and conditions? Finally, what are the actor's key idealized cognitive models? What does an actor think it means to be a human being? To be a good citizen or neighbor? To be happy and fulfilled? How does this relate to the actor's sense of what comprises desirable behavior?

All of these influences will give specificity to an ethical framework. The nature of the specific content and how it is entered into the actor's ethical framework then produce the actor's general ethical perspective. We can locate an ethical perspective on a moral continuum, much as we locate a person on a moral continuum. (He's a good person, or he's a cad.) Each individual has a kind of median position or ethical perspective, but individuals can fluctuate and relocate along this continuum according to stimuli from the external environment. Oskar Schindler provides a well-known example of this point. A self-professed gambler, a drunkard, a womanizer, a Nazi, and a war profiteer, Schindler was not someone who would ordinarily be judged morally commendable or expected to risk his life for other people. Yet something happened to give Schindler a different way of viewing certain Jews, and he performed extraordinary deeds to keep them alive. The movie, *Schindler's List*, uses an interesting device to convey this image. Shot in black and white, the movie has two moments of color. The first is the moment when Schindler—riding a horse on the bluffs of Kraków with one of his mistresses—looks down to see the Nazis clearing the ghetto. His eyes focus on a little girl wearing a coat shown as bright red in color. This color, I believe, is intended to signal the awakening of a tie Schindler feels, a moment when his sense of moral salience clicks in and he becomes someone who will help Jews, not benefit from their persecution as he had before. It is interesting that the color red was chosen, since that is the color visual cognitive psychologists often use in a set of classic experiments on visual perception.[41]

So the ethical framework works in conjunction with the external environment to produce an ethical perspective consisting of three factors that seem essential: cognitive classification or categorization, the relational self, and the moral imagination. The cognitive classification of others, which works through the framing of moral choice to set the boundaries of entitlement, effectively differentiates (a) those to whom we accord fellow feeling, (b) those to whom we deny fellow feeling, and (c) those to whom we feel indifferent. This has a great influence on what I call moral salience, the feeling that moves us beyond a generalized concern or sympathy in the face of another's plight to a felt imperative to act to alleviate the other's suffering. Beyond this, the ethical perspective contains what I think of as a relational self, our sense of self in relation to others. Do we see ourselves linked to the other person in any way, for any reason? Do we see ourselves as linked to all others, through bonds of a common humanity? As someone under threat from others? Each person will have a general, underlying sense of self in relation to others. But each of us also will have a shifting sense of self, depending on a wide variety of factors, from the behavior of the other person to how that person is viewed by others, by the society around the actor, the immediate framing of the situation, and so on. Finally, we need to consider the role played by the moral imagination. Are we able to conceptualize certain situations and certain possibilities? Can we distinguish between doing no harm and doing evil? Doing good? The possibilities we are able to imagine have a great influence on the next critical factor: the menu of choice options.

This ethical perspective works in conjunction with events in the external environment—such as the framing of critical situations by others, such as the Nazis—to produce the final two critical influences determining action: (1) a menu of choice options perceived as available, not just morally but cognitively; and (2) a sense of moral salience, the feeling that the suffering of another is not just sad or deplorable but is something that demands immediate personal action to ameliorate. The sense of moral salience provides the drive to act or the imperative to refrain from acting. The menu of choice determines the nature of that action. The result of the above will be a moral act, whether that act be one most of us would find morally commendable, one that is objectively speaking morally neutral, or morally evil.[42]

This theory itself proposes that our moral choices reflect our basic sense of who we are in relation to others. Identity constrains moral choice through setting the range of options we perceive as available, not just morally but cognitively. This distinction, for example, means we do not think of an option but reject it as ethically wrong; we do not think of that option at all. Assume you are in a new town and are mugged while sightseeing. You have no money and no way to get back to your hotel. Few of us would even think of mugging someone else to get money for a taxi, even though we must know in some objective sense that people get money by mugging others since it has just happened to us. Why not? Because mugging is not something *people like us* do. It is not on our cognitive menu. This example illustrates identity's ability to exert its influence by filtering an actor's sense of who the actor is in relation to others and operating in conjunction with the actor's worldview. This ethical framework will work, in this instance, in conjunction with the external stimuli to frame the situation so most of us would see ourselves as an innocent person harmed by a mugger; our cognitive classification or categorization system, our relational self, and our moral imagination will not produce a menu of choice options that includes the option of our mugging someone else to get back to the hotel. In this mugging example, that particular option is not a possible response to the situation since we do not put ourselves in the class of people who mug others, and hence do not attempt to mug someone to get money for a taxi to our hotel.

This theory is designed to explain that part of moral behavior that emanates in a psychological process that appears spontaneous, reflecting intuitions and emotions that affect how we see ourselves in relation to others at the time of action. It makes moral behavior not merely the result of conscious deliberation, although such conscious deliberations indeed may enter the equation. But it specifically allows for spontaneous forces that lie outside the realm of conscious deliberation or reasoning and assumes that what we say we have chosen may reflect who we are as much as—perhaps even more than—any conscious calculus based on reasoning.

This theory makes identity central to moral choice by providing a framework through which ethical situations are perceived, analyzed, and acted upon. Predicting moral choice requires us to understand both the actor's underlying ethical framework and the ethical perspective of the actor at the moment action is taken. It is the ethical perspective that constitutes the link between the social and the individual influences on behavior.

To understand moral choice, we need to understand how these influences in turn relate to the critical role played by identity perceptions in driving ethical behavior and moral choice. The particular choice may take the form of helping and peaceful cooperation or it may involve us in the stereotyping and prejudice that deteriorates into ill treatment based on any kind of difference: ethnic, religious, racial, gender or sexual preference, sectarian groups, etc. The resulting behavior from this choice can range from rescue and bystander behavior to the ethnic cleansing and genocide that result from prejudice based on perceived differences.

This conceptualization of the moral psychology makes our sense of who we are phenotypic. Our sense of self is composed of genetic factors that constitute a predisposition toward a certain personality—shy, aggressive, risk taking, and so on—plus those cultural and environmental factors—such as socialization via parents and schools—that shape our initial genetic predispositions.[43] It assumes every person has an ethical framework through which we view the world and ourselves in it as we think about and relate to others. This ethical framework includes cognition and emotion, intuitions, predispositions, habits, and sentiments.[44] Deciphering the critical parts of an individual's ethical framework will help us understand how that individual's particular ethical perspective at the time of action influences how the individual will respond to situations that call for a moral choice.

As analysts try to build this general theory into more specific models of moral choice, we should begin by focusing first on the actor's underlying ethical framework as the entry point for detecting the importance of the actor's perceptions. The next challenge is to specify the ways in which the actor's ethical perspective works with external stimuli to contribute to the ways in which choice options are analyzed, again drawing heavily on the concept of identity and how that filters through the subconscious forces that constitute identity. Finally, we need to specify the factors that lead to action, chief among them being the categorization system and the sense of moral salience that is established and will influence action. Our scientific knowledge of identity and how the brain processes and operates is at an exciting time, and much of our current knowledge will—I suspect—be surpassed and corrected in the years ahead. I offer the above theory as a starting point for political science work in what will be an exciting new frontier in understanding the importance of political psychology for political behavior. I encourage others to correct and build upon my work.

FURTHER EMPIRICAL EVIDENCE RELEVANT TO MORAL CHOICE

Let us now consider further scientific evidence that speaks to critical parts of my theory. Such a consideration is important for two reasons. First, it reveals certain psychological processes others have overlooked. Second, it is reasonable to ask about the limits of a theory of moral psychology developed on the basis of only one person's narrative interpretive analysis of interview data with a few individuals. If, as I claim, this theoretical framework can address broader themes about moral psychology, then there should exist other empirical work that supports this theory. Such evidence does exist, and in the rest of this chapter I highlight work relevant to the critical parts of my theory and suggest areas in which future analysis might profitably move. In particular I focus discussion on the following critical research questions: What is identity's ability to constrain and set choices? What do we know about the political significance of perceptions of ontological security? Of an actor's sense of self more generally? What is the relationship between group and individual beliefs, and how does the structuring of in-groups versus out-groups affect the categorization process that appears so critical in our perceptions and treatment of others? How do empathy, perspective, and moral insensitivity relate to our ethical perspective? To our sense of ontological security? Our attachment to others? Finally, might there be a biological underpinning for our moral acts?

Critical Parts of the Moral Psychology

IDENTITY'S ABILITY TO SET AND CONSTRAIN CHOICE

Empirical explanations of specific genocides often stress individual identity and personality. Psychoanalytic analyses of leaders, for example, focus attention on the neurotic-psychopathic personality of genocidal leaders, such as Hitler[45] or Milošević,[46] arguing that genocidalists have a deep-seated and psychopathological need that leads them toward genocide, either by setting in motion genocidal policies through the elite manipulation of masses or the actual committing of genocide. Other scholars[47] emphasize the individual personality by focusing on the extent to which an entire society can exhibit patterns of behavior, such as child rearing or authority relations in school, that result in certain kinds of psychodynamics, such as the authoritarian personality that facilitates acts of genocide. Steven Baum's (2008) is the most recent work to stress individual personality traits as critical to understanding behavior during genocides.

Others have expanded the notion of personality into a larger, cultural explanation[48] but most analysts[49] note that culture is complex and multifaceted. To speak
in terms of a *German* or an *American* culture, or even to speak of a *democratic*
culture, is to oversimplify complex realities. Beyond this, social psychologists[50]
have shown another aspect that makes the situation further complex; situational
factors can—and in most, but not all, cases do—bring out different parts of our
complicated and multifaceted individual identities. These studies reach the disturbing conclusion that given the right context and stimuli most albeit not all ordinary, decent individuals will engage in dubious ethical behavior. The fundamental
assumption for these social psychologists is a median personality around which
there is a great deal of variance. What analysts in this school focus on are external
stimuli and understanding how situational or contextual effects can trigger genocide in ordinary people.[51] Such works look at the interstices between individual
schemata and collective social knowledge.

There is a wide variety of theoretical literature that suggests why identity would
have political significance. Social cognition theory,[52] for example, assumes we acquire our knowledge by observing others within the context of social interactions
and experience. It suggests that how people think about themselves and the social
world—especially how people select, remember, interpret, and use social information to make judgments and decisions—has a tremendous impact on their political behavior. Work on social role theories suggests how the social role into which
the individual is cast can take over, leading the individual into behavior he or she
would otherwise not do.[53] Hence, the explanation that "I was only doing my job"
or "I was only following orders" that we find offered to excuse individual responsibility for one's actions during the Holocaust. This emphasis resonates with the
narratives of Beatrix, Fritz, and Kurt, all of whom implied that the situation for the
Jews was none of their concern, in part, because the role of concerned person had
not been assigned them.[54]

The importance of perceptions of reality, as opposed to reality defined more
objectively, is also underscored by social representations theory, a literature that
emphasizes the collectively held explanations of reality that are continually reproduced in interactions with others.[55] The role that intersubjective interaction plays
in the interpretation of events puts a high emphasis on the cognitive. It explains
why people often give a privileged place to the interpretation of reality, as opposed
to reality itself. In particular, this literature can help us understand the processes
and motivations that cause individuals to process information and act in accordance with the identity categories to which they belong and which are deemed
salient by the context.

A critical link here is provided by schema theory, which describes identity in
terms of mental structures that we all use. Schemas themselves are defined as the
highly organized and generalized structures in memory that guide cognition and
memory recall to efficiently manage the massive amounts of information that
bombard us daily.[56] Schemas do this by offering templates for interpretation.
These templates then reduce the amount of cognitive processing an individual has
to undergo in order to account for events. (Political parties, political platforms,

and the "friends and neighbor" phenomenon[57] can be understood in this context, as simplifying mechanisms to help us make a decision without taking the time to survey massive amounts of information about the positions, histories, and personalities of individual candidates.)

We can incorporate the concept of schema into identity research to explain the cognitive components and normative expectations that certain identities assume. Identity can be treated as a system of salient schemas about the self that are unique and fundamental self-defining elements.[58] Once in place schemas both define the self and maintain identity through selective processing of information. People have categories for themselves, just as they have schemas for others. Having multiple schemas leads to a "self-complexity" that may act as a buffer against threats to one's identity.[59] Once activated or "cued," schemas can result in distorted perception because they offer ready-made pathways for interpretation of incoming stimuli.[60] Events that fit into an individual's self-schemas are more likely to be processed and accepted than contrary information, which may be distorted or even ignored. Individuals also may engage in distorted perception because they need to maintain self-esteem or a consistent view of themselves. The cognitive hoops that Kurt and Fritz created to avoid thinking about the concentrations camps accords well with the type of explanation offered by schema theory. But the fact that rescuers insisted their acts were "nothing special" or just "normal" also may be related to underlying differences in schema, as they are to canonical expectations.

We can take our knowledge of Kurt and Fritz and use that to think about how an entire nation of bystanders and supporters allowed the Holocaust to happen if we further place our analysis in the broader context of social representations, the collectively held explanations of reality that are continually reproduced in interaction.[61] These social representations serve as a bridge between an individual's schemata and the collective social knowledge about the social world. These hegemonic representations become the foundation on which new events are interpreted to produce more specific social representations. These hegemonic social representations may be nonconscious schematic frameworks, as they seem to have been for Beatrix. Or they can be elevated to consciousness when an individual's understanding is challenged or confronted with otherwise inexplicable social events, as they were for Fritz, after the war.

The powerful ethical overtones of these cognitive processes underline a direct relationship between ethics and political psychology. Certainly, they explain a common phenomenon in politics: groups and individuals genuinely seem to perceive the same reality differently. This is hard to grasp at some level emotionally. How can Beatrix not have figured out that her husband's acquisition of her beautiful new home was not related to the sudden departure of the doctor who sold it to them, a doctor who "maybe" was "Jewish or something"? How can Florentine claim, with a straight face, that there was no Holocaust, and that the Jews made it up? It is easier for most of us to assume Florentine is simply lying, covering her guilt and complicity with justifications. Accepting Florentine's depiction of reality as genuine given her ethical perspective is more difficult to accept. The conclusion that she truly sees the world so differently boggles the mind, and skepticism sets in. But if we consider the psychological process of framing and schema described by cognitive psychologists, we begin to get purchase on how such self-deception might occur.

This psychological relationship between self-deception and moral choice becomes even more overt if we think of social attribution, the intuitive process by which individuals attribute causality to social events. Research in this area holds that when we make decisions on attribution, we consistently succumb to cognitive distortions that are self-serving. Such bias should not be seen merely as the failure of an individual to correctly account for his or her social environment, although there may be elements of that; it also may be an essential tool in maintaining and, indeed, defining positively, both personal and social identity.[62] We know that maintaining self-esteem is crucial for most individuals. People will go to extraordinary lengths to maintain a positive image of themselves in comparison with others. If and when the salient attitudes that make up identity are threatened in social interaction, a dissonance between self-image and social validation of that self-image arises. In these instances individuals will attempt to achieve consonance through manipulative cognitive procedures, such as social attribution and social comparison. Fritz's discussion of his response to National Socialism is but one obvious illustration of this phenomenon.

Attitudes, schemas, and social representations all offer ways in which the definition of social identities of self and others might be conceptualized and provide the building blocks upon which more detailed theories of sociopolitical identity and prejudice are built. Social role theories focus on the internalized role designations matching the social location of individuals and stress the shared behavioral expectations that become salient.[63] Such explanations have been offered to explain the traditional "I was just following orders" excuse for genocide.

This is the point at which boundaries and categorization enter into the psychological equation to influence conflict and the ethical response to it. Perhaps the single most important theory buttressing my work on the ethical perspective—certainly the most highly developed in terms of its specification of the psychological forces driving ethnic prejudice and discrimination—is social identity theory.[64] Rooted in the "minimal group paradigm," social identity theory[65] argues that groups that exist only in name, with no prior history or interaction, and even when created artificially and randomly by the experimenter and with no real material stakes, nonetheless can take on profound significance. In situations of group decision making, people tend to favor their own membership group (their in-group) over out-groups, even when these groups are artificial laboratory constructions and competition for resources between groups is absent.[66] Unlike previous perspectives in group psychology, which explain group differentiation primarily in terms of real or perceived competition between in-group and out-groups,[67] research in what is now known as the Bristol School of social psychology showed that the mere formation of otherwise meaningless groups produced in-group favoritism in regard to the out-group. How do we account for this phenomenon?

Groups provide members with positive self-esteem, and, as such, group-members are motivated to enhance their image of the in-group in relation to relevant out-groups.[68] Self-categorization theory is an important offshoot of social identity theory, suggesting the formation of psychological groups is driven by the cognitive elaboration of one's self-identity by comparing one's self with others.[69] Because social groups provide members with social identities and because the desire to maintain positive self-esteem is a fundamental human motivation, derogation of out-groups thus becomes a likely outcome of in-group tendencies to enhance self-evaluations.[70] The salient level of self-categorization and the determination of which schemas and categories are evoked by any given political object will interact to shape a person's political preferences in relation to that political object.

PERSONALITY PREDISPOSITIONS

The above-cited theoretical literature links individual to group identity in looking for the self's relationship to genocide, racism, and prejudice. Individual personality predispositions have a longer, if more controversial, history of influence on political behavior. An authoritarian personality, characterized by a number of traits, including submissiveness to authority, intolerance, and aggression, was famously offered as an explanation for attraction to fascism.[71] Similarly, dogmatic, closed belief systems—be they politically conservative or radical—were explained by a psychological need to avoid anxiety and make sense of the world.[72] More controversially, political conservatism has been traced to underlying motives to reduce uncertainty,[73] with the adoption of conservative values—punitiveness, authoritarianism, and intolerance of minority groups—explained as the individual's attempt to impose order, simplicity, and predictability on an uncertain world. Recent work[74] supports the idea that human needs to avoid uncertainty and threat are specifically associated with conservatism rather than with ideological extremism in general. This work underlines the association between conservatism and a number of personality traits, including dogmatism; avoidance of uncertainty; fear of threat and loss; and the need for order, structure, and closure. The desire for certainty appears relevant for political attitudes,[75] as it was in the stories told by Kurt and—in contrast—Tony,[76] who demonstrated remarkably little dogmatism, avoidance of uncertainty, or fear of threat.

VULNERABILITY AND "THE OTHER"

Racism in general has been found closely linked to both identity and ethics, following a psychological process similar to that found during the Holocaust. Pumla Gobodo-Madikizela's work with the South African Truth and Reconciliation Commission (1998) found bystanders fitted the same pattern I found during the Holocaust. In both instances widespread and shared fears of "the other" led racists to see themselves as victims of circumstance and fate and hence forced to take preemptive action to protect themselves.[77] Analysis of the South African situation suggests individuals' own feelings of vulnerability were constantly mushroomed by a systematic de-legitimization of the "other" and the creation of the enemy as a force to be feared.[78] In this process the importance of the environment's ability to frame and limit individual choice is critical. Individuals living in a totalitarian environment that rewards evil and immoral behavior—such as the Third Reich or South Africa during apartheid—find few resources to assist individuals hoping to withstand societal pressures to acquiesce.[79] Constraints from the environment closely influence an individual's ability to perceive the availability of certain moral choices and emphasizes the society's influence on our choices.

> How can conscience get suppressed to the point where people can allow themselves to commit horrible acts against others? Should one ask as well what kind of society or ideology enables such suppression? . . . In a community of people depressed by their circumstances, beset by life's struggles, thwarted in their hopes, how do you bring such an act into the range of possible choices? How do we even make it thinkable?[80]

In this instance, individual personality factors are acted upon—via framing or reinforcement—by the environment to constrain choices perceived as available.

PRIMING AND SETTING A COGNITIVE MENU

The traditional social psychological view of rescue-bystander-and-perpetrator behavior, in which the individual's psychology is molded by the environment, is further supported by work in neuroscience and psychology revealing the importance of priming for political and moral choice.[81] It has long been known[82] that racial stereotypes, applied to black and white faces, produce different activations in the amygdala.[83] Previous theorizing has treated this relationship as largely inevitable. Susan Fiske and Mary Wheeler disputed this hypothesis.[84] Their experiments had subjects view black and white faces under a neurobiological experimental setting. Depending on what "social-cognitive goal" was being addressed, the amygdala responded differently, especially during the different tasks of "social categorization" (putting the person in the photo in a particular group) or "individuation" (seeking traits beyond such categorization). The importance of this study for us is that even fast, automatic, subconscious responses to stereotyped groups—such as those we classify as other races—can be altered depending upon goal-directed mental activity. Priming can shift what might otherwise appear to be inevitable racist responses. This suggests identity can constrain choice but that identity itself is complex, multiple, and that the environment—whether through manipulation in a scholarly experiment or via massive Nazi propaganda—can tap into different aspects of identity and hence elicit different ethical treatment of others.[85]

This, in turn, suggests that an important part of identity's ability to constrain choice is related to cognitive stretching, the moral imagination, and the setting of a cognitive menu. The ability to move beyond—to stretch—the traditional parameters of the existing cultural norms and imagine other possible responses to others' suffering is an important part of responses to political repression. As during the Holocaust, South Africa's experience with apartheid suggests cognitive stretching can work to expand the moral imagination, or it can lead to a numbing, a sense that the political reality is surreal and thus leads people to view real human suffering at a distance, just as we view suffering in a play or a movie.[86] The importance of a cognitive menu for racism appears to hold both for racists and for more passive participants in the perpetuation of racism.[87] Gobodo-Madikizela argues that the families of apartheid racists tacitly (if not openly) supported the South African regime of terror because their lives were good, just as the lives of Nazi supporters like Fritz were materially enriched by the displacement and eventual eradication of the Jews and other enemies of the Reich:

> White society had a good life. They were quite happy with what they got . . . I mean, how many whites *really* voted against the National Party? Whites say they didn't know, but did they want to know? As long as they were . . . safe and they had their nice houses and their second . . . and their third cars and their swimming pools and kids at good government schools and university, they had no problem with cross-border raids or other counterinsurgency operations of the security [system] . . . why did they never question this?[88]

The eerie echoes of Beatrix's moral blindness concerning the origin of her living situation are repeated in other bystander interviews and in innumerable survivors' stories of lost homes with new owners who refused to acknowledge the returning Jews' property rights. The analogies with South Africa's racist apartheid regime are striking. Just as with the bystanders during the Holocaust, many white South Africans lived in a kind of twilight between knowing and not knowing. They refused full realization of facts and suspended or suppressed their suspicions or doubts because they were unable to face the implications of these facts. This South African parallel to Hitler's Germany is apt and captures the ubiquitous aspect of racism and prejudice that are central to genocide.

> In spite of the varied possibilities for information, most Germans didn't know because they didn't want to know. Because, indeed they wanted not to know. . . . [T]hose who knew did not talk; those who did not know did not ask questions; those who did ask questions received no answers; and so, in this way, the average German citizen won and defended his ignorance. . . . Shutting his mouth, his eyes and his ears, he built for himself the illusion of not knowing, hence not being an accomplice to the things taking place in front of his very door.[89]

This psychological process of denial seems an integral accompaniment to racism. The psychological process behind Fritz's self-described ostrich behavior, in which he feigned ignorance to avoid responsibility, is part of a broader pattern. It is not restricted to genocide.

COGNITIVE STRETCHING

Some of the psychological process that accompanies racism and genocide can be accounted for by cognitive stretching. The concept of cognitive stretching initially was developed—and is still most frequently utilized—by child developmental psychologists[90] to explain how children expand their cognitive abilities through playing games, organizing shapes, visualizing certain objects, and such. But cognitive stretching is a useful ethical construct if we expand it to include the way in which the cognitive parameters of the normal sociopolitical world expand. It relates closely to work on the moral imagination.[91] An especially creative instance is Robert J. Lifton's psychoanalytic work on Nazi doctors. Lifton suggests that when the horror of political events—or, indeed, of life in general—becomes so incredible that the imagination refuses to accept its reality, something inside certain individuals simply fails to click and some conclusions are simply not drawn. The cognitive boundaries for acceptable behavior will not stretch far enough to include the new reality, and the person finds himself clicking off, going numb.[92] Some of this numbing may originate in the slow, incremental aspect of the change.[93] For people living in political regimes that have broadened the parameters of acceptable political behavior, the terror tactics eventually can come to be seen as divinely sanctioned acts, defended in much the same terms that Florentine justified her efforts on behalf of Nazis.[94]

Alternatively, a person living in this terrorist, totalitarian regime can find other options. Axel von dem Bussche, one of the few members of the 1944 plot to assassinate Hitler to survive World War II, described realizing what the Nazis were doing as a moment when the bottom dropped out of everything, and he had to recalculate the parameters of his existence. The choices he found available, as a soldier loyal to Germany, were clear. (1) He could die in battle. (2) He could desert. (3) Or he could rebel against the government that ordered the kind of massacres that lie outside the boundaries of acceptable political behavior.[95] Von dem Bussche chose the latter, agreeing to blow himself up along with Hitler when Hitler came to inspect new uniforms. When Hitler canceled the visit at the last minute, the assassination was aborted and von dem Bussche was sent to the eastern front where he was badly injured in January 1944. He thus spent July 20 in a hospital, recuperating from his wounds. None of the other July 20 Claus von Stauffenberg plotters revealed his role in their activities, and thus von dem Bussche survived.

PERCEPTIONS AND ONTOLOGICAL SECURITY

Part of identity's ability to constrain choice works through differences in felt ontological security, the feeling that my very sense of who I am is—or is not—threatened by another person, group, or even by more diffuse sources in the environment.[96] The relation of ontological security to our treatment of others is found in experimental work.[97] One experiment manipulated a subject's sense of security by telling a subject he (a) would end up alone later in life or (b) that other participants in the experiment had rejected him. Responses varied according to what subjects were told. Subjects who were excluded socially during the experiment gave less money to a student fund and were less helpful when one of their cohorts was in trouble. The ontologically insecure subjects also demonstrated less cooperation with fellow students in a mixed-motive game. The effects of this experimental manipulation were mediated by empathy but not by "mood, state, self-esteem, belongingness, trust, control, or self-awareness."[98] This experiment suggests a sense of rejection can constitute a transient interference with affective responses and can cripple the ability to empathically understand others. Rejection, then, reduces the person's inclination to help or cooperate with others. It can lead to increased aggression and antisocial sentiments.[99]

These experimental findings confirm the psychological importance of security noted in my naturalistic data; the rescuers demonstrated remarkably little anxiety by being condemned to death and wanted by the Nazis, while the bystanders (Kurt, Beatrix) seemed much more susceptible to fear. The concept of security echoes in the disease metaphor employed by Nazis as they explained how they needed to take preemptive action to protect the good German body politic against infestation from foreigners who were described as dirty and threatening. Kurt's description of the Slavs as dirty people who spit on the streets provides a striking illustration of this disease metaphor's political appeal.[100] The biological metaphor associating "the other" with disease that can infect the health of the body politic is a central metaphor for genocide and ethnic cleansing.[101] Indeed, the term *ethnic cleansing* is itself a revealing choice of terminology for the killing that is part of genocide. Interestingly, we find discussions of immigration also contain this linkage between the fear of disease and chronic and contextually aroused feelings of vulnerability to disease with negative feelings toward foreigners.[102]

ATTACHMENT THEORY

One explanation for the psychological link between ontological security and treatment of others comes from work on attachment theory. This experimental work supports the claim that secure attachment is closely related to treatment of in-groups versus out-groups,[103] empathy, open-mindedness, tolerance, care giving, and altruism.[104] As initially proposed by John Bowlby (1969), attachment theory developed a framework to describe interpersonal human relationships.[105] Infants seek proximity to an identified *attachment figure* when they sense danger, distress, or alarm, becoming attached to adults who are sensitive and who respond positively to the infant as consistent caregivers. The period between six months to two years old seems of particular importance in this process, with the way in which parents or caregivers respond to the infant influencing the development of patterns of attachment that, in turn, develop internal working models that guide the child's thoughts, expectations, and feelings in later relationships. All children use these attachment figures as a secure base from which to explore the world.[106] If we have the ability to form bonds, then we can move beyond narcissism and see the world from a perspective that is not just our own. We can see the world from another's point of view. Doing so may facilitate our empathy for another's situation.

If secure attachment fosters the ability to see the world from another's perspective, this may resonate and help explain why empathy is so important for ethics.[107] Psychologists focusing on prosocial behavior[108] note that individuals who demonstrate high levels of prosocial behavior tend to show greater levels of secure attachment in early childhood through early adulthood.

Further links among empathy, cognitive models, and the moral imagination exist in other experimental works. Scholars building on object relations theory[109] have constructed studies suggesting internal representations play a critical role in the link between empathy and affective and cognitive processes.[110] More explicit political analyses suggesting the importance of mental representations and perceptions come from work on voting and psychological attachments.[111] All of this research—some experimental, some utilizing realistic data and focused on quite different dependent variables—underlines the importance of understanding how we view ourselves and how we see others. Our perceptions of both self and others affect our treatment of others.[112]

Further, the relationship among attachment, self-esteem, and worldview seem closely interrelated.[113] Threats to one will activate the defensive reaction of the other two. Individual differences in attachment style affect such defenses.[114] The implication of this for our study are intriguing but not definitive. The link between their wartime behavior and the kind of psychological security found in Tony versus the insecurity of Beatrix and Kurt finds support in experimental work, yes. But on the other hand, I found no expression of weak attachment in Florentine's interview, so the evidence is mixed here. These links justify further study to determine whether there exists a loose relationship between attachment, self-esteem, and ethical behavior. Tolerance of differences seems closely related to empathy, altruism, and attachment.[115]

TERROR MANAGEMENT THEORY

If attachment touches on deep-seated psychological forces that relate to treatment of others, another, closely related factor that influences our treatment of others is the fear of death. An intriguing, albeit controversial, body of literature comes from terror management theory, a synthesis of contemporary psychoanalytic and existential thought, arguing that the fear of death is a primary motivator in all spheres of human activity. Terror management theory asks about the implicit emotional reactions of people when they are forced to face the psychological terror of knowing we all eventually will die.[116] Much of terror management theory is designed to address the existential angst of making meaning out of our lives and deaths. It thus asks what drives human behavior when life is threatened, as is the case when moral courage is required, as it is during genocides. The theory offers a creative link between culture and the worldview of others and links our tendency to think and feel about life and death to our group identities.[117] In particular, terror management theorists argue that our cultural worldview acts as a kind of symbolic protector between the reality of life and the inevitability of death. Hence, humans need to have their own cultural worldviews confirmed by others. Doing so reinforces the belief that we have made the correct choice and gives us the community's esteem. When our own worldview is threatened by the worldview of another, we can easily interpret this as a threat to our own self-respect. When this happens, people not only will try to deny or devalue the importance of others' worldviews, they also will try to controvert others' ideas and worldviews, as often happens in conflicts that get cast in terms of holy wars or a clash of civilizations.[118] All of this results in increased stereotypic thinking and intergroup bias among groups.

Terror management theorists[119] focus empirical work on what they call the mortality salience hypothesis. This hypothesis argues that because cultural worldviews and self-esteem provide protection from the fear of death, increased fear of death will increase people's need to value their own cultural worldview and self-esteem and to denigrate those who seem to challenge that worldview. Laboratory results have largely supported this model. For instance, McGregor et al. (1998) found that simply reminding subjects of their own mortality—by asking them to write about their own deaths—increased the amount of punishment that they chose to allocate to a target who threatened their worldview.[120] Greenberg et al. (1990) found that after being exposed to the mortality salience prompts, Christian subjects rated a fellow Christian more positively and a Jew more negatively than did subjects in the control condition. Subjects in a mortality salience condition were also more likely to negatively evaluate a target who expressed anti-American views. In another study,[121] subjects reminded of their own mortality were more likely to support aggressive foreign policy against potential enemy states.

Other parts of terror management theory suggest that people in a state of emotional distress will be more susceptible to the allure of charismatic leaders. When events—wars or economic depressions—remind people of their own inevitable death this, in turn, leads them to cling more strongly to their own cultural worldviews, feeling threatened by alternate views. Experiments find that people who have been traumatized by political events, such as 9/11 or World War I and the punitive Treaty of Versailles, produce greater tendencies toward right-wing authoritarianism and toward strong leaders who express traditional, proestablishment, authoritarian worldviews.[122] Such individuals become hypersensitive to the possibility of external threats and more hostile to those they believe threaten them.[123] The links seem clear between these experimental findings by terror management theory's adherents and the importance of the ties between ontological security, self-esteem, worldview, and ethics that I found in the narratives of threat (Fritz, Kurt, and Florentine) versus Tony's much more open, trusting narrative.

PERSPECTIVE TAKING

The importance of perspective in the process by which moral choice is made is supported by literature on a field addressing the process of perspective taking. The concept of perspective taking was first advanced in the 1930s by Jean Piaget (1928, 1932) and George Herbert Mead (1934, 1982), who argued that humans have the unique ability to take on the perspective of other actors toward objects. For Mead this perspective taking is what enables complex human society and subtle social coordination. (Both buyer and seller adopt each other's perspective toward the object being exchanged, for example. Minus this mutual perspective taking, the act of economic exchange cannot occur.) Given Mead's importance for social psychology—he is recognized as one of the founders of the field—this concept of perspective taking is so widespread that it has become an unremarked upon part of both cognitive and social psychology.[124] Operating on a distinctly different conceptualization of identity than the Cartesian view of identity—"I think therefore I am"—this view posits a social self.

> The human capacity to coordinate roles is both the source of a sense of self [as a social entity] and the core of social intelligence. . . . [P]utting oneself in another's position and the subsequent consideration of one's own actions from that alternative position is the operation, uniquely human, that allows for the existence of a [social] self.

This process seems not to be culturally bounded,[125] with the literature on perspective taking underlining the universal importance of perceptions of both self and the other for ethics.

Although one might find individual criticisms of any one of the experimental studies noted above, taken as a whole, they constitute an important body of evidence confirming the importance of perceptions of ontological security as factors critical in understanding the psychological responses to genocide and confirming the significance of this factor as found in my work as well as in related work[126] on the Holocaust.

HAPPINESS AND OTHERS

The importance of ontological security for treatment of others may seem obvious. It is, after all, normal to protect oneself. The rescuers suggest an intriguing, if perhaps a more nonintuitive, link between ontological security and happiness. More specifically, rescuers suggest emotional well-being actually emanates from the care of others. There is a surprisingly diverse body of literature supporting this finding. Aristotle famously noted that man is a social being, and he linked happiness with virtue. Contemporary studies on health and happiness, such as the Framingham Heart Study[127] and the Harvard Study of Adult Development,[128] highlight the critical importance of friends for health and happiness. These studies draw on extensive medical and psychological tests as well as social science testing and find that warm connections with others are critical to aging and health; indeed, the director of the Harvard study described the link among friendships, happiness, and aging, saying that "the only thing that really matters in life are your relationships to other people."[129] The recognition that both self-interest and sociability are critical to our well-being suggests human selfish desires are balanced by less self-centered, though often still individual, yearnings for social respect, affection, memberships in groups, and similar needs. These needs provide limits to the selfishness that may accompany self-interest and constitute important limitations on rational choice models.[130]

The benefits of sociability are evident in studies in a wide range of other fields. Baboon studies measured the amount of time females spent socializing (sitting near and grooming others) and found offspring of females with more elaborate social networks had the best chance of surviving.[131] An analogous pattern was found for human mothers, where interviews with 247 pregnant women found higher-weight babies were delivered to mothers receiving the most support from friends and family.[132] My favorite personal example comes from work on friendship and stress by Shelley Taylor and associates.[133] While investigating the neuroendocrine underpinnings of female responses to stress, Taylor and her colleagues noted significant differences in male/female reactions. Of special interest are gender differences in neuroendocrine reactivity, memory, anxiety, and sociability in response to stress, and the moderation of these responses by estrogen, oxytocin, and vasopressin. Women are more likely to draw on social support, which Taylor dubbed a "health-protective affiliative response," and are less likely to respond to stress with aggression or substance abuse, such as drugs and alcohol. For Taylor and her colleagues this suggests women's neuroendocrine and/or their psychological responses to stress (such as anxiety) may be down regulated, relative to men's. Further, women show greater longevity than men in all the developed countries Taylor examined. Taylor concluded that the well-known "fight or flight" response to stress is male. In contrast, women turn to friends, and the bonds women establish in doing so actually may help women live longer. (Estimates range from three to six months, providing as important an increase in life expectancy as not smoking or being overweight.) Further, this female stress response—"tend and befriend" in Taylor's phrase—may originate in biochemistry. The hormone oxytocin— released into a woman's bloodstream most noticeably during orgasm, childbirth, and nursing—facilitates bonding. But Taylor and her colleagues found increased levels of oxytocin also occur when women engage in socializing and nurturing. Thus oxytocin may produce a calming effect that accounts for less stress and increased longevity. Estrogen enhances oxytocin's effect but testosterone, which men produce at high levels during stress, reduces oxytocin's effects. This biochemistry may explain why women live longer than men, and why on average men have fewer friends than do women. It certainly offers biochemical support for theories that assume human sociability is important. To Thomas Hobbes's man, with his solitary, nasty, brutish, and short-lived pursuit of naked self-interest, political scientists thus must add Taylor's sociable, happier, less stressed, and longer-living woman to our foundational theories of human behavior.

For my purposes all these studies underline the extent to which sociability may aid self-interest. (If those who live longer are those with more friends, this seems an important link.) Scholarly discussions that juxtapose self-interest and sociability, and scholarly models that build on this juxtaposition, may be ignoring the more intricate relations between self-interest and cooperation/sociability/altruism and thereby miss something critical in the self-interest dimension. Little of this work has filtered into political science.[134]

GROUP BELIEFS, INDIVIDUAL BELIEFS, AND THE STRUCTURING AND FRAMING OF GROUPS

Much of the critical psychological pressure points have to do with the relationship between individual and group behavior. Is there a crowd mentality that can sweep along an individual—let us call her Sandra—effectively pressuring Sandra into doing something that otherwise she would not do if acting alone? The empirical literature on this is vast, with social psychology as a field developed to explain the interactions between individuals and groups and asking how social conditions affect human beings. At one level social psychologists ask how individuals such as Sandra have their thoughts, feelings, and behaviors influenced by others. The other part of the equation—emanating from more sociological concerns—asks about the behavior of groups, with a focus on interaction and exchanges at the microlevel and what the dynamics among and between the group are at a more macrolevel. This more sociological approach thus is concerned with the individual (Sandra) but mostly within the context of larger social structures and processes— such as Sandra's race, class, social roles—and the socialization processes that influenced Sandra's development.

Social psychologists thus might ask how Sandra's particular mental processes shape her as an individual. For example, how does Sandra make her decisions? What kind of decision calculus does she use? Does a particular process shape Sandra as an individual who is decisive, hesitant, etc.? They would ask further how Sandra interacts with various groups, for example, how she communicates with others and what kind of impression she makes. Finally, they would ask how this interaction in turn sets the social structure within which Sandra lives, for example, what norms her individual and group behavior produce, whether these norms result in an authoritarian political structure within the family, the school system, the polity, and so on. Working down from the broader social structures, social psychologists would ask how the broader social structures operate—through processes such as overt socialization—to influence the interaction effects on Sandra. (Is the society one that encourages Sandra to be independent? To choose her own mate? Or is it one that fosters female obedience to male norms? To church dominance? To a tribal leadership?) The interaction effects in turn will influence Sandra's social perception and her internalization of the group norms. (Does Sandra believe it is proper for a woman to be cremated with her husband after he dies? Does she accept female circumcision as a critical part of induction into the social group?) These in turn will have an influence on Sandra's individual mental processes, shaping how—or whether—she thinks independently.

The analysis I have presented in this book concentrates on individual beliefs and values, presenting a microanalysis of individual choice. Most social psychological analyses dwell on the link between individual ethical political acts and the explanation of group beliefs and ask how individual behavior can become dictated by those beliefs.[135] Group beliefs are traditionally defined as "convictions that group members (a) are aware that they share and (b) consider as defining their 'groupness.'"[136] Scholars argue that these beliefs differ from individual to individual depending on the extent to which a person has confidence in them, the extent of a belief's centrality (how relevant it is for decision making), how closely related beliefs are to other beliefs (as in an organized, coherent structure), and with regard to the function that the beliefs fulfill, in terms of social adjustment, a sense of worthiness, meaningfulness, importance, hope, and so on.[137] Group pressures for uniformity can become compelling or even coercive when control mechanisms are invoked, as they frequently are through regular meetings, newsletters, or mass media information reminding members about group beliefs,[138] and when group beliefs, such as the dehumanization of the "enemy," become embedded. This type of social psychological explanation explains key aspects of behavior during both the Holocaust and the Rwandan genocides.[139] For example, Christopher Browning (1992) explains perpetrator behavior during the Holocaust, in part, by arguing that ordinary men were turned into killers through social isolation, dependence on the group, and indoctrination sessions emphasizing their in-group ties and vulnerability. Gourevitch's (1998) discussion of the Rwanda-Burundi massacres notes the ability of critical radio broadcasts both to create an appeal to group identity and to make group members believe their identity was under attack.

To consider how critical beliefs serve the important function of guiding societal action and become the determinant of group behavior,[140] we can review our interviews in light of the German de-legitimizing beliefs about Jews from 1933 to 1945. Florentine's interview is particularly striking in illustrating the cognitive process by which others are de-legitimized and cast out of the human family via a process of dehumanization, negative trait characterization, use of political labels, and negative group comparison between Jews and Aryans.[141] Florentine's discussion of how the Nazis literally threw a deviant Nazi from the train is a dramatic and quite literal casting out of someone. Nor is Florentine an isolated illustration; de-legitimizing group beliefs became an important part of German identity in the Third Reich. Such de-legitimizing beliefs were legally enshrined and enforced. The functions of these beliefs was to "enhanc[e] feelings of superiority, increas[e] group uniformity, and scapegoating."[142] There is thus more general, cultural evidence for the psychological connection I found in the individual interviews presented here.

COGNITIVE CLASSIFICATION AND CATEGORIZATION

Both my interviews and more social psychological works on the Holocaust suggest the connection between the frustrations of Nazis and the ease with which Nazis and their supporters adopted or accepted, and acted upon, anti-Semitism. A critical part of group hostility arises from the cognitive framing of group interests as conflictual. When groups perceive their interests in a zero-sum conflict with others, they feel threatened and justified in striking back or even in striking first in what is viewed as a kind of preemptive strike. Florentine explained World War II using this cognitive model, as she revised history to have the Germans going into Holland to free it from the English invaders.

Much of this psychological process is aptly captured and documented by thousands of experiments in social identity theory, which emphasizes the in-group/ out-group dynamic. As initially formulated by Henri Tajfel (1981), social identity theory focuses on the kind of prejudice and discrimination that fuels genocide. It builds on the human propensity to categorize, identify, and associate with certain groups, which Tajfel called in-groups. This process of group identification is critical to our self-esteem and our need for distinctiveness. We compare our in-groups with other groups and exhibit favorable bias toward the group to which we belong. By establishing a clear link between the individual and the group, social identity theory effectively links the microlevel psychological need to distinguish, categorize, and compare groups with the broader, social phenomenon of group behavior.[143] It thus offers a valuable jumping-off point for understanding the importance of both real and perceived differences. It is critical for analysts to understand how encounters between individuals will be conceptualized as encounters between group members and the nature of this encounter.

The moral implications of in-group bias and its power via the link such bias provides to self-esteem can be found in innumerable experiments. I note only one example to suggest how this works. Piercarlo Valdesolo and David DeSteno (2007) argue that our assessment of our own moral shortcomings is more generous than our assessment of the same failings in others. Their study extends this finding to the group level. They argue that "group affiliation might stand as a limit on the radius of one's 'moral circle,' qualifying in-group members for the same leniency that individuals apply to their own transgressions. To the extent that the group stands as an important source of self-definition, one may have an interest in protecting the sanctity of that entity."[144] In test 1, subjects were asked to distribute assets (that is, time, effort, etc.) to oneself and another. They could do so fairly or unfairly. They then were asked to evaluate the fairness of their own actions. In test 2, participants witness their confederate acting unfairly. Participants then were asked to judge the morality of their confederate's act. Test 3 was designed to judge the confederate's unfair action by varying the confederate's membership in an in-group or an out-group. The results indicate that hypocrisy toward oneself/one's in-group is present at the individual and the collective level. A foundational bias in moral cognition thus appears to be at work, with our own transgressions accorded less weight than those of the "other," regardless of whether the self is individual or collective. Unfairness or immorality thus is more likely to be excused when found in one's own group. As we review Fritz's narrative and his discussion of Hitler, the hopes he put on Hitler, and his later assessment of both National Socialism and Hitler after Fritz later learned more about the Holocaust, we find echoes of these experimental results.

Social identity theory also underpins later work[145] outlining how this process makes each group the enemy of the other. The key is the extent to which groups limit individual choice by telling members what is appropriate behavior. One contention is that genocide and ethnic cleansing erupt when ethnic identities become reified and boundaries harden into politicized identities, as opposed to less polarizing cultural identities.[146] Still other analysts find that merely the creation of a group can result in members becoming caught up in a genocidal dynamic,[147] with this process heightened when identities are codified into formalized power sharing arrangements.[148]

This phenomenon occurred in postcolonialism, when colonial elites frequently played off different indigenous groups, often creating a group identity when such group boundaries had been porous in precolonial times. Mahmood Mamdani notes that it was the Belgian classification of the Hutu as *indigenous* Bantu and the Tutsi as *alien* Hamites (who were racially different and superior) that resulted in this clash between "natives" and "nonnatives," even though in reality the Tutsi were just as indigenous to Africa. Indeed, Hutu politicians used this ideology to justify their monopoly of power; this, in turn, gave rise to the impulse to eliminate the settler (here, the Tutsi). This production of bipolar racial and political identities was derived from the Hamitic hypothesis, which "explained away every sign of civilization in tropical Africa as foreign import."[149] The Tutsi thus were cast as the cursed descendants of Caucasoid Ham (son of Noah). But as Mamdani demonstrates, it was the Belgians who created a binary political identity formation. The more natural identity based on ethnicity and culture was one the Hutu and Tutsi actually shared:

> It is when political identities do become polarized that they become most unlike cultural identities . . . whereas cultural identities tend to share into one another, with plenty of middle ground to nurture hybridity and ambiguity, there is no middle ground, no continuum, between polarized identities. Polarized identities give rise to a kind of political difference where you must be either one or the other.[150]

The colonial power thus encouraged construction of identities in which various ethnic groups of the kingdom became Hutu, and what could have been many
ethnic tribes became socially constructed by the colonial power into only two
groups. These notions of racial difference then became embedded in and reproduced through institutions that further reinforced the opposing political identities. This is a classic illustration of how "political identities are the consequence
of how power is organized . . . acknowledged in law and thus legally enforced."[151]
Once your race, as defined by law, becomes this central defining fact for the individual and his or her group—regardless or whether that definition entitles or
restricts political rights—then race comes to be understood as a political identity
not as a cultural construct. The implications of this argument—if accurate—for
multiculturalism are sobering and suggest that the mere creation of binary ethnic, racial, and religious categories sets us one step closer toward the creation of
political identities that too frequently relate to genocide. (There is an irony in this
insofar as multiculturalism in the United States originated not to create or impose
categories so much as recognize their existence and address the inequalities and
injustice subjected on people in such categories.)

It is easier to persuade one group to envision annihilating another if those to be
killed are understood to be outsiders, foreigners, and racially distinct, as they were
so viewed in Rwanda, because of the process outlined above.[152] The argument
that much ethnic conflict arises out of arbitrarily imposed boundaries, created by
colonial powers with too little knowledge of the actual ethnic or cultural or historical differences is a common theme in the postcolonial literature and serves to
emphasize the importance of boundaries in the categorization of others. (Indeed,
Mamdani [2001] attributes the Rwandan genocide to these postcolonial racialized
political identities.)

The existence of multiple group category possibilities and the importance of
porous boundaries in group categorization is found in literature on nonhuman
aggression, considered later in the chapter. But all of the work on bystanders and
perpetrators[153] supports the findings here concerning the importance of the classification of "the other" in genocide. Psychological distancing is key. As Tony said,
"It is easier to kill a yellow gook than to kill another farm boy like yourself." Thus
the phenomenon we noted during the Holocaust is one that can be applied to a
vast variety of instances of prejudice and group violence, not just the Holocaust.

CATEGORIZATION BOUNDARIES

Much of the critical political punch from group identity comes via the classification
of others into distinct groups.[154] This is illustrated in analyses of the ethnic wars
that plagued Europe throughout the twentieth century. If we ask what made so
many individuals commit acts against neighbors belonging to other ethnic groups,
we find ourselves considering the patterns that led to the critical contention of
who makes up what ethnic group. In part, what happens is that in times of conflict,
ethnic identities become reified and ethnic boundaries more or less impermeable:
"While identities are multiple and malleable, identities can crystallize when one
is in [the] grasp of a powerful emotion. [In times of conflict] . . . brutal simplicity

comes to frame outlooks and motivate actions." This work supports my empirical findings about the centrality of ontological security and psychological boundaries for the Nazis and their supporters. The concept of ontological security draws on work about the emotions that coordinate the actions of many people, chief among these fear, hatred, resentment, and rage.[155] Fear occurs during periods of weakened institutional constraints and results in attacks on potentially threatening groups. Hatred is expressed by repeated attacks against the same group, using similar justifications over an extended time period. Rage is a noninstrumental emotion that can best be described as lashing out against any available target once the level of frustration becomes unbearable. Finally, resentment emerges when members of a group perceive the existing ethnic status hierarchy to be unjust and decide to attack.[156] Although these four emotions—fear, hatred, rage, and resentment—are not mutually exclusive, resentment has been found to be the most frequent cause of ethnic violence in twentieth-century Eastern Europe.[157]

Although my data do not allow me to speak directly to the distinction between these four specific emotions and ontological security as a more general concept, elements of their general linkage are evident in Kurt's and Florentine's interviews. Both speakers express a hierarchical worldview and resentment toward the Jews, foreigners, and non-Aryans. This link seems worth exploring in future work. Such analysis might ask whether these emotions all reflect some basic sense of ontological insecurity on the part of perpetrators and, to a lesser degree, bystanders, or if they emanate from different sources.

PERCEPTIONS OF OTHERS

I have argued that it is not simply character or self-view that influences behavior toward others but also our perceptions of others in relation to ourselves. This effectively keeps identity as an independent input into ethical considerations while also allowing for identity to enter not as defined objectively but in other, more subtle and shifting ways in which people view both themselves and others. There is a rich literature in social psychology that both buttresses this claim and provides experimental findings suggesting why and how this phenomenon occurs. Indeed, one could think of social psychology as a field that was designed specifically to understand how individual behavior is influenced by our perceptions of the others around us. (Certainly two of the most famous experiments in social psychology— the Milgram experiments on the influence of authority figures and the Zimbardo Stanford prison experiments—provide dramatic evidence that most people are heavily influenced by others.[158])

Consider just one example, *The Roots of Evil*, one of the classic social psychological analyses of genocide that builds on social identity theory. Ervin Staub (1989) highlights the importance of identity and perceptions in discussing group identity during genocide. Staub characterizes the relationship that develops between conflicting groups engaged in mass murder and genocide as "ideologies of antagonism" in which each group defines the other as an enemy bent on the other's destruction. Each group creates and develops an identity as the enemy of "the other."[159] Daniel Bar-Tal elaborates on this theme, suggesting group beliefs guide group members' behavior, telling group members what they should (or should not) do, and prescribing appropriate behavior. Often for those individuals who have been driven by a particular ideological view of the world in their society there are few options available. This again underlines the importance of the moral imagination.

Perceptions of others seem closely related to the moral imagination, which affects choice for all involved in genocide. Victims are often unprepared for genocide, leaving them unable to adopt countermeasures. For victims, striking back is not something that frequently crosses their minds. Bruno Bettelheim's *Informed Heart* (1960), a fascinating intellectual autobiography by a psychologist placed in a concentration camp, relates how Bettelheim's camp experience shifted him from Freudian analysis to work emphasizing the environment's impact on our psyches. Bettelheim tells the story of an inmate in the camp who is being led to the gas chamber. A guard recognizes her as a well-known dancer and taunts her, in an act that seems gratuitously cruel, even during these times. The guard makes the emaciated, naked woman dance for everyone while he ridicules her, noting the contrast between her current pathetic state and her previous existence as a celebrated dancer. As the woman dances, she gets close enough to the guard to get his gun and kill him. She herself is immediately killed. But she was on her way to die anyway and, at least as Bettelheim describes the event, her act was a last defiant assertion of her identity. Because the dancing put her in touch with her sense of her self—a former self, in Bettelheim's analysis—she was able to reimagine the situation in a manner that presented her with a choice, in this case the choice to go down fighting. Bettelheim treats this incident as evidence supporting his interpretation of the Nazi method of arrest and interrogation, with its often senseless beating of the victims, not as mere sadism but rather as a well thought out attempt to control people by breaking the psychological links with the past lives of those arrested. He argues that the Nazi plan was to create more docile prisoners, since people who disassociated themselves with their former lives and their former selves became turned into people against whom a broader range of actions could be taken than the previous self would have permitted. The Nazis thus created a different sense of self for an inmate, and this new group could be more easily dominated.

Staub's work suggests that being able to cultivate an independent perspective may be an important precondition for moral courage in times of conflict. Himself a Holocaust survivor, Staub points out that a "fair percentage of rescuers of Jews during the Holocaust were in some way marginal to their communities."[160] In thinking about the discrepancy between the behaviors of bystanders and rescuers, Staub focuses us on different cultural patterns, especially patterns of child rearing. The Oliners (1988) also highlight the importance of raising children so that the practice of caring becomes ingrained in them, taking on the structure of habits that eventually crystallize into personality characteristics. This involves children being raised in an environment that encourages connectivity to a group, thus making them care for everyone, and autonomy, so they can think independently and speak against the passivity of their group in the face of violence.

Other scholars note that passive bystanders distance themselves from victims, often by justifying the actions of the perpetrators.[161] Both Staub and Bar-Tal suggest that people living under authoritarian or totalitarian systems, in which an ethnocentric-nationalistic ideology is fostered, tend to derive their basic motivations by devaluing other groups, scapegoating, joining authoritative groups, and adopting nationalist ideology. These developments encourage the motivation to harm other groups and diminish inhibitions against such acts; they hence work to discourage interventions by bystanders and lead to further bystander silence. The psychological process whereby bystanders are discouraged from intervention becomes critical for continuing ethnic violence since bystanders have a unique power to stop genocidal and ethnic violence:

> Bystanders, people who witness but are not directly affected by the actions of perpetrators, help shape society by their reactions. . . . Bystanders are often unaware of, or deny, the significance of events or the consequences of their behavior. . . . [T]o remain unaware they employ defenses like rationalization, motivated misperception, or avoid information about the victims' suffering. . . . Bystanders can exert powerful influences. They can define the meaning of events and move others toward empathy or indifference. They can promote values and norms of caring, or by their passivity of participation in the systems, they can affirm the perpetrators.[162]

Commenting on rescuers, Staub suggests most were independent individuals who refused to follow the crowd. Rescuers also had a history of performing good deeds and did not perceive rescue work as anything out of the ordinary. These are all factors related to perceptions: of themselves, of what was normal, and of the people in need. We do not know the extent to which shifts in these perceptions—especially of ourselves and of our relation to others—relate to an initially small commitment—perhaps agreeing to hide someone for a day or two—and *then* lead to further involvement but there is some evidence for this, and future scholars should explore it further.

EMPATHY AND PERSPECTIVE

We need to know more about the relation between perspective and empathy, especially insofar as empathy drives moral choice. Evidence from neuroscience suggests there actually may be a neural connection. For example, seeing another person being touched commonly triggers a neural response in the viewer that is similar to that of actual touching of their "own" bodies.[163] Those with "mirror-touch synesthesia" can actually produce a vicarious touch sensation on their own bodies. This trait is shown to be linked to empathy.[164] "Experiencing aspects of affective empathy may particularly depend on shared interpersonal representations."[165] Recent work[166] uses FMRIs to examine what happens in the brain while subjects donate to—or oppose giving to—charity organizations dedicated to large-scale social issues. This work discovered that the mesolimbic reward system was engaged by donations in the same way they were when awards of money are acquired. The medial orbito-frontal/subgenual and lateral orbito-frontal areas, which seem to contribute to social attachment and social aversion, accounted for many choices to donate to or oppose social causes. More forward sections of pre-frontal cortex were tied to instances where, when subjects were forced to choose between an altruistic response and a self-interested choice, they chose the altru-istic response.[167] Such work, while in early stages, suggests the value of research exploring the psychophysiological and neuroscientific foundations of ethics.

The links among ethics, empathy, and agency also seem worth exploring in fu-ture work. An intriguing study by Gail Zucker and Bernard Weiner (1993) used attribution theory to tie people's causal explanations for poverty to positive or negative affect, as well as their behavioral intent.[168] Given the links among agency, empathic involvement, and moral salience found in the narratives of bystanders in particular, and given the importance of bystanders for genocide, this relationship seems an important one to pursue in future work.

In this process, however, power seems to limit our ability to see the world through another's eyes. In one study, Galinsky et al. (2006) found participants primed with high power were less willing to take another's visual perspective.[169] In another study, "high-power" subjects were less self-aware of asymmetric knowl-edge on their part vis-à-vis "low-power" individuals, and were less willing to ad-just to the epistemic stance of the other. High-power subjects anchored heavily on their own vantage point. A third study found high-power participants exhibit decreased accuracy versus controls in discerning others' emotional expressions. All of these experiments suggest power may reduce our ability to experience em-pathy since the common theme, consistent across all experiments, was the inverse relationship between power and the ability to comprehend how other people see, think, and feel.[170] This empirical finding underscores the importance of philo-sophical works that ask readers to construct a political system behind the veil of ignorance[171] and suggests holding power may interfere with the ability to put one's self in the place of another.

If perspective is so important, can we use this knowledge to increase empathy for another? Will seeing the world through another's eyes lead to increased under-standing for the other's situation and to better treatment of them, or at least foster forgiveness? Relations among different races and religious groups are two areas in which we find the influence of perspective. P. J. Henry and Curtis Hardin (2006) conducted two studies; one between whites and blacks in the United States, the second between Christians and Muslims in Lebanon. Henry and Hardin asked whether intergroup status differences impede the efficacy of contact effects on im-plicit prejudice. They found intergroup contact reduces implicit prejudice among low-status groups. Their experiments showed that implicit prejudice of blacks to-ward whites was decreased as a result of friendly contact; however, the same did not hold for prejudice of whites toward blacks. Analogous results were reached in studies in Lebanon, where implicit prejudice of Muslims toward Christians went down, but not that of Christians toward Muslims.

Seeing things from another's perspective is generally held to influence our treat-ment of those nearest and dearest to us.[172] Ximena Arriaga and Caryl Rusbult (1998) inquired about influences from partners on perspective taking. They conducted four experiments on the role of "partner-perspective-taking" in influencing reactions to situations in which a partner undertakes a behavior that could be destructive.[173] For all four studies, adopting a partner's perspective during such dilemmas led to a more positive emotional response, with relationship-enhancing attributions more likely to productively respond. Adopting a partner's perspective also reduced negativity and led to less blaming of the partner and less inclination toward unproductive response. Three of the studies revealed that partner-perspective-taking leads to independent effects on emotions known to play key roles in accommodation as well as to attributions and preferences for behavior in line with the same.

MORAL INSENSITIVITY AND PSYCHIC NUMBING OF THE SELF

Is empathy related to sensitivity? The stories presented in the second part of this book document several eerie instances of the link between lack of empathy and moral insensitivity, with bystanders and supporters of genocide figuratively standing, as Fritz noted, with their heads in the sand like ostriches. This may be related to psychic numbing or the loss of the capacity to feel. Lifton describes this as "a form of desensitization . . . refer[ring] to an incapacity to feel or to confront certain kinds of experience, due to the blocking or absence of inner forms or imagery that can connect with such experience."[174] This critical part of the moral imagination suggests the importance of cognitive or mental models for the lack of choice among all groups I interviewed.

In *The Nazi Doctors* (1986), Lifton argues that doctors in Auschwitz had to relate to their environment as if it were some kind of fantasy and not part of the real world so that they could carry out the Nazi medical experiments. This is disconcertingly reminiscent of children watching violence on television. The violence is not experienced as real, in part because the children lack mental models for comprehending such violence.[175] Lifton argues that the Nazi doctors experienced a related absence of awareness of the reality around them, a psychological process that corresponds to what Gobodo-Madizikele calls a "psychological cutting off of one's sense of reality."[176] For example, Nazi doctors knew that they were participating in the policy of selection of Jews for gas chambers, but they did not interpret selection as murder.[177] Lifton utilizes the concept of "doubling," where the perpetrator operates in a sort of double self, one part of the self disavowing the other. (Or, to use Gobodo-Madizikele's term, perpetrators *compartmentalize* their existence with their actions.) Beatrix demonstrated some aspects of this in her inability to connect her own good fortune and ability to participate in the good life with the fact that she fell heir to some of the material goods of a Jew forced to emigrate. Nor does Fritz connect his good fortune during the war with the suffering of others. This obliviousness—the failure to make the connection between the situation for bystanders and supporters of genocide with the situation of the victim—is a phenomenon noted by other scholars.[178] Consider an excerpt from *The Nazi Doctors*, which illustrates this compartmentalization among the doctors who worked with the SS.

They [the SS doctors] did their work just as someone who goes to an office goes about his work. They were gentlemen who came and went, who supervised and were relaxed, sometimes smiling, sometimes joking, but never unhappy. They were witty if they felt like it. Personally I did not get the impression that they were much affected by what was going on—nor shocked. It went on for years. It was not just one day.[179]

Crimes of War[180] expands Lifton's work on psychic numbing and bystander denial, raising a difficult question via an inquiry about the identical nature of the American population's response to the My Lai massacre and that of the Germans to reports of World War II atrocities. In both cases, Lifton finds three main reactions. The first is denial, defined as an insistence that the massacres didn't really happen or were exaggerated. (This process is evident in Kurt's narrative, where Kurt first says he knew nothing of the concentration camps then says that after the war his men were stationed near Auschwitz, but that it was a prisoner of war camp. Still later Kurt suggests the Holocaust was vastly exaggerated, noting a friend— "Mr. Louis"—whom Kurt had been told was killed but whom Kurt later met in the United States.[181] Florentine and her Nazi friend also denied and minimized the Holocaust.) The second response is rationalization, as in the excuse that "all war is hell" or "everyone engages in torture." (This rationalization response is illustrated by Florentine's insistence that the British and American Allies did worse than the Germans did during the war.) The third reaction is the mobilization of self-righteous anger. Florentine insisted that Hitler asked the British politely three times to stop their invasion of Holland and only then did Hitler have to respond to stop what Florentine viewed as British aggression. Falk notes the same self-righteous anger among Americans concerning Vietnamese and Americans who criticized US foreign policy during the war. Americans felt the Vietnamese "had it coming to them" and that critics of US foreign policy "ought to be sent to Vietnam to fight." He concludes that all "groups, and even nations, distance themselves from—refuse to feel—their own atrocities; we have the experience of Nazi Germany for that."[182] In refusing to feel, bystanders partake in the same psychic numbing experienced by the perpetrators, but in a less extreme form.

IDENTITY AND THE NEED FOR PREDICTABILITY AND CONTROL

One reason identity plays such a central role in moral choice concerns identity's feedback relation to choice. As outlined in my theory of moral choice, decisions emanate from one's sense of self. But these choices also feed back into one's identity, shaping and altering it. This phenomenon is noted in sources as diverse as psychological experiments and works of literature. In *War and Peace*, Tolstoy describes how Napoleon's quest to spread the ideals of the French revolution led Napoleon into a war that undermined these very ideals. Tolstoy is no fan of Napoleon, and Tolstoy's portrait of Napoleon paints Napoleon as having to choose between world conquest based on the slaughter of war or honor and truth and humanity. Napoleon could not keep both.[183] "He could not renounce his actions, extolled by half the world, and therefore he had to renounce truth and goodness and everything human."[184]

Experimental literature in psychology offers a rigorous foundation for Tolstoy's impressionistic depiction of the feedback nature of identity and action. Cognitive dissonance theory,[185] for example, was developed to explain the psychic discomfort people feel when they hold contradictory beliefs. Elliot Aronson's (1969) reformulation of Festinger's basic theory linked it to the self-concept and argued that cognitive dissonance arises primarily *not* because people experience dissonance between conflicting cognitions but rather when people believe their actions conflict with their normally positive view of themselves.[186] It is difficult to think of one's self as gentle and kind and yet act mean and cruel. This now vast literature thus makes clear that a key source of an individual's psychic comfort and the maintenance of identity emanate in the desire for cognitive consistency. These needs for cognitive consistency are especially critical for actions that touch on our sense of who we are. Holding contradictory beliefs is troubling. But it is holding beliefs that challenge our own positive self-image that keeps us up at night. The need for consistency in behavior is reinforced in philosophical works on identity, where scholars[187] find that minus consistency in both behavior and cognition, our sense of self as a unitary being over an extended time period becomes a meaningless concept. As a philosophical concept, identity requires consistency.[188]

IS MORALITY INNATE?

Finally, let me consider evidence relevant to what some may find a controversial claim inherent in my theory: the innate aspect of morality. I claim that ethical acts emanate not so much from conscious choice but rather from deep-seated instincts, predispositions, and habitual patterns of behavior that are related to our central identity. These emanate and manifest themselves in diverse factors, such as genetic predispositions, social roles, or culturally inculcated norms. I further argue that culture provides a range of self-images but that actors gravitate toward the image(s) that strikes a chord with their genetic propensities, with a powerful push coming from situational or contextual factors. The actor need not be consciously aware of this process although conscious recognition is part of the process; but our moral sense is instinctual and powerful, often more influential than conscious calculus.

These claims are consistent with psychological experiments and theories of decision making that do not rely on conscious, deliberative analysis.[189] The nature/nurture debate over the origins of moral values seems more a red herring than a useful debate, and I prefer the concept of a phenotype to refer to behavior or characteristics resulting from the expression of an organism's genes as well as the influence of environmental factors and the possible interactions between the two. Indeed, I am prepared to believe human beings may be programmed to have certain innate moral senses.[190] The extensive literature supporting this claim is too hard to ignore, ranging from recent scientific work in child development (Jerome Kagan), evolutionary biology (Frans DeWaal), neuroeconomics (Paul Zak), primatology (Robert Sapolsky), and linguistics (George Lakoff). Haidt's work suggesting people have natural disgust for certain behaviors such as incest is but one illustration of this literature. Given its potential significance and its relative obscurity among current philosophical discussions among ethicists, let us consider the literature on an innate moral sense more carefully, focusing on just a few questions that relate directly to our concerns.

What if people are born with a moral sense built into their neural circuitry?[191] If they are, does this provide any content to the ethical framework? In other words, do human beings have any kind of innate moral sense or is the ethical framework I have posited simply a neutral scaffolding on which culture and socialization impart values, much as we have the innate capacity for grammar that waits to be filled in by culture and socialization? If so, how might this work?

Essentially, moral sense theory holds that morality is grounded in moral sentiments or emotions, born within us much as our sense of smell or taste or touch is innate. While moral sense theory as a body of philosophical literature was soon eclipsed by Kant's magisterial ethical analysis that privileges deliberative reason, the stories presented here make clear that there is an important part of ethics that *cannot* be explained solely by conscious choice and reason, and that the Kantian picture needs to be complemented by a theory of moral choice that allows more fully for identity, including that part of identity that is composed of innate forces and influences. A closer look at both the philosophical origins of moral sense theory and the contemporary empirical work revealing how these innate forces might be manifested and work thus is in order. Part of my intention in linking these two literatures is to encourage closer cooperation among political theorists and empirical social and biological scientists.[192]

The Original Moral Sense Theory

As a philosophical theory, moral sense theory holds that we are able to distinguish between right and wrong through a distinctive moral[193] sense.[194] Although human nature is a perennial philosophical theme, dating from Plato, the idea of an innate moral sense reflects the Enlightenment's attempt to explain how human psychology might justify political and moral theories.[195] As part of the Enlightenment's quest for the scientific analysis of moral issues, moral sense theory inquires about the realities of human nature in order to construct our disquisitions on government and moral conduct on this nature and, presumably, construct polities that then can more realistically hope to achieve an ethical politics and society. In this regard we discern the influence of both Locke and Hobbes.

In *An Essay concerning Human Understanding* (2000 [1690]), Locke attempted to develop a mental science much as Isaac Newton had developed a physical science. Locke was not the only scholar to reject the scholasticism and rationalism of his time and to eschew the approach in which we deduce "truths" from abstract premises that were otherwise unavailable to ordinary experience. In this Locke followed the scientific tradition of both Newton and Bacon in stressing an approach that attempted to discern the nature of human beings through an empirical method that was systematic and available to anyone who had ordinary powers of perception and unprejudiced judgment.[196]

This scientific approach to morality rejected the approach in which abstract rationality reduces the senses to a minor role. It generated a school known as moral sense theory, also sometimes referred to as British sentimentalism.[197] Moral sense theorists argued that moral terms must refer to something that is ultimately observable. The reference of such terms is a sentiment or a feeling of revulsion or approval. The moral quality of any act is the sentiment it elicits, and the core of morality is a distinctly human nature that is inclined toward social and political forms of connection. This makes the moral sense a substrate of all human behavior. At its core it remains the same, despite cultural variations.

Hobbes's influence on moral sense theory is less direct than Locke's but nonetheless powerful. Perhaps we best discern Hobbes's influence by noting that moral sense theory attempts to answer both the questions left unanswered by theorists who find reason the driving force behind moral action and the questions left unanswered by the intuitionists who opposed the primacy of reason. The problem for those who argue in favor of moral intuitions—as opposed to reason—as the impetus for morality is the following: If reason does indeed tell us it would be wrong to be immoral—to lie, for example—how does this discernment provide a *motive* to be moral? Is merely recognizing that something is wrong enough to move us to do the right thing, even when our desires suggest otherwise? For example, why would we not lie anyway, if lying is in our self-interest in a particular instance? The intuitionist position separates our moral knowledge from the forces that motivate us. Intuitionists make moral knowledge a matter of reason, but they locate our drive toward selfishness—such as lying or other forms of immorality—in the passions. This then raises obvious questions: Will reason dominate the passions? What happens if it does not?

An answer from religion is the blessing and sanction of God; the deity will react punitively in the absence of control of our selfish passions. Others (Émile Durkheim) found an answer in the socializing role of community. Hobbes answered this same question via the strong sovereign of social contract theory. In all these explanations we are compelled to act morally by an external force—whether sacred (God) or secular (society or the political authorities). The external thus provides the impetus to do good. These answers were unacceptable to the intuitionists who wanted to demonstrate that morality had innate bases within human beings and that it is reasonable to do good *regardless* of threats from any external power, divine or human. It is the attempt to construct such a demonstration that lies behind moral sense theory. Although the initial discussion occurred during the seventeenth and eighteenth centuries, the debate touches on an issue still under contention today: does the drive toward morality lie in conscious reasoning or in affective processes?

SHAFTESBURY

The term *moral sense* was first used by Shaftesbury, who argued we are able to distinguish between right and wrong by a distinctive moral sense that provides a special type of affective response.[198] For Shaftesbury the ability to sense virtue was akin to an aesthetic act, comparable to sensing beauty in art. Both senses have much to do with whether an act contributes to the general harmony of mankind. Therefore the moral sense as such is closely related to considerations of the general welfare.

Shaftesbury (1977) argued against the Hobbesian view that the prime motivation driving human behavior is self-interest. For Shaftesbury, Hobbes erred in privileging self-interest as an explanation; Shaftesbury agreed that self-interest is a natural passion in humankind but held that self-interest is but one of many passions. Shaftesbury claimed that self-interest is joined (and often superseded) by other passions, such as benevolence, sympathy, gratitude, and generosity. For Shaftesbury, these feelings create an "affection for virtue," which then naturally leads to the promotion of public interest. This affection, which Shaftesbury thought created a natural harmony between virtue and self-interest, was called the moral sense. Shaftesbury thus recognized that people had contrary desires, of the kind made central by Hobbes, and did not expect people to be virtuous at all times. But he contended that the pleasures of virtue are superior to those of vice and expected that the dual motives of self-interest and the social interest would work together in perfect adjustment.

The originator of the theory thus set it up as a distinctive moral sense. It is a feeling-response, analogous to sensing beauty. For Shaftesbury, the test of a proposed action was whether it contributes to the general harmony of mankind, which Shaftesbury identified as the general welfare. This harmony of the senses follows the Greek tradition (for example, Plato) in which the harmony of the two drives in human nature—that of self-interest and social interest—work together in equilibrium. For moral sense theorists, as for other Enlightenment thinkers, morality does not require supernatural sanctions and religion. Nonetheless, while religion is not critical for moral sense theory, the early moral sense theorists were at least nominally Christian and did allow that it may be God who implanted this moral sense in man. Moral sense theory thus is not antithetical to religious views of a moral sense and might be said merely to substitute nature for God as the key agent, as the Deist responses of the Enlightenment made plain. But the spurs to moral activity have their base in human nature, extraneous to religious sanction and prior to deliberative reason.

HUTCHESON

Shaftesbury's general ideas are expanded upon by Francis Hutcheson, whose analysis of human nature claimed there were a great number of special senses.[199] Essentially, Hutcheson argued that humans possess more than just the five external senses that allow us to smell, taste, see, hear, and touch. We also have a variety of internal senses. These internal senses include a sense of honor, of beauty, a sense of the ridiculous, and, more important for our purposes, what Hutcheson called a "public sense" that entailed the feeling of being pleased by the happiness of others and uneasy over human misery.

According to Hutcheson these internal senses are implanted in us, much as are the senses of taste, smell, etc. These internal senses cause us to react immediately and instinctively to the character of actions. The moral sense causes us to approve of acts that are good and virtuous and to disapprove of those that are bad or vicious, much as humans exhibit disgust at foul odors or salivate in the presence of food. Hutcheson went even further than the original intuitionists in asserting that moral judgment is not based on reason. He held that our moral sense does not simply, or even predominantly, find pleasing those acts that benefit our own interest. For Hutcheson, moral sense seems based on a disinterested benevolence, with the ultimate desideratum "the greatest happiness for the greatest number." (This argument anticipates the Utilitarians in both phrasing and in its concern to promote the general welfare à la Jeremy Bentham.)

Hutcheson suggested the moral sense is an internal reflex, responding both to external and internal precepts. While custom, education, and example may refine and even extend this sense, a natural substrate or protosense must exist in order to perceive the moral right and wrong. Hutcheson based part of his argument on the fact that benevolence is pleasing to man. He maintained that since man's power to reason is, in general, too weak to match his moral perceptiveness, there must be a moral sense to which benevolent activity is pleasing. This approach later appeared in work by Hume and Adam Smith (1976a [1759]), Hutcheson's most famous student.[200]

HUME

David Hume agreed that reason cannot constitute the foundation for morality since reason, for Hume, is the slave of the passions.[201] Reason cannot determine our ultimate desires and cannot move us toward action unless there is a prior desire; all it can do is tell us how best to achieve these desires. For Hume, all substantive knowledge ultimately must be derived from sense experience. But Hume broke with his predecessors who sought to provide a rational warrant for most of our original beliefs and held that many beliefs had no such warrant. Instead, Hume contended, they should be explained in psychological terms. They were the results of mental processes of a nonrational, though practically irresistible, kind. Hume drew particular attention to the role played by the imagination and the importance of the imagination as a source of conventional rules and custom.

Contemporary work in neuroscience and cognitive psychology confirms many of Hume's claims. Among philosophers, however, Hume's argument—that ethics is rooted in emotion or feelings instead of reason—moved the debate away from the specific claim of a moral sense, and Hume is conventionally understood to be arguing primarily for the predominance of emotion as the foundation of ethics rather than to be arguing in favor of a specific moral sense. In this regard Hume's heirs are the students of human nature and the historical development of society, and we find the concept of a moral sense surfacing most prominently among developmental psychologists concerned with ethics[202] and ethologists concerned with the extent to which human beings resemble other animals in having an inborn sense of morality, much as they have an instinct for survival.[203]

Moral sense theory was strongly criticized,[204] and the main currents in Western philosophy have largely ignored ideas linking[205] morality with natural, affective faculties. For example, Marx and Engels (2004) reduce morality to a kind of ideological reflex that is the epiphenomenal by-product of the concrete, material life and the relations of production. Certain varieties of analytic philosophy attempt to rigorously distinguish values from facts and question whether moral statements have any validity at all.[206] Certainly, Kant helped make deliberative reason the privileged site of moral judgment. Contemporary Anglo-American ethics[207] generally argues that reason provides the foundation for moral duty, helps us discover what morality is, and constitutes the tool by which we reach agreement when we disagree over or are torn by the particulars of moral choice.

Contemporary Evidence of a Moral Sense

Despite this lack of attention to the idea of an inborn moral sense among philosophers and political scientists, the idea nonetheless perseveres in other disciplines. Arguments that human beings have an inborn sense of morality, much as they have an instinct for survival, surface prominently in the contemporary literature of a wide variety of quite diverse disciplines. Ethology and anthropology, for example, share a concern for human sociability and ask whether there are behaviors, such as mothering, that are socially constructed or if such behaviors contain an innate element. Anthropologists ask about human behavior in the ancestral environment to discern the role of culture in influencing moral behavior. Animal ethologists ask if the ethical nature of human beings is rooted in the biological nature we share with other species. Developmental psychologists examine children in their earliest years, before culture and language have shaped what might be innate tendencies toward certain kinds of behavior. And, increasingly, moral psychologists and neuroscientists are making inroads into the biological substrates of moral behavior not only in animals or infants but also in adults throughout the life cycle.[208]

Some of the empirical research described below can be fragmentary and elusive; it occasionally involves questions about the scientific reliability of certain findings.[209] Nonetheless, this evidence is salient enough to justify a reconsideration of the existence of an innate moral sense. We need to ask if this assumption, or at least its possibility, should be built into our political models.[210]

DEVELOPMENTAL PSYCHOLOGY

Contemporary psychologists build on Piaget[211] who, while not explicitly proposing a moral sense, did assume people have a built-in capacity for morality. Piaget's heirs[212] privilege reason in constructing cognitive-developmental models that tie the idea of an innate moral sense to developmental reasoning as they ask how people progress through different stages of moral reasoning and, later, ask how factors such as gender influence a general developmental process that exists innately in all humans. Analysts such as Kohlberg[213] and Gilligan,[214] however, made moral development an extended process, wherein moral reasoning continues to develop well into adolescence and adulthood. Because their work emphasized reason, not an innate moral sense, it thus has only a tangential relevance for us.[215] Other child psychologists (Kagan, Lamb) provide clearer illustrations of developmental work arguing for an innate moral sense, work that does not rely on more complex cognitive processes of reasoning of the kind found only in adolescents or adults.[216] Let us thus turn to work on child development, treating research by Kagan, one of the most important developmentalists, as illustrative of the genre.

Kagan's lifetime of experiments with children asks whether human action is motivated by a desire for sensory pleasure. He finds the emergence of a moral sense in children by the end of the second year is universal and, perhaps more than language or reason, distinct to people. Humans seem biologically programmed with an innate moral sense of ethics and morality, much as we are programmed for language. As with language, the form this ethics takes in practice will vary according to external factors. In making this argument Kagan juxtaposes what he considers an innate moral sense in children with the kind of explanation offered by Utilitarians, who root the drive for ethics in the desire to maximize pleasure and minimize pain. Kagan concludes that the conscious feeling of pleasure that originates in one or more of the sensory modalities—those found in the sensory pleasure of eating food, touching something that appeals to us, or in sexual arousal—are indeed innate. But it is not this kind of pleasure that Kagan makes critical in his conceptualization of a moral sense. Instead, Kagan locates a moral sense in the "conceptual consonance between an idea, called a standard, and the chosen action. When that consonance occurs, the person momentarily experiences a pleasant feeling because his behavior is in accord with a standard he has categorized as good."[217]

This distinction is critical for our purposes. Kagan claims the pleasures of sensory experience discussed in Utilitarian thought can be confirmed with laboratory investigations. This particular sensory pleasure is found in a variety of animals, not just in humans. In the mammalian brain, this sensory pleasure centers in a set of neurons that, when excited, create a state of sensory enjoyment. Biological tests confirm the existence of such neuronal transmitters and reveal activity in the centers of the brain in which such sensory stimuli originate. For theorists who locate the drive toward morality in such a sensory pleasure, then, scientific evidence seems to validate the existence of such pleasure centers.[218] Nonetheless, Kagan notes, attempting to root morality in sensory pleasure still involves us in difficulties. "The traditional argument that moral standards are derived from sensory pleasure or the reduction of pain cannot explain the universal fact that people become angry when they see others violate standards they believe are right."[219] Does this mean we must abandon the idea of a moral sense? Not for Kagan, who argues that the biological foundation of this moral sense is critical and emerges from our primate ancestry. But the good feelings, the pleasures that come when we experience consonance with our standards, *these* are what Kagan argues drive us toward moral action, and these are as difficult to measure as they are critical for morality. Kagan proposes that these more complicated good feelings consist of five unique abilities that humans inherit genetically, much as both humans and other primates inherit the tendency to be attentive to the voice, face, and actions of others. For Kagan these five components constitute the moral sense: (1) the ability to infer others' feelings and thoughts,[220] (2) the capacity for self-awareness, (3) our penchant to categorize events and our selves as good or bad, (4) our capacity to reflect on past actions, and (5) our capability to know that a particular act could have been suppressed. These five abilities exist in all human beings. They merge to form a moral sense around the second year in children, thus making the human moral sense a biologically prepared competence.

These developmental arguments about our moral sense correspond to arguments about our innate mathematical abilities. The human ability to conceptualize numbers and grasp the rules of arithmetic is innate,[221] but an innate mathematical ability does not necessitate the particular set of mathematical principles that has been conceptualized and passed on to us as children. The form of the mathematics is arbitrary; other particular principles could equally well have been generated and transmitted.[222] Thus, although a foundation for a moral sense *does* exist, the mere existence does not necessarily imply that a *particular* ethical system is more natural than others. The wide "variety of moral standards across cultures in history" supports Kagan's claim that it is "very difficult to argue that one inherits a tendency for certain morals."[223] In this regard, ethics resembles language.

> Because we're humans, we inherit a capacity to learn a language. But the language that we learn could be Swahili, French, English, Japanese. The same thing [is true] with morality. We inherit, because we are humans, a concern with right and wrong, and empathy with others. But the specific actions that we regard as moral, can vary with culture, just as the specific language you learn can vary with culture.[224]

The proclivity toward ethical behavior thus is innate, but the particularities of the ethical action are not. Accordingly, a cultural relativist could accept the concept of an innate moral sense while still arguing that what some ethicists find an innate prohibition—a taboo against incest or murder, for example—is socially constructed. Despite this conclusion Kagan argues against cultural relativism when discussing the stages reached by normal children.[225] These stages include the cognitive sophistication necessary to integrate the past, present, and future in what Piaget calls reversibility, a process necessary for the assumption of responsibility for one's actions.[226] Most two-year-olds have a capacity to "infer the thoughts and feelings of another and will show signs of tension if another person is hurt, or may offer penance if they caused another's distress."[227] The ability to anticipate the feelings of another is linked with the suppression of the child's desire to hurt that person. This connection between empathy and anticipation of another's feelings, however, is the result of speculation and inference, not the result of experiments. Nonetheless, the "appearance of empathy in all children by the end of the second year implies that two-year-olds are prepared by their biology to regard hurting others as bad—that is, [as] a moral violation."[228] At the same age, most children become aware of themselves as individuals with specific characteristics, intentions, and feelings. They recognize that they can be labeled "bad" or "good" and will try to avoid creating unpleasant feelings in others since they know that if they do so, they in turn will be avoided.[229]

> That insight is a seminal origin of the moral motive, although it will not be the only basis for morality in later years. A desire to avoid or to deny the labeling of self as bad

increases in intensity as the child matures; in time, it will take precedence over fear of disapproval or punishment as the primary governor of behavior. This means "shame and guilt are biologically prepared, developmentally timed emotions."[230]

Child developmentalists such as Kagan do not take us to specific morality, just to our need to classify acts as "good" or "bad." We find little in his system to distinguish an Oskar Schindler from a Nazi genocidalist. Nor do they totally separate morality from a developmental process that controls out the influence of reason and culture, although references to cross-cultural studies allow for many cultural factors. For this we turn to literature in primatology that attempts to achieve both these goals and that suggests animals other than human beings have a moral sense that is expressed in specific behaviors. Such works are not referring to the kind of consonance between act and standard that Kagan makes his hallmark of morality. Further, Kagan himself would take strong exception to classifying other animals in the same category as humans, since Kagan holds humans the only species to have the particular form of a moral sense that moves beyond the pleasure principle or psychological egoism.[231] This view from one of the key child developmentalists, then, is that the human moral sense is biologically prepared, that it develops early, and that it is adaptive, a product of evolution unique to human beings. "That's why a lot of the animal research that tries to inform the human condition has limited value because we, only we, not chimpanzees, are aware of right and wrong, and we wish to do the right thing."[232]

EVOLUTIONARY BIOLOGY AND BEHAVIORAL ECONOMICS

Other scholars take strong exception to Kagan's insistence on the unique human claim to a moral sense. In searching for biology's ability to encode behavior, they focus on primitive behaviors that do not require the cognitive development Kagan required for his moral sense as consonance. (For example, Darwin [1889] embraced the concept of a moral sense but did not specify what he meant by it.) Do animals exhibit behavior that corresponds with what we humans think of as "moral"? Do nonhuman animals feel the kind of sentiments that Hume made the impetus for morality? Do animal possess the cognitive abilities necessary to engage in the relatively sophisticated developmental processes underlying Kagan's concept of morality as consonance? If so, which animals? Where do we draw the line in terms of cognitive development? Is animal behavior that looks moral to us the product of more primitive stimulus-response patterns that occur without the complex neurotransmitter responses of the neocortex? A host of questions remain to be answered, but the preliminary evidence is intriguing.

Relatively few works by evolutionary biologists focus on morality among human beings. Consequently, this literature does not often find its way into discussions of human morality, and evolutionary biological analyses of a human moral sense seldom are found in contemporary political science.[233] For empirical, albeit still controversial, evidence on the idea of a moral sense, we turn to scholars studying animal behavior, especially primatology. These animal behavioral scientists do not adopt Kagan's conceptualization of a more cognitively developed consonance;

yet Kagan and animal ethologists share one important theme: disputing the idea that the only drive behind behavior is psychological egoism. Their success in this endeavor has salience for political science, since psychological egoism is the sole or dominant force for many political theorists (Hobbes) and evolutionary biologists[234] who argue that human beings resemble other animals in being born selfish and lacking in true generosity and altruism. Animal behavioral scientists[235] challenge this view and offer intriguing evidence to support their view that animals have an innate moral sense.

Much of this literature is designed to demonstrate that morality is not merely man's cultural invention but is instead the product of millions of years of evolution. These evolutionary biologists concede that the strong have an advantage in any society built on individual strength. But this advantage shifts once additional factors relevant for survival are introduced. Any complex society, they argue, will make cooperation a valued form of behavior and thus evolutionarily adaptive. Working together helps individuals—be they capuchin monkeys or human beings—do better than they would alone. In game theoretic terms, joint efforts produce joint payoffs; with cooperation comes increased sensitivity concerning who gets what for their efforts. Thus some evolutionary biologists find the Hobbesian world mischaracterizes empirical reality. Instead, animal behavioral economics turns to the Adam Smith of *A Theory of Moral Sentiments*, emphasizing the way in which kindness begets kindness. They argue that human beings have a concern with fairness and justice.[236] These animal behavioral economists argue that humans come from a long line of social primates and believe there are concrete advantages associated with fairness in our primate past.

These conclusions are supported by a host of empirical studies, from animals as diverse as chimpanzees and lions to fish and humans.[237] Chimpanzees will groom in exchange for food, for example, suggesting memory-based and partner-specific exchanges that mimic what humans call gratitude.[238] Research on capuchins suggests they demonstrate cooperation, communication, and even obligations, as when two monkeys work together to get the reward of individual bowls of food.[239] Monkeys demonstrate a sense of fairness, protesting when one monkey gets grapes (a preferred food) while the others get cucumbers, even going on strike until they all get grapes.[240] The monkeys thus seem to reject unequal pay, behavior at variance with the fitness maximization, which stipulates they should take what they can get and not let another's resentment or envy interfere with maximizing behavior.

Behavioral economists argue that the evolution of emotions serves to preserve the spirit of cooperation. Caring what others get might seem irrational to some schools of economics, but it keeps us from being taken advantage of in the long run.[241] Discouragement of exploitation, free riding, and cheating thus is evolutionarily advantageous. Such empirical work has been developed into a sophisticated theory of cooperation, mutual aid, gratitude, reciprocity, and sharing.[242] Mammalian preferences for equity have been found among dogs, not just among primates.[243] These experiments in animal behavior conclude that the source of the fairness principle is conflict avoidance. It begins with individual animals noticing resentment and their concern about how others will react if one animal gets more. It ends with more complex declarations proclaiming inequity a bad practice in general. Human beings thus "embrace the golden rule not accidentally, as Hobbes thought, but as part of our background as cooperative primates."[244] In this sense, animal behavioral scientists might provide one answer to an important criticism posed to the original moral sense theorists: How do we choose between the various and conflicting behaviors that people judge moral? One plausible answer is to favor whatever behavior is more evolutionarily adaptive.

But what if we reject this route as too simplistic? Is the literature on animal behavior still relevant for us? Yes. If we are asking about an innate moral sense, and whether or not human beings possess this sense, then an important way to approach the problem is to conceive of humans as a subset of the animal kingdom. If other animals, especially primates—of which humans are a subset—demonstrate behavior that appears to correspond to what we would conceptualize as moral, then that constitutes inferential evidence suggesting human beings possess this moral sense as part of our animal biology.

HUMANS AND THEIR PRIMATE NATURE

Drawing on more than twenty-five years of experiments with primates, primatologists such as Frans DeWaal argue that an innate moral sense exists in all primates, and that animals have both culture and emotions.[245] This work challenges the philosophical tendency to privilege human beings and the premise that self-interest drives our animal nature.[246] "Morality is as firmly grounded in neurobiology as anything else we do or are."[247] Indeed, DeWaal finds a wide range of ethical acts among primates, from reciprocity and cooperation to helping those who are hurt or feeding the hungry. Such acts, for DeWaal, indicate the ability of animals to feel sympathy. "Survival of the weak, the handicapped, the mentally retarded, and others who posed a burden was depicted as the first appearance on the evolutionary scene of compassion and moral decency."[248] He cites numerous examples of animal succoring demonstrating the "functional equivalent of human sympathy" in animals as different as whales and macaques.[249] DeWaal further argues that animals respond to social rules to help one another and to share food and resolve conflicts. He does not argue that animals are morally good, but he does claim they exhibit behavior that looks like cooperation, altruism, sharing, helping, and similar acts that could be said to partake of morality. Overall, DeWaal finds a wide range of activity that suggests animals do not just demonstrate the kinds of behavior that ensures survival. His picture of animals, then, is a more complex picture of morality than that usually attributed to animals in a simplified model of Darwinian "survival of the fittest." Whether this behavior in animals corresponds to what we think of as moral, and whether we should further infer from this behavior that there is an underlying animal emotion that corresponds to the human emotions that drive similar behavior on our part are two important questions DeWaal does not address directly.

DeWaal does provide extensive evidence from animal behavior, however, that suggests animals exhibit behavior suggestive of an inborn sense that corresponds closely to what we might think of as morality. He provides numerous illustrations suggesting all social mammals—from elephants and dolphins to primates including humans—share four distinct characteristics that constitute the roots of a moral system. These traits are sympathy, hierarchy, reciprocity, and reconciliation.

1. *Sympathy*. DeWaal's observations of primates suggest all social mammals recognize one another as individuals and have feelings for one another. These feelings include sadness at long separations, happiness on being reunited, and the drive to help members who are in trouble in their community. Demonstrations of sympathy and concern include dolphins supporting an injured companion at the water's surface to keep it from drowning, an elephant returning to the spot where his mother died and touching her skull sympathetically, or an elephant herd trying to revive a young female elephant who was shot by a poacher and then, when their helpful efforts proved unsuccessful, spreading earth and branches over her body before they leave it. DeWaal argues that sympathy is the cornerstone of morality. It is sympathy that leads us to recognize the existence of others and to treat others with the consideration we would like to have shown us.

2. *Hierarchy*. DeWaal next suggests animals exhibit an inborn drive for hierarchy, another characteristic of morality he finds shared by animals and humans. Generally, DeWaal notes, all social mammals live in hierarchies and follow the rules enforced by the dominant group. Once the social order is established, breaking this order leads to the anticipation of punishment.[250] Primates will administer beatings, among other forms of punishment, to group members who break group rules.[251] DeWaal finds such behavior resembles the human need to enforce the rank and order of a community through the institutions of law, politics, and government. For DeWaal this demonstrates a sense of culture and a society that has rules and regulations that must be abided by. For the animals DeWaal studied, when behavior deviated from the norms of the group, punishment was effective and the established order was maintained.

3. *Reciprocity*. DeWaal notes a phenomenon closely related to dominance and hierarchy: reciprocity, a kind of *quid pro quo* that exists in all primate communities. Male chimpanzees, for example, pursue dominance and form coalitions that depend on mutual support during confrontations with their rivals. Repeated failure to support a partner destroys the coalition. Moreover, DeWaal finds some primates appear to remember who has hit them and will take revenge on these individuals afterward. Even in sharing food, primates tend to share food with those who have shared food with them in the past. For DeWaal this parallels the human need for fulfillment of obligations and keeping agreements. DeWaal concludes that primates have the intuitive ability to be generous and to expect a similar show of generosity in return.

4. *Reconciliation*. Finally, primates appear to resolve communal conflict over food, resources, and other social incidents in a similar manner. Reconciliation has to occur, and third parties play an important role in eliminating the conflict. Primates do this through grooming, embracing, or kissing in patterns that DeWaal finds evocative of forgiveness and mediation to maintain the peacefulness in the human community.

Space constraints limit fuller discussion of this research, but DeWaal's work illustrates the trends among primatologists to view human beings in evolutionary terms, not as a distinct moral species.[252] What we find in human beings, they argue, is a difference in degree, not a difference in kind. Thus, nonhuman animals share distinct aspects of a moral system that are akin to that of their human cousins. In particular, primatologists have gathered clear and striking scientific evidence that suggests psychological egoism is *not* all there is to our inherent primate nature. If our social nature exists as part of our primate genotype, our political theories should recognize this. When broken down to its most essential indicators—culture, language, and politics—morality can be found in animals. If it exists in all primates, the conclusion then must be that it exists in man as well, as part of our primate nature.[253]

Behavioral economics also sheds light upon how the presence of basic "moral emotions" could lead to cooperative economic outcomes. Samuel Bowles and Herbert Gintis have modeled a public goods game whereby in addition to personal material payoffs, subjects' utility functions can incorporate one's valuation of the payoff to others, one's "degree of reciprocity," and moral emotions such as guilt or shame at one's own or another's deeds; these factors can promote cooperation in a group setting. This tendency, they propose, points to the role of internalized norms building upon the moral emotions to construct socially optimal results. Such an "internalization of norms" serves to "eliminate(s) many of the cost-benefit calculations and replaces them with simple moral and prudential guidelines for action."[254] This means norm-internalizers are more "biologically fit than those who do not [internalize norms] so the psychological mechanisms of internalization are evolutionarily selected."[255]

The evolutionary and genetic implications of these findings have been plausibly modeled as well.[256] Such an approach provides a valuable addendum to the self-interest-based models[257] and its cognate parallels in biology.[258] In experimental situations, drives toward social motives—such as equality—have also been noted. Dawes and his colleagues (2007) found that in constructing a game isolating egalitarian motives, participants would alter the incomes of other players even at a cost to themselves, given a chance, when inequality was perceived. In other words, players' negative affect at inequality drove them to "reduce above-average earners' incomes and to increase below-average earners' incomes."[259] Dawes and his colleagues believe such behavior points to the evolutionary development of strong reciprocity."[260] This is an exciting area and I expect much work in this field in the future.[261]

A MORAL GRAMMAR

Recent work builds on this analogy but substitutes Chomsky's[262] model of innate linguistic grammar for math[263] and links this to Rawls's 1972 work on justice.[264] This work draws on evolutionary psychology, biology, linguistics, neuroscience, and primate cognition to argue that humans are endowed with a moral faculty that pronounces on right and wrong based on principles of action that are unconsciously derived.[265] The moral grammar consists of a set of principles that operate on the basis of the causes and consequences of action. Hence, just as we humans are endowed with the innate capacity for language, we also possess a moral faculty. We are born with a sense of abstract rules or principles. Nurture enters the picture to set the parameters and guide us toward the acquisition of particular moral systems. Empirical research distinguishes the principles from the parameters to discover limitations on the range of possible moral systems. It may be that the brain acts as a switchboard, lighting up when it recognizes certain problems as relevant for ethics. Many of the experiments noted here try to delimit stages in child development. For example, Marc Hauser finds three-year-olds already are aware of intention. They judge less severely acts that cause harm when the intention is good. Hauser deems this ability an innate way to detect cheaters who violate social norms.[266] Hauser rejects the Kantian perspective on morality as relying too exclusively on reason and principles, finding this Kantian view undermined by research[267] into the emotions.[268] This suggests people do not act by principled reasoning alone. Indeed, when questioned after an action, people frequently cite gut feelings or intuitions as their motivating force. Hauser also rejects the Humean position, however, which predicates the validity of a moral judgment on how one feels. If morality simply resides in how one feels—that is, it is grounded in individual self-reference—then, Hauser claims, moral pronouncements would be infinitely heterogeneous, atomistic, and internally inconsistent with a concept of morality as a referential behavior for a collective.[269]

Different locations (attitudes toward a moral dilemma) can be explained as variation from some mean. This is where the innate grammar analogy comes into play.

> Paralleling the story of language, one path to discovering whether our moral faculty consists of universal principles and parameters that allow for cultural variation is to tap into the anthropological literature with its rich descriptions of what people across the globe do when confronted with selfish and beneficent options.[270]

This suggests we might expect something akin to linguistic variation, that is, systematic differences among cultures based on parametric settings. These parametric settings explain diverse cultural responses in behavior and principles of harming and helping others.[271] "All societies have a normative sense of fairness. What varies between cultures is the range of tolerable responses to situations that elicit judgments of fairness. In essence, each culture sets the boundary conditions, by tweaking a set of parameters for a fair transaction."[272] For Hauser our moral judgments also reflect "intuition percolating up from unconscious and inaccessible principles of action."[273]

Hauser's work thus suggests we have a moral faculty that leads us to judge situations based on notions of fairness. This moral faculty is modeled after innate grammar: there are both strong and weak forms. The strong or nativist form argues that all content (rules, values, meaning, application) is innate. The weak form posits that a general principle is combined with some acquisition mechanism, which in turn provides content specificity. A hybrid form would argue that some content is innate but other content is acquired.[274] This makes the universal moral grammar a "theory about the suite of principles and parameters that enable humans to build moral systems. It is a toolkit for building a variety of different moral systems as distinct from one in particular. The grammar or set of principles is fixed, but the output is limitless within a range of logical possibilities."[275]

When applied to moral behavior, moral principles may be gleaned from anthropological sources. For instance, the edict "thou shall not kill" is a principle holding of many religions. Yet killing in the form of infanticide or honor killing is accepted by some cultures. These are exceptions to the rule. Hauser's moral faculty approach holds that examples of killing are permissible deviations (parametric settings according to culture). Thus Hauser accounts for societal and cultural variation of norms by positing an absolute norm that is universal but with local departures based on specific sociohistorical conditions.

> Underlying the extensive cross-cultural variation we observe in our expressed social norms is a universal moral grammar that enables each child to grow a narrow range of possible moral systems. When we judge an action as morally right or wrong, we do so instinctively, tapping a system of unconsciously operative and inaccessible moral knowledge. Variation between cultures in their expressed moral norms is like variation between cultures in their spoken languages. Both systems enable members of one group to exchange ideas and values with each other, but not with members of another group.[276]

He continues, "To say that we are endowed with a universal moral grammar is to say that we have evolved general but abstract principles for deciding which actions are forbidden, permissible, or obligatory. There are no principles dictating which particular sexual, altruistic, or violent acts are permissible."[277]

MORAL PSYCHOLOGY AND NEUROSCIENCE

Related advances in moral psychology also shed light upon the substrates of moral behavior in human evolution and on its legacy on the neuroscientific level. Building on Robert Trivers and Edward O. Wilson,[278] several research programs have converged upon results lending support to the moral sense hypothesis as features of the pressures of natural selection upon our human ancestors. Human selfhood likely arose as a pragmatic measure for perceiving and relating to objects (and fellow members of the species) in the external environment, making selfhood inherently relational. What likely arose originally as a "motor system ontology"[279] increasingly became a social "embodied simulation."[280] This simulation meant the actions of others were mimicked by the subject, to the point that the same neurons coding for the appropriate action would fire when either carrying out *or* observing the action concerned. This form of action and behavioral mimicking, first for physical behavior and eventually for facial expressions and affective empathy, depended upon specialized portions of the cortex dubbed "mirror neurons"[281] and led to what Gallese (2006) dubs "intentional attunement," an affective and social synchronization of behavior and mental states between two or more human subjects. This affective repertoire proves highly salient for accessing the emotions underpinning moral sentiments and behavior, including general empathy[282] and more specific feelings like disgust.[283] More specific findings about the emotional role provided in moral behavior pinpoints the ventromedial prefrontal cortex (VMPC), especially as assessed by tests of moral cognition of patients subject to VMPC damage.[284] Research into the neural bases of perceived fairness reveal that fairer offers in game-based experiments lead to greater activity in the ventral striatum, the VMPC, and the left amygdala, areas known to be "reward centers."[285] Reactions against unfairness also have physiological markers, such as increased skin conductance.[286] Cooperation can provoke similar neural reward responses, including the ventral striatum, rostral anterior cingulate cortex, and the medial orbitofrontal cortex.[287] Charitable donations similarly seem tied to frontal-mesolimbic structures, relying upon two parallel reward systems, one linking the ventral segmental area with mesolimbic areas and the ventral striatum (typically involved in pecuniary reward) and one including the subgenual area for donations. This is noteworthy since the subgenual area (at the nexus of the posterior part of the medial orbitofrontal cortex, the ventral cingulated cortex, and septal region) is tied to "social attachment and affiliative reward mechanisms in humans and other animals."[288] Decisions to donate similarly have their roots in measured compassion and anger. The opposition to donation had its own network of brain regions, comprising a network between the lateral-orbitofrontal cortex, the anterior insula, and the dorsolateral cortex; some of these have been previously implicated in the experience of disgust.[289] Altruism has often been linked to empathy,[290] and the neural mechanisms of empathy appear to be recruited for altruistic feelings. Perceiving the actions and intentions of others has been found to involve the posterior superior temporal cortex, particularly in the right hemisphere; variable activity in these regions has been linked to variation in levels of self-reported altruism.[291] Empathy itself also has correlates in the cerebral cortex; its perspective-taking manifestation results in activation of "middle insula, aMCC, medial and lateral premotor areas, and selectively in left and right parietal cortices."[292]

Additional studies have implicated key brain structures contributing to moral affect. When these are personal dilemmas in which danger or moral violation happens to immediate subjects, heightened activity arises in the medial frontal gyrus, posterior cingulate gyrus, and the bilateral superior temporal sulcus, while impersonal dilemmas activate more "working memory" segments, including the dorsolateral prefrontal cortex and the parietal cortex.[293] The superior temporal sulcus is particularly interesting since previous research implicates it in representations of "personhood" to which the subject socially responds. Hormonal elements likewise appear to support a human "moral sense," particularly that of oxytocin, the presence of which encourages trust in others,[294] as well as generosity.[295] The roots of oxytocin in human physiology also are clear for vicariously witnessing "morally elevating" stimuli. Breastfeeding women seeing a morally uplifting video were more likely to nurse their babies; they posit that "moral elevation may involve the release of oxytocin, a hormone affiliated with lactation and affiliation."[296] Other neurotransmitters also mediate reactions to perceived unfairness, such that serotonin-selective reduction of 5-HT levels in tested subjects made them more prone to retaliate against unfairness in a structured ultimatum game.[297] There are further reasons to suppose predispositions for a variety of moral emotions are directly genetic. In examining iterations of the classic "trust game," using two studies in Sweden and the United States, between monozygotic and dizygotic twins, researchers discovered that heritability explained a significant variance in the choice "to invest, and to reciprocate investment."[298] Recent work in social psychology also lends credence to elements of a moral sense, particularly the work of Haidt and his colleagues.[299] In constructing his social intuitionist model of moral judgment, Haidt makes explicit his debt to the Scottish Enlightenment scholars such as Hume: "Where do moral beliefs and motivations come from? They come from sentiments which give us an immediate feeling of right and wrong, and which are built into the fabric of human nature. Hume's answer . . . is our answer too."[300] Haidt's social intuitionist model draws upon previous work in social psychology[301] pointing to a "dual process" system in which an "intuitive" system responds quickly, effortlessly, and automatically, with its contents seldom available to introspection, and affectively laden. A second system is more ponderous, deliberate, linear, and devoted to serial reasoning, with limited computing power to bear on immediate objects of attention. The relative inaccessibility of such automatic processes to conscious thought[302] and the contribution of such automatic processes to moral behaviors like altruism[303] have been previously documented, and have laid the groundwork for social intuitionist models and experiments. Like others before him, Haidt proposes that the affective system is what leads in moral judgments and that much of what is deemed "moral reasoning" (à la Kant, Kohlberg, and others) is often in fact post hoc rationalizing of judgments already made. If moral reasoning does enter into the process, it is secondarily. Further, the social intuitionist model[304] identifies five repeatedly illustrated transcultural moral substrates for which human beings are likely innately prepared from birth. These five clusters include (1) harm/care, (2) fairness/reciprocity, (3) authority/respect, (4) unity/sanctity, and (5) in-group loyalty. According to Haidt and his colleagues:

> Moral development can now be understood as a process in which the externalization of five (or more) innate moral modules meets up with a particular set of socially constructed virtues. There is almost always a close match because no culture can construct virtues that do not mesh with one or more of the foundations.[305]

The emotions underlying the repertoire of social intuitions fall under four general "families" or clusters of emotions.[306] The first might be termed "other-condemning," including anger, contempt, and particularly disgust. The second consists of "self-conscious" emotions such as shame, embarrassment, and guilt. The third grouping of "other-suffering" emotions broadly includes those construed as compassion. Finally, "other-praising" emotions include affects such as gratitude, awe, and elevation. Each of these serves as a precursor to the moral prompts and decisions dealing with their appropriate targets.[307]

Conclusion

In this chapter I have presented both my own theory of moral choice and convincing evidence from a wide range of disciplines and methodologies that supports that theory. As we step back and take a theoretical reflection on this evidence and the theory of moral choice, we find several important contributions to political science. (1) Setting my empirical analysis of Holocaust behavior in the broader field of moral psychology reveals how knowledge gained by my analysis applies to other instances of prejudice and racial, ethnic, religious, and sectarian violence. Moral psychology as a field provides a lens through which we can discern surprising patterns and common themes in political situations that might otherwise seem unrelated. (2) Thinking about these patterns and common themes then reveals a broader theory of moral choice that suggests moral choice emanates not from conscious calculus but rather from the actor's sense of self in relation to others. (3) Findings in disciplines traditionally assumed tangential to political science point us to insightful evidence that makes sense of empirical findings that initially seem counterintuitive. The spontaneous aspect of moral choice provides just one illustration of this phenomenon. By setting this finding in the context of work suggesting how emotions focus our decision-making processes, however, the counterintuitive becomes clear and understandable. (4) The empirical evidence from a wide range of fields supports the claim that people have an innate ethical framework, much as we have an innate predisposition for language. Further, this empirical evidence fleshes out the underlying ethical framework I presented here and suggests other specific areas of fruitful future work scholars might explore to further our understanding of how people make moral choices. (5) Finally, the empirical evidence suggests Mother Nature may encode some ethical content on our ethical framework, actually predisposing us toward certain moral choices. The range, direction, and extent of this predisposition is far from clear, and I am not arguing in favor of moral sense theory as the definitive moral theory. Nonetheless, the analysis presented here does illustrate how political science can benefit from a more empirically based analysis of ethical issues. By drawing attention to the possible sources of such intuitions and promptings to act morally and thinking about the theoretical implications of these works, the intellectual payoff is clearly evident, not only in the form of the theory of moral choice presented here but also—I hope—in the development of other theoretical approaches that will further our understanding of ethics and moral choice.

Arguments derived from Utilitarianism (and buttressed by modern economics, at least in a simplified form) suggest humans adopt a calculative prompting of self-interest. Arguments developed from Kantian approaches suggest a role for obeying categorical rules. Both moral sense theory and my theory of moral choice draw attention to an alternative to these two important ethical theories, not necessarily in terms of normative implications but in terms of explanatory power. Empirically grounded theories provide scientific evidence about how it is humans are prompted to be moral, not why they should be moral. These are large and important questions and ones political scientists and ethicists should be addressing using all the evidence of science at their disposal.

The Psychology of Difference

IN 1937 A POLITICAL SCIENCE GRADUATE from the University of Chicago published a series of stories about a fictional immigrant named Hyman Kaplan,[1] an enthusiastic student of English taking night school classes with a Mr. Parkhill to obtain American citizenship.[2] Incapable of grasping the rules of English, Kaplan nonetheless exhibits a rare flair for logic and a joy of life that is infectious, if occasionally frustrating for his teacher. On the final examination, the students are asked to write an essay to demonstrate their grasp of basic grammatical principles. Kaplan's essay is titled *T*H*I*N*K*I*N*G A*B*O*U*T* and is punctuated, as is Kaplan's name on all his themes, with green stars between red letters outlined in blue. In this final essay, Kaplan explores the mysteries of grammar as they apply to the difference between "It is I" and "It is me." He does so by describing a stranger knocking on the door.

> If somebody is in hall besides my door, and makes knok, knok, knok; so I holler netcheral "Whose there"? Comes the anser "Its Me." A fine anser!! Who is that Me anyhow? Can I tell? No! So is "Its Me" no good.
>
> Again is knok, knok, knok. And again I holler "Whose there"? Now comes the anser. "Its I." So who is now that? Still can I (Kaplan) tell? Umpossible! So is "Its I" rotten also.
>
> So it looks like is no anser. (Turn around paige)
>
> As Mr. Parkhill turned the page "around" (Mr. Kaplan had interpreted "a one-page composition" with characteristic generosity), he could see how, put that way, the problem of "Its Me" or Its I" was a very Gordian knot.
>
> But must be som kind anser. So how we can find him out??? BY THINKING ABOUT. (Now I show how Humans isn't Enimals)
>
> If I am in hall and make knok, knok, knok; and I hear insite (insite the room) somebody hollers "Whose there"? I anser strong—"Its Kaplan"!!
>
> Now is fine! Plain, clear like gold, no chance mixing up Me, I, Ect.
>
> By Thinking is Humans making big edvences on enimals. This we call Progiss T-H-E E-N-D.
>
> Only after he had read the composition twice did Mr. Parkhill notice that there was a post-script to this expedition into the realm of pure logic. It was like the signature to a masterpiece.
>
> ps. I don't care if I don't pass, I love the class.[3]

Most scholars resemble the fictional Mr. Kaplan. We love our work and have great enthusiasm for it, even as we concede that we frequently miss much that is critical in our analyses. Like the ebullient Kaplan, we are grateful to the reader who allows us the privilege of *T*H*I*N*K*I*N*G A*B*O*U*T* these topics as we step back at the end of our studies to try to make sense of the broader themes that underlie our work and give meaning to our professional lives, acknowledging that much of what we do is more for ourselves than for the reader. As with Kaplan, passing the exam is not as important as loving the class.

As I think about my work I can see how events in my personal life influenced my work and how my work, in turn, changed me, leading me to view the world differently, making me aware of limitations in the traditional approaches to the discipline I love and heightening my commitment to interdisciplinary work and methodological pluralism as I search for fresher approaches to studying the normative bases of politics. It is to these themes that I now turn as I review what I have learned about altruism, moral choice, and the psychology surrounding the ethics of difference.

REFLECTING ON ALTRUISM AND MORAL CHOICE

Altruism and Moral Choice

In 1988 I was lucky enough to begin a project on altruism. My wish for every young scholar is to find such a research project, for it has taken me places I never knew existed, forcing me to reexamine the theoretical foundations of my parent discipline and the parameters of the dominant paradigms in social science, bringing together parts of my personal, professional, and intellectual life in ways I could not have anticipated and challenging me to see the world differently.

After a traditional introduction to the study of governmental institutions, political history, and international relations at Smith College, I encountered the neobehavioral revolution at the University of Chicago, where I fell in love with social science thanks to some extraordinary teachers in the political science department. Additional study in econometrics and political economy left me a rational actor theorist who approached the world intellectually by assuming people do what they perceive is best for them, subject to information and opportunity costs.

My rational approach to life crashed when my brother died from leukemia and I realized reason frequently left unexplained the most important issues in life, such as why good people die too early and what causes such deaths. Having my first child further reinforced the limitations of a rational, self-interested approach to human behavior. (People kept telling me I just had to let the baby cry himself to sleep. My reason told me it was cruel to let another person cry when all I had to do was pick him up to make him happy. But I soon realized reason had little to do with it. I simply was not programmed to let a baby cry.) I realized then that my rationalist, Enlightenment approach to life, while valuable, carried severe limitations. I needed alternate models to fully understand human behavior. (Why this realization was so long in coming is perhaps another interesting question.)

My personal and intellectual life converged professionally when I began examining the foundational assumptions of social science. I realized that neither altruism nor collective behavior—the stuff of politics—fit easily into the rational model, and I set out to figure out why this was the case. I began with altruism, reviewing the literature on altruism in social science and in fields as diverse as biology, religion, neuroscience, psychology, and philosophy. I found most scholarly analyses simply did not take seriously behavior that challenged the core assumptions of their own disciplinary paradigms. These theoretical paradigms included rational actor theory, psychological egoism, benefit/cost analysis, and evolutionary biology inter alia. Most explanations of altruism in these fields were simply veiled attempts to smuggle altruism into self-interest-based approaches.

Being empirically oriented, I designed a survey to test the diverse explanations for altruism.[4] This survey produced a range of questions to examine. Can you explain altruism through reciprocity, in which I help you now so you will help me later? Am I nice to you because doing so makes me feel good, as Hobbes supposedly posited? Do groups with altruists fare better in the long run, and hence deliberately protect their altruistic members? These were some of the questions I addressed by interviewing entrepreneurs (individuals who pursue their own self-interest) and altruists, arranged along a continuum from philanthropists to Carnegie Hero Commission recipients and rescuers of Jews during the Holocaust. To my surprise, none of the traditional explanations captured the critical influences driving the behavior of the people I interviewed.

The Altruistic Perspective

To understand the altruists I came to know, I gravitated to psychology and cognitive science for cues. Indeed, *The Heart of Altruism* argues that the critical explanation for altruism is psychological, a phenomenon I called the altruistic perspective to describe the particular way altruists have of viewing the world. Essentially, altruists see themselves as individuals at one with all humanity. Where the rest of us see a stranger, an altruist sees a fellow human being. I was further struck by the extent to which altruists' choices were limited by their perceptions of themselves in relation to others, perceptions that limited and constrained altruists' choice options, not just morally but cognitively. I concluded that identity sets choices for altruists, much as a menu in a restaurant limits the dinner choices.

I expanded my initial analysis of altruism with a more detailed consideration of rescue behavior as illustrative both of moral courage during war and genocides and of the psychological process driving moral choice. *The Hand of Compassion* used interviews with rescuers of Jews to consider some of the difficult but fascinating and important questions raised by the fact that identity works to constrain moral choice among altruists. (The title comes from a quote by a Czech rescuer, who said, "The hand of compassion was faster than the calculus of reason.") *The Hand of Compassion* related my empirical findings to the literature on identity at both the group and individual level to suggest the psychological process through which this empirical phenomenon may operate. I drew on the literature in social psychology to determine what causes shifts in perspective as individuals change the boundaries of those included in their communities of concern. I then set the empirical analysis of these rescuer narratives in the context of the literature on identity to construct a theory of moral choice that drew on identity, perspective, and categorization. This theory built on social identity theory and virtue ethics but relied more closely on two literatures not traditionally the domain of moral theory: (1) psychological work on the human need for consistency and self-esteem and (2) linguistic and psychoanalytic arguments regarding categorization.[5]

The Ethical Framework

The current volume expands my previous work to focus on two main questions. (1) What are the critical distinguishing psychological characteristics that explain the differential behavior of rescuers, bystanders, and supporters of genocide? (2) Does everyone have an ethical perspective, that is, does identity work its influence only for altruists or is there an analogous psychological process for everyone? Answering these questions proved critical in understanding the psychology surrounding genocide and ethnic cleansing.

I again found identity the central psychological variable with rescuers, bystanders, and Nazi supporters exhibiting dramatically different self-concepts. Identity constrained choice for all individuals, not just rescuers. Understanding identity helped decipher the speaker's ethical perspective and revealed how self-image provided content and moral specificity to a general ethical framework through which we think about moral choices. The critical parts of this ethical framework also became clear. Character and self-image are not all. A critical ethical aspect of identity is relational, having to do with the speaker's sense of self in relation to others and to the world in general. Hence, we need to decipher the speaker's worldview. (What is the actor's sense of agency? What does the actor think of as activities that constitute *normal* behavior? About what constitutes *proper* behavior? About what the good life is? About what it means to be a human being?) The ethical importance of values works through the fashion in which values are integrated into the speaker's sense of self and worldview. Personal suffering, in the form of past trauma, heightened awareness of the plight of others for rescuers; for bystanders and Nazis, however, it increased a sense of vulnerability that manifested itself in a defensive posture that served to heighten existing in-group/out-group distinctions. Finally, speakers' cognitive categorization systems carry strong ethical overtones. The dehumanization that accompanies genocide works through the reclassification of the "other" and is closely related to a sense of moral salience, the felt imperative to act to help another because of a feeling that another's suffering is relevant for the actor.

These findings provided an answer to my first question: What are the critical psychological differences found among rescuers, bystanders, and supporters? I found the three groups had critically different perceptions of themselves in relation to others. Rescuers see themselves as people strongly connected to others through bonds of a common humanity. This difference made them sensitive to the suffering of others and more inclined to try to help alleviate this suffering. One frequently offered explanation of bystander behavior suggests bystanders rationalize their lack of action through linking their initial refusal to help to a sense that the victims of genocide might have done something to deserve their plight. While I found shades of this, what was more critical was bystanders' striking sense of helplessness and low efficacy, suggesting bystanders felt it simply was beyond their ability to do anything to stop the Nazis. This less overtly conscious explanation was coupled with an incredible moral insensitivity expressed in many subtle ways, perhaps most strikingly in the surprising fact that only one bystander expressed remorse for their failure to help during the Holocaust. Finally, supporters of the Nazi genocide saw themselves as superior Aryan people who were under attack and therefore needed to strike preemptively to protect themselves and their community. It was the Nazi supporters and sympathizers who saw the world in terms of in-groups versus out-groups and saw those who were different as threats to their ontological security. The moral imagination was critical for all three groups. Rescuers were able to see and accept the tectonic shift in the political landscape ushered in by Hitler and to take action to counteract it, if only in a small way. Bystanders either were like ostriches, in denial about the Holocaust threat or were people who were slow to grasp what was happening and who minimized its existence. Nazis seemed remarkably unaware that they had done anything wrong and showed little repentance, shame, or even awareness of the reality of the Holocaust.

Perspective plays a critical role here. Perspective seemed to affect how all groups—rescuers, bystanders, and Nazi supporters—classified or categorized people. Tremendous moral implications for political and moral behavior resulted from this categorization. In part, rescuers seem to have adopted superordinate categories, thinking of all people as the same and thus deserving of equal treatment. This extensive rescuer categorization process searched for the common ties, not distinctions that separated people. The rescuers' categorization schema were broad and porous, such that all people could exhibit individual and group differences but also could still be placed into the common category of human being. This common category took on a superordinate moral status in which all people deserve to be treated with respect and dignity.

Bystanders and Nazi supporters did not employ this same broad categorization schema, being more comfortable in the cognitive world of "us and them" with the exclusive in and out-group categories that social identity theory captures so aptly. Nazis had rigid and hierarchical categorization schema, with Nazis at the top. For all individuals, however, the cognitive process by which the people in this book viewed others—their categorization and classification of others and their perspective on themselves in relation to these others—played a critical role in identity's influence on moral action. This cognitive process included an affective component that served as a powerful emotional reaction to another's need. This reaction in turn provided the motive to actively try to effect change. This appeared to work through the evoking of a particular self-concept. A critical part of the process by which perspective influenced moral choice involves the manner in which the external environment taps into the actors' core self-concept. For rescuers the self-concept was distinguished by a self-image as people who were connected to others through a common humanity. For bystanders the self-image was as people who had no control over their actions, who were weak, passive, and low in efficacy. For Nazis the self-image was as a superior people under attack from lesser beings.

This discussion of the importance of perspective returns us to the second question: Does everyone have an ethical framework? Yes, and the basic ethical framework we all possess acts as a kind of cognitive scaffolding through which we process ethical choices. This scaffolding gets filled in by life experiences for each individual to produce a particular ethical perspective, a way of viewing the world and ourselves in it that is unique to each of us. The altruistic perspective I first noted for rescuers thus is only a small part of a broader cognitive framework possessed by all people.

I believed it important to use my findings on moral choice during the Holocaust to construct a more general theory. Existing scientific knowledge of the workings of the human brain make it difficult to specify precisely when and how different factors influence acts that are as complex as moral choice, and I expect future work will both build upon and correct my initial theoretical thoughts. Nonetheless, to understand moral choice it seems clear we need to consider two critical psychological components: (1) the ethical framework and (2) the ethical perspective. Doing so suggests the following theory of moral choice, one I can summarize succinctly: Our moral choices reflect our basic sense of who we are in relation to others. Identity constrains moral choice through setting the range of options we perceive as available, not just morally but cognitively. Identity is created by some combination of nature and nurture, with the relevant ethical identity being constructed by how an innate ethical framework gets filled in by life experiences unique to the individual. Thus life experiences and innate personality characteristics work together to produce the actor's sense of who he or she is in relation to others, the actor's worldview, sense of agency and ontological security, and the values integrated into the actor's sense of self. All of these forces then produce an ethical perspective through which the actor views the world, others around her, and the situations demanding a moral choice. Cognitive classification or categorization, canonical expectations, idealized cognitive models, the moral imagination, and the menu of choice options effectively are produced from this ethical perspective through which the actor views the world.

This general psychological process results in moral acts that often appear spontaneous. Moral behavior does not result merely from conscious deliberation, although such conscious deliberations indeed may enter the equation. But our moral acts also reflect intuitions and emotions that affect how we see ourselves in relation to others, generally and at the time of action. What we say we have chosen consequently may reflect who we are as much as—perhaps even more than—any conscious calculus based on reasoning.

This theory makes identity central to moral choice. Predicting moral choice requires us to understand the ethical perspective of the actor at the moment action is taken. It is the ethical perspective that constitutes the link between the social and the individual influences on behavior. It creates the sense of moral salience that determines the felt imperative to act and it sets the menu of available choices that determines the specific type of action we will follow, whether that choice takes the form of helping and peaceful cooperation, standing by and doing nothing, or the stereotyping and prejudice that deteriorates into ethnic, religious, racial, and sectarian violence, including ethnic cleansing and genocide.

The Value of an Interdisciplinary Approach

My examination of the empirical link between identity and moral action utilizing extensive narrative interviews from the Holocaust highlighted three critical psychological phenomena: (1) the desire for self esteem and the need for continuity of self image; (2) core values stressing the sanctity of life and human well being, values that then are integrated into our underlying concept of who we are; and (3) external stimuli that trigger critical aspects of our multifaceted and complex identity in a way such that we notice and accord moral salience to the suffering of others.

These findings further illuminate the psychology underlying responses to the suffering of others. They suggest it is the critical parts of the ethical perspective—categorization, worldview, canonical expectations, idealized cognitive models, the moral imagination, but above all identity—that constitute the forces moving us beyond generalized feelings of sympathy, sorrow, or even outrage to a sense of moral imperative, a feeling that another's distress is directly relevant for us and thus requires our intervention and assistance. Deciphering an actor's ethical perspective suggests why some people take positive action to help when most of us ignore others' misery, thereby providing indirect or tacit support for the conditions that engendered such misfortune. This discovery can lend insight into the psychological forces driving responses to both other genocides and to the forms of ethnic violence and prejudice that precede and foster genocides. When such work is set in the broader context of research on moral choice, it can bring into focus the psychological dimension of ethics to shed light on one of the central themes in normative political science: how we treat others.

I was aided in my efforts to understand these questions by adopting an interdisciplinary approach, which left me free to draw on findings from a wide range of fields. Using narrative interviews, which allowed the speaker to reveal his or her own mind and thought process, also was immensely helpful and I encourage political scientists to break free of the overreliance on survey research, just as I encourage journal editors to be more willing to extend scholars the larger amount of precious journal space necessary for a narrative analysis. I am convinced I would not have been able to detect the more subtle influences on moral choice without following the less traveled routes in my research.

Importance of Narrative

I have already suggested the insights that stories can yield on the causes of genocide, including their ability to highlight critical differences between bystanders and supporters of genocide and rescuers. These stories also offer insight into the popular notion that genocide is the result of ancient hatreds that simmer to the surface or that genocide results from an ignorant, naive populace being manipulated for the leaders' own political ends. It seems clear that genocide results from some interplay between identity and the contextual or situational factors that tap into certain aspects of our complex identities, sometimes making us feel trapped and hostile, primed to strike against those we believe threaten us while at other times responding without such animosity, with sympathy for the other guy, understanding that we all are in the same boat and can help one another.[6] In general, psychological factors are crucial. The key to unlocking the puzzle of genocide is the particular type of cognitive categorization processes employed by those who participate in genocide. If we feel connected to those with whom we feel bonds, we will respond differently to their suffering than if we see ourselves as removed, distinct, different, and apart from them. There is a dissipation of our moral energy, and distancing facilitates the dehumanization that occurs with genocide.

Narratives are not only a research methodology. People need narratives to make sense of their own and others' acts and to describe the foundations of their group's collective identity. Narratives are created through dialogue, through relationships. They supply frameworks in which people are positioned differently. People will construct narratives centered on themes that help them confront fundamental life issues. Framing these narratives can have a strong impact on the ethical component of our interactions.[7] It is evident that each person who lived through the Holocaust had his or her narrative and these narratives related closely both to their acts at the time and to their remembrance of the Holocaust. One important part of individual narratives relates closely to the critical assumption of social identity theory: the assumption that group memberships create self-categorization in ways that naturally favor in-groups at the expense of out-groups. The Holocaust narratives I heard suggest social identity theory's conceptualization of how people think about social identity may lead to an overly deterministic view of identity development, one that does not allow sufficiently for identity's ability to shift and thus alter our choices. Underscoring the importance of perspective—and the emphasis on relationality that perspective captures—can perhaps yield more flexible understanding of how people respond to group differences than one that assumes an automatic in-group identity preference. The in-group/out-group categories are not necessarily rigid entities; they can shift.

Further, we must ask not just how people construct categories but how they accord moral salience to these categories and how the framing of categories can result in more ethical treatment of others. Rescuers, for example, clearly drew distinctions between Jews and Nazis; indeed, they had to in order to engage in rescue acts. But they did not accord moral salience to these categories. Both Jews and Nazis were supposed to be treated as human beings. Instead, rescuers constructed a broader or an alternative category that was deemed morally salient. For rescuers, the morally salient category was the human race, not ethnicity, religion, political affiliation, etc.

This raises a further important question: Is it the recognition of common membership in a category that is necessarily relevant, as social identity theory would seem to suggest? Or is it merely that shared membership in a category makes it *more* likely that one will treat other members of the same category well? It may be that the cognitive recognition of a shared category tends to accord moral salience, but this may not necessarily be the case. The empirical evidence offered in the stories analyzed here suggests the need to modify and build on social identity theory to incorporate the according of moral salience to identity categories. It is not enough to say that people divide the world into divisions of in-group/out-group. We must ask both how the categories are first constructed and then how the categories are accorded moral salience.

Perspective as the Link among Treatment of Others, the Lack of Choice, and Identity

How can we explain the surprising lack of conscious choice described in all our narratives? The important role played by our ethical frameworks and perspectives can perhaps best be illustrated by focusing on the altruistic perspective as an example. Perspective links altruists' self-images to the circumstances of those in need by highlighting the needy person's situation in a way that then accords a moral imperative to the plight of others. By tapping into this particular self-concept, the suffering of others became morally relevant for the rescuers, in the way the plight of one's child, spouse, or parent would be salient for most of the rest of us. Because the value of caring for others is so deeply integrated into altruists' self-concepts, it forms self-images that constitute the underlying structure for their identities. This self-concept translates and transforms altruists' knowledge of another's need into a moral imperative requiring them to take action. It did so by linking the self-concept to certain types of behavior that were considered acceptable on the moral menu.

The fact that the rescuers felt a moral imperative to help is evident most strikingly in rescuers' canonical expectations (the statements that revealed rescuers' implicit assumptions about what ordinary decent people should do) and rescuers' implicit cognitive models (their ideas about what it means to be a human being or what constitutes the good life). These unspoken expectations about what is acceptable behavior are deeply embedded in an altruist's psyche. They reflect the rescuers' idealized cognitive models about what it means to be a human being. They are revealed in rescuers' description of what is—and what is not—in their repertoire of behavior. As one rescuer (Margot) said, "You don't walk away. You don't walk away from somebody who needs real help." Or Margot's statement capturing her idea of what it means to be human: "[The] ability to help and alleviate the pain of fellow human beings . . . is the ultimate goal of our short existence on this earth." Other rescuers expressed similar phrases linking their idealized cognitive models to behavior, almost as if reading from a common menu of moral behavior available to them. Witness Madame Trocmé's question: "How can you refuse them?" John's insistence that "when you have to do right, you do right." Or his belief that happiness is the goal of life, and that happiness comes from helping others. And all the rescuers' insistence that "there is no choice" when clearly objectively there indeed *was* an alternative choice that existed; truth be told, if such an option had not existed, there would have been no need for rescue behavior in the first place.

But for rescuers—as for other altruists—all people within the boundaries of their community of concern were to be treated the same, and their circle of concern included all human beings. This perception of a shared humanity triggered a sense of relationship to the other that then made the suffering of another a concern for the rescuers. Significantly, this extensivity included Nazis, with the rescuers demonstrating extraordinary forgiveness of Nazis. It is this role of perspective to classify and categorize people and then to work through a cognitive process of moral salience that provides the link between the lack of choice and identity on the one hand and the variation in our treatment of others. It is what makes the bystanders' much-touted claims "not to know" so critical. I believe it cracks the code that Primo Levi refers to in depicting how ordinary people became accomplices to genocide.

> In Hitler's Germany a particular code was widespread: those who knew did not talk; those who did not know did not ask questions; those who did ask questions received no answers. In this way the typical German citizen won and defended his ignorance, which seemed to him sufficient justification of his adherence to Nazism.[8]

It is this pernicious code that allows genocide to exist. Shift the perceptions and the categorization, and the code crumbles.

The Importance of Categorization

The tremendous power of the human mind to limit our choices is stamped everywhere in our genocide narratives. Nowhere is this more important than in the ethical significance of categorization. The ethical consequences of this categorization process were evident in all of the people interviewed. Categorization is something everyone does. It is a fundamental part of our psychological make-up as human beings. The way in which we see the world and others in relationship to us in the world is defined by this categorization process. The differences in this ethical perspective are closely related to differences in behavior.

Genocidalists and their supporters—such as Florentine—see themselves as a people under attack. There is an outlandish and bitter irony to this, for in the genocidalists' worldview, victims are seen as threats. Florentine genuinely seemed to believe that the Jews were threatening her world and hence had to be destroyed. At some level, I had difficulty believing her interview and similar Nazi statements to this effect. Only when I translated the situation into terms closer to home could I fully comprehend the ethical role played by categorization, and the subtle, insidious way in which categorization influences our behavior. A personal anecdote may help me explain this process.

My family and I moved back to California in the fall of 1993. Then, as now, the university was in the midst of a massive period of construction of faculty homes.[9]

All the homes were the same, tending toward the undistinguished beige for which Irvine has become so justly famous. And all the yards were brown mud. Those familiar with Southern California will know that yards do not grow; they arrive on trucks. Our truck had arrived slightly ahead of most of our neighbors' and it was picnic time for the local beasties at my new household. The snails were particularly happy with our truck's arrival, feasting on the newly planted zinnias and marigolds.

I was sitting in our new garden one day, seven months pregnant with our third child, working on a review essay on genocide. As I sat, book balanced on belly, reading about the Holocaust, my then husband came out of the house and began to pick up snails and put them into a plastic bag.

"What are you doing?" I asked him.

"I'm putting the snails in a bag so they'll suffocate," he replied. "It'll be safer for the baby not to have all that poison around from the snail bait. And it's more humane than stepping on the snails."

My mind had been preoccupied with reading arguments among German public health officials during the Holocaust. Some medical officials wanted to avoid culpability and guilt by putting the Jews into ghettoes where they would die slowly and naturally from starvation and diseases induced by malnutrition. Others argued it was more humane to kill the Jews quickly.

The similarities were striking. "Can we talk about this a minute?" I asked.

We discussed our dilemma and decided to let the snails enjoy our zinnias; we would plant flowers the snails wouldn't want to eat.

In my more whimsical moments, I wonder if perhaps the little girl that was to become Chloe heard our conversation. Whatever the cause, three years later, I returned home to find Chloe had brought in all her little snail friends from the garden and was enjoying snail races with them in our family room. Most of the snails were concentrated on the glass doors facing onto the patio, just a few paces from the spot where Chloe's parents had once plotted the destruction of the ancestors of Chloe's new pets.

Deep-seated prejudices die hard, but I did permit Chloe to keep her newfound friends in the house for the rest of the evening. I recoiled, however, at letting her kiss them good night. (I shamefully retreated into Mommy-speak, suggesting Chloe's germs in her mouth could hurt the snails.) Certainly, I was less surprised than my daughter to learn that the snails had mysteriously figured out how to open the door and had returned to the garden while Chloe was safely asleep.

Some years later, when Chloe was in sixth grade, she had to do a science project. Chloe chose to work with snails. It was the wrong time of year for snails in Irvine and we soon discovered that pet stores do not sell ordinary snails. So I found myself spending my walking time looking carefully for snails. I was lucky and what I now viewed as three extremely precious snails participated in Chloe's science experiment testing whether snails prefer walking on grass, wood, or dirt.[10]

The point of this story? How we categorize snails has much to do with our treatment of them. For the three-year-old Chloe, snails were her friends. They were classed in the category of family pets, to be loved just as we loved our cat, Peppermint. To me, initially snails were slimy and disgusting things that ate my flowers. They were subhuman, not to be mourned if crushed beneath a human foot. Only when I saw someone I love value snails did I begin to see the snails' value, too. What led me to overcome my existing classification was reconceptualizing snails through my daughter's eyes; I then saw the snails' worth because of this shift in their place in my ethical perspective. It was my affection for my daughter that pushed me to construct an alternative conceptualization, a different narrative about the snails in relation to myself. Emotion, not logic, caused me to recategorize.

How do we draw on this experience for modification of intolerant attitudes and behavior in our daily lives? I am not sure, although I have conducted several years of a class experiment designed to use empathic involvement, via extensive narrative interviews with someone who is "different," as a way to increase tolerance of differences.[11] Without in any way suggesting human beings are on a par with snails, I wonder if a similar categorization process may explain some of our ethical and political treatment of other human beings. I try to relate what I learned about my response to snails—and how I shifted my attitudes, however subtly, in response to the affection held for snails by someone I love—and apply that to my academic work, to provide a more personal context for reading my interviews and thinking about genocide, ethnic cleansing, and the prejudice that too frequently accompanies differences. Doing so reminds me of a time when women were classified into separate categories, deemed inferior beings to men, unable to handle their own legal affairs or to make their own decisions. Indeed, this remains the case in too much of the world today. I am further embarrassed and baffled as I recall that African Americans were classed as only three-fifths people by the founding fathers, denied the human, civil, and legal rights of other Americans.[12] Or how gay Americans are still denied that most fundamental right—to marry the person you love—in most American states today. Reading about animal behavior prepared me to be equally ashamed as we learn more about the cognitive and emotional lives of the beasts we capture and use for the welfare of human beings, secure in our knowledge that these animals are in a separate category. "They" are "different" and thus somehow "less than" we are.

This categorization explains what can only be viewed as a legacy of exclusion in liberalism's universal ethic. Scholars have noted that liberalism talks a great deal about the rights of man but ignores the fact that the universal ethics of liberalism effectively excluded half the people (all the women) living in the world.[13] Scholars have similarly noted liberalism's mission to civilize the colonial world—white man's burden, Christianity's mission to convert the heathen—effectively relegated members of certain groups to second-class status because of their differences, be these religious, sectarian, ethnic differences, or so on.[14] This sidestepping around differences seems precisely the kind of categorization problem that my theory of moral choice addresses. I do not believe differences need to present either the exclusion of classical liberalism or the harsh group politics that identity politics unfortunately has come to mean in contemporary American society, in which groups frequently are pitted against each other in a zero-sum game that ignores the shifts and multiplicity of identity.[15] Some of what changes attitudes toward political differences—some of what shifts a difference once deemed politically important into a category where it is no big deal politically or ethically—is legal and political work traditionally defined. But some of it is simply a reflection of ordinary people who know members of the different group, who come to feel affection for individual members of the "different" group, and hence reclassify members of the discriminated-against group without being aware of doing so. (The current response to gay marriages seems such a transition with the public, especially young people, simply not understanding why gay marriage is seen a threat to the American way of life.[16])

If an analysis of rescue behavior suggests anything it is that what we want to foster is the recognition of differences, allowing—indeed, encouraging—all individuals to experience and cherish all of the multitudinous facets of their complex personalities, from the individual ethnic, religious, and racial differences to all the other characteristics that make one human being distinct and unique. People should be able to pick up and take off these diverse identities as they—not society—choose. Nor do we want to deny people rights because of these differences or to trap people in a special category, expecting or forcing them to act certain ways because of who they are: a woman, a Muslim, a Chinese, a homosexual, a Jew, etc.[17] The trick is to encourage differences as the individual—and group—expression of identity, while cherishing those variations as part of the flourishing of individual uniqueness within the context of our shared humanity. This seems to be the model provided for us empirically by the rescuers.

I wonder about the importance of categorization when I think about the Holocaust. I have argued that the basic idealized cognitive models for people who rescued Jews was such that "human-being" functioned as a basic level category for rescuers, while for the Nazis a specific set of people ("Germans" or "my family" or "my nation") functioned as their most basic level of categorization for sociopolitical life. What does this suggest about the categorization and dehumanization that occurs in other forms of ethnic and racial violence? Does a process of declassification and recategorization occur *before* people feel justified in mistreating and eventually killing other human beings? Is it the cognitive shift in reclassification that is key in shifting behavior, or are there other, more material causes for ill-treatment of a group—such as the desire for a group's land, its material goods or jobs—that lead to the reclassification as a justification? That is, does the cognitive reclassification occur *after* the fact, as a justification for acts desired for more materialistic ends, or does it lead to the seeing of possible gains from the reclassification? Analysts are only now beginning to address such issues. But logically, if we can declassify people, we also should be able to reclassify in an upward manner. The process, in other words, should work both ways.

Recategorization and Ethics

This fact brings us to the topic that drives most scholars of genocide: how do we stop genocide and prevent genocides from even starting? If we categorize, we can recategorize. We do not live in a world in which categories are inevitable or fixed. We socially construct them and then make them politically and ethically relevant.

This means that we can shift them or reconceptualize them so these categories do not have political or ethical relevance. All of which raises the question: how anchored are we to our original conceptual categories? What makes us change? What causes us to recategorize in ways that increase the ethical context, shifting people closer to the altruistic part of the ethical continuum? If certain categorizations lead us to different types of ethical behaviors, then how do we get to these categorizations? All of these questions are important if we wish to decipher the moral psychology.

Categories serve to legitimate social relations[18] and the tendency to categorize is an inherent part of human nature. But the boundaries of categories are often porous, shifting, and not all are morally salient. Critics of social identity theory[19] have argued that the original Tajfel studies were based on the minimal group paradigm, which assumes that there is only one set of categories through which participants in the experiment could make sense of the situation. Further, these categories were imposed by the experimenters. So, for example, in an experiment on classification of eye color, the categories offered meant that respondents could classify a student as a blue-eyed student or a brown-eyed student, but not as a student with hazel eyes. The social categories that were offered as salient were given an unchangeable nature.

In reality, of course, things are much more complex. Most of us have lived through a historical time period when Europeans moved from thinking of themselves as French or German or English with competing interests to Europeans united against the United States or Asia in order to gain economic well-being. Many of us have historic memory of problems in the Balkans, where feuding seemed endemic until Tito united the area into Yugoslavia. Indeed, many of us grew up thinking the "Balkan problem" that had given us World War I was a thing of the past. Then, after Tito's death, the area disintegrated into the Balkans again and the world saw the Bosnian ethnic cleansing, linked to old memories of rivalries that Tito had suppressed. Why did this happen? How did it happen? Was the peaceful Yugoslavia just a temporary process, imposed by the powerful personality of one individual? A geopolitical identity reaction against two powerful external forces, with the Yugoslavs not wanting to be Western but not wanting to be simply another Communist state in the Soviet orbit? How did identity relate to this situation and to the peaceful nature of the conflict? Did Yugoslavia revert to prior identities—some of which warred against each other—once the Cold War ended and there was no longer a reason to be united in order to avoid being swallowed up by the Soviet bloc?

This illustration suggests a critical factor in alleviating ethnic conflict may be the creation or the presentation of alternative identity categories for people. People who rescued Jews during the Holocaust, for example, consistently described themselves in terms and categories that made it clear that their identity and their salient identification was with all humanity. They did not act on the basis of an identity that was Christian or Jewish, Dutch or Pole, or even as Nazi or Nazi opponent. They had multiple identities, yes; but the superordinate identity was the one that was morally salient.

The permeability of group boundaries may be relevant ethically; so might the existence of cognitive alternatives to the status quo, the actions of common group members, the legitimacy of inequalities, and practical constraints on claiming valued resources. Each of these factors may complicate the simple us-versus-them group dynamic.[20] Better empirical work is required here. A basic question concerns whether or not—and under what circumstances—group membership gets translated into in-group cohesion and divisive intergroup behavior, such as ethnic political violence. If we want to understand why groups sometimes conflict and other times cooperate in peaceful group coexistence, this is a critical question that must be addressed.

Empirical findings in this area are vast and occasionally contradictory. Much more empirical work, especially on group behavior outside the laboratory, is required to provide both theoretical and empirical insight into group political activities. For example: How much do individuals differ in their willingness to internalize group membership? To vilify members of the out-group? It seems obvious that there is tremendous variation in group prejudice, among many groups: among whites in their support of racism,[21] among men in their exhibition of sexism,[22] among non-Jews in their expressions of anti-Semitism,[23] and so on. Asking about individual variation in identification with groups would seem to be a critical question insofar as it touches on the extent to which an individual's behavior is influenced more by societal pressures and group membership or is a product of free agency. My finding on the lack of choice suggests this psychological process works through identity and thus returns us to the need to understand identity and how it shifts in response to external stimuli.

A closely related question concerns the extent to which people who dislike one group tend to also dislike and discriminate against members of other groups as well, in which case we may need to look at the individual for an explanation—as did authors writing on the authoritarian personality.[24] Social identity theory does not speak to these differences in individuals and how these individual differences impact intergroup behavior. It relies more on the minimal group situation in which group membership is assigned in the laboratory experiment. But because experimenters seldom ask how deeply this group identity is integrated into the participants' sense of self, it is hard for researchers to get a good hold on the importance of individual differences in terms of the roles they play in the adoption of the group identity once they leave the laboratory setting.

The analysis of findings in this book attempts to speak to this concern. The work on rescuers showed that integration of values (and their subsequent role in creating an altruistic personality) was critical; this suggests we need to know more about this integrative process among the individuals who are *not* morally exemplary. The particular comparison of matched cases examined here was constructed to hold constant (as much as one ever can) these individual background variables and then look at the importance of group membership and membership in exclusionary versus cosmopolitan or universal groups.

The sense of fatalism that runs through the worldviews of all the people featured in this book—other than Tony—is closely linked to a lack of choice described by all these speakers. Blood bonds, the movement of history that an individual cannot escape, the lack of a concept of individual agency, all these constitute a striking part of the Nazi worldview. This worldview can be characterized as an us-versus-them mentality: if you are not with someone you are against them. This worldview, and its us-versus-them mentality, was reflected in the arguments for cultural separatism that we saw in extreme form in Florentine and in a milder form in both Kurt and Beatrix. The idea that there are separate races, and that these races correspond to ethnicity or geography or nation, is more widespread perhaps than we would like to acknowledge. In the contemporary political world, people frequently speak, for example, of the Caucasian or the African race. Biology is often used as a touchstone for people who engage in discussions of cultural separatism. Yet biologically every human being is a member of the same race. Cultures do differ, of course, and should be respected for their differences. But these cultures, nations, and ethnic groupings are man-made; they are socially constructed. They are not differences created by biology, Mother Nature, or any divine being. They are not immutable.

The rescuer self recognized this and refused to accept the Nazi's political form of categorization, even when forced into law by the Third Reich. The rescuer's sense of self and the rescuer categorization schema is evident in discussions about the rescuers' sense of their community. Contrary to what many analysts suggest, strong community ties are more frequently associated with the genocidalist than with the rescuer. Community is used more often to exclude people, providing the members of the in-group a status that then seems to offer a justification for—if not a contributing factor in—excluding nonmembers, even so far as designating them "life unworthy of life,"[25] as is done in genocide and ethnic cleansing.

Rescuers have a larger sense of community. Their community is open. It is porous. It is not limited to a nation, a religion, a political affiliation, or to any other subcategory. In thinking about the rescuers and the implications of their particular ethical perspective for understanding the political important of differences—and the prejudice and violence that often accompanies such differences—we can learn from anthropologists and animal ethologists whose work reveals the importance of a fission-fusion social structure in which boundaries between groups are permeable and malleable.[26] The experiences of human hunter-gatherers suggest small bands often merged, split, or traded members for a while and that this kind of fluidity helped solve social and environmental resource problems. The suggestion is that fluid group boundaries can increase familiarity and cooperation instead of the all or nothing groups we associate with the aggressive male chimps, where we have only our own group and that of the enemy.

Is it possible to maximize the interactions across group lines, thus encouraging the kind of fluid boundaries that work on primates suggests might help encourage cooperation among human beings? Again I return to work in social identity theory and to recent work on categorization that describe experiments that suggest the mere designation of groups leads to distancing. These somewhat pessimistic findings are supported by recent work on brain imaging, which suggests that humans may be hardwired to respond negatively when they see people of other races. The amygdala—a part of the body that plays a critical part in fear and aggression—becomes very active when people see faces from different races. But Susan Fiske conducted experiments that show that if you subtly bias the subject beforehand to think of people as individuals rather than as members of a group, then the amygdala does not budge.[27] "Humans may be hard-wired to get edgy around the Other, but our views on who falls into that category are decidedly malleable."[28]

The possibility of this is clear from our analysis of rescuers' categorization schema. All people are part of the human race for rescuers. The rescuers' boundaries and categorization schema do not fit easily into an us-versus-them mentality. This is closely related to the rescuers' sense of self and the rescuers' values. We find this reflected in Tony, who had an incredibly resilient personality, as witness his reaction to the trauma of war. War freed Tony from the need to cling to past moorings. It freed him of the need for bourgeois distinctions and status. It let him see people—including himself—in a different way. It is hard to determine whether the other people analyzed here exhibited varying degrees of fear because of the war or because of more internal, innate parts of their psychological makeup.[29] What is clear is that the values held by Tony, particularly his incredible commitment to the sanctity of life, entered strongly into his sense of self. This value did not enter into the self-image of anyone else featured in this book. The sense of self that is triggered for the rescuer because of the integration of this one critical value into the rescuer self-image thus differs in important ways from the self-image of other people interviewed here. It is this factor, I believe, that explains the feeling of moral salience. This moral salience is the sense that another's suffering is relevant for me, and therefore this necessitates an act on my part to help alleviate that suffering because I am not the kind of person who ignores injustice and suffering. The sense of moral salience is the critical variable that explains the drive to act on the part of rescuers. It worked much as the fatalism and sense of helplessness worked to limit choice for the bystanders, and as the genocidalists' self-image as a people under attack led them to strike out in a preemptive strike, killing the "other" before "they" kill us "us."

As I constructed my identity theory of moral choice and thought about why categorization and classification of others would exert such strong influence on our treatment of them, I turned to work in religion and work in animal behavior on fairness. I was surprised by some of the experiments I found, suggesting animals, not just human beings, become disturbed at differential treatment of members in the same group. Dogs asked to shake hands do so willingly and are happy with a pat on the head, until other dogs are rewarded with treats, at which point the first group of dogs will refuse to shake hands with the experimenters.[30] Monkeys exhibit the same behavior, performing happily for cucumbers until one of their members gets a grape, considered a tastier and preferred reward.[31] The psychological mechanism at work here is actually quite simple. Each of us—even monkeys and dogs—wants to be treated well. Recognizing that others have similar needs leads us to extend these universal rights of entitlement reciprocally, treating others as we ourselves wish to be treated. The moral psychology thus is reminiscent of tenets found in religious teachings and philosophical systems of ethics. ("Do unto others as you would have them do unto you.") Insofar as this ethical reciprocity is a fundamental correlate of the human capacity for intersubjective communication and the need to distinguish boundaries via categorization, ethical reciprocity resembles an innate moral grammar and is more fundamental than an intellectualized sense of duty or religion. Indeed, the power of religious and philosophical admonitions actually may emanate from their resonance with the basic moral psychology.

Perhaps the ethical framework originates in a kind of innate moral sense, born into all people, which then develops differentially in phenotypic fashion, depending on external forces in the environment. There is convincing scientific evidence supporting the idea of universal drives that can be said to constitute a biologically prepared moral architecture within human nature. Not limited to self-interest, these include what might be called a moral sense, akin to the olfactory lobes that provide us with a sense of smell or the hard wiring for a kind of moral grammar. This evidence suggests all human beings are born with the prototypes of a sense that fosters anxiety when they witness others in distress and, similarly, promotes positive feelings when that distress is alleviated. This empirical evidence suggests human beings are born with substrates of a moral faculty hard wired into their neural circuitry. The normative implication is that agents of socialization traditionally said to inculcate ethics actually may be reinforcing parts of an instinctive moral sense. I expect to see more extensive documentation of this in the years to come. All scholars concerned with ethics—political psychologists, political scientists, philosophers, policy makers—need to take such findings into consideration as they construct theoretical work and build accurate models for empirical research on political behavior.

My own work on this topic barely scratches the surface. It is suggestive and prelusive; I hope it is helpful for others who will follow. Like our friend Hyman Kaplan, I have loved the journey even if I have not taken us very far. I have delighted in work that forced me to think about the ethical foundations of political psychology and political science as disciplines. Studying altruism and the kind of moral courage demonstrated by rescuers and having to consider the less morally uplifting forms of ethical behavior by others during the Holocaust highlighted the sharp contrasts necessary to bring into relief the critical aspects of moral choice. This, in turn, revealed an alternative way of viewing ourselves, a way that does not pit individual self-interest against others' but one that underlines the importance—for ourselves—of how we relate to others.[32] How we form more inclusive groups raises interesting questions for me—for all of us—concerning our ties to others and what we need to flourish as individual human beings. Deciphering the ethical importance of identity thus leads us to consider our needs for human connection and human flourishing. This work forces us to think about what it means to be a human being and what we want as we live in a world with others. It shows us that our need for others is more than a longing for their cooperation in our own individualistic enterprises or even for their help in ensuring individual survival in a harsh world. It reminds us that it is a fundamental part of our human nature to crave acceptance, validation, and affirmation from others. We can find self-esteem and self-respect only when others help us claim it. And we can fully attain the humanity in ourselves only by honoring it in others.

Methodological Afterword

APPENDIX A

༄

What Is Narrative and How Reliable a Tool Is It?[1]

With the assistance of K. Fyfe, N. Lampros, and A. Martin

WHAT IS NARRATIVE? Since Aristotle's *Poetics*, the concept of narrative has involved an order, a temporal sequencing of events, starting with a beginning, plot action, and conclusion to the story.[2] In previous work[3] we defined narratives as the stories people tell and argued that narratives provide an especially rich source of information "about how people make sense of their lives. Narratives yield insight on how people collect and assemble the myriad disparate facts with which we all are bombarded."[4] These stories illuminate the cognitive landscape and help us understand how people see themselves, how they see others, and how their cognitive perceptions of others relate to their treatment of them.[5] In this sense narratives constitute one of the most important tools for analyzing political psychology, defined as the study of how the human mind works to influence our political behavior.[6] Narratives thus constitute both a methodology and a conceptual way of understanding the personality.

Narratives are subject to diverse interpretations by different listeners. Much of the power of a narrative emanates from its complexity;[7] the listener has to listen carefully, try to put aside preconceived ideas, and understand what the speaker is saying, catching unspoken nuances and implicit meanings. It thus follows that especially the strongest political narratives will be susceptible to a number of interpretations as the site of controversial contestation. How are we to know which interpretation is correct? What do we do when we have more than one plausible interpretation? And what are the consequences? One response is to publish the full interview, as in the present work. But that does not alter the fact that interviews are intersubjective—a human encounter with the speaker that involves necessary compromises, approximations, unpredictable interactions, and imperfect attempts at understanding and recording what the speaker said and what they meant (or chose not to say). Because of this I present this appendix as part of a methodological afterword designed to address certain issues with narrative as a tool for political science generally and more specifically dealing with issues concerning my own data analysis.[8]

A brief background concerning methodology may situate my discussion in a broader intellectual context. Political science has experienced many methodological vogues. Dominant historical and institutional approaches of the early twentieth century were rejected by behavioralist political scientists, advocating the utilization of statistical data and other indicators to measure political phenomena through actual behavior. These were applied with the view—and the hope—that such methods would be more "scientific" and "objective." Behavioralists ushered in the post–World War II era of mass public opinion surveys, aggregate data utilizing government statistics, and models designed to clarify the assumptions of the analyst.[9] After initial success, behavioralism in turn was criticized for its rigid positivism, an overemphasis on quantitative methods, and its treatment of cognition as an empirically inaccessible "little black box" beyond the analyst's purview.[10]

While some departments with a predominantly behavioralist orientation still exist, and remnants of the approach remain in most departments, the 1970s saw the discipline as a whole move to a kind of post-behavioralism and the advent of rational choice theory.[11] In classic Kuhnian fashion the underlying rational choice assumptions then eventually underwent challenge and revision,[12] and by the century's close, the contest between the behavioralists and the rational choice proponents had been replaced by one in which behavioralists, rational choice theorists, and formal modelers were often poised against scholars identified as postmodernists, constructivists, and political theorists, in addition to students of newly rediscovered area studies and interpretive data.

The latest phase of this debate was intensified in October 2000, when a small group of political scientists organized against what they deemed the narrow parochialism and methodological bias favoring quantitative, behavioral, and rational choice approaches to American political science.[13] Establishing an untraceable e-mail address, they issued a call for change under the name *Perestroika-Glasnost*,[14] drawn from the term in Soviet politics and chosen to suggest political science should be more welcoming, as a "warm house" is welcoming, to diverse kinds of political science. The core of the Perestroika challenge was methodological. Perestroikans argued that diverse methodologies were legitimate, and that qualitative forms should be accorded as much scientific authority as other, more quantitatively oriented varieties. The Perestroika debate tapped into deep-seated dissatisfactions in the discipline, and one result of the Perestroika movement was an increased interest in qualitative data, with a qualitative section of the American Political Science Association formed in the summer of 2003.

With the increased interest in qualitative and interpretive analysis, scholars—whether they eschew or utilize such data analysis—now must consider the "scientific" properties such data pose for political analyses. How reliable are these data? How objective can the interpretation of qualitative data be? Can interpretive results be replicated—in some general manner—by other analysts? Despite political science's increasing use of interpretive data, questions concerning the reliability of such data have not yet been addressed fully. In this appendix, I want to address such questions by inquiring into the reliability of one of the most important forms of qualitative data: interpretive narrative analysis.

AN EMPIRICAL EXAMINATION OF ORAL TESTIMONY AND WRITTEN WORK

I do so by focusing on the consistency and variation in narrative interviews. Methodologically, narrative interviews are not new, representing one of the oldest and most important tools for research in law and social science. Indeed, interviews constitute a staple in disciplines from history and anthropology to sociology and psychology. Long a staple of psychological therapy (especially "talk" therapy), narratives also gained attention in psychology in reaction to an emphasis on situational factors to explain behavior, a trend in which the question of personality was largely ignored. Psychologists such as Dan P. McAdams developed the concept of narrative identity, understood as a dynamically evolving story about the self, told by the self, situated within a particular social environment and cultural/historical context. McAdams identifies three possible levels of analysis or description of the personality. The first is understood as relatively context-free "traits," corresponding to characteristics such as the "Big Five" personality traits easily assessed with survey research; the second are more context-driven life projects that are specific to particular life tasks or goals; and the third (which McAdams finds most salient) concentrate on narrative identity assessed through a life-story interview in which the self is narrated over time, with key themes, patterns, and "morals" in the story that prove essential to defining who a person is and hopes to be. Such narratives are often highly culturally informed and provide a useful tool for getting at the way in which culture enters into an individual's behavior.[15] This methodology has been used successfully to study family metaphors in the narratives of liberals and conservatives,[16] conservatives' and liberals' usage of God-concepts in their moral universe,[17] and how Americans found meaning in their experiences of September 11, 2001.[18] Using this technique in political science, narrative interviews can provide critical information on a range of topics, from those cited above to foreign policy decision-making or the psychological portraits of altruists and genocidalists I have presented in this book.

The use of narrative interviews involves at least two important questions concerning reliability: (1) Do narrative accounts reflect the actual events that occurred? And (2) how consistent are the narratives produced by the same speaker at different points in time, speaking with different interviewers and in different contexts? I address the second of these questions here.

Because of narratives' significant ability to tap into memory, one of the most critical human capacities,[19] discussion of the interpretation of narrative data as a scientific tool is not new, although scientific work on objectivity in humans remains in its infancy.[20] Hermann Ebbinghaus (1885) first demonstrated that memory can be investigated objectively via experimental study.[21] This experimental work suggests that repetition and highly arousing emotional experiences make long-lasting memories, researchers now believe, because of hormonal activity and brain systems activated by emotional experiences. It is becoming clear that memory is not just recollection, but a re-performance, a re-creation involving a synthesis of various elements, entailing possible errors and omissions.[22] Much of what scientists know about how neurobiological systems create memories, however, comes from animal studies, and since memory is not directly observed but is instead inferred from animal behavior, the need for work based on human beings is especially acute.

To provide such an initial foray into the reliability of narrative interviews, I construct an empirical, comparative analysis of the narratives of two individuals, using two different sources of information for each individual: oral interviews and books written by the person interviewed. My choice of data set grew out of the interviews for this book, and hence owes as much to serendipity as to the research design. The narratives utilized in this book are emotionally charged and, as such, tap into a critical debate concerning memory and the reliability of oral testimonies versus written narratives, especially when important and traumatic political events are involved. The significance of the topic is relevant not only for political science but also for legal testimonies (Loftus[23]), work in cognitive psychology,[24] personality and social psychology,[25] neurobiology,[26] and philosophy.[27] The resurgence of narrative methods in this field is, in certain respects, a return to Gordon Allport's (1937, 1942) call for an emphasis on "ideographic" in addition to "nomothetic" methods, with the nomothetic allowing for greater descriptive depth and detail in individual cases as opposed to instruments such as surveys.[28] (For a review of the "idiographic" versus "nomothetic" debate, see Runyan [1983].)

When I began my work using narratives, their use in political science was limited. Indeed, narratives remain a difficult methodology in political science, in part because space limitations in professional journals restrict the ability to present detailed data analysis of this kind of data. Fortunately, the situation is beginning to change, and recent work by political scientists has raised broad questions about narratives' ability to reveal critical political insight. In *Shaping History: Narratives of Political Change* (2007), Molly Andrews makes a strong case for the ability of stories to link us to the political frameworks within which we operate. The "stories of our lives . . . implicitly communicate to others something of our political worldviews, our *Weltanschauung*."[29] Andrews directs us to ask why people choose one set of facts to emphasize, why the speaker weaves together events as they do, and why they see themselves in relation to those particular events in a particular fashion. Andrews also raises the question of the listener. Why is one particular person chosen as the repository of stories? How does the listener influence the telling of the story? All of these are excellent questions on which narrative interpretive analysts should focus. In my case I believe many of the people I interviewed for this project were at what psychologists called "talk stage." In the immediate aftermath of World War II, many of them had, in effect, put "Do not disturb" signs on their memory in order to block out the pain or horror of war and go on to build lives independent of the misery they had both witnessed and suffered. We can speculate that as they approached the ends of their lives they wanted to reach some closure of their own, make sense of their experiences, and leave their stories with someone they could trust. As such I was a sympathetic listener at an opportune moment, possessing the means and willingness to listen and to record.

Narratives are especially helpful in deciphering the political significance of identity, a major concern in this work as in many other works in political science. First, such narratives are particularly useful in showing us how people place themselves in the political world. Second, these narratives help get at the normative aspect of politics, the part that deals with values. Third, one can think of identities themselves as narratives, "stories people tell themselves and others about who they are [and who they are not]." But identity is something that is always in transition, "always producing itself through the combined processes of being and becoming, belonging and longing to belong. This duality is often reflected in narratives of identity."[30] Narratives of identity are both personal and political insofar as they reflect "the positionality" of the speaker.[31]

The issues concerning identity, politics, and interpretation become especially acute once we turn to the Holocaust and focus on critical arguments concerning reliability and memories of events that are emotionally tinged and traumatic.

Oral Testimony versus Written Work

In *Holocaust Testimonies*, Lawrence Langer (1991) makes a strong argument that oral testimonies constitute a more complex and nuanced depiction of the speaker's experience than written work can, precisely because oral testimonies do not contain a central narrative. They amble and wander; they exhibit contradictions and display ambivalence. In doing so the oral testimony includes the speaker's multiple stories, portraying a range of experiences that happened to the same person but that convey the speaker's varied responses to the political events. Langer argues that it is the very contradictions of oral testimonies that more accurately capture the contradictory aspect of complex reality than written narrative, especially since writers traditionally are taught to develop and follow a central and directed plotline. Langer analyzes oral testimonies of concentration camp survivors and argues that the Holocaust constitutes an arena in which the normal conceptualizations of the self simply do not hold. In part this is because victims of the camps were robbed of the agency necessary to make it meaningful to speak of moral choice. Traditional moral systems, Langer thus contends, cannot explain the Holocaust because the agent had no control over the results of his action. But—and this is directly relevant for the interpretive analyst—Langer further argues that the Holocaust often broke the connections to and with the self, leaving a prewar, a wartime, and a postwar person, with little to connect these selves. The integration necessary to return someone to the world of ordinary moral discourse was impossible for camp inmates. Langer constructs a compelling case that it is oral testimonies, not written works, that most effectively capture these contradictions in the face of a bewildering series of events. Some of this is evident in a volume edited by Peter Suedfeld (2001), in which survivors and refugees from the Holocaust were asked to describe how their Holocaust experience later influenced their later lives as social scientists. The written works differed significantly from the oral presentations I attended at two different conferences. The oral presentations were extremely moving and left many in the audience in tears. The written work was much more restrained, as if the speaker needed some protection against the memories. I suspect many traumatic memories exhibit the same properties, and what we find in Holocaust testimonies is a reflection of a deeply ingrained human propensity to protect one's self from the pain involved in traumatic memories.

Langer's book deals with the Holocaust, and one of his central claims is that the Holocaust represents a plane apart from contemporary moral theories. Moral theory cannot explain the Holocaust, Langer argues, since moral theory is based on choice, and camp inmates had no choice. Analogous arguments might apply to other documents dealing with retrieved memory, especially memories of traumatic political events that limit choice. There are many complex issues at hand; most I cannot address here. Recent psychological and neurobiological works on emotion and cognition suggest emotion has a far stronger impact on memory and cognition than had been thought.[32] Scientists also tell us there are different kinds of memory. How susceptible are these diverse forms to such concerns? How can we attempt to address this problem in a careful scholarly manner? How do we best capture and convey the complex individuals we all are and the complex reality in which we live? Is one format or conversation a better indicator than another one? Here we encounter sampling problems analogous to those of the temporal changes encountered by a doctor charting a patient's blood pressure or the survey researcher polling on an important public opinion at different points in time.

Our efforts here compare the oral testimony with written works by the same individuals. Like Langer, I consider individuals during a war and the Holocaust. And all of the people I interviewed insisted they had little choice in their actions, although this is surely not objectively as true for the people I interviewed as for the Jews on whom Langer focuses.

I begin by analyzing an extensive narrative interview describing the wartime experiences of Irene Gut Opdyke, who rescued Jews in Poland between 1939 and 1945. This narrative interview (published in Monroe 2004) is then compared with a book (Opdyke and Armstrong 1999) about the same experiences, written by Irene at or around the same time as my interviews with her. For contrast, I performed a similar comparison of oral interviews (Chapter 7) and a book written by Florentine Rost van Tonningen (1990), an ardent and unrepentant Nazi supporter. Florentine's does not identify any help from a research assistant or professional writer, but Irene's book was written with a professional writer. This introduces an obvious limitation to the comparison: Are differences between Irene's oral interview and her book the result of her ghostwriter? There is no way to answer this question. With this caveat in mind, I nonetheless felt it would be useful to construct an analysis to ask if we find critical differences between the spoken and the written narratives in the following dimensions, chosen because of the importance they are said to have in the literature, especially the arguments made by Langer:

1. Congruence of the factual events, e.g., who did what, when, where, and to whom.
2. Basic values and attitudes of the speaker.
3. Self-perceptions.
4. Categorization schema of others, e.g., Jews and Nazis.

COMPARISON OF FINDINGS FROM DIFFERENT INTERPRETIVE SOURCES

The transcripts and autobiographies were read independently by three coders who then compared their findings. Our findings confirmed Langer's claims that oral interviews amble more and are less temporally chronological. It seems impossible to evaluate Langer's claim that the self presented in these rambling oral interviews is more "real," a more accurate representation of the speaker's "true" self than the self presented in the more traditional, written narrative. But we can ask if the self represented in interviews differs in significant ways from the self presented in the book. This evidence is clear. For both our speakers there is little difference on this dimension. Overall, all coders found remarkable consistencies in values/ attitudes, categorization schema, and self-perceptions. This may suggest that these factors are so much a part of the speaker's psychological makeup that they do not differ significantly according to which type of methodology is utilized; or it may be that these are simply factors that are best captured in both narrative formats. The main differences found were those of factual descriptions, with the interviews describing factual events more succinctly and with less concern for chronology, as Langer suggests should be the case. Both books showed subtle differences in tone, with more self-conscious concern for creating an impression or making a case or a point. These findings are summarized in table A.1 for Irene and table A.2 for Florentine.

Factual Correspondence: Irene

In both documents, the interview transcript and the autobiography, Irene describes being beaten and raped by Russian soldiers during the partition of Poland. She recounts then being taken to Russia, cared for by a female doctor, and eventually returned to Poland where she later helped the partisans and rescued Jews. These basic facts are the same but are recounted, our coders felt, in a different tone and with interesting differences in detail. For example, the interview offers a more cursory account (roughly 3 percent of the interview time versus 20.6 percent of the book) and provides different ages when she was raped: eighteen in the interview (p. 3) versus seventeen in the book (p. 33). The date of the rape differs as well. In the book Irene dates the rape as January 1940; in the interview, the rape occurs just before Christmas of 1939.

Overall, coders found Irene often would relate the same facts but with a slightly different tone and minor variation in details. Certain images in the book are expressed more dramatically, even poetically, than in the interview. For example, Irene tells of a Jewish baby being shot by a Nazi. The imagery of this event differs. In the book the officer makes killing the baby a sport, implying both that he enjoys the killing and doesn't see the baby as human; in the interview the officer kills the baby in a more mechanical fashion, simply to carry out orders. The change may have been created intentionally or subconsciously,[33] perhaps to have a greater effect on the reader's emotions so that the reader might empathize with Irene. However, the impact of the baby's death on Irene is the same; in both documents it shocks Irene and compels her to take action to help.

> Book: As I pressed against the glass, I saw an officer make a flinging movement with his arm, and something rose up into the sky like a fat bird. With his other hand he aimed his pistol, and the bird plummeted to the ground beside its screaming mother, and the officer shot the mother, too. . . . But it was not a bird. It was not a bird. (p. 104)

TABLE A.1

	Irene		
	Interview	*Book*	*Conclusions*
Facts	Shorter Less color Not chronological order More focus on rescuing Jews, less on own personal events	More detail Romanticized Temporal chronology Fuller description of personal events	Function of time Different purposes: Book—Irene's life Interview—helping others
Values	Religious Raised to help others Felt that helping was necessary, not an option Gives credit to God and circumstance	Religious Raised to help others Felt that helping was necessary, not an option Gets more credit for her own actions, more admiring tone	Same battle with God Same sanctity of life
Worldview	Was protective of the helpless, the innocent Fought against the German aggressors as a group but was able to see good in individuals	Was protective of the helpless, the innocent Fought against the German aggressors as a group but was able to see good in individuals	Consistent impressions: same worldview
Self-perceptions	Identified with the Jews, who were relatively in the same boat as she Took advantage of her outward German appearance and name, and her sexuality to gain an edge in survival and protecting those she cared about	Identified with the Jews, who were relatively in the same boat as she Took advantage of her outward German appearance and name, and her sexuality to gain an edge in survival and protecting those she cared about	Consistent impressions: same view of self

TABLE A.2

Florentine

	Interview	Book	Conclusions
Facts	Familiar with information regarding her own life, her husband's career and death; Many unsubstantiated assertions about Nazi ideology and history	Provides fuller historical account of Germany on grander scale than own life	Consistent: History on grander scale than her life
Values	Family social status key Women subservient	Family social status key Women subservient	Consistent: Elitist, socially conservative in both Clings to past
Worldview	Some cultures worthy of respect, but believes they should be kept separate, especially in marriage; Keep blood "pure"	Obsequious praise for other cultures in a Social Darwinian sense, as long as they stay "pure." Aryans and other species should not mix.	Consistent: values certain cultures so long as they don't trespass into hers, keep racial purity
Self-perceptions	Wants to be part of an elite, exclusive group Identity and self-esteem come mainly from husband's power	Wants to be part of an elite, exclusive group Identity and self-esteem come mainly from husband's power	Consistent: Elitist, self-esteem reflection of husband's power

Interview: Then I saw a young woman with a baby in her arms. It was hard to hear what transpired, but the SS man pulled the baby and threw it with its head to the ground. The mother's scream penetrated even to my hiding place. I will never forget her inhuman scream. She leapt to save her child, and one bullet went to her head. She was dead, lying next to her child. It was unbelievable (p. 5).

How do our two speakers remember the aftermath of traumatic events? Psychologists argue that emotionally tinged events are better remembered and in more detail than ordinary events, and suggest this is because of increased hormonal activity, particularly as concerns the centrality of the memory to their sense of self.[34] Langer's work suggests the emotional fallout of traumatic events, such as the Holocaust, should lead to a jumbling of factual recounts of such events, as speakers try to make sense of something that is—at bottom—senseless. Findings on Irene are consistent with both views. In both documents Irene remembers her rape in detail although the coders found a chronological sequence in the recitation of the rape's aftermath in the book that is lacking in the interview. (This may be the result of the ghostwriter.) Interestingly, the narratives vary in Irene's recollection of what happened after the traumatic rape. In both documents Irene tells of being cared for after her rape by a kindly Russian doctor, Dr. Olga. But in the interview Irene does not tell about Dr. Olga's being transferred to the Finnish front or about a new protector (Dr. David) to whom she runs for help after the new hospital administrator attempts to rape her and Irene has to defend herself with a glass bottle. The book says Dr. David finds Irene a place to hide with his friend Miriam Svetlana, who is described as a village doctor, and for whom Irene is also able to put her medical skills to good work.

The book says Irene stays with Miriam just short of a year before leaving to attempt to return to Radom. Little of this is discussed in the interview. Irene remembers most vividly her rape by the Russian soldiers and the events that occurred immediately afterward, including her introduction to Dr. Olga. After that, her interview presents an Irene who has difficulty ordering the events in her head chronologically. There is the random jumping from one time period to another that Langer describes. For example, Irene talks about things that occurred while in the hospital, but she does so after she's already described being out on her own trying to return home. As Langer predicts, the interview becomes difficult to follow at that point, and there is no mention of either Dr. David or Miriam.

What can explain these differences? Coders concluded that Irene's memory might be more accurate about the rape because it was such an emotionally jolting incident.[35]

Interview: [Before that,] I was not even kissed by a boyfriend (Monroe 2004, 141).
Book: I was shy with men; I had never had a boyfriend, never been kissed, I was a good Catholic girl (Opdyke and Armstrong 1999, 33).

In contrast, the time spent waiting her return to Poland was less traumatic and more jumbled in Irene's memory. This would accord with the most recent findings in cognitive psychology, suggesting traumatic events are remembered more clearly than normal events.

All coders noted areas of divergence and omission in the different narratives. Some characters in Irene's autobiography are missing entirely from the account in her oral interview. For example, Father Joseph, Pasiewski, Janek, and Irene's reunion with her family after escaping from the Russian hospital are discussed in the book but not in the interview.

> *Book*: It was on my way back to Ternopol that day that I stopped at the church in Janówka. . . . I bowed my head and closed my eyes as though in prayer, but truly, I was both exhausted and overexcited. I let the priest's gentle Ukrainian accent wrap around me like a tender hand, and at first I did not pay much attention to his words. But then I began listening, and I realized that he was encouraging his flock to resist the Nazis and to help the Jews. . . . What he was saying could well bring him punishment from the Germans (Opdyke and Armstrong 1999, 130).

There was no mention at all of Father Joseph in the interview. Some of these differences could be the natural result of the longer time period spent with a professional biographer who provided a linear chronology in the book. A more startling and less explicable divergence is the interview's omission of any discussion of a love affair that seems highly significant in the book, a love affair that culminates in her engagement to Janek Ridel and Irene's desolation when he was killed shortly before their planned marriage.

> *Book*: Love at first sight is a girl's dream. By March of 1944 I was almost twenty-two years old; I had long since stopped thinking of myself as a girl—and I had no faith in dreams. But suddenly, every sweet song I had ever heard made perfect sense to me. I loved Janek . . . without question . . . followed him without question, and joined partisans without question. I did it for Poland, yes. And I did it for me, because I had sworn to keep fighting the enemy. But even more, I did it for Janek (pp. 212–13).
> "I know I should not be happy," I admitted, twining my fingers through his. "Our country is still dominated by our enemies. My family is far away. And yet I am happy."
> "Happy with me." Janek turned me to face him, and put his hand under my chin. "Mala, my little bird, I know exactly what you are you saying, because it is what is in my heart, too. I love you. I want to marry you."
> I pressed my forehead against his heart. "I want to marry you, too."
> We returned to Kielce that evening to tell his parents. The Ridels were overjoyed at our news, and urged us to set a date. We settled on May 5, my birthday, which was just under a month away. That evening, I could barely look at Janek across the dinner: I was afraid that my emotions would overpower me if our eyes met. I had been accustomed to hiding my true feelings for a long time. It was hard to believe that I could be happy (Opdyke and Armstrong 1999, 214–15).
> And then he left.
> Janek was killed in the ambush. We buried him in the forest (p. 216).

Did Irene omit discussion of Janek because she didn't think it would be of interest to the interviewer? For the sake of brevity? Because she simply "forgot" a piece of the story in her sessions with us? Because losing Janek was too painful to discuss? Because it made her look as if her partisan activities had been because of her romance, and not her own strength of character? Because I met her at her home, where her husband was nearby? No definitive answers are possible here, and Irene is no longer living so I cannot ask her. Since my interviews with Irene lasted many months, concerns with brevity seem unlikely. The evidence is consistent with a view that self-presentation might be involved, but this conclusion can only be speculative.

Beyond this striking omission, all coders further classified the book's discussion of Irene's involvement with the Polish partisan group in the forest as a much more driven, scheming account than the one presented in the interview.

> *Book*: I knew members of our fighting unit had assassinated Nazi officers, stolen weapons, made bombs, executed collaborators. I knew this. I understood that I was participating in death. I can't say how I reconciled it with everything I had done before, with all the pains I had taken to protect lives. But I did. From time to time, I would look across the campfire while we cooked our meager dinner in the forest. Perhaps I would see Jerzy spit on a whetstone and sharpen his knife—the knife he used to cut sausages—and know without being told that he had used the same knife on a man. Or I might see Aaron study the map of a nearby town, and know that he was planning a backstreet ambush. And the memory of a baby thrown into the air would flood my mind, hurtling me down into darkness, and I would think, "Yes, sharpen your knife." Sharpen it. Lay your traps (pp. 213–14).
>
> *Interview*: I joined the partisans because that was the only way I could go. So we were fighting the retreating Germans and the Russians who were advancing. We were right in the middle. Naturally, I was not fighting. I was just a messenger girl sometimes, but that's all (p. 23).

The brevity of Irene's description of her partisan activities in her interview is consistent with the view that she presented herself differently, playing up her altruistic activities when discussing her life, perhaps because she knew I was interested in altruism. But the differences also could be explained by reference to Irene's ghostwriter. Did the ghostwriter dramatize certain events for effect? All coders found the book a more romanticized version of Irene's involvement in partisan activities but drew no further conclusions on this issue. Certainly, our coders suggested, introducing Janek into that period of her life gives that part of Irene's story an idealized tone, a tone missing in the interview, where her partisan activities are summed up almost dismissively.

Fortunately, the problem of attribution that clouds the comparison of Irene's written narrative is not evident for Florentine's.

Factual Correspondence: Florentine

In both her single-authored book and her interview, Florentine is presented as a virulent Nazi who takes great pride in her marriage to one of the top Dutch Nazis and in her contacts with Himmler and Hitler. In both narratives, Florentine's Nazi ties are the high point of her life. Psychologists note that repetition strengthens memory, and Florentine's ongoing public speaking to Nazi audiences about World War II may account for the striking similarities between her book and her interview. Whatever the cause, the similarities were remarkable on critical dimensions.

All coders found that Florentine—like Irene—struck a slightly different tone and emphasis in her book than in her interviews. For example, Florentine's interview contains little discussion of her childhood. In contrast, her book provides extensive stories about a magical childhood of privilege, high social standing, and a keen interest and involvement in the NSB in Florentine's young adulthood. In her interview, Florentine's life story begins with her involvement in Nazi activities and culminates in her marriage to Meinoud Rost van Tonningen. In both narratives, however, Florentine has all the facts consistent and speaks in the same worshipful tone that depicts Meinoud as a central figure in the Nazi period.

> *Book*: He began his successful career at the League of Nations as a trainee at the International Labour Office in Geneva. In 1923 he became an assistant of the General Commissioner for the League of Nations in Vienna. . . . It was his goal to help Austria recover from the war. . . . In the fall of 1931 he was appointed General Commissioner for the League of Nations in Vienna, with a mandate to restore the Austrian economy (pp. 57–58).
>
> Himmler came upon another idea. My husband was to take the position of SS leader in the Netherlands. After hearing this, he laughed and replied: "Of course, Reichsführer, it would be a great honour for me to be a leader of the SS. But I do believe a younger man should do this, I know a capable young man, W. J. Heubel [my brother]" (pp. 96–97).

This grand view of her husband is also evident in Florentine's interview.

> *Interview*: [M]y husband goes to the League of Nations. He was working there… for Holland…. He was representative for Holland for Financial and Economic Affairs (p. 163).
>
> Mussert was not considered the right person for a leadership position in our country. . . . They wished to have a National Socialist movement under strong leadership. Himmler wanted my husband to be that leader. . . . He had already printed flyers and wanted to drop them by airplane over the country. His disappointment was great when my husband firmly stated that this would be a breach of loyalty to Mussert, and politely declined. . . . [T]hey said to my husband, "Do you want to take it [control] here in Holland? Mussert is away, you can do it." But my husband said, "No. Mussert is a good man. I don't want to have his position."
>
> So Mussert is staying there [as head]. So then Hitler and Himmler asked my husband to be head of the SS. "No," my husband said, "this is for young people." So he suggested my brother [Wim]…. So then they asked him to be leader of the Netherlands Bank, the Bank of Holland. . . . Of course he had a lot of jobs (pp. 165–66).

Even her husband's political vicissitudes signify his political importance to Florentine. This is evident in both narratives.

Book: For days Rost van Tonningen had noticed his car being followed by the police. On May 3 he was arrested in front of his house in The Hague. . . . Rost van Tonningen was taken to Flushing to be shipped to England from there. Because of the rapid German invasion, however, these plans could not be carried out. . . . After the men had spent thirty-six hours on the front line, they were finally rescued by German troops. At peril to his own life, Rost van Tonningen was given the opportunity to meet with General Rommel to request a marching order back to the Netherlands. Rommel showed him a ring and asked: "Do you recognize this?" Rost van Tonningen answered, "Yes, certainly, that's the Death's Head ring of the SS." Thereupon Rost van Tonningen received papers for himself and the other prisoners (pp. 77–78).

Interview: My husband was in prison, *before* the Germans came in. . . . The Dutch [Reina] queen . . . noticed that my husband had good relations with Hitler. So he was a dangerous man, of course. There was a move to take him to London, as a prisoner. But it was not possible because the Germans came so quickly through Holland, Flanders, and France. So all those who were outside, it was not possible to take the prisoners to England. So he had to walk to Collette, and there was Rommel already. Rommel was a big [great] man who was making the way inside to France. Then my husband tried to come into Rommel, to let Rommel see his SS ring and [once he did] that, he was okay. That meant my husband was free, and could come back to Holland with his other friends, these 33 people [fellow prisoners] (p. 165–66).

The coders found little factual divergence in the narratives although all coders noted that Florentine consistently refers to her husband by his full name in the book. This introduces an odd note of formality missing in the interview, which seems more natural and less overtly for public consumption or propaganda purposes.

Book: After the surrender of the German forces in Holland on May 5, 1945, my husband was taken prisoner by the Canadians (p. 155). . . . When Prince Bernhard came to visit the camp in Elst, he once again stood face to face with my husband. The Prince quickly realized that Rost van Tonningen was a danger, because he knew too much. He had to be removed.

Shortly after finishing his political testament, my husband was transferred to the Scheveningen prison. . . . With him being the president of the Bank of the Netherlands, it was considered particularly gratifying to humiliate him as much as possible. . . . He was continually beaten with truncheons (p. 159).

Wim Kreischer, one of my husband's cousins . . . was taken to a shed. To his horror, he found the barely recognizable remains of my husband lying on a pile of garbage. The sight shocked him (p. 161).

The interview's description of Meinoud's death is essentially the same, although the book provides more detail. Florentine does tell me that she does not know how she found out what happened to her husband; this statement conflicts with the book's account, which suggest she learned of her husband's death from his cousin. Do the inconsistencies concerning her husband's death suggest Florentine did not understand the question fully, perhaps because the interview was in English or because she was so elderly [age 84] when we spoke? Does the time factor involved in writing a book account for the clarity and the textbook quality of that narrative? Certainly, the book sounds far more like a Nazi history of the war than did Florentine's life story when she related it to me in 1999. But both accounts reflect the extent to which Florentine's sense of self is wrapped up in the idealized glories of the Nazi period.

Interview: Prince Bernhard came from the other side. Of course, Bernhard knew our name very well, Rost van Tonningen, and of course my husband knows too much. So Prince Bernhard says [Florentine slapped her hands together in a gesture, as if saying, "It is finished, just so"], "This man had to go out, he had to go to prison." So my husband alone they took away, and brought to Utrecht in the prison . . . so my husband came to Utrecht for three days, and he wrote his testament in Utrecht. The Canadians took that. The Canadians did that. Then all the people gets money and they put my husband in prison and said, "You can do with this man what you want but not [let him] alive, back out of prison." He had to go to die. Then they did terrible things, for ten days with my husband. Oh, terrible things. . . . The guards . . . invited women to the prison camp. To have fun. And my husband has to suffer this indignity. The president of the Bank of Holland! My husband has to put out his clothes, and he had to sing the rounds, with this rope on his penis (pp. 172–73).
Q. *How did you find out what happened to him?*
[Florentine sighed.] Nobody knows.
Q. *But you were telling me that they made him be naked and sing the national anthem. . . How did you know this? [Florentine ignored the question.]*
Yes. I have met my husband on the third of March '45 on the front (p. 173).

As the above excerpt demonstrates, when I pushed Florentine on points that were troubling, Florentine simply ignored the question or became unclear or evasive; in this example, Florentine insists she knew that her husband had been humiliated and beaten to death but then claims she does not remember or know the details. This pattern supports Langer's claim that oral interviews are more fragmentary and broken, especially when dealing with painful events.

Values and Attitudes: Irene

All coders remarked on the striking consistency both speakers demonstrated in values or attitudes. Consider Irene's narratives. In both documents, Irene is driven by deep-seated convictions about the value of human life and her responsibility as a decent person. All coders agreed that in both the interview and the book there is no question about Irene's core value: the sanctity of life. This core value meant there was no question as to whether or not Irene would help the Jews.

Book: I did not ask myself, Should I do this? But, how will I do this? Every step of my childhood had brought me to this crossroad; I must take the right path, or I would no longer be myself (p. 126).
Interview: I felt it so strongly that God put me there, in the right time, and the right moment, and the right place. Now I have a place for my friends (Monroe 2004, 147).

I wanted to help, but I didn't think. I didn't plan ahead. I was like when you see a child drowning in the water; you don't think if you can swim; automatically, you want to do something. You jump. That was exactly my way. I knew it was wrong what they did, the Germans. I knew that I had to help. I wanted to help so bad, but I just didn't make plans (Monroe 2004, 149).

In both accounts, Irene describes an inescapable urgency whenever she learns about danger to others, revealing what I describe as a strong sense of moral salience.[36] Another striking point of correspondence concerned the origin of Irene's values. In both documents Irene credited her mother's kindness and care of the less fortunate with instilling Irene's altruism and her desire to help those in need. This desire predated Irene's wartime experiences, as illustrated in Irene's choice of a career in nursing and her care for animals.

Book: Cats, dogs, rabbits, birds—we brought our small patients home to Mamusia, who tended them expertly. . . . My mother once raised a baby blackbird we had found fallen from its nest, and it always lived nearby and would fly in through the open window when she whistled for it (p. 8).

Mamusia urged us to direct our energy into useful . . . projects. Along with my sisters, I helped her prepare baskets of food for the poor and the sick. . . . In every charitable act we performed, Mamusia and Tatu were our models; they were generous and kind to everyone, even to the Gypsies who camped in the woods outside town and made people suspicious with their strange costumes and language. Wounded animals, out-of-luck neighbors, sick strangers—Mamusia and Tatu welcomed them all (pp. 14–15).

Interview: Mother was a wonderful woman. She was a saint. That may be why I was able to do the things I did later during the war, because Mama never sent anyone needy from her door. There were gypsies in the forest near our home. I remember one time my mother took a gypsy woman into our home for two weeks because the woman had pneumonia. There was always someone coming home with us. We all, all five of us children, always brought home from school, a bat, a dog, or cat, whatever needed help. My mother always knew what to do (Monroe 2004, 140).

Values and Attitudes: Florentine

Florentine's values and attitudes differ significantly from Irene's; yet both women demonstrated a remarkable consistency on this dimension, regardless of which narrative we examined. For Florentine the concept of cultural purity was key, and her preference for Aryan culture was abundantly clear in both documents. Any respect given other cultures was contingent upon these cultures refraining from trying to intermix. Florentine criticizes a top Dutch Nazi for putting politics above racial purity.

Book: I felt he just wanted a lot of members, no matter who or what they were. Rigorous racial hygiene was not a topic at this time. I felt disappointed and left the NSB (p. 65).

This criticism of a Nazi because of insufficient support for racial purity, and her deep-seated attachment to so-called racial purity, are again evident in both narratives.

> *Interview*: You must respect it, the culture from Aryans. So it is very foolish to say that we don't want to work with the Negro, etc., etc. I have nothing against the Negro but he has his own situation. We have our own situation. I don't like to be married with the Negro. . . . When I write to the Indonesian, I respect the Indonesian culture. I have very good friends in the Chinese. They took me into the Chinese culture but as Dutch woman. No more. Nothing more than that. Not that we should marry together or something like that (p. 169).

Nonetheless, the coders agreed that throughout her book, Florentine exhibits a tone that is absent in the interview. There is an ingratiating, cloying quality to the book, especially when she describes her husband. Her discussion of her time in Bali is almost obsequious about the Balinese culture even as she is clear she would not want anyone "like them" in her racially exclusive club. In the interview Florentine seems cognizant that she could be criticized for her beliefs; perhaps because of this she emphasizes that she respects cultures she'd only care to observe. The difference is one of tone, not substance, however, and in both narratives Florentine claims some groups of people have superior souls. In both documents, Florentine expresses longing for the Golden Age of Aryan culture. She accuses the Jews of being responsible for the Nazis' current infamy, and looks back to a distant past when the Aryan race dominated the world.

> *Book*: Where does the contemporary world get the right to accuse a country like Germany of every conceivable evil deed, which it never committed? . . . The German soldier—together with many European volunteers—fought for high ideals. Killing for the sake of killing was something entirely foreign to him. One should rather speak of him as a soldier of peace, for he sacrificed himself for his country and his people to gain peace, the holy flame and honour. These fighters felt bound to their culture, something plainly recognizable in their magnificent songs. How beautiful they were! (p. 204).
>
> *Interview*: We had our special culture. We had to be pure. . . . I am thinking that Jews have no culture so they don't respect us . . . Himmler . . . said, "When we win the war, . . . then all the American people who had German blood, would come back to Europe, to put them in beautiful housing, or something, farms or something. So you are together. But today, everyone is lost. Everyone is alone" (pp. 169–71).

In both narratives, Florentine clings fast to pride in her past and feels that today's society—with its mixing of different cultures—is lost. The racist element of this is clear in both documents.

Self Perceptions: Irene

All coders noted that both of Irene's narratives exhibit what has been called a *Gemeinschaftsgefuhl* view of the world.[37] Irene identified with the Jewish people under her watch in the laundry because they too were helpless under German control and had lost or been separated from family and loved ones. Her ties are to these people and to all human beings. In both documents, Irene significantly and consistently fails to distinguish herself from Jews. She demonstrates a special closeness to those who had suffered as she had. Her world was divided for the most part into aggressors and those trying to defend themselves, rather than into categories of race, nationality, or religion. The consistency of these aspects in both the book and the interview indicate that this self-view runs deeply embedded in Irene's cognitive worldview.

> *Book*: In my home, there had never been any distinction made between people. Many of our friends were Jewish, but we did not say to ourselves, "Our Jewish friends . . ." It had never occurred to me to distinguish between people based on their religion. But this was precisely what Hitler was doing a mere six kilometers away (p. 17).
>
> *Interview*: Some were Polish, some were German and some were Jewish and Russian. They had children, so we children all played together. All kinds of mischief we did together. But we learned to live together. They were my friends. There was not the difference that "this is Jewish" or "this is Catholic" or "this is whatever." We lived and played together (Monroe 2004, 140).

Another constant theme in both of Irene's narratives is her view of herself as a woman and her self-awareness of being perceived as a sexual being. All coders observed that the book depicts Irene as more consciously using flirting and flattery to play up her feminine advantage; but this self-image exists in both narratives. This similarity in self-image and the subtle differences in depiction are captured in the following excerpts. Consider first a chapter in the book. Here Irene describes her interactions with the SS officer (Rokita) who focuses on the sexual relationship between Irene and the Major (Rügemer), a focus that blinds the SS man to the fact that Irene is able to help Jews because of this relationship.

> *Book*: "What a pretty girl, Major," Rokita said. "And what an old dog you are."
>
> Major Rügemer flushed. "Don't be absurd, Rokita."
>
> I stood there, feeling like a prize mare, hot with embarrassment. Coming upon the cruel SS chief unexpectedly had rattled me.
>
> "Fräulein Gut, I don't bite," Rokita teased.
>
> I glanced at him, appalled. Was he flirting with me? Did he think I was blushing because I wanted him to like me? (p. 109).
>
> Steiner was right: I was only a girl. Nobody paid much attention to me. While I served dinners in the evenings, I came and went among the officers and I was an invisible servant, a pair of hands bringing and removing plates. The officers talked as if I were not there: I did not count. I was only a girl.
>
> But I listened to the officers discuss the progress at the front. I listened to the secretaries' gossip about Berlin. I listened especially when Rokita dined with Major Rügemer, which was quite often, and if he thought I lingered because I had a crush on him, so much the better (p. 110).
>
> And in this way, I made my weakness my advantage. If I happened to overhear plans for a raid on the ghetto, it never showed on my face. If I passed a table when a

disciplinary action was being scheduled for the Arbeitslager, no one suspected I cared. And when Rokita came to dine, I was always polite to him, and let him flatter himself that I lingered by his table because I was awed by his beauty and his power.

After all, I was only a girl (p. 111).

If I was assumed to be the major's girlfriend, then it would cause no comment to find me in his office. If I was assumed to be the major's girlfriend, there was no place at HKP that I could not go (p. 142).

Another time, as I wheeled my bicycle across a guarded bridge, an officer stopped me and flirted with me. I used my best German on him, flirting back, promising to return after I visited my mother. Meanwhile, a wrapped parcel containing thousands of British pounds lay in the basket between the handlebars. I played with my golden hair as we spoke, knowing that he would stare at it, and he never even noticed the parcel. . . . If we were stopped and questioned, I always smiled at the officers, and they always smiled back. In my heart, I was seeing them dead. But on my face, I was an open invitation.

If you are only a girl, this is how you destroy your enemies (p. 217).

In the interview, Irene describes the same self-image but without the emphasis on using flirtation to eavesdrop. And what seems a literary device—"only a girl"— is absent.

Interview: When I was serving dinner, I noticed quite often that the local head of the Gestapo was sitting by the table with the Major. So I start making sure that I would be serving the table where the Major and the Gestapo man were sitting. I began to listen to their conversation. Even after I started to listen to the conversation, I at first did not know what I was hearing, but then I started to make sense of it (Monroe 2004, 144).

After the Major discovered Irene was hiding Jews in his villa, Irene had to agree to be his mistress in return for his silence.

Interview: About midnight the Major came home. He was so drunk. He went to his room. I had to go and face him. There was not any other way. I was standing in front of him, and he reached and pulled me onto his lap. He started opening my clothes and he said, "I will keep your secret but you have to be mine, willingly." There was nothing I could do. I was trapped. So many lives depended on me (Monroe 2004, 154).

The book recounting of this places greater emphasis on Irene's active participation in creating this self-image, while the interview portrays her affair with the Major as just another trial she had to suffer through and does not mention her flirting to trick officers. While some of this may be the result of the ghostwriter (book) or desires for brevity (interview), the self-images seem largely consistent, with only subtle differences.

Another similarity in self-image centers on Irene's identity as a German speaker, with a German name. In both documents Irene is aware of her German appearance and its advantages but describes using it for the benefit of her Jewish friends rather than to improve her own standing among the Germans. When it was for her own benefit to lie about being German, Irene seems concerned that her parents would not approve. Irene is willing to deceive to fight or thwart her enemies, but not to assimilate. Both the book and the interview thus show Irene as defiantly Polish under her quiet Germanic-looking guise.

Book: Because of our name, Gut, many people assumed that we were of German descent, but my parents were fiercely patriotic. We were Polish. I was raised to be proud of that fact (p. 12).

Here was another, shorter line. At the head of this line, above a table, was a sign in both German and Polish: "Registration for German Citizens and Polish Citizens of German Descent."

Fear and excitement bolted through me, leaving my fingertips prickling. I was blond and blue-eyed, I spoke German, and I had a German name. I could pass myself off as of German descent. My cheeks flamed with heat as I took my place at the end of the line. I told myself that the ends justified the means. I knew I was not German, but they would not know I was not German. I had already spent a year lying and deceiving everyone in Svetlana—one more lie meant nothing, and I wanted to go home. I wanted to go home!

In front of me, several people were chatting together, talking conspicuously about their relatives in the Fatherland, dropping names and making admiring comments about Hitler. I thought it was shameful that they would deny their Polishness, but I wondered if they were only acting, playing a part, as I was about to do, if they were doing anything they could just to get home. We must pretend to be German, so we could finally be Polish again (p. 51).

In both the book and the interview, Irene describes an incident in which she did not deny her Polishness, even though she had the opportunity, and in which her honesty rebounded to her credit.

Book: "Wie heisst du?" he asked.[38]

My hands shook as I took the cup. "My name is Irene Gut." I noticed his surprise that I had understood German, and that I spoke it well. "Before the war, I lived in Oberschlesien."

He took a handkerchief from his pocket and blew his nose. "You must be of German descent, with that name."

"I don't know—I don't think so. I am Polish." I sipped the coffee, which was rich with milk and sugar, luxuries I hadn't tasted in months.

"So, you don't claim to be German—you'd be surprised how many people do," he said. He gave me a cynical smile. "I must admire your honesty for not attempting to do so" (p. 85).

This incident is similarly described in the interview.

Interview: When I came to, I was scared. I started using my best high school German to explain that I want to work but I am just returned from the Russian side and I am weak and sick. I guess he took pity on me. Maybe because I was blonde and blue-eyed, maybe because my name was Gut. Because I remember, he asked me, "Are you of German descent?"

"No, I don't know about that. My name is Miss Gutowna."

And he said, '"You are very honest." Because I did not jump to say, "Oh yes," you know, to save myself (pp. 4–5).

I was always playing on the fact that my name is "Irena Gut," a German name, and because I spoke German in those days. Now I cannot speak it [German]. Psychologically, I just cannot make myself do it (Monroe 2004, 143).

In both narratives, Irene relates how her German appearance contributed to her appeal to the German officers, but—again in both documents—even though she discovers the respect and special treatment that came with being mistaken for German, she refuses to give up her Polish identity except in cases where she lies in order to get back to her family quickly or to save lives.

Self-Perceptions: Florentine

In contrast to Irene, Florentine's self-image is elitist and exclusive. But like Irene's characterizations of her self-perceptions, Florentine's narratives also are consistent in this depiction. In both narratives Florentine depicts the Aryan race as an exclusive, superior club, with Rost van Tonningen's position at the top of it. This identity appears to be the main appeal of the Nazi dream for Florentine. All coders agreed that both narratives capture this view.

Book: [I] would never have been allowed to marry one of these young men, however— my mother did not want her daughter to marry below her social level (p. 27).

We enjoyed our endless conversations with the German youth. They shared so much comradeship, pride and devotion. Everyone seemed happy and full of hope for their country. This kind of love for the nation was missing in the Netherlands. We did have a group called the AJC in Holland, which organized dances and fairs. Their members, however, were mainly children from lower-class families who did not feel any nationalism, but were taught class struggle and free love. This was something we could not relate to (p. 31).

Interview: Then we had a few thousand girl [in the Hitler Youth], it was quite a number, heh? I think my boss has boys, our Dutch Hitler Youth, in German is BDM, we called Youth Storm in Holland. This was the female branch of the Hitler Youth (p. 163).

Categorization Schema: Irene

In both documents, Irene rejects stereotyping and differentiates between members of the same group; this is particularly evident in her discussion of the Germans. Irene judged the Germans by their actions and was able to see good in some Germans. The book reveals the process that she went through trying to understand how people could be part of a group involved in such evil things and yet still remain, at least in some respects, good people. In the book Irene also expresses her feelings of confusion and gratitude, while in the interview she simply describes what people did and reflects on it with mature hindsight.

> *Book*: I soon found out that my impression of him was not wrong. Schulz was a good, friendly man. To be sure, he was in the Wehrmacht, but he was a cook, not a soldier, and he had none of the ferocity and malevolence that I had come to expect of the Germans. And although he was a perfectionist and liked everything to be done just so, he was quick with praise and gentle with rebukes (p. 88).
>
> When I returned to work the next day [after witnessing a massacre], I could not look at Schulz. As good and kind as he was, he was a German, and I could not reconcile those two things in my mind. I was so confused and heartsick that I could barely speak (p. 93).

After hearing of the massacre at the Glinice ghetto, Schulz warns Irene about the danger of being a "Jew-lover."

> When he returned a few minutes later, he carried a tall stack of blankets in his arms— many more than just two extra blankets. "Irene, if you need anything—anything at all—you must not be afraid to ask me," he said in a low voice.
>
> At once, my heart began hammering behind my ribs, and my face felt hot, as though I had been caught at something. He knew. Schulz knew what I was doing.
>
> "After all," he continued in his usual cheerful tone, "I can't have my girls shivering now, can I? That would reduce our efficiency."
>
> Confusing emotions chased one another through my heart. I was grateful, and I was relieved, and yet I was almost angry at Schulz for being so kind and for helping me help the Jews without admitting it—he made hating Germans a complex matter, when it should have been such a straightforward one (pp. 118–19).

Irene expresses similar views in her interview.

> *Interview: Q. Do you think the Major knew that you were going to hide Jews when he asked you to be in charge of the villa?*
>
> No . . . I don't think he knew what I was doing. He knew that I was sympathetic to the Jews. He knew that it hurt me that I could not help. I did not sit with him and talk, like you and I do now, but I talked with one soldier. His name was Schulz. Short, fat, with red cheeks. He was Wehrmacht. He showed me his wife's picture, and his children. He was always saying, "That dumb war. I want to go home and see my children." When he saw that sometimes the Gestapo did something wrong, he'd say, "They're fighting the women and children instead of going to Russia and fighting" (pp. 10–11).
>
> Schulz brought a little cot for me to sleep on at the villa. I know Schulz knew something. He never spoke of it. But he brought me food, water, bread, everything. He'd say, "Instead you running back and forth to the diner, you have it here" (p. 17).
>
> *Q. So what you're also saying is that there are a lot of other people there who gave tacit help, like the German soldier Schulz?*
>
> Yes, although he really didn't do much, still he did know. Many in that time found the courage to help (p. 29).
>
> It is such a story that I wanted to tell. That there are bad and good people. I am not trying to put hate on any particular group. The time is for us to reach to each other. That's the only way we can be safe, even now (Monroe 2004, 147, 162).

Both narratives reflect Irene's similar feelings toward Germans and convey how Irene was able to judge people as individuals based on their actions rather than their nationality. All coders found Irene consistent in her categorization schema, which rejected the narrow classification of human beings into national, ethnic, or religious categories.

Categorization Schema: Florentine

Although Florentine's categorization schema differs strikingly from Irene's in substance, Florentine resembles Irene in being consistent in the categorization schema presented in her two narratives. In both documents Florentine classifies people according to definitive and rigid categories, all arranged on a hierarchical scale. Nowhere is this more evident than in her discussion of, and her attraction to, her husband.

> *Book*: The great distinction that Mr. M. M. Rost van Tonningen achieved in Austria was recognized by the Austrian government, which presented him upon his departure with the Grand Cross of the Austrian Order of Merit. His superiors at that time spoke about him with high esteem. For even the most difficult problems, he always found a satisfactory solution. His chief, Dr. Zimmerman, repeatedly praised him for this ability.
>
> After Meinoud returned to the Netherlands, numerous papers proclaimed: "A GREAT DUTCHMAN RETURNS TO THE NETHERLANDS" (p. 61). . . . Moreover, he was much older than me and a born orator, surrounded by many admirers (p. 63).
>
> *Interview*: But my husband saw not only Holland but he saw all of Europe (p. 6).
>
> He was too big for Holland, too cosmopolitan to think only of this little country. He tried to do it but it was not so easy. So we had our little movements. My husband was a very good speaker so he was going around speaking to the youths, to the workers. He was the best speaker of Holland, I think (p. 8).

It is noteworthy that Florentine's only qualifications about her husband concerned differences of a hierarchical fashion: age and a rumor that he was not of pure Aryan blood.

> *Book*: I wanted to be his wife with all my heart, but . . . Wasn't the age difference too great? Then there was the rumour that there was some East Indian blood in the Rost van Tonningen family (p. 98).

Interestingly, this issue was not raised during the interview.

The coders found that these differences seemed less important to Florentine than her desire to be at the top of a political hierarchy. This was evident in her discussion of the wedding reception the Rost van Tonningens received from Hitler and Himmler.

> *Book*: When we arrived in Berlin, we got our biggest surprise yet. Not only were we greeted at the station by a grand delegation, but we also had a beautiful reception at the Hotel Adlon given by Heinrich Himmler. . . . Then Hitler himself took my hand

and wished me luck. What an aura surrounded this man! Also present were many officials of the highest rank (p. 102).

Interview: We had 2,000 people; it was a very big marriage of course. [Later] we were
invited to Berlin to the Adlon Hotel where Hitler and Himmler wanted to congratulate us. We nearly missed the train but just at the last minute, we catch the train. And
we came to the Adlon Hotel for the reception that Hitler and Himmler give for us.
Then we went on a horse-drawn bridal sleigh to . . . a wonderful house of Himmler. We went in the snow. And my husband and I get a large mountain goat from
Himmler (p. 168).

So for this reason, just the last year, I put the Rost van Tonningen genealogy into
the Aristocratic Blue Book to say how marvelous our family was, you know (p. 174).

All coders noted that Florentine identifies with the elite and powerful. She
strives to rise to the top socially and economically, which is why her belief that she
was married to one of the top political leaders of the elite race of the world carries
such appeal in both narratives. Her sense of identity makes it necessary for others
to be inferior to her, and to be distinguishable as such. Her book and interview are
similar in this regard, although her interview seems less cautious and diplomatic
in expounding these beliefs. Her categorization schema also seems connected to
Florentine's belief that the world is so morally depraved now that she is not looked
upon with reverence and respect as much as she was in the past.

Conclusion

To inquire about the reliability of narrative interpretation as a methodological tool
for social scientists I focused on one aspect of this issue: the consistency of narratives by the same person describing similar events. To further focus on arguments concerning the dependability of memories of emotionally tinged events, I
contrasted the narratives of two women who lived through World War II and the
Holocaust. Each woman wrote about these events in their autobiographies and
also gave interviews about their lives. Independent coders examined these narratives, looking for consistency on four dimensions: (1) congruence of the factual
events, (2) basic values and attitudes of the speaker, (3) self-perceptions, and (4)
categorization schema.

Three independent coders found remarkable consistency on the last three dimensions but found slight variation in the presentation of basic facts. While this
analysis is an imperfect and an initial one, it suggests that narratives provide consistent reliable tools for capturing the inner psychology of a speaker, but that analysts wishing to use narratives for historical or legal documentation need exercise
a certain caution.

APPENDIX B

Glossary of Terms and Central Concepts

THE TERMS LISTED BELOW fall into two categories: (1) terms I developed to explain key psychological phenomena that seem critical for understanding the psychology surrounding genocide, such as canonical expectations and moral salience; and (2) terms (such as identity) that are used so widely—and differently—from one scholar to another that some description of my own usage of these particular concepts is in order. My intent here is not to present a full discussion of the concept but rather to provide more specificity on how I use the term.

Canonical expectations refers to the actor's expectations about what is normal and ordinary and the actor's expectations about what should occur in the normal course of human behavior, including the actor's sense that such normal behavior is right and proper. It is not merely expectations; it carries the important overtone of something being the way it should in a normative sense.

Categorization refers to the process by which ideas and objects are recognized, differentiated, or distinguished from one another and then understood. Categorization or classification—I use the terms interchangeably—suggests objects are grouped into categories or classes, usually for some specific purpose. Ideally, a category or classification will illuminate a relationship between the subjects and objects of knowledge.

Conceptually, categorization is utilized in work on language, inference, prediction, and decision making. There are three general and slightly different approaches to categorization, beginning with the classical concept found in Plato and Aristotle. The classical Aristotelian notion of categorization posits categories as discrete entities characterized by a set of properties shared by their members. In analytic philosophy these properties then are assumed to set conditions that are both necessary and sufficient to describe meaning. These categories or classes are meant to be clearly defined, mutually exclusive, and collectively exhaustive. The implication of this is that an entry in the designated classification category belongs unequivocally to one, and only one, of the proposed categories.

In contrast to the classical Aristotelian categorization, we find conceptual categorization, designed to explain how knowledge is represented. The conceptual approach assumes classes (sometimes called clusters or entities) are generated initially by formulating their conceptual descriptions; the entities then are classified according to these descriptions. This approach emerged during the 1980s as a machine paradigm to explain unsupervised learning. It is frequently differentiated from ordinary data clustering by first generating a concept description for each generated category. Categorization in which the category labels are made available

to the learner for certain objects are called supervised classification, concept learning, or supervised learning. A categorization task in which labels are not provided
is called unsupervised classification, unsupervised learning, or data clustering.

The type of categorization/classification I have used in this book draws most
closely from the third type of categorization theory: that based on the 1970s research of Eleanor Rosch and George Lakoff and often referred to as involving the
process of grouping things based on prototypes. In this type of categorization the
idea of necessary and sufficient conditions is almost never met and the categories
refer to naturally occurring things. (Lakoff in particular emphasizes the concept of
embodiment for categorization learning.)

All these approaches accept the idea that natural categories are graded. (They
are often fuzzy at their boundaries, a metaphor that seems ideally fitted for politics.) I assume these systems of categories do not exist objectively, that they are not
"out there" in the world but instead tend to be rooted in people's experience. This
means critical conceptual categories—the good leader, the loyal subject—are not
identical for different cultures. Indeed, they may well differ for each individual in
the same polity or culture.

The research on the ethical and political implications of categorization are
largely unexplored, and I hope future work will move far beyond my initial attempts to formulate how categories might influence political and ethical acts.[1]

Ethical framework refers to the innate cognitive scaffolding that is filled in by
life experiences to help us process our responses to situations touching on ethical concerns. It comprises an individual's underlying sense of self, worldview,
agency, attitudes, and the integration of critical values into the actor's self-image.
The ethical framework works with external stimuli to produce the individual's ethical perspective at any one point in time. It is akin to our innate cognitive capacity
for language or math insofar as everyone has such a cognitive edifice; but how the
structure gets filled in is what determines whether the framework is one that produces acts and choices that are morally commendable, neutral, or evil.

Ethical perspective refers to the way the actor sees the world and him or herself
in it at the moment of action. The ethical perspective is determined by both the
actor's underlying ethical framework and the way events are framed for the actor
by the external world. The critical components are the actor's relational self, moral
imagination, canonical expectations about what is right and good in the world,
and idealized cognitive models, all of which work together to create the actor's
way of seeing the world and him or herself in it. The ethical perspective produces
the menu of choice options perceived as available and the moral imperative to act.
Understanding the ethical perspective will help us understand many moral acts,
whether these acts are ones most of us would find morally commendable, ones
that are objectively speaking morally neutral, or morally evil.

Ethics and morality. No clear scholarly consensus exists on the distinction between ethics and morality. In general, *morality* may be more personal and *ethics*
may be said to refer to a system of principles by which one lives one's life within
a certain social structure. (Hence we speak of personal morality or personal ethics but also talk of business ethics, situational ethics, and such.) But, as Ronald

Dworkin says, "We can—many people do—use either "ethical" or "moral" or both in a broader sense that erases this distinction, so that morality includes what I call ethics, and vice versa."[2] It is noteworthy that Dworkin, one of the pre-eminent legal moral theorists, defines these terms "in what might seem a special way. Moral standards prescribe how we ought to treat others; ethical standards, how we ought to live ourselves."[3] One could make a plausible argument that this distinction blurs the earlier distinction, but an equally credible argument might be made suggesting that Dworkin's distinction is in harmony with what seems to be the general usage, in which the term *ethics* tends to refer to rules of conduct recognized in regard to a particular class of human actions or a particular culture, group, etc.as in business ethics, medical ethics, religious ethics and *morality* tends to refer to an individual, as in *Her personal morality forbade betrayal of a confidence*. Since resolving this issue is probably impossible, and certainly would require a much more lengthy exposition than can be made here, it seems more prudent to simply note that the terms *ethics* and *morality* tend to be used interchangeably in the field of moral psychology. Certainly there are differences that have occurred at different points in time and according to discipline, but these differences are not consistent. Hence, I use the terms interchangeably.

Framing refers to how facts are presented to us. Frames consist of a schema or a collection of stereotypes that people rely on to understand and respond to events, hence the term "frame the event." We also might think of frames as schema of interpretation or as a series of mental emotional filters developed throughout our lifetimes that we use to understand and make sense of the world. Any given choice we make will be influenced by the frame or the emotional filter through which we view and process the choice. Framing is influenced by how a choice is worded and the background or context for the choice options.[4] The frame of reference frequently influences how the event is interpreted. Most individuals are unaware of the frames of reference they bring to an event, but these frames have been found to determine the choice made in critical ways. Framing has an influence over the individual's perception of the meaning attributed to the word, phrase, or act that defines the packaging of an event in a manner that encourages certain interpretations and discourages other interpretations.

Idealized cognitive models, frequently abbreviated as ICMs, are defined as the mental representations by which we organize our knowledge. The category structures and prototype effects are by-products of that organization. The idea for idealized cognitive models comes from several sources in cognitive linguistics: Charles Fillmore's frame semantics (1982), George Lakoff and Mark Johnson's theory of metaphor and metonymy (1980), Ronald Langacker's cognitive grammar (1986), and Gilles Fauconnier's theory of mental spaces (1985). The concept is widely utilized to explain language development, suggesting that people have a mental representation of, for example, a chair and then use this concept to fill in what an armchair is or an easy chair, deck chair, rocking chair, and so on. Culture enters the cognitive process here in ways we do not yet fully understand.

The concept of an idealized cognitive model is seldom discussed in ethics; it nonetheless provides a useful concept for further exploration since it is possible that these more primitive representations may develop into more complex schema or scripts about how we should behave in certain situations. We can trace the origins of this concept to Plato's (370 BCE) theory of forms, which are rough archetypes or abstract representations of the many types and properties or universals of things we see all around us. Plato's work suggests how these forms are represented in our mind and how they carry ethical overtones. How we fill in the general form for our concept of justice, for example, differs for individuals, cultures, and polities; these differences affect our dispensing of justice as we conceptualize it. But even simpler idealized cognitive models carry ethical overtones.[5] For example, the narratives in this book illustrate the extensive influence that emanated from the actors' idealized cognitive models of what constituted the good life or of what it meant to be a human being. Some of these were discussed in chapter 8.[6]

Identity is an umbrella term used throughout the social sciences, most frequently to describe an individual person's conceptualization and expression of individuality or group affiliations, such as cultural or national identity. In psychology, identity most often refers to an individual's sense of him- or herself as an entity that is discrete and separate from others. In practice, identity is used interchangeably with concepts such as *the self* and *character*, and I have adopted this practice here rather than parsing fine distinctions among the three different terms. An important part of this conceptualization of identity is its emphasis on the individual's own comprehension or self-concept. In philosophy, identity is often used interchangeably with the term *sameness* to define whatever it is that makes an entity recognizable and definable, as for example, over time. Both of these conceptualizations can refer to either micro- or group-level identity, as can cultural identity or an individual's self-affiliation as a member of a cultural group. While individual identity can shift as the individual likes, an individual's cultural identity can be designated by the categorization by others. This cultural identity then can feed into the individual identity, as it did for many secular Jews during World War II.

Identity is a concept utilized in a wide variety of fields, from computer science to business accounting. My discussion of it draws on diverse traditions in social science, not political science, since the most frequent use in political science tends to refer to group politics, as in various national group identities—Asian American, African American, etc. While political scientists thus highlight the important aspect of identity politics that refers to political arguments concentrating on the self-interest of groups and the perspectives of self-identified social interest groups or minorities, this political science approach tends to ignore the fact that individual people have multiple identities that are fluid and intersect. I use the term in a more individual way to refer to one person's sense of self. I assume identity forms in some kind of nature-nurture way that will vary and that identity formation refers to the process through which the distinct personality of an individual develops.

Moral psychology is a newly emerging field at the intersection of ethics, social and biological science. Interdisciplinary in nature, contemporary moral psychology was initially narrowly defined to refer to the study of moral development, with the emphasis on the study of moral reasoning. In the last two decades of the twentieth century, however, this conceptualization expanded, as psychologists increasingly recognized the importance of emotions, intuitions, and innate predispositions for action. Reason still figures in accounts of moral psychology and plays a role in moral judgment, but reason now is frequently said to operate in a space that is prefigured by affect. An important shift in recent work in moral psychology thus is the move away from the emphasis on logic and reasoning.

Contemporary moral psychology draws heavily on the conceptual resources of philosophical ethics and the empirical resources of the human sciences concerned with the philosophy of mind that inquires about how we think and feel about ethics and morality. This conceptualization makes moral psychology a subfield of political psychology, itself defined to refer to the study of how the human mind thinks about politics and how these psychological processes then in turn influence political behavior. This broader conceptualization makes the domain of moral psychology include, but not be restricted to, research on moral decision making, choice, responsibility, character, luck, courage, imagination, disagreement, virtue ethics, forgiveness, and work on psychological egoism and altruism and their behavioral manifestations at both the individual and group level.

Moral salience is the sense or feeling that moves us beyond feeling a generalized sympathy at the plight of others to create a felt imperative to take action to alleviate the others' suffering. Moral salience emanates from a particular cognitive process of categorizing others—friends or foe, innocent or guilty—that then creates (or fails to create) a feeling that another's suffering is relevant for the observer. The key is the relational bond between the sufferer and the observer. Once a bond is established, another's suffering becomes relevant, much as the suffering of our children, spouse or parents is experienced as directly relevant for most of us and requires us to take action to remedy the situation causing our loved ones' pain. Experiencing moral salience means we feel another's suffering requires action to alleviate it; it is not sufficient to experience just a generalized feeling of concern or sympathy. The preconscious or subconscious aspect of moral salience sets it apart from duty-bound acts of moral courage found in the more traditional, Anglo-American approaches to ethics, which frequently assume that moral choice involves actors who recognize the existence of a morally relevant situation, deliberate or reflect on the options and moral principles and then finally act in accordance with or on the basis of this conscious deliberation.

Ontological security refers to the stable mental state that is derived from a sense of order and continuity concerning events and experiences in one's life. Anthony Giddens (1991) relates this sense of ontological security to an actor's ability to give meaning to his/her life. This meaning is derived from avoiding chaos and anxiety and from experiencing a positive view of one's self, the world, and the future.[7] Events that are inconsistent with the existing meaning of an individual's life will trigger anxiety and will threaten that individual's sense of ontological security.[8]

Schemas are structured parcels of knowledge that can include several concepts: (1) organized patterns of behavior or thought, (2) structured clusters of pre-conceived ideas, (3) mental arrangements representing different aspects of the world, (4) specific cognitive representations of the self, (5) mental frameworks focusing on specific themes that help organize social information, and (6) cognitive organizations of both our knowledge and assumptions about a particular thing that then are used to interpret and process information. Schema influence attention; we are much more likely to notice things that fit into our existing schematic framework. Information that contradict our schema may be interpreted as exceptions or unique. Our schemas give rise to scripts, or "conceptual representations of action sequences associated with particular social situations."[9] Even if the actor is not aware of these scripts or schema, their influence still is felt, thus possibly providing the route for behavior that appears spontaneous, as was the case for so much behavior during the Holocaust.

Worldview refers to the basic cognitive orientation of an individual or society, the essential view or the fundamental outlook the actor possesses. It includes the framework of ideas and beliefs through which the actor perceives, interprets, and interacts with the world. The concept of worldview encompasses the actor's values, emotions, ethics, natural philosophy, and the fundamental existential and normative postulates or themes. (Weltanschauung might be a close synonym.)

Worldview partakes of critical aspects of ideology but can be distinguished from ideology as a concept in critical ways. Ideology is a system of abstract thought that is applied to public matters primarily via a set of aims and ideas that directs the actor's goals and expectations and the actions designed to obtain those goals. While ideology does include a comprehensive vision or way of looking at things, a fundamental part of an ideology is the desire to change society or the political world and to present a set of ideals having to do with politics. (As an example, Marxism is an ideology.) A worldview does not have to include a political agenda; for example, it can simply be an optimistic worldview, as when we say someone sees the world through rose-colored glasses or sees the glass as half full.

In deciphering the cognitive construals that relate to worldview, group identity, ontological security, and cognitive classification we need to understand how much of an actor's ethical perspective remains static and how much will shift as a result of changes in external stimuli and framing, as is suggested by thousands of experiments in social psychology.[10] What are the critical triggers for different individuals? We know worldviews differ from one individual to another. But does this difference occur by chance? How and what triggers a shift in worldview for any one individual? Of particular interest should be concern to understand how these filters shift the actor's sense of self into a cognitive categorization and classification of the "other" so that the other is seen in a way that encourages a psychic move beyond sympathy for the other's plight to a felt imperative to turn that sympathy into an act of help. This is in contrast to an ethical perspective that allows the actor to remain indifferent to the suffering of another, to feel sympathy but not to feel an imperative to help, or to even feel that the other person is a threat and must be destroyed before he can kill you. These will all be critical questions to answer as we attempt to understand more about *how* moral choice works through the ethical perspective.

∾

ACKNOWLEDGMENTS

1. In most cases, I have changed names and minor details of speakers' narratives to camouflage identities for privacy and, in a few instances, for security reasons. When speakers or their families specifically asked me to use their full names, I have done so.

2. Sometimes this assistance had unanticipated results. Before a talk at Trinity College in Dublin, I asked my beautiful fourteen-year-old daughter to "fix up" my PowerPoint presentation, hoping she could tone down the color of the backdrop for the slides. Chloe interpreted my mundane request creatively, and as I stood before a large audience, the fifth slide appeared with dancing letters flying in from all directions and buzzing around on the screen in glorious patterns. People have long since forgotten the content of my talk but a surprising number of ISPP scholars still come up to me at meetings and tell me how much they enjoyed Chloe's PowerPoint presentation design.

CHAPTER 1
INTRODUCTION

1. Because these perspectival differences are so important, subtle, and difficult to detect, I document the variety of perspectives through extensive presentation of the "raw data," the narrative interviews with the people I interviewed, as I did in previous work. Except for Tony and Florentine, all speakers are given different names, and certain descriptions of them have been modified to protect their privacy. Tony and Florentine explicitly asked to have their real names used.

2. I use the terms *ethical* and *moral* interchangeably, though I note (1) that many scholars define the two differently and (2) that there is far from uniform agreement over the acceptable distinctions between the two terms/concepts. (See Appendix B for further discussion of terminology.) The concept of an ethical framework has an applicability that extends far beyond the Holocaust. It can be utilized to explain behavior in a wide range of circumstances, as I discuss in chapter 9.

3. Monroe (1996).

4. Monroe (1995, 2008).

5. A group of scholars, headed by Michael Spezio, are already using some of these data as they construct their cognitive models of moral exemplars. See Spezio and Adolphs (2007). My data will be given to museums of tolerance and Holocaust museums and will be made available to all scholars at www.ethicscenter.uci.edu, the website of the UCI Interdisciplinary Center for the Scientific Study of Ethics and Morality.

6. My independent research on Florentine's husband's confirmed her description of him. Meinoud Rost van Tonningen was an extremely important person in the Nazi movement. In particular, he played a major role with regard to the Waffen-SS in the Netherlands. He and Henk Feldmeijer were the founders of the Mussert-Garde in 1939. This paramilitary youth organization of the National Socialist Movement (Nationaal-Socialistische Beweging) (NSB) developed into a pre-SS and laid the foundations for the Dutch SS and recruiting

Dutch volunteers for the Waffen-SS. Some historians credit Rost van Tonningen with giving Dutch National Socialism its virulent anti-Semitic tone.

7. Florentine described this position as equivalent to being both the US Secretary of the Treasury and head of the Federal Reserve Board.

8. These terms are employed in a wide variety of disciplines and, as a result, are utilized differently by various scholars. A glossary (Appendix B) clarifies my use of these key terms.

CHAPTER 2
THE HOLOCAUST AND GENOCIDE

1. I use the word *gypsy* since it is better known in the West, but the preferred term is *Roma*. The term refers to wanderers (called Romany) and is probably of Hindu origin. According to the *Oxford English Dictionary*, the term first appeared in English in the sixteenth century and was used, by people like Shakespeare, to refer to people who roamed around but came from Egypt. The Roma had been persecuted in central Europe long before the Nazis, but the Nazis decided the Roma were both social inferiors (outside normal society) and had "alien" blood. The Nazis thus stepped up the persecution under the direction of Dr. Robert Ritter, a child psychologist at the University of Tübingen and a chief proponent of criminal biology, the idea that genetics determines crime. Ritter became the chief expert on classifying Roma. Some 500,000 Roma were killed during the Holocaust because, according to Nazi race doctrine, despite their Aryan roots, the Roma had intermingled with other people and diluted their blood, hence making it impure.

2. I am indebted to Shimon Samuels, director of the Simon Wiesenthal Center in Paris, for suggesting this description of the Holocaust. The concept of the *first among equals*, or *first among peers* is a Latin phrase usually suggesting that a person is the most senior of a group of people sharing the same rank or office. When the phrase is not being used to refer to a specific title, it may imply that the person is technically equal but looked on as an authority of special importance by his/her peers or is the group's unofficial or hidden leader. In terms of the Holocaust, I believe the phrase is designed to retain a sense of the unique nature of the Holocaust for the Jewish people while recognizing that the Holocaust takes on an additional importance insofar as studying it can teach us about other instances of genocide and ethnic cleansing. This seems the current resolution to a long-standing and often-heated scholarly debate over whether the Holocaust was unique.

3. Definitional clarity is necessary but should not detract us from the fact that even if an event does not fall into the technical category of a genocide—however defined—it nonetheless may be an evil that should be extinguished and lamented. For example, one of the controversies in the scholarly debate over what constitutes genocide concerns the question of intent. For example, were the Native Americans who were wiped out by Europeans through war and disease killed as the result of a genocide? How many of the deaths that came as a result of disease were intended, a deliberate part of the Europeans to conquer the New World and subdue the native peoples, even when this meant deliberately giving small-pox infected blankets to Indian tribes? How much were the deaths a natural and inevitable part of contact among different groups with different health immunities? Again in terms of intent, does an official government have to be involved in planning an event for the event to constitute a genocide? What if there are no supporting documents? What nature of proof do we need to label something a genocide? These issues are all fascinating and important but lie beyond the scope of this volume.

4. The precise date and document are unclear, varying according to the source.

5. Lemkin (1933, 117–19).

6. See Cooper (2008) for a biography of Lemkin.

7. Lemkin (1944, ix).

8. *Sunday Times*, October 21, 1945.

9. Lemkin (1944, 80).

10. Lemkin (1944, 79).

11. Office of the High Commissioner for Human Rights (1951).

12. Fein (1993, 24). Fein argues that genocide is not only a one-sided mass murder but also a violation of the life-integrity principle since it negates the biological and social integrity of people and groups that transcends culture and ages.

13. Fein makes these distinctions clear in her work (1990, 1993) and discusses them in more detail.

14. Fein makes this distinction between ideological and retributive genocide. Fein also tends to explain genocide as a more rational act, insofar as the perpetrators calculate the likelihood of success and view genocide as a legitimate tool to attain their desired ends. She also finds that state leaders anticipate, on the basis of past experiences, that more powerful states and bystanders (patrons or allies) either will aid the *genocidaires* or fail to check them. Goldhagen (2009) also assumes a rational component of genocide in which politicians pursue eliminationist policies to enhance their own goals or power; Goldhagen advocates a cost/benefit response in which the world unites to make genocide too costly a policy for elites to pursue.

15. *Untermenschen* was used in Nazi ideology to describe people the Nazis considered inferior. It most frequently referred to those "masses" from the East, and included Jews, gypsies or Roma, Slavs, homosexuals, Bolsheviks and any others not considered Aryan. In Yiddish, *Mensch* literally means human being but with the connotation of a person of decency, honor, and integrity, someone to admire and emulate. We might use it in slang to refer to a stand-up kind of guy or what my Grandpa Bob would have called a prince among men.

16. I cannot determine the origin of the term *white* for this event but am guessing it is to distinguish it from the bloodiness—and hence red—of genocide that involves murder.

17. See Petrovic (1994).

18. Hayden (1996, 727–48).

19. According to international law, as enshrined in the acts of the International Court of Justice (ICJ), *ethnic cleansing* on its own is not enough to establish that a genocide has occurred. See the Bosnian Genocide Case in the judgment of *Jorgic v. Germany* on July 12, 2007, at the European Court of Human Rights.

20. Ferdinandusse (2004, 1042n7).

21. See Article 7 of the Rome Statute of the International Criminal Court or Article 5 of the Updated Statute of the International Criminal Tribunal for the former Yugoslavia.

22. Shraga and Zacklin (2004).

23. Baum (2008).

24. Estimates on genocide vary according to source and conceptual subtleties in defining genocide. For example, Rummel (1996) estimated 38.6 million deaths from genocide in the twentieth century. (This calculation was made in 1994 and hence before later genocides, such as the 800,000 believed murdered in Rwanda.) Beyond this, the legal definition of genocide does not include mass killings of political groups (sometimes referred to as politicide), indiscriminate state-supported massacres or other state-sponsored killings, or deaths from the bombing of civilian populations. When Rummel tallied up these killings—a phenomenon he called democide—he found that (by 1994) the twentieth century

had 169 million who died by government killings. This calculation is some 93 million less than Baum's. Does this difference matter? At some level, murdering innocent people is an important problem regardless of the number of people killed. At another level, a difference of 93 million people is too great for most of us to fully comprehend. For my purposes the critical factor is not how many died from genocide but what causes genocide, so I leave this discussion aside.

25. There are many ironies here. From a biological point of view, we are all members of the human race, and hence the racial divides the Nazis found immutable cannot exist. Beyond this, the logic of the Nazi classification system is elusive, at best. Religion is hardly a category into which one may not shift; yet being born into the Jewish religion was said to constitute a racial classification. Further, many homosexuals would argue that sexual preference is not a matter of choice so much as of birth. Yet the Nazis considered this an act of volition. Bedwetting was a category that was persecuted for a time period, and being Polish was deemed something that was not a "stable" category even though one could argue that nationality should be just as immutable as ethnicity.

26. According to the *Whitaker Report* (1985), the first genocide of the twentieth century occurred in 1904 when the German military tried to kill members of two native groups in Southwest Africa, members of the Herero and Nama. According to this report, water holes were poisoned and the peace emissaries sent by the African tribes were shot. Estimates are that three-quarters of the Herero Africans were killed by the Germans colonizing what is now present day Namibia, reducing the Hereros from 80,000 to 15,000 starving refugees. See Fraenk (1985) or Crawford (2002, chap. 2).

27. Lerner (1992).

28. Rwanda was a German colony in 1910, awarded by the League of Nations to the Belgians to administer in 1923. In July 1962, Rwanda achieved independence from Belgium. The Tutsi (the people of the north, who are lighter skinned, taller, and hence judged more "European" looking) constituted 15 percent of the populace but under the Belgians had enjoyed a privileged status over the 84 percent who were Hutu and 1 percent of a small minority called the Twa. This changed with independence, when the Hutu dominated and reversed the earlier discrimination imposed by Belgians. The Tutsi thus became systematically discriminated against and periodically subjected to waves of killing and ethnic cleansing. From 1963 to 1994, there was increasing tension, which exploded in 1994 with a Hutu plot and arming of Hutu civilian population during early 1994. The "Dallaire fax," by the Canadian lieutenant general and UN peacekeeper Romeo Dallaire, was sent to New York. In it Dallaire claimed that Hutu extremists "had been ordered to register all the Tutsi in Kigali" (Des Forges 1999, 150). Fearing the extermination of the Tutsi, Dallaire asked for more troops to stop possible violence. Instead, his force was reduced from 3,000 to 500 men. This set the stage for genocide, which involved Hutus from all backgrounds. On April 6, 1994, the airplane carrying President Juvenal Habyarimana and President Cyprien Ntaryamira of Burundi was shot down, killing both men. From April 7 on, the Hutu controlled the army, the gendarmerie, and the militias, all of which worked together to wipe out Rwanda's Tutsi. Radio transmissions inciting fear among the Hutus were critical to the success of the genocide and are credited with making the Hutus feel they were under attack and needed to strike first to avoid being killed. Radio Mille Collines, the Hutu station, broadcast a wave of inflammatory propaganda urging the Hutus to "kill the cockroaches." Hutus responded, using surprisingly primitive weapons—knives, axes, machetes—and Tutsi fled their homes en masse, in panic, only to be trapped and butchered at checkpoints by the Hutu secret squads, the *interahamwe*, who used guns and clubs to kill the fleeing Tutsi civilians. The women and

younger men were especially targeted as they represented the future of the Tutsi minority. Women were raped in large numbers and then frequently killed, a pattern reminiscent of the Armenian genocide.

29. Some analysts include as genocide the murder of the 500,000 Indonesian Communists during 1965–66 by Indonesian army units and militias under Suharto. In 1971, during the East Pakistan—now Bangladesh—struggle for independence, the Muslim Pakistani Army killed between 1.5 and three million people, with the presumed goal of eliminating the eight to ten million Hindus living in the area. In the 1970s the Ugandan dictator Idi Amin killed nearly 400,000 Ugandans, and the Khmer rouge killed 1.7 million Cambodians. These deaths are reprehensible but seem to fall outside the commonly accepted category of genocide. Similarly, some abortion opponents refer to abortion as genocide. I also exclude that from genocide, adopting the more frequently and widely accepted definition employed by the United Nations.

30. Although Iraq is more usually discussed as a civil war, as of June 21, 2007, the UN High Commissioner for Refugees nonetheless estimated that 2.2 million Iraqis had been displaced to neighboring countries, and two million were displaced internally, with nearly 100,000 Iraqis fleeing to Syria and Jordan each month.

31. Slobodan Milošević was president of Yugoslavia (1997–2000) and Serbia (1989–97). A controversial figure, whose detractors called him the "Butcher of the Balkans" and accused him of starting four wars, Milošević's followers dubbed him a peacemaker who did everything in his power to prevent war. Milošević was arrested by Serbian authorities early on April 1, 2001, on suspicion of embezzlement, corruption, and abuse of power. An initial investigation faltered due to a lack of hard evidence; Serbian Prime Minister Zoran Dindic then sent Milošević to The Hague to stand trial on charges of war crimes. The War Crimes Tribunal at The Hague charged Milošević with crimes against humanity, with violating the laws or customs of war, grave breaches of the Geneva Convention, and genocide for his role during the wars in Croatia, Bosnia, and Kosovo. Milošević protested these charges and conducted his own defense. The trial ended without a verdict after Milošević died from a heart attack.

32. See Fein (1993); Staub (1989); or Monroe (1995) for a review.

33. Walzer (1977).

34. Crawford (2002).

35. Donnelly (2003).

36. Sears, Sidanius, and Bobo (2000).

37. Gourevitch (1998).

38. Valentino (2004); Fein (1993); Walter (1999); Rudolph and Rudolph (1993).

39. Staub (1989); Post (1999).

40. Staub (1989).

41. Hiebert (2008).

42. Gobodo-Madikizela (2003).

43. Petersen (2002).

44. The Bush administration's policy of declaring enemy combatants extraordinary instances that fall beyond the pale of ordinary treatment under Anglo-American law, or even the Geneva Convention on war, was yet another troubling instance of this approach.

45. Koenigsberg (2005a).

46. Kaufman (2000, 2001).

47. Although these concepts carry diverse meanings, the empirical work on genocide uses them interchangeably. See Monroe (2004) or Lebow (2003) for discussions of terminology.

48. Anscombe (1958); Nussbaum (1986); Slote (1983).

49. Smith (1976b [1759/1853]). Smith's term *sympathy* corresponds to contemporary notions of empathy. The word *empathy* itself was not invented until the nineteenth century as a term in art to denote entering into the artist's way of seeing the world. In the twentieth century empathy became employed among psychologists to refer to entering another's head in order to understand the other person.

50. See any article or book by Batson (e.g., 1991) or Monroe and Martinez (2007) for a review.

51. Reykowski (2001).

52. Dovidio (1984); Macaulay and Berkowitz (1988).

53. Axelrod (1984).

54. Alford (2001).

55. McFarland (2006); McFarland and Webb (2004).

56. Blasi (2003); Colby and Damon (1992).

57. Monroe and Martinez (2007).

58. Kinnvall (2004); Staub (1989, 2003).

59. Glass (1997).

60. Alford (1997); MacIntyre and Grant (2006).

61. Federn (1960).

62. Baum's (2008) analysis of the psychology of genocide, for example, uses trait theory in combination with social psychology to discern psychological patterns that suggest that how people respond during genocide will reflect their everyday behavior. Baum draws on eyewitness accounts to suggest common mental and emotional traits in everyday life that predict how all the participants will arrange themselves on a moral continuum, from rescuers and bystanders to perpetrators. Baum finds less of a break between traits in ordinary life and traits that are critical during genocide.

63. Fogelman (1994).

64. Le Bon (1952 [1896]).

65. Tajfel (1970, 1981).

66. Presumably, Tajfel survived in part by denying his Jewish identity and pretending to be a member of another ethnic group. After the war, Tajfel first spent his time helping rebuild the lives of orphans and concentration camp survivors. In this capacity, he worked for international relief organizations such as the United Nations' International Refugee Organization. But in 1946 Tajfel began studying psychology. After receiving his degree in 1954, Tajfel applied for British citizenship. He began his work at the University of Oxford in social psychology, with a focus on prejudice and nationalism. He is most closely associated with the University of Bristol, where he was made Chair of Social Psychology in 1967 and where he remained until his death from cancer in 1982.

67. Tajfel and Turner (1979); Turner (1982); Turner and Hogg (1987).

68. In this sense, Tajfel opposed the approach of realistic group conflict theorists, such as Sherif. Indeed, Tajfel's studies reject the idea that explicit and objective conflicts of interest are necessary for conflict to emerge (Sherif 1962 [1953]; Sherif et al. 1961).

69. Sometimes participants were told they were grouped according to preference for abstract art, with one group preferring work by Paul Klee and another preferring art by Wassily Kandinsky. Sometimes they were told to estimate the number of dots on slides and then were divided into groups who consistently overestimated or who consistently underestimated the accurate number of dots. Sometimes participants were told they were assigned by a toss of a coin. The random nature of the assignment was critical since the group identification was not something that would ordinarily be associated with a natural interest that would serve as a basis of group conflict.

70. Much of the power of this theory as initially constructed by Tajfel comes from the emphasis on self-esteem as a fundamental need in human nature (Tajfel and Turner 1979, 40). Marilyn Brewer's work (1999, 2007) shifts this need slightly from self-esteem to a human need for security, with the rituals and symbolism of group life playing an important part of the "profoundly social nature of human beings as a species" (2007, 730). In-groups thus become "bounded communities of mutual cooperation and trust" (2007, 732). Later social identity theorists differ over the extent to which in-group solidarity is necessarily related to hostility toward out-groups. See Gibson and Gouws (2000); Perreault and Bourhis (1999); and Kinder and Kam (2009, 18–24) for a review.

71. Tajfel and his students thus rejected both individualistic explanations of group behavior (e.g., Allport et al. 1950) and theories that reified the group (as in theories emphasizing the madness of crowd behavior [Le Bon 1952]). Tajfel argued that we have complex identities and can choose from a wide array of our identities at any one moment. The social context will influence this choice, sometimes evoking personal identities, in which case the individual will relate to others in an interpersonal manner, depending on the other's character traits and any personal relationship existing between the individuals. But under other conditions, a social identity, Tajfel argued, would become more important. In this case, behavior will be qualitatively different and will be group behavior.

72. Staub (1989). Staub's moving, disturbing tour de force analyzes the psychological underpinnings of both the Holocaust and related and equally disturbing events, such as the mass killings in Cambodia by the Khmer Rouge or the disappearances in Argentina under the colonels. Staub concludes with a consideration of positive psychology and the role of groups that can secure justice and more positive connections. His solution emphasizes the important socialization done by parents, family, and schools and the role of language and the ability of ideas to effect change. Since then, Staub has been a leader in the effort to understand and build on scholarly understanding of reconciliation after genocide and ethnic cleansing. His work is the first stop for those interested in the topic. See Staub (2011).

73. Bar-Tal (1990); Bar-Tal and Teichman (2005).

74. Kinder and Kam (2009) find Tajfel's work a major explanation of ethnocentrism.

75. Petersen (2002, 3–4); Mamdani (2001, 22).

76. Fujii (2006).

77. Mamdani (2001). There has been too little work asking why such formalized power-sharing arrangements sometimes work, as they did in Lebanon for many years, and why they fail, as they have done in Lebanon since the late 1970s (see Lijphart 1969, 1977).

78. Browning (1992); Fujii (2006). Fujii notes that a focus on bystanders-rescuers-perpetrators obscures acts of killing and rescue that do not originate with people who fall squarely into these categories. It allows scholars to avoid confronting the "grey zones of activity during genocide where people often elide, straddle and violate standard categories of analysis" (Fujii no date: Manuscript titled "Rescuers and Killers during the Rwandan Genocide: Rethinking Standard Categories of Analysis." In the author's possession.)

79. Ten Boom (1974); Gies (1987).

80. London (1970).

81. Tec (1986); Oliner and Oliner (1988); Rittner and Myers (1986); Monroe (1996, 2004).

82. Staub (2003).

83. Ophüls (1971).

84. Tanay in Rittner and Myers (1986).

85. This documentary was produced and directed by Robert Gardner.

86. Abramson (1999); Langer (1991); McGaugh (2003); Monroe (2004).

87. I have discussed the issue of reliability of memory, especially of traumatic events, extensively in *The Hand of Compassion* (2004). Without reviewing that argument here, I believe the cognitive portraits painted here are the same ones that were in existence during World War II and are not the result of a process that occurred fifty years after the event. The fact that survivors agree with me on this is significant evidence supporting this conclusion. For the best summaries of issues of traumatic memory and their reliability, see McGaugh (2003) or Langer (1991).

88. Oliner and Oliner (1988).

89. Nussbaum (1986).

90. Reykowski (1987, 2001).

91. Fogelman (1994).

92. McFarland (2006); McFarland and Webb (2004).

93. Hamer and Gutowski (2006).

94. Staub (1989); Bar-Tal (2000); Glass (1997).

95. Bar-Tal (1990).

96. Giddens (1991); Kinnvall (2004).

97. Afrikaners' attitudes toward the blacks illustrate the broader notion that bystanders also see themselves as victims of circumstance, poverty, or fate. See interviews with Eugene de Kock (Gobodo-Madikizela 2003).

98. Hochschild (2005).

99. I am grateful to an anonymous referee for pointing out Kressel's work. I found Kressel's distinction between crimes of initiative and crimes of submission intriguing but note that his *Mass Hate* (the 2002 revised version) takes frequent ideological potshots at respected scholars, such as Altemeyer and Sidanius, accusing them of leftist or liberal bias.

100. Lakoff (1987); Monroe (1995).

101. Gaertner et al. (1989).

102. Kreidie and Monroe (2002).

103. Monroe (2001, 2009).

104. Staub (1989).

105. Lerner (1992).

106. Sapolsky (2006).

107. Staub (2003)

108. What Staub calls blind patriots, for example, say "I love my group no matter what," while constructive patriots say "because I love my group, I will critique it so it will become even better." Sapolsky's (2006) work on porous boundaries also includes animal altruism.

109. "In a community of people depressed by their circumstances, beset by life's struggles, thwarted in their hopes, how do you bring such an act into the range of possible choices? How do we even make it thinkable?" (Gobodo-Madikizela 2003, 75). "How can conscience get suppressed to the point where people can allow themselves to commit horrible acts against others? Should one ask as well what kind of society or ideology enables such suppression?" (2003, 52).

110. Andreas-Friedrich (1947, 116–17).

111. Gobodo-Madikizela (2003).

112. Lifton (1976, 27).

113. Gobodo-Madikizela describes perception of events during the entire apartheid period as "something happening outside the boundaries of reality" (2003, 75). This underlies the broader importance of this phenomenon.

114. Gobodo-Madikizela (2003, 76).

115. Arendt (1963 [1968]). I use the concept of cognitive stretching to refer to both (1) society's ability to get its members to accept horrible acts that were previously unimaginable and (2) the process whereby an individual realizes the boundaries of ordinary political behavior have been breached and one's moral imagination has to stretch to accommodate the new political reality. In the second case, the individual can respond either by accepting the new political reality (as most Germans did) or refuse to accept it and become an émigré, a political dissident, or a rescuer, for example.

116. Gobodo-Madikizela (2003, 111).

117. Yahil (1990, 545).

118. Levi (1993 [1965], 215).

119. Lifton in Falk et al. (1971, 419–29).

120. Adorno et al. (1950); Bullock (1962, 1991).

121. This approach follows Blasi's (2003) work on the integration of values, Reykowski's (2001) work on worldview, and my own earlier findings (2004) on the relational aspect to self-perceptions as an influence on moral choice.

122. I have discussed the concept and use of narrative extensively in *The Hand of Compassion*, from which sections of the following are drawn. The original work on narrative was written with Molly Patterson (Patterson and Monroe 1998).

123. See Patterson and Monroe (1998).

124. Readers interested in narrative should consult many of the excellent works in this area, such as those by Molly Andrews (2007). For an overview, see my appendix on narrative in *The Hand of Compassion* (2004), which discusses the development of narrative as a tool in social science, asks if there are universals in human behavior that can be detected via narratives, discusses how witness is born in an oral culture, and provides a cognitive view of narrative and ordinary discourse. I also address the importance of narratives as sites of cultural contestation and in the construction of social science theory and discuss some of the cautions in interpreting narratives. Because of all this, I encourage journal editors to expand their use of narratives, which are powerful tools for analysis but which require more journal pages to craft the careful analysis than do other methodologies in social science.

125. Monroe et al. (2009).

126. Coles (1989); Patterson and Monroe (1998); Bar-On (2006); Andrews (2007).

127. Geertz (1973).

128. Thacher (2006); Williams (1986).

129. There are many complications for social scientists seeking methodological purity using real-life or natural data. For example, there is no way that anyone could ever draw a technically random sample of rescuers, perpetrators, or bystanders, since that would require compiling a complete list of all the individuals in those categories and then taking a random subsample from that. This would be impossible. I began with the Yad Vashem list of certified rescuers and sampled randomly from this list, adjusting the sample only to avoid overconcentration in terms of characteristics such as gender or nationality. Interviewing bystanders and Nazi supporters is perhaps even more complicated, and with rare exception one relies on self-identification. In methodological terms, these participants would most appropriately be called a target sample—some researchers might refer to them as a non-probability sample or a sample of convenience—of people willing to speak with researchers about their activities, motivations, etc. during the war. Although it is impossible to ascertain how representative they are of the population of bystanders/Nazi supporters as a whole, all the individuals in these two groups provide extremely useful information about an understudied group that rarely comes forward for research.

130. See Thacher (2006) for a discussion of the ability to generalize from case studies when addressing normative issues. The kind of "matched" case studies utilized here are particularly revealing of the worldview of the people speaking (Geertz 1973), with such case studies widely held to be especially valuable in illuminating the subjective meaning people's actions carry for them. For a more general discussion on the value of case studies in social science, see Max Weber's discussion of the value of interpretive case studies in contributing to our understanding (*verstehen*) through identifying the motivations and worldview that inform social action (Weber 1978, 7–8). Thacher argues that the normative case study is especially useful for analyzing "thick" ethical concepts, such as moral courage, that will carry both descriptive and evaluative dimensions that are difficult to disentangle (see also Williams 1986, 129–44). Essentially, I paired these case studies in order to obtain a level of nonexperimental design control that we don't usually find in studies using naturalistic data. There is a fine line to walk between experimental and natural data. There is an inevitable messiness inherent in analyzing data in the "real world," just as there is a sterility and artificiality potential in experiments that can control for such background factors. Further, experimental data must omit the kind of extreme altruism or moral courage that much of the literature has focused on (Oliner and Oliner 1988) and institutional review boards quite properly prohibit. To address these related methodological problems, I began with a sample of rescuers certified by Yad Vashem. (The Oliners and Fogelman also used this technique, which is now widely accepted.) To obtain bystander and Nazi supporters, I then used a combination of respondent-driven/nominee samples, where the person sampled provides the name of someone who resembles them on certain background characteristics but who differs in one critical regard, in this case activity toward Jews during World War II. This provided a way to find "comparable" bystanders and Nazi supporters who had at least a few critical background characteristics in common with the rescuer. This is an imperfect technique but probably the best way to control for background similarities in a nonexperimental context.

I also was curious to learn how much of the self-serving justification of memoirs/autobiographies would exist in the narrative interviews obtained through an interview process when there were personal introductions made and a more neutral context provided. I tried a number of techniques to determine how extensive was the overlap between interviews and others forms of data from bystanders, rescuers, or perpetrators; for example, I was able to test for differences between memoirs and my interviews in the few cases where rescuers or Nazis had written memoirs. I made a close textual analysis—again using different coders—and found differences in tone and emphasis but not substance. In general, the memoirs were simply more self-conscious and self-serving. This issue has been addressed by others, most eloquently by Lawrence Langer (1991), who makes a strong case that oral testimonies provide a truer reflection of the moral ambiguity that exists in situations of incredible moral and physical stress, such as the Holocaust. See Appendix A for fuller exposition of some of these issues.

131. The technique utilized to obtain these interviews resembles a respondent-driven (sometimes called a nominee) sample, a special form of snowball sampling. Snowball sampling is a technique commonly used in sociology to develop a research sample through asking existing study subjects to recruit future subjects from among their acquaintances. (Hence the name snowball, since the sample group appears to grow like a rolling snowball.) It is widely accepted for use with politically controversial or hidden populations that are difficult for researchers to access, for example, drug users, commercial sex workers, or, as in this case, people who might not like their Nazi or bystander past to become widely known. Because sample members are not selected from a sampling frame, snowball samples are

subject to numerous biases. (For example, people who have many friends are more likely to be recruited into the sample.) The question thus becomes: Can we make unbiased estimates from snowball samples? The variation of snowball sampling known as respondent-driven sampling has been shown statistically to allow researchers to make asymptotically unbiased estimates from snowball samples given certain conditions. The respondent-driven sampling also allows researchers to make estimates about the social network connecting the hidden population. On these technical, statistical issues, see Salganik and Heckathorn (2004) or Heckathorn (1997, 2002). Because of the small size of my sample, and because this technique is not widely used in political science or political psychology, I have referred to this smaller sample as simply a "matched case study" obtained through a respondent-driven/nominee sample. Nor do I make claims about statistical estimates for this case study. My thanks to Roxane Cohen Silver for her advice concerning the methodological issues involved in such a sample.

132. Results from the Dutch cases accord with findings from the broader set of interviews from respondents in all countries.

133. The role of sex and romance in this sequence of events is ironic.

134. This position is equivalent to both US Secretary of the Treasury and head of the Federal Reserve Board.

135. Another Nazi sat in on the interview with Florentine, and he occasionally made comments as part of the interview. I differentiate his remarks from Florentine's by labeling them as "Young Nazi," the "young" denoting that he was born after World War II.

136. *The Authoritarian Personality* (Adorno et al. 1950) represents early work in this vein. *Hitler's Willing Executioners* (Goldhagen 1996) represents recent work following the same tack.

137. Ghitis (2005).

138. All quotes come from the thirty formal interviews plus two quotes from Florentine's autobiography (Rost van Tonningen 1990).

139. I have modified identifying characteristics of Kurt—a pseudonym—as I did with most other interview subjects.

140. N-Vivo is simply a tool designed to handle large amounts of qualitative data in a systemic manner. It facilitates the examination of texts by topic and assists in more rigorous and systematic searching for patterns. It also helps compare coding by different analysts, and aids in testing theories or explanations that are grounded in the data. This system was used for all the matched or targeted case study interviews as well as for all the formal interviews.

141. There are two interesting methodological arguments to note. (1) Does the Holocaust constitute an event so dreadful that ordinary language and the conceptual categories of traditional ethics cannot adequately address it? (2) Can we generalize about ethical behavior by studying a small group of participants in just one genocide? While recognizing that analyzing any genocide demands sensitivity when making normative statements about participants, and recognizing that contextual influences will vary from incident to incident, just as they do from one individual to another, the essence of social science nonetheless argues that close analysis of participants in one genocide can inform our understanding of participants in related events, just as understanding the linguistic structure of one Spanish speaker can inform us about the language patterns of other Spaniards. Furthermore, as data from other genocides or genocidal activity suggest, the Holocaust was not unique. This topic is addressed more fully in chapter 9. Ongoing genocides and instances of ethnic cleansing demand our best efforts to crack the code of genocide. Close attention to cognitive processes makes smaller case studies critical in completing our knowledge of how psy-

chological shifts can move individuals from rescuers to bystanders, or from bystanders to perpetrators. See Arendt (1963), Levi (1989, chap. 1), Monroe (1996, 2004), Abramson (1999), or Langer (1991) inter alia for discussions of methodological issues involved in interviewing Holocaust participants or even constructing moral dialogues about the Holocaust and related genocides.

CHAPTER 3
TONY: RESCUER

1. James Lovelock, the geoscientist who pioneered Gaia theory, held that "life at an early stage of its evolution acquired the capacity to control the global environment to suit its needs and that this capacity has persisted and is still in active use. In this view the sum total of species is more than just a catalogue, 'The Biosphere,' and like other associations in biology is an entity with properties greater than the simple sum of its parts. Such a large creature, even if only hypothetical, with the powerful capacity to homeostat the planetary environment needs a name; I am indebted to Mr. William Golding for suggesting the use of the Greek personification of mother Earth, 'Gaia.'" See Lovelock (1972).

2. Jews and Roma were assembled at Westerbork, where they then were shipped to other Nazi concentration camps. Anne Frank passed through Westerbork en route to Auschwitz.

CHAPTER 4
BEATRIX: BYSTANDER

1. Beatrix may be referring to the delta island of Goeree-Overflakkee, off of the coast of the province of South Holland.

2. I have listened to the tapes many times and am still unsure whether Beatrix says "I knew everything, on the minute exactly about my news" or "exactly about my Jews" or "the Jews."

CHAPTER 5
KURT: SOLDIER FOR THE NAZIS

1. Theodoric "the Great" (471–526) ruled the Ostrogoths through their conquest of Italy and central and eastern Europe. See Grun (1991).

2. Roderich was king of the Visigoths (ca. 711) in what is now Spain. See Collins (2004).

3. The Battle of Sedan, on September 1, 1870, was the decisive battle of the Franco-Prussian War in which Napoleon III himself was taken prisoner. See Bagdasarian (1976).

4. Augusta Viktoria of Schleswig-Holstein (1858–1921) was Empress of Germany and wife to Kaiser Wilhelm II.

5. Kurt may be referring to the Schloss Charlottenburg (Charlottenburg Palace), one of the largest palaces in Berlin, originally the residence of the Hohenzollern dynasty.

6. Józef Klemens Piłsudski (1867–1935), was commander-in-chief of the Polish armed forces and, in effect, ruler of the 2nd Polish Republic from 1918 to 1922, and then again from 1926 to 1935, when he served as the authoritarian ruler of the 2nd Polish Republic. As best I can ascertain, Piłsudski was born in what is now Lithuania but which was part of the Russian Empire from 1795 to 1914. It is doubtful that Piłsudski would have considered himself Russian, as Kurt claims.

Poland has a long history as a state, emerging as a sovereign state around 1000. Poland's rich land and few protected borders made Poland a prey to geopolitical shifts, however, and the Polish state has morphed into many different forms. In the late sixteenth and early seventeenth century, the Polish-Lithuanian Commonwealth was a large, sovereign state that included the land where Piłsudski's family are believed to have lived. In 1795 the last of three military partitions of what we think of as modern Poland ended the existence of the Polish-Lithuanian Commonwealth. A major goal of Piłsudski's life was the reestablishment of an independent Poland.

However he conceived of his identity, Piłsudski was a major influence in Polish politics and the central European political scene from mid–World War I until his death in 1935. He is widely considered a key player responsible for Polish independence in 1918, after 123 years of partitions. Early in his political career Piłsudski was a leader of the Polish Socialist Party. He argued that Poland's independence would be won only by force and hence created the Polish Legions. In the period immediately before World War I, Piłsudski seems to have correctly anticipated the outbreak of a wider European war. As part of that war Piłsudski accurately predicted both the Russian Empire's defeat by the Central Powers, and the Central Powers' defeat by the western powers. Piłsudski worked carefully so that his Legions would fight with the Austro-Hungarian and German forces to help defeat Russia, thus accomplishing Polish independence. On November 5, 1916, Polish "independence" was declared. Polish troops were then to be sent to the eastern front to fight against Russia and relieve German forces on the western front. Piłsudski was serving as the minister of war in the incipient Polish Regency government and opposed the demand that the Polish units swear loyalty to Germany and Austria. Because of this, in July 1917, Piłsudski was arrested and imprisoned in M——, Germany. After the Central Powers lost the war—as Piłsudski had predicted—he headed the Polish forces in the brief war between Poland and the Soviets (1919–21). When the National Democrats took over the Polish government in 1923, Pilsudski withdrew from active politics but returned to power in the May 1926 coup d'état, becoming de facto dictator of Poland.

Many of Piłsudski's political acts remain controversial, but his memory is held in high esteem by most Poles. For more information on Piłsudski's life, career, and times, see Garlicki (1995) and Jędrzejewicz (1982).

7. The Harz Mountains refer to the highest mountain chain in northern Germany occupying parts of the German states of Lower Saxony, Saxony-Anhalt, and Thuringia.

8. The Rumpler Taube was one of the first German fighter planes; soon after World War I began, it was taken out of service due to maneuvering difficulties and was turned exclusively into a training aircraft.

9. Edgar Meyer (1907–1969) was one of Einstein's fellow physicists at the University of Zurich. See Isaacson (2007).

10. Einstein fled Germany in December 1932, narrowly escaping Hitler's "Law for the Restoration of the Professional Civil Service," which would have banned Jews like himself from academic positions. He renounced German citizenship in 1933. See Isaacson (2007).

11. A suburban town of Charing Cross, in East London.

12. It's difficult to determine what region or municipality Kurt is intending to describe here; the city or region may be Haskovo, in central Bulgaria.

13. Asparuh was one of the Bulgarian khans who founded the 1st Bulgarian Empire, circa 680. See Fine (1983).

14. The capital and largest city of Bulgaria. Hitler initially had an agreement with the USSR, but as he turned his attention East to begin his invasion of the USSR, Hitler moved to bring in other states in Eastern Europe. After World War I ended, Bulgaria felt itself deprived of provinces in Macedonia; it is believed that Hitler gave his permission to the Bul-

garian government to occupy provinces in Macedonian territory. The Bulgarians believed that these territories were theirs, but they were in Yugoslavia and Greece around the period Kurt discusses. Sometime in 1940, shortly after the period to which Kurt refers, King Boris of Bulgaria seems to have acceded to Hitler's demands, and both Romania and Bulgaria functioned as Axis satellites after March 1, 1941. See Miller (1975).

15. Kurt may be thinking of Georges Courteline, 1858–1929, the French author and satirist. See Haymann (1990).

16. Castle of Malbrouck, seized by John Churchill, 1st Duke of Marlborough.

17. Kurt may be mistakenly referring to the Spanish Volunteer Forces, the "blue brigade" that fought alongside the Germans in World War II under Franco. See Krammer (1973).

18. I believe Kurt may be referring to the Ludendorff Bridge in Remagen, which originally was built during World War I to move troops over the Rhine to reinforce the western front. See Hechler (1998).

19. The Battle of Passchendaele—also known as the 3rd Battle of Ypres—was one of the most disastrous and important battles of World War I, beginning in June of 1917 and lasting until November 1917. It was fought for control of the Belgian village of Passchendaele near Ypres. See Evans (2005).

20. A "stuka" was a Junkers Ju 87, a two-man attack bomber. Known for its characteristic siren call, it came to prominence through its devastatingly effective use in the blitzkrieg of 1939. See Griehl (2001).

21. Kurt seems to be insinuating that the French provoked the armed conflict.

22. Verdun was the scene of one of the critical battles during World War I, fought between the Germans and the French from February 21 to December 15, 1916, on hilly terrain north of the city of Verdun-sur-Meuse in northeastern France. The battle was technically a French victory since the Germans failed to capture Verdun and were pushed back to the right bank of the Meuse River, at the end of 1916. With more than a quarter of a million battlefield deaths, more than half a million wounded, and over forty million artillery shells exchanged, Verdun was one of the most devastating battles in World War I and, indeed, in human history. In popular memory, Verdun represents the worst horrors of war for both France and Germany, and is often likened to the Battle of the Somme for the British, Stalingrad for the Russians, Gallipoli for the Australians, or Gettysburg for the United States. See Brose (2010).

23. The Treaty of Verdun, in 843, divided the Carolingian Empire among the three grandsons of Charlemagne—Lothair, Louis the German, and Charles the Bald. Squabbling among their descendants further fractured the empire. See Ganshof (1971).

24. I believe Kurt refers to the Moselle River, which flows through France, Luxembourg, and Germany. (In French it is *Moselle*, in German *Mosel*, and in Luxembourgish Musel.)

25. Marshal Henri Pétain (1856–1951), formerly the army chief of staff of France, eventually headed the provisional French government under the Nazis headquartered in Vichy.

26. Henri Philippe Benoni Omer Joseph Pétain was convicted in August 1945 for his wartime accommodation with the Nazis and was sentenced to death by firing squad. In light of his advanced age—he was already eighty-nine years old—and his service during World War I, Pétain's sentence was reduced by Charles de Gaulle to life in prison. He died in 1951 of natural causes. His name is not widely honored in France today but is instead associated with collaboration, with *pétainisme* usually denoting a reactionary, authoritarian ideology. See Williams (2005).

27. I believe Kurt is lapsing into French and refers to the bridges (*ponts*).

28. Omar Pasha Latas (Greek: Ομέρ Πασάς) was born in Serbian Krajina in 1806 in what is now Croatia. Initially called Mihailo Latas, he was sent to military school then joined a regiment and fled to Bosnia in 1823 because he was charged with embezzlement. While

there, he converted to Islam and eventually served with distinction for the Turks. During the Russian War he successfully defended Kalafat (1853), entering Bucharest (1854) and eventually defeating forty thousand Russians at Eupatoria in the Crimea. See Jelavich (1983).

29. During the Russo-Turkish war (1877–78) there were four successive battles fought between the Russians and their Bulgarian allies against the Ottoman Empire for access to the Shipka Pass, a key passage through the Balkan mountains. Kurt is referring to the historical past encroaching on the present again. See Genov (1979).

30. Also called Thessaloniki, Thessalonica, or Salonica, Salonika is the second-largest city in Greece and the capital city of Macedonia. I believe Kurt refers to that part of Greece where an extended battle took place during World War I. See Palmer (1965).

31. The Iskar River runs 368 kilometers, making it the longest river that runs solely in Bulgaria. It is a tributary of the Danube.

32. Approximately 18 degrees below zero Fahrenheit.

33. I'm not sure whom Kurt refers to here since General Model committed suicide as the war was ending and Model had learned that he had been indicted for war crimes by the Soviets. (Model was charged with killing 577,000 people in Latvian concentration camps and with deporting 175,000 more as slave laborers.) As best I can determine, Model apparently tried to get killed on the front but ended shooting himself in the head on April 21, 1945. Other generals were killed in mysterious plane crashes. See D'Este (1989).

34. Kristallnacht, or the Night of the Broken Glass (literally "crystal night"), refers to the November 9–10, 1938, anti-Jewish pogrom in Germany. (It is also called *Novemberpogrom* or *Reichspogromnacht*.) The immediate trigger for Kristallnacht was the assassination of Ernst vom Rath by Herschel Grynszpan, a German-born Polish Jew. Ironically, vom Rath was not a Nazi, and most historians argue that his murder was a pretext for Nazi persecution that would have occurred anyway. Kristallnacht involved coordinated attacks on Jews and their property with the police standing by doing nothing. With ninety-one Jews murdered, twenty-five to thirty thousand arrested and sent to concentration camps, over two hundred synagogues destroyed, and thousands of homes and businesses ransacked, Kristallnacht is often cited as the beginning of the Final Solution. For more information, see Berenbaum (1997), Marino (1997), and Gilbert (2006).

35. The Fasanenstrasse synagogue was one of the largest in the city of Berlin. Closed by order of the Nazis in 1936, its burning was personally ordered by Joseph Goebbels, who is said to have watched its conflagration from his hotel. See Goebbels (1992).

36. I am not an expert but as best I can determine, Kurt is wrong on his historical facts. The Spanish Inquisition held roughly 49,000 trials between 1500 and 1700 and executed approximately three thousand to five thousand people. A reliable figure for the number of people involved in the Inquisition—whether arrested and questioned, tortured, or killed—is probably impossible to determine, given the unreliability of the data. See Rawlings (2006).

37. To protect his identity I have deleted the specifics of Kurt's description of what he did after the war.

CHAPTER 6
FRITZ: NAZI PROPAGANDIST

1. Gerardus Johannes Petrus Josephus Bolland (1854–1922) was a Dutch Hegelian philosopher noted for being "at odds with women, Jews, democracy, socialism, division of labor and positivistic science." Some of his followers formed the Union of Actualists, a fascist political party. See http://www.siebethissen.net/Wijsbegeerte_in_Nederland/1994_Dutch _Hegelianism_(English).htm.

2. The Allies invaded Holland on September 17, 1944.

3. The Dutch National Socialist Party (NSB) had a nationalist agenda that included a plan for "Greater Netherlands" (Groot-Nederlands project—a.k.a. Dietsland ("Dutch-land"). Their political ambition was for a unified Flanders and Netherlands. The Flemish in this scheme thus were identified as "Dutch-speaking" Belgians.

4. I assume the reference is to the Dutch admiral, Michiel de Ruyter, who occupied Sheerness, England, on June 21, 1667, and hence would be another one of Fritz's heroes from the Golden Age of Holland.

5. I am not sure which Rene Kok Fritz refers to here. The only author I can find is the author of Jewish Displaced Persons in Camp Bergen-Belsen, 1945–1950: The Unique Photo Album of Zippy Orlin, edited by Erik Somers and Rene Kok (Seattle: University of Washington Press with the United States Holocaust Memorial Museum).

CHAPTER 7
FLORENTINE: UNREPENTANT POLITICAL NAZI

1. I circulated the book manuscript to several colleagues and received mixed responses to this chapter. One person felt I was too judgmental of Florentine; for example, describing her as "unrepentant" implies she did something for which I believe she should atone. Other readers suggested I needed to put more of my own judgment in the interview itself. I decided to try to present the interview data in as unadorned a form as possible, free from editorial comment. I describe Florentine as unrepentant because I believe she saw herself as someone who was criticized by the world but who was not sorry for anything she had done.

I had no personal introduction to Florentine, unlike the other people whose interviews are presented here. I believe she opened up to me as much as she did because I had gotten her husband's death certificate for her. In places during her interview I have added words for clarification. Some of the spellings of names or places may be incorrect since Florentine did not return the copy of the transcript I sent her. I have used her full name at her request.

2. *Nationale Jeugdstorm*, or "National Youthstorm," was founded by Cornelis van Geelkerken in 1934. Its peak membership during the German occupation was estimated at close to twelve thousand. Modeled on the Hitler Youth, it featured a uniformed sports/youth activities regimen designed to build civic identity via songs, rituals, and such. It may be somewhat analogous to the American Boy Scouts and Girl Scouts. See Jong (1973).

3. Anton Mussert was the leader of the Dutch Nazi Party, the National Socialist Movement or Nationaal-Socialistische Beweging in the Netherlands, NSB. The NSB was successful during the 1930s and was the only party the German Nazis allowed to operate legally in the Netherlands during most of World War II. Anton Mussert and Cornelis van Geelkerken were the two founders, in Utrecht in 1931. They based the party on Italian fascism and German National Socialism. The party was not initially anti-Semitic and even included Jewish members at first. The party's first meeting in Utrecht was attended by six hundred party militant enthusiasts and received 8 percent of the votes in provincial elections in 1935, due mostly to the perception that Mussert was a pragmatic and reliable politician not interested in violence but in a democratic and legal route to power. After Florentine's husband, Meinoud Rost van Tonningen, became more important in the party, around 1936, the NSB became more openly anti-Semitic. Rost van Tonningen's challenge of Mussert led to internal fighting within the party and a decrease in support for the party as a result of an antifascist reaction among trade unions, churches, and political parties. Also during this period the NSB representatives in Parliament drew attention to themselves for their physical and ver-

bal violence, suggesting to many that the NSB claim to a peaceful route to democracy was illusory. Once World War II began, the NSB's ties to the Germans led to the arrest of some eight hundred members and sympathizers by the Dutch government, immediately after the German invasion. This is when Rost van Tonningen was arrested. Once the Dutch were defeated on May 14, 1940, however, the Germans freed him and the other detainees. The German occupation government outlawed all other Socialist parties and the Communist Party in 1940 and in 1941 made the NSB the only legal party allowed to function in Holland. Mussert had thought he would be named the leader of an independent Dutch state in close alliance with Germany but was unsuccessful, receiving only the honorary title of "leader of the Dutch People." He had little real power, and the Austrian National Socialist Arthur Seyss-Inquart effectively led the occupation government in Holland. Once the Allies took Antwerp (September 4, 1944) the NSB leadership fled to Germany on what is called Dolle Dinsdag (Mad Tuesday), September 5, 1944. When the Germans signed the surrender (May 6, 1945), the NSB became outlawed and Mussert, along with many of the NSB members, was arrested. Mussert was tried in 1945, convicted, and eventually executed on May 7, 1946. For information on Mussert, Meinoud Rost van Tonningen, and the events surrounding both in World War II–era Dutch politics, please consult the following sources, some of which are in the original Dutch: Barnouw (1994), Havenaar (1983, 1985), M. Rost van Tonningen (1967, 1993), F. Rost van Tonningen (1999), and *The SS and the Netherlands*, documents from the SS archives 1935–45, published by NKCA in 't Veld (1976), State Publishing, The Hague. See also online resources from the Netherlands' Huygens Institute for Dutch History at http://www.inghist.nl/Onderzoek/Projecten/BWN/lemmata/bwn1/bwn1/rost; *De Volkskrant*, March 24, 2007, "Rost van Tonningen was National Socialist," http://www.volkskrant.nl/vk/nl/2686/Binnenland/article/detail/836840/2007/03/24/Rost-van-Tonningen-bleef-nationaalsocialiste.dhtml; and *De Volkskrant*, March 27, 2007, "Quiet funeral for Black Widow," http://www.volkskrant.nl/vk/nl/2686/Binnenland/article/detail/839112/2007/03/27/Stille-begrafenis-van-Zwarte-Weduwe.dhtml.

4. Florentine's diction is slightly hard to discern at this point, but the word she was looking for may be the German word "größt," meaning alternately "large," "main," or "sovereign."

5. Dutch Queen Wilhelmina (1880–1962) fled to the United Kingdom during the Nazi invasion of the Netherlands. See Wilhelmina, Queen of the Netherlands (1960).

6. Wim Heubel, Florentine's brother, a former member of the German Sturmabteilung and an active member of the NSB, served in the Dutch SS and later fought in the Waffen-SS in Germany's campaign in Russia. He died in battle, April 1945.

7. Prince Bernhard of the Netherlands (1911–2004), Prince Consort to Princess (later Queen) Juliana, served as commander of the Dutch armed forces in the liberation of the Netherlands under Allied command. He was also there for the negotiations for cease-fire and surrender of the Germans in the Netherlands. See http://www.go2war2.nl/artikel/1072.

8. Further insight into how Florentine's mind works can be found in her autobiography, *Triumph and Tragedy: Some Personal Remembrances of Dutch and European History in the 20th Century*, by Florentine S. Rost van Tonningen, published by Consortium de Levensboom in the Netherlands (published originally in Dutch in 1990 and translated into English in 1998). One question of interest to social scientists, especially those using narrative interpretive theory, concerns how typical the narrative analyzed actually is of the speaker. Florentine's book and interview are compared in Appendix A, along with the autobiography and the narrative interview of a rescuer. I am grateful to Jane Guo, Kristin Fyfe, and Sarah Ubovich for their independent comparisons of these two documents.

Henry Ford was alluded to in my conversation with Florentine and her young Nazi admirer. Ford was admired by Hitler and was awarded the Grand Cross of the German Eagle.

Ford owned a newspaper—the *Dearborn Independent*—during the 1920s. This controversial periodical printed, among other anti-Semitic material, the *Protocols of the Elders of Zion*. The "Eternal Jew" publication to which Florentine and her admirer refer is probably *The International Jew, The World's Foremost Problem*, which consisted of reprints of articles from the *Dearborn Independent*, later published in four volumes. Some of the individual articles/chapters in this collection include titles such as "Historic Basis of Jewish Imperialism," "Jewish Degradation of American Baseball," and "The All-Jewish Mark on 'Red Russia.'" Ford received many complaints, public protests, and a major libel suit related to this work and eventually was forced to end publication of the paper in 1927, at which point he publicly disavowed the anti-Semitic views represented in its contents. At the time of the lawsuit, Ford was allegedly horrified at the anti-Semitic contents of his own paper, suggesting his employees had published such material without his knowledge. This explanation does not seem entirely plausible and remains controversial. For information on Ford's involvement in the *International Jew* affair, see Baldwin (2001), Bryan (1993), and Lee (1980).

9. What do we make of Florentine's claim? Is there any historical evidence in support of it? The claim finds voice in the work of the Canadian writer James Bacque in *Other Losses*, which claims General Dwight D. Eisenhower reclassified several thousand German refugees as "Disarmed Enemy Forces" to skirt Geneva Convention–prescribed rights for their treatment. It is also alleged that as a result of such deliberate action, perhaps a million people died of preventable starvation and malnutrition. Bacque's thesis has been hotly contested, however, by more mainstream historians, with controversy focused on Bacque's treatment of Allied statistics (in which he possibly misstates how many actually died in such conditions), whether or not there was an actual food shortage during that period in 1945 (if there was no shortage, excessive civilians deaths might be an indication of deliberate starvation on behalf of the Americans), and whether any such deaths were the result of a calculated, deliberate policy. The term "other losses," used to describe otherwise-unclassified deaths in the Allied casualty records (all not combat-related, etc.) has been alleged to be bureaucratic code for such "disarmed enemy forces" casualties under such circumstances. Bacque's critics allege that this term could mean any number of casualties, not just a cryptic reference to subjects of extermination, as he insinuates.

The proposition that there wasn't a real food shortage in Europe under Allied control at the time has generally been widely criticized by numerous respected historians, including James F. Trent and Stephen Ambrose. Few of these historians dispute the existence of Allied desires to "get back" at the Germans following the war, and most admit that there were episodes of prisoner abuse by Allies. But both Stephen Ambrose and Brian Loring Villa insist that any such abuses or atrocities were separate and arbitrary incidents, not the results of a coordinated policy. For fuller discussion of this topic, see Beaumont (1995).

10. The firebombing of Dresden by the Royal Air Force and the US Air Force between February 13 and 15, 1945, is one of the more controversial actions taken by the Allies during World War II. Over 1,300 bombers dropped more than 3,900 tons of high explosive bombs and incendiary devises and caused a firestorm that destroyed most of the German capital of Saxony. The casualties—between 25,000 and 40,000—have long been a topic of humanitarian controversy. The body count and how much of the loss of life was due to the conscious goal of terror bombing on the part of the Allies are both disputed. Air Chief Marshal Arthur Harris has been quoted in a memo from that time, claiming, "I do not personally regard the whole of the remaining cities of Germany as worth the bones of one British Grenadier." Neo-Nazi groups have since memorialized the Dresden bombing as a "bomb holocaust," claiming death totals far in excess of what historians have recently judged. Churchill and other leaders have been alleged to use Dresden as a demonstration to the Soviets of what

Allied firepower was capable of, in order to prompt greater concessions in postwar negotiations. (Some sources indicate, however, that "the Soviet Chiefs requested the Allies to deliver massive attacks on German communications in the Berlin-Leipzig-Dresden area and specifically to bomb those cities urgently.") For more information, see http://www.guardian.co.uk/world/2008/oct/03/secondworldwar.germany; Taylor (2004); http://www.spiegel.de/international/germany/0,1518,607524,00.html; and Probert (2001).

11. For more information and Florentine Rost van Tonningen-Heubel's obituary in the Dutch news media, see http://nos.nl/artikel/61335-weduwe-rost-van-tonningen-overleden.html.

CHAPTER 8
THE POLITICAL PSYCHOLOGY OF GENOCIDE

Acknowledgement: An earlier, abbreviated version of this chapter formed part of my presidential address to the International Society of Political Psychology in 2008 and appeared as an article in *Political Psychology*. I am grateful for the permission to reprint those parts here.

1. This approach follows Blasi's (2003) work on the integration of values, Reykowski's (2001) work on worldview and extensivity, and my work (2004) on the relational aspect of self-perceptions in influencing moral choice.

2. Extensivity is a concept developed by the Oliners (1988) and Reykowski (2001). It was developed by using a principal components analysis of a set of nineteen questions about moral obligations. The empirical findings suggested certain individuals have a constricted moral sense; these people feel stronger obligations toward family members and friends than they do toward strangers. According to the Oliner study, rescuers demonstrate an extensive moral sense and thus feel compelled to help both those to whom they are close and people they do not know or know only slightly. Such people are also more likely to engage in charitable giving and in volunteer work.

3. Proposed by James Lovelock, this theory views the earth as a single organism and stresses the interconnectedness of all of life on earth.

4. The moral courage demonstrated by rescuers is perhaps an extreme expression of the altruistic perspective. But the formulation of the self-concept in which rescuers found themselves closely related to everyone in the universe, including all living things, was evident among all rescuers. My work on altruism (1996) examined altruists in less exceptional, more everyday situations and found this same self-concept, in a less intense form, among all altruists. Based on this examination I concluded that this altruistic perspective existed in all altruists but varied in form and intensity depending on the person and the situation (Monroe 1996). I encourage other scholars to study this phenomenon in situations that require less extreme demonstrations of moral courage than the Holocaust to determine how widespread this altruistic perspective is.

5. It is important not to confuse two closely related concepts: (1) the sense of efficacy expressed by the speaker and (2) the speaker's comments about connections with other people. The link between the two is subtle, with rescuers feeling compelled to help people because of their connection with them. The sense of felt moral salience—discussed later in this chapter—that arose in response to the feeling that another's pain and suffering was a rescuer's concern that was closely related to a sense of efficacy.

6. This confirms prior findings (Falk, Kolko, and Lifton 1971; Lifton 1976; Koeningsberg 2005a, 2005b; Staub 1989).

7. Koenigsberg (2005b) argues: "At the core of Nazi ideology was the idea of Germany as an actual body suffering from a potentially fatal disease caused by Jewish-organisms. Just as a human body might contract a disease and die, so might the German body politic" (2005b, 2).

8. This influence corresponds to that described theoretically by virtue ethics and identified empirically as a critical factor by Oliner and Oliner (1988).

9. Blasi (2003).

10. Other scholars and commentators find other themes common among bystanders (Ophüls 1971; Reykowski private communiqué 2009). My comments are based only on the people I interviewed.

11. Emanuel Tanay, "Courage to Care," in Rittner and Myers (1986, 52).

12. Kristallnacht, or the Night of the Broken Glass (literally "crystal night"), refers to the November 9–10, 1938, anti-Jewish pogrom in Germany. (It is also called *Novemberpogrom* or *Reichspogromnacht*.) The immediate trigger for Kristallnacht was the assassination of Ernst vom Rath by Herschel Grynszpan, a German-born Polish Jew. Ironically, vom Rath was not a Nazi, and most historians argue that his murder was a pretext for Nazi persecution that would have occurred anyway. Kristallnacht involved coordinated attacks on Jews and their property with the police standing by doing nothing. With ninety-one Jews murdered, twenty-five to thirty thousand arrested and sent to concentration camps, over two hundred synagogues destroyed, and thousands of homes and businesses ransacked, Kristallnacht is often cited as the beginning of the Final Solution. For information, see Berenbaum (1997); Marino (1997); Gilbert (2006).

13. Gourevitch (1998, 18).

14. Suedfeld and de Best 2008. Suedfeld and de Best defined universalism as a "value category" that includes the values "social justice" and "equality" (2008, 34). Benevolence is a category that includes the values "helpful" and "responsible" and is in accord with the Oliner and Oliner (1988) findings that rescuers would feel a strong responsibility for others because they had been taught the habits of caring from an early age. Suedfeld and de Best also find benevolence provided the "internalized motivational basis for cooperative and supportive social behaviors (for example, working for the welfare of others, being genuine and sincere, being a close, supportive friend; and valuing emotional intimacy" (2008, 38) Finally, Suedfeld and de Best found spirituality was an unexpected difference between rescuers and resistance workers. Spirituality is not the same as religion, and it is possible it corresponds closely to what I am identifying as worldview. This hypothesis could be studied more systematically using the kind of thematic content analysis employed by Suedfeld and de Best, but lies beyond the scope of the present study. The Suedfeld–de Best study considered national differences and found their findings held across national boundaries.

15. Colby and Damon (1992).

16. Blasi (2003); Colby and Damon (1992); Tec (1986).

17. Neither Blasi nor Colby and Damon analyze rescuers.

18. Verdun was the scene of one of the critical battles during World War I, fought between the Germans and the French from February 21 to December 15, 1916, on hilly terrain north of the city of Verdun-sur-Meuse in northeastern France. See note 22 in Chapter 5 for details.

19. Levi (1993 [1965], 215).

20. See Fillmore's frame semantics (1982), Lakoff and Johnson's theory of metaphor and metonymy (1980), Langacker's cognitive grammar (1986), and Fauconnier's theory of mental spaces (1985). I have relied heavily on the work of Rosch (1978); Varela, Thompson, and Rosch (1991).

21. A glimpse of the potential significance for political analysis is evident if we consider the normative connotations attached to a word such as "mother" as an idealized cognitive model versus "working mother, single mother, and welfare mother." Each term conveys different normative overtones and suggests something potentially normatively significant about the individual speaker and the speaker's culture.

22. Monroe (1996, 11).

23. No one identified him- or herself as a religious person, but no one self-identified as an atheist either. All the speakers were about the same on this dimension. In the larger pool of interviews, I found no predictive pattern from religious influence.

24. Philip Gourevitch notes the same phenomenon in the 1994 Rwanda-Burundi genocide. "People do not engage in genocide as if it were a crime. . . . People don't go forward to kill saying "This is the end of the world and I'm a pig and I will kill you." They go forward and they say "This is the beginning of a better world and I am a purifier and I will kill you. This is going to bring harmony." It's an exercise in community building, it's this us-and-them and we will purify ourselves by eliminating you" (2002 interview with Gourevitch by Harry Kreisler of the Institute of International Studies at the University of California, Berkeley. At http://globetrotter.berkeley.edu/people/Gourevitch).

25. Blasi (2003); Colby and Damon (1992).

26. These quotes come from Florentine's autobiography (Rost van Tonningen 1990), not our interviews.

27. See Monroe and Martinez (2008) for an empirical test of this idea.

28. Tajfel (1981); Turner (1982); Turner and Hogg (1987).

29. Lakoff and Johnson (1999).

30. Prejudice based on difference continues today, with skin color, gender, sexual preference, and many other differences that need not logically be associated with differential political and legal rights.

31. Bystanders make genocide a crime of submission, not one of initiative, a result of weakness, role-playing, and passivity. Kressel (2002).

CHAPTER 9

A THEORY OF MORAL CHOICE

1. For the scientific analysis of storytelling, scientists must perhaps first define what is meant by a story. Is a story or narrative—the two terms are used interchangeably—simply exposition, in which a lists of facts are related? Does narrative include some sense of causality as events are linked as they unfold over time? And can we infer motivation and intentions of the actors from stories? All of these are questions worthy of fuller exposition and hence are discussed in Appendix A to avoid distracting from my central purpose here. See Patterson and Monroe (1998), Andrews (2007), or Langer (1991) on the methodological issues involved.

2. See Hsu (2008) for an eminently readable overview of how stories tie to crucial parts of our social cognition.

3. No one scholar can conduct a comprehensive empirical analysis of ethical behavior, and my own work is as limited by the particularities of the research, as any scholar's would be. But careful empirical analysis can yield broader theoretical insights that others can test later, using a wide variety of techniques and in a multitude of situations. This is what I offer here, in the hope that others can build on my theory to achieve a broader, scientific understanding of the psychology underpinning moral action.

4. In proposing this theory I recognize that all research inevitably entails limitations, and that my own work is no exception. Issues of traumatic memory, the reliability of oral versus written narratives, the representative nature of case studies, how far we can generalize from a few individuals, difficulties in deciphering what people mean as they speak of their experiences, focusing on the micropsychology versus the group dynamic or an institutional approach to genocide, all of these factors are choices a researcher makes. Each choice offers new insights; each entails limitations. Some of these issues of research methodology, often of immediate interest to only a handful of researchers in the specialized area, are discussed in the Methodological Afterword to the book. But no research can answer all questions, no one account can satisfy all our concerns, and the careful scholar concerned with substantive causes more than research design itself can simply note the important caveats involved in the research and then move on to the more substantive questions posed by the work.

5. Here I argue for a more catholic conceptualization of this subfield of political science and psychology than other scholars might adopt.

6. I believe I could argue convincingly that all of normative politics concerns moral issues and hence this is also a theory of political choice, but developing that argument fully lies beyond the scope of the present volume.

7. I hesitate to make too great a personal digression into my own intellectual journey, but I have learned that students often find such knowledge helpful.

8. Hirschman (1970); Myers (1985); Mansbridge (1990); Monroe (1991a).

9. The precise dates concerning *The Prince* are uncertain, with best estimates suggesting *De Principatibus* (*About Principalities*) was originally written in 1513, but the full document was published only in 1532, five years after Machiavelli's death. See Myers (1985) for an overview; Hobbes (1651); Locke (2000 [1513]); Machiavelli (2003 [1690]).

10. Economics has a long history of intellectual imperialism, with Marxism being the most obvious other economic approach that made serious incursions into social science. See Cropsey (2001); Mansbridge (1990); Monroe (1991) for further discussion.

11. The best-known economic model is the Downsian model, built on the 1957 work by Anthony Downs that explains democratic behavior through assuming people attempt to maximize their self-interest subject to information and opportunity costs when they vote. An "Economic Theory of Democracy" was Downs's dissertation and revolutionized political science by setting forth a model with precise conditions specifying when economic theory could be successfully applied to nonmarket political decision making. Downs's work inspired a whole generation of research that eventually became integrated into what is known as the Public Choice School. Downs did not make normative claims about public policy choices, focusing instead on what is deemed rational, given the relevant incentives built into the economic approach.

12. Easton (1965).

13. Monroe (1991a); Riker (1991).

14. I am effectively rejecting the dichotomy between nature versus nurture in favor of the concept of a phenotype, arguing that values and identities, for example, are born in us in some core sense and then are acted upon by the environment to be shaped and developed in particular ways that are unique to each of us.

15. Monroe and Kreidie (1997).

16. Hamer and Gutowski (2006, 2009); McFarland (2005).

17. Coles (1967); Kohlberg (1981a, 1981b); Piaget (1928).

18. Zajonc's 1980 paper, "Feeling and Thinking: Preferences Need No Inferences," presented as his lecture for the 1979 Distinguished Scientific Contribution Award from the American Psychological Association, argued that cognitive and affective systems are largely

independent, with affect being both more powerful and preceding cognition. Zajonc's paper stimulated much interest in affect among psychologists and was critical in bringing the study of emotion and affective processes into the forefront of psychology in both the United States and Europe. See also work by Kahneman, Tversky, and Slovic (1982) or Nisbett and Ross (1980) for a review.

19. Marcus (2004).

20. Schnall et al. (2008).

21. Hauser (2006); Mikhail (2007).

22. Scholars (Mikhail 2007) often distinguish the universal moral grammar from the dual-process model of moral judgment. Haidt argues that morality involves post hoc reasoning to justify what we already have decided what we want to do. Moral reasoning is used primarily to find the arguments to justify our judgments arrived at via intuition and to encourage others to reach the same conclusions we have reached. Haidt further specifies morality as focusing on five principle concerns: fairness/harm, harm/care, in-group loyalty, authority/respect, and purity/sanctity. Margolis (1984); Greene and Haidt (2002).

23. Sunstein (2005).

24. Lakoff and Johnson (1980, 1999).

25. Full discussion of this important work deserves a volume of its own. See work by Damasio or Haidt or for an easily accessible summary, the Brain Series on the human mind produced by Charlie Rose.

26. Moral sense theory holds that we are able to distinguish between right and wrong through a distinctive moral sense. This theory is examined more systematically later in the chapter.

27. Despite this philosophical and political theoretical lack of attention to the idea of an inborn moral sense, the idea nonetheless perseveres in other disciplines. Arguments that human beings have an inborn sense of morality, much as they have an instinct for survival, surfaces prominently in the contemporary literature of several disciplines. Anthropologists ask about human behavior in the ancestral environment to discern the role of culture in influencing moral behavior. Animal ethologists ask if the ethical nature of human beings is rooted in the biological nature we share with other species. Developmental psychologists examine children in their earliest years, before culture and language have shaped what might be innate tendencies toward certain kinds of behavior. And, increasingly, as we have seen, moral psychologists and neuroscientists are making inroads into the biological substrates of moral behavior not only in animals or infants but also in adults and throughout the life cycle. This empirical research on an innate moral sense can be fragmentary and prelusive; it occasionally involves questions about the scientific reliability of certain findings. Nonetheless, this evidence is salient enough to justify a reconsideration of the existence of an innate moral sense and whether this assumption, or at least its possibility, should be built into our political models.

28. Reimer et al. (2009, 7).

29. Ibid.

30. Damasio (1994); Haidt and Bjorklund (2008); Scherer (2003); Reimer et al. (2009, 7).

31. For a trivial example, when Sarah Palin winked during the 2008 vice-presidential debate, did she have dust in her eye, in which case the blink was involuntary and of little significance, or was she signaling something different? If we interpret her wink as purely physical or in a frame of nature, then we will interpret her wink differently than if we assume a different social frame.

32. See Kahneman, Tversky, and Slovic's (1982) work on heuristics, or mental short cuts that people use to make decisions.

33. Reimer et al. (2009, 11).

34. Haidt and Bjorklund (2008).

35. No clear scholarly consensus exists on the distinction between ethics and morality. In general, morality may be more personal and ethics refers to a system of principles by which one lives one's life within a certain social structure. (Hence we speak of personal morality or personal ethics but also talk of business ethics, situational ethics, and such.) But, as Ronald Dworkin says, "We can–many people do–use either "ethical" or "moral" or both in a broader sense that erases this distinction, so that morality includes what I call ethics, and vice versa" (Dworkin 2011, 41). It is noteworthy that Dworkin, one of the preeminent legal moral theorists, defines these terms "in what might seem a special way. Moral standards prescribe how we ought to treat others; ethical standards, how we ought to live ourselves" (Dworkin 2011, 41). One could make a plausible argument that this distinction does capture what seems to be the general usage, in which the term *ethics* tends to refer to rules of conduct recognized in regard to a particular class of human actions or a particular culture, group, etc., as in business ethics, medical ethics, religious ethics and *morality* tends to refer to an individual, as in *Her personal morality forbade betrayal of a confidence*. But it seems more prudent to simply note that the terms *ethics* and *morality* tend to be used interchangeably in the field of moral psychology. There are differences that have occurred at different points in time and according to discipline, but these differences are not consistent. I use the terms interchangeably.

36. Representatives of psychologists in this field thus include those initially designated moral psychology using the older conceptualization that focuses on moral reasoning—Jean Piaget and Lawrence Kohlberg—but also include psychologists such as Bibb Latané and John Darley (1970), C. Daniel Batson (1991), Jonathan Haidt (2001), Haidt and Joseph (2007), and Marc Hauser (2006). Philosophers are represented by Stephen Stich, John Doris, Joshua Knobe, Shau Nichols, Martha Nussbaum, Thomas Nagel, Bernard Williams, and R. Jay Wallace (for illustrations, see Batson [1993]; Monroe [1996]; Nussbaum [1986, 2001]; Toulmin [1958] inter alia; Williams [1981]; Wilson [1993a, 1993b]).

37. There has been a virtual explosion of work suggesting happiness relates closely to our relations with others and thus calling into question the traditional distinction between behavior designed to further our self-interest versus behavior designed to help others (Vaillant 2002; Taylor 2002).

38. Festinger (1957); Aronson (1997).

39. This leaves open the extent to which imposed identities fit into this picture, a subject worthy of future study. Consider just one of the many fascinating aspects of this topic I cannot address here: What if a person—call her Louisa—thinks of herself as non-Jewish but the society in which Louisa lives designates her Jewish because she has a Jewish grandmother? This was the situation for many Jews in the Third Reich, individuals who were highly assimilated and did not think of themselves as of any particular faith. Does Louisa become Jewish once she is designated and treated as such by the society? Analogous situations can occur for many other categories: race, ethnicity, sexual preference, age, and so on. My theory is designed to alert us to the importance of the extent to which notions of individuality, the self, and relations to others are all culturally inflected and culturally variable.

40. The terms are used interchangeably depending on the discipline and speaker.

41. The experiments are designed to show how our eyes focus on a bright color in a beige room. The room is beige. The walls, the furniture, the rug, everything is beige. Except a pot of red flowers. The eye automatically goes to the flowers. So it was with Schindler's ethical perspective; something clicked so that Schindler felt that the Jews' suffering was relevant for him and demanded his help.

42. I use moral choice not to refer only to acts that are considered morally commendable but to refer to all acts that touch on ethics.

43. Studies involving twins offer evidence for the genetic basis of certain personality characteristics, including the "Big Five" factors of neuroticism, extraversion, openness, agreeableness, and conscientiousness (Jang, Livesley, and Vernon 2006), as well as attitudes and belief systems, such as political ideology (Alford, Funk, and Hibbing 2005), religiosity (Waller et al. 1990), and attitudes toward some social issues and recreational activities (Olson et al. 2001). Critics have asserted that similar environments, rather than genetics, account for these perceived likenesses between monozygotic twins (Beckwith and Morris 2008). For more on child socialization processes in a political context, see Dennis, Easton, and Easton (1969); Greenstein (1965).

44. Even in scholarly parlance, analysts frequently use intuitions, predispositions, and sentiments interchangeably so the distinctions in the literature—which does, after all, cover works written over several centuries—are not clear cut. All phenomena can be thought of as content-laden domains that are evolutionarily programmed and get triggered by external stimuli. But the content is there waiting to be activated by the external environment.

45. Bullock (1962).

46. Langholtz and Stout (2004).

47. Adorno et al. (1950); Altemeyer (1981, 1988).

48. Goldhagen (1996).

49. Sen (2005).

50. Milgram (1974); Zimbardo (2007).

51. Browning (1992).

52. Bandura and Walters (1963).

53. I define social role theory to refer to theories in social psychology that assume much of everyday activity results from the acting out of roles that are socially defined, such as parent, teacher, policeman. Each of these roles will carry with it certain expectations, norms, duties, and rights, and people tend to act in accordance with these roles. See Mead (1934), Parsons (1951), or Merton (1949) for foundational work.

54. Lifton's (1986) work on the Nazi doctors was intriguing because it turned the concept of social roles upside down by asking: How could doctors and health officials, dedicated to *saving* lives, suddenly utilize their medical knowledge to perfect mechanisms for killing? The answer—a desire to protect the German body politic from infestation by inferior and diseased *untermenschen*—suggests how even traditional social roles can be utilized to lead people to genocide.

55. Moscovici (1961).

56. Morgan and Schwalbe (1990).

57. Matthews (2000).

58. Markus and Nurius (1986).

59. Linville (1987).

60. Neurobiologists now hypothesize that schema may actually form physical pathways of neurobiological material, making them akin to well-traveled roads. Conversation with Dr. Robert Keller.

61. Moscovici (1988).

62. Tetlock (1985).

63. See Stryker and Burke (2000).

64. This is perhaps not surprising, given that its founder, Henri Tajfel, was the son of a Polish businessman who was Jewish. While studying in Paris, Tajfel was drafted into the French army and later captured by the Germans. Hiding his Jewish identity was neces-

sary to survive. After the war Tajfel discovered all of his immediate family and most of his friends in Poland had perished. One can only wonder at how these events might have influenced Tajfel's theory. Whatever the personal psychodynamic at work, it seems fair to say that social identity theory owes much to the Nazi period. See chapter 2 for fuller details on the development of social identity theory.

65. Tajfel (1970).
66. Hogg and Abrams (1988).
67. Sherif (1962).
68. Hogg and Abrams (1988).
69. Turner and Hogg (1987); Turner et al. (1994).
70. Hogg (1992).
71. Adorno et al. (1950).
72. Rokeach (1960).
73. Wilson (1975).
74. Jost et al. (2003).
75. Jost et al. (2007).

76. The contention that political ideology is rooted in personality traits has not gone unchallenged, and the extent to which both personality and ideology may be rooted in one's genes is an open one. Alford and Hibbing (2007) report "a surprisingly weak relationship" among political ideology, the "Big Five" personality factors, and generosity (2007, 209). Instead, using attitudinal data from twin studies, these researchers suggest that ideology has a genetic basis (Alford, Funk, and Hibbing 2005).

77. See also Bar-Tal (2000, 129) on genocide and Gobodo-Madikizela (2003) on Afrikaner attitudes to the Africans.

78. As further reading will show, this could also be fear of facing consequences after resistance.

79. For example, the South African government interpreted any religious objections to the war as inconsistent with spiritual conviction. Soldiers who refused to participate in apartheid's war on the grounds of conscientious objection thus were severely punished. In addition to prison terms, stiff fines were imposed on those who refused military service. A maximum of six years' imprisonment and a fine of six thousand rand could be reimposed each time military service was refused. The sociopolitical hurdles working against helping others thus were great, as they were during the Holocaust.

80. Gobodo-Madikizela (2003, 75).

81. Work by Susan Fiske and her colleagues is some of the most creative and important in this field and should be more widely read by political scientists.

82. See Wheeler and Fiske (2005) as illustrative of these studies.

83. The amygdala is composed of almond-shaped groups of nuclei located deep in the medial temporal lobes of the brain in humans, as in other complex vertebrates. Amygdalae have been shown in research to perform a primary role in the processing and memory of emotional reactions, hence their interest for political and social scientists.

84. Wheeler and Fiske (2005).

85. A slightly tangential study by Amodio, Devine, and Harmon-Jones (2007) suggests guilt also may follow a similar psychological process. The basic hypothesis of the Amodio study was that guilt has a dynamic role in giving negative reinforcement cues tied to reduced approach motivation and leading to approach-motivated behavior when subjects are given the chance to make up for their past offenses. Amodio and his colleagues tested this hypothesis in cases of racial prejudice. White subjects looked at multiracial faces while cortical activity was monitored through EEGs. When given false feedback illustrative of "an-

tiblack" responses, participants reported experiencing greater feelings of guilt, which were tied to changes in frontal cortical asymmetry (that is, showing lessened approach motivation). When given a chance to behave in prejudice-reducing ways, the guilt was significantly associated with heightened interest in prejudice alleviation, that is, it was tied to "approach-related" change in frontal asymmetry in the brain. This appears to support a model of guilt tied to "adaptive changes in motivation and behavior."

86. Consider the description of his acts by a perpetrator of apartheid, Eugene de Kock. De Kock's description of the killing is telling. De Kock uses phrases such as "in that second or two seconds, you are on automatic" and "you are in an emotional block" and "you cross the border and enter the surreal . . . everything becomes a sort of a blur, but you have to move" (Gobodo-Madikizela 2003, 76).

87. Gobodo-Madikizela argues that wives, such as de Kock's, were happy to remain "officially" in the dark even though they had their suspicions about what their husbands were doing.

88. De Kock interview, Gobodo-Madikizela (2003, 111).

89. Levi (1993, 215).

90. Piaget (1932).

91. Lakoff and Johnson (1999); Scott and Monroe (2008).

92. Bruno Bettelheim's *The Informed Heart* uses this argument to explain the Nazi system of brutalizing arrests as designed to create such disassociative behavior, breaking the link between the arrested person's past—when they were independent—and the person they became after the arrest, docile and willing to do anything to survive.

93. The boiling frog metaphor captures this inability of people to notice slow incremental change. The story is that frogs put into boiling water will hop out. But if frogs are placed in water that is room temperature, they will stay in the water and die as the water is slowly boiled since the change is so slow the frogs do not notice that they are being slowly cooked. As best I can determine, this metaphor is stronger than the scientific evidence supporting it.

94. Gobodo-Madikizela quotes P. W. Botha as arguing that reporting for military duty was answering God's call to fight the Antichrist. The echoes of this in the Bush administration's approach to the war on terror in the United States strike an eerie chord.

95. The person usually referred to as Axel von dem Bussche in English was a German nobleman, born April 24, 1919 to a German father and a Danish mother. He enlisted in the professional army and became a member of the German resistance, volunteering to assassinate Hitler in November 1943. The assassination was arranged but Hitler's plans changed and Hitler did not attend the event. Von dem Bussche then was sent to the eastern front, where he was wounded and lost a leg. He spent the next months recuperating in an army hospital and, because of that, did not participate in the July 20 plot. After the plot failed, most of the conspirators were arrested, tortured, and many killed. Von dem Bussche escaped this fate since he was still in the hospital and because he was not exposed by any of the other plotters. I have seen filmed interviews with him when he movingly describes how he felt when he first witnessed what he eventually realized was a massacre of Jews. He describes how this event made the bottom fall out of his world and he had to readjust his world and his place in it.

96. I initially came across the concept in theoretical work by Anthony Giddens (1991) and have seen it utilized in applied work successfully by Catarina Kinnvall (2004).

97. Twenge et al. (2007).

98. Ibid., 56.

99. These conclusions seem to hold cross-culturally based on experimental tests in the United States, Belgium, the Netherlands, and Hong Kong (Warburton, Williams, and

Cairns 2006; Richman and Leary 2009; Lok, Bond, and Tse 2009; Stouten, De Cremer, Van Dijk 2007).

100. Faulkner et al. (2004) examined this disease hypothesis in four studies: "Chronic disease worries" successfully predicted associations of foreigners with danger and negative reactions to immigrants. A focus on infectious disease was a likely trigger for malevolent attitudes toward immigrants and prompted approval of immigration policies to restrict entry by those of unfamiliar races and ethnic groups.

101. See Lerner and Rothman's (1995) work on the Nazi public health officials.

102. Faulkner et al. (2004).

103. Mikulincer and Shaver (2001) test the effects of priming one's secure base attachment schema to look at how it influences biases toward in-groups and out-groups. Studies 1 and 2 look at effects of dispositional attachment style while Studies 2–5 look at a mood interpretation, while Study 3 examines the role of threat appraisal, and Studies 4–5 induce threats to one's self-esteem or cultural worldview. They found secure base priming produced reduced negative evaluations of out-groups. This took place even when self-esteem or cultural worldview was threatened.

104. Mikulincer and Shaver (2001), Gillath et al. (2005), Mikulciner et al. (2003), Mikulincer et al. (2005), and Mikulincer et al. (2001) broadened and expanded Mikulincer's prior research in light of recent scholarship suggesting dispositional and experimentally manipulated attachment security contributes to open-mindedness and empathy, bolstering self-transcendent values, and promoting tolerance. They found two apparent behavioral systems at work—attachment and care giving. Two studies were run in three different countries (Israel, the Netherlands, and the United States) to examine whether contributions of attachment insecurity—anxiety and avoidance—are linked to real-world altruistic volunteer activity. In both studies, in all locations, avoidant attachment was linked to less volunteering, and when volunteering was present such volunteering was less altruistic and exhibited fewer "exploration-oriented motives," while anxious attachment was linked to "self-enhancing" motivations (Gillath et al. 2005, 425). Anxious attachment was linked to self-enhancing motivations for volunteering. Additional findings indicated that volunteering reduces interpersonal problems of individuals high in anxiety and that volunteering has more beneficial effects if done for selfless, prosocial reasons.

Mikulincer et al. (2003) also conducted three studies to monitor the effects of ongoing or context-dependent activation of a sense of a secure base attachment on endorsement of self-transcendence values, as measured by Schwartz's Value Survey (Schwartz 1992), especially the subscales of benevolence and altruism. The sense of secure base was primed by asking the subjects (Israeli undergraduates) to recall personal memories or watch pictorial depiction of supportive others. This condition was compared against priming of unrelated positive affect or neutral control issues. Participants then reported on the importance of two self-transcendence values, benevolence and universalism (in Studies 1–2), or were asked to list their own most important values (in Study 3). Finally, a chronic sense of attachment security was measured along dimensions of avoidance and anxiety. Results suggested secure base- priming and lower scores of attachment avoidance were significantly tied to higher endorsement of self-transcendence values. The effects were not explained by inducted or self-reported mood.

In another study, Mikulincer et al. (2005) conducted five experiments over two countries (Israel and United States) to test the hypothesis that increases in attachment security (manipulated both explicitly and implicitly), promote compassion and altruistic behavior. This hypothesis was supported across all five studies, independent of rival explanations. Dispositional attachment styles of anxiety and avoidance inversely were related to exhibited compassion, personal distress, and altruistic behavior. The authors concluded that attachment security provides the basis for caring feelings and care-giving behavior, while forms of insecurity repress or interfere with the same.

Finally, Mikulincer et al. (2001) conducted five studies to examine effects of chronic and contextual activation of attachment security on reaction to the needs of others. A sense of attachment security was contextually primed through asking subjects to recall personal memories, read a story, look at a picture of supportive others, or subliminally expose to proximity-related words. This condition then was compared against "the priming of neutral themes, positive affect, or attachment insecurity schemas." Reports of empathy and personal distress memories or availability of empathy and personal-distress memories also were measured. Mikulincer and his colleagues concluded that attachment security boosted empathic responses and reduced personal distress. Self-reports of anxiety and avoidance were tied to reduced empathy, and anxiety was positively related to personal distress.

105. See Bowlby (1999, 1958, 1973, 1952, and 2005).

106. Bowlby's theories were published in "Attachment and Loss" between 1969 and 1980. His theory of attachment rejected the then dominant theories of early relationships and drew on a wide range of work in fields as disparate as evolutionary theory, object relations theory in psychoanalysis, and cognitive psychology. Attachment theory was initially criticized by academic psychologists and psychoanalysts but has now become a major theory of early social development and understanding of children's social relations, in part because of the empirical tests conducted by Mary Ainsworth, which not only tested Bowlby's theory but also expanded it and provided it with empirical specificity. The major criticism of attachment theory today centers on claims that attachment theory overlooks the complexity of social relationships within family settings and the variation of discrete styles for classifications.

107. Smith (1976a); Batson (1991).

108. Van Lange et al. (1997).

109. Psychoanalysts use object relations theory to explain the process by which we develop a mind as we grow in relation to others. The "objects" referred to in the theory can be both real people in our world as well as our internalized images of these others. The object relationships are formed initially during our early interactions with our primary care givers. The patterns of interactions may alter and shift with experience but usually continue to influence us throughout life. See Ronald Fairbairn (1952) on the initial use of the concept, which was active in shaping psychoanalysis from 1917 on. See also work by Melanie Klein, Donald Winnicott, Harry Guntrip, and Scott Stuart among others. Somewhat controversial, object relations theory is perhaps most useful for our purposes as it relates to our ability to tolerate ambiguity, to see that both the "good" and the "bad" mother are a part of the same care giver, as Tony was able to see that there was good and bad in all people. I did not explore the psychoanalytic aspects of genocide and leave explorations in this area to others.

110. Westen (1995) and Niec and Russ (2002) examined the relationships between internal representations, measured empathy, and "affective and cognitive processes in fantasy play." To discern the validity of the Social and Cognition and Object Relations Scale Q-Sort (SCORS-Q) developed by D. Westen (1995), Niec and Russ (2002) administered eight Thematic Apperception Test cards, a play task, and a self-reported empathy measurement instrument to eighty-six children ages eight to ten. Teachers responsible for rating students' empathy and "helpfulness" also took part in the experiment. The internal representations were related to empathy, helpfulness, and the quality of the fantasy play of the children. The variance in SCORS-Q scores was in line with object relations theory and with previous results from the original SCORS. For Niec and Russ, these findings affirm the value of us-

ing internal representations as a way of discerning children's interpersonal functioning and serve as further indication of the usefulness of SCORS-Q.

111. Weber and Federico (2007) extend the intellectual link between interpersonal attachment and ethics. By focusing on ideology, they ask whether two dimensions of sociopolitical beliefs, right-wing authoritarianism (RWA) and social dominance orientation (SDO), are the products of insecure psychological attachment. Their findings from structural equation models of an undergrad sample (N = 255) show that "anxious" attachment leads to right-wing authoritarianism with this effect mediated by the conviction that "the world is a dangerous place." "Avoidant" attachment leads to social dominance orientation, tied to the attitude that the world is a hostile, competitive jungle in which people try to maximize their own personal utility.

In their words, "working models of anxious and avoidant attachment heighten the individual's concern about danger and competition, respectively, which are regulated by the adoption of ideological beliefs related to either social conformity (RWA) or social dominance (SDO). In doing so . . . [the] model allows political psychologists to go beyond one-dimensional focus on consequences of generalized threat and make sense of how different types of aversive relational concerns—linked to anxiety and avoidance—may give rise to conservatism" (Weber and Federico 2007, 406).

112. See Mikulincer and Horesh (1999) for studies on attachment style variance in perception of others. This work suggests that projective processes are behind these differences in attachment style. Mikulincer and Horesh asked subjects to report on their attachment style and generate "actual-self" traits and "unwanted-self" traits. In the next session, tests were conducted to detect impression formation concerning new people, ease of retrieval of memory of known individuals, and memory inferences about learned features of made-up individuals. The results show anxious-ambivalent persons' impression formation, memory access, and inferences about other people reflected projection of *actual-self* traits and that those of avoidant persons indicated influence of the projection of *unwanted-self* traits.

113. Hart, Shaver, and Goldenberg (2005).

114. In Studies 1 and 2 attachment threats resulted in worldview defense among those subjects who were anxiously attached, and motivated self-enhancement (in particular, among avoidantly attached individuals), similar to mortality-salience effects already observed in Terror-Management Theory. Studies 3 and 4 found that worldview threat, paired with self-esteem threats, prompts attachment-related "proximity seeking" in fearful subjects and avoidance of the same in dismissive subjects.

115. Mikulincer and Florian (2000) later conducted five studies to examine influence of attachment style on mortality salience, in light of Pyszczynski, Solomon, and Greenberg's Terror Management Theory (TMT). Terror Management Theory suggests that since awareness of one's eventual death is the ultimate goad to stress, anxiety and dysfunctional status, individual projects (including in-group status, worldview defense, etc.) help to alleviate this distress and even buffer against ever feeling it. In Study 1, Mikulincer and Florian found that making subjects aware of their mortality resulted in harsher judgments of transgressions only from individuals with anxious-ambivalent and avoidant attachment styles, but not secure people; while anxious-ambivalent subjects showed both immediate and delayed increases in the severity of judgments; avoidant individuals displayed such a response only after a delayed period of time. In Study 2, anxious-ambivalent individuals exhibited both immediate and delayed increases in ease of access to death-related thoughts being reminded of mortality; individuals with avoidant- and secure-attachment patterns showed such an effect only after a delayed interval. In Study 3, worldview defense in response to death-salience reduced death-thought availability only among avoidant-attachment-style

individuals. In Studies 4–5, mortality salience prompted an increase in sense of "symbolic immortality as well as in desire of intimacy" only for securely attached individuals, but not among avoidant or anxious-ambivalent individuals. All of this suggests that responses to death vary among individuals with different attachment styles, and that this has pivotal consequences for their psychological behaviors in enforcing their values, defending their worldviews, and, by extension, engaging in their politics.

116. Inspired by Ernest Becker's work (1973) but associated most closely with Jeff Greenberg, Tom Pyszczynski, and Sheldon Solomon (1986), terror management theory builds on the premise that knowledge of our own mortality is a uniquely human trait. Greenberg, Pyszcynski, and Solomon cite Becker's *The Denial of Death* as the psychological and philosophical forerunner of terror management theory.

117. The link between existential threat and posttraumatic distress with extremist political positions and exclusionist attitudes is not unique to terror management theory (Canetti-Nisim et al. 2008). I am grateful to Rony Berger (private correspondence, August 5, 2009) for alerting me to work on this area. Phil Zimbardo and Berger are working on projects to promote prosocial behavior and social virtue (Zimbardo) and enhancing resiliency (Berger), drawing on some of this research on trauma to create communities of healing in Israel and Palestine.

118. Huntington (1993).

119. Schimel, Wohl, and Williams (2006); Rosenblatt et al. (1989).

120. The punishment was measured by the amount of the hot sauce subjects received.

121. Pyszczynski et al. (2006).

122. Chanley (2002); Landau et al. (2004); Bonanno and Jost (2006).

123. Bonanno and Jost note: "Almost three times as many participants reported becoming more conservative than those who reported becoming more liberal in the 18 months following 9/11. What is more, conservative shift occurred across political party lines; that is, a shift toward conservatism was reported by sizeable proportions of self-identified Democrats and Independents, as well as Republicans, and within each group conservative shift was always more prevalent than liberal shift. These results are consistent with the notion that the appeal of conservatism is generally enhanced by psychological needs to manage uncertainty and threat" (Jost et al. 2003; Jost et al. 2004; Bonanno and Jost 2006, 320–21).

124. This is especially true among psychologists who break with contemporary cognitive psychological accounts of child development. See Harris (1989), Selman (1980).

125. Wu and Keysar (2007) explored the role of culture in perspective. A stated difference in the literature exists between the perspective-taking responses of subjects in "collectivistic" cultures and those in "individualistic" cultures. An experiment thus was devised to test the influence of culture upon this crucial social ability. Chinese and American subjects played an interaction game in which perspective taking was required. Measurements of eye gazing illustrated that Chinese participants were more attuned to partners' perspective than American participants were. Perhaps more to the point, Americans "often completely failed to take the perspective of their partner," whereas Chinese subjects "almost never failed to do so." The implication here is that cultural norms of interdependence condition the focus of attention upon the "other," illustrated here by the ability of the Chinese subjects to be better "perspective takers" than the American subjects (605).

126. Staub (2002, 2010).

127. Christakis and Fowler (2007).

128. Vaillant (2002).

129. Vaillant in Shenk (2009). For example, 93 percent of the men in the Harvard study who were flourishing at age sixty-five had experienced close relations with siblings. The

Harvard study, like far too many other experimental studies in science, is based only on male subjects.

130. Haidt and Keyes (2002), Margolis (1984), Mansbridge (1990), Monroe (1991). Margolis argues that we have dual utility functions and alternate between them, achieving a balance between fulfilling or self-interested needs and our needs for sociability and caring for others. Haidt's moral foundations theory examines the cultural variation in morality and identifies five fundamental moral values that Haidt believes all societies and individuals share to a greater or lesser degree. These include caring and protecting others from harm; fairness; loyalty to one's group, family, and nation; respect for tradition and authority; and a sense of purity that avoids disgusting things, including acts that are morally repugnant. Haidt found self-identified conservative Americans valued these five things equally whereas self-identified liberals tend to put care and fairness higher in their list of traits (Haidt and Keyes [2002], Haidt and Graham [2007], Haidt and Hersh [2001]).

131. Silk, Altmann, and Alberts (2006a, 2006b).

132. Feldman et al. (2000).

133. These are fascinating studies and I encourage people to read more than the short summary I can provide here. See especially Taylor (2002); Taylor, Dickerson, and Klein (2002); Taylor et al. (2006).

134. This work is having some impact in economics via what is becoming known as the study of happiness economics, which effectively studies a country's quality of life by utilizing some combination of economic and psychological techniques and a more expansive notion of utility than that found in conventional economics. Some of the key scholars are Andrew Oswald (1997), Bruno Frey and Alois Stutzer (2001). See also Luigino Bruni and Pier Luigi Porta (2005), Renaud Gaucher (2009), Bernard Van Praag and Ada Ferrer-i-Carbonell (2004), and Daniel Kahneman and Ed Diener (2003).

135. For an excellent discussion of how situational variables interact with individual and structural factors to turn good people into evil ones, and back, see Phil Zimbardo's *The Lucifer Effect: Understanding How Good People Turn Evil* (2007). Zimbardo draws on his own famous Stanford prison experiments, as well as recent actual instances of prison abuse, such as the events at Abu Ghraib, to decipher the causes of evil, in order to suggest how public and communal actions can contain and transform it. His analysis is a comprehensive tri-partate exposition, drawing on both individual and structural influences, not merely the group social psychological factors that emphasize the interaction effects of the situation on individuals.

136. Bar-Tal (1990, 16).

137. Ibid., 16–20. The variability in this could explain why some people can resist and others can't and is in line with Staub's theories of child rearing.

138. Bar-Tal (1990, 73).

139. Fujii (2009).

140. During the Holocaust, the group behavior/action was that of a bystander.

141. Bar-Tal (1990, 94).

142. Ibid., 102

143. Tajfel and his students thus rejected individualistic explanations of group behavior (e.g., Allport 1968) and theories that reified the group (as in theories emphasizing the madness of crowd behavior [Le Bon 1952]). Tajfel argued that we have complex identities and can choose from a wide array of our identities at any one moment. The social context will influence this choice, sometimes evoking personal identities, in which case the individual will relate to others in an interpersonal manner, depending on the other's character traits and any personal relationship existing between the individuals. But under other conditions,

Tajfel argued that a social identity would become more important. In this case behavior will be qualitatively different and will be group behavior.

144. Valdesolo and DeSteno (2007, 689).

145. Bar-Tal (1990); Bar-Tal and Teichman (2005).

146. Petersen (2002, 3–4); Mamdani (2001, 22).

147. Fujii (2006).

148. See Mamdani (2001). There has been too little work asking why such formalized power sharing arrangements sometimes work, as they did in Lebanon for many years, and why they fail, as they have done in Lebanon since the late 1970s. See Lijphart (1977, 2002).

149. Mamdani (2001, 16).

150. Ibid., 23.

151. Ibid., 22.

152. Mamdani also discusses the importance of looking at regional dynamics in understanding the Rwandan genocide, such as events in neighboring Uganda, where many Tutsi sought refuge. When the Ugandan government established an ancestry requirement for Ugandan citizenship in 1990, it forced the refugee Tutsi there to reestablish themselves in Rwanda. Hence, Uganda exported its own political crisis to Rwanda in the form of the Rwandan Patriotic Front, which began a series of invasions into Rwanda in 1990 and was followed by the death of the prime minister and the genocide.

153. Barnett (1999); Staub (1998a, 1998b).

154. *Understanding Ethnic Violence* (Petersen 2002) speaks directly to my findings on the importance of categorization of others. In contrast to Bar-Tal and Gobodo-Madizikela, both of whom focus on specific instances of genocide and ethnic violence, Petersen takes a broader tack, identifying four emotions as being the causes for the ethnic conflict as acted out in the violence that wreaked havoc on Eastern Europe during the twentieth century.

155. Petersen (2002, 17).

156. Here Petersen delves into social dominance theory, a social psychological theory formulated by Jim Sidanius and Felicia Pratto, which argues that societies are stratified by age, sex, and group, with the critical group divisions based on group identities, such as those corresponding to ethnicity, religion, and nationality. Sidanius and Pratto find human social hierarchies, consisting of a hegemonic group at the top and negative reference groups at the bottom. The more powerful social roles are likely to be occupied by a hegemonic group member, such as an older, white male. Prejudiced beliefs such as those associated with racism, sexism, nationalism, or class status are reflections of this principle of social hierarchy. For social dominance theorists, the origin of social hierarchies takes on an evolutionary explanation, with groups that have a tendency toward social hierarchies having a competitive edge in the struggle for survival. See Pratto et al. (1994), Pratto, Sidanius, and Levin (2006), Thomsen, Green, and Sidanius (2008) inter alia. Petersen sees society as a group-based hierarchy, and points to a variety of empirical evidence from twentieth-century violence.

157. Petersen (2002).

158. See Zimbardo (2007) for an overview or Milgram (1974).

159. Petersen presents evidence that positive in-group appraisal must involve negative out-group appraisal and even out-group denigration (2002, 48).

160. Staub (2003, 5).

161. The importance of legitimating the demonization of victims is attested to in a somewhat offbeat set of experiments by Bushman et al. (2007). Bushman had participants read a gruesome excerpt said to come from either (a) the Bible or (b) an "ancient scroll." For half of the participants, the passage indicated that the depicted violence was condoned by God. Next, subjects competed in a task for which the winner gets to "blast the loser with loud

noise through headphones." (This was defined as aggression.) In Study 1, participants came from Brigham Young University students, 99 percent of whom said they believed in "God and the Bible." Study 2's sample consisted of students from Vrije University in Amsterdam: 50 percent of whom were theists, but only 27 percent of whom were self-identified believers in the Bible. Results from Study 1 suggested aggression went up when the passage was "biblical" or mentioned "God." In Study 2 aggression went up when the passage mentioned God—especially for those believing in God and the Bible. The relevance of these findings—notably for indicating that scripturally sanctioned violence may increase aggression, especially in those who believe in God—seem especially troubling when we consider how much of contemporary genocide and ethnic sectarian violence is related to religion.

162. Staub (1989, 86–87).

163. Banissy and Ward (2007).

164. "Empathic ability of mirror-touch synesthetes (n = 10) was compared with those of nonsynesthetic controls (n = 20) and of controls (n = 25) reporting other types of synesthesia but not mirror touch . . . empathy quotient has three main subscales: cognitive empathy, emotional reactivity and social skills. Mirror touch synesthetes showed significantly higher scores on the emotional reactivity subscale of the EQ relative to controls, but not on the other subscales" (Banissey and Ward 2007, 816).

165. Banissy and Ward (2007, 816).

166. Moll et al. (2006).

167. The ventral striatum appears important for donations other than just monetary rewards. Two types of reward systems appear to be active in charitable giving: (1) The VTA-striatum mesolimbic network, also a feature of money rewards, but also (2) the subgenual area, an area specific for donations and also known to be involved in social attachment or what the authors call "affiliative reward mechanisms." (This held for species both human and non-human.) The lateral-orbitofrontal cortex, as well as where it meets the anterior insula and the dorsolateral cortex, is apparently triggered by opposition to certain social causes—the anterior insula is known to be involved in anger and moral disgust.

168. In Study 1, participants rated thirteen causes of poverty by importance, controllability, blame, pity, anger, and help giving. Two measures also were taken: conservatism and belief in a just world. Causal attribution was divided into three types: individualist, societal, fatalistic; thus, believing what was and wasn't within an individual's control. Conservatism correlated with a belief in the importance of individualistic causes, controllability, anger, and blame, while having an inverse relationship with the importance placed on "social" causes, pity, and one's intent to help. No systematic effects emerged associated with belief in a just world. Personal help intentions appeared to be emotionally influenced, while welfare appraisals were directly tied to questions of personal responsibility and ideological orientation. Study 2 reproduced the results of Study 1 with a nonstudent population.

169. The willingness to take on another's perspective was measured by being more or less likely to draw the letter *e* on the forehead in a self-oriented versus other-oriented direction.

170. A large literature suggests evolution favored prosocial and antisocial behavior. The logic is that natural selection may have produced human cooperative behavior as a way for rival human groups to compete more effectively. Such logic might apply especially to male members of the species. Van Vugt, de Kremer, and Janssen (2007) performed three tests. In step-level "public goods" activity, men give more to their group if that group is in competition with other groups, as opposed to no intergroup competition. Female cooperation seemed to have no link to the presence or absence of competition. Men seem to react more intensely to intergroup threats.

Wheatley, Milleville, and Martin (2007) look at the roles of mirror neuron system and social-network hypotheses. The mirror-neuron hypothesis argues that social understanding focuses on action simulation, while social-network theory proposes that these are linked with factors such as faces and affect, expression, and so on. Wheatley's study assesses which brain regions become active as subjects interpret and visualize moving shapes as either "animate" or "inanimate," that is, as "living" or "nonliving." Observing and imagining links up with the mirror neuron system, but only the social network system linked to perceptions of animation, such as the lateral region of the fusiform gyrus while animation was inferred, and the STS and the medial prefrontal cortex while animation was imagined.

Recent studies in behavioral economics use psychological experiments to test critical economic assumptions. In a test of a classic philosophical dilemma in moral choice, Waldmann and Dieterich (2007) asked: To save five lives, would you redirect a trolley to a track where it would kill only one? This classic dilemma is designed to examine when utilitarian strategies (emphasizing the greatest good for the greatest number) are deployed, and when they are more likely to be superseded by other considerations. For example, few think it moral to have a hospital visitor killed in order to ensure that five patients would live. Experiments show that "moral intuitions are influenced by the locus of intervention in the underlying causal model" (Waldmann and Dietrich 2007, 247). When the action taken influences the agent on a path of harm (that is, the train is about to hit someone), utilitarian moral judgments are more likely to hold than when the intervention influences the path of a potential "patient" (that is, the victim). Shleifer and Murphy (2004) are two economists who devise a model of the origins of social networks via discussion and mutual persuasion. Members were influenced by those within the network, but not external to it. These networks may be "rented out" to politicians seeking their votes and sympathy for their platforms, but may have little to do with the actual beliefs of the network. The outcomes of such a model suggest political competition leads not to preferences of voters in the center being "maximized" as Downs suggested in his classic study (1957), but instead suggests messages become distinct as parties try to segregate their networks from one another and inhibit contact with those from the rival party. See also Haidt (2003).

171. Rawls (1972).

172. I address this topic directly through an empirical experiment in Monroe and Martinez (2007).

173. Study 1 looked at the relations between spouses, while the remaining studies looked at the interactions between dating partners. Studies 1, 3, and 4 examine already-existing inclinations toward partner-perspective taking, while 2, 3, and 4 also had manipulations of perspective.

174. Lifton (1999, 3).

175. I first noted this in my eldest son, watching *The Lion, the Witch, and the Wardrobe* on a video. I had never seen the video and was watching it with Alex on his second pass. As I realized the lion was going to die, I became concerned for my son, alarmed that he might be upset at the lion's death. I whispered to my husband something to the effect that perhaps we should turn off the video. Alex looked up and said, totally nonchalantly, "Oh, yeah. The lion's going to die." He showed the same lack of concern when Bambi's mother died in that childhood video. Later, when he was twelve or fourteen, he watched *Schindler's List* without showing any emotional distress, something that surprised me since I had great difficulty getting through the movie. As the movie ended, and the film switched to color, Alex asked who these people were putting stones on the grave. "They're the actors with the people they

played in the film," I told Alex. He looked at me, aghast. "You mean this is REAL?" he exclaimed, and started to sob. This is but one homey illustration of the importance of mental structures for comprehending violence.

176. Refer to Gobodo-Madizikela for more on this absence of awareness.

177. Lifton (2000, 445).

178. Staub (1989, 2010).

179. Lifton (1986, 193).

180. Lifton was an editor of the volume.

181. Or, as another quote showed: "Our boys wouldn't do this. Something else is behind it."

182. Falk, Kolko, and Lifton (1971, 427).

183. The full quote is: "And not only for that hour and day were reason and conscience darkened in this man who, more than all the other participants in this affair, bore upon himself the whole weight of what was happening; but never to the end of his life was he able to understand goodness, or beauty, or truth, or the meaning of his own actions, which were too much the opposite of goodness and truth, and too far removed from everything human for him to be able to grasp their meaning. He could not renounce his actions, extolled by half the world, and therefore he had to renounce truth and goodness and everything human" (Tolstoy, translated by Richard Pevear and Larissa Volokhonsky, 2007, 815).

184. Tolstoy (2007, 815).

185. Festinger (1957).

186. I am grateful to David Sears for first pointing this out to me.

187. Elster (1986).

188. Rorty (1986).

189. Kahneman, Tversky and Slovic (1982); Simon (1982). Even extreme rational choice theorists (Friedman 1953, 22) allow that economic actors may rely on habit or random chance rather than conscious rational calculation as long as the outcome produced corresponds to the outcome that would have occurred "as if" they had followed the rational calculus (Friedman 1953). Work in neurobiology linking emotions to cognition is moving toward expanding our understanding of why and how this process works, but the work remains in early stages.

190. Interestingly, the modern concept of the self originated with John Locke, who conceptualized a tabula rasa self in which people are born without any innate ideas. Locke's patron was Anthony Ashley Cooper, the 1st Earl of Shaftesbury. Locke arranged the marriage of Cooper's son, the 2nd Earl, and thus was indirectly responsible for the birth of the 3rd Earl, the man most closely associated with the origin of moral sense theory, arguing for an innate moral sense. The young man was tutored by Locke who, we may infer, was an excellent tutor who taught his young charge to think for himself.

191. Much of the rest of this chapter represents joint work done with Adam Martin and Priyanka Ghosh, two extraordinary students with whom I have been fortunate enough to work. I would like to acknowledge their assistance, stimulation, encouragement, and their permission to reprint part of this work here. Parts of this section appeared in Monroe, Martin, and Ghosh (2009).

192. Some ten years ago I was asked to participate in an APSA panel on whether political theorists and empirical political scientists should work together. The question struck me as unusual since the answer seemed so obvious. Political theorists are extraordinarily smart and well educated and have worked out details of distinctions among concepts that are incredibly useful; why wouldn't we want to read and learn from them? On the other hand, there has been a lot of amazingly good science since then; why wouldn't a theorist want to

know about empirical work that could inform their theoretical statements? My position on the panel was a minority one, and the two groups surprised me by how they spoke in planes that were largely tangential. Unfortunately.

193. I use the terms *ethics* and *morality* interchangeably, both because this is the common practice in everyday language and because there is no one commonly accepted distinction among the scientists working in the diverse fields we have discussed here. Nonetheless, there are basic, albeit subtle, differences that moral philosophers or ethicists would recognize. In general, morals refer to personal character while ethics tends to refer to a social system in which those personal morals are applied. This means *ethics* tends to point to standards or codes of behavior expected by the group to which individuals belong. Further discussion of the myriad other intricate subtleties lies beyond the scope of this chapter. See the glossary for a short discussion.

194. Other theorists—from Plato to Hannah Arendt—often allude to elements of moral sense theory. The description just presented focuses on theorists who explicitly concentrated on the theory and identified themselves as moral sense theorists. Late Enlightenment thinkers found much to criticize in moral sense theory. These critiques cluster in four areas.

(1) *Feelings and a moral imperative.* Critics argued that there is more to morality than feeling, and that a feeling, as such, cannot create a moral imperative to action. They argued, further, that the mark of moral responsibility is the actor's freedom to reach a moral judgment and to choose a moral course of action. Given this, they find moral sense theory reduces the human being to an instrument of his own dispositions if the moral dimensions of life arise by sentiments, and if "right" and "wrong" are only the consequences of a kind of emotional reflex over which the moral agent has little control.

(2) *Reason versus emotions.* Closely related to this critique is Kant's (1991 [1797]) argument that if an action is impelled by any desires emanating from the psychological or biological facts of life, then it is determined by these factors and cannot be considered moral. Hence, as rational beings—this criticism continues—we occupy the "intelligible" realm, and actions are determined in this realm not by causes but by reasons. Actions are morally right to the extent that they instantiate a moral maxim.

(3) *Sentiment versus reasoned judgment of worthiness of the sentiment.* Critics who grant that the moral side of life does include emotions—such as anger and love— raise a further question: Does moral action have to do just with the emotions themselves? Is not the object to which we feel emotionally disposed also relevant? In other words, should not the critical issue be more than *just* the sentiments of approval or approbation but also the *judgment* of what and who deserve such attitudes and feelings? This view also argues that such judgment comes from deliberative processes, and therefore the moral life cannot be separated from reason.

(4) *Resolving difference in innate moral senses.* Finally, critics ask about the difficulties in resolving different moral senses. If morality is determined by sentiment and feelings and does not reflect any objective state in the world, what happens when these feelings vary from person to person? How are these disputes resolved? By reason? Force? Convention? By what is evolutionarily adaptive? If the moral

sense is a feeling common to all, then these moral sentiments should retain a kind of objectivity. Even if they do not reflect anything in the universe apart from human feelings, our moral judgments may be true or false, depending on whether they capture the universal human moral sentiment. But if feelings vary from one individual to the next, moral judgments become entirely subjective, leaving no acceptable way to adjudicate competing moral claims. Alternative choices and preferences may be irreconcilable. How does moral sense theory propose to resolve such disagreements?

195. Porter (2001).

196. Myers (1985).

197. This school included Francis Hutcheson, Anthony Ashley Cooper (a.k.a. the 3rd Earl of Shaftesbury), Adam Smith, Bishop Butler, and David Hume as its best-known advocates. While these men did not always agree on fundamental principles, they nonetheless shared a common outlook that distinguishes them from other ethicists.

198. See Shaftesbury (1999 [1711]).

199. Hutcheson's ethical theory is expressed in three works: *Inquiry into the Original of Our Ideas of Beauty and Virtue* (1971 [1725]), *An Essay on the Nature and Conduct of the Passions and Affections, with Illustrations upon the Moral Sense* (1969 [1728]), and *System of Moral Philosophy* (1968 [1755]). First written in 1738, this book was expanded and revised throughout Hutcheson's life and was published after his death. It contains the fullest expression of Hutcheson's philosophy, ranging from discussions of our human nature, duties to God and to each other, the rights and duties of parents, civil liberty, rights and contracts, and laws of peace and war. It contains an argument against slavery that was influential in providing academic legitimacy to the antislave movement. Reprinted in colonial Philadelphia, it supposedly influenced authors of the US Constitution.

200. Smith maintains the basis of morality in the sentiment but moves toward the device of an impartial spectator. He thus shifts from reliance on an innate moral sense and is not considered a moral sense theorist. Other more minor moral sense theorists, however, such as Joseph Butler, emphasize harmony between morality and enlightened self-interest, though Butler claims that happiness is a by-product of the satisfaction of desires for things, not just the desire for happiness in and of itself. Such direct and simple egoism was a self-defeating strategy for Butler, who argued that egoists would do better for themselves if they adopt immediate goals other than their own interests and then live their everyday life in accord with these more immediate goals.

201. Hume (1978 [1777], 1999).

202. Piaget (1932); Kohlberg (1981a, 1981b, 1984).

203. DeWaal (1996, 2001); Goodall (1986, 1990).

204. See Monroe, Martin and Ghosh (2009) for a review.

205. Hume's emphasis on the consequence of an act as the test of morality, however, was accepted by many theorists. Hence the split between deontologists and consequentialists.

206. Wittgenstein (1963).

207. Rawls (1972).

208. See Narvaez and Lapsley (2009).

209. See Geertz (2001) on the debate over observer contamination and fabricated data in anthropology. The 2010 investigation into the reliability of Marc Hauser's empirical work is one illustration of the general criticisms of this work but should not call into question the reliability of the entire field.

210. Moral sense theory, as generally construed, assumes it is grounded in sentiments or emotions. Hence our basic sense of what is good or bad is neither inferred from nor based upon any propositions. Such noninferential moral knowledge is based on a priori nonempirical knowledge such as mathematical truth. What is often referred to as "ethical intuitionism" is distinguished from moral sense theory and is said to model the acquisition of such noninferential knowledge about right and wrong on empirical grounds, in the manner that we acquire knowledge of the color of objects. Since our interest here is not in constructing an extended discussion of the concept of morality, we define it simply as behavior designed to further the well-being of others. See Monroe (2004) for fuller discussion.

211. Piaget (1932).

212. Kagan (1981).

213. Kohlberg (1976).

214. Gilligan (1982).

215. See Monroe (1996 and 2001) for a discussion of such work.

216. Kagan (1981, 1989); Kagan et al. (1979); Kagan and Lamb (1987).

217. Kagan (1998, 151). While Kagan finds no English word for this concept and refers to it as virtue, his elaboration on this consonance appears to correspond closely to what Freud called the superego.

218. Research dating from the 1950s found that mice that had stimulus applied to the pleasure centers of their brains would ignore food in preference for behavior that triggered such stimuli. See *Inside the Animal Mind* (1999) for a fascinating, visual overview of these experiments, which includes excerpts from experiments on many kinds of animals, not just laboratory mice.

219. Kagan (1998, 158).

220. This resembles Smith's concept of empathy in many regards.

221. Gladwell (2000, 80).

222. That the specific forms of mathematics can vary is evidenced by different mathematical systems, such as the Mayan, Egyptian, or the Babylonian number systems. Perhaps a simpler more whimsical illustration comes from the mistakes all of us have made on mathematics tests.

223. Kagan (1998, 12).

224. Ibid., 13.

225. The entire discussion is directed at what might be considered the normal pattern and ignores pathology or extremes.

226. Kagan (1998, 175).

227. Ibid., 173.

228. Ibid.

229. Ibid.

230. Ibid., 175.

231. "What is biologically special about our species is a constant attention to what is good and beautiful and a dislike of all that is bad and ugly. These biologically prepared biases render the human experience incommensurable with that of any other species" (Kagan 1998, 191). Kagan does not discuss the link between moral superiority of humans and keeping slaves. "The biological imperative for all animals is to avoid hunger and harm and to reproduce, and adult chimps spend much of each day doing just that. But humans in ancient societies established cities, wrote laws forbidding certain behaviors, built ships, wore finery, used slaves, attended plays, and, in Greece, admired the Parthenon" (Kagan 1998, 191).

232. Kagan (1998, 11).

233. Wilson's APSA presidential address and his subsequent book were an exception. Wilson asked whether "people everywhere have a natural moral sense that is not entirely the product of utility or convention" (1993a, 13). Wilson defined moral sense as "a directly felt impression of some standards by which we ought to judge voluntary action. The standards are usually general and imprecise. Hence, when I say that people have a moral sense, I do not wish to be understood as saying that they have an intuitive knowledge of moral rules. Moral rules are often disputed and usually in conflict; but the process by which people resolve those disputes or settle those conflicts leads them back to sentiments that seem to them to have a worth that is intuitively obvious" (1993a, 13). Unfortunately, Wilson's own demonstration of a moral sense left much to be desired. We need greater specificity and testable ideas for political scientists to reexamine moral sense theory as a plausible account of moral behavior.

234. Dawkins (1976)

235. DeWaal (1986); Goodall (1986, 1990).

236. Some (Hauser [2006]) critique political theorists (Rawls [1972]) for focusing on how much we care about fairness when we should be asking *why* primates came to care about justice and fairness in the first place.

237. Crawford (1937); DeWaal (1982 [1998]).

238. Bonnie and DeWaal (2004).

239. In one experiment, for example, a monkey called Sammy was in such a hurry to get her food reward that she released the tray before her co-worker (Bias) got her reward. When Bias realized that her tray had bounced out beyond her reach, she screamed. Sammy then approached her own pull bar and released it so Bias could get Bias's cup of food. Sammy did so despite the fact that her own food cup was now empty (DeWaal 1996).

240. Brosnan and DeWaal (2003).

241. See *Animal Spirits* by Akerlof and Shiller (2009) as one illustration of this work.

242. DeWaal (1997b); Clark and Grote (2003); Smaniotto (2004); Brosnan, Schiff, and DeWaal (2005).

243. Range et al. (2009).

244. DeWaal in Markey (2003).

245. See DeWaal (2001) for arguments on animal culture and DeWaal (1982, 1989a and 1989b, 1996, 1997a) on animal emotions.

246. DeWaal's recent work (2001) focuses more on the ability of animals to learn behavior, much as humans do, but since that is not directly relevant to my argument here, I do not pursue the line of inquiry it suggests about the possibilities of shaping the moral sense.

247. DeWaal (1996, 217).

248. Ibid., 7.

249. Ibid., 40.

250. Interestingly, Kagan also notes this phenomenon in very young children.

251. DeWaal notes the example of two chimpanzees who did not come when they were called by their keepers at feeding time. Because these two stayed out late, the other members of the group were not fed at the normal feeding time, and the entire group remained hungry. The rest of the group retaliated and beat the two miscreants. The next night, these two were the first to come in at feeding time, and they never again dallied when called for food (1996, 89).

252. Goodall (1986, 1990); Sapolsky (2002).

253. DeWaal himself raises a further possibility by suggesting morality ought to be universal and holistic. Other primatologists do not go this far in their argument, however, and I am not making such a claim here, even though such an argument could plausibly be made (see Monroe 2001 or DeWaal et al. 2009).

254. Bowles and Gintis (2002, 21).

255. Ibid., 21.

256. Gintis (2003).

257. Axelrod (1984).

258. Trivers (1971).

259. Dawes et al. (2007, 794).

260. Such results corroborate "public goods" experiments such as that of Fehr and Gachter (2002).

261. See work by Bruno Frey (Frey and Stutzer 2001) and Andrew Oswald (1997) entering happiness into the economic calculus or Amartya Sen's creative work on introducing the concept of capabilities into our estimates of a nation's wealth.

262. See Chomsky (1965) for the distinction between competence and behavior.

263. Ironically, the main proponent of this approach—Marc Hauser—refers neither to the original work on an innate moral sense nor to Kagan's work.

264. Hauser (2006); Young et al. (2007).

265. Hauser (2006).

266. Hauser focuses on traditional perspectives of morality as they confront archetypal moral dilemmas. He then outlines three main moral philosophical approaches: the Kantian, Humean, and Rawlsian perspectives. (Hauser ignores the extent to which Rawls's work is based on Kant's.) He finds strong forms of Kantian and Humean moral philosophy unable to account for the diverse behavior of those entangled in moral quandaries.

267. Damasio (1994, 1999); Kahneman and Tversky (2000).

268. "Reasoning and emotion play some role in our moral behavior, but neither can do complete justice to the process leading up to moral judgment" (Hauser 2006, 11).

269. Hauser blends evolution and moral psychology, classifying Piaget and Kohlberg as Kantian and arguing (1) that neither psychologist offers a convincing account of how children or adults move from one stage to the next, and (2) that both psychologists conflate correlation with causation. Thus while Hauser finds their stage theories of moral development interesting, he finds both theorists offer a map rather than a progression of moral development.

270. Hauser 2006, 131.

271. Ibid., 129.

272. Ibid., 99.

273. Ibid., 121.

274. Hauser seems to favor three models of the Rawlsian creature: weak, temperate, and staunch. He considers these as phenotypic expressions of a genetic potential set in different contexts. A weak Rawlsian "as a species, distinct from all others . . . has the capacity to acquire morally relevant norms, but nature hasn't provided any of the relevant details" (2006, 198). A temperate Rawlsian is "equipped with a suite of principles and parameters for building moral systems. These principles lack specific content, but operate over the causes and consequences of action" (2006, 198). Finally, the staunch person "is equipped with specific moral principles about helping and harming, genetically built into the brain and unalterable by culture" (2006, 199).

275. Hauser (2006, 300).

276. Ibid., 420.

277. Ibid., 420.

278. Trivers (1971); Wilson (1975, 1978, 1998).

279. Metzinger and Gallese (2003).

280. Ibid.

281. Gallese, Keysers, and Rizzolatti (2004); Iacoboni (2008).

282. Iacoboni et al. (2003); Singer et al. (2004).

283. Wicker et al. (2003).

284. Young and Koenigs (2007).

285. Tabibnia and Lieberman (2007).

286. van 't Wout et al. (2007).

287. Rilling et al. (2002).

288. Moll et al. (2006, 15624).

289. Moll et al. (2006).

290. Batson et al. (2002).

291. Tankersley, Stowe, Huettel (2007).

292. Lamm, Batson, and Decety (2007, 42).

293. Greene and Haidt (2002).

294. Zak, Kurzban, and Matzner (2005).

295. Zak, Stanton, and Ahmadi (2007).

296. Silvers and Haidt (2008, 291).

297. Crockett et al. (2008).

298. Cesarini et al. (2008, 3721).

299. Haidt (2001, 2007); Haidt and Bjorklund (2008).

300. Haidt and Bjorklund (2008, 185).

301. Bruner (1986); Pyszczynski and Greenberg (1987); Zajonc (1980).

302. Nisbett and Wilson (1977).

303. Bargh, Chen, and Burrows (1996).

304. Haidt (2007) recently dubbed his model the "new synthesis in moral psychology."

305. Haidt and Bjorklund (2008, 204–5).

306. Haidt (2003).

307. Wheatley and Haidt (2005).

Conclusion
The Psychology of Difference

1. Leonard Q. Ross was the pseudonym for Leo Rosten. An obituary in the *Independent People*, written by Chaim Bermant and appearing Friday, February 21, 1997, suggests Rosten may have been the model for Mr. Parkhill and that Kaplan actually existed.

Leo Rosten wrote a torrent of books of which two have remained classics, *The Education of Hyman Kaplan* (1937), and *The Joys of Yiddish* (1968). The first was the product of an unhappy phase in his life during the Depression when, although he had two degrees, one from the University of Chicago and the other from the London School of Economics, he was out of work and he taught English to immigrants at night school. It was there that he met Kaplan, lately from Poland, who thought he knew English—as he thought he knew everything—but hoped to perfect it, and who tortured the language as readily as he tortured his teachers.

Rosten captured his experience in a succession of short stories which he wrote for the *New Yorker* under the name Leonard Q. Ross. They reappeared in book form in 1937 as *The Education of Hyman Kaplan* and were an instant success. . . . The book was enjoyed even by the most English of English literati such as P. G. Wodehouse and Evelyn Waugh. The Nurses Association of America asked for a warning wrapper to be put round it because patients who read it were in danger of bursting their stitches. . . .

Some Jews, however, were not amused, and one of them, Nathan Ausbel, an authority on Jewish folklore and Jewish humour, wrote: "Jewish dialect jokes are not Jewish at all, but the confections of anti-Semites who delight in ridiculing and slandering Jews." The book was in fact an affectionate portrait both of the immigrants and their teachers. . . .

Rosten was born in Lodz in Poland, and came with his family to the United States in 1911; he grew up in Chicago . . . He produced a spate of novels (many of them turned into films . . .), thrillers, screenplays . . . and essays. . . . Although Rosten relished popular acclaim he was basically a scholar and taught political science and sociology at Chicago, Columbia, Yale and the New School for Social Research in New York. During the Second World War he was Deputy Director of the Office of War Information in Washington, and in 1945 he became a special consultant to the Secretary of War and was sent on missions to France, Germany and England.

2. Ross (1937).
3. Ibid., 144.
4. My original survey is available on request.
5. See *Stumbling on Happiness* (Gilbert 2006) for a discussion of how critical certainty and predictability are to happiness.
6. Note that I am analyzing the microlevel influences on genocide, not the macrolevel influences (wars, economic depressions) or the institutional factors (lack of a free press, effective democratic opposition).
7. McAdams (2006b); Salvatore, Dimaggio, and Semerari (2004); Scuzzarello, Kinnvall, and Monroe (2009); Coles (1989); Andrews (2007).
8. Levi (1995 [1963], 215).
9. Students joke that UCI stands not for the University of California at Irvine but Under Construction Indefinitely.
10. It may be of interest to note that snails do not travel in straight lines or on command, and that the experiment—designed to learn on which surface snails would travel farther—was not a complete success. I am grateful to my daughter for letting me tell this story of her snails and for her many other lessons on ethics.
11. Monroe and Martinez (2009).
12. Representatives to the US House of Representatives are allocated in the Enumeration Clause of the Constitution, which gives every state a number of representatives based on its population. In this document, slaves are referred to as "other persons" and are counted as three-fifths of a whole person. Arriving at this compromise involved some political discussion, but not necessarily along the lines one might initially have expected. Northerners wanted to consider slaves as legal property and have them uncounted, in the same way that horses or dogs would not be counted. Southerners objected to this, not because they valued slaves as equals but rather because they knew that the higher proportion of slaves were in their states and that counting each slave as "a whole person" would increase the Southern states' political power in the House. (Estimates vary but it is believed that at the time this clause was written that 43 percent of South Carolina's population was enslaved, 32 percent of Maryland's, 26 percent of North Carolina's, and 39 percent of Virginia's.)
13. Pateman (1988); Brown (1995); Okin (1989).
14. Mills (1997); Bodane (2009).
15. Recent work in what is called intersectionality is designed to capture the extent to which one individual may have identities that pull and conflict with each other, as a black woman might have felt conflicted during the Democratic political primaries for US presi-

dent in 2008, unsure whether she should vote as a woman or as a black person. This work recognizes the phenomenon I refer to, where individuals have more than one aspect to their identity. I laud work on intersectionality as an important first step, but we still need a much more complex psychological portrait of political identity in order to capture what is the empirical reality.

16. One of the jokes circulating on the Internet around the time of the Defense of Marriage Act listed all the Republican politicians who were divorced and concluded with the punch line "Don't let gays destroy marriage—that's the job of the Republicans." I can joke about such issues in my more optimistic moments when I believe there indeed is a shift in attitudes toward gays, lesbians, and transgendered citizens. On weeks when I read of yet another suicide by a young person who was bullied, stigmatized, or treated cruelly because of his or her gay identity, the jokes do not seem funny.

17. An athlete does not have to be a dumb jock, as my Phi Beta Kappa son who plays water polo can attest. A beautiful blonde does not have to be a dumb blonde, as is demonstrated by my daughter with her straight As. Fathers who choose to stay at home with their children should not be relegated to the category of Mr. Mom. Women who are wonderful mothers can still be excellent professionals, as is demonstrated by innumerable numbers of women in professional life. And so on. I deliberately use stories about my children and family in my work to remind my students of these facts. We can all fall too easily into stereotypes.

18. Reicher (2004).

19. Karp et al. (1993).

20. Although Tajfel himself does not introduce the notion of a dominant group's legitimate superiority into the equation, the concept of power seems implicit within his theory, although others have criticized him for not speaking directly to the issue of power (Brown and Lunt 2002).

21. Dovidio and Gaertner (1986).

22. Swim et al. (1995); Glick and Fiske (1996).

23. Smith (1993).

24. Adorno et al. (1950); Altemeyer (1988); Sanford (1973).

25. Glass (1997).

26. Sapolsky (2006).

27. Fiske and Cox (1979); Fiske (1982). See chapter 9 for details.

28. Sapolsky (2006, 119).

29. Baum (2008).

30. Range et al. (2009).

31. DeWaal and Brosnan (2006).

32. I must acknowledge the generosity of Joe Cropsey in helping me learn this, as I believe he did for other students. At Joe's Festschrift, Paula Wolff said—as I recall—"Joe always made us think about how we are with others, and how we are with ourselves."

APPENDIX A
WHAT IS A NARRATIVE AND HOW RELIABLE IS IT?

1. Parts of this appendix were written in conjunction with Kristin Fyfe and Adam Martin, and edited by Nicholas Lampros. I am grateful for their assistance and happy to be able to list them as my coauthors on this Appendix.

2. Dienstag (1997, 18).

3. Monroe (2004).

4. Monroe (2004, 266).

5. Readers interested in narrative should consult many of the excellent works in this area, such as those by Molly Andrews (2007). For an overview, see my appendix on narrative in *The Hand of Compassion* (2004), which discusses the development of narrative as a tool in social science, asks if there are universals in human behavior that can be detected via narratives, discusses how witness is transmitted in an oral culture, and provides a cognitive view of narrative and ordinary discourse. I also address the issue of narratives as sites of cultural contestation and in the construction of social science theory and discuss some of the cautions in interpreting narratives. My plea here would be for journal editors to expand their use of narratives, which are powerful tools for analysis but which require more journal pages to craft the careful analysis than do other methodologies in social science.

6. Monroe et al. (2009).

7. Polletta (2006, vii).

8. Another interesting issue concerns the use of case studies as a tool, a topic I wish to address here briefly. In part 2 of this volume, the narratives reveal the mind of the rescuer, the mind of a bystander, and the minds of three people who supported the Nazis in various ways, either through propaganda, military service, or intense political conviction. I have argued that deciphering the political psychology of these five individuals can help us understand the differences in their wartime treatment of others. This enterprise raises a methodological question: How generalizable are the results of an empirical analysis of one small group of people?

To answer that question, think about how we learn about languages. We have general categories of languages, such as French, Spanish, and Italian. If we then can find a person who is representative of speakers in that category, we can make a close examination of how that one person speaks in order to learn about the rules of the grammar, syntax, pronunciation, etc. for the speaker's language. So, for example, we can find and analyze a Spaniard and learn about Spanish, a French speaker to learn about French, and so on. This does not mean the speaker may not be unusual, as was the fabled king of Castile, whose lisp is claimed to influence the pronunciation of European Spanish today. (As best as I can determine, this story is an urban legend; I note it here because it nonetheless illustrates my point so dramatically.) But focusing on one person is a legitimate activity and can provide valuable knowledge of a pattern that then can be compared with others in the same category. When we extend the analysis to contrast the differences in language among French, Spanish, and Italian speakers, for example, we gain further insight on what French speakers share and what distinguishes them from speakers of other languages, what these three languages have in common, and how they differ from non-Romance-based languages, and so on.

So it is with our rescuers. Tony is emblematic of the morally praiseworthy rescuers. Beatrix illustrates bystanders. Fritz provides an example of the Nazi supporters, and Florentine represents the Nazi elite. Kurt falls somewhere along this continuum; indeed, the very ambiguity in his interview and the difficulties in easily placing him along the moral spectrum actually may serve to make him a fairly typical representative of the many Germans whose attitudes toward Hitler were mixed but whose actions provided at least tacit support to the Nazi regime, if only through their military participation in the war or their failure to challenge the Nazi regime.

How typical of these representative groups is each of our individuals? In the case of the rescuer, the question of Tony's typicality is answered by extensive empirical evidence from other rescuers I interviewed. *The Hand of Compassion*, for example, presented detailed evidence that other rescuers demonstrated both a worldview and a self-image similar to

Tony's. The same is true of Beatrix, whose somewhat helpless sense of self and fatalistic worldview parallels that of other bystanders with whom I spoke.

My formal analysis of Nazi supporters is far more limited. It is difficult to obtain entrée to living Nazis. It is difficult to determine who actually was a Nazi and equally difficult to conduct the kind of interview that is both free of heavy propaganda and the legal maneuvering that can distort the analysis. Finally, there is a certain moral repugnance and aversion to interviewing Nazis, and I found it difficult always to suspend the judgment necessary to conduct an interview properly. Hence, my claims as to Florentine's representativeness are weaker and are based on my readings of secondary sources, not my own interviews. I know from personal experience that one's own empirical examination of a phenomenon often results in conclusions that differ significantly from the conventional wisdom. So even though my reading of speeches, memoirs, and biographies of Nazis suggests Florentine is typical, I do not have an extensive firsthand knowledge of the genocidalist mentality. On the basis of my readings of such material from the Holocaust, and based on my prior narrative interpretive analysis of interviews with participants in ethnic violence in Lebanon during the Civil War, however, I believe it is accurate to say that Florentine is at least not atypical of the Nazi mindset and psychology, and that the analysis of her psychology can lend at least initial insight into the genocidalist mental framework.

I thus conclude that the analysis of the patterns detected here can produce useful knowledge about the more general psychological patterns that are relevant to more general issues of prejudice, discrimination, bigotry, sectarian and ethnic violence, ethnic cleansing, and genocide. In this conclusion, I am supported by other academic works corroborating my findings on the importance of the ethical perspective, even though these findings may not have brought together the disparate parts of the process in the same fashion that I have depicted here. Three literatures are of special interest. The first literature asks what causes good behavior; the second asks what causes evil, and the third addresses the causes of forgiveness. All this literature focuses attention on the importance of the self-concept.

With these caveats in mind, let us review my findings with an eye for broader generalizations and put them in the context of earlier works.

9. Behavioralism originated in psychology in the early twentieth century with the work of John Watson. Behavioralists argue that the observation of behavior is the most reliable and convenient way to investigate psychological and mental processes. Some behavioralists hold that studying behavior is the *only* way to investigate such processes, and that commonly used psychological terms (such as *belief* or *goals*) have no referents. These scholars eschew such concepts and refer only to behavior. Those taking this point of view sometimes refer to their field of study as behavior analysis or behavioral science rather than psychology. Watson's work constituted a significant break from structuralist psychology, which relied heavily on the method of introspection.

Behavioralists owe much to experimental psychology and to work in animal psychology, such as that by Pavlov. Many followers of Watson have gone into experimental psychology, consider themselves part of the natural sciences, and distrust all methods of investigation that are not experimental in design. They thus reject the case studies and interview methodology frequently utilized in clinical and developmental psychology. Contemporary cognitive psychologists study the mental processes that are hypothesized to underlie behavior. They thus study subjects such as attention, creativity, memory, perception, reasoning, representation of knowledge, and problem solving. Cognitive psychologists tend to reject introspection (as found in Freudian psychology) but do posit the existence of internal mental states and thus try to allow for the importance of beliefs, motivations, and desires for behavior. In this they differ with the radical behavioralist psychologists, such as B. F. Skinner.

10. Easton (1997); Monroe (1991a, 1991b) for an overview.

11. Easton's 1968 presidential address to the APSA trumpeted the beginning of the end of behavioralism in political science (Easton 1969, 1997; Monroe 1991, 1997).

12. Mansbridge (1990); Monroe (1991a); Green and Shapiro (1994).

13. Another part of the Perestroika movement was concerned that the American Political Science Association (APSA) system of governance systematically underrepresented critical groups. This issue lies outside the domain of this manuscript.

14. I italicize *Perestroika* when referring to the Russian movement but not when referring to the Perestroika movement within American political science. Two ideals are central to the American Perestroika movement: "the idea of restructuring American political science and the desire to welcome new ideas and new participants into the political process, as is suggested by the term 'warm house'" (Monroe 2004, 5).

15. McAdams spends a great deal of time elucidating and giving support for the prototypical American narrative being that of the "redemptive self," a theme of overcoming obstacles, learning from hardship, and self-actualization. Aspects of McAdams's work draw heavily from developmental themes found in Erik Erikson's work, *Identity and the Life Cycle* (1959).

16. McAdams et al. (2008).

17. McAdams and Albaugh (2008).

18. Adler and Poulin (2009).

19. McGaugh argues that memory is one of our most important possessions, which enables us to "value everything else we possess. Lacking memory, we would have no ability to be concerned about our hearts, hair, lungs, libido, loved ones, enemies, achievements, failures, incomes or income taxes. Our memory provides us with an autobiographical record and enables us to understand and react appropriately to changing experiences. Memory is the 'glue' of our personal experience . . . [M]emory is the consequence of learning from an experience" (McGaugh 2003, 2–3).

20. See Patterson and Monroe (1998) for a history of narrative analysis and its use in political science.

21. It is ironic that many of the arguments now being reexamined with a finer scientific eye date, in their philosophical tone, to earlier debates at the turn of the twentieth century. See McGaugh (2003, chap. 1) for details on this early work. Political theorists have suggested my own work might benefit from the concept of spiritedness, which Plato conceptualizes as a phenomenon between emotion and reason. A consideration of this lies beyond the present work.

22. Schacter and Addis (2007).

23. Loftus's widely cited but controversial work (see 1997 or Loftus and Ketcham 1994) conducted experiments challenging the reliability of memory, suggesting that memories can be changed by things that people are told. Her work focuses on how facts, ideas, suggestions, and other forms of postevent information modify memories. This work, and that of other scholars doing related work, has had strong and divisive implications for legal research and practice.

24. Bruner (1957, 1992).

25. McAdams (1996); McLean, Pasupathi, and Pals (2007). Personality psychology has begun to take narratives much more seriously as evidence of personality studies. McAdams's "narrative identity" (1996) is seen as a macrolevel organizing "story" that supersedes and integrates lower-level factors such as discrete personality traits usually addressed via quantitative or survey methodologies.

26. McGaugh (2003).

27. Nussbaum (2001).

28. "Nomothetic" (or proposition of the law) is a term used in philosophy, psychology, and in law with differing meanings. In psychology, nomothetic measures are contrasted to ipsative or idiothetic measures, and nomothetic measures are said to be those that can be made by an outside observer directly (weight or how many times a particular behavior occurs), while ipsative measures are self-reports such as a rank-ordered list of preferences. To illustrate, Carl Jung's psychological types, the Big Five personality traits, and the Myers Briggs type indicator all would be categorized as nomothetic theorieshttp://en.wikipedia.org/wiki/Sociology. In sociology, nomothetic explanation presents a generalized understanding of a given case and is contrasted with idiographic explanation that presents a full description of a given case.

29. Andrews (2007, 2).

30. Yuval-Davis (2006, 201), quoted in Andrews (2007, 9).

31. Andrews (2007, 9).

32. Much of this work is technical, dealing with neurophysiological work such as brain imaging. See McGaugh (2003), Nussbaum (2001) for accessible reviews.

33. I cannot determine whether this was created by Irene or by her ghostwriter.

34. Berntsen and Thomsen (2005); Peace and Porter (2004); Adolphs, Tranel, and Buchanan (2005).

35. In a third document, an early draft of a book Irene was writing about her life and which only Irene had written, there were further discrepancies.

36. Coder 1 did note some slight differences in nuance, with the book portraying Irene as taking all of this responsibility upon herself, and as a quick thinker, able to coordinate the lives of six other people. Coder 1 felt the book's narrative shows Irene as taking a much more proactive approach to helping the Jews and Poland in the book, often describing herself as "cooking up" ideas on her own. For Coder 1, the Irene in the interview was more at the mercy of God and her circumstances, with her actions more the effect of what situation she confronts. Other coders found no difference on this dimension.

37. Term coined by Sam McFarland (2005) to describe my concept of individuals who feel at one with all humanity.

38. "What do you call yourself?" he asked.

Appendix B
Glossary of Terms and Central Concepts

1. My examination of altruists (1996) suggests the existence of an altruistic perspective. Examining the political psychology of bystander and Nazi interviews suggests the altruistic perception was part of a more general psychological phenomenon that could be explained by drawing on the above-described work in linguistic and cognitive science to explicate the ethical implications of how the human mind processes information (see especially Rosch 1978; Lakoff 1996; Lakoff and Johnson 1999; Taylor 1995). We have seen how categorization theory can be utilized to analyze in-depth interviews with rescuers, bystanders, and Nazi supporters to identify the psychological process driving their actions. A subtle process of recategorization transformed ordinary citizens into perpetrators or Nazi supporters, if only through their inaction and sticking their heads in the sand, like the ostrich Fritz describes when asked to characterize his own self-image. This process entails the distancing and dehumanization which slowly turns a neighbor into the "other," someone eventually seen

as threatening and against whom violence then becomes justified—even necessitated—as self-defense.

This psychological categorization process is not unique to my data. Other scholars analyzing the Holocaust or related instances of ethnic cleansing and sectarian violence (Kreidie 2000; Fujii 2009) collected analogous narratives. Interviews with perpetrators of sectarian violence during the Lebanese civil war (Kreidie and Monroe 2002) and among American converts to Islamic fundamentalism are two instances in which I was closely involved in the research (Kreidie 2000; Kreidie and Monroe 1997). My reading of analyses by other scholars analyzing South African apartheid (Gibson and Gouws 1999, 2003; Gouws and Gibson 2001) or racism (Blascovich et al. 1997; Gobodo-Madikizela 1998, 2003; Tajfel 1969, 1981) provides further empirical evidence that the ethical perspective is a broad phenomenon influencing many important types of political behavior. The link between cognitive categorization and ethnic violence appears close, with recategorization providing the psychological fuel to flame old hurts and underlying prejudice into open acts of willful violence and brutality. The initial work on cognitive classification and perceptions (e.g., Rosch's work on visual perception) or the linguistic analogue that finds moral overtones in such classifications (Lakoff 1996; Lakoff and Johnson 1999) thus has direct relevance for moral psychology. This is illustrated by the use of derogatory terms during genocide and ethnic cleansing, as when Radio Rwanda referred to the "cockroaches" in a deliberate effort to reduce human beings to vermin that should be destroyed.

As a note in the history of science, it is important to recall how much theoretical work is informed speculation based on empirical observations, creative if educated guesses about the internal psychological processes that we do not yet have the tools to detect scientifically. The prospect of scientific advance is greatened with sharing across disciplines. My own experience accords with this view. A sophisticated team of scholars, trained at Caltech and headed by Michael Spezio, subjected some of my data to a latent semantic analysis that captures the role of emotions in decision making via recurrent multilevel appraisal and drawing on work in appraisal theory (Ellsworth and Scherer 2003; Lazarus 1991; Scherer 2003) and somatic markers (Damasio 1994; see Spezio and Adolphs 2007 or Reimer et al. 2009 for overview). Their work moves us forward on our quest to decipher the biochemical links that might accompany emotion's role on appraisal that happens mostly beyond deliberate awareness (Damasio 1994; Haidt and Bjorklund 2008). The Spezio team used this knowledge to build a model to explain voter turnout in the Iraqi elections of 2005 and the Pakistani elections of 2008, elections in which moral courage was required to vote. In both instances, what I call the ethical perspective came into play. I expect more advances in future years and will make my interview data available online at the UCI Ethics Center website (www.ethicscenter.uci.edu) and the ISPP website for the Caucus of Concerned Scholars: Committee on Ethics and Morality so any scholar who wishes to use an already collected data set may do so. I encourage others working in this area to share their data. Too often science is competitive. If working on altruism teaches us anything, it is that we all can frequently gain when we share.

2. Dworkin (2011, 41).

3. Ibid.

4. For example, decision theorists, such as Daniel Kahneman and Amos Tversky, discovered that people respond differently to a choice option when told there is a 90 percent chance of failure than they do when they are told there is a 10 percent chance of success. Or, consider different ways we might explain an event, bearing in mind that the understanding of the event can depend on the frame referred to. If we see a girl rapidly closing and open-

ing her left eye, we respond differently if we attribute the eye blinking to a purely "physical" frame (she blinked because there was something in her eye) or to a social frame (she winked to denote a joke or flirtation).

5. There are clear political overtones to the terms *welfare mother, working mother, soccer moms*, and, most recently (2010), *Mama grizzlies.*

6. For example, the ethical behavior of the bystander (Beatrix) was limited by her belief that "the good life" meant having the leisure time to play tennis and squash. This was provided by the economic affluence of a husband who could afford "help in the house." But Beatrix also noted that having household help meant Beatrix could do nothing to rescue Jews since the help might turn her into the Gestapo. In poignant contrast, when I asked rescuers why they risked their lives to save strangers, rescuers also referred to their idealized cognitive models about what it means to be a human being. For rescuers the idealized cognitive model of what it meant to be a human being related closely to the ability to help others. (This echoes Aristotle's link between happiness and virtue.) Most rescuers noted, as did a Dutch rescuer on the Gestapo's Most Wanted List, that the purpose of life is to help others. Rescuers frequently also added that it is not money that brings happiness but helping others. This example is but one of the more dramatic illustrations of how the idealized cognitive models—the mental representations—of what it meant to be happy, to be a rich, full human being, resulted in different ethical treatment of others. Thus do idealized cognitive models carry critical ethical overtones.

7. Elias (1985); Giddens (1991).

8. We noted the importance of ontological security—the political importance of the actor's sense of being protected, threatened, or falling at another point on a continuum between these two extremes—in the wartime narratives in this book. Kurt (the soldier who fought for the Nazis) spoke of being threatened and vulnerable, referring to an experience as a child after World War I and then later in the field during World War II. But he also spoke of the danger to his security as a member of a German Reich, which Kurt viewed as besieged. Kurt viewed others through this filter of fear. Interestingly, Kurt's discussion of the French stressed noble soldiers whom Kurt described as similar to himself, soldiers who had fought valiantly and deserved to be treated with respect when they were defeated. This view contrasted sharply with his discussion of Polish civilians. Yet it was not the Polish civilians who had tried to kill Kurt; it was his "fellow soldiers" who fought for France, and whose ancestors killed Kurt's father at Verdun and wounded his grandfather during the Franco-Prussian war. Nonetheless, it was the Poles whom Kurt described in derisive terms. Why? This categorization reflected Kurt's worldview as divided into "us versus them" with a world of Slavic people versus more Nordic Europeans who must defend themselves against the out-groups who were close to being *untermenschen.* Kurt's narrative is vague on the reasons for this classification, but this categorization seemed closely related to his sense that the Germans were under threat from the less civilized people from the East; hence the Slavs as a whole are cast as less civilized, more barbaric and "different." This classification system meant Kurt had to "be with his people" even if doing so risked his life, as it did during the Battle of Stalingrad, when Kurt was seriously wounded but left the hospital early and against doctors' orders, with his white head bandages painted green as camouflage, in order to fight "with his boys" against the Slavs.

Kurt's narrative illustrates how the cognitive filters—this one dealing with ontological security—shift the actor's sense of self into a cognitive categorization and classification of the "other." The shift can cause the other to be viewed in different ways: (1) to encourage sympathy for the other's plight; (2) to move beyond sympathy and toward an act of help; (3)

in contrast, this filter can allow the actor to remain indifferent to the suffering of another; (4) to feel sympathy toward but not to feel an imperative to help; or finally, (5) to even feel that the other is a threat and must be destroyed before he can kill you. This is but one illustration of how moral choice works through the ethical perspective.

9. Reimer et al. (2009, 7).

10. Milgram (1974); Zimbardo (2007); Zimbardo and Leippe (1991).

〜

Abramson, H. 1999. *A Prayer for the Government: Ukrainians and Jews in Revolutionary Times, 1917–1920*. Cambridge, MA: Harvard University Press.

Ackerman, Joshua, Jenessa Shapiro, Jon Maner, Mark Schaller, et al. 2006. "They All Look the Same to Me (Unless They're Angry): From Out-Group Homogeneity to Out-Group Heterogeneity." *Psychological Science* 17: 836–40.

Adler, J., and M. Poulin. 2009. "The Political Is Personal: Narrating 9/11 and Psychological Well-Being." *Journal of Personality* 77 (4): 903–32.

Adolphs, R, D. Tranel, and T. W. Buchanan. 2005. "Amygdala Damage Impairs Emotional Memory for Gist but Not Details of Complex Stimuli." *Nature Neuroscience* 8 (4): 512–18.

Adorno, T. W., E. Frenkel-Brunswik, D. J. Levinson, and R. N. Sanford. 1950. *The Authoritarian Personality*. New York: Harper. Reprinted in 1958.

Akerlof, G., and R. Shiller. 2009. *Animal Spirits: How Human Psychology Drives the Economy and Why It Matters for Global Capitalism*. Princeton, NJ: Princeton University Press.

Alford, C. F. 1997. *What Evil Means to Us*. Ithaca, NY: Cornell University Press.

———. 2001. *Whistleblowers: Broken Lives and Organizational Power*. Ithaca, NY: Cornell University Press.

Alford, J. R., C. L. Funk, and J. R. Hibbing. 2005. "Are Political Orientations Genetically Transmitted?" *American Political Science Review* 99 (2): 153–68.

Alford, J. R., and J. R. Hibbing. 2007. "Personal, Interpersonal, and Political Temperaments." *Annals of the American Academy of Political and Social Science* 614 (1): 196–212.

———. 2008. "The New Empirical Biopolitics." *Annual Review of Political Science* 11: 183–203.

Allport, G. W. 1937. *Personality: A Psychological Interpretation*. New York: H. Holt.

———. 1942. *The Use of Personal Documents in Psychological Science*. New York: Social Science Research Council.

———. 1950. "Prejudice: A Problem in Psychological and Social Causation." *Journal of Social Issues* 6 (S4): 4–23.

———. 1968. *The Person in Psychology: Selected Essays*. Boston: Beacon Press.

Altemeyer, B. 1981. *Right-Wing Authoritarianism*. Winnipeg: University of Manitoba Press.

———. 1988. *Enemies of Freedom: Understanding Right-Wing Authoritarianism*. San Francisco: Jossey-Bass.

Amodio, David, Patricia Devine, and Eddie Harmon-Jones. 2007. "A Dynamic Model of Guilt: Implications for Motivation and Self-Regulation in the Context of Prejudice." *Psychological Science* 18: 524–30.

Amodio, D., J. Jost, et al. 2007. "Neuro-Cognitive Correlates of Liberalism and Conservatism." *Nature Neuroscience* 10 (10): 1246–47.

Andreas-Friedrich, R. 1947. *Berlin Underground, 1938–1945*. Translated by Barrows Mussey. New York: H. Holt.

Andrews, Molly. 2007. *Shaping History: Narratives of Political Change*. New York: Cambridge University Press.

Anonymous editor. 1976. *The SS and the Netherlands, Documents from the SS Archives, 1935–1945*. Published by NKCA in 't Veld. The Hague: State Publishing.

Anscombe, G.E.M. 1958. "Modern Moral Philosophy." *Philosophy* 33 (124): 1–19.

Arendt, H. 1963. *Eichmann in Jerusalem: A Report on the Banality of Evil.* New York: Viking Press. Reprinted in 1968.

Aristotle. 350 BCE. *Nicomachean Ethics.* Translated by W. D. Ross. MIT Internet Classics Archive. http://classics.mit.edu/Aristotle/nicomachaen.html.

Aronson, E. 1969. "The Theory of Cognitive Dissonance: A Current Perspective." In *Advances in Experimental Social Psychology,* vol. 4, edited by L. Berkowitz, 1–34. New York: Academic Press.

———. 1997. "The Theory of Cognitive Dissonance: The Evolution and Vicissitudes of an Idea." In *The Message of Social Psychology: Perspective on Mind in Society,* edited by C. McGarty and A. Haslam, 20–35. Cambridge, MA: Blackwell.

Arriaga, X., and C. Rusbult. 1998. "Standing in My Partner's Shoes: Partner Perspective Taking and Reactions to Accommodative Dilemmas." *Personality and Social Psychology Bulletin* 24 (9): 927–48.

Axelrod, Robert. 1984. *The Evolution of Cooperation.* New York: Basic Books.

———. 2008. "Political Science and Beyond: Presidential Address to the APSA." *Perspectives on Politics* 6: 3–9.

Ayala, Francisco J. 1987. "The Biological Roots of Morality." *Biology and Philosophy* 2 (3): 235–52.

Bagdasarian, Nicholas Der. 1976. *The Austro-German Rapprochement, 1870–1879: From the Battle of Sedan to the Dual Alliance.* Rutherford, NJ: Fairleigh Dickinson University Press.

Baker, W. 2005. *America's Crisis of Values: Reality and Perception.* Princeton, NJ: Princeton University Press.

Balakian, Grigoris. 2009. *Armenian Golgotha: A Memoir of the Armenian Genocide, 1915–1918.* Translated by Peter Balakian with Aris Sevag. New York: Knopf.

Baldwin, N. (2001). *Henry Ford and the Jews: The Mass Production of Hate.* New York: Public Affairs.

Bandura, A., and R. Walters. 1963. *Social Learning and Personality Development.* New York: Holt, Rinehart, and Winston.

Banissy, M., and J. Ward. 2007. "Mirror-Touch Synesthesia Is Linked with Empathy." *Nature Neuroscience* 10: 815–16.

Bargh, J., M. Chen, and L. Burrows. 1996. "Automaticity of Social Behavior: Direct Effects of Trait Construct and Stereotype Activation on Action." *Journal of Personality and Social Psychology* 71: 230–44.

Barnett, P. 1999. *Bystanders: Conscience and Complicity during the Holocaust.* Westport, CT: Greenwood Press.

Barnouw, D. 1994. *Rost van Tonningen: Fout tot het bittere eind* (Rost van Tonningen: Mistake to the Bitter End). Zutphen: Walburg Press.

Bar-On, D. 2006. *Tell Your Life Story: Creating Dialogue among Jews and Germans, Israelis and Palestinians.* Budapest; New York: Central European University Press.

Bar-Tal, Daniel. 1990. *Group Beliefs: A Conception for Analyzing Group Structure, Processes, and Behavior.* New York: Springer-Verlag.

———. 2000. *Shared Beliefs in a Society: Social Psychological Analysis.* Thousand Oaks, CA: Sage.

Bar-Tal, Daniel, and Yona Teichman. 2005. *Stereotypes and Prejudice in Conflicts.* Cambridge: Cambridge University Press.

Batson, C. D. 1991. *The Altruism Question: Toward a Social-Psychological Answer.* Hillsdale, NJ: Erlbaum.

———. 1993. "Experimental Tests for the Existence of Altruism." In *Stanford Encyclopedia of Philosophy, PSA, 2,* edited by D. Hull, M. Forbes, and K. Okruklik, 69–78. East Lansing, MI: Philosophy of Science Association.

Batson, C. D., N. Ahmad, D. A. Lishner, and J. Tsang. 2002. "Empathy and Altruism." In *Handbook of Positive Psychology*, edited by C. R. Snyder and S. L. Lopez, 485–98. New York: Oxford University Press.

Baum, Steven K. 2008. *The Psychology of Genocide: Perpetrators, Bystanders, and Rescuers.* New York: Cambridge University Press.

Beaumont, J. 1995. "Eisenhower and the German POWs: Facts against Falsehood." *Journal of Modern History* 67 (4): 976–78.

Becker, E. 1973. *The Denial of Death.* New York: Free Press.

Beckwith, J., and C. A. Morris. 2008. "Twin Studies of Political Behavior: Untenable Assumptions?" *Perspectives on Politics* 6 (4): 785–91.

Bekoff, Marc, and Jessica Pierce. 1965. *Wild Justice: The Moral Lives of Animals.* Chicago: University of Chicago Press.

Bentham, J. 2002. *Works.* Charlottesville, VA: InteLex Corp.

Berenbaum, M. 1997. "The November Pogroms: Kristallnacht and Its Aftermath." In *Witness to the Holocaust*, edited by M. Berenbaum, 40–68. New York: HarperCollins.

Bermant, C. 1997. "Obituary: Leo Rosten." *The Independent*, London, February 21.

Berntsen D., and D. K. Thomsen. 2005. "Personal Memories for Remote Historical Events: Accuracy and Clarity for Flashbulb Memories Related to WWII." *Journal of Experimental Psychology: General* 134: 242–57.

Bettelheim, Bruno. 1960. *The Informed Heart.* New York: Free Press.

Blascovich, J., N. A. Wyer, L. A. Swart, and J. L. Kibler. 1997. "Racism and Racial Categorization." *Journal of Personality and Social Psychology* 72 (6): 1364–72.

Blasi, A. 2003. "Character, Moral Development, and the Self." In *Character Psychology and Character Education*, edited by D. K. Lapsley and F. C. Power, 52–82. Notre Dame, IN: University of Notre Dame Press.

———. 2004. "Moral Functioning: Moral Understanding and Personality." In *Moral Development, Self, and Identity*, edited by D. K. Lapsley and D. Narvaez, 335–47. Mahwah, NJ: Erlbaum.

Blight, James, 1990. *The Shattered Crystal Ball.* Savage, MD: Rowman and Littlefield.

Blight, James, and Peter Kornbluh, eds. 1998. *Politics of Illusion: The Bay of Pigs Invasion Reexamined.* Boulder, CO: Lynne Rienner.

Bodane, M. 2009. Presentation in Ethics Workshop. University of California, Irvine, June 5.

Bonanno, G. A., and J. T. Jost. 2006. "Conservative Shift among High-Exposure Survivors of the September 11th Terrorist Attacks." *Basic and Applied Social Psychology* 28: 311–23.

Bonnie, K. E., and F.B.M. DeWaal. 2004. "Primate Social Reciprocity and the Origin of Gratitude." In *The Psychology of Gratitude*, edited by R. A. Emmons and M. E. McCullough, 213–29. Oxford: Oxford University Press.

Bowlby, J. 1952. *Maternal Care and Mental Health; a Report Prepared on Behalf of the World Health Organization as a Contribution to the United Nations Programme for the Welfare of Homeless Children.* Geneva: World Health Organization.

———. 1958. "The Nature of the Child's Tie to His Mother." *International Journal of Psychoanalysis* 39: 350–73.

———. 1960. "Separation Anxiety." *International Journal of Psychoanalysis* 41: 89–113.

———. 1969. *Attachment and Loss.* New York: Basic Books.

——— 1973. *Separation: Anxiety and Anger, Attachment and Loss.* New York: Basic Books.

———. 1999. *Attachment*, 2nd ed. New York: Basic Books.

———. 2005. *The Making and Breaking of Affectional Bonds.* New York: Routledge.

Bowles, S. and H. Gintis. 2002. "Prosocial Emotions." Santa Fe Institute Working Paper #02-07-028.

Brewer, Marilynn B. 1999. "The Psychology of Prejudice: Ingroup Love and Outgroup Hate?" *Journal of Social Issues* 55 (3): 429–44.

———. 2007. "The Importance of Being We: Human Nature and Intergroup Relations." *American Psychologist* 62: 728–38.

Brose, E. 2010. *A History of the Great War: World War One and the International Crisis of the Early Twentieth Century.* New York: Oxford University Press.

Brosnan, S. F., and F.B.M. DeWaal. 2002. "A Proximate Perspective on Reciprocal Altruism." *Human Nature* 13: 129–52.

———. 2003. "Monkeys Reject Unequal Pay." *Nature* 425: 297–99.

———. 2004. "Reply to Henrich and Wynne." *Nature* 428: 140.

Brosnan, S. F., H. Schiff, and F.B.M. DeWaal. 2005. "Tolerance for Inequity Increases with Social Closeness in Chimpanzees." *Proceedings of the Royal Society B* 272: 253–58.

Brown, S., and P. Lunt. 2002. "A Genealogy of the Social Identity Tradition: Deleuze and Guattari and Social Psychology." *British Journal of Social Psychology* 41 (1): 1–23.

Brown, W. 1995. *States of Injury: Power and Freedom in Late Modernity.* Princeton, NJ: Princeton University Press.

Browning, C. R. 1992. *Ordinary Men: Reserve Police Battalion 101 and the Final Solution in Poland.* New York: HarperCollins.

Bruner, J. 1957. *Contemporary Approaches to Cognition: A Symposium Held at the University of Colorado.* Cambridge, MA: Harvard University Press.

———. 1986. *Actual Minds, Possible Worlds.* Cambridge, MA: Harvard University Press.

———. 1991a. *Acts of Meaning.* Cambridge, MA: Harvard University Press.

———. 1991b. "The Narrative Construction of Reality." *Critical Inquiry* 18 (1): 1–21.

———. 1992. A Psychologist and the Law. *New York Law School Law Review* 37: 173.

Bruni, Luigino, and Pier Luigi Porta. 2005. *Economics and Happiness: Framing the Analysis.* Oxford: Oxford University Press.

Bryan, F. 1993. *Henry's Lieutenants.* Detroit: Wayne State University Press.

Bullock, A. 1962. *Hitler: A Study of Tyranny.* New York: Harper and Row.

———. 1991. *Hitler and Stalin.* London: HarperCollins.

Bushman, Brad J., Robert D. Ridge, Enny Das, Colin Key, and Gregory Busath. 2007. "When God Sanctions Killing: Effect of Scriptural Violence on Aggression." *Psychological Science* 18: 204–7.

Butler, Bishop. 1900. *The Works of Bishop Butler.* Edited by J. H. Bernard. London: Macmillan.

Cahill, L. 1997. "The Neurobiology of Emotionally Influenced Memory Implications for Understanding Traumatic Memory." *Annals of the New York Academy of Sciences* 821 (June): 238–46. Special issue on the psychobiology of posttraumatic stress disorder.

Canetti-Nisim, D. E. Halperin, K. Sharvit, and S. Hobfoll. 2008. "A New Stress-Based Model of Political Extremism: Personal Exposure to Terrorism, Psychological Distress, and Exclusionist Political Attitudes." *Journal of Conflict Resolution* 53: 363–69.

Cesarini, D. et al. 2008. "Heritability of Cooperative Behavior in the Trust Game." *Proceedings of the National Academy of Sciences* 105 (10): 3721–26.

Chakrabarty, D. 2008. *Provincializing Europe: Postcolonial Thought and Historical Difference.* Princeton, NJ: Princeton University Press.

Chanley, V. 2002. "Trust in Government in the Aftermath of 9/11: Determinants and Consequences." *Political Psychology* 23 (3): 469–83.

Chomsky, N. 1965. *Syntactic Structures.* The Hague: Mouton.

Christakis, N., and J. Fowler. 2007. "The Spread of Obesity in a Large Social Network over 32 Years." *New England Journal of Medicine* 357 (4): 370–79.

Clark, M. S., and N. K. Grote. 2003. "Close Relationships." In *Handbook of Psychology: Personality and Social Psychology*, edited by T. Million and M. J. Lerner, 447–61. New York: John Wiley.

Coan, James, Hillary Schaefer, and Richard Davidson. 2006. "Lending a Hand: Social Regulation of the Neural Response to Threat." *Psychological Science* 17: 1032–39.

Colby, A., and W. Damon. 1992. *Some Do Care: Contemporary Lives of Moral Commitment*. New York: Free Press.

Coles, R. 1967. *Children of Crisis: A Study of Courage and Fear*. Boston: Little, Brown.

———. 1989. *The Call of Stories: Teaching and the Moral Imagination*. Boston: Houghton Mifflin.

Collins, R. 2004. *Visigothic Spain, 409–711*. Malden, MA: Blackwell Publishing.

Connolly, Kate. 2008. "Panel Rethinks Death Toll from Dresden Raids." *The Guardian*. Accessed October 3. http://www.guardian.co.uk/world/2008/oct/03/secondworldwar .germany.

Connolly, W. 2002. *Neuropolitics: Thinking, Culture, Speed*. Minneapolis: University of Minnesota Press.

Cooper, John. 2008. *Raphael Lemkin and the Struggle for the Genocide Convention*. New York: Palgrave Macmillan.

Crawford, M. 1937. "The Cooperative Solving of Problems by Young Chimpanzees." *Comparative Psychology Monographs* 14: 1–88.

Crawford, N. 2002. *Argument and Change in World Politics: Ethics, Decolonization, and Humanitarian Intervention*. New York: Cambridge University Press.

Crockett, M. J., L. Clark, G. Tabinia, M. D. Lieberman, and T. W. Robbins. 2008. "Serotonin Modulates Behavioral Reactions to Unfairness." *Science* 320(5884):17–39.

Cropsey, J. 2001. *Polity and Economy: With Further Thoughts on the Principles of Adam Smith*. South Bend, IN: St. Augustine's Press.

Cunningham, William, Marcia Johnson, Carol Rayel, Chris Gatenby, John Gore, and Mahzarin Banaji. 2004. "Separable Neural Components in the Processing of Black and White Faces." *Psychological Science* 15 (12): 806–13.

Dahrendorf, Ralf. 1960. *Homo Sociologicus*. Cologne: Westdeutscher Verlag.

Damasio, Antonio M. 1994. *Descartes' Error: Emotion, Reason, and the Human Brain*. New York: Putnam.

———. 1999. *The Feeling of What Happens: Body and Emotions in the Making of Consciousness*. New York: Harcourt Brace.

Darwin, Charles. 1889. *The Origin of Species*. New York: Appleton.

Dasen, P. R. 1977. "Cross-Cultural Cognitive Development: The Cultural Aspects of Piaget's Theory." *Annals of the New York Academy of Sciences* 285: 332–37.

Dawes, C., J. Fowler, T. Johnson, R. McElreath, and O. Smirnov. 2007. "Egalitarian Motives in Humans." *Nature* 446: 794–96.

Dawkins, Richard. 1976. *The Selfish Gene*. New York: Oxford University Press.

Dennis, J., D. Easton, and S. Easton. 1969. *Children in the Political System: Origins of Political Legitimacy*. New York: McGraw-Hill.

Des Forges, Alison. 1999. *Leave None to Tell the Story: Genocide in Rwanda*. New York: Human Rights Watch.

D'Este, C. 1989. "Model." In *Hitler's Generals*, edited by C. Barnett. London: Phoenix.

DeWaal, Frans. 1982. *Chimpanzee Politics: Power and Sex among Apes*. Baltimore: Johns Hopkins University Press. Rev. ed. 1998.

———. 1986. "The Integration of Dominance and Social Bonding in Primates." *Quarterly Review of Biology* 61 (4): 459–79.

DeWaal, Frans. 1989a. "Food Sharing and Reciprocal Obligations among Chimpanzees." *Journal of Human Evolution* 18: 433–59.

———. 1989b. *Peacemaking among Primates*. Cambridge, MA: Harvard University Press.

———. 1996. *Good Natured: The Origins of Right and Wrong in Humans and Other Animals*. Cambridge, MA: Harvard University Press.

———. 1997a. *Bonobo: The Forgotten Ape*. Berkeley: University of California Press.

———. 1997b. "The Chimpanzee's Service Economy: Food for Grooming." *Evolution and Human Behavior* 18: 375–86.

———. 2001. *The Ape and the Sushi Master: Cultural Reflections of a Primatologist*. New York: Basic Books.

DeWaal, Frans, and M. L. Berger. 2000. "Payment for Labour in Monkeys." *Nature* 404: 563.

DeWaal, Frans, and S. F. Brosnan. 2006. "Simple and Complex Social Reciprocity in Monkeys and Apes." In *Cooperation in Primates and Humans: Mechanisms and Evolution*, edited by Peter Kappeler and Carel van Schaik. New York: Springer.

DeWaal, F., S. Macedo, and J. Ober. 2009. *Primates and Philosophers: How Morality Evolved*. Princeton, NJ: Princeton University Press.

Dienstag, J. 1997. *"Dancing in Chains": Narrative and Memory in Political Theory*. Stanford, CA: Stanford University Press.

Donnelly, J. 2003. *Universal Human Rights in Theory and Practice*. Ithaca, NY: Cornell University Press.

Dovidio, J. 1984. "Helping Behavior and Altruism: An Empirical and Conceptual Overview." In *Advances in Experimental Social Psychology*, edited by Leonard Berkowitz et al., 362–428. New York: Academic Press.

Dovidio, J. F., and S. L. Gaertner. 1986. "The Aversive Form of Racism." In *Prejudice, Discrimination, and Racism*, edited by John F. Dovidio and Samuel Gaertner, 61–89. San Diego: Academic Press.

Downs, A. 1957. *An Economic Theory of Democracy*. New York: Harper.

Durkheim, Émile. 1954. *The Elementary Forms of Religious Life*. New York: Free Press.

Dworkin, R. 2011. "What Is a Good Life?" *New York Review of Books* 58 (3): 41–43.

Easton, D. 1965. *A Systems Analysis of Political Life*. New York: Wiley.

———. 1969. "The New Revolution in Political Science." *American Political Science Review* 63 (4): 1051–61.

———. 1997. "The Future of the Postbehavioral Phase in Political Science." In *Contemporary Empirical Political Theory*, edited by Kristen Monroe, 13–46. Berkeley: University of California Press.

Ebbinghaus, H. 1885. *Memory: A Contribution to Experimental Psychology*. New York: Teachers College, Columbia University.

Ekman, P. 1992. "An Argument for Basic Emotions." *Cognition and Emotion* 6: 169–200.

Elias, N. 1985. *The Loneliness of the Dying*. Oxford: B. Blackwell.

Ellsworth, P., and K. Scherer. 2003. "Appraisal Processes in Emotion." In *Handbook of Affective Sciences*, edited by Richard J. Davidson, Klaus R. Scherer, and H. Hill Goldsmith, 572–95. New York: Oxford University Press.

Elster, J. 1986. *The Multiple Self*. New York: Cambridge University Press.

Erikson, E. 1959. *Identity and the Life Cycle: Selected Papers*. New York: International Universities Press.

European Court of Human Rights. 2007. Judgment in *Jorgic v. Germany*, July 12. Application no. 74613/01, ECtHR.

Evans, M. 2005. *Passchendaele: The Hollow Victory*. London: Pen and Sword Books.

Fairbairn, W.R.D. 1952. *Psychoanalytic Studies of Personality*. London: Routledge and Kegan Paul.

Falk, Richard, Gabriel Kolko, and Robert Jay Lifton. 1971. *Crimes of War.* New York: Random House.

Fauconnier, G. 1985. *Mental Spaces: Aspects of Meaning Construction in Natural Language.* Cambridge, MA: MIT Press.

Faulkner, Jason, March Schaller, Justin Park, and Lesley Duncan. 2004. "Evolved Disease-Avoidance Mechanisms and Contemporary Xenophobic Attitudes." *Group Processes and Intergroup Relations* 7: 333–53.

Federn, Ernst. 1960. "Some Clinical Remarks on the Psychopathology of Genocide." *Psychiatric Quarterly* 34 (3): 538–49.

Fehr, E., and S. Gachter. 2002. "Altruistic Punishment in Humans." *Nature* 415: 137–40.

Fehr, E., and K. M. Schmidt. 1999. "A Theory of Fairness, Competition, and Cooperation." *Quarterly Journal of Economics* 114: 817–68.

Fein, Helen. 1979. *Accounting for Genocide: Victims and Survivors of the Holocaust.* New York: Free Press.

———. 1990. "Social Recognition and Criminalization of Genocide." *Current Sociology* 3 (1): 1–7.

———. 1993. *Genocide: A Sociological Perspective.* London: Sage.

———. 2007. *Human Rights and Wrongs: Slavery, Terror, Genocide.* Boulder, CO: Paradigm.

Feldman, L. G. 1984. *The Special Relationship between West Germany and Israel.* Boston: Allen and Unwin.

———. 1999. "The Principle and Practice of 'Reconciliation' in German Foreign Policy: Relations with France, Israel, Poland, and the Czech Republic." *International Affairs* 75 (2): 333–56.

Feldman, P. J., et al. 2000. "Maternal Social Support Predicts Birth Weight and Fetal Growth in Human Pregnancy." *Psychosomatic Medicine* 62: 715–25.

Ferdinandusse, W. 2004. "The Interaction of National and International Approaches in the Repression of International Crimes." *European Journal of International Law* 15 (5): 1042.

Festinger, L. 1957. *A Theory of Cognitive Dissonance.* Stanford, CA: Stanford University Press.

Fillmore, Charles J. 1982. "Frame Semantics." In *Linguistics in the Morning Calm,* edited by the Linguistics Society of Korea, 111–37. Seoul: Hanshin.

Fine, J. 1983. *The Early Medieval Balkans.* Ann Arbor: University of Michigan Press.

Fiske, S. T. 1982. "Schema-Triggered Affect: Applications to Social Perception." In *Affect and Cognition: The 17th Annual Carnegie Symposium on Cognition,* edited by M. S. Clark and S. T. Fiske, 55–78. Hillsdale, NJ: Erlbaum.

Fiske, S. T., and M. Cox. 1979. "Person Concepts: The Effect of Target Familiarity and Descriptive Purpose on the Process of Describing Others." *Journal of Personality* 47 (1): 136–61.

Fiske, Susan, Juan Xu, Amy Cuddy, and Peter Glick. 1999. "(Dis)Respecting versus (Dis)Liking: Status and Interdependence Predict Ambivalent Stereotypes of Competence and Warmth." *Journal of Social Issues* 55 (3): 473–89.

Fogelman, E. 1994. *Conscience and Courage.* New York: Anchor Books.

Fowler, J., L. Baker, and C. Dawes. 2008. "Genetic Variation in Political Participation." *American Political Science Review* 102 (2): 233–48.

Fowler, J., and C. Dawes. 2008. "Two Genes Predict Voter Turnout." *Journal of Politics* 70 (3): 579–94.

Fowler, J., and C. Kam. 2007. "Beyond the Self: Social Identity, Altruism, and Political Participation." *Journal of Politics* 69 (3): 813–27.

Fraenk, P. 1985. *The Namibians.* London: Minority Rights Group.

Freud, A. 1966. *The Ego and the Mechanisms of Defense.* Translated by Cecil Baines. London: Hogarth Press for the Institute of Psycho-Analysis.

Frey, B., and A. Stutzer. 2001. "What Can Economists Learn from *Happiness* Research?" Working papers 503. CESifo.

Friedman, M. 1953. *Essays in Positive Economics.* Chicago: University of Chicago Press.

Frost, Samantha. 2008. *Lessons from a Materialist Thinker: Hobbesian Reflections on Ethics and Politics.* Stanford CA: Stanford University Press.

Fujii, L. 2006. "Genocide." Paper presented at the UCI Center for the Scientific Study of Ethics and Morality, Irvine, CA.

———. 2009. *Killing Neighbors: Webs of Violence in Rwanda.* Ithaca, NY: Cornell University Press.

Gaertner, S. L., J. Mann, A. Murrell, and J. F. Dovidio. 1989. "Reducing Intergroup Bias: The Benefits of Recategorization." *Journal of Personality and Social Psychology* 57: 239–49.

Galinsky, Adam, Joe Magee, M. Ena Inesi, and Deborah Gruenfeld. 2006. "Power and Perspectives Not Taken." *Psychological Science* 17: 1068–74.

Gallese, V. 2006. "Intentional Attunement: A Neurophysiological Perspective on Social Cognition and Its Disruption in Autism." *Brain Research* 1079: 15–24.

Gallese, V., C. Keysers, and R. Rizzolatti,. 2004. "A Unifying View of the Basis of Human Social Cognition." *Trends in Cognitive Sciences* 8 (9): 396–403.

Ganshof, F. 1971. *The Carolingians and the Frankish Monarchy: Studies in Carolingian History.* Ithaca, NY: Cornell University Press.

Garlicki, A. 1995. *Józef Piłsudski, 1867–1935.* Brookfield, VT: Ashgate Publishing.

Gaucher, Renaud. 2009. *Bonheur et économie: Le capitalisme est-il soluble dans la recherche du bonheur?* Paris: Harmattan.

Geertz, Clifford. 1973. *The Interpretation of Cultures: Selected Essays.* New York: Basic Books.

———. 2001. "Life among the Anthros." Book review of Patrick Tierney's *Darkness in El Dorado: How Scientists and Journalists Devastated the Amazon. New York Review of Books* 48 (2): 18–21.

———. 2002. "The Last Humanist." *New York Review of Books,* 49. Accessed May 30, 2008. http://www.nybooks.com/articles/15671.

Genov, T. 1979. "Military Operations in the Balkan Theater during the 1877–78 War." *Southeastern Europe* 6: 136–53.

Ghitis, F. 2005,. "The Dutch, Too Tolerant for Their Own Good? A Country Caught between Tradition and Terrorism." *Washington Post,* October 30, B4.

Gibson, J. L., and A. Gouws. 1999. "Truth and Reconciliation in South Africa: Attributions of Blame and the Struggle over Apartheid." *American Political Science Review* 93 (3): 501–17.

———. 2000. "Social Identities and Political Intolerance: Linkages within the South African Mass Public." *American Journal of Political Science* 44:278–292.

———. 2003. *Overcoming Intolerance in South Africa: Experiments in Democratic Persuasion.* Cambridge: Cambridge University Press.

Giddens, A. 1991. *Modernity and Self-Identity: Self and Society in the Late Modern Age.* Cambridge: Polity.

Gies, M. 1987. *Anne Frank Remembered: The Story of the Woman Who Helped to Hide the Frank Family.* New York: Simon and Schuster.

Gilbert, D. 2006. *Stumbling on Happiness.* London: HarperPress.

Gilbert, M. 2006. *Kristallnacht: Prelude to Destruction.* New York: HarperCollins.

Gillath, Omri, Philip Shaver, Mario Mikulincer, Rachel Nitzberg, Ayelet Erez, and Marinus Van Ijzendoorn. 2005. "Attachment, Caregiving, and Volunteering: Placing Volunteerism in an Attachment-Theoretical Framework." *Personal Relationships* 12: 425–46.

Gilligan, Carol. 1982. *In a Different Voice: Psychological Theory and Women's Development.* Cambridge, MA: Harvard University Press.

Gingeras, Ryan. 2009. *Sorrowful Shores: Violence, Ethnicity, and the End of the Ottoman Empire, 1912–1923.* New York: Oxford University Press.

Gintis, H. 2003. "The Hitchhiker's Guide to Altruism: Genes, Culture, and the Internalization of Norms." *Journal of Theoretical Biology* 220 (4): 407–18.

Gladwell, M. 2000. "Baby Steps." Review of Jerome Kagan's *Three Seductive Ideas. New Yorker* 80 (January 10).

Glass, J. 1997. *"Life Unworthy of Life": Racial Phobia and Mass Murder in Hitler's Germany.* New York: Basic Books. Reprinted in 2001.

Glick, P., and S. Fiske. 1996. "The Ambivalent Sexism Inventory: Differentiating Hostile and Benevolent Sexism." *Journal of Personality and Social Psychology* 70 (3): 491–512.

Gobodo-Madikizela, Pumla. 1998. "Healing the Racial Divide? Personal Reflections on the Truth and Reconciliation Commission." *South African Journal of Psychology* 27: 271–72.

———. 2003. *A Human Being Died That Night.* New York: Houghton Mifflin.

Goebbels, J. 1992. "Diarist Goebbels on the Night of Broken Glass. *Der Spiegel* 29 (July 13): 126–28.

Goldhagen, D. 1996. *Hitler's Willing Executioners.* New York: Knopf.

———. 2009. "Ending Our Age of Suffering: A Plan to Stop Genocide." *New Republic* 240 (4,870) (October 21, 2009): 26–28.

Goldman, Daniel. 1993. "Scientist at Work: Ervin Staub; Studying the Pivotal Role of Bystanders." *New York Times,* June 22, C1.

Goodall, Jane. 1986. *The Chimpanzees of Gombe: Patterns of Behavior.* Cambridge, MA: Belknap Press of Harvard University Press.

———. 1990. *Through a Window: My Thirty Years with the Chimpanzees of Gombe.* Boston: Houghton Mifflin.

Gourevitch, P. 1998. *We Wish to Inform You That Tomorrow We Will Be Killed with Our Families: Stories from Rwanda.* New York: Farrar, Straus and Giroux.

Gouws, A., and J. L. Gibson. 2001. "The Study of Political Tolerance in the South African Context." *Social Dynamics* 27 (2): 109–33.

Grant, R., ed. 2006. Foreword by A. MacIntyre. *Naming Evil, Judging Evil.* Chicago: University of Chicago Press.

Green, Donald, and Ian Shapiro. 1994. *Pathologies of Rational Choice Theory.* New Haven, CT: Yale University Press.

Greenberg, J., T. Pyszczynski, and S. Solomon. 1986. "The Causes and Consequences of a Need for Self-Esteem: A Terror Management Theory." In *Public Self and Private Self,* edited by R. F. Baumeister, 189–212. New York: Springer-Verlag.

Greenberg J., T. Pyszczynski, S. Solomon, A. Rosenblatt, M. Veeder, and S. Kirkland. 1990. "Evidence for Terror Management Theory II: The Effects of Mortality Salience on Reactions to Those Who Threaten or Bolster the Cultural Worldview." *Journal of Personality and Social Psychology* 58: 308–18.

Greene, J., and J. Haidt. 2002. "How (and Where) Does Moral Judgment Work?" *Trends in Cognitive Sciences* 6 (12): 517–23.

Greenstein, F. I. 1965. *Children and Politics.* New Haven, CT: Yale University Press.

Griehl, M. 2001. *Junker Ju 87 Stuka.* London and Stuttgart: Airlife Publishing/Motorbuch.

Grun, B. 1991. *The Timetable of History,* 3rd ed. New York: Simon and Schuster.

Haidt, Jonathan. 2001. "The Emotional Dog and Its Rational Tail: A Social Intuitionist Approach to Moral Judgment." *Psychological Review* 108: 814–34.

———. 2003. "The Moral Emotions." In *Handbook of Affective Science*, edited by R. Davidson, K. Scherer, and H. Goldsmith, 852–70. Oxford: Oxford University Press.

———. 2007. "The New Synthesis in Moral Psychology." *Science* 316: 998–1002.

Haidt, Jonathan, and F. Bjorklund. 2008. "Social Intuitionists Answer Six Questions about Moral Psychology." In *Moral Psychology*. Vol. 2, *The Cognitive Science of Morality*, edited by W. Sinnott-Armstrong, 181–217. Cambridge, MA: MIT Press.

Haidt, Jonathan, and J. Graham. 2007. "When Morality Opposes Justice: Conservatives Have Moral Intuitions That Liberals May Not Recognize." *Social Justice Research* 20 (1): 98–116.

Haidt, Jonathan, and Matthew Hersh. 2001. "Sexual Morality: The Cultures and Emotions of Conservatives and Liberals." *Journal of Applied Social Psychology* 31: 191–221.

Haidt, Jonathan, and C. Joseph. 2007. "The Moral Mind: How 5 Sets of Innate Moral Intuitions Guide the Development of Many Culture-Specific Virtues, and Perhaps Even Modules." In *The Innate Mind*, vol. 3, edited by P. Carruthers, S. Laurence, and S. Stich, 367–91. New York: Oxford University Press.

Haidt, Jonathan, and C.L.M. Keyes. 2002. *Flourishing: Positive Psychology and the Life Well Lived*. Washington, DC: American Psychological Association.

Hamer, K., and J. Gutowski. 2006. "Identification with All Humanity in Poland." Paper presented at the annual meetings of the International Society of Political Psychology, Barcelona.

———. 2009. "Social Identifications and Pro-Social Activity in Poland." In *On Behalf of Others: The Psychology of Care in a Global World*, edited by S. Scuzzarello, C. Kinnvall, and K. R. Monroe, chap. 7. New York: Oxford University Press.

Harcourt, Alexander H., and Frans B. M. DeWaal. 1992. *Coalitions and Alliances in Humans and Other Animals*. Oxford: Oxford University Press.

Harris, P. 1989. *Children and Emotion*. Oxford: Blackwell.

Hart, Allen J., Paul J. Whalen, Lisa M. Shin, Sean C. McInerney, Hakan Fischer, and Scott L. Rauch. 2000. "Differential Response in the Human Amygdala to Racial Out-Group vs. In-Group Face Stimuli." *Neuroreport* 11 (11): 2351–54.

Hart, J., with P. Shaver and J. Goldenberg. 2005. "Attachment, Self-Esteem, Worldviews, and Terror Management: Evidence for a Tripartite Security System." *Journal of Personality and Social Psychology* 88 (6): 999–1013.

Hauser, Marc D. 2006. *Moral Minds: How Nature Designed Our Universal Sense of Right and Wrong*. New York: Ecco.

Havenaar, R. 1983. *The NSB between Nationalism and "Folk" Solidarity: The Pre-War Ideology of the National Socialist Movement in the Netherlands*. The Hague: State Publishing.

———. 1985. *Anton Adriaan Mussert: Verrader voor het vaderland—Een biografische schets* (Anton Adriaan Mussert: Traitor to the Fatherland—A Biographical Sketch). Den Haag: Kruseman.

Hawley, Charles. 2009. "'Post-War Myths': The Logic Behind the Bombing of Dresden (Interview with Frederick Taylor)." *Der Spiegel* (online international edition), February 13. http://www.spiegel.de/international/germany/0,1518,607524,00.html.

Hayden, Robert M. 1996. "Schindler's Fate: Genocide, Ethnic Cleansing, and Population Transfers." *Slavic Review* 55 (4): 727–48.

Haymann, E. 1990. *Courteline*. Paris: Flammarion.

Hechler, K. 1998. *The Bridge at Remagen: The Amazing Story of March 7, 1945, the Day the Rhine River Was Crossed*, 3rd ed. Novato, CA: Presidio.

Heckathorn, D. D. 1997. "Respondent-Driven Sampling: A New Approach to the Study of Hidden Populations." *Social Problems* 44: 174–99.

———. 2002. "Respondent-Driven Sampling II: Deriving Valid Estimates from Chain-Referral Samples of Hidden Populations." *Social Problems* 49: 11–34.

Henry, P. J., and Curtis Hardin. 2006. "The Contact Hypothesis Revisited: Status Bias in Reduction of Implicit Prejudice in the United States and Lebanon." *Psychological Science* 17: 862–68.

Henry, P. J., and Christine Reyna. 2007. "Value Judgments: The Impact of Perceived Value Violations on American Political Attitudes." *Political Psychology* 28: 273–98.

Hiebert, M. 2008. "The Three 'Switches' of Identity Construction in Genocide: The Nazi Final Solution and the Cambodian Killing Fields." *Genocide Studies and Prevention* 3 (1): 5–29.

Hing, Leanne Son, Ramona Bobocel, Mark Zanna, and Maxine McBride. 2007. "Authoritarian Dynamics and Unethical Decision-Making: High Social-Dominance Orientation Leaders and High-Right-Wing-Authoritarianism Followers." *Journal of Personality and Social Psychology* 92: 67–81.

Hirschman, A. (1970). *Exit, Voice, and Loyalty: Responses to Decline in Firms, Organizations, and States.* Cambridge, MA: Harvard University Press.

Hobbes, T. 1651. *Philosophical Rudiments concerning Government and Society.* London: Printed by J. C. for R. Royston, at the Angel in Ivie-Lane.

Hochschild, A. 2005. *Bury the Chains: Prophets and Rebels in the Fight to Free an Empire's Slaves.* New York: Houghton Mifflin.

Hodson, Gordon, and Kimberly Costello. 2007. "Interpersonal Disgust, Ideological Orientations, and Dehumanization as Predictors of Intergroup Attitudes." *Psychological Science* 18: 691–98.

Hogg, M. A. 1992. *The Social Psychology of Group Cohesiveness: From Attraction to Social Identity.* New York: New York University Press.

Hogg M. A., and D. Abrams. 1988. *Social Identifications: A Social Psychology of Intergroup Relationships and Group Processes.* New York: Routledge.

Hsu, J. 2008. "The Secrets of Storytelling." *Scientific American* (August/September): 46–49.

Hume, David. 1902. *An Enquiry concerning the Principles of Morals.* Oxford: Oxford University Press. Original work published in 1751.

———. 1978. *Enquiries concerning Human Understanding and concerning the Principles of Morals.* Edited by P. H. Nidditch. Oxford: Clarendon. Originally published in 1777.

———. 1999. *An Enquiry concerning Human Understanding.* Edited by Tom Beauchamp. Oxford: Oxford University Press.

Huntington, Samuel P. 1993. "The Clash of Civilizations?" *Foreign Affairs* 72 (3): 22–49.

Hutcheson, Francis. 1971. *Inquiry into the Original of Our Ideas of Beauty and Virtue.* New York: Garland. Originally published in 1725.

———. 1969. *An Essay on the Nature and Conduct of the Passions and Affections, with Illustrations upon the Moral Sense.* Gainesville, FL: Scholars' Facsimile and Reprints. Originally published in 1728.

———. 1968. *A System of Moral Philosophy.* New York: A. M. Kelley. Originally published in 1755.

Iacoboni, M. 2008. *Mirroring People: The New Science of How We Connect with Others.* New York: Farrar, Straus and Giroux.

Iacoboni, M. et al. 2003. "Neural Mechanisms of Empathy in Humans: A Relay from Neural Systems for Imitation to Limbic Areas." *Proceedings of the National Academy of Sciences* 100: 5497–502.

Inglehart, R., and P. Norris. 2004. *Sacred and Secular: Religion and Politics Worldwide.* Cambridge: Cambridge University Press.

International Criminal Court. 1992/2002. Rome Statute: Article 7, "Crimes against Humanity." http://untreaty.un.org/cod/icc/statute/romefra.htm.

International Criminal Tribunal for the Former Yugoslavia. 2008. Updated Statute, Article 5. http://www.icty.org/x/file/Legal%20Library/Statute/statute_sept08_en.pdf.

Isaacson, W. 2007. *Einstein: His Life and Universe.* New York: Simon and Schuster.

Jang, K. L., W. J. Livesley, and P. A. Vernon. 2006. "Heritability of the Big Five Personality Dimensions and Their Facets: A Twin Study." *Journal of Personality* 64 (3): 577–92.

Jędrzejewicz, W. 1982. *Piłsudski: A Life for Poland.* New York: Hippocrene Books.

Jelavich, B. 1983. *History of the Balkans.* New York: Cambridge University Press.

Johnson, Kareem, and Barbara Fredrickson. 2005. "We All Look the Same to Me: Positive Emotions Eliminate the Own Race Bias in Face Recognition." *Psychological Science* 16 (11): 875–81.

Johnson, M. 1994. *Moral Imagination: Implications of Cognitive Science for Ethics.* Chicago: University of Chicago Press.

Jong, L. de. 1973. *German Fifth Column in the Second World War.* New York: H. Fertig.

Jost, J. T., J. Glaser, A. W. Kruglanski, and F. Sulloway. 2003. "Political Conservatism as Motivated Social Cognition." *Psychological Bulletin* 129: 339–75.

Jost, John, Jaime Napier, Hulda Thorisdottir, Samuel Gosling, Tibor Palfai, and Brian Ostafin. 2007. "Are Needs to Manage Uncertainty and Threat Associated with Political Conservatism or Ideological Extremity?" *Personality and Social Psychology Bulletin* 33: 989–1007.

Jost, J., et al. 2004. "The Ideological Animal: A System Justification View." In *Handbook of Experimental Existential Psychology*, edited by J. Greenberg, S. L. Koole, and T. Pyszczynski, 263–82. New York: Guilford Press.

Kagan, Jerome. 1978. *The Growth of the Child: Reflections on Human Development.* New York: Norton.

———. 1981. *The Second Year: The Emergence of Self-Awareness.* Cambridge, MA: Harvard University Press.

———. 1984. *The Nature of the Child.* New York: Basic Books.

———. 1989. *Unstable Ideas: Temperament, Cognition, and Self.* Cambridge, MA: Harvard University Press.

———. 1998. *Three Seductive Ideas.* Cambridge, MA: Harvard University Press.

Kagan, Jerome, and Sharon Lamb, eds. 1987. *The Emergence of Morality in Young Children.* Chicago: University of Chicago Press.

Kagan, Jerome, and Howard Moss. 1962. *Birth to Maturity: A Study in Psychological Development.* New York: Wiley.

Kagan, Jerome, et al. 1979. *A Cross-Cultural Study of Cognitive Development.* Chicago: University of Chicago Press.

Kahneman, D., and Amos Tversky, eds. 2000. *Choices, Values, and Frames.* New York: Cambridge University Press.

Kahneman, D., Amos Tversky, and Paul Slovic. 1982. *Judgment under Uncertainty: Heuristics and Biases.* Cambridge: Cambridge University Press.

Kahneman, D., E. Diener, and N. Schwarz. 2003. *Well-Being: The Foundations of Hedonic Psychology.* New York: Russell Sage Foundation.

Kant, I. 1991. *The Metaphysics of Morals.* Introduction, translation, and notes by Mary Gregor. Cambridge: Cambridge University Press. Originally published in 1797.

Karp, D., et al. 1993. "Raising the Minimum in the Minimal Group Paradigm." *Japanese Journal of Experimental Social Psychology* 32 (3): 231–40.

Kaufman, S. J. 2000. "Peace-Building and Conflict Resolution." Conference on "Living Together after Ethnic Killing." Rutgers University, New Brunswick, NJ.

———. 2001. *Modern Hatreds: The Symbolic Politics of Ethnic War.* Ithaca, NY: Cornell University Press.

Keech, W., and D. Matthews. 1976. *The Party's Choice.* Washington, DC: Brookings Institution.

Kegan, Robert. 1982. *The Evolving Self.* Cambridge, MA: Harvard University Press.

Kinder, Donald R., and C. D. Kam. 2009. *Us against Them: Ethnocentric Foundations of American Opinion.* Chicago: University of Chicago Press.

Kinnvall, C. 2004. "Globalization and Religious Nationalism: Self, Identity, and the Search for Ontological Security." *Political Psychology* 25 (5): 741–67.

Kirkpatrick, Lee. 1997. "A Longitudinal Study of Changes in Religious Belief and Behavior as a Function of Individual Differences in Adult Attachment Style." *Journal for the Scientific Study of Religion* 36: 207–17.

Kirkpatrick, Lee, and Wade Rowatt. 2002. "Two Dimensions of Attachment to God and Their Relation to Affect, Religiosity, and Personality Constructs." *Journal for the Scientific Study of Religion* 41: 637–51.

Kirkpatrick, Lee, Daniel Shillito, and Susan Kellas. 1999. "Loneliness, Social Support, and Perceived Relationships with God." *Journal of Social and Personal Relationships* 16: 513–22.

Klinesmith, Jennifer, Tim Kasser, and Francis McAndrew. 2006. "Guns, Testosterone, and Aggression: Experimental Test of a Mediational Hypothesis." *Psychological Science* 17: 568–71.

Koenigsberg, R. A. 2005a. "Civilization and Self-Destruction: The Psychology of War and Genocide." Lecture presented at the Institute for Conflict Analysis and Resolution, George Mason University.

———. 2005b. "Genocide as Immunology: The Psychosomatic Source of Culture." *Ideologies of War and Terror* 25 (November): 1–4.

Kohak, Erazim V. 1984. *The Embers and the Stars: A Philosophical Inquiry into the Moral Sense of Nature.* Chicago: University of Chicago Press.

Kohlberg, Lawrence. 1976. "Moral Stages and Moralization: The Cognitive-Developmental Approach." In *Moral Development and Behavior*, edited by T. Lickona, 31–53. New York: Holt, Rinehart and Winston.

———. 1981a. *Essays on Moral Development.* San Francisco: Harper and Row.

———. 1981b. *The Philosophy of Moral Development.* San Francisco: Harper and Row.

———. 1984. *Essays on Moral Development*, vol. 2. New York: Harper and Row.

Krammer. A. 1973. "Spanish Volunteers against Bolshevism: The Blue Division." *Russian Review* 32: 388–402.

Kreidie, L. H. 2000. "Deciphering the Construals of Islamic Fundamentalism." PhD diss., University of California, Irvine.

Kreidie, L. H., and K. Monroe. 2002. "Psychological Boundaries and Ethnic Conflict: How Identity Constrained Choice and Worked to Turn Ordinary People into Perpetrators of Ethnic Violence during the Lebanese Civil War." *International Journal of Politics, Culture, and Society* 16 (1): 5–36.

Kreisler, H. 2000. "Conversations with History: Philip Gourevitch—Reporting the Story of a Genocide." http://globetrotter.berkeley.edu/people/Gourevitch/gourevitch-con0.html.

Kressel, N. 2002. *Mass Hate: The Global Rise of Genocide and Terror.* Cambridge, MA: Westview Press. Originally published in 1996.

Kurzban, Robert, John Tooby, and Leda Cosmides. 2001. "Can Race Be Erased? Coalitional Computation and Social Categorization." *Proceedings of the National Academy of Sciences* 98 (26): 15387–92.

Lakoff, G. 1987. *Women, Fire, and Dangerous Things: What Categories Reveal about the Mind*. Chicago: University of Chicago Press.

―――. 1996. *Moral Politics*. Chicago: University of Chicago Press.

Lakoff, G., and M. Johnson. 1980. *Metaphors We Live By*. Chicago: University of Chicago Press.

―――. 1999. *Philosophy in the Flesh: The Embodied Mind and Its Challenges to Western Thought*. New York: Basic Books.

Lamm, C., C. D. Batson, and J. Decety. 2007. "The Neural Substrate of Human Empathy: Effects of Perspective-Taking and Cognitive Appraisal." *Journal of Cognitive Neuroscience* 19 (1): 42–58.

Landau, M. J., S. Solomon, J. Greenberg, F. Cohen, T. Pyszczynski, J. Arndt, C. H. Miller, D. M. Ogilvie, and A. Cook. 2004. "Deliver Us from Evil: The Effects of Mortality Salience and Reminders of 9/11 on Support for President George W. Bush." *Personality and Social Psychology Bulletin* 30: 1136–50.

Langacker, Ronald W. 1986. "An Introduction to Cognitive Grammar." *Cognitive Science* 10 (1): 1–40.

―――. 1987. *Foundations of Cognitive Grammar*, vol. 1. Stanford, CA: Stanford University Press.

Langer, L. 1991. *Holocaust Testimonies: Ruins of Memory*. New Haven, CT: Yale University Press.

Langholtz, H., and C. Stout, eds. 2004. *The Psychology of Diplomacy*. Santa Barbara, CA: Greenwood Publishing.

Latané, B., and J. M. Darley. 1970. *The Unresponsive Bystander: Why Doesn't He Help?* New York: Appleton-Century-Crofts.

Lazarus, R. 1991. "Cognition and Motivation in Emotion." *American Psychologist* 46 (4): 352–67.

Le Bon, G. 1952. *The Crowd: A Study of the Popular Mind*. London: E. Benn. Originally published in 1896.

Lebow, R. N. 2003. *The Tragic Vision of Politics: Ethics, Interests, and Orders*. Cambridge: Cambridge University Press.

Lee, A. 1980. *Henry Ford and the Jews*. New York: Stein and Day.

Lemkin, R. 1933. "Acts of Barbarism and Vandalism under the Law of Nations." *Anwaltsblatt Internationales* 19 (6): 117–19.

―――. 1944. *Axis Rule in Occupied Europe: Laws of Occupation—Analysis of Government—Proposals for Redress*. Washington, DC: Carnegie Endowment for International Peace.

―――. 1945. Editorial, *Sunday Times*, October 21.

Lerner, B. H., and D. Rothman. 1995. "Medicine and the Holocaust: Learning More of the Lessons." *Annals of Internal Medicine* 122 (10): 793–94.

Lerner, R. 1992. *Final Solutions: Biology, Prejudice, and Genocide*. University Park: Pennsylvania State University Press.

Levi, P. 1989. *The Drowned and the Saved*. New York: Vintage International.

―――. 1995. *The Reawakening*. New York: Collier Books. Originally published in 1963.

Libby, Lisa, Eric Shaeffer, Richard Eibach, and Jonathan Slemmer. 2007. "Picture Yourself at the Polls: Visual Perspective in Mental Imagery Affects Self-Perception and Behavior." *Psychological Science* 18: 199–203.

Lifton, Robert Jay. 1976. *The Life of the Self: Toward a New Psychology*. New York: Simon and Schuster.

―――. 1986. *The Nazi Doctors: Medical Killing and the Psychology of Genocide*. New York: Basic Books.

————. 1999. "Evil, the Self, and Survival." Conversations with History, Institute of International Studies, University of California, Berkeley. Interview with Robert J. Lifton by Harry Kreisler, November 2.

————. 2000. *The Nazi Doctors: Medical Killing and the Psychology of Genocide*. New York: Basic Books.

Lijphart, Arend. 1968. "Consociational Democracy." *World Politics* 21 (January): 207–25.

————. 1977. *Democracy in Plural Societies: A Comparative Exploration*. New Haven, CT: Yale University Press.

————. 2002. "The Wave of Power-Sharing Democracy." In *Architecture of Democracy: Constitutional Design, Conflict Management, and Democracy*, edited by Andrew Reynolds, 37–54. Oxford: Oxford University Press.

Linville, P. 1987. "Self-Complexity as a Cognitive Buffer against Stress-Related Illness and Depression." *Journal of Personality and Social Psychology* 52: 663–76.

Locke, John. 2000. *John Locke: An Essay concerning Human Understanding*. Edited by Gary Fuller, Robert Stecker, and John P. Wright. Routledge Philosophers in Focus Series. London: Routledge.. Originally published in 1690.

Loftus, E. 1997. "Creating False Memories." *Scientific American* 277 (3): 70.

Loftus, E., and K. Ketcham. 1994. *The Myth of Repressed Memory: False Memories and Allegations of Sexual Abuse*. New York: St. Martin's Press.

Lok, M. H., A. J. Bond, and W. S. Tse. 2009. "Contrasting Effects of a Hot and a Cool System in Anger Regulation on Cooperative Behaviors." *International Journal of Psychology* 44 (5): 333–41.

London, P. 1970. "The Rescuers: Motivational Hypotheses about Christians Who Saved Jews from the Nazis." In *Altruism and Helping Behavior*, edited by J. Macaulay and L. Berkowitz, 21–50. New York: Academic Press.

Lovelock, J. 1972. "Letter to the Editors: Gaia as Seen through the Atmosphere." *Atmospheric Environment* 6: 579–58.

————. 1979. *Gaia, a New Look at Life on Earth*. Oxford: Oxford University Press.

Luigino, Bruni, and Pier Luigi Porta. 2005. *Economics and Happiness: Framing the Analysis*. Oxford: Oxford University Press.

Machiavelli, N. 2003. *The Prince*. Translated by Rufus Goodwin. . Boston: Dante University Press. Published in 1513 and 1532.

Macaulay, J., and L. Berkowitz, eds. 1988. *Altruism and Helping Behavior*. New York: Academic Press.

MacIntyre, A., and R. Grant. 2006. *Naming Evil, Judging Evil*. Chicago: University of Chicago Press.

Mamdani, Mahmood. 2001. *When Victims Become Killers*. Princeton, NJ: Princeton University Press.

Manchester, William. 1968. *The Arms of Krupp*. Boston: Little, Brown.

Mansbridge, Jane, ed. 1990. *Beyond Self-Interest*. Chicago: University of Chicago Press.

Marcus, G. F. 2004. *The Birth of the Mind: How a Tiny Number of Genes Creates the Complexities of Human Thought*. New York: Basic Books.

Margolis, Howard. 1984. *Selfishness, Altruism, and Rationality*. Chicago: University of Chicago Press.

————. 1991. "Incomplete Coercion: How Social Preferences Mix with Private Preferences." In *The Economic Approach to Politics: A Critical Reassessment of the Theory of Rational Action*, edited by K. R. Monroe, 353–70. New York: HarperCollins.

Marino, A. 1997. *Herschel: The Boy Who Started World War II*. Boston: Faber and Faber.

Markey, Sean. 2003. "Monkeys Show Sense of Fairness, Study Says." *National Geographic News*, September 17.

Markus, H., and P. Nurius. 1986. "Possible Selves." *American Psychologist* 41: 954–69.

Marx, K., and F. Engels. 2004. *The Communist Manifesto*. Hauppauge, NY: Barron's.

Maslow, A. 1982. *Toward a Psychology of Being*. New York: Van Nostrand Reinhold. Original work published 1968.

Matthews, D. and Prothro, J. (1963). Social and economic factors and Negro voter registration in the South. *American Political Science Review*, 57(1), 24–44.

Matthews, D. 2000. *U.S. Senators and Their World*. New York. Random House.

Mazower, Mark. 2009. "The Evil That Men Do." *New Republic* 4,862 (July 1): 35–40.

McAdams, D. P. 1996. "Personality, Modernity, and the Storied Self: A Contemporary Framework for Studying Persons." *Psychological Inquiry* 7: 295–321.

———. 2006a. *The Person: A New Introduction to Personality Psychology*. Hoboken, NJ: John Wiley.

———. 2006b. "The Role of Narrative in Personality Psychology Today." *Narrative Inquiry* 16 (1): 11–18.

———. 2008. "Personal Narratives and the Life Story." In *Handbook of Personality: Theory and Research*, 3rd ed., edited by O. P. John, R. W. Robins, and L. A. Pervin, 242–62. New York: Guilford Press.

McAdams, D. P., and M. Albaugh. 2008. "What If There Were No God? Politically Conservative and Liberal Christians Imagine Their Lives without Faith." *Journal of Research in Personality* 42: 1668–72.

McAdams, D. P., M. Albaugh, E. Farber, J. Daniels, R. L. Logan, and B. Olson. 2008. "Family Metaphors and Moral Intuitions: How Conservatives and Liberals Narrate Their Lives." *Journal of Personality and Social Psychology* 95: 978–90.

McDermott, Rose. 2007. "Genetic and Hormonal Differences in Aggression in a Computer Simulation Game." Talk presented at the UCI Ethics Center, Irvine, CA, April 20.

McFarland, S. 2005. "All Humanity Is My Ingroup: Oneness with All Humanity." Paper presented at the annual meetings of the International Society of Political Psychology, Boston, July.

———. 2006. "A Test of a Maslovian Model of 'Oneness with All Humanity.'" Paper presented at the annual meetings of the International Society of Political Psychology, Barcelona.

McFarland, S., and M. Webb. 2004. "Measuring *Gemeinschaftsgefuhl*: Identification with All Humanity." Paper presented at the annual meetings of the International Society of Political Psychology, Lund, Sweden.

McGaugh, James. 2003. *Memory and Emotion: The Making of Lasting Memories*. New York: Columbia University Press.

McGregor, H., J. Leiberman, J. Greenberg, S. Solomon, J. Arndt, L. Simon, and T. Pyszczynski. 1998. "Terror Management and Aggression: Evidence That Mortality Salience Promotes Aggression against Worldview-Threatening Individuals." *Journal of Personality* 74: 590–605.

McLean, K., M. Pasupathi, and J. Pals. 2007. "Selves Creating Stories Creating Selves: A Process Model of Self-Development." *Personality and Social Psychology Review* 11 (3): 262–78.

Mead, George Herbert. 1934. *Mind, Self, and Society*. Chicago: University of Chicago Press.

———. 1964. *Selected Writings*. Edited by A. J. Reck. Indianapolis: Bobbs-Merrill.

———. 1982. *The Individual and the Social Self: Unpublished Essays by G. H. Mead*. Edited by David L. Miller. Chicago: University of Chicago Press.

Merton, Robert K. 1949. *Social Theory and Social Structure*. Glencoe, IL: Free Press.

Metzinger, T., and V. Gallese. 2003. "The Emergence of a Shared Action Ontology: Building Blocks for a Theory." *Consciousness and Cognition* 12: 549–71.

Mikhail, J. 2007. "Universal Moral Grammar: Theory, Evidence, and the Future George-town University Law Center." *Trends in Cognitive Sciences April 2007*. Georgetown Public Law Research Paper No. 954398.

Mikulincer, Mario, and Victor Florian. 2000. "Exploring Individual Differences in Reactions to Mortality Salience: Does Attachment Style Regulate Terror Management Mechanisms?" *Journal of Personality and Social Psychology* 79: 260–73.

Mikulincer, Mario, Omri Gillath, Vered Halevy, Neta Avihou, Shelly Avidan, and Nitzan Eshkoli. 2001. "Attachment Theory and Reactions to Others' Needs: Evidence That Activation of the Sense of Attachment Security Promotes Empathic Responses." *Journal of Personality and Social Psychology* 81: 1205–24.

Mikulincer, Mario, Omri Gillath, Yael Sapir-Lavid, Erez Yaakobi, Keren Arias, Liron Tal-Aloni, and Gili Bor. 2003. "Attachment Theory and Concern for Others' Welfare: Evidence That Activation of the Sense of Secure Base Promotes Endorsement of Self-Transcendence Values." *Basic and Applied Social Psychology* 25: 299–312.

Mikulincer, Mario, and Netta Horesh. 1999. "Adult Attachment Style and the Perceptions of Others: The Role of Projective Mechanisms." *Journal of Personality and Social Psychology* 76: 1022–34.

Mikulincer, Mario, and Philip Shaver. 2001. "Attachment Theory and Intergroup Bias: Evidence That Priming the Secure Base Schema Attenuates Negative Reactions to Outgroups." *Journal of Personality and Social Psychology* 81: 97–115.

Mikulincer, Mario, Philip Shaver, Omri Gillath, and Rachel Nitzberg. 2005. "Attachment, Caregiving, and Altruism: Boosting Attachment Security Increases Compassion and Helping." *Journal of Personality and Social Psychology* 89: 817–39.

Milgram, S. 1974. *Obedience to Authority: An Experimental View*. New York: Harper and Row.

Mill, J. S. 2002. *The Basic Writings of John Stuart Mill: On Liberty, The Subjection of Women, and Utilitarianism*. Introduction by J. B. Schneewind; notes and commentary by Dale E. Miller. New York: Modern Library.

Miller, M. 1975. *Bulgaria during the Second World War*. Stanford, CA: Stanford University Press.

Miller, R. 2005. "Professional Distrust of Altruism: Lessons from Living Unrelated Kidney Transplant Donation." Workshop presented at the UCI Interdisciplinary Center for the Scientific Study of Ethics and Morality.

Mills, S. 1997. *Discourse*. Florence, KY: Routledge.

Moll, Jorge, Frank Krueger, Roland Zahn, Matteo Pardini, Ricardo de Oliveira-Souza, and Jordan Grafman. 2006. "Human Fronto-Mesolimbic Networks Guide Decisions about Charitable Donation." *Proceedings of the National Academy of Sciences* 103: 15623–28.

Monroe, Kristen Renwick. 1984. *Presidential Popularity and the Economy*. New York: Praeger.

———. 1991a. *The Economic Approach to Politics: A Critical Reassessment of the Theory of Rational Action*. New York: HarperCollins.

———. 1991b. "John Donne's People: Explaining Differences between Rational Actors and Altruists through Cognitive Frameworks." *Journal of Politics* 53 (2): 394–433.

———. 1995. "The Psychology of Genocide: A Review of the Literature." *Ethics and International Affairs* 9: 215–39.

———. 1996. *The Heart of Altruism: Perceptions of a Common Humanity*. Princeton, NJ: Princeton University Press.

Monroe, Kristen Renwick. 2001a. "Morality and a Sense of Self: The Importance of Identity and Categorization for Moral Action." *American Journal of Political Science* 45 (3): 491–507.

———. 2001b. "Paradigm Shift: From Rational Choice to Perspective." *International Political Science Review* 22 (2): 1151–72.

———. 2004. *The Hand of Compassion: Portraits of Moral Choice during the Holocaust.* Princeton, NJ: Princeton University Press.

———. 2008. "Cracking the Code of Genocide: The Moral Psychology of Rescuers, Bystanders, and Nazis during the Holocaust." *Political Psychology* 29 (5): 699–736.

———. 2009. "The Ethical Perspective: An Identity Theory of the Psychological Influences on Moral Choice." *Political Psychology* 30 (3): 419–44.

Monroe, Kristen Renwick, ed. 2002. Introduction and chapter 21. In *Political Psychology.* Hillsdale NJ: Lawrence Erlbaum.

Monroe, Kristen Renwick, W. Chiu, A. Martin, and B. Portman. 2009. "What Is Political Psychology?" *Perspectives on Politics* 7 (4): 859–82.

Monroe, Kristen Renwick, and C. Epperson. 1994. "'But What Else Could I Do?' Choice, Identity and a Cognitive-Perceptual Theory of Ethical Political Behavior." *Political Psychology* 15 (2): 201–26.

Monroe, K. R., and L. H. Kreidie. 1997. "The Perspective of Islamic Fundamentalists and the Limits of Rational Choice Theory." *Political Psychology* 18: 19–43.

Monroe, Kristen Renwick, A. Martin, and P. Ghosh. 2009. "Politics and an Innate Moral Sense: Scientific Evidence for an Old Theory?" *Political Research Quarterly* (September) 62: 614–34.

Monroe, K. R., and M. L. Martinez. 2009. "Empathy, Prejudice and Tolerance." Chapter in *On Behalf of Others: The Morality of Care in a Global World.* Sarah Scuzzarello, Catarina Kinnvall and Kristen Monroe, Editors. Oxford University Press, 2009. Chapter written with Maria Luisa Martinez. Chapter 7, pages 201–222.

Morgan, D., and M. Schwalbe. 1990. "Mind and Self in Society: Linking Social Structure and Social Cognition." *Social Psychology Quarterly* 53 (2): 148–64.

Moscovici, S. 1961. *La psychanalyse, son image et son public.* Paris: P.U.F.

———. 1988. "Notes towards a Description of Social Representations." *European Journal of Social Psychology* 18: 211–50.

Myers, Milton L. 1985. *The Soul of Modern Economic Man: Ideas of Self-Interest, Thomas Hobbes to Adam Smith.* Chicago: University of Chicago Press.

Narvaez D., and D. K. Lapsley, eds. 2009. *Personality, Identity, and Character: Explorations in Moral Psychology.* New York: Cambridge University Press.

Newman-Norlund, Roger D., Hein T. van Schie, Alexander M. J. van Zuijlen, and Harold Bekkering. 2007. "The Mirror Neuron System Is More Active during Complementary Compared with Imitative Action." *Nature Neuroscience* 10: 817–18.

Niec, L., and S. Russ. 2002. "Children's Internal Representations, Empathy, and Fantasy Play: A Validity Study of the SCORS-Q." *Psychological Assessment* 14: 331–38.

Nisbett, R. E., and L. D. Ross. 1980. *Human Inference: Strategies and Shortcomings of Social Judgment.* Englewood Cliffs, NJ: Prentice-Hall.

Nisbett, R. E., and T. D. Wilson. 1977. "Telling More Than We Can Know: Verbal Reports on Mental Processes." *Psychological Review* 84 (3): 221–49.

Nussbaum, M. 1986. *The Fragility of Goodness: Luck and Ethics in Greek Tragedy and Philosophy.* Cambridge: Cambridge University Press.

———. 2001. *Upheavals of Thought: The Intelligence of Emotions.* New York: Cambridge University Press.

Oakes, P. J., J. C. Turner, and A. Haslam. 1991. "Perceiving People as Group Members: The Role of Fit in the Salience of Social Categorizations." *British Journal of Social Psychology* 30 (1): 25–44.

Office of the High Commissioner for Human Rights. 1951. Convention on the Prevention and Punishment of the Crime of Genocide. http://www2.ohchr.org/english/law /genocide.htm.

Ohman, Arne, and Susan Mineka. 2001. "Fears, Phobias, and Preparedness: Toward an Evolved Module of Fear and Fear Learning." *Psychological Review* 108 (3): 483–522.

Okin, S. 1989. "Reason and Feeling in Thinking about Justice." *Ethics* 99 (2): 229–49.

Oliner, S., and P. Oliner. 1988. *The Altruistic Personality: Rescuers of Jews in Nazi Europe.* New York: Free Press.

Olson, J. M., P. A. Vernon, J. Aitken, and K. L. Jang. 2001. "The Heritability of Attitudes: A Study of Twins." *Journal of Personality and Social Psychology* 80: 645–60.

Opdyke, I. G., J. Elliot, and M. Burgess. 1992. *Into the Flames: The Life Story of a Righteous Gentile.* San Bernardino, CA: Borgo Press.

Opdyke, I. G., and J. Armstrong. 1999. *In My Hands: Memories of a Holocaust Rescuer.* New York: Knopf.

Ophüls, M. 1971. *The Sorrow and the Pity.* Motion Picture.

Oswald, Andrew. 1997. "Happiness and Economic Performance." *Economic Journal* 107: 1815–31.

Oxley, Douglas R., Kevin B. Smith, Matthew V. Hibbing, Jennifer L. Miller, John R. Alford, Peter K. Hatemi, and John R. Hibbing. 2008. "Political Attitudes Are Predicted by Physiological Traits." *Science* (September 19).

Page, G. 1999. *Inside the Animal Mind.* New York: Doubleday.

Palmer, A. 1965. *The Gardeners of Salonika.* New York: Simon and Schuster.

Parker, S. T., and M. L. McKinney. 1999. *Origins of Intelligence: The Evolution of Cognitive Development in Monkeys, Apes, and Humans.* Baltimore: Johns Hopkins University Press.

Parsons, Talcott. 1951. *The Social System.* Glencoe, IL: Free Press.

Pateman, C. 1988. *The Social Contract.* Stanford, CA: Stanford University Press.

Patterson, M., and K. Monroe. 1998. "Narrative in Political Science." *Annual Review of Political Science* 1: 315–31.

Peace, K. A., and S. Porter. 2004. "A Longitudinal Investigation of the Reliability of Memories for Trauma and Other Emotional Experiences." *Applied Cognitive Psychology* 18: 1143–59.

Perreault S., and R. Y. Bourhis. 1999. "Ethnocentrism, Social Identification, and Discrimination." *Personality and Social Psychology Bulletin* 25: 92–103.

Perry, S., and L. Rose. 1994. "Begging and Transfer of Coati Meat by White-Faced Capuchin Monkeys, *Cebus capucinus.*" *Primates* 35: 409–15.

Petersen, Roger D. 2002. *Understanding Ethnic Violence.* Cambridge: Cambridge University Press.

Petrovic, D. 1994. "Ethnic Cleansing: An Attempt at Methodology." *European Journal of International Law* 3: 342–59.

Phelps, Elizabeth, Kevin O'Connor, Christopher Gatenby, John Gore, Christian Grillon, and Michael Davis. 2001. "Activation of the Left Amygdala to a Cognitive Representation of Fear." *Nature Neuroscience* 4: 437–41.

Piaget, Jean. 1928. *The Moral Development of the Child.* Glencoe, IL: Free Press.

———. 1932. *The Moral Judgment of the Child.* London: Kegan Paul, Trench, Trubner.

Piaget, Jean. 1952. *The Child's Conception of Number*. London: Routledge and Kegan Paul.

Plato. 370 BCE. *Parmenides*. Translated by Benjamin Jowett. MIT Internet Classics Archive. http://classics.mit.edu/Plato/parmenides.html.

Polletta, F. 2006. *It Was Like a Fever: Storytelling in Protest and Politics*. Chicago: University of Chicago Press.

Porter, Roy. 2001. *The Enlightenment*. New York: Macmillan.

Post, Jerrold M. 1999. "The Psychopolitics of Hatred: Commentary on Ervin Staub's Article." *Peace and Conflict: Journal of Peace Psychology* 5 (4): 337–44.

Praag, Bernard M. S. van, and Ada Ferrer-i-Carbonell. 2004. *Happiness Quantified: A Satisfaction Calculus Approach*. Oxford: Oxford University Press.

Pratto, F., J. Sidanius, and S. Levin. 2006. "Social Dominance Theory and the Dynamics of Intergroup Relations: Taking Stock and Looking Forward." *European Review of Social Psychology* 17: 271–320.

Pratto, F., J. Sidanius, L. Stallworth, and B. Malle. 1994. "Social Dominance Orientation: A Personality Variable Predicting Social and Political Attitudes." *Journal of Personality and Social Psychology* 67 (4): 741–63.

Probert, H. 2001. *Bomber Harris: His Life and Times*. London: Greenhill Books.

Pyszczynski, T., and J. Greenberg. 1987. "Toward an Integration of Cognitive and Motivational Perspectives on Social Inference: A Biased Hypothesis-Testing Model." *Advances in Experimental Social Psychology* 20: 297–340.

Pyszczynski, T., et al. 2006. "Mortality Salience, Martyrdom, and Military Might: The Great Satan versus the Axis of Evil." *Personality and Social Psychology Bulletin* 32 (4): 525–37.

Range, F., L. Horn, Z. Virányi, and L. Huber. 2008. "Effort and Reward: Inequity Aversion in Domestic Dogs?" *Proceedings of the National Academy of Sciences* 106 (1): 340–45.

———. 2009. "The Absence of Reward Induces Inequity Aversion in Dogs." *Proceedings of the National Academy of Sciences* 106 (1): 340–45.

Rawlings, R. 2006. *The Spanish Inquisition*. Malden, MA: Blackwell Publishing.

Rawls, John. 1972. *Theory of Justice*. Oxford: Oxford University Press.

Reicher, S. 2004. "The Context of Social Identity: Domination, Resistance, and Change." *Political Psychology* 25 (6): 921–45. Symposium: Social Dominance and Intergroup Relations.

Reicher, S. D., S. A. Haslam, and R. Rath. 2008. "Making a Virtue of Evil: A Five-Step Social Identity Model of the Development of Collective Hate." *Social and Personality Compass* 2/3: 1313–44.

Reimer, K., M. Spezio, W. Brown, G. Peterson, and J. Van Slyke. 2009 (under review). "Political Courage: New Methods for the Interdisciplinary Study of Virtue." *Political Research Quarterly*.

Reykowski, J. 1987. "Sociopsychological Aspects of the Polish Crisis." In *The Polish Dilemma: Views from Within*, edited by L. S. Graham and M. K. Ciechocinska, 180–90. Boulder, CO: Westview Press.

———. 2001. "The Justice Motive and Altruistic Helping: Rescuers of Jews in Nazi-Occupied Europe." In *The Justice Motive in Everyday Life*, edited by M. Ross and D. T. Miller, 251–70. New York: Cambridge University Press.

Richman, L. S., and M. R. Leary. 2009. "Reactions to Discrimination, Stigmatization, Ostracism, and Other Forms of Interpersonal Rejection: A Multilevel Model." *Psychological Review* 116: 365–83.

Riker, W. H. 1991. "The Ferment of the 1950s and the Development of Rational Choice Theory." In *The Economic Approach to Politics: A Critical Reassessment of the Theory of Rational Action*, edited by K. R. Monroe, 191–201. New York: HarperCollins.

Rilling, J. K., et al. 2002. "Neural Bases of Social Cooperation." *Neuron* 35: 395–405.

Rittner, C., and S. Myers. 1986. *The Courage to Care*. New York: New York University Press.

Rokeach, M. 1960. *The Open and Closed Mind: Investigations into the Nature of Belief Systems and Personality Systems*. New York: Basic Books.

Rorty, A. 1986. "Self-Deception, Akrasia, and Irrationality." In *The Multiple Self*, edited by J. Elster, 115–32. New York: Cambridge University Press.

Rosch, Eleanor N. 1973. "Natural Categories." *Cognitive Psychology* 4: 328–50.

———. 1975. "Cognitive Representation of Semantic Categories." *Journal of Experimental Psychology* 104 (3): 192–233.

——— 1977. "Human Categorization." In *Studies in Cross-Cultural Psychology*, edited by Neil Warren, vol. 1: 1–72. New York: Academic Press.

———. 1978. "Principles of Categorization." In *Cognition and Categorization*, edited by E. Rosch and B. B. Lloyd, 27–48. Hillsdale, NJ: Lawrence Erlbaum.

———. 1983. "Prototype Classification and Logical Classification: The Two Systems." In *New Trends in Cognitive Representation: Challenges to Piaget's Theory*, edited by E. Scholnick, 73–86. Hillsdale, NJ: Lawrence Erlbaum.

Rosch, Eleanor N., with C. Mervis. 1981. "Categorization of Natural Objects." *Annual Review of Psychology* 32: 89–113.

Rosch, Eleanor N., with Francisco Varela and Evan F. Thompson. 1991. *The Embodied Mind*. Cambridge, MA: MIT Press.

Rose, L. 1997. "Vertebrate Predation and Food-Sharing in Cebus and Pan." *International Journal of Primatology* 18 (5): 727–65.

Rosenblatt, A., J. Greenberg, S. Solomon, T. Pyszczynski, and D. Lyon. 1989. "Evidence for Terror Management Theory I: The Effects of Mortality Salience on Reactions to Those Who Violate or Uphold Cultural Values." *Journal of Personality and Social Psychology* 57: 681–90.

Ross, L. Q. 1937. *The Education of Hyman Kaplan*. New York: Harcourt, Brace and World.

Rost van Tonningen, F. 1990. *Triumph and Tragedy: Some Personal Remembrances of Dutch and European History in the 20th Century*. Arnhem: Consortium de Levensboom.

Rost van Tonningen, M. 1967. *Correspondence, Part 1, 1921–May 1942*. Introduced and edited by E. Fraenkel-Verkade with A. J. van der Leeuw. The Hague: Nijhoff.

———. 1993. *Correspondence, Part 2, May 1942–May 1945*. Introduced and edited by David Barnouw. Zutphen: Walburg Press.

Rost van Tonningen-Huebel, F. 1990. *Looking for My Wedding Ring*. Belgium: De Krijger, Erembodegem.

Rousseau, J. 1754. "Discourse on the Origin and Basis of Inequality among Men." http://www.constitution.org/jjr/ineq.htm.

Rudolph, Susanne Hoeber, and Lloyd I. Rudolph. 1993. "Modern Hate: How Ancient Animosities Get Invented." *New Republic* (March 22): 24–29.

Rummel, R. J. 1996. *Death by Government*. New York: Transaction Publishers.

Runyan, W. M. 1983. "Idiographic Goals and Methods in the Study of Lives." *Journal of Personality* 51 (3): 413–37.

Salganik, M. J., and D. D. Heckathorn. 2004. "Sampling and Estimation in Hidden Populations Using Respondent-Driven Sampling." *Sociological Methodology* 34: 193–239.

Salvatore G., G. Dimaggio, and A. Semerari. 2004. "A Model of Narrative Development: Implications for Understanding Psychopathology and Guiding Therapy." *Psychology and Psychotherapy* 77 (Part 2): 231–54.

Sanford, N. 1973. "Authoritarian Personality in Contemporary Perspective." In *Handbook of Political Psychology*, edited by J. N. Knutson, 139–70. San Francisco: Jossey-Bass.

Sapolsky, Robert. 2002. *A Primate's Memoir*. New York: Touchstone Books.

———. 2006. "A Natural History of Peace." *Foreign Affairs* (January/February): 104–20.

Schacter, D. L., and D. R. Addis. 2007. "The Cognitive Neuroscience of Constructive Memory: Remembering the Past and Imagining the Future." *Philosophical Transactions of the Royal Society, London—B. Biological Sciences* 362: 773–86.

Scherer, K. R. 2003. "Introduction: Cognitive Components of Emotion." In *Handbook of Affective Sciences*, edited by R. J. Davidson, K. R. Scherer, and H. Hill Goldsmith, 563–71. Oxford: Oxford University Press.

Schimel, J., M. Wohl, and T. Williams. 2006. "Terror Management and Trait Empathy: Evidence That Mortality Salience Promotes Reactions of Forgiveness among People with High (vs. Low) Trait Empathy." *Motivation and Emotion* 30 (3): 214–24.

Schnall, S., J. Haidt, G. L. Clore, and A. H. Jordan. 2008. "Disgust as Embodied Moral Judgment." *Personality and Social Psychology Bulletin* 34: 1096–109.

Schwartz, S. H. 1992. "Universals in the Content and Structure of Values: Theoretical Advances and Empirical Tests in 20 Countries." In *Advances in Experimental Social Psychology*, edited by M. Zanna. San Diego: Academic Press.

Scott, J. V., and K. R. Monroe. 2008. "The Political Imagination: Establishing Dialogue between Political Psychologists, Literary Theorists, and Cognitive Scientists." Paper presented at the Annual Meetings of the International Society of Political Psychology, Paris.

Scuzzarello, S., C. Kinnvall, and K. Monroe, eds. 2009. *On Behalf of Others: The Psychology of Care in a Global World*. Oxford: Oxford University Press.

Sears, D. O., J. Sidanius, and L. Bobo, eds. 2000. *Racialized Politics: The Debate about Racism in America*. Chicago: University of Chicago Press.

Selman, R. L. 1980. *The Growth of Interpersonal Understanding*. New York: Academic Press.

Sen, Amartya. 1990. "Development as Capability Expansion." In *Human Development and the International Development Strategy for the 1990s*, edited by K. Griffin and J. Knight. London: Macmillan.

———. 2005. *The Argumentative Indian: Writings on Indian History, Culture, and Identity*. New York: Farrar, Straus and Giroux.

Shaftesbury, 3rd Earl of (Anthony Ashley-Cooper). 1977. *An Inquiry concerning Virtue, or Merit*. 1714 edition with Toland's 1699 edition and bibliography. Edited by David Walford. Manchester: Manchester University Press. Originally published in 1699.

———. 1999. *Characteristics of Men, Manners, Options, Times*. Edited by L. Klein. Cambridge: Cambridge University Press. Originally published in 1711.

Shenk, J. W. 2009. "What Makes Us Happy?" *Atlantic Monthly* (June 2009). http://www.theatlantic.com/doc/print/200906/happiness.

Sherif, M. 1962. "The Self and Reference Groups: Meeting Ground of Individual and Group Approaches." *Annals of the New York Academy of Sciences* 96: 797–813.

Sherif, Muzafer, and Carolyn W. Sherif. 1966. *Groups in Harmony and Tension*. New York: Octagon Books. Originally published in 1953.

Sherif, Muzafer, O. J. Harvey, B. Jack White, William R. Hood, and Carolyn W. Sherif. 1961. *Intergroup Conflict and Cooperation: The Robbers Cave Experiment*. Norman, OK: University Book Exchange.

Shleifer, Andrei, and Kevin Murphy. 2004. "Persuasion in Politics." NBER Working Paper 10248. http://www.nber.org/papers/w10248 (January).

Shraga, Daphna, and Ralph Zacklin. 2004. "The International Criminal Tribunal for the Former Yugoslavia." *European Journal of International Law* 15 (3).

Sibley, C. G., and J. Duckitt. 2008. "Personality and Prejudice: A Meta-Analysis and Theoretical Review." *Personality and Social Psychology Review* 12 (3): 248–79.

Silk J. B., J. Altmann, and S. C. Alberts. 2006a. "Social Relationships among Adult Female Baboons (*Papio cynocephalus*) I: Variations in the Strength of Social Bonds." *Behavioral Ecology and Sociobiology* 61: 183–95.

———. 2006b. "Social Relationships among Adult Female Baboons (*Papio cynocephalus*) II: Variation in the Quality and Stability of Social Bonds." *Behavioral Ecology and Sociobiology* 61: 197–204.

Silvers, J., and J. Haidt. 2008. "Moral Elevation Can Induce Nursing." *Emotion* 8 (2): 291–95.

Simon, H. 1982. *Models of Bounded Rationality*, vols. 1 and 2. Cambridge, MA: MIT Press.

Singer, Peter. 1975. *Animal Liberation: A New Ethics for Our Treatment of Animals*. New York: Random House.

Singer, T. et al. 2004. "Empathy for Pain Involves the Affective but Not Sensory Component of Pain." *Science* 303: 1157–62.

Skyrms, Brian. 1996. *Evolution of the Social Contract*. Cambridge: Cambridge University Press.

Slote, M. 1983. *Goods and Virtues*. New York: Oxford University Press.

Smaniotto, R. C. 2004. "'You Scratch My Back and I Scratch Yours' versus 'Love Thy Neighbour': Two Proximate Mechanisms of Reciprocal Altruism." PhD diss., University of Groningen.

Smart, R. L., and M. R. Leary. 2009. "Reactions to Discrimination, Stigmatization, Ostracism, and Other Forms of Interpersonal Rejection: A Multi-Motive Model." *Psychological Review* 116 (2): 365–83.

Smith, Adam. 1976a. *The Correspondence of Adam Smith, 1723–1790*. Edited by Ernest Campbell Mossner and Ian Simpson Ross. Oxford: Clarendon Press.

———. 1976b. *The Theory of Moral Sentiments*. Introduction by E. G. West. Indianapolis: Liberty Classics. Originally published in 1759 and 1853.

Smith, T. 1993. "Actual Trends or Measurement Artifacts? A Review of Three Studies of Anti-Semitism." *Public Opinion Quarterly* 57: 380–93.

Somers, E., and R. Kok. 2004. *Jewish Displaced Persons in Camp Bergen-Belsen, 1945–1950: The Unique Photo Album of Zippy Orlin*. Seattle: University of Washington Press with the United States Holocaust Memorial Museum.

Spezio, M., and R. Adolphs. 2007. "Emotional Processing and Political Judgment: Toward Integrating Political Psychology and Decision Neuroscience." http://emotion.caltech.edu/papers/SpezioAdolphs2007Emotional.pdf.

Spivak, G. C. 2007. *Other Asias*. Malden, MA: Wiley-Blackwell.

Staub, Ervin. 1978. *Positive Social Behavior and Morality*. Vol. 1: *Personal and Social Influences*. New York: Academic Press. 1979. Vol. 2: *Socialization and Development*. New York: Academic Press.

———. 1989. *The Roots of Evil: The Origins of Genocide and Other Group Violence*. New York: Cambridge University Press. Also printed in 1992.

———. 1998a. "Bystander Psychology: Studying the Pivotal Role of Bystanders." In *Deathly Silence Guide*.

———. 1998b. "Halting and Preventing Violence: The Role of Bystanders." In *The Friends of Raoul Wallenberg*, edited by R. H. Walker. Spring Valley Ranch, CO: R. H. Walker.

———. 2002. "The Psychology of Bystanders, Perpetrators, and Heroic Helpers." In *Understanding Genocide: The Social Psychology of the Holocaust*, edited by Leonard S. Newman, Ralph Erber, 11–42. New York: Oxford University Press.

———. 2003. "Notes on Cultures of Violence, Cultures of Caring and Peace, and the Fulfillment of Basic Human Needs." *Political Psychology* 24 (1): 1–21.

Staub, Ervin. 2010. *Overcoming Evil: Genocide, Violent Conflict, and Terrorism*. New York: Oxford University Press.

Staub, E., and Daniel Bar-Tal, eds. 1997. *Patriotism in the Lives of Individuals and Nations*. Chicago: Nelson-Hall.

Staub, E., D. Bar-Tal, J. Karylowski, and J. Reykowsk, eds. 1984. *Development and Maintenance of Prosocial Behavior: International Perspectives on Positive Morality*. New York: Plenum Press.

Staub, E., Nancy Eisenberg, and Janusz Reykowski, eds. 1989. *Social and Moral Values: Individual and Societal Perspectives*. Hillsdale, NY: L. Erlbaum.

Stouten, J., D. De Cremer, and D. Van Dijk. 2007. "Managing Equality in Social Dilemmas: Emotional and Retributive Implications." *Social Justice Research* 20, (1): 53–67.

Stryker, Sheldon, and Peter J. Burke. 2000. "The Past, Present, and Future of an Identity Theory." *Social Psychology Quarterly* 63 (4): 284–97.

Suedfeld, P., ed. 2001. *Light from the Ashes: Social Science Careers of Young Holocaust Refugees and Survivors*. Ann Arbor: University of Michigan Press.

Suedfeld, P., and S. de Best. 2008. "Value Hierarchies of Holocaust Rescuers and Resistance Fighters." *Genocide Studies and Prevention* 3 (1): 31–42.

Sunstein, C. R. 2005. "Moral Heuristics." *Behavioral and Brain Sciences* 28 (4): 531–42.

Surowiecki, J. 2003. "The Coup De Grasso." *New Yorker*, October 5.

Swim, J., et al. 1995. "Sexism and Racism: Old-Fashioned and Modern Prejudices." *Journal of Personality and Social Psychology* 68 (2): 199–214.

Tabibnia, G., and M. Lieberman. 2007. "Fairness and Cooperation Are Rewarding: Evidence from Social Cognitive Neuroscience." *Annals of the New York Academy of Sciences* 1118: 90–101.

Tajfel, Henri. 1969. "Cognitive Aspects of Prejudice." *Journal of Social Issues* 25: 79–97.

———. 1970. "Aspects of National and Ethnic Loyalty." *Social Science Information* 9: 119.

———. 1981. *Human Groups and Social Categories*. Studies in Social Psychology. New York: Cambridge University Press.

Tajfel, Henri, and John Turner. 1979. "An Integrative Theory of Intergroup Conflict." In *The Social Psychology of Intergroup Relations*, edited by William G. Austin and Stephen Worchel, 94–109. Monterey, CA: Brooks-Cole.

Tankersley, D., C. J. Stowe, and S. A. Huettel. 2007. "Altruism Is Associated with an Increased Neural Response to Agency." *Nature Neuroscience* 10 (2): 150–51.

Taylor, F. 2004. *Dresden, Tuesday, February 13, 1945*. New York: HarperCollins.

Taylor, J. 1995. *Linguistic Categorization: Prototypes in Linguistic Theory*. Oxford: Oxford University Press.

Taylor, S. E. 2002. *The Tending Instinct: How Nurturing Is Essential to Who We Are and How We Live*. New York: Holt.

Taylor, S. E., S. S. Dickerson, and L. C. Klein. 2002. "Toward a Biology of Social Support." In *Handbook of Positive Psychology*, edited by C. R. Snyder and S. J. Lopez, 210–45. London: Oxford University Press.

Taylor, S. E., G. Gonzaga, L. C. Klein, P. Hu, G. A. Greendale, and S. E. Seeman. 2006. "Relation of Oxytocin to Psychological and Biological Stress Responses in Older Women." *Psychosomatic Medicine* 68: 238–45.

Tec, N. 1986. *When Light Pierced the Darkness: Christian Rescue of Jews in Nazi-Occupied Poland*. New York: Oxford University Press.

Tedeschi, J. T., B. R. Schlenker, and T. V. Bonoma. 1971. "Cognitive Dissonance: Private Ratiocination or Public Spectacle?" *American Psychologist* 26: 685–95.

Ten Boom, C. 1974. *The Hiding Place*. New York: Bantam Books.

Tetlock, P. E. 1985. "Accountability: A Social Check on the Fundamental Attribution of Error." *Social Psychology Quarterly* 48: 227–36.

Thacher, D. 2006. "The Normative Case Study." *American Journal of Sociology* 111 (6): 1631–76.

Thiele, L. P. 2006. *The Heart of Judgment: Practical Wisdom, Neuroscience, and Narrative*. Cambridge: Cambridge University Press.

Thomsen, L., E.G.T Green, and J. Sidanius. 2008. "We Will Hunt Them Down: How Social Dominance Orientation and Right-Wing Authoritarianism Fuel Ethnic Persecution of Immigrants in Fundamentally Different Ways." *Journal of Experimental Social Psychology* 44: 1455–64.

Tolstoy, L. 2007. *War and Peace*. Translated by R. Pevear and L. Volokhonsky. New York: Random House.

Toulmin, S. E. 1958. *The Uses of Argument*. New York: Cambridge University Press.

Trivers, R. L. 1971. "The Evolution of Reciprocal Altruism." *Quarterly Review of Biology* 46: 35–57.

Turner, J. C. 1982. "Towards a Cognitive Redefinition of the Social Group." In *Social Identity and Intergroup Relations*, edited by H. Tajfel. Cambridge: Cambridge University Press.

Turner, John C., and M. A. Hogg. 1987. *Rediscovering the Social Group: A Self-Categorization Theory*. Oxford: Basil Blackwell.

Turner, J. C., P. J. Oakes, S. A. Haslam, and C. McGarty. 1994. "Self and Collective: Cognition and Social Context." *Personality and Social Psychology Bulletin* 20 (5): 454–63.

Twenge, Jean, Natalie Ciarocco, Roy Baumeister, C. Nathan DeWall, and J. Michael Bartels. 2007. "Social Exclusion Decreases Pro-Social Behavior." *Journal of Personality and Social Psychology* 92: 56–66.

Vaillant, G. 2002. *Aging Well: Surprising Guideposts to a Happier Life from the Landmark Harvard Study of Adult Development*. Boston: Little, Brown.

Valdesolo, Piercarlo, and David DeSteno. 2007. "Moral Hypocrisy: Social Groups and the Flexibility of Virtue." *Psychological Science* 18: 689–90.

Valentino, B. 2004. *Final Solutions: Mass Killing and Genocide in the 20th Century*. Ithaca, NY: Cornell University Press.

Van den Bos, Wouter, Samuel J. McClure, Lasana T. Harris, Susan T. Fiske, and Jonathan D. Cohen. 2007. "Dissociating Affective Evaluation and Social Cognitive Processes in the Ventral Medial Prefrontal Cortex." *Cognitive, Affective, and Behavioral Neuroscience* 7 (4): 337–46.

Van Honk, Jack, and Dennis Schutter. 2007. "Testosterone Reduces Conscious Detection of Signals Serving Social Correction." *Psychological Science* 18: 663–67.

Van Lange, Paul, Wilma Otten, Ellen De Bruin, and Jeffrey Joireman. 1997. "Development of Pro-Social, Individualistic, and Competitive Orientations: Theory and Preliminary Evidence." *Journal of Personality and Social Psychology* 73: 733–46.

van 't Wout, M. et al. 2007. "Affective State and Decision-Making in the Ultimatum Game." *Experimental Brain Research* 169 (4): 564–68.

Van Vugt, Mark, David de Kremer, and Dirk Janssen. 2007. "Gender Differences in Cooperation and Competition." *Psychological Science* 18: 19–23.

Varela, F., E. Thompson, and E. Rosch. 1991. *The Embodied Mind: Cognitive Science and Human Experience*. Cambridge, MA: MIT Press.

Waldmann, Michael, and Jorn Dieterich. 2007. "Throwing a Bomb on a Person versus Throwing a Person on a Bomb: Intervention Myopia in Moral Intuitions." *Psychological Science* 18: 247–53.

Waller, N. G., B. A. Kojetin, T. J. Bouchard Jr., D. T. Lykken, and A. Tellegen. 1990. "Genetic and Environmental Influences on Religious Interests, Attitudes, and Values: A Study of Twins Reared Apart and Together." *Psychological Science* 1 (2): 138–42.

Walter, B. F. 1999. "Designing Transitions from Civil War." *International Security* 24 (1): 127–55.

Walzer, M. 1997. *Just and Unjust Wars: A Moral Argument with Historical Illustrations*. New York: Basic Books. Reprinted in 2006.

Warburton, W., K. Williams, and D. Cairns. 2006. "When Ostracism Leads to Aggression: The Moderating Effects of Control Deprivation." *Journal of Experimental Social Psychology* 42 (2): 213–20.

Weber, Christopher, and Christopher Federico. 2007. "Interpersonal Attachment and Patterns of Ideological Belief." *Political Psychology* 28: 389–416.

Weber, M. 1978. *Economy and Society: An Outline of Interpretive Sociology*, 2 vols. Berkeley: University of California Press.

Westen, D. 1995. *Revision of Social Cognition and Object Relations Scale: Q-Sort for Projective Stories (SCORS-Q)*. Unpublished manuscript, Department of Psychiatry, Cambridge Hospital and Harvard Medical School, Cambridge, MA.

Weyl, E. Glen. 2006. "Overconfidence in Neural Networks." Unpublished paper.

Wheatley, T., and J. Haidt. 2005. "Hypnotically Induced Disgust Makes Moral Judgments More Severe." *Psychological Science* 16: 780–84.

Wheatley, T., S. Milleville, and A. Martin. 2007. "Understanding Animate Agents." *Psychological Science* 186: 469–74.

Wheeler, M., and S. Fiske, 2005. "Controlling Racial Prejudice: Social-Cognitive Goals Affect Amygdala and Stereotype Activation." *Psychological Science* 16 (1): 56–63.

Whitaker, Benjamin. 1985. Revised and Updated Report on the Question of the Prevention and Punishment of the Crime of Genocide. UN Doc. E/CN.4/Sub.2/1985/6.

Wicker, B. et al. 2003. "Both of Us Disgusted in My Insula: The Common Neural Basis of Seeing and Feeling Disgust." *Neuron* 40: 655–64.

Wilhelmina, Queen of the Netherlands. 1960. *Lonely but Not Alone*. Translated from the Dutch by J. Peereboom. New York: McGraw-Hill.

Williams, B. 1986. *Ethics and the Limits of Philosophy*. Cambridge, MA: Harvard University Press.

Williams, B. 1981. *Moral Luck*. Cambridge: Cambridge University Press.

Williams, C. 2005. *Pétain*. New York: Palgrave Macmillan.

Wilson, E. O. 1975. *Sociobiology: The New Synthesis*. Cambridge, MA: Harvard University Press.

———. 1978. *On Human Nature*. Cambridge, MA: Harvard University Press.

———. 1998. *Consilience: The Unity of Knowledge*. New York: Alfred A. Knopf; Random House.

Wilson, G. D., ed. 1973. *The Psychology of Conservatism*. New York: Academic Press.

Wilson, James Q. 1993a. *Moral Sense*. New York: Free Press.

———. 1993b. "The Moral Sense." *American Political Science Review* 87 (1): 1–11.

Wittgenstein, L. 1963. *Tractatus logico-philosophicus*. London: Routledge and Kegan Paul.

Wu, Shali, and Boaz Keysar. 2007. "The Effect of Culture on Perspective Taking." *Psychological Science* 18: 600–606.

Yahil, L. 1990. *The Holocaust: The Fate of European Jewry*. New York: Oxford University Press.

Yardley K, and T. Honess. 1987. *Society and Identity: Psychosocial Perspectives*. New York: Wiley.

Young, L., and M. Koenigs. 2007. "Investigating Emotion in Moral Cognition: A Review of Evidence from Functional Neuroimaging and Neuropsychology." *British Medical Bulletin* 84: 69–79.

Young, Liane, Fiery Cushman, Marc Hauser, and Rebecca Saxe. 2007. "The Neural Basis of the Interaction between Theory of Mind and Moral Judgment." *Proceedings of the National Academy of Sciences of America* 104: 8235–40.

Zajonc, R. 1980. "Feeling and Thinking: Preferences Need No Inferences." *American Psychologist* 35 (2): 151–75.

Zak, P., R. Kurzban, and W. Matzner. 2005. "Oxytocin Is Associated with Human Trustworthiness." *Hormones and Behavior* 48: 522–27.

Zak, P., A. Stanton, and S. Ahmadi. 2007. "Oxytocin Increases Generosity in Humans." *PLoS One* 2 (11): 1128. http://doi:10.1371/journal.pone.0001128.

Zimbardo, P. G. 2007. *The Lucifer Effect: Understanding How Good People Turn Evil.* New York: Random House.

Zimbardo, P. G., E. B. Ebbesen, and C. Maslach. 1977. *Influencing Attitudes and Changing Behavior*, 2nd ed. Reading, MA: Addison Wesley.

Zimbardo, P. G., and M. Leippe. 1991. *The Psychology of Attitude Change and Social Influence.* New York: McGraw-Hill.

Zucker, Gail Sahar, and Bernard Weiner. 1993. "Conservatism and Perceptions of Poverty: An Attributional Analysis." *Journal of Applied Social Psychology* 23: 925–43.